INSIDERS' GUIDE® TO

BALTIMORE

FIFTH EDITION

MARY K. TILGHMAN

INSIDERS' GUIDE®

GUILFORD, CONNECTICUT
AN IMPRINT OF THE GLOBE PEQUOT PRESS

The prices and rates in this guidebook were confirmed at press time. We recommend, however, that you call establishments before traveling to obtain current information.

INSIDERS' GUIDE®

Text design by Nancy Freeborn
Maps by XNR Productions, Inc. © Morris Book Publishing, LLC

ISSN 1529-5893
ISBN 978-0-7627-4553-1

Printed in the United States of America
10 9 8 7 6 5 4 3 2 1

CONTENTS

CONTENTS

Directory of Maps

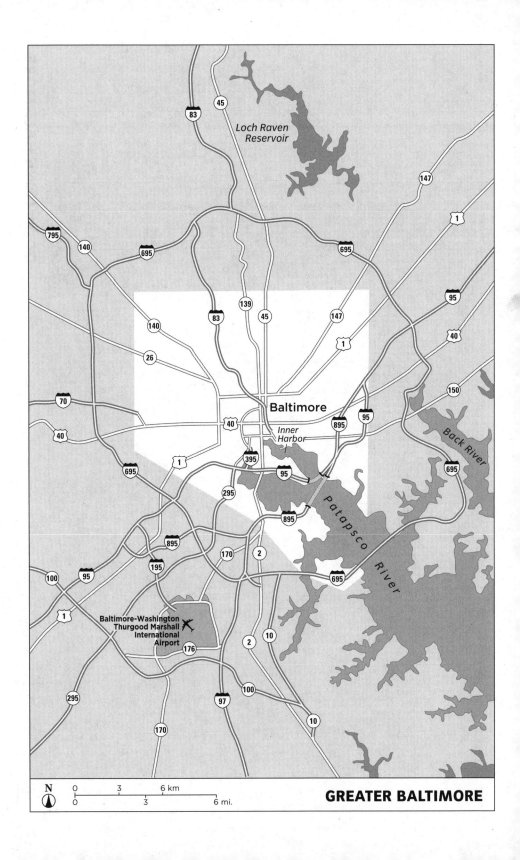

Loch Raven Reservoir

Baltimore

Inner Harbor

Back River

Patapsco River

Baltimore-Washington
Thurgood Marshall
International
Airport

N

| 0 | 3 | 6 km |
| 0 | 3 | 6 mi. |

GREATER BALTIMORE

DOWNTOWN BALTIMORE

NORTH BALTIMORE

SOUTH BALTIMORE

PREFACE

Welcome to Baltimore, hon! You've arrived at a city that emphasizes friendliness and treasures civility, honors tradition and encourages innovation.

Baltimoreans are quick to say hello when they meet you on the street. They don't even have to know you. They apologize when they get in your way—or you get in theirs. They say thank-you and please. Need something? Ask anybody; they'll help you out. They'll also hold the door for you. An older Baltimorean might even tip his hat.

Charm City's citizens celebrate their good fortune in all sorts of festivals, fairs, and neighborhood events. If you want to get to know the town, stop by the Irish Festival, the Fells Point Fun Festival, or the Flower Mart (where hats are optional but quite traditional). In Little Italy, residents still get together to play bocce or watch *Moonstruck* on a screen painted on the side of a house. Hampden's Christmas decorations are so over the top, they're famous. Stop by and you'll see homeowners sitting on the porch or welcoming you in to see their train garden. Who wouldn't want to be part of such hospitality?

Baltimoreans may be considered southerners to those north of the Mason-Dixon Line (and after all, Federal troops had to train their guns on the city to keep Maryland part of the Union during the Civil War). But we don't really think of ourselves as southerners. And, obviously, we're not northerners, either. No, we like to think of ourselves as Baltimoreans— individuals with diverse backgrounds and plenty of charm.

Baltimore City is a city of firsts, and we continue to encourage the sort of innovation that has led Baltimore to give the nation its first railroad, its first shopping center, its first Ouija board, its first African-American newspaper chain. Baltimore has been lucky enough to have some of the world's finest medical facilities, including the Johns Hopkins Hospital, the University of Maryland Medical and Dental Schools, and the Shock Trauma Center. The fervor for innovation continues today at the city's many hospitals, universities, and research centers. The first umbrella was made here—who knows what technology will come next?

Meanwhile, as Baltimoreans await the future, they treasure the past. The city's icons are the Washington Monument, the country's first monument to the first president; the *Constellation*, the U.S. Navy's last all-sail ship; and the *Pride of Baltimore*, a replica of the famous Baltimore clipper ships. The city is dotted with history. Fine art collected during the last century by Henry Walters and the Cone sisters are housed in magnificent museums. The B&O Railroad Museum's roundhouse is filled with trains from all of railroading history. We wander the streets of Fells Point, listening to stories of ghosts. Baltimore is home to the first Methodist church in America, the city's first Catholic cathedral and Catholic seminary, and the first convent for African-American women religious.

One thing to remember: Baltimore is never stodgy, never stuck-up. If you come for the day or the rest of your life, welcome. We're always glad to see you, hon. Can we tell you where to get a good crab cake?

ACKNOWLEDGMENTS

Many people helped make this book possible. Hotel and restaurant staff, public relations staff of Baltimore's wonderful museums and attractions, and plenty of shopkeepers made sure my information was up-to-date and offered advice about other places to see around town. Tracey Baskerville of the Baltimore Office of Promotion and the Arts and Anthony Tornetta of the Baltimore Area Convention and Visitors Association as well as the helpful employees at the visitor center at the Inner Harbor supplied information and pictures. I have to thank Michelle Pendoley of the Baltimore Symphony Orchestra for sending great pictures of their new music director and Sara Pedroni and Anne Mannix of the Baltimore Museum of Art for their help with photos and information about Claribel and Etta Cone. I also must thank Anna Custer, executive director of Live Baltimore for her help as I wrote the chapter on Relocation.

I had lots of help and support from my family as well. I can always count on my husband, Ray Truitt, and my three children, Gina, Sean, and Brigid, to join me when I'm visiting sites to gather information and to understand when I spend yet another long evening in front of my computer as a deadline looms.

And I always want to thank Baltimore for being a great (and always underrated) city. I'm lucky to call this place home.

HOW TO USE THIS BOOK ?

The book you hold offers you so many opportunities to discover our city by the bay. Baltimore loves visitors and it welcomes newcomers. With gracious hospitality, the people here will be happy to show you around, tell you where to find a good crab cake, lead you to an amazing array of museums, shops, and neighborhoods. It is that spirit that permeates these pages. Every listing is designed to lead you to new discoveries about Charm City, memories you'll cherish; experiences you'll relate often (and happily, we hope).

But this requires several things from you. First, you have to use this book. It's a guide, after all. It's not meant to sit in your house while you trek through Baltimore. Take it with you, mark it up, highlight places you want to visit or things you've already seen. Put stars against the best stuff, or put Xs next to the places you didn't like. Use it as a diary of your visit, putting notes in the margin or on the inside front and back pages. Put it to use. Keep it close by for its maps, its insights, its selections, its ability to tell you more about where you are than you might find out on your own.

Second, you have to tell us if you find something you like, something you dislike, or if information contained within the pages becomes inaccurate. Our goal has been to present accurate information; if we have failed, either because of the usual changes in businesses and attractions or because we made an error of our own, tell us. We need to know so we can fix it for the next edition. You can reach us at: Insiders' Guide, The Globe Pequot Press, P.O. Box 480, Guilford, CT 06437, or visit our Web site, www.insiders guide.com.

WHICH WAY IS NORTH?

We have tried to make things easy to follow. Baltimore's city limits do not fully take into account the area we wanted this book to address, so instead we've concentrated on the Greater Baltimore area, which in most cases we have defined as the neighborhoods within and around Interstate 695, commonly known as the Baltimore Beltway.

We have made exceptions. They reflect a reality we cannot overcome—that people and places are not easily defined by geographic boundaries. To that end, we offer information about the area near Baltimore–Washington International Thurgood Marshall Airport, which is where many tourists stay in hotels and motels, attend conferences, or visit either on their way into or out of town. We have included information about Hunt Valley, an area about 15 miles north of Baltimore with hotels and conference facilities. Similarly, we have included information about White Marsh, a growing suburb where the tourist trade seems to be growing as well.

We have broken the area into four distinct geographic areas, named by their geographic location if you were to look down on the city from above. These areas—Northeast, Northwest, Southeast, and Southwest—are not consistent with the names people give the area. Baltimoreans discuss their city in terms of neighborhoods. However, one glance at just the sample of communities covered in the Relocation chapter makes it obvious why we could not expect to craft a well-organized book broken into neighborhoods and neighboring towns too numerous to count. The maps we've provided give the best indications of what our areas include. Insiders' Tips (indicated by an **i**), offer quick insights.

Basically, the east-west divider with which we chose to define our regions is Interstate 83 to Charles Street (Highway 139) from the north, extending down to Highway 2 (Hanover Street and Ritchie Highway) to the south. The north-south divider of our regions is Highway 150 (Eastern Avenue) from the east until you reach U.S. Highway 40, which extends west. It isn't a perfect crossing, nor would any other one be, but it works for our purposes here.

We made another exception as a concession to the realities of our area. A significant portion of Baltimore's tourist emphasis is on the area surrounding the Inner Harbor—including Harborplace, Oriole Park at Camden Yards, M&T Bank Stadium, Little Italy, and Fells Point. We've created a Downtown district that encompasses these areas. It's a sort of hole in the middle of the four-area system explained previously. Our Downtown district's boundaries include North Avenue to the north, Edison Highway and Highland Avenue to the east, Cross Street and the northwest branch of the Patapsco River to the south, and Interstate 395 (Martin Luther King Jr. Boulevard) to the west. For people visiting the city proper, this Downtown district offers activities, restaurants, and events that are either within walking distance of each other or a short bus or taxicab ride between.

The intersection of Charles and Baltimore Streets is where the north/south and east/west addresses generate. Streets running north to south in the city are north streets above Baltimore Street and south streets below it. An example would be Charles Street, our east-west divider throughout the book. Heading north from Baltimore Street, it's North Charles Street; heading south, South Charles Street. Similarly, Charles Street serves as the city's east-west divider. So if you are looking for West Eager Street, you know that you need to be west of Charles Street, because if you were on the east side of Charles Street, you would be on East Eager Street.

A typical listing in this guide has the name of the business or organization on the first line and the address, telephone number, and Web site (when available) on subsequent lines. If the address includes a town or city name after it, then it is outside the official city limits of Baltimore. If no town is listed after a street address, then it is within the city limits of Baltimore, but that does not necessarily mean that the establishment is in Downtown Baltimore. For instance, the B&O Railroad Museum is listed under Southwest in the Attractions chapter. You know it's in Baltimore because its address shows it as being on West Pratt Street, with no town name after it. It's listed as Southwest because it is outside of the Downtown district we created.

OTHER HINTS ABOUT THE BOOK

Telephone Numbers

In Maryland, callers must dial the three-digit area code to make any call. This additional dialing is required in Maryland because the phone company overlaid new area codes over the existing 410 area code. Most still use the 410 area code but you may see 433 or 240 area codes as well. There's no need to dial 1 first, but you have to dial all 10 numbers no matter what. By the way, these are still local calls; don't worry about long-distance charges.

Highway Numbers vs. Road Names

We've included the highway numbers for most main roads, although most people in the area refer to roads by their more common names. Just remember I-695 is the Baltimore Beltway with an inner loop running clockwise around the city and an outer loop running counterclockwise. I-83 is the Jones Falls Expressway inside the Beltway and, well, I-83 all the way to Harrisburg, Pennsylvania. If you have to ask for directions, give the place you are trying to get to and the street address, whenever possible. Based on this information you should be able to find the right way, probably using common road names rather than the highway numbers.

(See the Getting Here, Getting Around chapter for more information.)

Have Fun

As a native Baltimorean, I've done my best to introduce you to the city. I hope you find all the listings helpful. I hope they lead you where you really want to go: to good food, beautiful sights, new friends.

Go ahead, wear out this book; I hope you'll carry it everywhere, stash it in the car just in case you need the name of a restaurant, a spot to stop for a few minutes or hours of fun. It is my hope this book will help you enjoy your visit to Baltimore. Baltimoreans are always glad to see someone new taking delight in the places we love.

AREA OVERVIEW

Baltimore is a fascinating mixture of old and new. Its buildings, its businesses, its people, and its image run the gamut from progressive to old-fashioned—sometimes all in the same block. In this chapter we provide a general overview of some of these people and places as well as tell you other chapters in which you'll find more information about these subjects.

THE PEOPLE

Baltimoreans are good neighbors. We're the kind of folks who will stop to give you directions, who'll help you find your lost cat. We might not agree with our neighbors' politics, but that won't stop us from watching their house while they are away on vacation.

We like to get together. In addition to all the citywide festivals that are held every year, neighborhood bazaars, flea markets, bingo nights, crab feasts, ham and oyster suppers, and dances abound. Even though we're a big city, we gather like small-town folks at our churches and our schools and we love to linger over dinner at our local restaurants.

We get together for group yard sales, block parties, and just talking over the backyard fence. Baltimore is not a place where people walk by with their heads down and their eyes averted, fearing to speak. We are congenial. Philosophical dissertations with a stranger while standing in line at the grocery store are not uncommon. Strangers walking up to touch a pregnant woman's distended stomach and ask when she's due are not all that out of the ordinary.

We come in all colors, shapes, and sizes. Overall, we're a good group.

THE PLACE

Perhaps one of the reasons Baltimoreans are such good neighbors is that most of us are clustered together in neighborhoods. Each major area of Baltimore (Downtown, Northeast, Northwest, Southeast, and Southwest) is broken down into neighborhoods. Very few of these neighborhoods were intentionally laid out, so geographic boundaries sometimes overlap. Yet, each neighborhood exudes a distinct character that is often defined by both its historic origin and its population.

The general ethnic mix of Baltimore and its neighborhoods continues to change, but many of the neighborhoods retain their original flavor and, in some cases, the descendants of their original resident populations. Just the names of the local places of business will sometimes tell you what the main industry of the original community was or what its ethnic origin is.

Places such as Little Italy, Little Lithuania, and Greektown are the easiest to figure out. There are also Butchers Hill, Brewers Hill, and Pigtown. No misunderstandings there either. Many of the neighborhoods in Baltimore were culled from the estates of prominent citizens. Homewood, Guilford, Bolton Hill, Mount Clare, Mondawmin, Walbrook, and many others carry the names of their original estates. (See the Relocation chapter for more information.)

Cities and towns in Baltimore County to the north, east, and west of Baltimore City as well as Howard and Anne Arundel Counties to the southeast and southwest, respectively, took their names directly from the people who originally settled the land. That's why we have Jonestown, Towsontown (now just Towson), Reisterstown, Ellicott City, Cockeysville, Catonsville, and Dickeyville, to name only a few.

Fun on the Web

If you find yourself with some downtime, by all means, go Downtown. Two Web sites are devoted to having fun Downtown. The Downtown Partnership, a nonprofit organization that promotes the Downtown area for business and pleasure, maintains a good Web site, www.godowntownbaltimore.com. Anything going on in the next couple weeks is usually listed here. Look for concerts, lectures, festivals, and restaurant promotions. The Greater Baltimore Cultural Alliance produces www .baltimorefunguide.com. This is a pretty comprehensive guide to the goings-on at the museums, stadiums, and other fun places around town.

Some neighborhoods sprang up because of some industry that drew workers. Fells Point in Downtown was established in 1730 by shipbuilder William Fell and his family and became the hub of shipbuilding (and privateering) in Baltimore during the Revolution (see the History chapter). The streets he named and the area he laid out are still here, populated with local crafters, great little shops, and lovers of old things. (See the Antiques and Collectibles chapter.) Baltimore has many neighborhoods that were once mill towns. Hampden, in Northwest Baltimore, is one of those, as are all the neighborhoods that cluster around the Jones Falls Valley. The valley was once lined with mills that were powered by the swiftly running waters of the Jones Falls.

Baltimore does have a few neighborhoods, however, that were specifically designed as residential tracts. Peabody Heights, established in the 1890s and renamed Charles Village in the mid-1970s, is one of these areas. You can see the original tracts in the different housing styles that were constructed by each builder: porch fronts in the 2800 block of Maryland Avenue and bowed fronts in the 2600 block; five-story, 20-foot-wide houses on Charles Street; two-story, 13-foot-wide houses on Howard Street. There were houses for every income and every size family in the original Peabody Heights, and Charles Village continues today as one of Baltimore's most eclectic areas.

Interestingly, Baltimore also boasts the first neighborhood ever designed specifically as a suburb. Walbrook was laid out in 1870 but did not have a long suburban life span— it was annexed by the city in 1888, as was Hampden.

One truth, then, about Baltimore is woven throughout the city and its neighborhoods: It is an area of history, and it is because of that history that much of Baltimore was built in the first place.

BIG BUSINESS

Baltimore's location prompted the growth of Baltimore's business interests. Because we boast the best protected harbor in the world and, at the same time, are central to the Eastern seaboard (as close to New York and Massachusetts as we are to Norfolk and the Carolinas), Baltimore was an obvious choice for businesses that needed to touch both North and South and reach West.

The cotton mills that made Baltimore the largest supplier of southern cotton duck canvas in the entire world were a natural. Balti-

i If you're moving to Baltimore, you must exchange your valid out-of-state driver's license and your car registration for their Maryland counterparts within 60 days. Call MVA at (800) 950–1682 for how to go about it or be prepared to pay the fines.

Selected Baltimore Firsts

In 1800 Alexander Brown opened the first investment banking house in America in Baltimore. The original building, which miraculously survived the Great Baltimore Fire, still stands at the southwest corner of Baltimore and Calver Streets. Now known as Deutsche Bank Alex. Brown, the company is still going strong.

In 1803 Thomas More invented the first icebox refrigerator.

Samuel Morse inaugurated the first commercial telegram service here in 1844—which was appropriate, since the first telegraph line in America was erected here that same year.

—*Excerpted from* Baltimore—America's City of Firsts, *a pamphlet published by Baltimore Bicentennial Celebration, Inc.*

more, an industrialized city with plenty of water for power, was just a hop, skip, and a short rail commute to the raw cotton suppliers of the South. As for customers, they were right here, as long as most ships that came to port were under sail.

It was this ability to get products to market just about anywhere in the United States that made Baltimore boom, and much of its current economy still revolves around the transportation industry. The port has a huge economic influence, with 32.4 million tons of cargo in 2005. Railroads, warehousing, and distribution are a rapidly growing sector of business in Baltimore, and Baltimore–Washington International Thurgood Marshall Airport has become one of the busiest airports in the country.

Baltimore also has retained a solid manufacturing base. General Motors, McCormick Spice Company, and Under Armour Apparel all have facilities in Baltimore. We also claim a growing number of high-tech, defense industry manufacturers, perhaps, in part, due to our proximity to the nation's capital. Being near Washington, D.C., also spurs some of the smaller businesses in Baltimore, particularly those related to real estate and tourism. A great many people who come to visit Washington also make the short trip north to Baltimore, and many residents of the Washington area come here regularly to shop at the Inner Harbor, see the sights, and attend sporting events. Some former residents of D.C. have settled in Baltimore because of the relatively short commute by car or train (about 60 minutes) and because the real estate is cheaper and the quality of life higher.

The growing business focus in Baltimore, however, is on service industries. Education, medicine, international banking and investment, international trade, real estate, and tourism are all big business in Baltimore.

Maryland rates as the best-educated workforce in the country due largely to the many hospitals and research universities in town. World-renowned colleges and research universities like Johns Hopkins and the University of Maryland are home to some 45 top federal research labs, and our state houses the highest percentage of professional and technical workers, the second highest number of doctoral scientists, and the third highest concentration of doctoral engineers. As a result, Maryland receives 10 percent of national research and development monies.

Once a state known primarily for its blue collar and its blue crabs, Maryland is now home to a burgeoning high-tech and biotech industry. Unlike other states that primarily support Internet companies, Maryland has laid the groundwork for broad technology growth. Some of the most exciting research in the areas of genetics and biotechnology is taking place right in Baltimore's backyard.

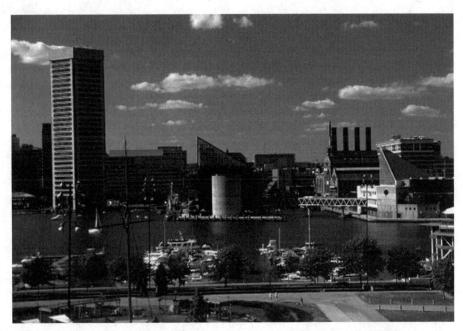

The view of Baltimore's Inner Harbor from Federal Hill. BALTIMORE AREA CONVENTION AND VISITORS ASSOCIATION

Maryland is home to 300 of the most vital, fastest-growing bioscience firms in the world, including Celera Genomics, Gene Logic, and Human Genome Sciences. Baltimore serves as the backbone to the state's high-tech rebirth. Visionaries, like local developers at Struever Bros. Eccles & Rouse, Inc., are reinventing old warehouse space by transforming the large, underdeveloped sites into wired workplaces. Deserted factories—like the American Can Company on the waterfront in Canton—now attract savvy business and retail clients with high-tech office space upstairs and high-end shopping and dining on the ground floor.

Baltimore has a comprehensive banking sector that began with the first mortgage banking house in the United States, Álex. Brown & Sons. Now known as Deutsche Bank Alex. Brown, it owns one of the largest market research staffs in its industry. Baltimore is also home to such financial industry giants as T. Rowe Price and Legg Mason.

THE COST OF LIVING

As cities go, Baltimore is not an expensive one. The real estate boom that skyrocketed rents and housing costs in most major cities certainly affected the housing costs locally, but Baltimore is significantly less expensive than neighboring Washington. The average home cost in Baltimore in 2005, according to the National Association of Realtors, was $265,300, more than double the price of a house in 2004. Housing runs the gamut from the exorbitant to the modest. A few years ago you could scoop up a fixer-upper in Canton for the low fifties; now those rehabbed beauties are selling for $500,000. There are still bargains to be found in the city, both for renting and buying (See the Relocation chapter for more information.)

Daily expenses like groceries and eating out are very reasonable. Groceries for a family of four will cost about $150 per week if that family buys brand names. Eating out is easy

How to Speak like a Native

If you've come to Baltimore expecting to be able to speak the language, you may have a more difficult time than you expected. Our location causes some problems. Because we are in the middle of the Eastern seaboard, just below that pesky Mason-Dixon Line, when it comes to our culture and our language, we take some of our cues from the South and some from the North.

Whereas in some areas of the country, all cola drinks are called Cokes or Pepsis even if they're Diet Rite, in Baltimore, we call a spade a spade. If you want a Pepsi-Cola, you must order "Pepsi," and a "Coke" is a Coca-Cola. And don't ask for a pop, unless you don't care what you get. We call anything that fizzes a "soda." If you ask for an orange pop, you're likely to get frozen orange ice on a stick!

There are some generic names that you might misconstrue as a simple mispronunciation. "Zinc" is one such word. "Sinks" were originally made of zinc. So when we put our dishes away at the end of a meal, we put them in the "zinc." (We are not mispronouncing "sink.") If you're used to having your hamburger or sandwich on a bun, ask your waitress for a "roll." If you want a sweet roll with your morning's breakfast, ask what type of "buns" are available.

In the summer, we don't barbecue, we "cook out." We live in row houses, or row homes, not town houses.

If you're hungry for a hoagie, you can find them in a few places, but if you want the Baltimore version, you'll need to go in search of a "sub" shop. "Sub" is the short version of "submarine sandwich," our name for hoagie.

On the other hand, if you want directions to the nearest sub shop, you may encounter a language barrier that is built of more than just the words you use. In Baltimore, we have our own language of sorts. We call it Bawlmerese. No one we know of has documented the origins of the language, though it shares similarities with a dialect spoken in Philadelphia and with England's Cockney. Bawlmerese is spoken mostly on the eastern, northeastern, and southern sides of Baltimore. You will also hear it in valley communities that were once teeming with cotton mills. Though most of the mills are now closed, many descendants of the original settlers remain, and they speak Bawlmerese.

The o's are broad, unless spoken before a consonant, and the t's often come out as d's, as in "wudder." (Wudder, by the way, is the clear, cool liquid that often rains on us. We spell it water.) Sometimes the t's get lost altogether, or syllables are simply left out, as in "Bawlmer," the town in which we live.

L's are often swallowed, and words tend to run together as if there were no space between them. "B'lair" is one of those. It is how we locals pronounce Bel Air, a nearby town in Harford County, and also a road in Bawlmer.

Some words become so Bawlmerized they are hardly recognizable. Take "styrofoam." In these parts it's pronounced, and sometimes even spelled, "skyraphone." On a cold winter night, smoke goes up our "chimbly." When school's out, we like to go "down-e o'shun" to "Ocean City, Murlin" (that would be Maryland), or "Rehoebet Beach, Delwaware." "The shure," on the other hand, is much closer. If someone you know in Baltimore is going "down-e shure" for the weekend, they're probably only going as far as Middle Fiver, about 25 minutes away. All shure places are on the Chesapeake Bay and the rivers that flow into it.

Baltimoreans go down to ("down-e") lots of places besides the shure and the oshun, even when they're north, east, or west. We often go down to the corner store: or down to a friend's house. Actual direction is of no consequence.

Bawlmerese plays havoc with pronoun references and adjectives as well as direction. Don't faint if you hear a native say that "Me and him went to see dem Birds last night." "Dem Birds" are also known as "dem O's" or "dem Orals"—our baseball team. In fact, a common greeting from a Baltimorean after a winning baseball game is "How about dem O's?" ("A great game!" would be an appropriate response.)

If you want to go to an Orioles game, don't ask the way to Oriole Park. Few people will know what you're talking about. You see, we had an argument over what to call our new stadium. The powers-that-be wanted to call it Oriole Park, the citizenry wanted to call it Camden Yards. So a compromise was reached, and the stadium's formal name is Oriole Park at Camden Yards. Baltimoreans, however, don't care what the formal name is. We call it "Camden Yards" or, more simply, "the Yard."

We're very stubborn like that. Although our airport was long ago renamed Baltimore–Washington International Thurgood Marshall Airport, or BWI, the native Baltimorean will often call it "Friendship." Friendship Airport was the original name.

Oh, and don't be surprised or insulted if someone calls you "hon." The waitresses do it. A woman on the street whom you ask directions from might do it. We mean nothing by it—in fact, it's a term of inclusion. We are a friendly people, and we want you to feel at home . . . hon.

If you're settling here, you can expect the local children to call you Miss Susan (if your name is Susan, that is). Children would never call someone Mr. Smith—too formal—but if he was Paul Smith, they would call him Mr. Paul. It is a show of respect. In fact, Baltimoreans are generally respectful and polite. Of course, the occasional obscenity is screamed from a car window when we're stuck in baseball traffic, but, generally, we are a please-and-thank-you kind of crowd.

If someone holds the door for you, "thank you" and a smile are expected. If you don't give it, don't be surprised if you hear a surly "you're welcome" as the door closes behind you. If you're driving in Baltimore and someone offers you his or her right-of-way, raise your hand as a thank-you as you pass. It's expected.

Thanks are often given to the store clerk who helps you or the antiques dealer who lets you look around the store. We thank our bus drivers and cabbies when they let us out at our stops, and often the response is not "you're welcome" or another "thank you," but "have a good one . . . ." "One" is the day, the afternoon, or the evening.

And you will, we hope. Have a good one, that is. Hopefully, knowing a little bit about the native tongue will help you get settled in. Enjoy Bawlmer, hon!

Economic Interests

Maryland is the center of the Boston-Atlanta Corridor on the Atlantic seaboard and borders on Washington, D.C., the nation's capital. Among the 50 states, Maryland ranks 42nd in size and 19th in population. Its per capita income is the fourth highest in the United States. Of Maryland's population age 25 and older, about 87 percent hold a bachelor's degree or higher, which is the third highest percentage among the states. Professional and technical workers constitute 25 percent of the state's workforce, the second highest concentration among states in the nation. In Baltimore there is increasing interest in recycling waterfront industrial buildings to house technology firms, as part of Baltimore's new "Digital Harbor." The Can Company in Canton, for example, is an old manufacturing plant transformed into a mixed-use space that couples high-end retail and restaurants with digitally wired office space for high-tech companies.

—Excerpted from the State Department of Business and Economic Development Web site, www.choose maryland.com.

with a laundry list of chains and a high volume of outstanding locally owned cafes and restaurants. (See the Restaurants chapter for dining-out options). Clothing and amenities can also be found at reasonable prices. We have all the big national stores, but one of Baltimore's best attributes is its plethora of little shops and specialty markets. There are neighborhood shops with bargains on everything from T-shirts to furniture. Some of our secondhand stores offer designer and vintage clothing for a steal (see the Shopping and Antiques and Collectibles chapters for specifics).

When it comes to making a living, Maryland has one of the country's lowest poverty rates and ranks among the top states in median household and per capita personal income. Staying on the job is easier, too, when you have some of the best child care in the country. Maryland was ranked fourth in the nation in the National Association of Child Care Resource and Referral Agencies' 2007 survey of child-care standards.

Baltimore earned a bad reputation for its high number of drug-related homicides in the mid-1990s, but the homicide rate dropped below 500 in 2000 for the first time in years.

Unfortunately, as of 2007, gang and gang-related violence has pushed the homicide rate back up for the first time since the 1990s. Baltimore's mayor and police force are dedicated to reducing crime on our city streets. Although Baltimore can feel like a small town, it is a city and it does have its share of muggers and panhandlers. There is no need to fear the city, but a level of awareness is required to successfully navigate Downtown. Common sense tells us not to leave items in our cars that might attract a burglar and to keep purses and shopping bags close when walking along the streets. The Downtown Partnership's Public Safety Guides patrol the 106-block Downtown area in an effort to keep the area safe and clean. Look for these friendly folks— you'll know them by their purple caps and yellow shirts—if you feel unsafe or if you need directions. They're always quite helpful.

CLIMATE

Being centered on the Eastern seaboard, we tend to get the tail end of cold fronts coming down from the north, followed by the top end of warm fronts coming up from Georgia. Every now and then we are affected by hurricanes, and small tornadoes occasionally touch down.

The fronts that typically drop feet-deep snow on Minnesota and the Midwest usually drop the rest of it in the Appalachian Mountains. Hence, Baltimore does not get very much snow from the west, unless a cold front meets moisture coming from the south. Then we can get foot after foot of very wet snow. There is sometimes significant snow or rain from the northeast. Nor'easters, as they're called, come rarely, but when they hit, they do so with a vengeance.

Besides the occasional messy travel conditions, the only real problem caused by Baltimore's weather is what to wear. Take one particular moment in time, in September. One morning temperatures started out in the 60s—normal for fall, but then, September is not quite fall until late in the month. By the end of the day, temperatures were in the 90s as a warm front moved through. The next day started out hot; then a thunderstorm brought a cool breeze.

You will hear a lot of Baltimoreans say, "It's not the heat, it's the humidity," and they would be correct. If it's 90 in Baltimore and the humidity is 30 percent, then it feels about 85. If it's 90 in Baltimore and the humidity is 95 percent—which is possible—then it feels about 120. The only places where it can be hotter than Baltimore when Baltimore is HOT is a steam bath or an oven.

We also take note of the windchill index in winter, which can make temperatures seem much colder. Normally (and we use that term

i The cobblestone circle around the Washington Monument on Charles Street has a regular traffic pattern: Cars simply split to either side of the monument rather than drive around the circle. But in suburban Towson, the busy traffic circle on York Road in the heart of town has a circuitous counterclockwise traffic flow.

loosely here), winter weather usually hits in late December and continues through early February. Daytime highs are normally in the upper 30s and overnight lows are in the low 20s to upper teens. In the spring and fall, temperatures tend toward the upper 50s and 60s, with lows in the mid-40s. Summer has highs generally in the low to mid-80s range, but there is always a week or so where temperatures are 95 or higher.

Baltimore also has what is often referred to as "Indian summer." The term describes periods of warm weather following the first freeze; however, Baltimoreans tend to use the term to refer to any warm period that occurs after we've had some cold, freeze or no.

When summer is at its sultriest, expect your hair to curl and your shirt to stick. Wear earmuffs and mittens in the winter, because the north wind doth blow. But always know that a beautiful day in Baltimore is just around the corner. When the weather is just right, Baltimore can be the most beautiful place in the world—hot sun, cool, flower-scented breezes, and clear blue sky. The birds sing, the crickets chirp, and just about all is right with the world.

Vital Statistics

Mayor: Sheila Dixon
Governor: Martin O'Malley
Outlying counties: Baltimore County, Carroll County, Harford County, Howard County, Montgomery County, Anne Arundel County
Populations:
  City: 635,815
  State: 5.6 million
Nickname: Charm City (most common), Monument City, Mob City
Average temperatures:
  July: High 88° F, Low 72° F
  January: High 41° F, Low 28° F
Average rain: 41 inches
  Snow: 20 inches
  Sun: 120 days
Major universities: University of Maryland System, Johns Hopkins University, Towson University, Loyola College, Goucher College, Morgan State University
Major area employers: Port of Baltimore; Johns Hopkins Institutions; The University of Maryland, Baltimore; General Motors; Deutsche Bank Alex. Brown; St. Paul Companies
Major airport: Baltimore–Washington International Thurgood Marshall Airport
Military bases: Aberdeen Proving Grounds, Fort Detrick, Fort Meade, Patuxent River Naval Air Station, United States Naval Academy, Andrews Air Force Base, United States Coast Guard Yard at Curtis Bay
Alcohol laws: DWI limit .08; DUI limit is .07; must be 21 years old to purchase or consume alcohol; bars open until 2:00 a.m.; liquor stores closed on Sunday, but bars can be open and packaged goods may be bought from bars on Sunday.
Daily newspapers: *Baltimore Sun, Daily Record*, the *Examiner*
Sales tax: 6 percent state sales tax, 11.5 percent tax on car rentals
Major interstates: Interstate routes such as I-68, I-95, I-70, I-695 are marked with a blue and red interstate shield-shaped sign.
  United States routes such as US 1, US 15, US 40, US 113, US 301, and US 219 are marked with a white US shield-shaped sign.
  Maryland State highways such as MD 2, MD 45, MD 140, and MD 404 are marked with a white Maryland rectangular sign.
  The Baltimore Beltway (I-695) is 51.59 center line miles.
Public transportation: Maryland Mass Transit Authority (410-539-5000, 800-543-9809, www.mtamaryland.com)—Light Rail, Baltimore Metro Subway, Maryland Rail Commuter Service (MARC) Train, Maryland Mass Transit Authority Buses.
Driving and Traffic Safety Laws (as provided by the Maryland State Highway Administration): Maryland law limits the extent to which speed limits may be raised or lowered. The most notable restrictions are those that prohibit any speed limit greater than 65 miles per hour and any limit above 55 miles per hour anywhere except on interstate highways or other expressways.
  Every child younger than four years old, regardless of weight, and every child weighing 40 pounds or less, regardless of age, must be secured in a U.S.

DOT–approved child safety seat. Children and young people up to 16 years of age must be secured in seat belts or child safety seats, regardless of their seating positions. It is strongly recommended that all children ride secured in the rear seat. Drivers and front-seat passengers, regardless of their ages, are required to wear seat belts. It is strongly recommended that all occupants wear seat belts.

Motorcycle operators and passengers are required to wear U.S. DOT–approved helmets. Operators must wear eye protection as well.

Stay alert and give driving your full attention.

Show courtesy to other drivers, pedestrians, and cyclists.

Comply with our traffic laws and heed all traffic signs, signals, and markings.

Avoid driving aggressively.

Vehicles must stop for school buses when the bus's red flashers are on (except when the bus is on the opposite side of a highway divided by a barrier or median strip).

After stopping and yielding to pedestrians and other vehicles, a right turn or left turn from a one-way street to another one-way street may be made on a red signal, except where prohibited by a sign.

Maryland has a mandatory adult seat-belt law that covers the driver and the front-seat passenger next to the door, if the passenger is at least 16 years of age. Maryland's law allows primary enforcement, i.e., police may stop a vehicle and issue citations to violators solely for violating the seat-belt law. Both the driver and an adult passenger may receive tickets for not wearing seat belts.

Chamber of Commerce and Visitors Bureaus:

Maryland Office of Tourism Development, 217 East Redwood Street, Baltimore 21202; (866) 639-3526; www.mdisfun.org

Annapolis and Anne Arundel County Conference & Visitor Bureau, 26 West Street, Annapolis 21401; (410) 280-0445, (888) 302-2852; www.visit-annapolis.org

Baltimore Area Convention and Visitors Association, 100 Light Street, 12th Floor, Baltimore 21202; (410) 649-7000, (877) BALTIMORE; www.baltimore.org

Baltimore City Chamber of Commerce, 3 West Baltimore Street, Baltimore 21201; (410) 837-7101

Baltimore Office of Promotion, 7 East Redwood Street, Suite 500, Baltimore 21202; (410) 752-8632; www.bop.org

Calvert County Department of Economic Development, Courthouse, Prince Frederick 20678; (800) 331-9771; www.co.cal.md.us/visitors

Carroll County Visitor Center, 210 East Main Street, Westminster 21157; (800) 272-1933; www.carrollcountytourism.org

Dorchester County Tourism, 2 Rose Hill Place, Cambridge 21613; (410) 228-1000, (800) 522-TOUR; www.tour dorchester.org

CONTINUED

Garrett County & Deep Creek Lake Chamber of Commerce, 15 Visitors Center Drive, McHenry 21541; (301) 387-4386; www.visitdeepcreek.com

Harford County Office of Tourism, 220 South Main Street, Bel Air 21041; (888) 544-4695 or (800) 597-2649; www.harfordmd.com

Howard County Tourism Inc., 8267 Main Street, P.O. Box 9, Ellicott City 21041; (410) 313-1900, (800) 288-8747; www.visithowardcounty.com

Kent County Office of Tourism, 400 High Street, Chestertown 21620; (410) 778-0416; www.kentcounty.com

Ocean City Convention & Visitors Bureau, 4001 Coastal Highway, Ocean City 21842; (410) 289-8311, (800) OC-OCEAN; www.ococean.com

St Mary's County Division of Tourism, 23115 Leonard Hall Drive, P.O. Box 653, Leonardtown 20650; (800) 327-9023; www.co.saint-marys.md.us

Talbot County Office of Tourism, 11 South Harrison Street, Easton 21601; (410) 770-8000; www.tourtalbot.org

Washington County Convention & Visitors Bureau, 16 Public Square, Hagerstown 21740; (301) 791-3246, (888) 257-2600; www.maryland memories.org

Time and temperature phone number: (410) 662-9225

GETTING HERE, GETTING AROUND

Baltimore serves as a hub for everything from Amtrak trains to Greyhound buses, regional commuter rail lines to national and international airlines. To meet the growing needs of these travelers, getting here and getting around the area can be simple and cheap or expensive and complicated. The choice is yours. Happy traveling.

GETTING HERE

By Air

Baltimore–Washington International Thurgood Marshall Airport
End of Interstate 195 East, Linthicum
(410) 859-7111, (800) I-FLY-BWI
www.bwiairport.com
The local airport's name isn't the only thing that's grown in the last couple of years. Now named Baltimore–Washington International Thurgood Marshall Airport in honor of the first African-American Supreme Court justice and a Baltimore native, BWI has added huge new garages—with a smart green and red lighting system that enables drivers to see exactly where parking spaces are—along with new curbside roadways and, most importantly, a new terminal for Southwest Airlines, which serves half of BWI's travelers. A new "cell phone lot" enables friends to park for free to pick up travelers. With all the security in place, it's still not very easy to get around BWI, but it's now a lot easier to drive and park there.

Getting to the airport is fairly easy. It's located in Linthicum, about 9 miles from Baltimore and 32 miles from Washington. It sits just off Interstate 95, at the eastern end of 195, a short spur off I-95 built specifically for the airport. It's also easily accessible from Interstate 295 (the Baltimore–Washington Parkway) and the Baltimore Beltway.

With nearly 21 million passengers in 2006, and forecasts for continued growth, BWI is one of the fastest-growing airports in the United States. Operated by the Maryland Aviation Administration of the Maryland Department of Transportation, the airport covers 3,596 acres with 1.976 million square feet of passenger terminals.

Four domestic concourses and one international concourse have 70 gates, including 12 for commuter aircraft. Thirty-three commercial airlines fly to BWI, with Southwest Airlines carrying more than half of the passengers who arrive at BWI every year. Every day more than 650 flights are scheduled at BWI, which sees more than 56,000 passengers daily.

In addition to Southwest, BWI is served by Air Tran, American, US Airways, and United, as well as five international carriers, Air Canada Jazz, Air Jamaica, British Airways, North American, and USA 3000. These airlines are taking people to destinations as close as Orlando, Boston, and Atlanta and as far as Accra, West Africa, and London.

BWI's excellent rail connections make the airport a great choice for passengers traveling throughout the Baltimore–Washington, D.C., area and beyond. Amtrak, Maryland Rail Commuter (MARC), and the Light Rail all serve the airport (see By Rail later in the chapter).

BWI recently completed an expansion project, which increased parking by 12,000 spaces, added new concourses, and improved access to terminals.

The airport features all the creature comforts that weary travelers seek, from restaurants and bars to observation decks, local cultural displays, and sitting areas. A master list of all departures and arrivals is available on the second floor at the center of the airport, near the large escalators. If you want to know which gate to go to, try there first. The wings each have names that start with A, B, C, and so on in alphabetical sequence from south to north (or right to left) as you look directly at the airport structure. The A and B wings are on the side you enter by car or bus. The center area is wing C; wings D, E, and the International Pier are to the north (or left, as you look from the parking structure).

Getting to the Airport

Access to the airport is convenient from I-95 using I-195, a feeder road designed to connect that major north-south highway with the airport.

The Light Rail system offers transportation to and from the airport for a fee of up to $1.60 one way. The Light Rail will take you to Downtown Baltimore or as far north as Hunt Valley (about an hour and 40 minutes away). Tickets are available at the Light Rail terminal on the south side of the airport terminal. Call (410) 539-5000 for more details.

i When driving within a 5-mile radius of BWI, tune in to 1040 AM for current roadway conditions and take note of variable message signs.

Once at the Airport

BWI has a two-story terminal, with check-ins on the second floor and pickups on the first level. Park on the third or fourth level of the four-story parking garage if you're departing, and have the folks greeting you park on the first level of the garage if you are being picked up. This saves a lot of energy, especially if you pack heavy (and who doesn't?).

The loading and unloading locations directly in front of each airline's check-in area are convenient spots for dropping someone off. If someone will be waiting for you to pick up your baggage on the first level upon arrival,

it's a good idea to send them around the half-mile loop outside the parking garage a couple of times. Don't even think of parking or having others park in the loop near the terminals; increased security at the airport means no cars are allowed to stop here.

Duty-free shops, gift counters, magazine stands, and candy stores are open during the day and early evening in the central terminal area, between gates B and C, and between gates C and D. Restaurants, coffee shops, bars, and several fast-food options also serve travelers in these corridors. There are arcade machines, fax phones, and a courtesy phone to contact taxicabs and hotel shuttles in these corridors. Large bathroom facilities with baby changing stations are also available. If you have kids, the observation deck is the perfect place for a good view of incoming and outgoing flights, and there's a scale model airplane that kids can climb on (see the Kidstuff chapter for more information).

Rental Cars at BWI

The airport has a new rental car facility at Stoney Run Road and New Ridge Road. Free shuttle services take customers to and from the airport. Arriving passengers should take the shuttle from the lower-level terminal. The ride takes about 10 minutes. Those returning rental cars should follow the signs on the way to the airport. A shuttle will take passengers to the terminal. Some of the rental car providers include Avis, (410) 859-1680; Budget, (410) 859-0850; Dollar, (800) 800-4000; Enterprise, (800) 325-8007; Hertz, (410) 850-7400; and National, (410) 859-1136. If you are calling to reserve a car from out of town, use the company number in your local telephone directory. Rates range from $30 to $80 a day, depending on the size and make of the car, the options you choose, and how long you are planning to rent.

Airport Security

Security has tightened at all U.S. airports, and BWI is no exception. The U.S. Transportation Security Administration has transferred the screening of selected passengers from the aircraft boarding areas to the security check-points at airports across the country. This can translate into long lines and delays, so plan on arriving at least two hours before your flight. Additionally, all passengers are now required to have their boarding passes before going through the security screening areas.

E-tickets enable some passengers to check their luggage curbside and bypass the ticket counter. Those not checking luggage can usually go directly to the gate. Check with your airline to be sure of its procedures. Also, remember to carry government-issued identification, such as a driver's license or passport, along with your e-ticket to get through security.

By Roadway

Interstates and Highways

Interstate 695, known locally as the Baltimore Beltway, forms a circle outside the city limits. No matter where you get on, you will end up in the same place in about an hour's driving time. (We don't recommend this, unless you are really, really bored.) The road varies in width from two lanes in each direction on the east side to five lanes in the Northeast quadrant. If you get on I-695 on the east side of the roadway, you'll have to drop $2 to cross the Francis Scott Key Bridge over the Patapsco River.

Interstate 83, the Jones Falls Expressway, heads south into the city from Pennsylvania, but its path can be confusing. From the Pennsylvania line to I-695 (the Baltimore Beltway), about 30 miles, it's a straight shot, but at the Beltway southbound traffic has to get onto the Beltway for one exit before veering right, then left onto I-83 again. Once back on I-83, southbound traffic will find itself dropped right near Little Italy, leaving a convenient trip of about 4 blocks west to reach the Inner Harbor. The northern section of the highway becomes icy in extremely cold weather; the southern portion in the city can be slow going during rush hour and storms.

I-95 runs north to Maine and south to Florida, passing on the southwest and east

i Confused about the Inner Loop and Outer Loop of the Baltimore Beltway? It's simple. The Inner Loop is closest to the city, with exit numbers going in ascending order, while the Outer Loop is outside the Inner Loop and has exit numbers going in descending order.

side of Baltimore. During rush hour, traffic backs up at the entrances to the Baltimore Beltway, both near White Marsh in the northeast and in the Southwest corner. The highway goes through the Fort McHenry Tunnel, one of two tunnels beneath the Patapsco River toward the Inner Harbor area. The tunnel costs $2 for cars and provides an easy connection to Interstate 395, aka Martin Luther King Jr. Boulevard.

Highway 295, the Baltimore–Washington Parkway, is an old, four-lane connector between Baltimore and Washington, D.C. Beautifully lined with trees (rather than the standard concrete, soundproof walls), the highway can be a good alternate route for travel between the two cities. Heavy trucks are barred from using this commuter road. Heading north, the highway passes the Capital Beltway (Interstate 495 in Washington), I-195 (which takes you to BWI Airport), and I-695 (the Baltimore Beltway) before dropping into the city near Oriole Park at Camden Yards, M&T Bank Stadium, and the Baltimore Convention Center. A right turn onto Conway Street leads you to the Inner Harbor. Heading south into Washington, the highway leads to New York Avenue, which can take you to the Capitol area. Past New York Avenue, Highway 295 turns into I-295 and takes motorists toward Richmond, Virginia. If you use this highway, watch out for police officers in the medians behind the trees. The speed limits are strictly enforced.

I-395 becomes Martin Luther King Jr. Boulevard after carrying motorists from I-95 into Downtown Baltimore near the baseball and football stadiums and the convention center. During morning rush hour the road into the city is bottlenecked; in the afternoon, the

EZ Pass

If you are likely to use the Chesapeake Bay Bridge, one of the harbor tunnels, or head north on I-95 on a regular basis, you might want to consider getting an EZ Pass. It may not give you any discounts on tolls, but it will allow you to breeze past the cash-paying drivers to a dedicated EZ Pass lane and whiz right through (although in Maryland, that whizzing will take place at about 10 mph.)

You can pick up the EZ Pass transponder at any Motor Vehicle Administration office and keep your account full by check or via electronic fund transfer.

Once you see all the traffic you're not sitting in, you'll be glad you got the pass. For details, visit www.ezpassmd.com.

lanes carrying motorists out of the city are filled. Also, if heading out of the city on this road, keep right to head north, following signs for northbound I-95 and New York. Heading south toward Washington requires motorists to stay to the left to feed into southbound I-95.

Interstate 795 heads from Reisterstown in northwest Baltimore County to the Baltimore Beltway (I-695). It serves as a major feeder route to and from bedroom communities in Owings Mills and Reisterstown and connects, via Highway 140, to Westminster, a community about 40 miles northwest of Baltimore.

Interstate 895 is a bypass for I-95, offering motorists a second tunnel under the Patapsco River near the Inner Harbor. The Harbor Tunnel Thruway, the older of the two tunnels beneath the river, costs $2 to go through and connects to the Baltimore Beltway. It also provides access to Interstate 97, which leads to Annapolis, the state capital, about 25 miles southeast of the city.

U.S. Highway 40 is a major east-west highway running through Baltimore. As the highway runs through the city, at times it takes on the names Pulaski Highway on the east side and Orleans Street downtown. It's the Baltimore National Pike in Catonsville and Ellicott City. However, the US 40 signs are clearly marked. It's a good alternate route to I-95 and I-895 that doesn't require a toll—you don't have to cross the Patapsco River. Instead, you'll catch lots and lots of traffic lights. Still, it's a

good route for seeing different parts of the city.

Interstate 70 comes into the Baltimore Beltway as the major route for traffic coming in from Pittsburgh or other points west. It does not reach the city limits.

By Bus

Baltimore Travel Plaza
6523 O'Donnell Street
(410) 633-6389
www.greyhound.com
Lots of free parking and bright, clean, inviting facilities are the lure of the Baltimore Travel Plaza, conveniently located off I-895 and I-95 in Northeast Baltimore. If you are planning to take a Trailways or Peter Pan bus heading to New York City, Atlantic City, or a variety of other locations up and down the East Coast and beyond, then this is the place to catch it in the Baltimore area.

Like the Greyhound terminal on Haines Street near Baltimore's Inner Harbor, the Baltimore Travel Plaza also offers access to Greyhound buses, traveling to New York City more than 10 times a day and to points farther north, south, and west. In addition, a number of tour buses heading to points all over the mid–Atlantic, especially Atlantic City, Pennsylvania Dutch Country, and western Maryland, also offer pickups and drop-offs at the Travel Plaza, which also sports more than 100 hotel rooms for travelers looking for a night's rest.

The plaza offers clean and open counters for purchasing tickets, plenty of wood tables and chairs for waiting for the bus, and a variety of time-killing ideas. Sbarro's, a pizza place; KFC; the Tradewinds Restaurant, a moderately priced buffet and sit-down restaurant; and Buckhorn's, a steak and potato and so much more restaurant across the street, provide the eats. Vending machines and a small shop feature magazines, newspapers, snacks, and touristy wares, such as T-shirts, Orioles caps, and Maryland mugs. There is also an array of video games for idling moments waiting for the loudspeaker's call for your bus.

It's about a 15-minute taxicab ride from the Travel Plaza to the Inner Harbor area. The plaza is also accessible by city bus.

Greyhound Lines
2110 Haines Street
(410) 752-1393
www.greyhound.com
From an out-of-the-way terminal off I-295, the Greyhound bus station still provides thousands of travelers with valuable and reliable service to myriad points at all hours of the day. Ocean City, Atlantic City, New York City, Atlanta, Miami, Boston, Indianapolis, and Chicago are all served from this station.

Tickets purchased two weeks or more in advance can be reserved with a credit card; tickets purchased within two weeks of departure must be obtained from the ticket window, but advance purchases are not required because Greyhound does not work on a reservation system.

By Train

Amtrak
Penn Station, 1525 North Charles Street
(410) 291-4261, (800) USA-RAIL
www.amtrak.com
Penn Station is a marvel, with beautiful light-wood benches with high backs waiting for weary travelers to sit on for a minute or a day. A major terminal between New York and Washington, Penn Station attracts a great many business travelers heading to those

cities on the Metroliner. Travelers can also take advantage of the Acela Express, Amtrak's high-speed train that travels between Boston and Washington, D.C. The station also draws people looking to head farther north, and south to Florida. Located conveniently on Charles Street and just off I-83 (the Jones Falls Expressway), the station's biggest challenge used to be parking for those picking up or dropping off passengers. However, a new parking garage has answered many a train traveler's prayers. During normal business hours, you can find a store selling juices, candy, and magazines, and it has a small sandwich counter.

Keep in mind, Amtrak also has a station at the airport, about 11 miles south of Baltimore. It offers free bus transfers to the airport terminal. It's just a small station but is open from about 5:00 a.m. to 10:00 p.m., with a ticketing office, a snack stand open during the usual business hours, restrooms, and an uncomfortable waiting area. There's plenty of parking, too. The MARC train stops here, too.

By Ship

Baltimore has become a popular starting place for cruises, so why not combine a visit to Hamilton, Bermuda, with a stop at Charm City? In 2007, 29 cruises, mostly Royal Caribbean, set sail from Baltimore's Locust Point terminal, built in 2006. Although there's no direct link to the Downtown area from the port, taxis are usually available to whisk passengers to hotels and attractions. Quite a few hotels offer Cruise Maryland packages. Check out the port's Web site at www.marylandports.com for all the details. For information about the port, call (866) 427-8963. For cruise information contact Royal Caribbean at (800) 398-9819 or see www.rccl.com.

By Water

Eastern Baltimore County's rivers and the Inner Harbor provide good boat access to the

Selected Baltimore Firsts

Edward Warren, reported to have been only 13 years old at the time, made the first American hot-air balloon ascension in 1784.

Even in 1806, our proximity to Washington had its benefits! It was in that year that the first federally financed road opened in Baltimore. Of course, that proximity and that road didn't seem so great when the British tried to land during the War of 1812!

The first horse-drawn streetcar line opened in Fells Point in 1859.

Not to be outdone, even by ourselves, the Baltimore Union Passenger Railway Company, the first commercial electric streetcar line in the Western Hemisphere, began service in Baltimore in 1885.

Baltimore ushered in the modern era when the first drive-in gas station opened for business in 1917. Baltimore got a treat in 1920 when Hubert Latham made the first nonstop airplane flight over a city. He circled Baltimore's skyline 22 times.

The first coal-burning, steam locomotive, the Tom Thumb—a stagecoach on wheels—was built here in 1830 by B&O as well as the first electric locomotive, built in 1894. The elevated electric railway to run it on was erected in 1893.

The first passenger train and the first commercial carrier left from Baltimore in 1830 and 1827, respectively.

The first train to operate at 30 miles per hour got on the B&O tracks in 1830.

The first train to have a center aisle boarded passengers in 1831, and the first air-conditioned train in the world, B&O's Columbian, left Baltimore in 1931.

We also lay claim to the first city railroad station, the President Street Station, which opened in 1853.

—*Excerpted from* Baltimore—America's City of Firsts, *a pamphlet published by Baltimore Bicentennial Celebration, Inc.*

area, and a number of local marinas offer daily, weekly, and monthly mooring rates. See the On the Water chapter for more information.

GETTING AROUND

By Car

Compared with other major East Coast cities, Baltimore's road system is in pretty good shape. Unlike its neighbor to the south, Washington, where roads seem to defy any logic, Baltimore's highway and road system is pretty easy to understand, and (believe it or not) readily available maps give fairly good descriptions of what you might encounter. One of the few challenges facing motorists is finding roads that go in the direction you want to travel; many streets run one way through the city, leaving visitors and the uninitiated perplexed.

Here's a simple approach to the one-way system: If the road you want to be on is going the opposite direction, head one street farther, make either a right or left turn (depending on the location of the road you're seeking), then another right or left as soon as possible. Before long you should see the road you want. It's that easy. As you get farther from downtown, the roads become less complicated. Unlike some East Coast locales, Baltimore's roads are well marked in most cases. Major highways and interstates heading in all directions are clearly posted with highway signs.

Remember, many of the people in our area have encountered the same confusion you might be running into. Therefore, don't be afraid to ask for directions or help. We tend to be friendly when approached the right way. When asking for directions, try to be (no pun intended) direct: Ask how to get from point A to point B. As in most big cities, rush hours and lunch hours can make traffic devilish, to say the least. When you want to be somewhere, the best route often varies with the time of day and the weather conditions.

Major north-south roadways include Belair Road, Harford Road, and Charles Street, and east-west roadways include Northern Parkway, North Avenue, and Frederick Road. Watch out for Hillen Road, which seems to pop up everywhere you look. It, along with many of the city's less traveled roads, come and go, as if someone erased a few blocks then drew it back in. It's confusing, but it gives you a feeling of pride when you overcome it.

Most people who drive in the Baltimore area follow the rules. We use our directional signals, we try to follow speed limits, and we appreciate people who don't indicate their lack of preparation, planning, or understanding of our roads. In other words, ask, ask, ask before you get lost, lost, lost.

Ice, sleet, and snow, any and all of which can occur on winter nights, can be a problem on Baltimore roadways. Even though schools and businesses close at the first sign of snow, those of us who have to or want to drive in inclement weather can often make a mess of things. This isn't the territory where chains are needed, but you do need common sense.

Part of the problem is that we don't often get enough snow for plowing; instead, local crews apply lots of sand and salt. It melts the snow and ice into a brown slush that often refreezes the following evening if temperatures again drop below freezing. Compounding matters is that many motorists don't respect the cardinal rule for driving in winter weather: Moving slow is fine in the snow. On the bright side, we can be grateful that these days usually

i During weekdays, WBAL 1090 AM has traffic reports at 11-minute intervals from 6:11 through 9:00 a.m. and from 3:44 to 6:00 p.m. Major traffic tie-ups are also reported during the station's hourly news reports.

only come a couple of times a month, normally from December to March, and most major highways are well cared for, even in the worst weather. Mass transit, which seems to operate remarkably well in these conditions, can be a safe, efficient, and prudent option. Remember, forewarned is forearmed.

RULES OF THE ROAD

There are several driving rules you need to observe in the state of Maryland.

• Seat belts are mandatory for all front-seat passengers. Police officers will pull over motorists and issue tickets to those who violate the law. Children younger than age four or weighing less than 40 pounds must be kept in a child safety seat.

• Right turns are permitted when the traffic light is red, except where posted otherwise. Left turns on red lights, when going from one one-way road to another one-way road, are also allowed, except where signs say "All Turns Prohibited" or "No Turn On Red."

• Speed limits are strictly enforced, using all means available, including VASCAR radar (which usually is not picked up by radar detectors), speed guns, and aerial surveillance. On highways, state troopers, operating olive-and-brown cars or in unmarked sedans, SUVs, minivans, or even red Ford Mustangs, make their fair share of speeding arrests, especially

i If you're listening to a traffic report in Baltimore, the "JFX" is the Jones Falls Expressway (or I-83); the Harbor Tunnel Thruway is on I-895; and the Fort McHenry Tunnel is on I-95. The "MLK" is Martin Luther King Jr. Boulevard (I-395), and the Northwest Expressway is I-795.

Baltimore's Horsepower

Mounted police are a magnificent sight; particularly when they are in pursuit. The larger than average horses with helmeted officers astride thunder through the city. Through lines of stalled cars, down narrow alleys or sidewalks, their on-the-hoof raw power is, to say the least, awe inspiring.

Their value in a pursuit is not only in the terror they can engender when riding full-tilt but also in their versatility. Rubber horseshoes allow for a comfortable run on city streets, but the horses can leave the streets if necessary to gallop across and through places where motorized vehicles can't go.

Baltimore's mounted police unit was formed in 1888, making it the oldest in the United States. The unit became necessary when Baltimore annexed adjacent county lands, almost doubling its size. Baltimore's police force up until then had been foot patrolmen, but these patrols simply could not cover the vast, new areas.

Permanent stables for the horses were built in 1899 at what is now the Northern District Police Station at 3858 Kesick Road in Hampden; the original stables and courtyard take up the entire block behind the cabled Victorian brick building.

The horses were moved from that location in 1923 and are currently housed at 411 North Holliday Street, under the Jones Falls Expressway. Call the barn at (410) 396-2343 to arrange a tour. There is no charge though a group, rather than a single person, is preferred.

The officers of the Mounted Police Unit volunteer for this duty and come from all areas of the city's police department. They must have at least three years of patrol experience before they can be considered. Once trained for the unit, each officer becomes responsible for his assigned mount, who is actually considered a fellow officer, right down to being assigned a badge number. The horses work an eight-hour day and get a 30-minute lunch break and a 15-minute break every hour.

In 1888 there were only 10 officers in the unit. Since then, the mounted police unit has grown or diminished over the years, depending on the city's needs and who's in control of overseeing them. In the 1990s the unit consisted of 23 men and horses. Their arrest unit record was one of the police department's highest. Today the unit has four officers, a supervisor, and six horses. Their duties take them all over the city. One day they may be patrolling the Inner Harbor and the next day be in a neighborhood wracked by drug trafficking. Although tourists may see the proud steeds pawing the ground as the police/rider bends over to answer a question, the mounted police remain a vital part of the Baltimore police department. They are still going after the bad guys— sometimes at a full gallop.

on holiday weekends and at busy travel times. Radar detectors are allowed.

The maximum speed limit in Maryland is 65 mph, but this speed is only allowed on major highways leading away from urban areas. Watch for speed limit signs. In rural areas where speed limits are not posted, motorists can travel at 50 mph; in urban areas, the unposted speed limit is 30 mph.

• Motorists must stop for all school buses with their stop signs out or flashing red lights and can be ticketed for violating the law based on the observation of the bus driver.

By Taxi

Baltimore boasts an array of options for people without wheels. For $1.80, plus $2.00 a mile, you can get just about anywhere with local cabbies who speak the language, know their way around, and are willing to share some personality and sightseeing suggestions with you. Many cab companies charge an extra dollar for radio-dispatched calls. If you find yourself needing to get somewhere in the Downtown area, it's probably more cost-effective and more efficient simply to hail a cab. Most major hotels as well as shopping areas and the train station have cabbies waiting nearby.

The following companies provide cab service.

Baltimore City

Arrow Cab, (410) 358-9697
Diamond Cab, (410) 947-3333
Raven Cab, (410) 945-2212
Royal Cab, (410) 327-0330
Yellow Cab, (410) 727-6237

Baltimore County

Arrow Cab, (410) 338-0000

Atwater Cab (based in White Marsh)
(410) 682-2100

County Cab,
(410) 284-3330, (410) 484-4111

Jimmy's Cab (based in Towson)
(410) 296-7200

Valley Cab (based in Pikesville)
(410) 486-4000

Baltimore–Washington International Thurgood Marshall Airport/Anne Arundel County

Airline Limousines and Sedan Services
(410) 768-4444

The Airport Shuttle
(410) 381-2772
www.theairportshuttle.com

Associated Cabs (Glen Burnie)
(410) 766-1234

BWI Airport Taxi
(410) 859-1103

Hotel Shuttles

Most of Baltimore's major hotels operate shuttle buses to take passengers to the airport, train station, bus station, and other points of interest. It's best to check in advance about whether the place where you are staying provides this free or discounted service.

By Bus

Mass Transit Administration Buses
(410) 539-5000, (866) RIDE-MTA
www.mtamaryland.com
The MTA operates 50 local and express bus lines throughout the Baltimore area. Exact fare is required. Practically all parts of Baltimore and most stretches of Baltimore County, Anne Arundel County, and Howard County are accessible by bus.

For many Baltimoreans, the bus is their transportation to work, to play, to sports events, to the theater, to just about everything. Most north-south and east-west roads into and out of the city are serviced by at least one bus line. If you're confused by the schedule, the routes, or some other aspect of travel on the white and blue buses, ask the first bus ℹ️ Planning to use public transportation often during a certain day or month? An all-day pass allowing unlimited travel on the buses, Light Rail, and Metro subway is $3.50. They're available at any stop. Buy a Transit Link Card (TLC) by adding $50 to your MARC monthly pass and get a month of unlimited travel on the MARC, Baltimore Metro, buses, and Light Rail as well as Washington's subway system. That's a lot of miles for your money.

driver who stops or call the previously listed number.

Customers pay when they board the bus, and exact change is mandatory. You're going to be putting your money into a machine that gobbles up extra change without a thought for returning the extra coins. Plan ahead. Really. Fares are $1.60 for a one-way pass or $3.50 for an all-day pass. A weekly pass costs $16.50.

Keep your eye out for your stop and press the yellow strip running above the windows of the bus to notify the operator of your stop. Drivers don't call out stops unless you request it, so either ask someone to remind you when your stop is coming or stay alert. Smoking, eating, drinking, and playing radios without earphones are all prohibited on MTA buses.

Bus routes are marked with small signs (white with blue trim) on the right side of roadways. Route numbers are on the signs. Schedules are available at most hotels, tourist attractions, and visitor centers. The MTA will also mail one to you. They are on the MTA Web site, too.

By Rail

It's only fitting that the city that was home to the first railroad places a major emphasis on rail travel. In the last decade, Baltimore's old rails have been put to significant use by the area's growing Light Rail and MARC (Maryland Rail Commuter) systems. Baltimore also is a stopping point for Amtrak trains.

MARC
(800) 325-RAIL
A total of 81 Maryland Rail Commuter trains operate on three lines running throughout the Baltimore–Washington corridor, eight Maryland counties, and northeastern West Virginia. In all, MARC serves some 25,000 commuters Monday through Friday.

For Baltimore, the Camden Line runs between Baltimore and Washington's Union Station (a major hub for transportation in all directions). The Camden Line stops near the Camden Station at Oriole Park at Camden Yards. In all, there are nine stops between Baltimore and Washington, D.C.

MARC's Penn Line starts about 50 miles north of the Inner Harbor in Perryville, off I-95 near the Susquehanna River in Cecil County, and continues south to Penn Station and on to Washington. Ten stops are along the way.

No matter which line you use, ample free parking is available at the stops, making it an affordable way to reach the city. Ride passes are available at the stops; prices vary depending on your point of origin and destination. A one-way fare from Penn Station in Baltimore to BWI Airport is $4, while the one-way fee to go from Camden Station to Washington's Union Station is $7. Unlimited weekly tickets and unlimited monthly tickets are available.

Light Rail Line
(410) 539-5000, (866) RIDE-MTA, ext. 2
Baltimore's Light Rail Line operates from Hunt Valley, about 25 miles from the Inner Harbor, through the Downtown area near Oriole Park at Camden Yards and on to Cromwell Station/ Glen Burnie, a small community about 10 miles south of the Inner Harbor in Anne Arundel County. This system is 30 miles long and serves 32 stops between Hunt Valley and Penn Station to the north. In late 1997, Light Rail service to BWI was added, but the time it takes to get from Timonium to the airport, about 90 minutes, is somewhat disconcerting given that by car it takes about 30 minutes to make the 25-mile trip. A stop at Penn Station,

where passengers can pick up Amtrak service, was also opened, making the Light Rail much more useful for out-of-town visitors. The line runs about every 17 minutes during normal hours and every 8 minutes during rush hour.

Hours of operation are from 6:00 a.m. to 11:00 p.m. Monday through Saturday, and 11:00 a.m. to 7:00 p.m. Saturday. The line also operates special service for baseball and football games (see the Spectator Sports chapter). Tickets cost $1.60 for one-way trips. If you are planning on riding more than twice a day or need to connect with their other MTA services, buy a day pass for $3.50. It includes unlimited travel that day on Light Rail, regular bus, or Metro Subway. Tickets can be obtained from machines at all stops. Tickets must be purchased before boarding the trains.

Metro Subway
(410) 539-5000, (866) RIDE-MTA, ext. 2
Baltimore's Metro provides service between Johns Hopkins Medical Campus to the east and Owings Mills in southwestern Baltimore County. The 15.5-mile subway system has 14 stations scattered east-to-west across the city. It takes about 25 minutes to reach the Downtown area from Owings Mills. Parking at most stops is free, and the parking at Owings Mills is close to a large mall, Owings Mills Town Center, that has more than 100 stores (see the Shopping chapter). If you want to head to the city for a day of sightseeing, the subway from Owings Mills is a fun, clean, and affordable way to go. It's also a great way to get to Johns Hopkins Hospital, which can be a tough place to find parking.

Ride passes are available (exact change only) at machines at each stop, and the cost is $1.60 for a one-way fare, or $3.50 for an all-day pass. Subway cars run about every 8 minutes during rush hour, every 10 minutes during the day, and every 15 minutes in the evening and on Saturday. The subway operates from 5:00 a.m. to 12:30 a.m. Monday through Friday and from 6:00 a.m. to 12:30 a.m. on Saturday. No service is available on

MARC trains now provide Quiet Cars for commuters in which cell phones, laptops, radios, and children are not allowed.

Sunday. Old Court and State Center Stations close at 8:00 p.m. daily. Bicyclists are welcome to bring bikes except when trains are crowded.

By Water
Seeing Baltimore's harbor area from the water provides insights into its industries and history. Several companies provide tourists with fun and entertaining ways to go from place to place by water; however, availability depends on the season, the weather, and whether tourist groups have made prior reservations. All services depart from the Inner Harbor. (See the On the Water chapter for more information about traveling Baltimore's waterways.)

Harbor Cruises
(410) 727-3113
www.harborcruises.com
The *Bay Lady, Lady Baltimore,* and *Prince Charming* offer a variety of cruises from the Inner Harbor either around the harbor or down to Annapolis (the trip under the Bay Bridges is an added bonus). There are lunch and brunch cruises, dinner buffet cruises, crab feast cruises, and a special fireworks cruise on the Fourth of July (a pretty cool way to see Baltimore's fireworks display). Harbor tours last an hour and cost $15 for adults and $10 for children age 3 to 10 and for seniors. Brunch tours cost $50 for adults and seniors and $26 for children. Dinner buffets and crab feasts cost about $70 for adults and and seniors and $35 for children. Reservations are required.

Harbor Sightseeing Shuttle
If you've got a couple of hours to kill, the shuttle offers a great view of the city as well as access to shopping and historical sites and cultural spots in Canton and Fells Point. You'll get the same water view of Fort McHenry that

the British and Francis Scott Key had. Don't forget that an evening trip on the shuttle in summer is enchanting and romantic—a great change of pace that provides a terrific view of the city's skyline.

Ed Kane's Water Taxi
(410) 563-3901
www.thewatertaxi.com
This service visits 12 stops in the Inner Harbor, Fells Point, Canton, and Fort McHenry. An all-day ticket providing unlimited use costs $8 for adults and $4 for children age 10 and younger. The pontoon boats have covers and bench seating.

In addition, the water taxi offers a "Letter of Marque," which combines the all-day ticket with discounts at restaurants and attractions near the water taxi stops. If you think commuting by water taxi would be fun, go ahead and buy an annual "frequent floater" pass for $80 and ride all the time.

HISTORY

Here in Baltimore, we like to think of ourselves as being on the Chesapeake Bay, but, in truth, we live on the Patapsco River. We're probably better off for it because the Patapsco provides us with many benefits.

Although it is removed from the Atlantic Ocean by about 150 miles, the Patapsco River is a tidal river. And even though the ebb and flow of the ocean can be seen in the Inner Harbor, the 5 miles of river between Baltimore and the bay insulate us from most of the major wave cycles and storms that move up the East Coast. The river has also discouraged attacks by sea.

In addition to protection, the Patapsco provides a connection. It ties Baltimore to trade in Europe, South America, and most everywhere else. That connection served as a lifeline and economic dynamo for the city as it grew from a settlement to a town to a city and emerged as an industrial powerhouse helping meet the needs of a growing nation.

DISCOVERING "FROTH"

Captain John Smith probably had only a small sense of the bounty he discovered in 1608 while exploring the Chesapeake Bay. He described in his journal the area he had found: "Thirtie leagues Northward is a river not inhabited, yet navigable." The river, one of four major waterways that flow into the Chesapeake Bay, was given its Indian name, Patapsco, which many believe meant "backwater" or "tidewater covered with froth." (More than three centuries later, a froth of a different kind, that produced by National Bohemian beer, "Natty Bo" to locals, would garner the attention of beer drinkers.)

What Smith found was vast, relatively flat, open land that the Susquehannock tribe had used for hunting. The Susquehannocks would venture down from northern Maryland on what would a century later become Charles Street in Baltimore. As impossible as it seems now, bears were abundant then. Over time, the bear proved to be less of an opponent to the Susquehannocks than smallpox and tuberculosis, new diseases brought to America by early colonists at the end of the seventeenth century. By 1700 only a few hundred surviving Indians lived in any part of Maryland.

DAVID (NOT DAVY) JONES SETTLES

In 1632 George Calvert, an advisor to King James I, was granted a charter to what is now the state of Maryland. Though he did not live to see his colony founded, his son Cecilius sent his son Leonard on the *Ark* and the *Dove* in November 1633 to establish Maryland. They arrived in their new capital, St. Mary's City, on March 25, 1634, to found a colony notable for its progressive policy of liberty of conscience and its decision not to have an established religion. The state, though founded by Catholics, became home to Protestants and Quakers as well. This tolerant stance—although it took a beating throughout the state's early years—became law when the Toleration Act was passed in 1649. By then colonists had sailed north on the Chesapeake Bay to settle what would soon become Maryland's state capital, Annapolis.

In 1659, the first settlers of the Baltimore region established Baltimore County. The county provided settlers with what they and their ancestors had come from England for—economic opportunity in a place where they could freely practice their chosen religion. Settlers soon began taking sites along the water. In the mid-1600s, they settled near where Fort

McHenry now stands and along Harford Road in the northeastern section of Baltimore, near Harford Run.

In 1661 one of Baltimore's first settlers, David Jones, moved onto 380 acres along a stream that would later be named Jones Falls in his honor. Today the Jones Falls Expressway, a six-lane highway running parallel to (and sometimes over) that stream, also refers to Jones, when it is not being called by its nickname, "the JFX."

WATER AND WHEELS

Activity on and around the waterfront began to grow. One of the first settlements, Whetstone Point, where Fort McHenry now stands, was named a port of entry by act of legislature in 1706. Five years later, the first mill for the area was built along the Jones Falls by Jonathan Hanson.

Transportation was primarily by water, though some roads had been cut in the woods. In 1704 a new law required trees to be cut down so the main road could be widened to 20 feet and, probably more important, marked. Since it was long before travel guides like this one, slash marks charted the course. There was one vertical slash on trees beside the road leading to the church; there were three horizontal lines (one higher than two others close together) on roads heading to the county courthouse.

Soon settlers began making iron for England and growing wheat for the British colonies in the West Indies. The Jones Falls and two other rivers, Herring Run and Gwynns Falls, provided the water power for

the iron furnaces and the mills that turned wheat into flour.

LOTS FOR SALE

With an economy in place, workers needed housing. In 1729, 60 acres of land in what is now Downtown Baltimore were approved for division into one-acre lots. Buyers would have to pay the owners, Daniel and Charles Carroll, either 40 shillings an acre or tobacco at the rate of one penny per pound. Philip Jones, a county surveyor, laid out the land. Three roadways, Calvert, Forest (now Charles), and Long (later Market and now Baltimore) Streets, were created. Nine narrow alleys ran between the three streets, and the lots were numbered and divided.

Land buyers agreed to either build a house of at least 400 square feet within 18 months or forfeit the land. The first 18 buyers, all of whom made purchases on the first day the land was available, bought land close to the Patapsco; Charles Carroll selected a lot at the corner of Calvert Street and the harbor basin on January 14, 1730. The surveyor Philip Jones, who selected second, picked land at the foot of Charles Street near the waterfront.

The growing port on the Patapsco became the outlet for sending wheat from fields in western Maryland and Pennsylvania to England and the Caribbean islands. But economic success bred frustration. Merchants chafed at British taxes and commercial policies. As intolerance for British interference continued to grow, Baltimore found its place in the political world of the colonies.

After representatives of the 13 colonies signed the Declaration of Independence in Philadelphia on July 4, 1776, Baltimore soon became a temporary national capital. Leaders feared a possible attack by British troops, so they fled from Philadelphia to Baltimore, where they convened in a newly built tavern named Congress Hall. For 68 days, from December 20, 1776, through February 27, 1777, the delegates handled big and small matters of state in Congress Hall. Delegates

i Fort McHenry, the five bastioned, pentagonal shaped fort, takes its name from Dr. James McHenry (1753–1816), who served as a medical officer with Gen. George Washington during the Revolutionary War. He later served on the Continental Congress and as secretary of war for presidents Washington and Adams between 1796 and 1801.

granted George Washington powers to pursue war, and they ordered that pigs and geese stay off Baltimore's unpaved streets.

HOME FOR PESKY PRIVATEERS

Baltimore's economy boomed during the Revolutionary War. Shipyards in Fells Point, named after the wharf's creator, William Fell, produced warships. Privateers from Baltimore, eager to make a buck by sinking British ships or seizing their assets, filled the waters of the Patapsco River and Chesapeake Bay. Between 1776 and the end of the Revolution, about 250 private ship owners armed themselves and were granted government commissions (called "letters of marque and reprisal") that empowered them to seize enemy vessels—and their assets—on planned attacks or in pursuit of trade. Everyone tied to these seizing ships—the sailors, owners, and financial backers—took their share of the booty from these missions.

During and after the war, Baltimore continued to be a commercial hotspot, benefiting greatly from the on-again, off-again trade wars between England and France. Local leaders decided to pursue status as a city. The commissioner who had been appointed to rule Baltimore County was picked in Annapolis, and merchants and businessmen wanted greater control of their own destinies.

Eventually, it happened. On December 31, 1796, the city of Baltimore was born. As the nineteenth century began, Baltimore's population swelled. Doubling by 1810 to 27,000 people, Baltimore passed Boston to become America's third-largest city, trailing only Philadelphia and New York.

"A NEST OF PIRATES"

In 1812 Baltimore again would find itself in the middle of a war with England, and again it would prove to be a financial boon. President James Madison's declaration of war on Great Britain was a problem for the U.S. fleet, which

numbered 17 ships. Privateers, whose success in the Revolutionary War had provided good training and income more than 30 years earlier, helped increase the U.S. fleet's numbers. Still, at about 1,000 ships, the British fleet significantly outnumbered America's. During the war, the 126 privateers led the water attack, either seizing or sinking more than 550 British ships. Frustrated by this successful tactic, the British war leaders called Baltimore "a nest of pirates" and "the great depository of the hostile spirit of the United States against England."

As successful as the privateers were, British troops, led by Admiral Sir George Cockburn, ruled the Chesapeake Bay in the summer of 1814. By the dog days of August, British forces sailed up the Patuxent River on their way to Washington. On August 24, 1814, Baltimoreans could see the smoke on the horizon as the British burned Washington's Capitol, the White House, and other public buildings 40 miles away. In Baltimore residents took the smoke as a signal that they would be next. Under the leadership of Mayor General Samuel Smith, a veteran of the Revolution and a popular politician, the city quickly prepared for an attack.

With Smith's guidance, the newly created militia fortified Fort McHenry, a strategic location guarding the city and its harbor from invasion up the Patapsco River. The 16,000 men, 90 percent of whom were untrained citizens, were ready for battle, though they had practically no realistic chance of winning. On September 12, about 4,700 British troops took the shore on the west side of North Point, a section of the Patapsco River about 8 miles southeast of the fort, as they prepared to take over the city. The Battle of North Point lasted for more than two hours, as the hometown militia held off the British by land. The next day the city shook as British troops bombarded Fort McHenry for many hours.

Francis Scott Key, a lawyer who grew up in Baltimore, watched the bombardment from 8 miles away, on the deck of a boat where truce negotiations were in progress. Fearing the

Important Dates in Maryland History

10,000 B.C.—First humans arrived by this date in the land that would become Maryland.

1498—John Cabot sailed along Eastern Shore off present-day Worcester County.

1608—Capt. John Smith explored Chesapeake Bay.

1620—Earliest appearance in Maryland of European objects in archaeological context.

1632—June 20, Maryland Charter granted to Cecilius Calvert, Second Lord Baltimore, by Charles I, King of Great Britain and Ireland. The colony was named Maryland for Queen Henrietta Maria (1609–1669), wife of Charles I (1600–1649).

1633—Nov. 22, English settlers on *Ark* and *Dove* set sail from Cowes, England, for Maryland.

1634–1644—Leonard Calvert, governor.

1659–1660—January 12. Baltimore County known to have been established by this date, when a writ was issued to county sheriff.

1663—Augustine Herrman, first naturalized citizen of Maryland.

1689–1690—Maryland Revolution of 1689. Protestant Associators overthrow proprietary officers.

1727—September, *Maryland Gazette*, first newspaper in the Chesapeake, published by William Parks at Annapolis (until 1734).

1729—Baltimore Town established by charter.

1744—June 30, Native American chiefs of the Six Nations relinquished by treaty all claims to land in colony. Assembly purchased last Indian land claims in Maryland.

1766—Sons of Liberty organized in Baltimore County.

1769—Maryland merchants adopted policy of nonimportation of British goods.

1772—March 28, Cornerstone laid for new State House in Annapolis.

1776—July 4, Declaration of Independence adopted in Philadelphia. Engrossed copy signed by Marylanders William Paca, Charles Carroll of Carrollton, Thomas Stone, and Samuel Chase.

1776—July 6, Maryland Convention declared independence from Great Britain.

1777—February 5, First General Assembly elected under State Constitution of 1776 met at Annapolis.

1777—March 21, Inauguration of Thomas Johnson, first governor elected by General Assembly.

1781—March 1, Maryland ratified the Articles of Confederation.

1784—December 30, St. John's College established at Annapolis. General Assembly designated it, with Washington College, as University of Maryland.

1787—September 17, U.S. Constitution signed by Marylanders Daniel Carroll, James McHenry, and Daniel of St. Thomas Jenifer, at Philadelphia.

1788—April 28, Maryland Convention ratified U.S. Constitution, making Maryland the seventh state to do so. Convention adjourned without recommending amendments.

1789—December 19, Maryland ratified federal Bill of Rights, first 10 amendments to U.S. Constitution.

1791—December 19, Maryland ceded land for federal District of Columbia.

1799—Construction began on Fort McHenry, Baltimore.

1814—September 12, British repelled by local militia at Battle of North Point.

1814—September 13, Bombardment of Fort McHenry inspired Francis Scott Key to write "The Star-Spangled Banner."

1827—February 28, Baltimore and Ohio Railroad chartered.

1829—Oblate Sisters of Providence opened school for black children, Baltimore.

1830—Baltimore & Ohio Railroad Station at Mount Clare, first in United States.

1832—In aftermath of Nat Turner rebellion in Virginia, Maryland laws enacted to restrict free blacks.

1837—May 17, *Baltimore Sun* began publication under Arunah S. Abell.

1838—Frederick Douglass escaped from slavery in Baltimore.

1845—Lloyd Street Synagogue constructed in Baltimore, first Maryland synagogue, a Robert Cary Long Jr. design.

1845—Frederick Douglass published narrative of his life in slavery.

1845—October 10, U.S. Naval Academy founded at Annapolis, when Department of the Navy established officers' training school at Fort Severn, Annapolis.

1849—Harriet Tubman escaped slavery in Dorchester County.

1859—October 16, John Brown launched raid from Maryland on federal arsenal in Harper's Ferry, West Virginia.

1861—April, James Ryder Randall wrote "Maryland, My Maryland."

1861—April 19, Sixth Massachusetts Union Regiment attacked by Baltimore mob.

1861—April 22, Federal troops occupied Annapolis.

1861—June 13, Congressional elections returned Unionist delegation.

1862—May 23, Marylanders opposed one another at Battle of Front Royal.

1862—September 17, Battle of Antietam (or Sharpsburg), 4,800 dead, 18,000 wounded.

1863—late June through early July, Lee's army passed through Washington County en route to Gettysburg and in retreat.

1864—November 1, Maryland slaves emancipated by State Constitution of 1864.

1865—Chesapeake Marine Railway and Dry Dock Company, first black-owned business in state, established by Isaac Myers.

1865—April, John Wilkes Booth assassinated President Lincoln, escaped through Prince George's and Charles Counties.

1870—Maryland Jockey Club sponsored racing at Pimlico track.

1872—General Assembly mandated separate but equal white and black schools.

1876—October 3, The Johns Hopkins University opened in Baltimore.

1885—Baltimore-Union Passenger Railway Company, first commercial electric street railway in country.

1887—Pennsylvania Steel (Maryland Steel, 1891) built blast furnace at Sparrows Point.

1888—October, Maryland flag of Calvert and Crossland colors flown at monument dedication ceremonies, Gettysburg.

1892—*The Afro-American* founded by John H. Murphy Sr.

1894—Baltimore Orioles won their first professional baseball championship.

1899—Building program began at Naval Academy, Ernest Flagg architect.

1904—Maryland Woman Suffrage Association led by Emma J. Maddox Funck.

1904—February 7–8, Baltimore fire, 70 blocks in heart of business district devastated.

1910—August 30, First statewide primary election in Maryland.

1913—Baltimore Chapter, National Association for the Advancement of Colored People (NAACP), formed, second oldest in country.

1914—Babe Ruth pitched for International League Orioles.

1916—February, Baltimore Symphony Orchestra organized under Gustav Strube.

1917—Aberdeen Proving Ground, first testing center of U.S. Army, established.

1920—November 2, Women voted for first time in Maryland.

1931—March 3, "The Star-Spangled Banner" adopted as national anthem.

1935—University of Maryland School of Law opened to blacks after NAACP lawyer Thurgood Marshall brought suit.

1941—April–September, Bethlehem-Fairfield Shipyard produced first Liberty Ship, *Patrick Henry*.

1941—December 7, USS *Maryland* among naval ships attacked at Pearl Harbor.

1944—Drs. Helen Taussig and Alfred Blalock of Johns Hopkins Hospital performed first heart surgery to save the lives of "blue babies," babies born with heart defects that deprive the blood of oxygen.

1946—First photograph of Earth from space is produced at Johns Hopkins Applied Physics Laboratory.

1950—June 24, Friendship International Airport, (now BWI), began operation.

1952—July 31, Chesapeake Bay Bridge opened.

1954—University of Maryland integrated, first state university below Mason-Dixon Line to do so.

1954—First black elected to House of Delegates, from Baltimore.

1954—May, Thurgood Marshall and NAACP won Brown v. Board decision.

1962—First phase of the Baltimore Beltway opened.

1967—Baltimore's Thurgood Marshall was named the first African American to serve on the United States Supreme Court.

1968—Riots followed the assassination of Martin Luther King.

1970—Colts won third Super Bowl.

1977—The 28-story World Trade Center, designed by renowned architect I.M. Pei, opened on the Inner Harbor and is the world's tallest pentagonal building.

1982—Cal Ripken's Oriole career began.

1983—Orioles won third World Series.

1984—Robert Irsay moved Colts to Indianapolis in the middle of the night.

1987—Dr. Ben Carson, director of pediatric neurosurgery at Johns Hopkins Medical Institutions in Baltimore, led a medical team that separated West German conjoined twins.

1992—Oriole Park at Camden Yards opens.

1996—Former Cleveland Browns became Baltimore Ravens.

2001—Ravens won the Super Bowl.

2007—Sheila Dixon became Baltimore's first woman mayor.

worst, with dawn emerging through fog and rain, Key trained a small spyglass on the fort and saw the tattered, 30-foot-by-42-foot American flag. The emotion of the moment stirred him to write a poem, "The Star-Spangled Banner," on the back of a sheet of letter paper. This original document is now housed at the Maryland Historical Society. (See the Attractions chapter for more information on the Maryland Historical Society.) It was Key's brother-in-law who suggested it be set to music. It was played first in Baltimore. The song later became the national anthem, but at the time served as a reminder of the militia's unlikely success in defeating a far superior British force. Baltimore's successful defense,

Fort McHenry. BALTIMORE AREA CONVENTION AND VISITORS ASSOCIATION

coupled with British losses in battles in upstate New York, helped to force the British to accept the Treaty of Ghent, signed on Christmas Eve in 1814.

BUILDING THE B&O

With another war behind them, Baltimore's leaders set out to make the city every bit as historical and cultural as the European cities of their ancestry. Some of the results of this effort remain today. Among them are the Roman Catholic Basilica of the Assumption on Cathedral Street, the first cathedral of American Catholicism; and the Battle Monument. The city also erected the first monument to honor George Washington, known—simply enough— as the Washington Monument. Baltimore soon became known as "Monument City."

In the late 1820s, word of construction of the Chesapeake & Ohio Canal—the first of its kind—running through Georgetown, south of Washington, D.C., challenged Baltimoreans. Fearing a devastating effect on commerce, Baltimorean Charles Carroll, grandson of the

Charles Carroll who obtained the 60 acres of land in Baltimore in 1729 and who at age 91 was the last surviving signer of the Declaration of Independence, began building the Baltimore & Ohio (B&O) Railroad. In 1853 the railroad finally reached its goal: the Ohio River at Wheeling, West Virginia. Besides speeding the movement of goods to the port in Baltimore for shipping, the railroad was responsible for bringing thousands of immigrants to the city, where they hoped to reestablish communities for their ethnic groups in a historically tolerant area. The rapidly growing area afforded them the opportunity to work on railroad and construction projects so they could earn a living. Some of the B&O railroad's tracks are still visible through the pavement in places on Key Highway and other sections of the city, although efforts lately have been made to pave over them for good.

Driven by economic hardships and political upheaval, immigrants streamed to the United States in increasing numbers in the 1830s, '40s, and '50s, and Baltimore received a large number of them, mostly German and Irish.

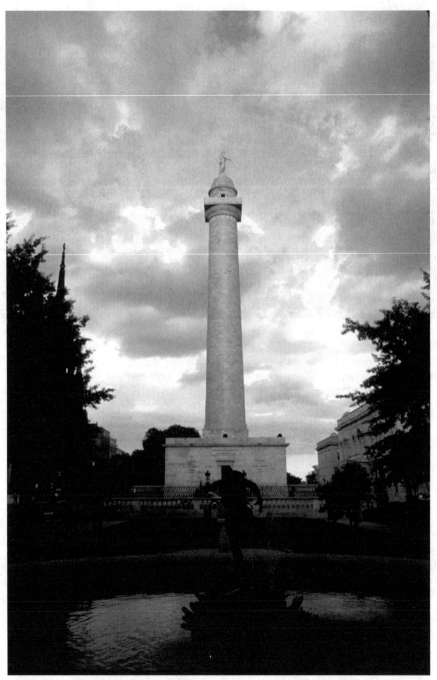

The Washington Monument houses a museum on its first floor. BALTIMORE AREA CONVENTION AND VISITORS ASSOCIATION

NORTH VS. SOUTH

With its location just south of the Mason-Dixon Line, the surveyed line between Pennsylvania and Maryland and the line separating North from South, Baltimore would find itself in a difficult position as the rumblings of Civil War became a reality. The city's commercial ties were increasingly to the North—ties that could significantly affect its commerce; its emotional ties were to the South, where many relatives of Baltimore and Maryland residents had moved to seek greater prosperity on land that was more open. Slavery had been part of Maryland's agricultural history, especially with its major cash crop—tobacco. Opposition to slavery grew as more merchants became successful in endeavors not requiring slaves for labor. By 1860 Baltimore, the city, would be home to more freed blacks than any other city in the state; of the 84,000 freed slaves, more than 25,000 stayed in Baltimore.

Despite efforts to ensure balance, in early 1861 Baltimore would again be the focus of a war. In fact, the first bloodshed of the Civil War occurred in the city. When 1,200 members of the Sixth Massachusetts Infantry passed through the city on their way to Washington to answer Lincoln's call for troops on April 19, 1861, a large group of Southern sympathizers attacked them. After a hail of insults, cobblestones, and pistol shots, the infantry returned fire, creating a riot and ending the lives of four soldiers and 12 Baltimoreans. After the incident, James Ryder Randall, a Marylander living in Louisiana, wrote a poem, "My Maryland," describing his outrage at the "gore that fleck'd the streets of Baltimore" during the riots. Set to the German tune "O Christmas Tree," it soon became Maryland's state song.

On May 13, less than a month after the riots, federal troops occupied Federal Hill, aiming their weapons at Baltimore's downtown. Other federal troops bringing weapons, barricades, and fear soon followed, making Baltimore an occupied city. Troops on both sides of the war came from Baltimore, and monuments and other reminders of the war reflect that dual role for the city.

> Baltimore grew from near obscurity at the time of the Revolution to become America's third-largest city by 1850.

RANDOM ACTS OF KINDNESS

After the Civil War, long before the phrase "random acts of kindness" became popular, several successful Baltimore businessmen demonstrated a new, private type of philanthropy. George Peabody, who came to Baltimore from Massachusetts in 1814, amassed his first million during the next 20 years, then moved to London to further his fortune. He gave $1.5 million to the city to establish the Peabody Conservatory of Music and Library, built on Mount Vernon Place between 1866 and 1878.

Peabody's donation impressed Johns Hopkins, a friend who had earned his money first as a wholesale commodities dealer, then as a financier and an early investor in the B&O Railroad. In 1867 Hopkins gave most of his $7 million estate for the creation of a university and hospital bearing his name—a fitting gift for a man who never married and whose own formal education ended when he was 12 years old. (For more on Johns Hopkins University, see the Education chapter.)

Enoch Pratt, a merchant and banker who would become one of the nation's leading hardware dealers, donated $833,000 in city bonds toward construction of an enormous free library bearing his name. He sensed that the Peabody Library, though impressive, was not large enough for the growing city and its increasingly affluent population. In 1886 Enoch Pratt Free Library opened with its shelves stacked with 28,000 books. Today it holds one of the best collections of books, music, periodicals, and other printed materials in the country.

During this era the magnificent Victorian City Hall was built, topped with a giant cast-iron dome, visible today (as then) from miles away. The building, designed by George Frederick, did something practically unheard of today—it came in 10 percent under its $2.27 million budget.

i On the way to his inauguration in
Washington, Abraham Lincoln had
to be smuggled through Baltimore in the
middle of the night for fear of assassination attempts by Southern sympathizers.

Coinciding with the enhancement of
appearances was an incredible population
increase. More than 60,000 immigrants
arrived at Baltimore Harbor from the 1870s to
1900, creating new enclaves in the city. To the
east was a Polish enclave, and to the west
near the harbor sprouted up an Italian
enclave, appropriately named Little Italy. It
remains today as one of the best areas to go
for an authentic Italian meal. Jews from Russia
also found their way to Baltimore, where
established Jewish communities helped them
overcome the fear of persecution. Baltimore
became a true community of neighborhoods,
each having a distinctive style, flavor, and feel
that carries over through today. (See the Relocation chapter.)

THE GREAT FIRE OF 1904

Heading into a new century, nothing
appeared able to stop Baltimore's growth. But
disaster loomed. Just before 11:00 a.m. on
Sunday, February 7, 1904, an automatic alarm
signaled fire at a six-story brick building containing dry goods at Hopkins Place and German (now Redwood) Street. Soon, other
alarms were howling, flames were billowing,
and strong winds in the cold, blustery day
were carrying flames to the northwest. The
fire quickly spread, and those same winds
challenged firefighters trying desperately to
extinguish the blaze.

The fire was so intense that dynamite was
used to block its spread. People in Washington
could see the fire's glow on the horizon. Contained more than 30 hours after it started, the
fire caused an estimated $150 million in dam-
age but, amazingly, no deaths. More than 70
blocks of prime Downtown space was
destroyed, and 15,000 buildings and 2,500
businesses were ruined. The clothes manufac-

turing district, an area containing wharves
from Light Street to the Jones Falls and 20
banks, was left in ruins.

People in the city quickly set about
rebuilding, and eight years after the fire, Baltimore played host to the contentious Democratic National Convention of 1912. It was held at
the Fifth Regiment Armory. After 46 ballots,
future President Woodrow Wilson, who
received his Ph.D. from Johns Hopkins University, prevailed. His selection by the Democrats
would be confirmed in the November election.

YET ANOTHER WAR

A few years later, the city would again play a
crucial role in a war. Protected from the open
seas, Baltimore provided a safe harbor, impen-
etrable by the feared enemy submarines that
lurked out in the Atlantic Ocean. It also provided a critical link to rail lines heading west
and water access to Europe.

When the United States entered World War
I in 1917, many Baltimoreans enlisted in the
Navy, while others were enlisted in 24-hour-a-
day operations to manufacture military uniforms, a task the city had performed effectively
during the Spanish-American War. By the end
of World War I, more than 55,000 Baltimoreans
had enlisted to help with the war effort.

By the time peace came in 1918, Baltimore had undergone a major transformation
into an industrial center. Leaders also had
seen the need for the city to become larger—
in 1918 they annexed 62 square miles of
largely undeveloped land, some in Anne Arundel County and Baltimore County. The city
had grown to 92 square miles. The new suburbs would see new homes popping up everywhere in the 1920s. More than 6,000 homes a
year were being built, doubling the previous
record. To the north of established row house
communities in Mount Vernon Place and
Bolton Hill would come the new developments of Guilford, Homeland, Roland Park,
and Peabody Heights (now Charles Village).
Farther north, into Baltimore County, came
the estates of Greenspring, Worthington, and

Dulaney Valleys, areas that, today as then, remain as residential areas.

SWEET TIMES

Fueling the economy was new business. American Sugar Company built a modern refinery in Baltimore County along the Patapsco River, opposite what would become the Inner Harbor, during the second decade of the century. The site remains today, although the company's name, emblazoned in large neon letters, is now Domino. McCormick, the spice manufacturer, and Black and Decker followed suit.

During the advent of air travel during the 1920s and 1930s, Baltimore housed one of the major airplane manufacturers, Glenn L. Martin Company, based in Cleveland. The factory, which was situated on Middle River just outside the city, built thousands of major aircraft and brought the need for new homes to house workers. Shoreline communities, many of which remain today, sprouted everywhere around the facility, and the factory's runways still serve as an airport for small planes and the Maryland Air National Guard.

On many of those new residents' doorsteps was the *Baltimore Evening Sun*, featuring the work of H. L. Mencken, a curmudgeon born in 1880 in a row house on Hollins Street in Southwest Baltimore. Arguably the most important journalist of his era, Mencken made sport of most everything he saw wrong with the world. One thing he liked was his hometown: "If the true purpose of living is to be born in comfort, to live happily and to die at peace, the average Baltimorean is infinitely better off than the average New Yorker."

THE CRASH HITS BALTIMORE

In New York the stock market crashed in October 1929, sending the country into the long and painful Great Depression. The toll on Baltimore would be great, but it was lessened slightly by the work of the Public Works Administration in Maryland. The organization spearheaded efforts to expand and improve the city's water supply through projects such as the construction of Prettyboy Reservoir in Baltimore County. The city continues to get most of its water from county reservoirs (Prettyboy and Loch Raven) along with the Big Inch, a water line created in the early 1960s running from the Susquehanna River, 40 miles north of the city, parallel to Interstate 95. Even with the Public Works Administration projects, about 100,000 Baltimoreans—about one in seven people—had no income during the Depression era.

Fortunately, many of the people who had purchased new homes in the Baltimore area prior to the crash had taken five-year mortgages, so even though they had no income, they were not forced onto the streets. A sign of the times came in September 1931, when the $85 million, 32-story Baltimore Trust Company building was closed. Still, in the face of growing concern, the Baltimore Association of Commerce said in the early 1930s, "Industry as a whole is in good shape." The city's diverse economy kept it better off than most cities, but by Christmas 1933, one in six families in the city was on relief.

Love would soon take Baltimore's thoughts away from the Depression and put the city at the center of the world's attention. On December 10, 1936, England's King Edward VIII renounced his throne (to the surprise of all of England), so he could be with Bessie Wallis Warfield Simpson, a twice-divorced Baltimore woman the king had fallen in love with. She became the Duchess of Windsor and a spectacle of public attention whenever she and the duke visited her hometown.

SUPPLYING WW II

In September 1939, when World War II began in Europe, Baltimore was providing much of the materials for battle. Overseas orders for Japanese ships were coming in to Bethlehem Steel, and Glenn L. Martin Co. was busy building airplanes. Another $5.5 billion in federal war contracts were soon heading to the city by the bay.

Before long, the Great Depression was forgotten. The 47,000 workers at Bethlehem Steel built 500 Victory and Liberty ships and, along the way, cut the assembly time from 110 to 52 days using automobile assembly line techniques. By 1943 Glenn L. Martin Co. was employing 37,000 people, and another 77,000 people were involved in shipbuilding in the city.

The growing workforce increased the city's population by an estimated 134,000, with another 28,000 families moving into new homes on the outskirts of the city. Baltimore's population eclipsed 1.5 million.

PEACETIME PURSUITS

In the 1950s the state spent $10 million on new schools and devoted $3 million to the construction of Friendship Airport (now Baltimore–Washington International Thurgood Marshall Airport), about 15 miles south of Baltimore and 20 miles north of Washington. Mass transportation and cars enabled suburbanites to get to their jobs in the city—moving to the more open county and beyond became feasible. Brick homes were being built by the hundreds. (If you don't have an idea when a certain house was built, odds are good that if you guess the 1950s, you'll be right.)

With the flight to the outskirts, city housing was decaying, and business leaders had to do something. They created the first housing court, a body empowered to crack down on the numerous housing violations that were ruining the city's appearance. Under Mayor Thomas J. D'Alesandro Jr., the new "Baltimore Plan" received praise and acclaim for its forward-looking approach. Beyond housing, the plan led to the improvement of bus routes and the construction of a new convention center in the city (now the Baltimore Arena), where entertainment, sporting events, and other activities could be held. A new plan for 33 acres in the center of the city called for the creation of Charles Center, a commercial and retail center on Charles Street, 3 blocks north of the Inner Harbor.

All was not about big business and urban issues in the 1950s. Several drive-in theaters opened, including the Bengies, still operating on Highway 150 in Essex. And in 1954 the Baltimore Orioles appeared on the scene, having moved from St. Louis, where they had been called the Browns. (Oddly enough, more than 40 years later the Cleveland Browns football team would move to Baltimore and become the Baltimore Ravens, succeeding the Colts, who left Baltimore for Indianapolis in 1984.) The Orioles played their home games at Memorial Stadium, a ballpark built in the northeastern part of the city as a large memorial to lost wartime soldiers. The Colts, with Johnny Unitas at the helm, also used the field for their incredible brand of play.

RACIAL STRIDES AND MISSTEPS

The exodus to the suburbs by middle-income whites in Baltimore and other big cities created racial tensions. Not since the Civil War had the nation's population been so divided, both emotionally and physically. But even though it was south of the Mason-Dixon Line, Baltimore was more racially integrated than most cities. In September 1952, two years before the Supreme Court's landmark ruling outlawing racial discrimination in public schools, the Baltimore City School Board voted to allow 12 black students to enroll in the city's Polytechnic Institute, a citywide college-prep engineering school. This act proved to be the start of desegregation in Baltimore.

Living in this environment was Baltimorean Clarence Mitchell Jr., chief Washington lobbyist for the National Association for the Advancement of Colored People and a persuasive leader in the passage of the civil rights acts of the late 1950s and early 1960s. He is honored as the namesake of Baltimore's City Courthouse. Despite its advanced stance on desegregation, the city became a home to rioting in April 1968, when Dr. Martin Luther King Jr. was assassinated.

AN URBAN RENAISSANCE

In September 1970 the first City Fair was held at Charles Center and the Inner Harbor in an effort to heal the city's wounds and bring people back together. Just two years after rioting, representatives of almost all of Baltimore's neighborhoods gathered under tents to share their heritages; more than 300,000 people attended. For many of these people, a trip to the city for something other than work was rare, if not unheard of, due to the lingering fear of racial clashes. In the following years the city played host to summers filled with ethnic festivals. To this day such events are common, spotlighting the food, music, arts, and other entertainment of diverse cultures, ranging from the Estonians to the Hispanics.

In 1971 Baltimoreans elected William Donald Schaefer mayor. Although the movement had actually started with several leaders before him, Schaefer quickly became the embodiment of Baltimore's urban renaissance. In 1973 a homesteading program began, allowing people to buy city-owned houses for $1 as long as they agreed to refurbish them. The program was an immediate success, leading to the restoration and renovation of more than 500 old homes. Some of the best examples are the 100-year-old homes in the Otterbein, Ridgely's Delight, and Reservoir Hill neighborhoods. (See the Relocation chapter for more information.)

Commercial improvements were also in the works. In time for the nation's bicentennial, the Maryland Science Center opened in a $10 million, four-story building on the Inner Harbor. In July 1976 the city held a giant fireworks display, where the rockets' red glare fell on eight beautiful "tall ships" visiting from faraway ports. In February 1977 the city launched its own goodwill ambassador vessel, the $467,000, 90-foot *Pride of Baltimore,* a replica of the clipper ships that had been popular on the area's waters more than a century earlier. Several years later, the ship sank during an Atlantic storm, taking with it several sailors. But the *Pride of Baltimore II* followed, a clipper ship replica with modern safety features that has sailed to all parts of the world.

In 1978 Baltimore voters approved the construction of Harborplace, a 3.1-acre complex of shops, restaurants, and food stalls to be constructed at the center of the Inner Harbor. Built for $10 million by the Rouse Company, Harborplace's opening in July 1980 was the crowning glory of the urban revitalization effort: a tourist attraction that would bring locals and visitors to the city's downtown area in droves for years to come.

Propelled by the city's newfound $625 million-a-year tourist industry, a new convention center opened just ahead of Harborplace in August 1979, and the 500-room, 13-story Hyatt Regency opened in 1980. With the Hyatt boasting that company's second-highest occupancy rate (92.3 percent) in its first year, other hotels soon followed. The Stouffer, Sheraton, and Harbor Courts were soon taking reservations from people hungry to visit a city that had been profiled in *National Geographic, Time, Newsweek,* and a host of travel articles in national and international newspapers. An enduring image of Mayor Schaefer, wearing an old-style striped bathing suit and sporting a yellow rubber duck, jumping into a tank at the National Aquarium, brought the city even more positive publicity.

BUILDING ON SUCCESS

Schaefer's own success led him to the State House, where he served as governor from 1986 to 1994. During his tenure as governor, he further fortified the city, leading trade missions to the Far East and other areas to woo businesses. His administration pushed for the construction of Oriole Park at Camden Yards, a new stadium for the Baltimore Orioles, that was within walking distance of the Inner Harbor. Camden Yards, as it is now referred to by most people, opened to sellout crowds in 1992 and played host to baseball's All-Star Game in 1993 and the American League Championship in 1997. A companion football stadium, now called M&T Bank Stadium, was built for the Baltimore Ravens and opened in

Mobtown

Baltimoreans tend to wear the town's "Mobtown" moniker as a badge of honor nowadays, but its history is really pretty dark. Although origins of the name are a little vague, three events seem to be at least partially responsible. Three nights of rioting in 1835 led Baltimore's citizens to call for order. The growing city up to this point had quite a mix of refined public spaces and boisterous unruly streets. Mobs rioted in the streets again in the 1850s during the rise of the Know-Nothing Party, a collection of anti-Catholic, anti-immigrant groups that led such riots in several American cities. Then, on April 19, 1861, as the Sixth Massachusetts Union Regiment marched between the President Street Station and the Camden Station on its way south, a mob of Southern sympathizers attacked the soldiers, shedding the first blood of the Civil War. Four soldiers an 12 Baltimoreans were dead. The term "Mobtown" stuck.

the fall of 1998 across the parking lot from the baseball-only park.

Schaefer and other leaders could not stop the May 1986 end of the *News American,* an afternoon newspaper that appealed to the area's blue-collar workforce. Less than a decade later, the last edition of the *Evening Sun,* the city's other afternoon newspaper, published by TimesMirror Co., which also publishes the morning edition of the *Sun,* would come, leaving the city with one major daily (see the Media chapter for more information).

In another medium, Baltimore would find growing success and visibility. Movies such as *Diner, Bedroom Window, Tin Men,* and *The Accidental Tourist* were shot in Baltimore, many made by local filmmaker Barry Levinson. In 1992 Levinson used his hometown as the setting for a television project—the dramatic series *Homicide: Life on the Streets.* The show garnered critical acclaim for its gritty portrayal of Baltimore's finest, using location shoots throughout the city and especially in Fells Point.

With Schaefer's departure for the governorship in Annapolis, the reins for Baltimore's municipal leadership were taken by mayors from the city's minority population. Clarence "Du" Burns took over as mayor when Schaefer

became governor and served the last 11 months of Schaefer's term. Burns was succeeded by fellow African American Kurt L. Schmoke, a Rhodes scholar from Yale and former prosecutor for the city, who served as Baltimore's mayor for 12 years.

THE FACE OF THE FUTURE

In 2000 Baltimore welcomed a young energetic mayor, Martin O'Malley, who asked us to "Believe." With bumper stickers and banners and signs all over the city, he launched a program to renew the city and boost morale. He was so dynamic he caught the attention of the national media. *Esquire* magazine named him "The Best Young Mayor in the Country" in 2002, and he appeared in *Time* magazine as one of America's "Top 5 Big City Mayors" in 2005. That same year, *Business Week* called him one of "Five Fresh Faces" to lead the Democratic Party. So it was no surprise when he won the election for governor in 2006.

As he left office in 2007, Sheila Dixon, the City Council president, stepped up to take the mayor's office and become the first African-American woman to lead Baltimore. She was elected to serve in her own right in the November 2007 elections. Dixon got to work, setting as her goals cleaner streets, opportunities for the city's youth, and smoke-free restaurants and bars, effective in January 2008.

Like so many urban centers, Baltimore suffered a loss of its manufacturing and corporate base as the economy shifted in the last millennium. While traditional sources of employment waned, new prospects emerged, and service sector employment, biotechnology, IT, and other tech-based employment opportunities grew. Baltimore has a low unemployment rate. Developments such as the Digital Harbor have created high-tech hubs for burgeoning businesses, while financial companies such as Legg Mason and T. Rowe Price, and major hospitals and universities remain solid employers.

Development in general is bustling throughout the city. Our West Side is seeing a massive overhaul, while the Inner Harbor continues to spread east along the water with new hotels, businesses, and housing. The national trend of young professionals and empty nesters moving back into cities can definitely be seen in Baltimore. It would seem our Downtown is primed for another renaissance. The city has already seen an influx of luxury high-rises Downtown, and empty office and corporate buildings are finding new life as resident buildings, bringing a whole new life to the heart of the city. Some of these new residents are D.C. transplants who realize they can buy a gracious city home for a quarter of what they would pay in our nation's capital. They are scooping up properties in Baltimore and using the MARC rail system to commute to work in D.C. The center of Baltimore increased its resident population by 50 percent in just five years, and the growth spurt does not look like it will slow anytime soon.

RELOCATION

Once upon a time . . . Baltimore City was a little pocket of industry and commerce nestled near the Patapsco River and surrounded by vast estates. Slowly but unerringly such estates were gobbled up, one by one, to create little towns and eventually larger neighborhood areas. The largest spurts of growth occurred after the Civil War, just after the turn of the last century, and in concert with World Wars I and II. By the 1950s most of the inner and midtown areas of the city had been filled in. Outside those areas, however, were still rolling green hills, horse farms, homemade ice cream, and country general stores. Those pockets can still be found, even though, in the intervening years, suburban cities and towns have reached out toward each other, paving and building in the spaces between. Out Falls Road, headed for Greenspring and Worthington Valleys, the city quickly becomes the country. Once past Joppa Road on north Harford Road, for a few miles before you reach the suburbs of Bel Air, there are cows grazing in fields, old frame houses, and waving fields of wheat. And in the suburban areas south and east of the city, the smell of salty water and the cry of the sea gulls are ever-present.

Baltimore is bracing for new growth in the next few years, too. With the Base Realignment and Closure (BRAC) bringing 13,000 new jobs to Maryland, the city expects about 10 percent of those families, up to 2,500 of them, to move here. Military jobs are being reassigned from Virginia and New Jersey to nearby bases, including Fort Meade in Anne Arundel County, Aberdeen Proving Ground in Harford County, and Fort Detrick in Frederick. Expansion of supporting services and defense contractors has followed the growth of the military in the past—and that is expected here, too.

If you're moving to Baltimore, relocating to this city is easy. There are many services set up to help newcomers get acclimated. Live Baltimore Home Center is an independent, nonprofit organization founded in 1997 to promote the benefits of city living. It produces an extensive relocation kit with up-to-date information including the latest homebuying incentives. You can order a catalog for $15 by contacting **Live Baltimore Home Center** at 343 North Charles Street, 1st Floor, (410) 637-3750. You can also visit the Web site, www.live baltimore.com, which offers a comprehensive list of neighborhoods, home values, real estate contact information, and more.

In this chapter we focus on greater Baltimore and the different neighborhoods you can choose from. We also look at how these environs are evolving. Some of our regional magazines publish extensive articles about city neighborhoods and the outlying suburbs. In 2003 for example, *Baltimore* magazine produced a piece called "Rating the 'Burbs," a look at the housing markets, amenities, and relocation opportunities of five Maryland counties. You can request back issues of *Baltimore* magazine by calling the editorial office at (410) 752-4200.

Generally, even the poorest among us often have active neighborhood associations that organize street fairs in summer and neighborhood block watches all year-round. Neighbors watch after latchkey children or babysit for those who have to work. Often, that neighbor is also a relative, because in many of Baltimore's neighborhoods, relatives live nearby. But whether your neighbors are real family or extended family, the sense of family is strong, possibly because our sense of history and the way we are connected to it is so much a part of our daily lives.

Newcomers to the area often talk about Baltimore's quality of life, about what a pleasant, easy place it is to live. One transplant we spoke with noted that he had lived all over the world and in all the major cities in this country, and after 17 years in Baltimore, it would "take a bomb" to blow him out of here. Natives feel the same way. A new friend who lives in Federal Hill is a great case in point. The original members of her family landed in Baltimore in the late 1700s to work in the shipbuilding industry. Since then, generation after generation has stayed on, and the current family boasts three generations of Baltimore firefighters and a Baltimore policeman. These kinds of families are the glue that holds Baltimore's neighborhoods together.

The great thing is that, unlike some small towns where distrust among the natives runs high toward newcomers, Baltimore tends to open its arms. We are always happy to have newcomers embrace the city and its way of life.

Most neighborhoods still have town squares or parks where neighborhood events are held. And, of course, there's always the corner bar that serves the function of a European pub, a place to get together with neighbors and relax. Often, there are also corner stores, where people meet as well as shop. In the counties, people gather for special events at the neighborhood mall or shopping centers.

Both in the city and the counties, schools and churches are important neighborhood fixtures, with solid outreach into the community. They are the institutions we look to to provide day care, after-school care, and places for bazaars, dances, and meetings.

Within the city limits, we try to "buy neighborhood." If there's a good drugstore on the corner, we don't go to one 3 blocks away, and if there's a good bakery 3 blocks away, we don't drive a mile to find another. This may account for the continuing success of our neighborhood grocery stores and restaurants. We often refer to even the chain stores by their neighborhood name. One doesn't just shop at the Giant, one shops at the Giant

Rotunda or the Giant York Road. One doesn't run down to the Eddie's but to the Roland Park Eddie's or the Charles Street Eddie's.

Some neighborhoods are eclectic, both in culture and population. Some neighborhoods were created by one ethnic group for that ethnic group, and the rest of us are just visitors. Some neighborhoods are blue collar, some white collar, some hippie, some yuppie.

Baltimore is the City of Neighborhoods. All you need to do is find the right one for you. In that regard, this chapter contains capsulized views of some of Baltimore's more sought-after or more historic areas as well as some of the neighborhoods that are trying to join one of those categories. There are a minimum of 280 neighborhoods within the city's limits alone; we simply cannot mention them all.

There are some great little neighborhoods contained within other larger, more well-known neighborhoods. We may not mention them either, even though some would be well worth mentioning if we had all the space in the world. A good example is Evergreen, a lovely enclave of small, single homes built for the railroad workers beside the B&O tracks that used to run through there. Its three streets sit smackdab in the middle of Roland Park. You will find Roland Park in this chapter; you will not find Evergreen.

We've tried to note both the positives and the negatives of living in certain areas. Also, we've mentioned the range of housing prices and general condition of living in an area. At the same time, we would mention here that in big cities, areas sometimes change block by block. One block is great . . . the next block, well . . . not so much. So, realize that the subsequent descriptions are general. If you want to know more, you'll just have to go and see for yourself.

For those neighborhoods beyond the city line but in the catchment area of greater Baltimore, we've tried to do the same. We're mentioning large areas in the suburbs, however, not the individual developments and settlements, not the tiny towns that are, no doubt, wonderful but are contained within a larger, more easily recognized area.

With that in mind, we apologize to those we've left out and hope we've done justice to those we've included.

BALTIMORE HOUSING 101

Before you take a look at the neighborhoods themselves, we thought it might be a good idea to introduce you to what it takes to buy housing in Baltimore—some of the restrictions, some of the perks, some of the history.

Dollar Houses

In the early to mid-1970s, Baltimore City was beginning a renaissance. Because of the increase in housing prices elsewhere, younger professionals had begun taking another look at city neighborhoods, mostly in the midtown areas. Charles Village, for instance, got its name then (changed from Peabody Heights). It was done strictly for publicity purposes and was the brainchild of one Grace Darin, a Charles Village resident and writer. This name change and an active civic league that spent hours at zoning and other meetings pleading the neighborhood's causes stopped, for a time, the encroachment of businesses and associations into its residential area and, in the process, renovated thousands of homes. In the inner city areas, however, decay continued.

William Donald Schaefer, our mayor at the time, was a no-nonsense kind of guy. If it needed to be done, he found a way. It was a time of creative solutions, and one of these became known as the Dollar House Project.

The project was based on a simple concept: If you made it cheap enough, people would take a chance. "Cheap enough" turned out to be one single dollar. So many people wanted to take the chance on those inner city neighborhoods that each targeted block of houses ended up having to be sold by lottery.

The people who were interested would tour the targeted block or blocks of houses. Then they would submit their name for the house they were interested in. Usually, there was more than one name in the proverbial hat, so drawings were held. The winner was not only given the house for a dollar but also guaranteed a low-interest renovation loan from the city.

The Dollar House Project succeeded in renovating not just blocks of houses, but whole neighborhoods in the inner city, most of which have retained not only their beauty but also their monetary value.

Renovator and Homeowner Loans and Tax Incentives

Although the Dollar House Project is no longer, Baltimore City continues to provide tax incentives to new homeowners as well as to homeowners who renovate and homeowners who maintain and improve their homes. Here is a sampling of some of the programs offered as of June 2007.

The **American Dream Down-payment Initiative** offers a $3,000 forgivable loan for down payment and closing costs. This is one of several down payment loan programs offered to new homeowners in Baltimore City.

Live Near Your Work provides grants for employees settling in certain neighborhoods near their jobs. Both employees and employers must be approved for this program, which offers a minimum of $2,000 for closing costs.

The **Single-family Construction Loan Program** is designed to assist families renovating any city property.

The **Healthy Neighborhoods Initiative** offers homeowners loans for purchase, rehabilitation, and home improvement in 10 specific neighborhoods, including Charles Village, Reservoir Hill, Patterson Park, and Mondawmin. See www.healthyneighborhoods.org for details.

A number of tax credits are also available for homeowners and rehabbers. These include the Historic District Tax Credit both for residential and income property. Homes must be either on the national register or in locally designated historic districts. Since improving a property also raises its value and thus its assessment, this program credits the property tax increase from rehab for 10 years. Improvements on homes in other areas can receive a five-year reduction in property values. Another tax credit is available for new construction, and one offers tax credits for owner-occupied previously vacant dwellings once they are inhabitable.

These tax credit programs ease the fears of homeowners who worry they won't be able to pay the property taxes on their newly renovated homes. Although this sounds impossible, it actually happened in Charles Village when original renovators in the 1960s and 1970s were forced out of the very homes where they put in so much time and effort and capital. The subsequent assessments were so high—in some cases up to 300 percent higher—the homeowners couldn't afford the taxes and had to move. These credits, which begin at 100 percent the first year, are designed to help in these cases.

For information on these programs, contact Baltimore Housing at (410) 396-3972 or visit www.livebaltimore.com.

Historic Designations

Many areas in Baltimore City and some areas in surrounding counties bear a historic designation. It is important to know what the designation is and what restrictions are put on your property because of it. Maryland Historic designations have different restrictions than National Historic District designations. Both require things like the facade of the building being kept in historic shape, i.e., it must look as if it is still the year that it was built. This would mean no awnings, no changes of window size, no turning double doors into single doors, and so on. On the positive side, however, it also means that a developer can't come into your neighborhood and tear down the row of homes next to you and build a high-rise.

Covenants

In both Baltimore City and surrounding counties, many neighborhoods bear covenants. For instance, all of the city communities noted as having been built by the Roland Park Company do. Covenants are strict rules about how your property can be used and what can be done to it in the way of renovation, add-ons, and sometimes even the colors it can be painted. When you are looking at property in a self-contained neighborhood, ask if there is a covenant before you fall in love with it. If there is, ask for a copy of the covenant to make sure you can live with the restrictions. You don't want to come to the settlement table not knowing what you're in for.

Real Estate Prices

Housing prices in Baltimore City were very low in the 1970s. It was the prices that brought people back in droves to renovate and rehabilitate Baltimore. Because of the renovation, housing prices soared over the next 10 years and probably would have gone higher if not for the double-digit interest rates of the 1980s. Once interest rates dropped, Baltimore properties got new attention and prices began rising slowly. Then the market took off and a number of Baltimore's neighborhoods saw prices skyrocket—at least until the market cooled in late 2006. Prices have stopped climbing, but they've stayed at all-new highs. A good example: A three-bedroom, Cape Cod home in the neighborhood of Evergreen was for sale in 1976 for $14,000. In 1981 that same house—with no improvements—sold for $58,000. In 1985 the property was again for sale . . . for more than $100,000. Today, it would probably sell for more than $200,000. So if you buy a house in Baltimore today in a stable neighborhood, you will pay close to top of the market prices for that area, although prices in Baltimore City are still excellent bargains when compared with the suburbs. Deals can still be found on estate sales or in areas that are less stable and still trying to make it. Taxes tend to be higher on these properties, and some are selling for the same price as a three-bedroom town house in the suburbs. In this chapter, the prices we have quoted are averages from 2006.

Community Development Corporations

Baltimore Housing, a joint venture of Baltimore City's Housing Authority and Department of Housing and Community Development, to help homebuyers and developers, 417 East Fayette Street, Suite 1339, (410) 396-3237, www.baltimorehousing.org

Maryland Center for Community Development, (410) 752–6223 or (800) 949–6223, www.mccd.org, a nonprofit homeownership referral hotline and resource center

St. Ambrose Housing Aid Center (for Baltimore City), 321 East 25th Street, (410) 366-8550, www.stambrose.org

Greater Baltimore Urban League (Baltimore City), 512 Orchard Street, (410) 523-8150, www.bul.org

Adopt-A-House Development Corporation (Coldstream-Homestead-Montebello communities), 1527 Gorsuch Avenue, (410) 235-6721

Belair-Edison Housing Service (Belair-Edison community), 3412 Belair Road, (410) 485-8422, www.belair-edison.org

East Baltimore Midway Community Development Corporation, 802 East North Avenue, (410) 243-0391

HarBel Housing Partnership Program, 5807 Harford Road, (410) 444-9152, www.harbel.org

Howard County Office of Housing and Community Development, 6751 Columbia Gateway Drive, (410) 313-6320, www.co.ho.md.us

Greater Baltimore Community Housing Resource Board, (410) 453-9500 or (800) 895-6302, www.gbchrb.org, housing information

Ground Rents

Ground rents are something unique to older cities. Renting the land was a way for people who owned land on which houses were built to retain income from the land, a sort of cash-only feudal arrangement. The builder/resident owned his house but paid rent on the land under it. Many of Baltimore City's properties still have ground rent, which may cost less than $100 a year. Homebuyers often can buy the ground at settlement for a few thousand dollars. Whenever you see a home advertised for sale "in fee" there is no ground rent. Otherwise, make sure to ask your real estate agent about the ground rent. New laws passed in 2007 outlaw new ground rents, make it easier

for homebuyers to convert a ground rent, and ban the use of ejectment, which enabled ground rent owners to take possession of houses in lieu of owed back rent.

Closing Costs for Homebuyers

Closing costs on housing in Maryland generally are a major expense. There are filing fees, bank fees, and property taxes to pay, among other things. In Baltimore City, however, programs that allow semiannual property tax payments can reduce closing costs, so don't forget to request that option. There is also a program usually referred to as a SELP loan. The acronym stands for Settlement Expense Loan Program, and what it basically does is lend you the money to pay your settlement costs, which then are figured into your mortgage and paid off over the life of your mortgage.

ORGANIZING THE CITY OF NEIGHBORHOODS

For your convenience, as we have in most of this book, we've broken the territory within the city's limits into Downtown, Northeast, Northwest, Southeast, and Southwest. Because of the large numbers of neighborhoods in the Downtown area, however, for the sake of this chapter only, we've also broken Downtown into Northeast, Northwest, Southeast, and Southwest. Also, the area that we have labeled as Downtown Baltimore includes some areas that others would label Southwest, South, and Southeast Baltimore. We have included these areas in our Downtown because they are within walking distance of the Inner Harbor, which is our central focus for the Downtown area. In the categories of Northeast, Northwest, Southeast, and Southwest, we have divided these regions into Within the City and Over the County Line in an effort to further clarify where these areas are located.

Special thanks for information about home price averages from Live Baltimore and the Greater Baltimore Board of Realtors. (GBBR's source is MRIS; information is reliable but not guaranteed.)

NORTHEAST DOWNTOWN

Baltimore's elegant past, its turn-of-the-twentieth-century boom days, are well characterized in one neighborhood, **Mount Vernon**, which straddles the east-west boundary of Charles Street, running east to Guilford Avenue, west to essentially Howard Street, and north to the train tracks below Mount Royal Avenue.

Originally part of the estate of John Eager Howard, it was given up to development in the 1850s. Those first residents were the cream of Baltimore society and philanthropy, and today, Mount Vernon is the hub of Baltimore's

i If moving to Baltimore is in your future, stop by the Live Baltimore Home Center downtown at 343 North Charles Street or visit the Web site at www.livebaltimore.com for a stack of resources and people to talk to. If you prefer to peruse papers, get one of their relocation kits for $14. Order it from the Web site or call (410) 637-3750.

cultural activity. Within its confines are the Peabody Conservatory of Music, the Walters Art Gallery, Center Stage Theatre, the Lyric Opera House, and the Joseph Meyerhoff Symphony Hall. It is the home of the Washington Monument, some of the most fabulous church buildings ever erected, and some of Baltimore's better restaurants, both old and new. Many of Baltimore's exclusive clubs are on Mount Vernon Square; the Women's Club and the Engineer's Club come to mind most often.

The neighborhood is tightly knit, serving both as gathering place and home to artists, actors, and students as well as the center of the gay community in Baltimore. Apartments and homes are fairly priced, with home prices ranging from $125,000 to 1.5 million. Understand, however, that the average house on the main streets of Charles, Calvert, and Cathedral is 25 feet wide and four to five stories high, not counting the basement, and most of them have 15- to 20-foot interior ceilings. You could put a typical suburban town house, including front and backyard, within the third floor of many of these buildings and still have room to walk around it. Hence, $450 a month for an apartment in Mount Vernon buys you plenty of space.

Oliver/Eastern Terrace is south of North Avenue, north of Biddle Street, and bounded by Broadway and Ensor Street on the east and west, respectively. Built on land that originally was known as the Green Mount Estate, owned by the Oliver family, one of its most notable attractions is the Greenmount Cemetery, dedicated in 1839, where both the Poe and Booth family plots lie. Most of the row homes in the area were constructed in the

Close-up

Mount Vernon Cultural District

Mount Vernon is one of Baltimore's richest neighborhoods, boasting some of the best architecture, culture, housing, food, and fun in the downtown area. The center of Mount Vernon is the Washington Monument on Charles Street, so much a part of the city it's featured on Baltimore's seal. The 178-foot Doric column that supports a statue of George Washington can be seen from many spots around town. American author Herman Melville once wrote, "Great Washington stands aloft on his towering mainmast in Baltimore, and like one of Hercules' pillars, his column marks that point of human grandeur beyond which few mortals will go."

Baltimore's statue is our country's first monument to George Washington, predating the one in Washington, D.C. by 55 years. The base of the monument offers an exhibit detailing the construction of the neoclassic sculpture begun in 1815 by Robert Mills, who also designed its D.C. cousin. Guests may wind their way up the dizzying 228 steps to the top of the monument for a bird's-eye view of the city (although you can get better views of the city from the top of the World Trade Center in the Inner Harbor or from the lounge and bar on the 13th floor of the Belvedere on Chase Street). Conservation sometimes prohibits visitors from climbing the column, but the exhibit on the ground floor usually remains open.

Around the statue is Mount Vernon Square, a primarily nineteenth-century neighborhood founded by Baltimore's elite. When the monument was first constructed, Mount Vernon lay far north of the burgeoning city, but by 1840 the city expanded to encompass the neighborhood. The town houses that border the Washington Monument range from Greek Revival to Italian Renaissance and Gothic Revival, with the oldest house in the square standing at 8 West Mount Vernon Place. These homes were the place to live in the 1800s, and urban revival has put them back in high demand. There are only four buildings built after 1900 in the square. A series of landscaped parks punctuated by sculptures and fountains add to the charm of this urban setting.

1880s and 1890s and were owned by German and Irish merchants and industrialists. During World Wars I and II, the density of the neighborhood increased as the city nearly burst to overflowing with people who came primarily from the South to work in Baltimore's defense plants. Later came the flight to the suburbs in the 1950s and '60s, and the neighborhood saw further decline. Since the 1970s, however, the neighborhood has been fighting its way back. Oliver/Eastern Terrace has seen some of its worst sections razed in recent years to be replaced by more modern row houses.

Now primarily an African-American working-class neighborhood, Oliver/Eastern Terrace has well-regarded parochial schools and active neighborhood churches. Oliver/Eastern Terrace homes average $40,000.

The circle of cobblestone and the adjoining parks that surround the Washington Monument are the site of many annual festivals and parades. Each winter the city kicks off the holiday by stringing the monument with strands of twinkling lights. Each May the Flower Mart ushers in spring and every September the Book Festival takes over the square with books, music, and visits from famous authors.

Within 3 blocks of the monument you will find the Maryland Historical Society Museum, the Contemporary Museum, the Walters Art Museum, the Enoch Pratt Free Library, and the Peabody Institute. You will also find commercial galleries, fine food, cafes, and unique shops. In recent years many cultural organizations and businesses in the neighborhood gelled to create the Mount Vernon Cultural District (MVCD), whose cooperative goal is to improve the physical amenities in the area and to help spread the word about the many cultural, historic, and social attractions. The organization touts that Mount Vernon is "one neighborhood with 100 things to do," and with more than one million people visiting Mount Vernon in 2000, it appears that word has spread. The MVCD is a good stepping-off point for a tour of the Mount Vernon area. Its Web site has a map with links to member organizations at www.mvcd.org.

The MVCD is housed in the same building as the Downtown Partnership, a nonprofit corporation dedicated to making Downtown Baltimore a great place to invest, work, live, and play. You may want to pop into the Downtown Partnership, located at 217 North Charles Street, for brochures, general information, and friendly advice from the informed reception staff. "It's easy to fall in love with Downtown Baltimore," explains the Partnership's Web site. "Few downtowns have as true a Little Italy as does Baltimore, or fresh seafood markets such as those found in Fells Point, Market Center, and Federal Hill, or cultural institutions, restaurants, and retail establishments as in Mount Vernon." The Downtown Partnership also offers a safety escort service for people working late or playing late who want someone to walk them to their car or hotel. The service, available within the 106-block area that comprises the core of Downtown, can be reached by calling (410) 244-1030.

NORTHWEST DOWNTOWN

One of the poorest areas in Baltimore City, with a population of more than 10,000 people, **Sandtown-Winchester** is a classic story of urban decay. A recent publication about Sandtown-Winchester noted 50 percent of its households earn less than $11,000 a year, and 44 percent of its adult residents are unemployed or underemployed. School performance standards are low; crime is high, as are drug use and HIV/AIDS infection. However, Sandtown-Winchester is undergoing a metamorphosis. Residents have decided to stay and fix it. The challenge would be astounding, even if it were just a government project; but what makes Sandtown-Winchester's challenge truly memorable is the fact that its residents sparked the beginnings of the 72-block neighborhood's rehabilitation, and they work for it every day at the grassroots level. Since 1990, when a partnership was formed between the city, the residents, and The Enterprise Foundation, that spark has begun to glow. By 1996, the more than 100 block clubs organized to fight crime had helped reduce crime by 20 percent. More than 3,000 housing units have been built or renovated; parks, festivals, and new community services have become part of the Sandtown-Winchester transformation. New recruits to Sandtown-Winchester's cause are being enlisted every day, and as they themselves note, Sandtown-Winchester is becoming a "national model for positive change." Homes in the neighborhood can be bought for as little as $5,500, with top prices falling in at about $60,000.

Seton Hill is an area of about 7 square blocks 10 blocks north of Camden Yard tucked above Franklin Street between Orchard and Eutaw Streets. On the National Register as a Historic District, Seton Hill took its name from Mother Elizabeth Anne Seton, now a saint, who opened the first boarding school for Catholic girls on the site. Another religious first occurred in Seton Hill when Mother Mary Elizabeth Lange, an African-American Catholic who is being championed for sainthood, founded the Oblate Sisters of Providence there in 1829. This mostly renovated neighborhood of some 300 homes grew up between 1800 and 1850 around St. Mary's Seminary, the first Catholic seminary in the United States, founded in 1791. The focal point of the neighborhood is now St. Mary's Park, where until 1975 the Seminary still stood, and where the Seminary Chapel—the earliest example of neo-Gothic design in the United States—still stands. One of the most interesting facts about the houses that front right at the sidewalk along busy streets is that many of them share common, landscaped garden space in the back. Though charming from the front, the difference between front and back can be as startling as when Dorothy stepped out into Munchkinland.

The average price of a single-family home in the area is $174,000 to $199,000.

Bolton Hill is bounded on the north by North Avenue, on the west by Eutaw Place, on the east by Mount Royal Avenue, and on the south by the Fifth Regiment Armory, where the original Bolton estate once stood. Development was begun in the 1850s at Eutaw Place by a member of the Tiffany family. After the Civil War development spread east and professional and merchant-class families moved in, as did a fair number of displaced Southerners. Robert E. Lee's aide-de-camp, Charles Marshall, moved to Bolton Hill at that time. Other former residents include Ottmar Mergenthaler, who invented the Linotype in 1885, and writers Christopher Morley, Gertrude Stein, Edith Hamilton, and F. Scott Fitzgerald. One of the few neighborhoods that maintained its population and its homeownership through the postwar flight to the suburbs, Bolton Hill today offers an eclectic mix of population and lifestyle within the ambience of old-world elegance. Houses range in price, with the average going for $430,000.

In 1977 **Madison Park** became Baltimore's seventh Historic District and its first African-American historic district. On the west side of Bolton Hill just below North Avenue, Madison Park was built from 1876 to 1894 by Baltimore's gentile elite. Subsequently taken over by the well-to-do Jewish population, then settled after World War I by professionals, Madison Park is still primarily an upper-middle income, professional neighborhood. Home prices average $162,000.

SOUTHEAST DOWNTOWN

Just east of the Inner Harbor is **Little Italy,** one of Baltimore's oldest and best-known neighborhoods. Bounded on the north by Pratt Street, on the west by President Street, on the east by Central Avenue, and on the south by the Harbor itself, Little Italy covers only 12 square blocks. Settled in the 1840s by Italian immigrants in search of work on the railroad, it is renowned for its 20 cozy Italian restaurants and its continuing observation of

The Enterprise Foundation

The Rouse Company that Jim Rouse created has been a fixture in Maryland for more than 30 years. A major developer in Maryland generally, the Rouse Company has been responsible for some of Baltimore's more impressive development, including Harborplace, which serves as the centerpiece for Baltimore's Inner Harbor Development. The Enterprise Foundation (www.enterprisefoundation.org), a nonprofit housing and community development organization begun in 1982 by Jim and Patty Rouse, supports an entirely different kind of development—the development of neighborhoods. They call the process "Neighborhood Transformation." Its goal is to literally transform neighborhoods from urban decay into safe, livable, cohesive communities.

Foundation funds go to support public housing redevelopment, assisted-living programs for low-income seniors, inner-city child-care facilities, neighborhood planning, job creation, neighborhood safety programs, and more.

As of 2007, Enterprise had raised and invested more than $8 billion in grants, loans, and equity to the process of neighborhood transformation. In 2006 alone, the foundation raised $1.2 billion and built or rehabilitated apartments and homes for 23,000 families.

Though begun in Baltimore, The Enterprise Foundation is not being stingy with with its expertise. Projects as far away as Texas have had the benefit of The Enterprise Foundation's direct intervention. Its outreach extends to just about anywhere people need help and right now that includes scores of networking organizations in 41 states.

Through an online site, Enterprise OnLine, the foundation shares practical how-to and model program information with other nonprofit organizations who seek to do the same nationwide.

A measure of its success is the fact that since its inception in 1982, the foundation has helped create some 200,000 homes for low-income people, including the development of "green" communities and new homes for Gulf Coast families affected by Hurricane Katrina. The Enterprise Foundation has a network of local organizations that stretches across the country. It maintains local offices in 16 areas of the country, including New York, Texas, and California.

the Italian way of life. This solidly Catholic community is very active in church, school, and neighborhood happenings. Its residents are family focused, and often three generations live in the small houses (all row houses and most only 10 feet by 13 feet and two rooms deep). A little piece of Little Italy averages $225,000.

Although an inner-city neighborhood, Little Italy is safe. It is also incredibly clean, thanks to the neighbors and business owners who come out each morning with broom and hose. You'll find plenty of formstone and white marble steps in Little Italy, as well as window boxes that drip with colorful flowers from spring through fall. The advantages of living in Little Italy include the short walking distance to Downtown, being right on the water, and, of course, the food.

Inner Harbor East didn't even exist a few years ago. This area right on the harbor was abandoned industrial properties for the most part, with decrepit low-income high-rise housing to the north. Certainly nobody wanted to live in this desolate area. But then developers gave the area a new look. First, a vacant chromium plant was demolished and the site was cleaned up. The high-rise projects were also razed and in their place went mixed-income town houses, one street prettier than the next. Soon, high-rise offices, hotels, condominiums, and shops were elbowing their way into the spaces left behind. The result is an exciting new neighborhood; some call it Baltimore's "Gold Coast."

Living here isn't cheap. The new apartments lease for approximately $1,300 to $6,000 a month. Condominium prices soar as high as the buildings, starting at just less than a million dollars but reaching the $5,000,000 mark. Town houses for sale in the neighborhood, most built in 2006 or 2007, hover in the mid $300,000 to $400,000 range.

Just beyond Little Italy and Harbor East is **Fells Point.** Established in 1730 by William Fell as a shipyard, Fells Point the town was actually laid out in 1773 by William's son, Edward Fell, for the families and artisans who worked at the yard. The names of its streets are decidedly British, such as Shakespeare Street and Thames Street. (Thames is pronounced as spelled, by the way.) Because of its ideal location near a deep, protected harbor as well as, at that time, a seemingly unlimited supply of hardwood, Fells Point quickly became the main colonial shipbuilding center. The first two ships in the American Navy, the *Wasp* and the *Hornet*, were commissioned at Fells Point in 1783. The Broadway Market, one of three original Baltimore markets, was built on land donated to

the town by William Fell and still stands in its original location. Most of the small, brick row houses date from those revolutionary days and have been highly coveted by renovators since the neighborhood was saved from demolition for a highway in 1967.

Prices can be high for the amount of house you get, but the ambience is worth it. And in today's housing market, prices actually fall in the low to normal range, between $100,000 for smaller, unrenovated properties on the area's borders to well over $850,000 for renovated properties in Fells Point's center. The average Fells Point home now sells for $279,000.

However, Fells Point is not just a bedroom community; it is a center of activity. During the day the area teams with shoppers who are interested in antiques and unusual craft items. Community theater, family restaurants, and bars with live music make parking hard to find in the evening, but since the water taxi can take you right to the foot of Broadway in Fells Point from the Inner Harbor, tourists really needn't worry.

On the other hand, if you're thinking of settling there, Fells Point has covered the parking problem by having two-hour parking limits for visitors on its mostly residential side streets. Residents park by permit.

The neighborhood is as eclectic as its history has painted it. The very wealthy, the middle class, the working stiff, and the homeless all live in Fells Point.

Originally part of Jonestown, settled in 1661 by David Jones, **Oldtown** is east of the Jones Falls and north of Fells Point and Little Italy. The neighborhood was originally settled by German and Irish immigrants.

Many of the original row houses in Oldtown were built prior to the Civil War. The area is now primarily an African-American community, a great many of whose ancestors crowded into Baltimore after the Civil War and during World Wars I and II, when defense work was plentiful in the area. In fact the first housing projects were built in the area to house defense workers.

i When you find yourself at the foot of Broadway in Fells Point, look east. You will see the old Recreation Pier, which you may recognize as the outside set for the police station on *Homicide*, the former NBC detective show filmed in Baltimore and produced by one of Baltimore's own, Barry Levinson.

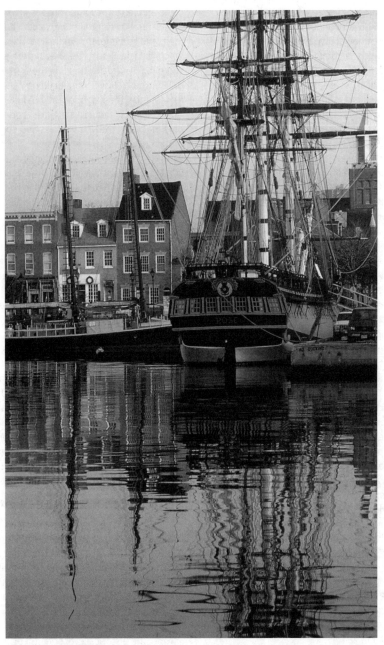

Boats dock in Fells Point just as they always have since the 18th century. BALTIMORE AREA CONVENTION AND VISITORS ASSOCIATION

Much recent renovation, demolition, and new building in the area, however, is due to the continuing influence of the Oldtown Plan, an urban renewal plan that was developed by the city and the community in 1968. This stimulated some renovation interest in the area and one of its jewels, **Stirling Street**. Originally scheduled for demolition, this block of 150-year-old row houses became instead Baltimore's first Dollar House Project of the mid-1970s. (See Dollar Houses earlier in this chapter.)

Above Little Italy and Fells Point and south of Orleans Street is a large area known as **Washington Hill**. Near the center of the community is Church Hospital, sometimes called Church Home by natives, where Edgar Allan Poe died after he was found drunk and beaten in a waterfront dive. The neighborhood, with some houses dating from the 1700s, is more currently noteworthy for the extensive renovation in its neighborhood that sparked Artisan's Row, an area within the community of stained-glass craftsmen, frame restorers and gilders, stone workers, woodworkers, and more.

Prices for restored homes average $242,000.

Still Downtown, southeast of Charles Street but across the Inner Harbor, is **Federal Hill**. The Federal Hill neighborhood is named for the promontory that has the distinction of being the tip of land Captain John Smith first sighted in 1606 as well as the area from which British ships were sighted during the War of 1812 and the site of a Union fort during the Civil War. It is said that from the observatory tower that once stood on the site ships could be seen 35 miles into the bay.

The area was first settled by factory workers, dock workers, watermen, and trainmen. It caught fire as a renovation neighborhood during the 1970s, when Inner Harbor development began and renovation fever was sweeping the city.

Federal Hill begins on the south side of the Inner Harbor at Key Highway and extends south to Cross Street. Most of its houses are row homes, usually two stories but some three and four. The larger houses are said to have been built for the supervisors and foremen, and sometimes owners and merchants, who originally settled the area. There is also some highly unusual housing there. When the old Southern High School building was closed, for instance, the neighborhood didn't want it razed. It was instead turned into condominiums that used the original halls and contours of the building wherever possible. The result can be a resident who lives in an area that used to be an entrance hall. These apartments boast cathedral ceilings, fan light windows, sunken living spaces, and lofts.

Like Fells Point, Federal Hill is not just homes. Many of the old corner stores have been turned into corner shops, antiques, and otherwise. There are many nice restaurants and there is Cross Street Market (see the Shopping chapter for more information). Like many inner-city neighborhoods, the streets are narrow, so if you're not used to parallel parking with only inches to spare, we suggest you make your first visit to Federal Hill a sunny day's stroll.

Federal Hill holds an eclectic mix of old-time residents as well as blue-collar and professional people. Properties may still be found in the area for $50,000, with large, upscale, renovated properties going for well over $450,000. The average price of a Federal Hill home is about $338,000.

SOUTHWEST DOWNTOWN

West of Federal Hill and the Inner Harbor is the small enclave of **Otterbein**, within which you will find the Old Otterbein Church, the oldest continuing congregation in the city and the site of the first Methodist congregation in the United States, begun in 1771.

Originally settled by German, Greek, Polish, and other immigrants from Eastern Europe, the historical preservation district continues to be a vital, eclectic area. Otterbein was another area saved in 1975 by the Dollar House Project; hence, most of its houses, though archaic on the outside, are thoroughly modern on the inside (see Dollar Houses earlier in this chapter). The neighborhood also has brick sidewalks, cobblestone alleyways, and its own swim club for those hot summer days.

Prices can be high: Although the houses themselves were bought for a dollar, the renovations weren't. Renovated homes in Otterbein sell for $375,000 to $466,000. If you like being where the action is—and walking distance from Camden Yards—Otterbein is just the place.

The west has zest! Or so the banners flying over Eutaw Street said as development got under way here in the early years of the new century. It has been slow going. The Hippodrome Theatre at the France Merrick Performing Arts Center was virtually alone on a dark and desolate street when the curtain rose on its first performance in about 40 years. But since that day in 2003, a lot has changed.

Loft apartments have brought two historic buildings, one across the street from the theater and another around the corner, back to life. Centerpoint, nearby, was also due to open in 2007. New town houses in Camden Crossing, near Oriole Park, were due to open in 2008. A 22-story apartment tower overlooking Pratt Street was also going up, set to open in late 2007. Most of the new housing will be rental property.

Meanwhile, University of Maryland Medical Systems and Medical School have been building, too, with new medical facilities and student residences.

So the dark, vacant streets have vanished as bit by bit the empty spaces begin to become a neighborhood. Since very little of this development was for sale at press time, no prices were yet available. The West Side is bounded by Howard Street to the east, Read Street to the north, Pratt Street to the south, and Martin Luther King Boulevard on the west. It connects with the Seton Hill and Mount Vernon neighborhoods.

Pigtown, also called Washington Village, is generally considered to be the area that borders Carroll Park on the south, along Washington Boulevard, and it is usually included as part of Southwest Baltimore. It falls, however, in our catchment area for Downtown, and so we note it here.

Pigtown was originally named "Kuh Viertel," German for "Cow Quarter." Historically home to stockyards and slaughterhouses, it was originally populated by Irish and German immigrants and, later, black freemen, who worked in the slaughterhouses and at Alexander Russell's brickworks.

Most residents there can trace their families' histories back three or four generations right there in those few square blocks. There are no slaughterhouses anymore, but there are plenty of white marble steps, plenty of formstone fronts, and some pretty good buys in housing, both renovated and unrenovated. Pigtown houses now sell in the $115,000 to $135,000 range.

Ridgely's Delight began as the combination of two properties. In 1732 Charles Ridgely married Rebecca Howard, daughter of General John Eager Howard. As dowry, he received a large estate that buttressed a smaller property owned by him. Upon his marriage, he combined the two into one grand plantation, Ridgely's Delight. Now, easy to find since it's directly opposite the west side of Camden Yards, the neighborhood forms a perfect triangle of land, bounded on the east by Russell Street, the north by Pratt Street, and the west by Fremont Street. By some calculations it is within the borders of Pigtown.

Another area where many of the historic row homes were reclaimed by the Dollar House Project (see previous section in this chapter), Ridgely's Delight is touched by all the main architectural styles used in Baltimore's homes. The earliest homes date from

i Need a new fridge? Energy efficient models—available from most major manufacturers—are tax exempt in Maryland, making a high-end purchase a cost saving prospect.

Getting to Know Baltimore Architecture

Throughout this book, we often refer to Baltimore's architecture because it is a reflection of the city's history and the city's place in history. As a character in the TV show *Homicide* noted, Baltimore is "drowning in history," and it is Baltimore's architecture that allows citizens and visitors alike to immerse themselves in the pool.

In a way, Baltimore is a working museum. Down every street where people live and work are architectural examples from almost every historical period that harmonize across Baltimore's landscape. Yet, even those of us who are used to the give and take of old and new are sometimes astounded by the contrasts.

The 50-story skyscraper that towers over, but somehow doesn't overshadow, a three-story, iron facade. The country mansion that is no longer in the country but surrounded by black macadam roads and the roar of traffic. As we go about our twenty-first-century lives, it's sometimes hard to remember that in Baltimore almost every brick and cobblestone bears some historic significance from the three centuries that came before.

Baltimore's original cityscape was created by architectural names like Latrobe, Cassell, and Pope. The people who hired them were the Peabodys, the Pratts, and the Hopkinses—city benefactors, philanthropists, businessmen.

Sadly, many of Baltimore's exciting and architecturally significant buildings have been excised from the cityscape over the years by 1960s urban renewal and the current city government's "fix it up or we'll tear it down" mentality. But, luckily, much of the work of Baltimore's builders remains to be appreciated.

If you are interested in visiting specific architectural sites such as the B&O Railroad Roundhouse, the Carroll Mansion, Evergreen House, Homewood House, or some of the architectural sites used as examples below, their exact whereabouts can be found in the Attractions chapter. In this brief Close-up, we're hoping to provide only some general information about architectural styles so that as you ride around town, you'll be able to tell what's what.

—Thanks to Mary Ellen Hayward and John Dilts for information about Baltimore's architecture and to John and his coauthor John Dorsey for A Guide to Baltimore Architecture, *3rd edition (Tidewater Publishers, Centreville, Maryland, 1997). Thanks also to John C. Poppeliers, et al., for their book,* What Style Is It? A Guide to American Architecture *(John Wiley & Sons, Inc., New York, 1995), which was consulted frequently while compiling this information.*

The Colonial Style and Georgian Revival

Anyone who has ever been to or seen pictures of restored buildings at Williamsburg, Virginia, has a good idea of what the colonial period wrought architecturally. Also known as English Georgian, the colonial style is characterized by white columned porticos, peaked roofs, red brick, and dormer windows that were multi-paned. Good examples of colonial-style buildings still visible in Baltimore include Mount Clare Mansion, Old Otterbein Church, and Captain John Steele House.

The desire to build in the colonial style ended with the Revolution, as old English trends fell by the wayside and new American trends stepped in to take their places. By the end of the nineteenth century, however, builders who sought to lend an old-world dignity and grace to their buildings revived the style. In fact, homes with a Georgian flavor continued to be built on through the twentieth century and, even now, you will find homes being erected that have two-story-high pillars under a peaked roof portico, multipaned windows, and redbrick walls.

You can tell the nineteenth century from eighteenth because later buildings tend to have exaggerated certain elements. Pillars are larger, taller; moldings are deeper and more multilayered. Also, we've noticed that eighteenth-century brick appears to be thinner top to bottom and smaller overall; newer red brick appears thicker and larger. It may, in fact, be that there is simply more mortar between the bricks in newer houses, but, for whatever reason, the observation remains.

The Federal and Jeffersonian Styles
The Federal style has much of the colonial in it, but scaled back. A more delicate rendition, one might say. Columns are narrower, their caps simpler with no more than one level of decoration. The Jeffersonian style, which was a simplification externally even on the Federal, often does not have any decoration at all. Rooflines are dotted with hound's-tooth molding or are without adornment. Dormers may be curved instead of peaked, and if peaked the pitch is not very steep. Windows have fewer panes. Overall, lines are simpler, coming as they do from a time when function was prized above frivolity.

Doors may have fan windows above and side windows as well. Interior ceilings of this style have simple relief decorations, such as carved roses or ceiling moldings. Round rooms and domes were also popular, as were flat, fluted decorative pillars.

An example of a Federal building in Baltimore is Homewood House, the restoration of which was completed by Johns Hopkins University on whose campus it sits and after which its Homewood campus was named.

Though the Federal period dates from 1776 to about 1795, the Federal style is well used in Baltimore over the past two centuries, particularly in the porchfront row homes in neighborhoods such as Charles Village that were built between 1909 and 1923, approximately. A takeoff on the Federal style may also be found in the row homes built as recently as the 1940s through the 1960s in neighborhoods such as Northwood, where redbrick houses sport white, peaked trim, multipaned windows, and flat, fluted pillars molding the main entranceways.

Classical Revival
At the turn of the nineteenth century, there was a return to the classical styles of Greece and Rome. Whereas a Federal-style portico might have, at most, four columns, the classically styled portico might have eight, and in place of a simple column cap, there might be swirls or copious foliage. The thinner one-story columns of the Federal style gave way to two-story-high, giant fluted columns. Rooflines include domed towers and central rotundas.

One of the most famous examples of Classical Revival architecture in Baltimore is the Basilica of the Assumption, which was designed by Benjamin Henry Latrobe, who also designed the U.S. Capitol in Washington, D.C. Later examples that adhere to this style are also visible in Baltimore, however. The War Memorial across from Baltimore's City Hall is

CONTINUED

noted as one of them, although it has some Art Deco elements as well.

Gothic Revival

To think of Gothic is to think of times when myth held the reins of terror in Europe. One tends to envision sorcerers and witch burnings. The original Gothic style was heavy, almost cumbersome, in its uses of tower and gargoyle, gray stone and ironwork. Gothic Revival of the late eighteenth and early nineteenth centuries uses these elements but to a much lesser degree. No columns or porticos grace the fronts of Gothic Revival buildings, only simple steps. Rooflines are punctuated with steep, peaked caps over doorways and windows. This was the beginning of bay and oriel windows with pointed caps or crenelated stone tops, which reflected the corner watchtowers of a castle.

A straightforward example of such style is the main gate at Greenmount Cemetery, which was designed by Robert Cary Long Jr., who also designed five Gothic churches in Baltimore as well as buildings reflecting other architectural styles.

Antebellum

Antebellum architecture in Baltimore was driven by one main economic engine, the railroad. By the time the B&O Railroad reached the fertile Ohio Valley in 1652, Baltimore was finding many uses for products such as iron ore dug from the Appalachians and returned to the city by rail. Iron was already big industry in Baltimore before the Civil War, and one of the forward-thinking items it produced was prefabricated ironworks. Facades for buildings, circular staircases, railings, window grills, balconies, and the like became part and parcel of the buildings of that time. The value of iron for such use was that it could be molded like plaster, yet it was stronger and more impervious to the elements than wood, brick, or stone.

One of the most astounding interior uses of iron prefabrication in Baltimore is the five-tiered interior of the George Peabody Library, built in 1857 and designed by Edmund George Lind. The facade of the main gallery of the City Life Museums on President Street is also all iron, as is the City Hall dome, which was designed and built here in Baltimore by Wendel Bollman.

Victorian Styles

After the Civil War and through the turn of the twentieth century, Baltimore was in its heyday. The railroad and the industries that had blossomed from it ruled the cityscape. Money was being made hand over fist in a time when there were no income taxes, no zoning laws, and still plenty of land to go around. It was, therefore, a time of building.

From the 1850s Gothic and Classical styles had given way to French and Italian Renaissance stylings. There are a great many examples of this type of architecture in Baltimore. The features include such items as broad verandas, formal gardens, and mansard roofs. Houses from this period are often made of wood, with shingle. The mansard roofs are decorated with gingerbread trim that looks like rows of thick lace. Towers, bowed walls, and bay windows add to the look, although the Italian Renaissance styles tend to be more square, with roofs pitched lower.

During the Victorian times, however, these styles and others were drawn together into an eclectic mix that picked up pieces from all styles that had gone before and brought them together into a mix that is sometimes called Second Empire style. Mansard roofs are deeper, including dormer windows or sometimes narrow, multicapped columns and balconies. Porches, porticos, and verandas are in evidence, and the overall feeling is busy because of so many visual forms being brought together in one place. The effect is, however, grand and imposing. One sure sign of Victoriana is a capped widow's walk, which you will see on many Baltimore buildings and in other port towns. The widow's walk is a cupola, either closed or open, on the roof of the building, where, reportedly, the wives of captains and sailors paced and waited for sight of their husband's ship to enter the harbor.

Examples of Victorian architecture are found in Roland Park, Lutherville, and other country neighborhoods of the time. More formal examples are easily seen at Mount Vernon Place and the Belvedere at Chase and Charles Streets.

Art Deco

As the 1920s roared into town, Baltimore, like most big East Coast cities, was ready to become thoroughly modern. Victorian evolved into what is called Nouveau. Nouveau was really an interior and fashion style more than a building style, but buildings that were rendered during this period tend toward smoother lines overall, with larger visuals and more glass, while still reflecting the gingerbread and visual clutter of the Victorian era.

By 1925, builders were ready for the cleaner, less cluttered appearance. The style is called modern decorative, Art Deco, or simply Deco. Deco style cuts off all corners . . . literally. A typical Deco building has rounded edges. If design was rendered in brick, designers tended to use yellow instead of red, and the bricks were larger. Other building choices included smooth stone or stucco. There was a lot of chrome and a lot of glass, including glass block, and interiors tended to be rendered in lighter woods such as oak and ash rather than cherry or mahogany.

Whereas Victorian and nouveau glass renderings tended to be intricate and three-dimensional like a Tiffany lampshade, Deco was rendered boldly and often two-dimensionally—three petals above a single stem etched into a blue glass mirror. You can, in fact, see that actual item over the water fountain inside of the decidedly Deco Senator Theater, which is across the street from the definitely Deco department store building that now houses a Pier One, a health club, and a Blockbuster. But an absolute favorite expression of Art Deco in Baltimore is the interior of Werner's Restaurant on Redwood Street, where the blond wood booths are still edged in chrome and surrounded by mirrored columns.

A Word About Formstone . . .

As you move through Baltimore, you will see a great many buildings—particularly marble-stepped, two-story, nineteenth-century row houses—covered with a substance that you may not be able to identify. It looks like multicolored stone from far away, but when you get up close it seems to be some kind of formed stucco.

The substance is called formstone, and it is not original to any of the buildings to which it adheres. It can be removed, blasted, and chipped away to uncover the original brick, and we are seeing more and more of this today.

We believe that formstone was originally sold as a way to waterproof and insulate homes. This supposition makes sense, for without formstone, an old brick house that was having leakage problems would have to repoint all the brick, an expensive process, and to insulate would require losing floor space by adding depth to interior walls, which, when your living room is only 10 feet by 13 feet, hardly seems practical.

the Federal period, around 1804. These are the smaller, two-story homes. The larger homes that were built later, mostly to house doctors from the University of Maryland Hospital nearby, are Victorian, Edwardian, and Georgian Revival, with the bulk of the homes being built between 1840 and 1860. One tiny home was the birthplace of Babe Ruth and is now a museum in his honor. When sold by lottery for $1, many of these homes had only two side walls and a crumbling facade. Millions of dollars and more than 30 years later, Ridgely's Delight is populated with middle- and upper-middle-income professionals who enjoy the proximity to the Inner Harbor, the downtown business district, and the MARC commuter train. Renovated properties average about $270,000. Ridgely's Delight is a Baltimore City Historic District and is posted on the National Register of Historic Places.

A little south and west, encircling Ridgely's Delight to our western Downtown boundary, are Barre Circle, Scott Circle, Washington Village, Mount Clare, and Union Square. All have undergone extensive renovation and continue to upgrade, renovate, and, generally, keep the areas moving forward— not that they aren't already in a pretty good place. **Barre Circle,** for instance, which is an area of fewer than 120 homes nestled between the 1000 block of West Barre Street, the 800 block of Lombard Street, the 700 block of McHenry Street, and the 700 block of Otterbein Street, has seen renewed interest in their renovated 1840 row houses, pushing prices up into the $284,000 range. Many of them have large backyards and gardens, and there are two large green commons for the enjoyment of all the neighbors. The houses tend to get bigger and fancier as you head west, but **Union Square** at the western border has not seen the same level of interest. Home prices average $180,000. The area is racially and economically diverse, with active community organizations.

NORTHEAST
Within the City

Across North Avenue from Oliver/Eastern Terrace, diagonal to Greenmount Cemetery, at the edge of our northern boundary, is **East Baltimore Midway.** Bordered by Harford Road on the east and Hargrove Street on the west, it stretches north to 25th Street, east of Charles Village. Housing here is mainly row houses, with only St. Ann's Avenue having individual homes. Most of the houses date from the turn of the twentieth century and are two- and three-story brick. A predominantly African-American community of approximately 6,000 households, the neighborhood boasts long-term residents and has 43 percent homeownership. There are also two recreation centers in the area and two small parks. The bane of the neighborhood is the increasing vacant properties, many of which have been simply abandoned by absentee landlords who decided that they didn't want to spend the time and money dealing with lead-paint problems. The positive side of this, of course, is that some of these properties can be picked up for about $60,000. Off the beaten track, but surrounded by it, residents of East Baltimore Midway are only three minutes by car from center city and only 10 minutes by bus. They are within walking distance of Penn Station, where they can pick up trains or Light Rail, and there are four main bus lines available to residents.

North of 25th Street, west of Harford Road across from the golf course, south of 32nd Street and Harford Road as it wraps around the community, and east of Loch Raven Boulevard is the community known as **Coldstream-Homestead-Montebello.** The area is technically three separate communities, but some time back they banded together. The area was initially developed at the turn of the twentieth century, although there is housing there that was built as recently as 1989. There are a fair number of apartment complexes in the area, but most of the homes are traditional two-story row homes, many of brown and yellow brick. There are also some freestanding homes.

Housing prices differ for each part of the community. In Coldstream, which is the area closer to 25th Street, houses tend to sell in the mid-$30,000s to $40,000 range. In Homestead, which is toward the western boundary, prices move into the low to mid-$40,000s. In Montebello, which is in the north near Montebello Lake, where houses get larger and there are more individual homes, prices rise. The average price for the area is $64,000. Primarily a middle-income, African-American community, Montebello had 64 percent homeownership in 2005. Insiders say the area is trying to increase that figure, while working on creating a better mix of community-related commercial establishments.

Contiguous to the southeast side of Clifton Park golf course is the area known as **Belair–Edison.** The Brehms Brewery once claimed 624 acres there, and an Insider notes that underground tunnels have been found under the community where the brewery once stored its brew. The neighborhood grew up between 1930 and 1960 and is primarily row after row of the typical, two-story, brick row homes from those times, although there are some duplexes and individual homes here and there. The neighborhood boasts 14 churches and four parochial schools. Neighbors are proud of nearby Herring Run Park, a soccer player's heaven. An eclectic area of working people, homes average $99,000.

A shoemaker's shop, a corn husk depot, a blacksmith, a wheelwright, and three small stone houses made up the original 1840s town that eventually became **Waverly.** The area where they stood is still a part of Waverly's business district, which extends from its southern border of 28th Street/Exeter Hall Avenue to within a few blocks of its northern border of 39th Street. The western border is Greenmount Avenue, contiguous to the eastern edge of Charles Village; its eastern borders are Loch Raven Boulevard below 33rd Street and Ellerslie Avenue above it. The homes are a mixture of early 1920s row

houses, stately Victorians, and both older and newer country shingle. It was, after all, a country town when it was annexed by Baltimore in 1888. More than a century later, its side streets still have that suburban, small-town feeling. An eclectic community of mostly lower-middle- to middle-class working people, it offers some excellent housing opportunities, with larger Victorian individual homes in the low $50,000s and an average price of $94,000.

The area north and east of the Memorial Stadium site on 33rd Street is named **Ednor Gardens/Lakeside.** Originally part of the 500-acre Montebello estate, the area matured in the late 1920s through the 1950s. The original row houses are the Tudor-style homes; the later postwar homes are the traditional redbrick, two-story porch fronts. There are also some individual homes and large duplexes that sit closer to, and on, 33rd Street across from City College. House prices average $174,000.

Mayfield begins just north of Erdman Avenue, on the other side of the public golf course from Montebello. It runs north from there to Chesterfield Avenue, which is the boundary to Herring Run Park, west to Montebello Lake and east to Crossland Avenue. It was developed just after the turn of the last century and is a quiet, pleasant tree-lined area of single homes, duplexes, and row houses. The residential areas are safe, and most of the residents have been there a long time. There's a mixed group of white-collar and blue-collar professionals. There are mostly individual homes—some large enough to be considered mansions—with some smaller row homes right on Chesterfield Avenue. The average house price is $265,000.

Lauraville is west of Harford Road, south of Echodale Avenue, and north of Herring Run Park. One of its particularly nice features is that it backs up to woods on its west side, giving it privacy that other neighborhoods with major roads running through them don't have. Its larger Victorian houses have been sought by renovators since the late 1970s and are still considered a bargain, although the prices keep rising, and now average $174,000.

Originally known as North Lauraville, **Hamilton** encloses the area west of Walther Boulevard and east of Perring Parkway, which extends northward from Echodale Avenue to the county line, where it runs into Parkville and Overlea. Hamilton is primarily a working-class neighborhood, with a solid community spirit and a history that dates from its days as a farming community. Its houses are mainly of the clapboard, shingle variety of individual homes—the kind that look small from the outside but are big on the inside. Yards are generous and properties well kept.

Prices for single homes can run into the upper $100,000s, with semidetached and row houses (of which there are some) hovering in the $70,000s. The overall average price for a home in Hamilton is $165,000.

Original Northwood is just across The Alameda from Ednor Gardens/Lakeside, in a triangle of land bounded on the east and south by Loch Raven Boulevard, which wraps around it, and on the north by Argonne Drive, although the houses on the north side of Argonne are also considered as being in Original Northwood. Developed in the 1920s by the Roland Park Company, the same developers who gave us Roland Park, Homeland, and Guilford, Original Northwood is a combination of individual, semidetached, and row houses. Like those neighborhoods, Original Northwood is adrift in foliage. Tall old trees, gardens, and any number of beautiful plantings line its few streets. Its row houses are of particular interest because they are not the traditional brick lineup that you see in most Baltimore neighborhoods, both older and younger. The rows were intentionally given an uneven face and a Tudor style. Similar homes are found only in Roland Park. They look small from the outside, but are in fact quite roomy inside. Though not a historic neighborhood, Original Northwood does have a covenant that governs how its houses may be painted and changed on the outside.

Prices in the neighborhood range from about $70,000 for row homes and semi-detached houses to about $200,000 for the individual homes. The average price in Original Northwood is $270,000.

Northwood is a pre– and post–World War II neighborhood of mostly brick row houses built to house the growing families of the 1950s. Originally a neighborhood with a predominance of Irish, Germans, and Italians, Northwood has grown into an eclectic neighborhood that is a prime location for teachers and students of nearby Morgan State University. The neighborhood is bound by Argonne Drive on the south, Woodbourne Avenue on the north, on the west by Hillen Road, and on the east by The Alameda. Although most of the houses look the same from the outside, some are larger than others and many end-of-groups have fireplaces. Another green area, with large trees, 20-to-30-foot front lawns, and fenced backyards, Northwood is a great family area. Houses sell in the $130,000 range. The neighborhood also claims one of the largest apartment complexes within the city's limits, the Northwood Apartments.

Above Northwood is a large area called **Perring Loch** that sits in the V between Hillen Road on the west and Perring Parkway on the east. Row houses of the 1950s are prevalent in this area, but they are considerably smaller overall than those in Northwood. Residents are particularly proud of the community's diversity, old and young, white and black, factory worker and professional. The average home sells for $155,000.

Just below the county line, down to Lake Avenue and west of York Road and east of Bellona Avenue, is the neighborhood of **Cedarcroft**, an area of longtime residents, quiet streets, and large, overhanging trees. An eclectic area featuring shopping and Baltimore's only remaining big-screen neighborhood theater, The Senator, and a short commute from Downtown or Towson, Cedarcroft blends convenience and comfort. Built in the 1950s, the area has a much wider choice of housing than many strictly row house

Selected Baltimore Firsts

In 1816 Rembrandt Peale introduced the first building to be lighted by gas in Baltimore.

In 1828 Columbus O'Donnell and the Canton Company chartered the first planned industrial and residential community in Fells Point.

Bogardus and Hopping designed the first known cast-iron building in the world at South and Baltimore Streets; it burned in 1851.

In 1896 Frederick Olmsted, the famed landscape architect, designed the first strip shopping center to serve the country community; he also designed Roland Park.

John H. B. Latrobe invented the first stove for use in indoor heating. Known as the Latrobe Stove, or the Baltimore heater, the first one was installed here in Baltimore in 1846.

In 1937 Albert Knight of Formstone Company received the first patent for form-stone. Formstone is the faux stone of different colors that has been plastered to the brick fronts of many Baltimore row houses. (Albert Knight was a good salesman!)

—*Excerpted from* Baltimore—America's City of Firsts, *a pamphlet published by Baltimore Bicentennial Celebration, Inc.*

neighborhoods of the same era. There are row houses in the area but also duplexes (two independently standing side-by-side row houses). Individual homes in the Cape Cod, Victorian, and colonial styles can also be found. Prices range from around $70,000 to more than $250,000.

Contiguous to Cedarcroft and Govans on the west, confined by Charles Street on the east, the county line on the north, and Homeland Avenue on the south are 391 acres of land that originally constituted the estate of David Maulden Perine known as **Homeland.** It continued as a working estate until 1922, when it was bought by the Roland Park Company for development. Most of the homes are individual (some are impressive mansions) and range in style from stone Tudor to brick Early American, although there are some modern ranch-style houses and large row homes as well. Streets are tree-lined, with wide expanses of green lawns and flowering shrubbery. Some of the original details from the estate still remain, such as the ponds along Springlake Way. (Baltimore's winters have been too mild in most recent years for a hard freeze, but we can remember throwing ice skates over our shoulders and heading out of our neighborhoods for the trek to Homeland and these man-made ponds that became our ice rinks.) Much of the public landscaping done by the Olmsted Brothers of Boston also remains and is tended with loving hands. Homeland is one of the most popular areas in Baltimore for the high-income professionals, because it is so close to the city and Towson, close to shopping and schools, both public and private, while saving for itself the feeling of a country estate. Housing prices now average $541,000.

Govans is named for its first owner, William Govane, a wealthy importer and shipping magnate who was granted the land by the last Lord Calvert. The growth of the community was spurred when the York Turnpike (York Road) was completed in 1786. Industrialists like W. Abell and philanthropists such as the Pratt family once settled there on country estates. With ready access, industry eventually began to locate there, and over the next hundred years the town grew steadily. Govans is now considered the area that sits above Cold Spring Lane, west of The Alameda and east of York Road. On the north, the boundary is sketchy, as it runs into the Belvedere area. Govans prides itself on a heterogeneous population. The housing is just as diverse. Large Victorians, small country frames, 1940s bungalows, and 1920s rows all can be found in Govans, with prices ranging from $86,000 to $103,000.

South of Cold Spring Lane to University Parkway, west of St. Paul Street, and east of Greenmount Avenue (York Road) lies **Guilford**, one of the most astoundingly beautiful communities in Baltimore. Another one of the Roland Park Company's development projects, the community was designed by Frederick Law Olmsted Jr., and its first lots were offered for sale in 1913. The lots were not so much simple building areas but land enough to be claimed as small estates. Six of the nine acres that constitute Sherwood Gardens, for instance, were originally part of the Sherwood Estate. And we're ever so glad for it. Baltimoreans flock to Sherwood Gardens every spring to walk among the 100,000 tulips, 10,000 pansies, and walls of azaleas planted there. But a simple walk through the community can have the same effect. Its 700 magnificent individual homes run the gamut from castle to chalet, but every one is a gem. Prices depend on the size of the home and land, and range from $150,000 to $2 million. The average price is $516,000.

Okenshaw is a tiny enclave of large, two-story row houses at the foot of Guilford, to the west of Waverly and north of Charles Village. We mention it because it is such a pleasant little pocket, only about 5 blocks in all, but filled with neighbors who know each other well and still do such things as have holiday cookie swaps. Tree-shaded and well-landscaped houses can sell for $275,000.

On the edge of Guilford facing onto Greenmount Avenue/York Road, both north and south of 39th Street is an area known as **York Courts**. Prices here are much lower because the 36 houses face the busy York Road corridor. They are unique, however, in that the row houses, rather than being in a line along the street as is true with most row house blocks in Baltimore, face onto a large, green, landscaped common.

Over the County Line

From Charles Street on the west, Loch Raven Boulevard to the east, and from the city line to the south to slightly above the Beltway on the north lies a gigantic area that is considered **Towson** (pronounced TOU-sun not TOW-zon). It started out as a small town, whose center was, and for the most part still is, at the convergence of York Road, Dulaney Valley Road, and Joppa Road (which was originally an old Indian trail). Today Towson is the county seat of Baltimore County. Within its boundaries are probably as many neighborhoods as are found within the city's limits. The ones closer to the city line developed mostly from summer estates held by city dwellers; farther out was farmland, and Towson's neighborhoods were in many ways developed a farm at a time. Most of the solid, older neighborhoods in Towson and around the county generally started out as simple suburban housing developments from the 1930s onward. They've grown, however, into unique enclaves that share a point of view and a way of life.

South of Towson's center, below Towson University and running up to the city line are the communities of **Rogers Forge, Stoneleigh, Idlewylde,** and **Anneslie.** They are among the most popular neighborhoods for city transplants because they offer quick access to Baltimore, while bestowing on the transplant lower taxes, better schools, and safer streets. Their histories began as the summer retreats of Beulah Land, owned by Joshua Regester; Anneslie Villa, the Birckhear Estate; and Stoneleigh, the Brown Estate. The communities grew when the streetcar and road building made them more accessible.

The houses in the area run the gamut from original frame farmhouses to 1950s rows. There are modern split levels, ranchers, and Cape Cods, and there is still the occasional free building lot.

North of Towson's center, past the humongous Towson Town Center shopping mall on its northeast corner, is the intersection of Goucher Boulevard and Providence Road. To the north of the intersection is an area called **Campus Hills,** where 119 acres of farmland were claimed for 369 brick, predominantly split-level, moderately priced houses in 1955. There were seven different models to choose from, with sizes up to five bedrooms and three baths. The neighborhood was much coveted at the time, being, as it was, totally modern. It is still a popular area because it has a well-landscaped setting with individual homes, but it is walking distance to virtually every major shopping area in Towson. Towson-area homes average $403,000.

Around the corner from Campus Hills, so to speak, to the east is **Loch Raven Village.** Very much a clone of Northwood, which is just a few miles south down Loch Raven Boulevard, Loch Raven Village boasts much larger homes, although still in the style of the postwar, two-story brick porch front.

Above the Beltway, where Charles Street ends—making this community just about dead north of Baltimore—is **Lutherville.** Lutherville is only about 1 square mile, but it holds some restored Victorian gems. Large lots, big porches, bowed windows and walls, and dormers galore mark these homes as desired. Lutherville is a pleasant Victorian village right smack-dab in the middle of everything. Its properties sell for an average of $526,000.

Above the Beltway, between York Road and Dulaney Valley Road, is the community of Hampton—not to be confused with Hampden. Hampton is particularly notable because it surrounds the Hampton Mansion, built in 1790 by the Ridgely Family and donated to the National Park Service in 1947. Hampton was developed beginning in 1949. The homes are large, with landscaped yards, woods, and streams, and have prices to match, but their convenience to the Beltway, and thus Downtown, and to Towson's center make it an ideal location. Average price is $400,000.

North of Hampton, Towson ends, although it doesn't seem to, at least on York Road. The endless strip malls, fast-food restaurants, and apartment complexes continue into **Timonium,** known for its race track and its fairgrounds where the Maryland State Fair is held every year. Above Timonium is the old town of **Cockeysville,** which is much built up, but where the vestiges of the old town center still remain in the form of antiques and specialty shops. Above Cockeysville is an area known as **Hunt Valley** that was, in fact, a valley through which the elite used to sound the horn, hit the saddle, and take off across hill and dale. A very new area, it is nevertheless very popular because of its proximity to Towson and downtown. By Beltway and Interstate 83 North, Hunt Valley is a brief 20-minute ride from Downtown. Light Rail also now goes to Hunt Valley Town Center. Prices around here range from $430,000, the average in Hunt Valley, to an average of $640,000 in Timonium. Many houses here cost well over $1,000,000.

Above Hunt Valley is still mostly country with a few new developments. We will not go there; but if you'd like a lovely ride, you should.

East of Loch Raven Boulevard, west and south of the Beltway as it circles around, and north of the city line are the areas of Hillendale, Parkville, and Overlea. There are many smaller neighborhoods and developments within these areas, but these are the names given generally to the area that begins east of Towson and wraps around the city line to the east. Hillendale is directly adjacent to Towson and continues the feel of Loch Raven Village, showing large row house developments as well as single homes from the late 1940s and '50s, although much of the area at Loch Raven Boulevard and Taylor Avenue was farmland and woods into the early 1960s. Memories are vivid of piling on the #3 bus and heading north from Northwood up Loch Raven Boulevard, all dressed for riding in jeans and leather boots. A large apartment complex was built on that horse farm in the mid-'60s, much to our disappointment, but south down Hillen Road, there is still an excellent golf course and a well-used skating rink.

Parkville is contiguous to Hillendale on the east and north of the city neighborhood of Hamilton. Parkville has always seemed like an extension of Hamilton, its neat little Cape Cod houses all tucked side by side among green lawns and large trees. And **Overlea** holds more of the same but also lays claim to Overlea Hall, which is still the site of many wedding receptions and high school dances. Houses in Overlea average about $200,000. They are mainly working-class neighborhoods and are still filled with the kind of folk who are happy to roll up their sleeves and help at the neighborhood church bazaar, the Girl Scout cookie drive, or the Little League game.

Right at the edge of the Beltway and beyond it are the very popular residential areas of **Carney, Perry Hall, Fullerton**, and **White Marsh**. Perry Hall, Fullerton, and Carney were all small towns that fanned out over the years, filling in farmland, to meet one another. Other towns around the area—Rosedale, Rossville, Poplar, and White Marsh—grew up around train stops.

White Marsh is particularly interesting, however, because although the shopping mall is less than 20 years old and much of the housing that surrounds it dates only to that time, the original community stood on land owned by Charles Ridgely, who named the area when he claimed it just after the American Revolution. Local historians say Ridgely named it White Marsh because of the white glare of the sun on the sands of the marsh. Although you'll find the occasional country farmhouse, the White Marsh area is filled mostly with new housing. Tract housing, condos, and apartment complexes from the small and simple to the grand and gracious are found there with prices ranging from $30,000 to $700,000.

NORTHWEST
Within the City

In 1896, 50 acres of land above the city line and then contiguous to some of the grander estates were bought for development. Blocks of land were turned over by the developer to individual builders who constructed exteriors and then finished the interiors to suit the buyers. Called "tract housing" now and a standard sales technique in suburban developments, **Charles Village**, as it is now known, is thought to be the first community to employ such tactics. Because of it, however, original interior details of Charles Village homes may be grand or sparse depending upon how much the original owner could afford or what he considered important. Some have simple woodwork and ceilings, only to have intricate parquet floors and marble fireplace mantels. Some have entrance halls framed by the classic Baltimore arches, intricate ceiling detail, and hand-inlaid designs in woodwork, only to show underfoot a simple, tongue-in-groove pine floor. Houses also come in all shapes and sizes. There are individual, rather country-looking homes in the 2600 block of St. Paul Street. Around the corner on 26th Street are two-story, 10-foot-wide bow fronts, Victorian "painted ladies" known for their pastel facades. On Calvert Street are large, three-story porch fronts; on Charles Street across from the Baltimore Museum of Art, four-story, 20-foot-wide individual behemoths and apartment buildings. Several apartment buildings, mostly student housing, are under construction. Once you cross Charles, the houses become smaller again, with Howard Street homes measuring typically 13 feet wide, 45 feet deep, with only 9-foot ceilings (as opposed to the typical 15-foot ceilings of Charles Street homes).

It may be the Village's eclectic housing that accounts for its eclectic population, or it may be the fact that Charles Village is right in the middle of everything—near the Johns Hopkins Homewood campus, all major bus routes to Downtown, two minutes by car to

Zoning

Don't forget to call the Zoning Commission in whatever area you want to settle down in, have an office in, or do business in. You may think that because you are a done-by-computer business that has no clients visit and has no need to hang out a shingle that you need not worry about zoning. And, you may not. New regulations are being written all the time in all divisions. So it's better to be sure.

Baltimore City Zoning Commission, (410) 396-4301, www.ci.baltimore.md.us

Baltimore County Zoning Commission, (410) 887-3391, www.co.ba.md.us

Howard County Planning and Zoning, (410) 313-2393, www.co.ho.md.us

Anne Arundel Zoning Enforcement, (410) 222-7446, www.aacounty.org

the Jones Falls Expressway, and seven minutes (not in rush hour) from Downtown. The neighborhood actually straddles the line of our east and west boundary of Charles Street, with its borders running to Greenmount Avenue on the east (thereby taking in parts of Waverly within its boundaries), Howard Street on its west, 21st Street to the south, and 33rd Street to the north. The area below 25th Street is often referred to as South Charles Village and on the east side also encompasses some of the neighborhood known as Harwood. Generally, it is a neighborhood of all colors and ethnic persuasions, primarily professionals. A great many writers, designers, artists, weavers, social workers, lawyers, and professors live in the Village. Real estate prices now average $283,000.

North and west of Charles Village is **Roland Park.** The neighborhood was the first development of the Roland Park Company and one of the first planned communities in the United States. It's home to the first strip shopping center in the country, designated with a historic marker. The development was built as summer housing for those who lived and worked in the city. It was typical of the times that during the summer months, those who could afford to took family out to the suburbs out of the pollution and the inner-city

heat and humidity. In Roland Park, the large shingle houses, with their wide wraparound porches and ceiling-to-floor windows, were built with air circulation in mind. The whole area is inundated with shade trees, and it is amazing the difference in summer's heat when one emerges from their canopy. Commonly called "affluent" Roland Park when referred to in the city's papers, the neighborhood is in fact a very middle-class area. Its new residents are young professionals with growing families, and its older residents are seniors living on pensions—many of whom came here themselves as young people. The wonderful thing about Roland Park is that little of its visage has changed. There are, however, pockets of new housing in Roland Park, mostly suburban-like town house condominiums, but they are behind walls of trees and do not change the overall look of the neighborhood. From the first, there has been a very active community organization, the Roland Park Civic League, and the community remains strong and cohesive. House prices average $520,000.

East of Roland Park on University Parkway, west of Charles Street, south and east of 39th Street, is another little pocket of homes named **Tuscany-Canterbury.** Densely populated because of the five large apartment complexes that are within its borders, Tuscany-Canterbury also offers large, two-story row houses, tree-lined streets, and the quiet confidence of a stable, safe area. Prices average $330,000.

Cold Spring Newtown is one of the city's newer planned communities with 300 homes. Tucked between the Jones Falls Expressway, Cylburn Arboretum, and Cold Spring Lane, the area was developed in the 1970s as "a town within a town."

The most striking feature—once you get past the tree-lined walkways, manicured lawns, and tot-lots—are the "deck houses." These mid-century style condos and town houses boast courtyards, large windows, and skylights. Another development, The Woodlands at Coldspring, has filled in the space closest to the arboretum with more traditional single-family homes. The average price for a house in this area is $176,000.

Hampden/Woodberry is one of the towns that grew up around the grist mills, cotton mills, and foundries of the Jones Falls Valley. The land was originally owned by a family named Ensor, and descendants of the original owners are said to still live in the community. The first cotton mill, Druid Mill, opened in 1865, followed by Mount Vernon Mills, Clipper Mill, and Woodberry Mills. Although idle now, many of the mills have been refurbished in recent years and are used for other purposes such as offices and shops. There is still industry in the Valley, and many of Hampden's citizens still work there.

About 20 years ago, the city rediscovered Hampden. South of Roland Park, north of Charles Village, and east of the Johns Hopkins Homewood campus, it had sat all those years pretty much as it had for a century, a small enclave of, for the most part, two-story, stoop-front and porch-front homes inhabited by generations of hardworking, blue-collar people. A self-sustaining community within the city limits, it kept to itself. But, by the late 1970s, people who wanted to buy in the city could no longer afford housing in the nearby renovation areas, and they began to look for other midtown areas that satisfied their commuting and housing needs, at a price they

could afford. At the time, perfectly livable houses could be bought in Hampden for around $15,000; ones that needed renovation could be bought for $5,000. Prices still hover in the bargain range, but with the recent housing market boom, the average is now $185,000.

South of Hampden and contiguous to Charles Village west of Howard Street is the community of **Remington**. Another mill town area, which dates from 1789, Remington grew with the railroad when the mainline of the B&O was laid. Remington had streetcar service by 1885, and by the turn of the last century, three separate lines ran through the neighborhood, connecting it east, west, north, and south. Most of the brick row houses were built around that time. There are some duplex homes and some larger porch-front row houses here and there, but most houses are 10 feet wide and two rooms deep, abutted to the sidewalk. A relatively eclectic community racially, it is still home to primarily lower income groups. Homes have an average sales price of $85,000.

Medfield, a neighborhood of middle-class working people, sits north and west of Hampden but contiguous to it. The neighborhood is a mixture of row homes and individual homes, most of which were built after World War II. Home prices run an average of $180,000. Most of the community sits on the highest hill around and one of the few that rises above the smog of the Jones Falls Valley. This smog is caused mainly by the continuous traffic on the Jones Falls Expressway. It is easily visible—some would say "palpable"—on a hot, muggy Baltimore day. But if you live in Medfield, you need only look down on it.

Mount Washington sits essentially at the north end of the Jones Falls Valley at the confluence of Western Run and the Jones Falls. It grew up around the Washington Cotton Manufacturing Company, which built a mill there in 1810. The mill itself has recently been rehabbed for alternate uses, one of which is a Whole Foods Market. Also near the mill is a swim club with one of the largest pools you'll ever see—Olympic swimmers have prepared here—and a well-used skating rink. Mount Washington Village sits above this area and has craft shops and some very nice restaurants. Mount Washington's older single homes are built above and around its center, climbing up the sides of the hills that lead out of the valley. Some of the more interesting ones are actually set into the side of a hill. Mount Washington does have a fair number of more modern apartment complexes outside of this original area. Prices average $342,000.

The land on which **Mount Royal Terrace** and **Reservoir Hill** stand—above the Jones Falls Valley but much farther back toward Downtown than Mount Washington—was originally owned by Jonathan Hansen, a Pennsylvania Quaker. It was called Mount Royal because it stood on one of Baltimore's highest hills. In 1720 Hansen acquired 340 acres that extended all the way down to the area just north of the harbor. In 1730 the Maryland Colonial Assembly acquired from Hansen a little 60-acre tract near the harbor and called it Baltimore Town. In 1789 Dr. Solomon Birckhead bought part of it and, on it, built a mansion that he called Mount Royal Mansion, Hansen's original name for the property. Unlike many areas where the mansions have been razed to make way for other buildings, Dr. Birckhead's mansion has been converted to alternative uses over the years. By 1862 land had been sold to the city to create Druid Hill Park, which is still essentially as it was in those days, with the added benefit of being the home of the Baltimore Zoo.

More than 100 years later, the neighborhoods of Mount Royal Terrace and Reservoir Hill are confined on the west by McCulloh Street, on the east by the Jones Falls Expressway, between the park on the north to North Avenue on the south—although Mount Royal Terrace extends beyond, down Mount Royal Avenue to the Maryland Institute of Art. These neighborhoods suffered all the effects of abandonment, subdivision, and poverty known to most of the city over time and faced

rebirth during Baltimore's 1970s renaissance. In fact, they were a prime target, because at the time only 12 houses in Reservoir Hill were valued at more than $20,000, yet the area owns some of the most beautiful and unique architecture in the city. Some of the original mansion houses and swank apartment complexes from the turn of the twentieth century still stand, and a plethora of three- and four-story brownstones, with windows bayed and walls bowed. Stone porches, cupolas, and tile fronts can be found there. Today, the area still teeters on the edge between elegance and poverty, with some blocks slowly being restored to their former glory and some boarded up, waiting for a savior. Homes and potential homes sell for an average of $212,000. Four years ago, the average price was half of that.

Within the confines of Reservoir Hill but worthy of its own space because of its separate historic designation, **Upper Eutaw/Madison** covers the 2300, 2400, and 2500 blocks of Madison Avenue and Eutaw Place. A publication of the Upper Eutaw/Madison Neighborhood Association described the area as "eclectic, elegant, and exciting, but not expensive." We think that says it pretty well. Prices for restored homes in the area fall between $110,000 to $350,000, depending mostly on size. There are unrestored but still livable houses selling for around $85,000. An Insider assured us, however, that there are still some vacant properties that might be bought for less.

Ashburton has tree-lined streets and magnificent individual houses, south of Wabash Avenue and north of Liberty Heights Avenue, that many of Baltimore's most prosperous African Americans have called home since the late 1950s. Only 10 minutes to Downtown from the Metro at Mondawmin Shopping Center and less than that by car, the setting recalls the large suburban estates that once surrounded the city. A typical Ashburton house sells for $190,000.

North of Wabash Avenue and the graceful homes of Ashburton, northwest of Druid Hill

Park, sits a large neighborhood of some 50,000 residents on a wedge of land bounded on the other side by Greenspring Avenue and on the west by Northern Parkway. **Park Heights** has had its problems over the years, primarily with crime, but a new program that is providing police officers to walk a beat again in the neighborhood is said to be making a difference. Regardless of its problems, however, Park Heights is one of the few neighborhoods that is not in the central city that receives thousands of visitors every year. They come for one thing—the Preakness, Baltimore's finest horse-racing event, which takes place at Pimlico Race Course, located on Park Heights' northern border. During racing season and particularly on Preakness Day, some neighbors turn their yards into parking lots, charging $10 and more to park for the day. Properties in Park Heights may be purchased for $25,000 up to $200,000.

Edmondson Village covers a 2.25-square-mile area in west Baltimore. Born like much of Baltimore from the estates that once claimed the land, the area began to grow with increased access and transportation. Edmondson Avenue was built in 1910, the streetcar came through a few years later, and neighborhoods began to spring up along its routes. In 1947 the first regional commercial development, Edmondson Village Shopping Center, was erected in and designed in the style of Colonial Williamsburg. The homes there range from the simple, brown-shingled cottage variety to large, Georgian mansions. There are a fair number of 1950s-type row houses and apartment complexes in the area. It is a primarily African-American area of mostly lower- to middle-income residents. Edmondson Village homes sell in the $45,000 to $80,000 range.

Walbrook is south of Gwynn's Falls Parkway, east of Gwynn's Falls Park, west of the Western Maryland Railroad tracks, and just north of North Avenue. Named after an estate that belonged to Galloway Cheston in 1853, Walbrook's actual development began in 1870, and it claims the distinction of being

Baltimore's first true suburb. Walbrook grew up neither because of a mill (though there was a mill nearby) nor because of the railroad (though the railroad tracks came through). Walbrook grew up around the Highland Park Hotel, which opened in 1874 after being built at a cost of some $400,000. It closed just two years later. Still, it was Walbrook's central focus in its day. Since then, Walbrook's center has been Walbrook Junction, a small town center where main streets cross. The area has some modern apartment complexes and shopping centers, but its quaint Victorian homes and diminutive junction create the feeling of country suburb. Homes in Walbrook average $30,000 to $85,000.

Harlem Park, the area between Lafayette Avenue, Monroe Street, Franklin Street, and Fremont Avenue, was subdivided in 1886 after being annexed by the city of Baltimore. The three-story brick row homes built there at the turn of the twentieth century still stand, and some retain their wood-grained mantels, stained-glass windows, high ceilings, and carved molding. You'll also find simple stone houses that were originally built for the servants of the great houses. Harlem Park was one of the first neighborhoods to catch renovation fever, with more than 2,000 buildings restored by the late 1970s. Today, Harlem Park homes are still bargains, with average home sales priced from $45,000 to $99,000.

Lafayette Square was first just that—a square of green lawn and landscaped shrubbery. It was acquired by the city in 1856 and was used as a bivouac area by Union troops during the Civil War. No houses were built around it until about 1876, although three churches and the first teacher's college in Maryland had already located at that site. Today, it shares the same problems of many city neighborhoods but counts itself lucky to be an eclectic community with a multitude of glorious nineteenth-century architecture at reasonable prices. In fact, Lafayette Square offers what many would consider bargain rates, with properties selling for an average price of $72,500.

West Arlington began in 1890 in an effort to create a "model suburban town." By 1896 there were 30 houses and a church, but fewer than 10 years later, the neighborhood claimed 1,000 people. Development continued, though more slowly, into the 1950s. Hence, the area represents many housing styles, large and small, freestanding and row, Victorian and modern. Over the years, the community has sought to preserve its original mandate—to maintain its suburban atmosphere. Home prices reflect that effort, with an average sales price of $133,500.

Windsor Hills was another area that grew because of water to turn mill wheels. The original grist mill was built in 1770 by seven brothers who had left Switzerland to find their fortunes in the colonies. By 1800, the area had become a center for industry. By the end of the nineteenth century, it was being considered for redevelopment as a summer resort community for Baltimore's industrial elite.

Like many of the western communities that began as suburbs, much of Windsor Hills' suburban character remains today. The community is tucked between Leakin Park, the largest natural park in the country within the limits of a city, and the Gwynn's Falls, Windsor Mill Road, and Forest Park Avenue. Homes in Windsor Hills sell for a$120,000 to $149,000.

One of the few almost totally unspoiled mill communities is the neighborhood of **Dickeyville.** Just 134 homes and the old Ashland Mill make up this neighborhood that faces Pickwick Road. It looks like something out of a book, with the kinds of pictures that allow you to peek through a gnarled tree at a white stone cottage. Perhaps one of the reasons that it stayed so true to its beginnings so long was that the mill operated there until 1967, when renovation fever was just around the corner. The mill was reopened as Dickeyville Mill and continues in use as office space, one of the first mills in Baltimore to open to a converted use. Both the mill and the village are on the National Register of Historic Places. Dickeyville home prices average $292,000.

Hunting Ridge/Ten Hills is the west side of Baltimore's answer to Homeland and Guilford. Located at the Baltimore County line along Edmondson Avenue, these two clusters of row houses and single-family houses sit on large, tree-filled lots, some half an acre. Most of the houses were built in the 1920s in every style from spacious Georgians and Tudors to more modest American Four-squares and even a few ranches built after World War II. Row houses are located in Hunting Ridge.

Hunting Ridge is nestled between Leakin Park and Edmondson Avenue. while Ten Hills stretches down to Frederick Avenue. Both neighborhoods are racially integrated. Housing prices in these two communities have soared over the years. Occasionally, one comes on the market for $100,000 or so, but the average house price is more like $400,000 for Ten Hills and $330,000 for Hunting Ridge.

Over the County Line

West of Towson, across Charles Street, are the very popular communities of Ruxton and Riderwood. They are often mentioned in one breath as Ruxton/Riderwood, but their characters are very different. Although both are popular because of their location—close to Towson, Downtown, and many private schools—**Ruxton** is very countrified. Among its wooded lots sit some of the loveliest Victorian homes around. Other homes are currently being built—some are small homes with small lots; others, big homes with large lots. There are colonials from the 1920s, ranch homes from the 1960s, and just about everything in between. There is a sense of status that goes with living in Ruxton—a sense of success. The neighborhood is eclectic, primarily upper-middle-class professionals, and real estate prices in the neighborhood average well over $400,000.

Riderwood was mostly developed in the 1960s. Most of its homes are ranch-style or split levels, with some simple bungalows and larger traditional colonials here and there. Individual communities within Riderwood are true developments in which the roads only go in and around the community, nowhere else.

The lovely homes in the area sell for more than $400,000.

Pikesville, Owings Mills, and Reisterstown are the main communities that form the **Reisterstown Road Corridor.** That is to say they are the main stops along Reisterstown Road, which juts out from the city to the northwest from Mount Washington. **Pikesville** is the accepted center of the Jewish community in Baltimore. You'll find interesting shops and great corned beef. One of this community's best-known places is Fields, which grew from Fields Pharmacy into a shop that now handles mainly cosmetics. The lunch counter where many a vanilla Coke was served is now a little more upscale. In fact, all of Pikesville is a little more upscale. The old town remains, but it's been built up and upon wherever space has permitted. Housing options run from the row variety to spacious ranch homes and elegant, older high-rises. Houses here sell for around $322,000.

As you cross over the Beltway on the way to Owings Mills, you pass through an area known mostly as Woodhome, then into McDonogh Township, named for McDonogh School, which was begun after the Civil War as a school for boys orphaned by the war. In just the last 20 or so years, this whole area has been built up from farmland. It's dripping with new suburban town house communities, single-house developments, shopping centers, and business centers. Development continues across McDonogh Road to Liberty Road, where the area becomes **Randallstown.** Prices are high, but worth it for the easy access to Greenspring Valley, which is a much nicer ride to the city than going down busy, overflowing Reisterstown Road.

Owings Mills is another sleepy area that has grown to a busy center over the last few years. Until the early 1970s, it seemed too far away from Baltimore to pay attention to, but a little theater in the round, Painters' Mill Theatre, brought it into the limelight around that time. The area grew steadily, then burst into major growth when the Owings Mills Corporate Campus and the Owings Mills

Town Center—a large, posh shopping mall— were built. Residences in the area include town houses, single-family houses, and apartments. The average house price here is $350,000.

Reisterstown used to be a day trip from Baltimore, a Sunday of antiquing. It is still an antiques center, but it has been built up all the way to the Carroll County line with housing developments. Even so, the town itself remains pretty much as it has been for the last 40 years.

In both Owings Mills and Reisterstown, you can find anything from a small country home to a large country estate, both of which will probably be surrounded by development housing. There are myriad apartment and condo complexes in this area, as well as developments of town houses and large individual homes. Prices for a single-family home average in the high $300,000 range and more, although some select properties may be purchased for less.

SOUTHEAST
Within the City

Patterson Park is a 155-acre park and the centerpiece for 18 Baltimore neighborhoods as well as the general name often given to the area that immediately surrounds it. (A few of those 18 neighborhoods are mentioned subsequently.) A publication of Southeast Development Corporation noted prices as little as $20,000 for small, unrenovated row houses, though new condominiums near the water can go for $1 million. The median price falls somewhere in the $185,000 range, but needless to say, such prices guarantee housing for virtually every income level, making it one of the most eclectic and stable communities in Baltimore.

West of Patterson Park, below Baltimore Street but above Fells Point, is the area known as **Butchers Hill.** The neighborhood was originally named Loudenslager Hill for Jacob Loudenslager, who operated both an inn and butchery near the corner of Baltimore Street and Patterson Park Avenue in 1810. Dozens of butchers eventually moved into the area because of its easy access to Broadway Market in nearby Fells Point. The area developed separately from Baltimore itself, with the bulk of its row house development occurring after the Civil War and through the turn of the twentieth century. By the time the last butcher closed up shop in 1925, the area was still largely occupied by German and Jewish residents. Like much of Baltimore, the 1950s and '60s saw a major downturn in fortune, and the 1970s saw an eclectic population interested in the area's history and beauty. Today, Butchers Hill maintains much of its 1970s population of renovators and innovators, while homes are also being snapped up by artists and empty nesters. It is a neighborhood united, and one that is becoming more popular. Butchers Hill homes sell for an average of $289,000.

On one of the highest points around Baltimore's harbor, above Canton and Fells Point and contiguous to the east corner of Patterson Park, is **Highlandtown,** which essentially includes the neighborhoods of Brewers Hill and Greektown. Highlandtown was once the site of the Union's Fort Marshall. Abandoned in 1866, after the Civil War, the area's development was begun by an Irish immigrant named Thomas McGuiness, with investment from the Philadelphia Land Company. McGuiness laid out streets, planted trees, and built one house—his own. For years he was the only resident, but as industry developed, others—mainly German brewers—joined him. The area was renowned for its taverns and beer gardens. By 1918 the area was still booming, and Baltimore City just couldn't resist the temptation to once again enlarge its city limits and its industrial base by annexing it in that year. By the 1920s a few slaughterhouses and meat-packing plants had located in Highlandtown, and with B&O's rail yards in Canton, employment for residents was not a problem. Highlandtown continued through the war years as a thriving blue-collar community. Unlike many of the neighborhoods that lost residents in the rush to the suburbs during the postwar years, Highlandtown has remained the same, with generation after generation staying on. It is a clean, safe area where the houses in the main are small row homes, with traditional white marble steps and flat fronts with corniced rooflines. Homes are selling for an average price of $90,000.

Canton is the waterfront area south and west of Highlandtown and east of Fells Point—part of Baltimore's new "Gold Coast." Its small workman's houses, warehouses, and other industrial buildings have been transformed over the last 20 or so years into some of the most expensive and exclusive real estate in Baltimore. The original land was purchased by an Irish sea captain named O'Donnell in 1785 with money he made selling tea, silk, and satin that he'd picked up in Canton, China. (Although named for that Chinese city, Baltimore's Canton is pronounced CAN-tin, not CAN-tawn.) By the mid-1800s O'Donnell still held the land, but built on it was a thriving industrial complex that included the B&O rail yards, the first charcoal ironworks, a copper-smelting plant, a cotton mill, a distillery, two shipyards, and, later in the century, a series of small oil refineries. Whereas the world wars decimated some areas, Canton's industry continued strong, and the blue-collar neighborhood primarily of Welsh, Germans, Poles, and Irish grew in population. By the 1970s, however, much of the industry had moved away, warehouses and factories lay abandoned, and it looked as if Canton might be headed for truly hard times. Then, as luck would have it, renovation fervor hit the city. Planners considered warehouse loft apartments, boat slips, and the wonderful advantages to living on the water. Today, Canton is a thriving area, architecturally and ethnically diverse, filled with innovative housing and upper-income professionals as well as traditional housing and blue-collar workers. Renovated homes can go in the $280,000 range, while unrenovated homes go for much less. The average Canton home price is about $377,000.

The point of land that divides Baltimore's Inner Harbor from the Patapsco River's Middle Branch, just south and east of Federal Hill, is known as **Locust Point.** Surrounding Fort McHenry, the neighborhood is composed mostly of small, brick row houses with traditional white marble steps. Originally inhabited by dockworkers, workmen in the shipbuilding and water-related trades, Locust Point is another area where people tend to stay. Some families boast six generations at the Point, many in the same house as it passed down from one generation to the next. The ethnic mix includes Germans, Irish, Poles, Bohemians, Hungarians, Austrians, Swedes, Norwegians, Russians, Scots, and Welsh. This is not odd when you consider that in 1706 Locust Point was made the official port of entry for Baltimore. Immigrants got off the boat and simply stayed where they landed. Like a small town unto itself, Locust Point has a strong sense of community focused on church and family. If you'd like to become a part of it, you might want to get to know someone in the neighborhood. Many of Locust Point's houses are sold by word of mouth. Homes in the area are going fast for an average price of $262,500, up nearly $100,000 from two years ago.

Over the County Line

Essex/Middle River is tucked between Back River and Middle River, south of U.S. Highway 40. Riding east on Eastern Avenue through Little Italy, Fells Point, Butchers Hill, and Highlandtown, you'll be in Essex once you've crossed Back River. Inundated at every opportunity by rivers, streams, and creeks, Essex began primarily as a watermen's community. Industry grew during the war years, and during the 1950s and '60s Essex was known mostly as a place to escape the city's summer heat. During those years many people in Baltimore bought cottages in Essex and Middle River. Used mostly on weekends, these cottages were known as the "shore" places; and, even now, many people from the city and northern suburbs spend their weekends at

these shores. Even more people, however, live permanently in these areas, working at the factories nearby or still plying the waters for their livelihoods. Many older homes are small, clapboard cottages that sit quietly by tree-shaded inlets. There are also old and new row house developments and apartment and condominium complexes. Essex/Middle River home prices average $212,000, but waterfront homes sell for much more.

Dundalk, named after the Irish city, is primarily a blue-collar, industrial area. Fairly large, it encompasses most of the land east of Dundalk Avenue to Old North Point Road and all the way to Bear Creek to the south. The whole area is crisscrossed by creeks and inlets, and many houses sport boats as part of their permanent backyard equipment. The individual houses are mostly clapboards, built in the war years to house defense workers. There are also row houses that date from the same era as well as some newer row house and apartment developments. Individual homes sell in the mid-$170,000 range, with prices increasing as you get closer to the water. Waterfront properties sell in the $200,000 range and above. But there are still bargains.

SOUTHWEST
Within the City

Cherry Hill sits on land that juts into mouth of the Middle Branch River where it meets the Patapsco. It is bounded on the south by Patapsco Avenue and on the west, essentially, by railroad tracks. A large park takes up almost one-third of the neighborhood on its east side, running the full length of the neighborhood's boundary along the Patapsco. Cherry Hill Park has softball, football, and soccer fields, basketball courts, and both indoor and outdoor swimming pools. On the northern boundary, Middle Branch Park and Harbor Hospital Center hem in the neighborhood. Originally a small planned community for veterans returning from World War II, by 1945 Cherry Hill Homes had 1,600 rental units and was growing. By the 1970s, Cherry Hill had more than 22,000 residents and some serious crime problems, but residents have worked hard to mitigate them. Cherry Hill still has individual home bargains for about $54,000.

Across the Patapsco River from Cherry Hill and the south Baltimore areas contiguous to the Inner Harbor is **Brooklyn**. It is that spit of land that looks like Baltimore's chin when you view the city's outline. With water on three sides and the Anne Arundel County line at its back, Brooklyn began as Curtis' Neck, the estate of Paul Kinsey, who took title to 200 acres of land there in 1663. For 200 years it was primarily a farming and fishing community, with access to market just a quick sail across the Patapsco to Fells Point. It had also had some claim to fame as a summer resort for Baltimoreans by the mid-1800s but became more of a part of the city in 1856, when a bridge was constructed that linked it directly to South Baltimore. By 1878 rail lines also extended to the area, spurring construction of shipping facilities for coal and iron ore. By 1892 there was also streetcar service to Brooklyn, and industry rushed to locate there. By the time the century turned, the area had everything from smelting furnaces to oyster packing plants mostly right on the water's edge at Curtis Bay. With industry came workers who needed a place to live. The community of Brooklyn grew up around the industry and continues as a blue-collar working community. Houses tend to cluster around the west side of the point. Property prices can vary, but average $48,000.

Transportation and ease of access have always been, and continue to be, the grist from which communities are made. So it was with **Irvington**. When the Frederick Turnpike was permanently carved out to link Baltimore Town and Frederick Town in the late 1700s, communities began to spring up along the road. The site of Irvington had been settled before that, however, by one Thomas Coale, a Quaker. His 450-acre estate, Maiden's Choice, dated from 1673. By the time the Civil War had ended, some two centuries later, the area was populated enough to support Mount

Saint Joseph's, which opened in 1873 and is still an active Catholic boys' high school. (See the Education chapter.) One of Irvington's well-known landmarks is Loudon Park Cemetery, created in 1876 on the original site of Maiden's Choice. In 1861 the federal government carved out a section for a federal cemetery where 2,300 Union and 275 Confederate soldiers were laid to rest. Irvington, named for Irving Ditty, one of the first builders in the area, today is an eclectic community that still boasts many of the original Victorian masterpieces built before the turn of the twentieth century. It also offers multifamily housing, brick-and-frame duplexes, and row houses. Housing lots are, on average, fairly large, and the whole area is very green. Giant trees overhang houses whose average price is $105,000.

Over the County Line

If you head out Frederick Road, west of the city, the first main area you will come upon is **Catonsville.** Catonsville's center at Ingleside/Bloomsbury Avenues and Frederick Road looks very much as it did a century ago, although spreading out from that center are convenience stores, gas stations, and fast-food places. Still, Catonsville seems to be able to maintain its charm. Down its side streets are grand homes that reflect the Victorian country estates and simple Cape Cod homes that were built in the 1940s. It has maintained a reputation as a good place to raise a family and is peopled with all colors and backgrounds. Right in Catonsville's back pocket, as it were, are Catonsville Community College, the University of Maryland, Baltimore County, and large expanses of Patapsco Valley State Park, which borders the Patapsco River, the county line between Baltimore County and Howard County. Catonsville home prices average $333,000.

Just over the Howard County line is **Ellicott City,** a brief 20 minutes from northwest Baltimore, and it is a treasure. Or, should we say, it's filled with treasures. Ellicott City is the antiques and collectible shopper's paradise (see our Antiques and Collectibles chapter), but the city itself is a postcard. It sits at the level of the Patapsco, which is hardly more than a wide stream there. All the buildings are made of brick and stone and rise up the hill from the river. This center looks much as it did in the middle of the nineteenth century, but in recent years because of its proximity to Columbia, Maryland, much of the open land around the city has been developed, and there are all manner of modern suburban town houses, single-family homes, and apartments available. But the houses that are truly prized are the ones that are within the old community. Property in Ellicott City sells for $200,000 to $2,000,000.

More south of the city, south and east of Catonsville, just above where the wandering Patapsco separates Baltimore County from Anne Arundel County, you will find **Arbutus** and **Halethorpe**. These areas, like most of the county, began as farmland and estates but grew when road and rail came to their communities. Halethorpe, which originated with a train stop, boasts some century-old Victorians among its housing stock. Some of the estate homes in Arbutus and Halethorpe still stand, but most of the land around them was filled in mainly after World War II. Lynnewood, the first planned development in the area, grew up in 1954. Its housing may be slightly unique for Baltimore in that its split-level and ranch houses were built on concrete slabs with no basements, similar to a typical house in California. (Most Baltimore row houses from the period are famous for their knotty-pine panelled basements.) Arbutus and Halethorpe are made up of single-family, freestanding homes. The twist is that in the 1960s many of them had one floor converted into an apartment. Hence, a great many homeowners have an apartment that they rent out on a continual basis. Most of the homes sit on average suburban lots with shrubbery and greenery, although one Insider noted that if you want giant oak trees, **Relay**, just to its west, is really the place to go. Relay also boasts a Victorian community hardly touched by the twentieth century. Prices for housing in Arbutus average $261,000, but historic Relay's Victorians are priced much higher.

LIVING IN THE BIG B . . .

Now that you have a handle on where you'd like to bed down, the questions become: "Apartment, condo, co-op, row house, or individual home?" and "Should you rent, purchase, or share?" Most of these housing opportunities are available in all areas in greater Baltimore, albeit at differing price levels and with differing housing stock. The organizations below can help you determine what you can afford and where you can get the most for your money, and the real estate companies, of course, can help you directly rent or purchase the property you want.

Apartments

In every area mentioned previously in this chapter, there are apartments. In Downtown you'll find traditional apartments cut from row houses or new and relatively new high-rise apartments, but you'll also find apartments in alternative-use buildings. Alternative-use buildings are those edifices that started their lives as a warehouse or a school but now function as apartments. In the counties garden apartments and apartment/town houses are more the order of the day, although in some areas such as Pikesville, there are many high-rise buildings—the kind where the doorman meets you. Some of these are condominiums, but there are still many elegant apartment complexes.

In racks as you leave most grocery stores or at places where travelers frequent such as hotels and the train station, you'll see published guides that list apartments for rent or sale in the area. These are good for contact information for the larger apartment complexes, but if you'd like to touch base with a person who can tell you generally what's available in the particular area, the organizations below will be able to help you.

Renter's Resources

Baltimore has many renting options, and it doesn't have the pressure-cooker issues of major metropolises like New York and Boston. It's not unreasonable to find a listing, see a place, and rent it on a handshake. Most places do require a one-year lease and a security deposit. Like every city Baltimore has its share of dubious landlords, the ones who take advantage of newcomers and their need to find a place fast. Tenant-landlord information resources are available and are worth consulting before signing any agreement. Baltimore Neighborhoods, Inc. provides a counseling hotline at (410) 243-6007.

Landlords also frequently require their tenants to carry renters' insurance. You can usually procure insurance through your auto insurance company and tack it on to your car premiums for a minimal monthly cost. If you do not own a car, try companies like American Skyline Insurance, 14 Light Street, Suite 200, (800) 711-4452.

Apartment Assistant.net
www.apartmentassistant.net
ApartmentAssistant.net combines a high-tech approach to apartment locating along with personalized knowledge of the individual apartment and condo communities. The site offers city-specific information that includes contact information for necessities like the telephone, cable, and water companies.

Apartment Search
www.apartmentsearch.com
The free service offers an online tool to look over apartments before hitting the actual streets. The service offers apartments all over the country. In the Baltimore area, the service offers both downtown apartments and garden apartments in the suburbs. Rents range from $500 to more than $2,000 a month.

Apartment Solutions
www.apartmentsolutions.com
Apartment Solutions focuses on providing comprehensive apartment solutions services in Pennsylvania, New Jersey, Delaware, Virginia, Maryland, and Washington, D.C. Apartment Solutions has more than 1.4 million apartment units and more than 4,000 owners and property managers participating in its system.

Southern Management
Apartment Locators
(800) 999-7368
www.southernmanagement.com
Apartment Locators is one of the oldest locator services in the Baltimore area. It has more than 65 apartment complexes in the Baltimore area.

Management Companies

Management companies may own the properties that they manage, or they may simply manage properties for others. Some do both. There are a great many management companies in Baltimore; we've only mentioned a few here.

Bridge Street Corporate Housing
(800) 278-7338
www.bridgestreet.com
Bridge Street has been in business for around two decades in the Baltimore area. The service provided deals in temporary housing, primarily for business travelers and corporate executives who are relocating. If you're just coming to town, expect to stay but need time to canvass neighborhoods and decide where you'd like to live, you might want to try out a place by renting temporarily. If the train carrying your furniture from California got derailed,

if your settlement's been delayed, if you've just been transferred, or if you're simply on an extended vacation and would like a base from which to take day trips all around the Mid-Atlantic area, then Bridge Street can provide fully furnished apartments and/or individual homes by the night, the week, the month, or the year. A lot of businesses use Bridge Street, but it also works with individuals. It has housing stock in such neighborhoods as Fells Point, Federal Hill, and other Inner Harbor areas as well as in Baltimore, Howard, and Anne Arundel Counties. Prices range from $55 to $200 a day, depending on the property, its location, and a 30-day minimum. Prices per day do vary, depending on length of stay, with shorter stays costing more per day and longer stays costing less. Rentals are fully equipped, right down to the towels, dishes, and the first few rolls of toilet paper. Cleaning services are available.

Houses/Condos/Co-ops

Baltimore has many options in housing. But to really understand the market takes an expert. There are simply too many qualifiers on some properties—ground rents, covenants, historic district designations, co-op/condo fees, settlement costs, inspections, and more. There are also a great many options on some properties. You might be qualified for a low-interest rehab loan or you might be able to receive a loan for closing costs or a VA or FHA mortgage. It's better to get help with questions that you might have before problems arise, which is why we've listed some community development corporations (see sidebar at the beginning of this chapter) that may be able to help you determine how much property you can afford and the best way to pay for it.

Real Estate Firms

Baltimore has some well-respected local and national real estate agents, and most have multiple locations. What follows is just a small sampling of those available.

Allen Realty
8314 Liberty Road, Randallstown
(410) 496-6700
www.allenrealty.net
This is a small, independently owned business formed in 1996. The Realtors focus on simplifying the process of homeownership to help low- to middle-income families find and select the best loan programs available. They specialize in HUD VA, and foreclosures.

Century 21 Horizon Realty
3117 East Joppa Road, Parkville
(410) 882-0021
www.c21horizon.com
Century 21 has been selling homes in the Baltimore community for a quarter century. Part of the largest real estate organization in the world, there are 6,600 offices and 110,000 agents around the world. This particular office has 42 agents selling property in northern Baltimore, as well as in the Parkville-White Marsh, northern Baltimore County area; a sister office in Dundalk has 17 agents. It serves the eastern part of the city and county.

Chase Fitzgerald & Company, Inc.
1 Village Square, Suite 131, Cross Keys
(410) 323-6000
www.chasefitzgerald.com
Chase Fitzgerald is a Baltimore company that traces its roots back to the Roland Park Company. The focus is in Roland Park, Guilford, Hampden, and points north. It's neither a high-end or low-end real estate company, selling row houses for $246,000 and country estates for $2,500,000. They specialize, as well, in north Baltimore condominiums.

Coldwell Banker Residential Brokerage
3301 Boston Street
(410) 563-7601
www.coldwellbankermove.com
With more than 2,800 agents throughout the state of Maryland and 4,000 agents serving the Mid-Atlantic, Coldwell Banker has Realtors in most neighborhoods throughout Baltimore City, including Fells Point, Federal Hill, and

Roland Park. The agency also covers the eastern shore and the Maryland suburbs around Washington D.C. With more than 90 offices total, Coldwell Banker provides services ranging from concierge and relocation services to mortgage and insurance advice. The firm handles a wide range of housing prices and options, and also services the bustling rental market downtown.

Fiola Blum Realtors, Inc.
110 Slade Avenue
(410) 484-4800, (800) 486-4038
www.fiolablum.com
Fiola Blum Realtors is one of Baltimore's independent realtors. It has been in business for more than 50 years and is still family-owned and -operated. The firm's 40 agents handle property primarily in the northwest and northern areas of Baltimore County, including condominiums and individual, single-family homes. Prices of its properties range from $80,000 to $2,500,000 and above. When you call, ask for Harry Blum or his wife, Phyllis.

Hill & Company
255 Village Square II, Cross Keys
(410) 435-2000
www.hillrealtors.com
Hill & Co. has been in business in the Baltimore area since 1923. It has a reputation for handling only high-end properties, and you will definitely see its signs in all of Baltimore's prestigious neighborhoods, including Guilford, Homeland, Roland Park, Mount Vernon, and Bolton Hill. Jake Boone, who's been with the company for more than 10 years, says that the company's 31 agents handle lower-priced properties as well, even though he admitted the bulk of the homes sold fall in the $200,000 to $5,000,000 range. The company also handles property out the Charles Street corridor, Inner Harbor homes, and farm properties and estates in the Greenspring and Worthington Valleys.

Long & Foster, Roland Park
4800 Roland Avenue
(410) 889-9800
www.longandfoster.com
Long & Foster is one of the largest real estate companies in the area, with offices in Maryland, Virginia, and Washington, D.C. Its first office opened in Virginia, but there are currently 50 offices in the greater Baltimore region doing business in virtually every neighborhood.

The Roland Park office handles properties primarily in Roland Park, Guilford, and Hampden and considers itself "Downtown oriented," even though most of its 25 agents also do business in Baltimore County. Homes sold range in price from $180,000 to $1,000,000.

O'Conor & Mooney Realtors
1414 Key Highway, Suite 101
(410) 385-8800
www.oconorhomes.com
This real estate company with 40 agents has offices in both Baltimore City and northern Baltimore County. Although the names keep changing, the O'Conor name has been part of the real estate scene in Baltimore for more than 40 years. Locally owned by Sean O'Conor and Tom Mooney, the company's listings range from mid-town town houses listed in the mid $100,000s to mansions in horse country for $2,500,000.

Otis Warren and Company
10 South Howard Street, Suite 110
(410) 539-1010
When Otis Warren started out nearly half a century ago, he managed rental properties and then expanded to sell real estate in his west Baltimore neighborhood. Now he has become a developer as well, with new projects dotting Baltimore city. His projects are both residential and commercial and include the $40 million City Crescent Office Building under construction in 2007. Still family-owned, the company continues to sell and lease residential properties.

RE/MAX Realtors
22 West Road, #100, Towson
(410) 337-9300
www.remaxgreatermetro.com
RE/MAX is the largest franchised real estate broker in the world, with more than 50,000 agents in the United States and Canada alone—1,100 of which are in the state of Maryland. Broker Mary Lou Kaestner has been in the real estate business since 1970. She opened her own office in 1981 and became affiliated with RE/MAX in 1994. She and her 27 full-time independent agents list and sell properties in Baltimore City and Baltimore, Anne Arundel, Howard, Harford, and Carroll Counties. One of the perks of being associated with a worldwide agency is the ability to reach people on the other side of the globe—real people with a name, a face, and a bio—and work with them to help clients who are looking to relocate or need to move people and companies. The bulk of the company's business, however, is home sales. Agents handle properties in all price ranges, from $30,000 to $2 million and more.

ACCOMMODATIONS

Only a few of the elegant, old-world hotels still serve Baltimore's guests. The others that once welcomed some of the most influential people in the world to their doors gave way first to the Depression, then war, urban blight, office towers, and urban renewal. A few were saved and turned into condominiums. The Belvedere Hotel in Mount Vernon is one of those. Its apartments are modern, but the lobby, main ballroom, and the Owl Bar, where H. L. Mencken liked to come after a hard day of curmudgeoning, are still much as they were at the turn of the twentieth century.

The urban renewal of the 1960s produced Charles Center and the Downtown Holiday Inn on Fayette Street. At the time the most modern and one of the tallest buildings in that area, the Holiday Inn is now dwarfed by the towers that have grown up around it in the last 40 years.

Once the Inner Harbor became the focus of Downtown events, there was a tremendous building spurt, both at the harbor itself and in the entire area near it, especially between the harbor and Camden Yards. As their business travelers have grown in number, Timonium and Towson have also added a fair number of new accommodations.

Being, as we are, on the main north-south truck routes of Interstate 95 and U.S. Highway 1 and essentially at the beginning of western U.S. Highways 40 and 50, we've always boasted a number of motels. (Well, since the invention of the automobile, anyway . . .) Up and down these well-used roads—every few feet, it seems—there are motels. Some of them are nothing more than a few cabins; some of them are pretty posh establishments. Most of them have been excluded from our list. We have included only those few that are close to Downtown or other major business areas. As for the others, we figure you're pretty much like us. When you're on a long drive and you get tired, you stop at the next vacancy sign.

Hotels are different. For them, we usually plan ahead. Here we've provided a sampling of these accommodations in the area, including the chains. Of course, most of the chains have more than one location. For instance, Holiday Inn still has its hotel in Downtown Baltimore, but it also has hotels at Baltimore–Washington Thurgood Marshall International Airport (BWI), in Towson, in Columbia, in Glen Burnie, and in Pikesville. You'll find Marriott Hotels at two locations in the Inner Harbor and also at BWI and Hunt Valley; the Sheraton has hotels at the Inner Harbor, BWI, and Towson.

All told, Baltimore has more than 75 hotels and motels in and around the immediate area. The accommodations we've presented in this chapter are in the Downtown area and around the Baltimore Beltway. Each is within easy access of the Inner Harbor or is convenient to expressways, Light Rail, subway, or bus service.

You can assume that every listed hotel is wheeelchair accessible. You can expect that you cannot have your dog with you (although a few do allow pets).

Cabs make a habit of parking outside of most Downtown hotels. Buses are also convenient to most Downtown locations, as is the MARC train to Washington, the subway, and the Light Rail (see the Getting Here, Getting Around chapter). These modes of transportation are less convenient to some of the suburban locations we mention, but if a suburban location does have access, we've noted it.

If you arrive in Baltimore by car, be it a rental or your own, expect hotels in the Downtown area to charge a daily parking fee. We've noted those that do. Hotels outside the city and around the Beltway tend to offer free parking.

Many hotels now include some kind of breakfast in the price of the room. The full American breakfast often includes a choice of eggs, pancakes, waffles, hot cereals, fresh fruit, milk, juice, and coffee or tea in the hotel's on-site restaurant. If it is included, we'll tell you, but more often than not you'll be offered a continental breakfast of some combination of muffins, biscuits, toast and the like, juice, and coffee or tea. You'll also find information about recent renovations, decorations, and amenities a particular hotel offers, such as swimming pools, exercise rooms or equipment, van service, etc.

Most hotels in Baltimore also have smoking rooms, but they now constitute a smaller percentage of total rooms available. So, if you're a smoker, you'll need to make your reservations well in advance.

Price Code

The room rate we've chosen to quote is the industry standard, known in the trade as the RACK rate. In cases where a hotel has seasonal rates, we've taken an average price to quote as the standard. For instance, a room that costs $129 during the hotel's off-season may cost $190 during its peak season. That hotel's price would then average out to $160. What we've provided here is meant to be only a guide for selecting an accommodation. For specific rates applied to a particular time of year, call the hotel.

```
$ . . . . . . . . . . . . . . . Less than $80
$$ . . . . . . . . . . . . . $80 to $125
$$$ . . . . . . . . . . . . $126 to $150
$$$$ . . . . . . . . . . . $151 to $199
$$$$$ . . . . . . . . . . $200 and more
```

There is a room tax in Baltimore City of 12½ percent; in Baltimore County, 13 percent. Most hotels require a major credit card to guarantee a reservation; some require you to confirm. If they don't, then they have a cutoff time after which your reservation is not held.

DOWNTOWN

Admiral Fell Inn $$$$
888 South Broadway
(410) 522-7377, (866) 583-4162
www.harbormagic.com
In the heart of historic Fells Point at the foot of Broadway is the Admiral Fell Inn. Eighty rooms are spread through eight buildings, some of which date from the 1770s. The inn reflects that period with Federal-style decorations and furnishings throughout. It is a very classy, old-world place and often used by Baltimoreans for wedding receptions, rehearsal dinners, and the like—pretty much in any case where image and ambience are the order of the day. In 1996 the Admiral Fell underwent a complete renovation and expansion, including the building of meeting and banquet facilities on the roof—now the fifth floor.

The room price includes a light continental breakfast. There is no exercise room or pool, but guests may request that exercise equipment be brought to their room, or, for an additional charge of $15, they may take advantage of the Gold's Gym at the Power Plant complex just about five minutes away by hotel van. (If you want exercise, however, we would recommend a good brisk walk through Fells Point's charming cobblestone streets.) A few specialty rooms run as high as $289 per night, such as the "attic room" in the oldest building. It's tucked up under the eaves, with the original hand-hewn beams gently rising to a peak. If you want a taste of Baltimore history and a short commute to the Inner Harbor, the Admiral Fell Inn is where you want to be. Valet parking is $25 per day.

**Baltimore Marriott Inner Harbor
at Camden Yards** $$$$–$$$$$
Pratt and Eutaw Streets
(410) 962-0202, (800) 228-9290
www.marriott.com
The Marriott Inner Harbor and its attached parking garage sit not quite on the harbor itself, but a block west, just across from

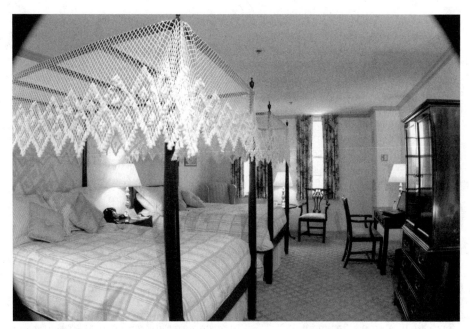

Rooms at the Admiral Fell Inn have colonial charm. ADMIRAL FELL INN

Camden Yards. Built in 1984, this 10-story modern hotel offers 490 traditional rooms as well as 34 suites. Amenities include an on-site restaurant, gift shop, full business center, secretarial services, and safe deposit box at the front desk. The rooms come equipped with a two-line phone, speakerphone, voice mail, and the dataports. The Marriot has seasonal rates that vary accordingly. Packages are available that include breakfast.

i If you'd like to stay at the Inner Harbor, but you're concerned about Downtown traffic, don't be. It only really gets crowded during rush hours (8:00 to 9:30 a.m.; 4:00 to 5:30 p.m.), or if there's a baseball or football game.

Baltimore Marriott
Waterfront $$$$–$$$$$
700 Aliceanna Street
(410) 385-3000, (800) 228-9290
www.marriott.com
The Marriott Waterfront is among the newest

near Baltimore's Inner Harbor. The hotel overlooks the harbor and is within walking distance to various shops and popular restaurants including the ESPN Zone, Hard Rock Cafe, and the popular neighborhood of Little Italy. There are three restaurants, a deli, and a lounge, either in the hotel or attached. This huge hotel offers 750 guest rooms, all with harbor view. The rooms come equipped with amenities that include climate control, two-line telephone with message light, dataport, and voice mail. In-room coffee and tea, hair dryer, iron, and ironing board are also included. There is on-site parking and the hotel is located at a water taxi stop—a truly great way to get around the harbor (see Getting Here, Getting Around chapter for information on the water taxi).

Brookshire Inner Harbor
Suites Hotel $$$$–$$$$$
120 East Lombard Street
(410) 625-1300
www.harbormagic.com
The Brookshire is a small corporate hotel,

with 97 guest rooms and 10 suites. Executive suites have a living room, wet bar, and separate bedroom with bath and are more expensive than the standard price; junior suites have the same except the separate wet bar. Some suites have a view of the harbor. Because the hotel is small, it does not have its own parking lot. Valet parking is provided for a fee of $25 a night. While the hotel has an exercise room you can also receive a pass to a nearby health club for a charge of $15. The hotel has remodled often in the less than two decades it's been at this location; its last update in 2006 included new beds. It is also pet friendly—for a fee. The Brookshire does not have seasonal rates, but it does run seasonal specials and offers special corporate rates as well as major discounts for members of the American Association for Retired Persons and AAA.

Courtyard by Marriott, Baltimore
Inner Harbor $$$–$$$$
1000 Aliceanna Street
(443) 923-4000
www.marriott.com
Situated in a new development of buildings and hotels known as Inner Harbor East, this Courtyard is across the parking lot from the towering Baltimore Marriott Waterfront and a few blocks from the Inner Harbor and Fells Point. Ten guest-room floors provide 205 rooms replete with two-line phones, dataports, and cable TV. Though they are all pretty new, the rooms were completely redone in 2007. There is an indoor pool and exercise room on-site, a conveniently located garage, and a nearby Whole Foods natural food market with a great salad bar, deli, and sushi stand.

Days Inn, Inner Harbor $$$
100 Hopkins Place
(410) 576-1000
www.daysinnerharbor.com
The Days Inn is only 3 blocks west of the Inner Harbor proper, directly across from the Convention Center. It offers 250 rooms with two double beds, 42 rooms with queen-size beds, and 8 oversize rooms on its nine floors. Renovations to the whole hotel were finished in 2007. Because the hotel is so close to Camden Yards, its busiest season is baseball season. Rental car service is available by asking the concierge. Guests are charged an additional $15 per day for parking. The hotel offers an outside swimming pool, open May through September, and a fitness center. There is also a restaurant, Hopkin's Bar and Grill, on-site. The hotel is smoke-free.

Harbor Court Hotel $$$$$
550 Light Street
(410) 234-0550
www.harborcourt.com
Architecturally, the Harbor Court, with its huge, twin, redbrick towers, is one of the most striking hotels in Baltimore. The English country interior is just as phenomenal. The grand staircase is reminiscent of ball gowns and footmen. The pickled oak paneling in the lobby was imported from England; and the 25 specialty suites sport canopy beds and marble bathrooms. The Harbor Court has 195 rooms and three restaurants. Guests may take advantage of 24-hour room service and a full-service health club, including tennis and racquetball courts, tanning salons, and massage. There's a concierge staff of three. All rooms must be guaranteed with a credit card. Package rates and corporate rates are available.

Hilton Baltimore $$–$$$$
401 West Pratt Street
(443) 573-8700
www.baltimore.hilton.com
When the new Hilton opens in Fall 2008, it will be Baltimore's largest hotel with 757 rooms. Ten suites will overlook Oriole Park at Camden Yards (with the luxury room rates to match). It will be located just west of the Inner Harbor. More importantly it will be directly across the street from Baltimore's Convention Center and linked to the center by a skybridge. Amenities will include an indoor pool, a whirlpool and fitness center, a restaurant, and

a business center. Rooms will have wi-fi access (for a fee), large-screen televisions, and work stations.

Holiday Inn Express at the Stadiums $–$$
1701 Russell Street
(410) 727-3400
www.holidayinn.com

This motel is 4 blocks south of Camden Yards, across Russell Street Bridge in an industrial area. The motel is, however, a clean place to call home for a time, particularly if you're traveling on a budget. It offers cable TV, complimentary continental breakfast, free parking, and a swimming pool in summer. It's only about 20 feet from the on ramps to I-95 and the Baltimore–Washington Expressway.

Holiday Inn Inner Harbor $$
301 West Lombard Street
(410) 685-3500
www.holiday-inn.com

The downtown Holiday Inn is two buildings containing a total of 375 rooms, with a two-level parking garage in between, and a breezeway connecting them. Built in 1964, the hotel was completely renovated in 2005. Rooms include such everyday amenities as free Wi-Fi, a voice mail system, iron and ironing boards, and gourmet coffee in every room. Suites also have whirlpools. There is an $18 daily parking fee. The hotel is only a block from Camden Yards and a seven-minute walk from the Inner Harbor. And get set to get wet—it boasts the largest indoor pool of any hotel in Baltimore.

Hyatt Regency $$$$–$$$$$
300 Light Street
(410) 528-1234, (800) 233-1234
www.hyatt.com

The glass-clad Hyatt sits on one of the Inner Harbor's prime spots, making it one of the city's most popular hotels. Its 2007 $20 million renovation will make it even more in demand. The new blue and gold decor goes well with the glittering water views just beyond the rooms' gigantic windows. All 488

rooms and suites were freshly redone with sleek modern furnishings, including chaise lounges by the windows—a great idea. Bathrooms also got a makeover and the amenities were updated, including iPod docks, wireless Internet, and flat-screen TVs. The location is still one of the city's best for visitors because of its proximity to the Inner Harbor and convention center, both accessible by skywalk, as well as Downtown and the two stadiums. Valet parking is available for $36 per day; self-parking is $29 per day; car rental is available at the hotel.

Inn at Henderson's Wharf $$–$$$
1000 Fell Street
(410) 522-7777, (800) 522-2088

Henderson's Wharf was built on the "point" of Fells Point. Built in 1894 for the B&O Railroad, the site is a registered National Historic Landmark. The 38-room inn takes up only the first floor of the building, with the second through sixth floors serving as private apartments. A gated parking lot is on the property, if you need a place to park a car; there is also a full-service marina right out the front door of the inn, if you need a place to park your boat. The water taxi is nearby. Half of the rooms have a view of the water; the others overlook the inner courtyard, with its cobblestone patio and wooden tables sheltered by white umbrellas. The hotel was renovated after it was flooded during a hurricane in 2003. The result is a soothing classic style. The hotel also has a 24-hour fitness center and free wireless internet. All reservations must be guaranteed with a credit card. Continental breakfast is included in the price of the room.

i Before the city gets busy and the offices and shops open is a wonderful time to soak in the scenery. Come out on your balcony or stroll around the Inner Harbor just after sunup. You'll enjoy the fresh smell of the air, the early morning sparkle of the sun on the water, and the occasional gust that carries the scent of bread baking.

Mount Vernon Hotel $$–$$$
24 West Franklin Street
(410) 727-2000, (800) 245-5256
www.mountvernonbaltimore.com

For more than 50 years, the downtown YMCA was housed at this address. When the Comfort Inn bought it and renovated it for a hotel, it traded the Olympic pools for parking under the building. The Baltimore International College took over the site in 1994 and completely renovated the building, redecorated the lobby and in-house cafe, appropriately, in the Victorian style. It offers 135 rooms on nine floors, including single, double, and wheelchair-accessible rooms as well as loft and Jacuzzi suites. This is a basic hotel, right in the center of everything. It's across the street from the central branch of the Enoch Pratt Free Library, the Basilica of the Assumption, and the First Unitarian Church. One block north is the Walters Art Museum; 2 blocks north is Mount Vernon Square. It is a 7-block walk from Pratt Street and the Inner Harbor and is accessible on major bus lines. Parking is available on site for an extra $13 a night.

Peabody Court Hotel $$$$$
612 Cathedral Street
(410) 727-7101, (877) 424-6423
www.choicehotels.com

Located in the heart of the Mount Vernon Cultural District, just 1 block from the Washington Monument and walking distance to all the galleries, restaurants, and shops along Charles Street, this Clarion property is an elegant boutique hotel with 104 warm and inviting guest rooms. Each room features heated towel warmers, glorious pillow-top mattresses, full marble bathrooms, and imported French marble-topped furniture. The in-house restaurant, aptly named George's On Mount Vernon Square, is in honor of the "Three George's" of Baltimore—George Washington, George Peabody, and George Herman ("Babe") Ruth. The hotel also offers a fitness room, and a business center with high-speed Internet access. Wireless Internet service is free. Valet parking is available for $29 a night and arrangements can be made for pets.

Pier 5 Hotel $$$$–$$$$$
711 Eastern Avenue
(410) 539-2000
www.harbormagic.com

The Pier 5 Hotel is the only hotel with an Inner Harbor location that sits right on the water. And it's right in the thick of things. Pier 6 Concert Pavilion is out the door to your right; the Hard Rock Cafe is out the door to your left; and both seafood and steak restaurants are on-site. The Inn offers 65 rooms on three floors, including seven suites. Guests can self park for $21 a day on two lots, next to and across the street from the hotel. Valet parking is available for $28 a day. The Pier 5 Hotel is smoke-free. Twenty-four-hour concierge service and room service are available. Even with all this, however, the Art Deco ambience and the sound of the water lapping up against the dock are probably the best features of the Pier 5 Hotel.

Radisson Plaza Lord Baltimore $$–$$$$
20 West Baltimore Street
(410) 539-8400, (888) 201-1718
www.radisson.com

Built in 1928, the Radisson Plaza Lord Baltimore is the city's only National Historic Landmark hotel. It's located right in the heart of the city, within walking distance from many attractions. The hotel was built in Baltimore's heyday, and the historic interior reflects the grand style of the roaring '20s. Plush carpet, warm wood, brass, and a three-story lobby compliment the 439 deluxe guest rooms, including suites with full kitchens, living rooms, and whirlpools. Some rooms even have "Sleep Number" beds; ask for one when you make your reservation. You can upgrade to a Plaza Level room and be lavished by private concierge attention, silver service continental breakfast, and evening cocktails and hors d'oeuvres.

While the hotel reflects the past, it is any-

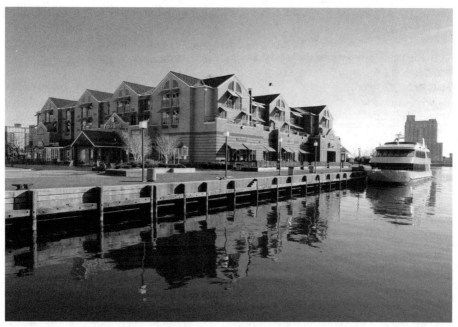

The Pier 5 Hotel has direct water access. PIER 5 HOTEL

thing but archaic. Modern amenities abound, including a gym, in-room fax and e-mail service, free Wi-Fi, and personalized concierge attention. Rooms can range drastically in price depending on the time of year, from $60 for a double to upwards of $260 for an executive suite. Valet parking is $25 per night.

Renaissance
Harborplace Hotel $$$$–$$$$$
202 East Pratt Street
(410) 547-1200, (800) HOTELS-1
www.renaissancehotels.com

The Renaissance Harborplace Hotel is directly opposite the Pratt Street Pavilion at Harborplace, the World Trade Center, and the National Aquarium. Built in 1988 and renovated in 1996 and 1998, its 622 rooms on 12 floors were completely renovated, along with the restaurant and public spaces, in 2007. Club Level rooms include a continental breakfast and other food amenities such as hors d'oeuvres and dessert in the evening. A few of the hotel's amenities include an indoor pool, an exercise

facility, Watertable Restaurant, and a lounge that overlooks the harbor (see the Restaurants chapter). There is a $27 daily self-parking fee and a $30 per day valet parking fee.

Sheraton City Center $$–$$$
101 West Fayette Street
(410) 752-1100

The Sheraton is one of the largest hotels in Maryland, with 707 rooms on 27 floors. All 707 rooms are undergoing renovation. It is actually not on the Inner Harbor but 3 blocks north and 2 blocks west of it. It's situated directly across Liberty Street from the Baltimore Arena. A subway stop is just beyond the cab stand, and the hotel is only a few blocks east of the Light Rail. The Sheraton offers singles, doubles, triples, quads, junior suites, and suites. There's an exercise room on-site. Unlike some hotels that base rates on season and availability, the Sheraton's rates are based strictly on availability, which can make it an excellent choice if you're looking for a bargain. The hotel includes two award-winning steak houses, Shula's Steak House and Shula's Steak 2.

Sheraton Inner Harbor Hotel $$$$
300 South Charles Street
(410) 962-8300, (866) 226-9330
www.sheraton.com

The Sheraton Inner Harbor offers 337 rooms and 20 suites in a high-rise building that is, essentially, right next door to Camden Yards. Amenities include two in-house restaurants, including the Orioles Grill and a Morton's of Chicago. An indoor pool and health club with sauna help you shed the unwanted pounds you might gain eating out. All Sheraton hotels offer discounts of up to 35 percent off their regular rates through their Sure Savers program. The special club rooms incorporate a small office space into the room that includes a fax/copier/printer. Call for information about special programs and rooms like the "Take me out to the ballgame" package that includes Orioles tickets. There is on-site parking in the Sheraton garage for $20 per day.

NORTHEAST

Burkshire Marriott Guest Suites &
Conference Center $$
10 West Burke Avenue, Towson
(410) 324-8100, (800) 435-5986

Adjacent to Towson University, the Burkshire Marriott's 135 guest apartments were originally meant to be retirement condominiums. This means that when we say the Burkshire has fully equipped kitchens, we're not talking about a microwave and a hot plate. The living rooms are living-room size, and each apartment even comes with its own washer and dryer. There are one-, two-, and three-bedroom apartments available. There is an on-site fitness room, but all guests of the Burkshire Marriott have access at no additional charge to the sports facilities at Towson University, which includes racquetball, tennis, and wallyball courts. Long-term parking is hard to find in Towson, so the hotel's free underground parking lot is an added bonus.

Discounts off already low prices are available for people who have business with the university, and Marriott reward points are honored here. Advance reservation with a credit card is suggested.

Chase Suite Hotel by Woodfin $$$
10710 Beaver Dam Road, Hunt Valley
(410) 584-7370, (800) WOODFIN
www.woodfinsuitehotels.com

The Chase Suite Hotel offers 96 suites that include one- and two-bedroom suites as well as single and double studios. All rooms come with full kitchens. Located in Hunt Valley, about 18 miles from the Inner Harbor, this hotel is convenient to the Light Rail and Maryland State Fairgrounds. The Chase Suite Hotel allows pets for an additional $10 charge per night. The accommodation offers its guests a homey atmosphere that includes a complimentary weeknight dinner. An outdoor pool and outdoor spa are part of the hotel's amenities.

Comfort Inn Baltimore East $
8801 Loch Raven Boulevard, Towson
(410) 882-0900, (800) 4CHOICE
www.choicehotels.com

This five-story, 185-room hotel offers free parking, an on-site restaurant and lounge, complimentary breakfast, and free HBO. It was completely redecorated when it became a Choice property in 2004. About 20 minutes from downtown Baltimore and minutes from Towson Town Center (see the Shopping chapter), the hotel is close to shopping, movies, golf, and bowling. Also within a short distance are Towson University, Morgan State University, Goucher College, Loyola College, the College of Notre Dame, and the Johns Hopkins University.

Days Hotel & Conference Center $–$$$
9615 Deereco Road, Timonium
(410) 560-1000, (800) DAYS-INN
www.daysinn.com

Days Hotel has 150 single and double rooms on six floors, above a floor of office and meeting room space that can be combined to create a large ballroom. Built in 1989, the hotel is constantly renovating, so that all rooms are kept up to date with the latest amenities. The hotel is one of the few in the area to offer a standard long-term stay rate. If you stay longer than 30 days, you are exempt from the 13 percent tax. Days Hotel offers some common, modern in-room amenities, such as refrigerators and free wireless, but it also offers guests free local phone calls, use of on-site washers and dryers, and complimentary continental breakfast. The best convenience, however, may be that the hotel is attached to a Chili's Grill and Bar, which has an on-premises lounge and provides room service to the hotel as well as a take-out service.

Days Hotel & Conference Center is about a 20-minute drive from Downtown Baltimore via I-83. It's also by a Light Rail station.

Embassy Suites
Baltimore Hunt Valley $$$–$$$$
213 International Circle, Hunt Valley
(410) 584-1400, (800) 362-2779
www.embassysuites.com
Embassy Suites, only a 25-minute drive or a short ride on Light Rail from the heart of Baltimore City, offers 223 newly renovated two-room suites over eight stories. All suites include a living room and bedroom. Some have king-size beds; others have two double-size beds. All have pull-out sofa and offer balconies that overlook a garden atrium, complete with waterfalls and a park-like setting, right in the heart of the business complex in Hunt Valley. The hotel has free wireless, a sauna, and an indoor pool. Breakfast, which is included in your room rate, is cooked to order. Rates vary based on availability.

Hampton Inn White Marsh $$–$$$
8225 Town Center Drive, White Marsh
(410) 931-2200
www.hampton-inn.com
White Marsh is a suburban shopping mall, surrounded by a bedroom community of the same name. But the mall has grown over the

years to include an industrial park and some unique shopping opportunities. (See the Shopping and Relocation chapters for more information.) With easy access to I-95, the hotel is at least 25 minutes from the center of Baltimore City. The four-story building has 131 rooms, most featuring two double beds or a king-size bed. Amenities include an outside pool during the summer, an on-site exercise room, and access to the Bally Total Fitness center next door.

Marriott Hunt Valley Inn $$–$$$$
245 Shawan Road, Hunt Valley
(410) 785-7000, (800) 228-9290
www.marriotthuntvalley.com
Marriott Hunt Valley Inn has 290 rooms, 8 suites, and 22 meeting rooms. It's right in the heart of the Hunt Valley business district near McCormicks and Procter & Gamble. You'll find a restaurant, indoor and outdoor swimming pools, a health club, whirlpool, and sauna all on-site. There's golfing nearby at Longview Golf Course and Pine Ridge Golf Course (see the Golf chapter for more information).

Red Roof Inn $–$$
111 West Timonium Road
(410) 666-0380, (800) RED-ROOF
www.redroof.com
Red Roof Inn has recently finished an extensive renovation of all of its 137 rooms. Off-season rates have fallen in the past to as low as $55, and there is no additional charge for a pet. This is a comfortable, clean facility 20 minutes north of the city by car, 10 minutes to Towson, and close to two Light Rail stops. It's right off Interstate 83 at exit 16a.

Sheraton Baltimore
North Hotel $$$–$$$$
903 Dulaney Valley Road, Towson
(410) 321-7400, (800) 433-7619
www.sheratonbaltimorenorth.com
Right in the heart of Towson, at the intersection of Dulaney Valley Road and Goucher Boulevard, you'll find the Sheraton Baltimore, a newly renovated 283-room, luxury hotel. Its

location is one of its best attributes—right in Towson, only 20 minutes from the center of Baltimore, not quite a mile from the Beltway and connected by skywalk to Towson Town Center, the largest shopping mall in the area (see the Shopping chapter). However, traffic can be relentless, particularly at rush hours, so keep that in mind if you need to be somewhere at a particular time. Although bus service does go out to Towson, main access is by car.

The Sheraton is another hotel that prices according to demand, so rates can fall precipitously depending on whether it's busy or not. All reservations must be guaranteed with a credit card. Pets are allowed with a security deposit.

Among the in-room amenities are two phones, voice mail, and modem accessibility. There is also an indoor pool, fitness center, restaurant, and lounge.

NORTHWEST

Baltimore Days Inn West—
Security Boulevard $-$$$
1660 Whitehead Court
(410) 944-7400, (800) DAYS-INN
www.the.daysinn.com/Baltimore 09351
Built in 1958 and totally renovated in 1997, this two-story Days Inn offers single rooms at prices as low as $75 and suites as high as $189. Right in the thick of west Baltimore's suburban business centers, the hotel is near the Social Security Administration headquarters, shopping, fitness centers, and tennis courts, and it has a pool, restaurant, and lounge on-site.

Doubletree Inn
at the Colonnade $$-$$$
4 West University Parkway
(410) 235-5400
www.colonnadebaltimore.com
The Colonnade is a luxury high-rise condominium building, directly across from the playing fields of the Johns Hopkins University's Homewood Campus, on the southern edge of the community known as Tuscany-Canterbury.

The Doubletree Inn takes up the first three floors of the building, offering 125 newly redecorated rooms, among which are a presidential suite and a honeymoon suite. Rates are based on availability, but if you're visiting Hopkins, ask if special rates are available. The Spice Company restaurant is in the lobby, as well as the Corbin Salon, a full-service hair salon. An indoor pool sits under a glass dome facing an inner landscaped courtyard.

Hilton Pikesville $$-$$$$$
1726 Reisterstown Road, Pikesville
(410) 653-1100, (800) 774-1500
www.pikesville.hilton.com
The Hilton Pikesville offers everything from single rooms to suites with full kitchens. Rooms have the usual amenities—phones, TV, alarm clock, and free wireless Internet. But this particular Hilton has some things that you won't find everywhere. The Hilton Pikesville offers a multilingual staff that speaks Spanish, German, Russian, French, and Italian—a true rarity among Baltimore lodgings. The Hilton Pikesville also offers an outdoor swimming pool, six lighted indoor tennis courts, and an on-premises health club with massage. Also located on the property is a hair salon, jewelry shop, travel agent, camera shop, and bank. There is also a restaurant and lounge on the premises.

Radisson Hotel at Cross Keys $$-$$$
Village of Cross Keys
100 Village Square
(410) 532-6900, (800) 333-3333
www.radisson.com/baltimoremd
The Radisson is located in the Village of Cross Keys, a relatively modern secured development within the bounds of one of the oldest developed neighborhoods in Baltimore, Roland Park. The inn has 148 rooms on four floors. It sits at the west end of the community shopping center, which boasts some of the more exclusive shops in the area. The inn serves mainly business travelers and neighborhood guests. One of the hotel's unique amenities is complimentary access to the

Cross Keys Tennis Club. Rooms have voice mail, free wireless Internet, and coffeemakers. Complimentary scheduled shuttle service to the Baltimore Inner Harbor is available. There is also a full-service restaurant on the premises.

SOUTHEAST

**Best Western Hotel &
Conference Center** $$–$$$
5625 O'Donnell Street and I-95
(410) 633-9500, (800) 633-9511
www.bestwestern.com/Baltimore
New owners recently took over this property at the Baltimore Travel Plaza and got to work redecorating all 175 sleeping rooms, the lobby, fitness center, and pool. In addition, the long-dark theater now has a new tenant, Toby's Dinner Theatre. A "Broadway in Baltimore" package combines a night at the hotel with tickets to the show. The hotel has a wide variety of room types, with a king-size bed or two double beds, a mini-suite with sitting area, and the always-popular Jacuzzi suites (which cost $300 a night). Amenities here include free Internet, a full-service restaurant, and a shuttle to the Inner Harbor. A continental breakfast is included in the room rate.

Hampton Inn Glen Burnie $$
6617 Ritchie Highway, Glen Burnie
(410) 761-7666, (800) HAMPTON
www.hampton-inn.com
Twenty minutes from BWI and from Camden Yards, the Hampton Inn Glen Burnie offers 116 rooms on five floors. It is actually a part of the Governor Plaza shopping center, so it's a short walk to restaurants, shops, and Bally's Fitness Club, to which guests have complimentary access. One of its unique features is 9-foot ceilings, which give an additional feeling of spaciousness to the relatively large guest rooms. Wireless Internet is available in every room, and copy and fax service are available. A complimentary continental breakfast is served. Built in 1989, the inn underwent a complete renovation that was completed in 2002. All room reservations must be guaranteed with a credit card.

During winter months, many of Baltimore's hotels have special packages that offer extra services while charging less. Many also offer business rates and group rates. Don't forget to ask.

SOUTHWEST

**Best Western Baltimore–
Washington Airport** $–$$
6755 Dorsey Road, Elkridge
(410) 796-3300, (800) WESTERN
www.bestwestern.com/bwiairport
The Best Western on Dorsey Road offers 133 rooms in a pleasant low-rise building that lies 7 miles from the Baltimore–Washington Thurgood Marshall International Airport. Children younger than age 17 stay free with a full-paying adult. On the premises you'll find a fitness center and spa, indoor heated pool, whirlpool, and sauna, as well as meeting and banquet facilities that can service affairs for up to 100 people. A welcome amenity is the free courtesy transportation to BWI and the Light Rail station nearby.

Comfort Inn–BWI $$–$$$
6921 Baltimore Annapolis Boulevard, Linthicum
(410) 789-9100
www.comfortinn.com
Comfort Inn offers singles (queen- or king-size beds), rooms with two double beds, a penthouse, and two executive suites, totaling 188 rooms on six floors. There is a large exercise area, which includes Jacuzzi and sauna, and a video game room. Wireless Internet service is free. Guests are treated to a full buffet breakfast. Pets are allowed with the proviso that guests notify the hotel in advance. There's a restaurant on-site. Shuttles take guests to the airport or train station. The Light Rail station is adjacent to the hotel. "Stay and Fly" packages are available.

Courtyard by Marriott Baltimore–Washington Airport $$–$$$$
1671 West Nursery Road, Linthicum
(410) 859-8855, (800) 321-2211
www.courtyard.com/bwica

This Marriott Courtyard is just a little more than 2 miles from BWI. A low-rise building with 149 rooms and 12 suites, it caters to the business traveler, as many of the airport hotels do. The positive aspect of this for tourists is that hotel rates are lower on the weekends and amenities are high. The Courtyard offers valet service, an indoor pool, and an exercise room, and there is a restaurant on the premises. There's also a shuttle service to BWI and the Light Rail station.

Embassy Suites Hotel Baltimore at BWI Airport $$$$–$$$$$
1300 Concourse Drive, Linthicum
(410) 850-0747, (800) 362-2779
www.baltimorebwiairport.embassysuites
.com

Weekend prices can be almost half of the week-day rate at this eight-story, atrium-centered facility near BWI. Amenities in its 251 suites include wet bar, refrigerator, coffeemaker, and microwave. The hotel features an indoor pool, Jacuzzi, sauna, exercise room, gift shop, newsstand, business center, and on-site steak house–style restaurant. Ten of the suites are wheelchair accessible. Transportation is also easy here, with free hotel transportation not only to and from BWI but also to the BWI Amtrak stop, the Light Rail, and MARC train. The hotel also offers an evening complimentary reception for hotel guests and complimentary breakfast.

Four Points by Sheraton BWI Airport $$–$$$$
7032 Elm Road, Linthicum
(410) 859-3300
www.fourpoints.com\bwi

The Sheraton at BWI offers 201 rooms freshly renovated in 2007 on the grounds of the BWI Airport. Other than sheer convenience, amenities include an outdoor pool, exercise room, jogging area, and room service, as well as an on-site restaurant. The best thing about this Sheraton location is its rates, which during low occupancy times can fall as low as $99. On-site parking is free. Rooms now have 32-inch flat-screen TVs and high-speen Internet access.

Marriott Residence Inn $$$–$$$$
1160 Winterson Road, Linthicum
(410) 691-0255, (800) 331-3131
www.marriott.com

The 120 one- and two-bedroom suites at the three-story Marriott Residence Inn are designed for comfort over the long term. In fact, each suite features a fully equipped kitchen; however, we doubt you'll ever have need to use it. There is no restaurant on-site, but every morning the house kitchen prepares a complimentary continental breakfast for guests. Selections on the menu vary, but you can always be assured of one hot item, such as waffles or sausage, and cold fresh fruit as well as pastries, breads, and other goodies. Evening socials feature a complimentary light dinner, which might be anything from a sandwich to the weekly guest barbecue. When you're not chowing down, you can take advantage of the outdoor pool, Sport Court, and exercise room. Rates change depending on the season, availability, and length of stay, with price breaks available at 5 nights, 12 nights, and 30 nights. Only 2 miles from BWI and within jogging distance of NSA and Martin Marietta, the Marriott Residence Inn is excellent as a home-away-from-home for the long-term business traveler or as a base for sightseeing in the Baltimore-Washington area. Pets are allowed for a fee. A shuttle will take guests to BWI or the Light Rail station.

Turf Valley Resort & Conference Center $$$–$$$$$
2700 Turf Valley Road, Ellicott City
(410) 465-1500, (888) 833-8873
www.turfvalley.com

Turf Valley could be considered outside the Baltimore area, in that it is on the outside edge of the area considered Ellicott City, about 30 minutes from Downtown. We include it, however, because it offers some accommodations and amenities not available anywhere else in the area. Before the hotel was opened at the site in the mid-1980s, Turf Valley was a country club, and its two 18-hole championship golf courses are open to hotel guests. Turf Valley offers 171 hotel rooms and suites, and 40,000 square feet of meeting space. Also offered are one-, two-, and three-bedroom villas with fireplaces. Some accommodations are pet-friendly, too. Golf is not the only thing for guests to do. There is a complete recreation area with tennis courts and fitness center. Wi-fi is complimentary. A European spa, two restaurants, a lounge, and both an indoor and outdoor swimming pool are here. If that's not enough, Turf Valley has more than 1,000 acres of beautifully landscaped grounds to stroll through.

BED-AND-BREAKFASTS

One of your best bets to really get an insider's sense of Baltimore's neighborhoods is to stay at one of our bed-and-breakfasts.

These owner-operated rest stops, nestled within communities such as Federal Hill, Fells Point, and Mount Vernon, offer a much more intimate picture of Baltimore than is available at other accommodations. The stories that flow from the walls, the innkeepers, the other visitors, and the communities that surround these establishments will color your stay. The owners and operators are part of their communities; therefore, they can provide insights into where to eat, what to do, how to get around—things that might not be available to you in any other way.

"If you want to see Baltimore, you need to stay in one of our bed-and-breakfasts," says Paul Bragaw, an innkeeper and past president of the Maryland Association of Bed and Breakfasts.

Practically every era of Baltimore's history is represented. Waterfront houses built in Baltimore's earliest years, Victorians with all their beauty and splendor, and converted row houses, acquired during the city's ambitious effort to bring people back to the cities in the 1970s are just some of the offerings awaiting those willing to pass on the familiar chains of hotels and motels dotting the area.

Of equal appeal to many who stay at inns and bed-and-breakfasts is the slower pace. TVs give way to conversation, radios give way to reading. Quiet, contemplative time in front of a fireplace or sipping tea and relaxing with others after taking in the sights are to be expected. Mere pleasantries exchanged over a shared, family-style breakfast lead to shared insights and discussions about how home and away are similar and different. Occasionally, visitors who meet at a bed-and-breakfast become long-term friends, often returning to the site of the blossoming of a newfound relationship year after year.

Price Code

Prices can range from $125 to more than $175, depending on whether it's a weekday or weekend, the size of the room, the location and the time of the year.

A safe average would be about $150 a night, which includes a full breakfast in the morning. Most rooms are not open to children or pets. Because many bed-and-breakfasts are often in older buildings, they usually offer poor wheelchair accessibility. Smoking is usually prohibited to satisfy nonsmoking visitors.

The price codes shown reflect the weekend rates. Rates do not include city and state taxes, which usually add about 15 percent to the bill.

$. . . . . $125 or less
$$ . . . . $126 to $175
$$$ . . . . $176 and more

Don't expect to make reservations for a weekend from April to November just a few days in advance. Home games for the Baltimore Orioles and/or the Baltimore Ravens as well as conventions in the area draw many visitors during these months, so rooms are booked well in advance.

A sizable portion of the bed-and-breakfast trade in the Baltimore area is geared toward businesspeople who visit the area, often with their spouses or other family members. A number of people staying at bed-and-breakfasts are friends or relatives of people living nearby. And you may be surprised by the number of locals who abandon their homes for a few nights in a bed-and-breakfast. After all, just because we live here doesn't mean we're not entitled to a little pampering.

Baltimore's bed-and-breakfast industry is still in its youth. The relative newness of the market has encouraged some illegal entrepreneurial spirit, so make sure that the place where you stay meets all of the local codes. The listings that are certified by the Maryland Bed and Breakfast Association are noted. Certification ensures that members meet parking, use, occupancy, and safety requirements. Be cautious of people who have large homes and "open them up" to people on the weekends.

DOWNTOWN

**Abacrombie Fine Food and
Accommodations** $$
58 West Biddle Street
(410) 244-7227
www.abacrombie.net
This row house from the 1880s provides 12 rooms with distinctive features in Mount Vernon. This site is convenient to the city's cultural center for the symphony, art galleries, or theaters. The first floor features an open parlor for relaxing. Each morning, guests select from the restaurant's continental breakfast. Dinner and Sunday brunch are served in the ground-floor restaurant (except Monday and Tuesday).

Single and double occupancy are available. The rooms all have private bathrooms, telephones, and televisions. Rooms also have their own temperature controls connecting to the central air system. Smoking is not permitted. Abacrombie Fine Food and Accommodations is a Maryland Bed and Breakfast Association member.

Ann Street B&B $
804 South Ann Street
(410) 342-5883
In 1988 Baltimore's innkeeping veterans, Joanne and Andrew Mazurek, opened Ann Street B&B in the house where Andrew had grown up.

More than 20 years ago, the city condemned the site and about 70 houses in preparation for the planned extension of Interstate 95 through the city. But community opposition sent the highway in another direction. In the mid-1980s the city offered the homes back to their last owners. The Mazureks bought the family row house and one next door. The result is a happy ending for the Mazureks and guests at their three-bedroom bed-and-breakfast. Restored to an earlier era when Andrew's ancestors lived there, the inn features double poster beds, original hardwood floors, and a country colonial charm. Each room has a private bathroom and two have fireplaces. The inn also features central air-conditioning. Twelve fireplaces help to keep the place warm in the winter as guests talk, snack, visit, and read. Another favorite feature of the house is the private garden, which from spring to fall is the ideal location to relax, away from the hustle and bustle of modern life. The Mazureks tend to it daily to ensure that guests always have an inviting outdoor spot in which to visit.

Located in the heart of Fells Point, there's no limit to the dining, dancing, and imbibing possibilities near the inn. The Mazureks are active participants in the Fells Point business community, offering guests insights into special-interest restaurants and stores in the area. According to Joanne Mazurek, their goal is to provide guests "not a real formal place to relax for a while."

**Celie's Waterfront Inn
Bed and Breakfast** $$
1714 Thames Street
(410) 522-2323, (800) 432-0184
www.baltimore-bed-breakfast.com
In the heart of the Fells Point waterfront, Celie's Waterfront Bed and Breakfast features open rooms, many with skylights, and lots of modern conveniences for a bed-and-breakfast. All seven rooms offer private baths, air-conditioning, and a choice of king-, queen-, or single-size beds. Rooms vary in their offerings, some with fireplaces,

whirlpool tubs, private balconies, and harbor views. Everyone can spy the city skyline from the rooftop deck and visit the private gardens maintained by innkeepers Kevin and Nancy Kupec. The Courtyard Room is wheelchair accessible and has its own courtyard.

Guests will find many antiques and collectibles, fresh-cut flowers, down comforters, flannel sheets, thick terry robes, and bath sheets in all of the rooms. They'll also find TVs, refrigerators stocked with soft drinks, juices, and mineral water, and even VCRs and coffeemakers are available. The most popular rooms are the Harbor Front rooms, where guests can have a king-size bed, wood-burning fireplace, wicker seating, a whirlpool tub, and three windows facing the harbor.

Although it's not close to the university, Celie's offers discounts to Johns Hopkins Hospital patients and "family members" during weekdays. Children older than age 10 are welcome, but smoking is prohibited. Private telephone lines are in all rooms, and breakfast is a combination of fresh fruits, juices, baked breads, and cereals. Celie's is a Maryland Bed and Breakfast Association member.

1870 Guest House $
21 South Stricker Street
(410) 947-4622
www.bbonline.com/md/1870guest house/
Located in a restored Italianate-style row home in Union Square, the 1870 Guest House offers accommodations complete with a fully equipped private kitchen and bath. Set in Southwest Baltimore, known as SoWeBo to insiders, the house faces the 1.3-acre Union Square Park that was established in 1847. About 15 blocks away from the Inner Harbor, the 1870 Guest House is a closer walk to the B&O Railroad Museum, H. L. Mencken House Museum, and Hollins Market. The market was built in 1836 and is Baltimore's oldest market still in use.

The third-floor suite features a queen-size bed, bath with tub and shower, AC, TV/VCR, and private phone. The kitchen is stocked with a substantial breakfast and guests may serve themselves at their leisure.

The Inn at Government House $$$
1125 North Calvert Street
(410) 539-0566
Set in the historic district of Mount Vernon, The Inn at Government House is a terrific cross between a bed-and-breakfast and hotel. With 19 rooms, the inn is larger than most bed-and-breakfasts in the area, but just as charming. Rooms come with a private bath, hair dryer, ironing board, iron, TV, and refrigerator. A continental breakfast and parking is included in the price of the room. Restoration of the Government House took place from 1983 to 1985, at a total cost of $2.5 million. Once the renovation was complete, the mansion was open to the public and has since served as the official guesthouse of the city of Baltimore. The mansion offers original woodwork and stained glass, as well as a Knabe square grand piano in the Music Room. More than 150 years old, it is probably one of the very few pianos of its kind left in existence. The mansion's library shows off detailed woodwork and a rounded bay windowseat with original stained glass. In the dining room guests are invited to have breakfast at the Potthast table. The table was manufactured in Baltimore and is nearly as old as the mansion, which dates from 1889.

Inn at 2920 $$$
2920 Elliott Street, Canton
(410) 342-4450, (877) 774-2920
www.theinnat2920.com
If you prefer sleek to quaint or modern to colonial, make your reservation at the Inn at 2920. This five-unit ode to modern design is hidden behind a Canton row house about 2 miles from the Inner Harbor. Set in a residential area just off the main thoroughfares, the inn is decorated in neutral tones (except for one deep-red wall in the public space) and keeps all the lines clean and simple. Local artists' work decorates the walls. Linens feel rich to the touch. Fans and open windows cool the rooms, although there is central air

for those soggy Baltimore summer days. The usual amenities are available, including wireless Internet and rain showers, though phones are not available. Queen-size beds are in four of the rooms, though the "Bordello" room has a king-size bed. A first-floor suite has a sitting room and a nonworking fireplace. The ottoman, believe it or not, turns into a twin-size bed. The second-floor sitting room is spacious and inviting, with deep modern seating and a traditional marble fireplace.

Scarborough Fair $$$
1 East Montgomery Street
(410) 837-0010
www.scarboroughfairbandb.com

New owners have purchased the Federal Hill bed-and-breakfast, which Ashley and Ellen Scarborough opened in 1997. It remains, as the Scarboroughs imagined it, a place where people from diverse backgrounds can gather to share everything from food to conversation to tips on the area they are visiting. Rooms are due to get some updating in late 2008 and a few packages have been added. Picnics on Federal Hill, massages, and trolley tours are among the offerings.

This house, built in 1801, was a rehabilitated office building in the 1980s and now has become a six-bedroom guesthouse, about 2 blocks from the Inner Harbor. The previous owners put six months of work into converting the office building into a guesthouse, and their time was well spent.

All of the rooms have different color schemes, colonial- and Victorian-era antiques, and queen-size beds, with the exception of one room that offers two twin-size beds that convert into a king-size one. Each room has a private bath adjoined to it. Four of the rooms have gas fireplaces.

A full breakfast is served in a 12-seat dining room. A greeting room and library, featuring a variety of books, is available to travelers. Because of the inn's easy access to the Inner Harbor area, Oriole Park at Camden Yards, M&T Bank Stadium, and the Baltimore Convention Center, reservations are recommended.

SOUTHWEST

The Wayside Inn $$
4344 Columbia Road, Ellicott City
(410) 461-4636
www.waysideinnmd.com

Nestled on the outskirts of Ellicott City, a historic mill town about 8 miles outside of Baltimore's city limits, the stone farmhouse offers guests the package of history and charm in four distinctive guest rooms. Margo's Suite is a romantic two-room suite with a queen-size bed, antique painted chests, floral blue wallpaper, and eyelid windows. The second room is a quaint sitting room, and the private bath offers an antique claw-foot bathtub. Betty's Suite is a two-room suite filled with Federal period antiques and reproductions. This suite offers a queen-size pediment bed, sitting room, and private bath with tub and shower. The Banneker Room offers a queen-size antique rice bed and coordinating dresser and nightstand. The Ellicott Room offers an artistic rendering of Main Street, Ellicott City, in the mid-1800s. The Banneker and Ellicott rooms share working fireplaces and spacious new baths with double Jacuzzis.

To recall the mid-1850s, the owners have maintained stately trees, flower gardens, and a small pond, giving the two-acre site a distinctly rural feel despite its closeness to urban life. One tradition of old inns that owners David and Susan Balderson maintain is the keeping of lighted candles in each window to signal the availability of rooms and the welcoming spirit of its owners.

For antiques lovers, historic mill enthusiasts, and people looking for a place out of the

> **i** Baltimore's bed-and-breakfasts are busiest in May. The Preakness Stakes, the second leg of horse racing's Triple Crown, is the third Saturday of the month, and numerous college graduation ceremonies draw relatives and friends from near and far throughout the month. Reservations are hard to come by through September without advance planning.

mainstream, the Wayside Inn is a good bet. (See the Antiques and Collectibles chapter for more information about Ellicott City.)

The Wilderness Bed & Breakfast $$
2 Thistle Road, Catonsville
(410) 744-0590
www.thewilderness.biz

Tucked at the edge of Patapsco State Park, The Wilderness seems like it's, well, nowhere. But it is, in fact, just a half-hour drive to downtown or Columbia, and about five minutes to historic Ellicott City. And in spite of its proximity to the busy modern world, its Victorian charms and leafy three-acre setting make guests feel a part of some place quiet and relaxing. The aroma of something sweet wafting in from the kitchen welcomes guests right away. A mix of comfortable furnishings and eye-catching antiques fill the sitting room, dining room, and three suites. Each suite has a separate sitting room and modern bath. If the outdoors beckon, there's a wide front porch, a screened porch in back, and a patio in the yard. TV and phones are available, as is wireless Internet. Two resident cats keep an eye on guests. Credit cards are accepted, and special rates are available for a multiple-night stay.

NORTH

Gramercy Mansion
Bed & Breakfast $$$
1400 Greenspring Valley Road
Stevenson
(410) 486-2405, (800) 553-3404
www.gramercymansion.com

Nestled in the middle of the Green Spring Valley, just 20 minutes from downtown Baltimore and the Inner Harbor, the Gramercy Mansion Bed & Breakfast is a step back in time. The Tudor style mansion and estate, which dates from 1902, is situated on 45 acres of bucolic countryside.

Built by Alexander J. Cassatt, owner of the Pennsylvania Railroad and brother of American Impressionist painter Mary Cassatt, the mansion was presented as a wedding gift to his daughter, Eliza. In the 1950s, the estate became home to the Koinonia Foundation, a predecessor of the Peace Corps. The present owners have since restored the mansion and its surrounding gardens.

This bed-and-breakfast offers 11 stylish rooms, including two suites. Aphrodite's Retreat is a sun-filled room with oriental carpets, French antiques, and a king-size bed. Aunt Mary's Suite has a Victorian flare with sitting room, fireplace, and extra large clawfoot tub with shower. The Ambassador's Room is furnished with elegant draperies, fireplace, and whirlpool tub with statuary shower. All rooms include TV, fresh flowers, robes, coffee, tea, soda, and full gourmet breakfast. Visitors can also take advantage of the Olympic-size pool and tennis court, stroll along a woodland trail, through the orchard, flower, or herb gardens, or visit the organic farm.

The Gramercy Mansion is a Maryland Bed and Breakfast Association member.

RESTAURANTS

Baltimore has an eclectic mix of restaurants. Although we are known primarily for our seafood—crabs, oysters, and shrimp—Baltimore's culinary scene has much more to offer than just crustaceans. Baltimore now gives neighboring metropolises Washington and New York a run for their money when it comes to fine dining. We now boast a number of innovative and traditional restaurants that offer five-star service and exquisite menus. Located on the water in Harbor East, Chef Cindy Wolfe's Charleston has a gorgeous menu of innovative Southern cuisine and an extensive wine list. Her well-trained staff can help anyone navigate both the food and the wine menus to create the perfect dining experience. Want Italian? Try Little Italy in the heart of the city for a number of traditional, Southern Italian pasta dishes, or head up Charles Street to Sotto Sopra, where the chef de cuisine hails from Milan and the carpaccio rivals that of the best Tuscan trattoria.

There are also more casual settings for good food, places to meet after work for a cocktail and an appetizer, or after the theater for cappuccino and dessert. Downtown is now dotted with wine bars, breweries, tapas restaurants, and small cafes with creative vegetarian dishes. Baltimore is still very much a big small town, and small neighborhood joints provide some of the best surprises. Friendly service, small but interesting menus, and a selection of local beers and artwork make these smaller, off-the-beaten-path places a great Baltimore experience. At Peter's Inn in Fells Point, the restaurant occupies the first floor of a small row house, and owners Bud and Karin change the menu weekly depending on what's fresh at the market. At tiny Ethel and Ramone's in Mount Washington Village,

one taste of their jambalaya will transport you to New Orleans. Nick's Fish House in Locust Point brings out the best in Chesapeake Bay seafood on a spot of waterfront nobody would go near a few years ago.

No trip to Baltimore would be complete without a trip to one of the many local diners, where some of the servers have waited tables for 30 years. The Sip 'n' Bite on the waterfront in Canton, for example, serves 24 hours a day, seven days a week, except Christmas Day.

Of course there is the great seafood. From sushi to paella, Baltimore is the best place on earth to find fresh seafood. Baltimoreans love their shellfish, and you'll see the counters of Nick's Seafood at the Cross Street Market in Federal Hill packed with locals year-round. You can belly up to the raw bar for oysters shucked on the half shell, or order one of the famous lump meat crab cakes.

With hundreds of restaurants in the area, we tried to list a diverse collection, designed to offer something for everyone. Not every restaurant in such places as Little Italy or Greektown or Fells Point, where there are more than a dozen eating establishments within a few blocks of one another, could be listed. In all cases, we have favored the tried and true or those that are newer and receiving high praise from all quarters. Just because a restaurant that's your personal favorite or one that others rave about isn't listed doesn't mean it's inferior and should not be visited.

We've tried to list specialty items, those entrees or appetizers or desserts that can't be replaced on the menu because they're in constant demand. We've also listed a few of our favorites (because we couldn't resist the temptation). One category you will not find too often is the chains, those restaurants that are in every city or town, serving the same food. You know what they have, how they serve it, what the seating is like. They're all around but not nearly as exciting as a locally owned restaurant.

Wherever possible, we've tried to give you a feel for what you might expect once inside an establishment's door. Just remember that things change; in the last few years, ownership has changed tremendously at many restaurants, as have menus, decor, chefs, and names. The fluid nature of the restaurant trade in Baltimore is a sign of success and innovation rather than a sign of failure.

In the listings that follow, casual means anything from jeans and a dress shirt to a shirt and tie for guys and everything from jeans and a blouse to a dress for the gals. Where it says formal, expect to wear good pants or a dress, a shirt with a collar, and, in some cases, a sport coat and tie. We've mentioned where coats are required of men, but you won't run across those instructions too often here.

We have also tried to clue you in on the peculiarities of the alcohol regulations, where they apply. Restaurants can have licenses to serve beer and wine and liquor, just beer and wine, or to allow people to bring in their own alcohol. Most of the smaller, non-dinner-oriented places don't serve alcohol (nor would you probably want them to).

Beginning in February 2008, Maryland has banned smoking statewide. That means absolutely no lighting up in any bar or restaurant.

If you want to avoid crowds, watch out for dinner hours on Thursday, Friday, and Saturday as well as brunch hours, say 11:00 a.m. to 3:00 p.m., on Sunday, when the after-church crowd makes way for a group or family get-together. In the tourist areas such as the Inner Harbor, Fells Point, and Mount Vernon, the crowds can get thick at just about any time, but your patience or planning can be rewarded with some great nectar from Baltimore's gods of the kitchen.

We have also tried to keep you posted on parking, which in the city can mean pumping quarters into a meter or paying top dollar for a private lot where they have control of your keys while you are dining. If you're in the city, you can expect to pay 25 cents per 15 minutes of parking at meters on the street and an average of $10 for two hours of parking at the underground or covered parking garages in the Downtown area. As you get farther away from the Downtown area, you'll find free and ample parking is more available. To make it easier, we've highlighted your best parking options wherever possible.

Wherever you park, make sure you remember the street and closest cross street. A friend of ours parked his car in the city, went to a meal, and then he—and the people who he had dropped at the restaurant's door before parking the car—couldn't find his car for more than a hour because he couldn't remember the names of the streets where it was parked. Don't laugh. It can happen, but hopefully not to you.

Price Code

To further explain what to expect, we have included a price code for the restaurants listed. It isn't foolproof, but we have tried to offer a good average, meaning some meals cost more and some less. But, in general, it should give you enough of a guideline to avoid sticker shock. The price code includes the cost of a dinner for two people, excluding appetizers and desserts, wine and spirits, taxes, and tips. Basically, it is the price of the entrees two people will have for the main meal served, usually dinner unless the restaurant doesn't serve dinner.

$.	$15 and less
$$	$16 to $30
$$$	$31 to $40
$$$$	$41 and more

The restaurants are grouped by geographic area—Downtown, Northeast, Northwest, Southeast, and Southwest—the same geographic areas we've used in most of the other chapters. If you refer back to the beginning of the book and the area maps, you can orient yourself to where you are staying and where you wish to go to eat. If there is no town or city listed after the street address, that means the eatery is within the city limits. If a town or city follows the street address, it means you will be leaving the city. We've provided you with clues on what restaurants are near or how to get to them, so you can focus on the thing you want to do most now—EAT!

DOWNTOWN

Amicci's $$$
231 South High Street
(410) 528-1096

The High Street location opened for fine dining in Little Italy in 1991. Neighborhood people, tourists, and businesspeople rave about the pane Rotundo appetizer, a round loaf of Italian bread hollowed out and covered with garlic butter to make room for six jumbo shrimp cooked in garlic sauce. For a main course, try the penne La Rosa—jumbo shrimp, mushrooms, and onions covered with pureed sun-dried tomatoes and garlic sauce.

The Little Italy location offers lunch and dinner seven days a week. The restaurant serves beer, wine, and cordials. Reservations are a good idea, especially on weekends or summer weeknights. Parking is available on the street, but you better have some change handy for the meters.

Attman's Delicatessen $
1019 East Lombard Street
(410) 563-2666

Like one of New York's best delis, Attman's features 10 cooks arguing and jockeying for position as they prepare deli sandwiches for the masses. Local favorites include hot corned beef, available in the three-quarter-pound variety, which is plenty for most people, or the "extra heavy," which costs an extra $2.30 for about a third-pound to a half-pound more meat. Like any self-respecting deli, this one offers a real deli pickle to go with the meal. A word of advice: Know what you want when

i Several restaurants validate parking. Check when you enter to see if this is the case. It doesn't hurt to ask, and it may even save you a few bucks.

you get in line because there isn't usually much time for waffling.

If you plan ahead, you can hit the deli on your way out in the morning, or you can go during lunch or the dinner hour. It's open every day. On-street parking is available.

Bagel Works $
The Belvedere,
1023 North Charles Street
(410) 347-2790

There's no place to sit at these works, located within The Belvedere condominiums complex. But if you're looking for a wide range of bagels, you won't notice. The most basic is the New Yorker, any style in the bins with cream cheese on top, and the most unusual, the Beast, which is roast beef, Swiss cheese, onions, and horseradish. Your eyes might water, but your taste buds will rejoice. Some less adventurous sandwich options, including turkey and ham, are also available, as are the usual toppings such as butter, lox, and flavored cream cheeses. And there's always a pot of coffee on. Bagel Works serves breakfast and lunch only and is closed on Sundays.

The Bay Atlantic Club $$
206 East Redwood Street
(410) 752-1448
www.bic.edu

There's no other lunch spot quite like The Bay Atlantic Club. Primarily, it's because the staff here, all students of the Baltimore International College, hope to become tomorrow's great chefs. And it shows in the food and the service. The menu varies widely depending on the day and, we guess, the curriculum. You'll find full dinners such as herb-crusted salmon or braised short ribs, as well as salads, sandwiches, and wickedly rich desserts. The ambience is elegant, with white tablecloths and chandeliers. And the staff, although young, earnestly tries to please. It's also fun to see these young people so proud of their work. Reservations are recommended, especially since the restaurant occasionally closes for student breaks.

Bertha's $$
734 South Broadway
(410) 327-5795

If you look on the bumpers of many Baltimoreans' cars, you'll see a sticker saying, "Eat Bertha's Mussels." It's a tribute to this family-run business that opened as a bar in the Fells Point area in 1972. Since then it's grown up to have two dining rooms for casual dining. The mussels are the mainstay of the menu, steamed with a choice of eight butter-based sauces, such as garlic sauce with capers. When basil is in season, in the late summer and early fall, try the basil-pesto sauce on the mussels. Other menu items have a Caledonia heritage, with a Scottish afternoon tea served every day except Sunday. You need to make a reservation for the teas, but otherwise, drop by when the green bumper stickers weigh heaviest on your mind. Parking is available on the streets of Fells Point.

The Bicycle $$$
1444 Light Street, Federal Hill
(410) 234-1900
www.bicyclebistro.com

A bicycle mounted on the outside of this brightly painted row house in South Baltimore announces the restaurant from the street. The caveat for this place is its small, linear interior. Tables can sometimes feel crowded (making it a poor choice for large parties), but the food and the bustle in the open kitchen make up for it. The new chef-owner has been putting his personal touch on the menu with great success. The self-described "global bistro" menu is exotic. East Asian red snapper has a Thai influence; Mongolian barbecued beef short ribs are tender and fiery. In summer months a garden patio is open for dining. The Bicycle serves dinner only, Monday through Saturday. Reservations are recommended. Parking is on

the street, or you can park in the Federal Hill Garage on West Street (about $6) and walk the 5 blocks to the restaurant.

Black Olive $$$$
814 South Bond Street
(410) 276-7141
www.theblackolive.com

Down a quiet side street you'll find this taverna that specializes in fresh, organic Greek foods. The menu is laden with fish choices served a variety of ways. Fish is filleted at tableside. Beef tenderloin is organic. Green village pie is made with sheep's milk and topped with homemade filo. You can count on baklava for dessert. The restaurant is open every day for lunch and dinner. Dinner reservations are recommended. On-street parking isn't too hard to find.

Blue Agave Restaurante y Tequileria $$
1032 Light Street, Federal Hill
(410) 576-3938
www.blueagaverestaurant.com

Blue agave is the plant that produces the nectar of Mexico: tequila. And this place has its share. The bar offers tequila tastings and delicious margaritas (served over ice, only—don't offend the traditionalist owners and ask for a frozen margarita from a blender). As for the food, you won't find canned refried beans or enchiladas drowning in cheese. The menu is true classic Mexican and Southwestern cuisine, featuring slow-roasted pork and the best fish tacos in town. The house salad is a signature dish, with a delicious mix of greens, avocado, and black bean salsa. Casual and fun, Blue Agave serves dinner every day but Monday. Parking is on the street or in the Federal Hill Garage on West Street.

Bo Brooks Crab House $$
2701 Boston Street
(410) 558-0202
www.bobrooks.com

This is easily Baltimore's most popular home for steamed crabs. Bo Brooks' reputation brings people from near and far for a chance to sit down for a platter of crabs served on paper-covered tables. What the place lacks in atmosphere (diners drop the picked-through crab shells in buckets on the floor), it more than makes up for in the taste of the steamed crabs. There's alcohol and some other entrees for those who don't partake, but the pickings are slim.

Bo Brooks is open seven days a week for lunch and dinner. The restaurant takes only a few reservations, so if you don't want to wait in the long, long lines, plan to arrive before 6:00 p.m. or after 8:00 p.m. You can call ahead to learn the prices and sizes of the crabs of the day; the best selection is from March to September, when crabs are typically in season. Free valet parking is available.

Boccaccio $$$
925 Eastern Avenue
(410) 234-1322
www.boccaccio-restaurant.com

This is one of Little Italy's priciest locales, but the service from the black-tie staff makes it worthwhile. The northern Italian dishes, including a rich mushroom risotto and a farfalle topped with crab, are as good as you can find in Baltimore, making the price seem that much more reasonable. The restaurant is open for lunch only on weekdays and for dinner seven days a week. Reservations are a real good idea, especially on weekends.

Brass Elephant $$$$
924 North Charles Street
(410) 547-8480
www.brasselephant.com

One of the Baltimore area's favorites since its opening in 1980 in the historic and arts-oriented Mount Vernon area, the Brass Elephant means fine dining in a restored nineteenth-century Victorian town house that's practically overrun with history and elephants (check out the elephant sconces— really!). Focused on northern Italian cuisine, the menu changes with the seasons. But you are guaranteed lots of entrees featuring lots of local, in-season produce and seafood,

especially crabmeat. This is a coat-and-tie establishment for professionals and people on important nights out who have a respect and appreciation for the restored building and for a four-course meal that might take more than three hours to enjoy.

An artisan cheese plate and trio of tortellini stuffed with shrimp, lobster, or cheese start the meal; cioppino with spinach linguini made here or New Zealand lamb are among the entree choices. Save room for the chocolate bread pudding or profiteroles. There's a full bar and an upstairs lounge that has a casual happy hour Monday through Friday. Free valet parking is available. The restaurant serves dinner seven days a week and lunch on weekdays. A jacket is required.

The Brewer's Art $–$$$
1106 North Charles Street
(410) 547-6925
www.belgianbeer.com

This place straddles the line between restaurant and bar. Upstairs, a gloriously majestic nineteenth-century space has been transformed into a restaurant and lounge. The dinner menu includes elaborate entrees and classic European-style country fare featuring meats, fish, seafood, pasta, and a vegetarian offering. Downstairs is a whole other world. The cavernous, dark, smoke-filled bar is popular with art students and local hipsters, and cozy alcoves are packed with friends commiserating over pints of the house brews. The Resurrection Ale, served in a Belgian Ale mug, is a favorite, but with a nearly 8 percent alcohol content, it can catch up to you quickly. A less expensive light-fare menu is served downstairs; the seasoned, shoestring pommes frites are the best in town. Dinner is served daily, and the light fare is available as late as 11:00 p.m.

Brighton's Orangerie $$$
Intercontinental Harbor Court Hotel
550 Light Street
(410) 234-0550
www.harborcourt.com

Now the main restaurant in the Intercontinental Harbor Court Hotel (the incomparable Hampton's is closed), Brighton's boasts a bistro menu and a casual atmosphere that's perfect for an impressive business meeting over a meal, but without all the pomp. Continental favorites and local favorites, especially such seafood specialties as heavy crab cakes, scallops, and rockfish (a local favorite known as "striped bass" by many), are the perfect companion to the great view of the Inner Harbor. This is one of the best places to see and be seen in the city.

Reservations are recommended at all times for this restaurant, which serves breakfast, lunch, dinner, and afternoon tea. During tea, scheduled between 3:00 and 5:00 p.m., a variety of homemade pastries and dessert fare is served with several types of tea. Brighton's is open every day but doesn't serve tea or dinner on Sundays. Valet parking is available, or you can park at the harbor and walk over.

Burke's Cafe and Comedy Club $$
36 Light Street
(410) 752-4189

Close enough to the Inner Harbor and its attractions but far enough away to not be perpetually crowded, Burke's Cafe offers gigantic burgers, homemade soups, sandwiches, oyster stew, and salads. A favorite for visitors, many of whom stop by after an Orioles' game, is the Burke's onion ring, a large, tasty, breathtaking, and breath-killing appetizer.

Reservations are a good idea on weekend nights or if you plan to go before an event, but otherwise you'll be seated for breakfast, lunch, or dinner pretty quickly. The bar is known for its frosty mugs of beer and soda; it's also a good place to wait for a table. Burke's is open 7:00 a.m. to 2:00 a.m. daily. Parking is available at several parking garages within a block of the restaurant. Try the garage at the Gallery shopping area, or if it's late at night or the weekend, park on the street.

Charleston $$$$
1000 Lancaster Street
(410) 332-7373

Charleston is a singular dining experience. A contemporary American restaurant set in Baltimore's Inner Harbor East development, this is the place to spoil yourself with rich, decadent food, phenomenal service, and an impeccable wine list. Educated servers guide you through the wine menu, which features more than 600 vintages, while famed chef Cindy Wolfe dazzles with her fabulous menu crafted from the finest seasonal seafood, game, and fresh produce. Everybody orders up three to five courses here. The menu has only three prices, depending on those courses. And don't worry, portions are large enough to thrill your taste buds but small enough to leave room for dessert. The seasons rule here. Tomatoes will be spotlighted in summer; root vegetables in winter. Cheese courses and desserts are always a knockout.

City Cafe $$–$$$
1001 Cathedral Street
(410) 539-4252

In addition to its American fare, focusing on pastas and traditional entrees, City Cafe offers a collection of vegetarian dishes on its ever-changing menu. There's always a vegetarian sandwich, a vegetarian pasta dish, and a vegetarian soup for customers to try. The casual-dining experience includes outdoor seating at tables with umbrellas during the warmer months. Because of its location, it attracts a large neighborhood clientele from Mount Vernon who return often to try the latest creation on the menu. It's open every day.

Since 1994 the restaurant, winner of several City Paper awards, has been serving breakfast, lunch, and dinner. There's also a coffee bar for your morning joe or last cup of the day and a bar where the martini rules and you can order from the menu. Parking is available at meters, which must be fed before 6:00 p.m. Reservations aren't needed for this restaurant, which can seat up to 170 people. You can call the listed number for daily lunch and dinner specials.

Da Mimmo $$$$
217 South High Street
(410) 727-6876
www.damimmo.com

Da Mimmo's offers a great selection of seafood and veal dishes as well as all the usual Italian specialties you'd expect in Little Italy. Shrimp dishes are among the best, while the collection of wines to choose from is equally impressive. Don't fill up on the breads or salads, because the pricey entrees offer super-large servings. The fine-dining atmosphere can be noisy; it just isn't a place for privacy. Open daily for lunch and dinner. Reservations are an absolute must. There's live piano music most nights. Free parking is available.

Ding How $$
631 South Broadway, Fells Point
(410) 327-8888

Fells Point and Chinese food really don't seem like a likely match, but Ding How is apt to change your mind. At this restaurant in a historic part of Baltimore, you can find the usual Chinese favorites as well as lots of vegetarian and local seafood specialties, including lobster, soft-shell crabs, and calamari. A favorite is the boneless orange roughy with vegetables served in a spicy sauce. The restaurant is open for lunch and dinner every day, and you can park on the streets of Fells Point pretty easily. Dress is casual.

Eichenkranz $$$
611 South Fagley Street
(410) 563-7577
www.eichenkranz.com

Eichenkranz has been offering true German food since it opened in 1934, and while ownership has changed a few times, with the latest owners taking over in 1992, the food has remained constant. Located off Fleet Street in Fells Point, the restaurant offers four types of schnitzel—Wiener schnitzel, Jager schnitzel, schnitzel Holstein, and the Eichenkranz schnitzel, which features veal, shredded ham, and Swiss cheese. The casual

i The 2900 block of O'Donnell Street in Canton, known as "The Square," has a number of great restaurants and bars concentrated on both sides of a small grassy park. If you're not sure what you're in the mood for, come here and walk around. You're sure to find something to please.

atmosphere, which tends to draw lots of couples, is enhanced by a number of pictures of Germany retained from its original owners.

The restaurant serves lunch and dinner every day. Reservations are recommended, even if you call on the day you wish to dine out, and parking is free on a lot at the restaurant. There's a full bar, too.

Helen's Garden Restaurant $$$
2908 O'Donnell Street
(410) 276-2233
www.helensgarden.com

Located in Canton Square, Helen's Garden is a cozy, intimate cafe with a great wine list and an equally wonderful menu. This is the kind of place where you can either dress casual and get away cheap with a bottle of vino for less than $20, or you can show up in black-tie attire and have an elegant meal. Grilled fish entrees, such as the tuna, are superb, and the weekend brunch menu is well loved by locals. Reservations are recommended. Open for lunch and dinner, Tuesday through Sunday; brunch is served Sunday. Valet parking is available Thursday through Sunday night.

The Helmand $$
806 North Charles Street
(410) 752-0311
www.helmand.com

There's seemingly every type of food at this Afghan restaurant that's fewer than 10 blocks north of the Inner Harbor. For a reasonable price, you can dine on ravioli filled with ground beef and topped with a creamy sauce made of split peas and yogurt. Lots of meals have yogurt in them, including the pumpkin with garlic yogurt sauce. The atmosphere is really casual for this dinner-only restaurant that's open nightly. This is a Baltimore favorite, and it fills quickly.

Henninger's Tavern $$$
1812 Bank Street
(410) 342-2172
www.hennigerstavern.com

Vintage photos and an antique china closet greet visitors at this Fells Point–area restaurant known for its seafood. Don't kid yourself: This is on the outskirts of Fells Point, removed by several blocks from the hubbub of the Fells Point area. No matter—pan-fried, breaded oysters and flounder stuffed with crabmeat make the trip worth it.

There's a full bar and a semiformal atmosphere. Parking is available on the street. Reservations are not taken, meaning you may spend a fair amount of time looking at the photos before being seated. To avoid the crowds, come early or late to this restaurant that serves dinner Tuesday through Saturday from 5:00 to 10:00 p.m. The bar stays open until 1:00 a.m.

Ixia $$$
518 North Charles Street
(410) 727-1800
www.ixia-online.com

Ixia is as cool as its blue walls. Located in an elegant Charles Street town house, the restaurant also features a lounge and offers an after-hours small plates menu and martinis. Service is smooth, the menu a fusion of flavors from around the world. Here's your chance to sample grilled octopus, cumin-scented rack of lamb, a variety of the world's cheeses, and carrot sherbet and walnut ice cream. The menu changes as quickly as the seasons, so it's always a surprise.

James Joyce Irish Pub
and Restaurant $$-$$$
616 South President Street
(410) 727-5107
www.thejamesjoycepub.com

Set in the up-and-coming Harbor East neighborhood, James Joyce has quickly become a popular spot for casual fare and live music several evenings a week. Baltimore has its share of Irish restaurants (no, not every one is listed here) but this one is notable for its convivial atmosphere and its varied menu. Traditional Irish fare is featured here, but the salads topped with meats and seafood are a delight, as are the hearty main courses available after 2:30. With so much variety, you can eat cheap or you can splurge. There's a children's menu here. Valet parking is available in the evening. Parking is also available in the nearby garage.

Kali's Court $$$$
1606 Thames Street, Fells Point
(410) 276-4700
www.kaliscourt.net

The grilled whole fish here has quite a following but the whole menu, with its Mediterranean style, has plenty to love. Halibut is baked in a feta crust. Bouillabaisse is scented with saffron. The crème brûlée is filled with chocolate chunks. Actually, the menu changes according to available ingredients, but you can count on a fresh grilled fish and plenty of creative options. Brunch is extravagant with three to five courses; caviar is optional. The space is swank, loud around the bar but intimate on the mezzanine upstairs. The restaurant is open every night for dinner and Sunday for brunch. Definitely make a reservation. Valet parking is available in the evenings.

La Tasca $$-$$$
201 East Pratt Street
(410) 209-2562

This local chain with, believe it or not, an English heritage, makes an art of sangria and small plates. The restaurant in the Pratt Street Pavilion of Harborplace occupies parts of both floors with plenty of space out on the deck. Tapas are in the spotlight here, with all kinds of ingredients. Plenty of seafood, classic serrano, and manchego cheese and meat choices should satisfy just about every appetite. If not, paella is a standout here, too.

A variety of sangrias are on the menu to wash it all down. It's a big place, but reservations will ensure you get a table without a long wait. The restaurant is open every day for lunch and dinner. Parking is available in area lots and garages. Harborplace offers valet parking in the evening.

Maggie Moore's $$$
21 North Eutaw Street
(410) 837-2100

What makes Maggie's worth a recommendation is its staff and its location. The waitstaff here understand you may have a show to get to—since it's just across the street from the Hippodrome Theatre—so they serve in a timely manner. There's even a theater menu to make things easier for everybody. They make room for late diners, as well, or those who just want dessert or a drink after the show. The location bears mentioning because this is the only restaurant (so far) within walking distance of the Hippodrome. The restaurant is located in a gracious old bank building with lots of wood molding, soaring ceilings, and enormous windows. A grand bar opens the way to dining rooms on two levels.

Oh, and the food is good, with some Irish standards, lots of steak and seafood, and heavenly desserts. There's live music four nights a week. Open for lunch and dinner every day, brunch is served on Sunday.

Matsuri $$
1105 South Charles Street
(410) 752-8561
www.masuri.us

There's plenty of Japanese cuisine to go around here. Take the two-page sushi and sashimi menu. Served from a long, long bar, the options include tuna, salmon, sari clams, eels, and quail eggs. Among the favorites is the nabeyaki udon, broth-laden noodles topped with shrimp and fish cakes.

The restaurant is open for lunch Monday through Friday and dinner every day. One-hour free parking at the Cross Street parking garage is available, and parking is also is avail-

able on the street. Dress is casual, and reservations are important on weekend nights, when the restaurant fills with regulars.

Minato $$
800 North Charles Street
(410) 332-0332
www.minatorestaurant.com

In the heart of Mount Vernon, Minato offers tasty Japanese food at a reasonable price. Portions are large, especially the tempura and teriyaki. The noodle soups, ramen, soba, and udon are also winners, served in portions that carry them from soup to meal in a few spoonfuls.

Dress is casual. The restaurant is open for lunch Monday through Friday and dinner every day, and parking is available on the street. Reservations are necessary for weekend nights.

No Way Jose Cafe $$
38 East Cross Street
(410) 752-2837

There's an unmistakable scent of Tex-Mex food once you enter this restaurant in Federal Hill, where shrimp and smoked ribs compete with pork dishes, and all are served with the mandatory side of slaw and fries. Lunch and dinner in beyond-ample portions are served daily.

Obrycki's Crab House $$$
1727 East Pratt Street
(410) 732-6399
www.obryckis.com

If you're eating steamed crabs, be prepared to sit at a table covered in paper with paper towels and mallets at the ready. But Obrycki's can be a cozy place for a crab cake, too. Brick and wood paneling make the room feel warmer, and with the friendly waitstaff here you're going to feel like family in no time. Be prepared—crab houses have all the trappings of a fire hall banquet. Obrycki's has that memorable name that sticks with you for hours, but it's the steamed crabs and crab cakes that will draw your attention, and they forge Obrycki's strong reputation for being the

How to Eat Crab

When you come to Baltimore, you will, no doubt, want to try our most famous local delicacy—the Chesapeake Bay blue crab. You can try them in a variety of ways.

Crab soup is a nice choice in cooler weather. We produce an assortment of local crab soups, from a mild, creamy bisque to the traditional Maryland hot-and-tangy kind, thick with floating claws. Pan-fried, backfin crab cakes are great plain, on crackers, or nestled in rolls with Maryland tomatoes and crisp lettuce, dripping with tartar sauce. If you're the adventurous type, you can have a soft-crab sandwich. This is a whole crab— that's right, shell and all—laid between two slices of the bread of your choosing. You can eat the shell because this pan-fried pleasure is a soft-shell crab. He's shed his hard shell and would have had to grow a bit before it hardened up again. Unluckily for him, but luckily for you, we plucked him from the bottom of the Chesapeake Bay before that could happen. If you're a little more conservative, there are multitudes of crab salads, crab imperials, and pasta and crab dishes. Somewhere in this town you can probably even find a crab burrito.

But the best way to eat crab is just to eat crabs. Smothered in Old Bay Seasoning (a product with salt and other spices made by McCormick, a local spice maker) their red shells heavy with sweet, white meat, a pile of crabs is hard to resist—although some newcomers do have a little difficulty eating food that is staring at them.

If you dare to eat crabs, you'll want to know what you're doing. So, let's begin at the beginning. Use this chapter to pick a crab restaurant that sounds good to you. Then, set aside some time. Crabs are not fast food at any stretch of the imagination.

As you're seated, most likely you'll notice that the table is covered with newspaper, brown paper, or tail cloth. This is your clue to the first truth about eating crabs: they are messy, so dress appropriately. If you're wearing your favorite silk blouse or you're just coming from the opera, don't eat crabs. Jeans and a T-shirt will do.

You will also see a bib in front of you on the table. Wear it. Even T-shirts can only stand so much! In addition to the bib, you'll find a wooden mallet and a knife. These and your two hands are the only tools you need to pick a crab. The mallet is used for cracking the claws—which, among crab connoisseurs, are eaten either first or last: never as you go. The knife is for removing the crab's shell and air sacs (or lungs, as they're sometimes called) and for cutting apart the crab so that you can reach the meat.

Now that you're appropriately bibbed and have your tools in hand, here's how it's done. Pull a crab from the pile and turn it over. On its white underside, you will see an outline that looks either like a tower on a hill or a Brownie's beanie. The tower configuration signifies a male crab; the beanie is a female. Take your knife, or fingernail if you'd prefer to be a totally hands-on crab picker, insert it along the edge of the outline, and lift the flap. You'll see, toward the back of the crab, a sort of indentation where the top shell is attached. Place your knife in that "V" and press down while gripping the body of the crab with your free hand. At this point, all you need do is lift. The body of the crab will peel away from its shell.

Discard the shell, unless you want to keep it for a souvenir. (A note on that: Crab shells, once cleaned and lacquered, make excellent ashtrays and candy dishes.) Now, turn the crab back over. First, take your knife and cut away the eyes and the "mouth."

Just two cuts, from the first claw to the center of the body—forming the two sides of an isosceles triangle—will do it. This may sound a bit yucky, but it's really not as bad as it sounds. Once you've cut the front part away, look at the back. At that little "V," you may see some yellow stuff. Some people like to scoop that out and eat it. (It's called mustard.) Personally, we suggest you scoop it out and discard it, but it's your call. Use your knife to scrape away the stringy, intestinal-looking material and to cut off the wedge-shaped, fleshy-looking sacs that are attached to the undershell. This is not an option. Some novices think these sacs are the meat and try to eat them. Don't. They may make you sick. What you want, the sweet meat, is inside the thin undershell upon which the sacs sit.

Once you're discarded the sacs, you're almost ready to eat. Take the crab in both hands, each hand cradling the crab's legs and firmly gripping each side of the body. With the upside of the crab still facing you, push your hands down and together, thus cracking the body in half. Now, look inside. That white stuff is what you're after. There are a few different ways to get at it, any of which will make you look like an old hand at crab-eatin'.

Option #1: Local experts suggest that you break off the claws at this point and use your knife to cut off the "knuckles," those little knobby things where the claws are attached. You can then use your knife or your finger to pull or push the meat out.

Option #2: Access it from the inside. Break off the claws and then cut away the thin shell that still protects the meat on the inside of the body, opposite the knuckles. Then scoop the meat out with your knife.

Option #3: The most difficult but most satisfying technique is to remove the meat as you remove the claws. Rather than just breaking off the claws, detach them with a gentle twist and pull. If you do it just right, the meat will come along. If it doesn't, Options #1 and #2 are still available.

Having finished this operation, you may now opt to tackle the claws, or you can set the claws aside for later and pick another crab from the pile. You have only picked and eaten about an ounce or two of meat, in—on your first try—about 25 minutes' time. So, you need to keep eating. You will, however, be full before you know it. When you get to the claws, simply crack the shell with your mallet, then break it away. The claw meat is resting on a thin piece of cartilage inside. All you need to do is put your fingers near the claw joint and slide the meat off.

Good drinks with crabs are beer or soda; good side orders are slaw and corn on the cob. Enjoy!

place in Baltimore to savor the local seafood specialty.

Between March and November, this place gets really, really busy as locals get the unmistakable hankering for steamed crabs. Reservations are a good idea at all times. It's closed in the winter, however, as there aren't any local crabs to steam. The restaurant serves lunch and dinner when it's open, and parking is available at a lot across the street.

Peter's Inn $$
504 South Ann Street
(410) 675-7313
www.petersinn.com
Owners Karin and Bud Tiffany run this small restaurant on the first floor of a row house, just a few blocks north of the hustle and bustle of Fells Point. The place seats less than 30 and has a long wooden bar that never seems to empty of neighborhood friends chatting away over beers. Hanging out at Peter's is kind of like hanging out at home—there is a comfortable couch in the back for larger parties to sit and eat at, and it seems everyone knows one another. Karin changes the menu weekly based on what's fresh in the markets and keeps the simple but exceptional offerings (usually including one soup, one appetizer, and five entrees) listed on a chalkboard at the back of the room.

Peter's is open for dinner only and is closed Sunday. Other important things to note: Peter's does not take reservations. It almost never offers dessert, and the bar is not separate from the dining area. You may want to turn off your cell phone before coming in. Peter's is a place to get away and catch up with friends and enjoy a good meal; a ringing phone may earn you dirty looks from the locals. Park on the street or at meters.

Phillips Harborplace Restaurant $$$
301 Light Street
(410) 685-6600
www.phillipsseafood.com
Located at the Inner Harbor, Phillips Harborplace Restaurant is actually three entities in one, seating as many as 870 people. The main dining room has indoor seating with a piano bar and outdoor seating along the water. The extensive menu offers traditional Maryland-inspired seafood such as spicy Maryland crab soup, steamed crabs, and Old Bay shrimp. Those who don't eat seafood still will find plenty to choose from, including steak and chicken entrees. Phillips Harborplace also houses Phillips Seafood Festival Buffet, a self-service buffet featuring seafood, chicken, soups, salads, sides, and desserts. And for those on the go, there is Phillips carryout and seafood market, serving crab cake sandwiches, soups, and salads.

Pierpoint $$$
1822 Aliceanna Street
(410) 675-2080
www.pierpointrestaurant.com
A bistro in Fells Point that focuses on local seafood dishes, Pierpoint is best known for its smoked crab cakes, a variation on an area favorite that gives it a hickory-smoked flavor like no other. You can also try owner Nancy Longo's homemade Eastern Shore rabbit sausage, the smoked duck quesadillas, or the Moroccan lamb. Save some room for the bread pudding, served just out of the oven and topped with a praline crust. Yum!

The restaurant serves lunch Tuesday through Friday by reservation only and dinner Tuesday through Sunday. Brunch is served on Sunday. With just 44 seats, reservations are required. Parking is available on the street, but the meters need to be fed.

Red Maple $$
930 North Charles Street
(410) 547-0149
www.930redmaple.com
A modishly sleek interior formed from teak-

wood, steel, and glass makes this one of the most architecturally stunning spots in the city. Opened in 2001, the modern lounge vibe fueled by the best resident and guest DJs earned the Red Maple a slot on *In Style* magazine's list of the top 60 nightspots in America. The patrons are as good-looking as the surroundings as they imbibe the bar's exotic cocktails. Linear benches offer seating for an Asian tapas menu created by chef Jill Snyder. Try the red maple mussels or the hazelnut-crusted tuna. There is usually a cover at the door in support of the music. Once inside, there's no smoking at all, but an outdoor courtyard (home to the namesake red maple) allows smokers to light up. The attire is hip, not formal, but tennis shoes are not allowed. The kitchen closes before the lounge, but it usually stays open late on weekends. Open daily after 5:30 p.m. Reservations for dinner are recommended. Park on the street or pay to park in a surface lot for about $6.

Robert Oliver Seafood
Restaurant $$$
1225 Cathedral Street
(410) 528-5950
www.robertoliverseafood.com

This corner site strategically situated across from the Meyerhoff Symphony Hall and down the street from the Lyric Opera House ought to be a great location for a restaurant. And it has been the home of a couple of really fine places, including the late, great Spike and Charlies. Robert Oliver is now in the house, a dark, romantic space, with candlelight and the strains of cool jazz. The menu includes some classic and unusual martini concoctions, "mezze" small plates such as lamb meatballs and persimmon with slivered ham and walnuts, and gorgeous seafood entrees, including filet mignon of tuna and pan-seared scallops. Steak and vegetarian options round out the menu, along with tantalizing desserts. Parking is available across the street in a paid lot, but if you aren't going to a concert or opera, you will probably have to find another

location or space on the side streets. If there is a concert in your immediate future, tell the server and they'll make sure you don't miss a single note.

Sascha's 527 $$$
527 North Charles Street
(410) 539-8880
www.saschas.com

Small plates are an art here at Sascha's. You can get full dinners, but why would you want to when you can share a variety of things, such as mini bison burgers, skewers of Carribean jerk chicken, and a cone of their perfect fries with peach ketchup. "Big plates" offerings include steak and seafood, as well as a daily pasta and stew special. The space, set in a Mount Vernon town house, is colorful, bright, and sophisticated. The restaurant is open every night for dinner. Parking is available on the street.

Sotto Sopra $$$
405 North Charles Street
(410) 625-0534
www.sottosoprainc.com

If you're in the Mount Vernon cultural district, figure this eatery to be Little Italy North, a place where you can find some great homemade northern Italian fare. Some of the staff's favorites are the homemade gnocchi and buckwheat ravioli and fettuccine. It's known for its special events, too, particularly dinners by guest chefs and Opera Night, a pairing of music and fine dining. Sotto Sopra is open for lunch and dinner every day. Valet parking is offered on weekends; during the week metered parking is available. This place is packed for dinner, so definitely make reservations.

Thai Arroy $
1019 Light Street
(410) 385-8587
www.thaiarroy.com

This casual, small restaurant serves traditional Thai dishes, such as red curry and Pad Thai, and it has quickly become a neighborhood staple. The food is delicious and well priced.

As of publication, the restaurant did not have a liquor license, but you are welcome to bring your own beer or wine (Smitty's liquor store is 2 blocks away—see the Shopping chapter for details). Or try the delicious Thai iced tea, made with coconut milk. If you find the place too packed for a seat on a busy weekend night, you can always get takeout. Lunch is available only on weekdays, and it's closed on Monday.

Thairish $
804 North Charles Street
(410) 752-5857
This authentic Thai restaurant is primarily for takeout, but there are a few seats in the small space located in the heart of Mount Vernon. The owner whips together a great Pad Thai. Thairish is open Tuesday through Friday for lunch and dinner, and for dinner only on Saturday and Sunday. It is closed on Monday. If you're curious about the name, the owner will tell you he chose it to honor his marriage: He is Thai and his wife is Irish.

Tio Pepe $$$$
10 East Franklin Street
(410) 539-4675
Baltimoreans are divided on this restaurant. Some consider it among the city's best, but others criticize the waiters or say the food isn't as good as expected for the price. I say if paella is your thing, or the idea of freshest flounder enrobed in bananas or creamy flan makes you weak, you'll want to find this slightly out-of-the-way basement restaurant. It's really just east of Charles Street. Head down the steps into a wine cellar–like space of whitewashed walls, dark brown wood trim, and white tablecloths. The menu is decidedly Spanish with Latin American touches. The sangria is fruity, the bread freshly made, and the waitstaff is either coolly professional or pretentious (you decide). Men are asked to wear jackets. Parking is available on the street and in the lot across the street.

Vaccaro's $
222 Albemarle Street, Little Italy
(410) 685-4905
www.vacarrospastry.com
Plenty of local restaurants tout the fact that their desserts come from Vaccaro's. So why not find an excuse to stop in at the tiny little bakery and cafe in Little Italy just for dessert. And what dessert! Tiramisu, crunchy cannoli filled with perfectly sweetened ricotta, three huge scoops of gelati (it's okay to ask for just one scoop), vanilla- or hazelnut-scented coffee, perhaps a liqueur-based after-dinner drink. It opens early enough for morning coffee and stays open late enough for opera and theater fans to cap off their night. If the tables are full and you don't want to wait (no reservations here), stop by the counter and take your treats home. On-street parking is usually easy to find for the after-theater crowd. Otherwise, be prepared to hunt or find your way to the garage around the corner.

Watertable $$$$
Renaissance Harborplace Hotel
202 East Pratt Street
(410) 685-8439
Located in the Renaissance Harborplace Hotel, Watertable offers contemporary American cuisine. From the fifth floor of the building, there are window views of the Inner Harbor, as well as crab cakes, salmon, and tuna served every day in new and traditional ways. Save room for dessert because they're all made in the hotel kitchen. But no matter how good the food is, the view's the thing that sticks in your mind and in your camera lens. Reservations are absolutely necessary; you can park in the hotel parking lot or walk over from the Inner Harbor area.

Ze Mean Bean Cafe $
1739 Fleet Street
(410) 675-5999
www.zemeanbean.com
This quaint little storefront eatery with an East

European atmosphere offers coffee, borscht, and pirogies as well as an assortment of tasty pastries and dinner entrees. The restaurant serves lunch and dinner Monday through Friday and brunch and dinner on the weekends. The wine list is surprisingly extensive. Jazz is played while you eat. Expect a wait, because this Fells Point find has been discovered by many. Park in the area and window-shop your way to and from the restaurant.

NORTHEAST

Angelina's $$$
7135 Harford Road
(410) 444-5545

Most restaurant sections start with Angelina's, not just because it's first in the alphabet, but because of this formal dining restaurant's reputation for great homemade crab cakes. What you pay for is a good deal—crab cakes made with lump crabmeat and backfin, the preferable parts of the crab, with little filler and clawmeat.

It will take you about 15 minutes to get from the Inner Harbor to Parkville, heading north on Harford Road, but it's worth the trip for Angelina's, which also offers a variety of other seafood and meat dishes. The restaurant serves lunch and dinner every day except Monday and has a full bar. Parking is available on the street, and reservations are a good idea on weekend nights.

An Poitin Stil (The Still) $$
2323 York Road, Timonium
(410) 560-7900
www.thestill.net

Cobbled together with bits of old Irish pubs, the building itself is worth a visit. You'll feel like you've entered a piece of the Emerald Isle. The outside replicates actual pub fronts with a castle-door entrance and a pulpit-style bar. Each of the dining rooms recalls a bit of Irish history: the cottage, a monk's cell, small-town shops. Oh yes, and the food. There's standard pub fare, as well as a few Irish selections such as corned beef and cabbage, fish and chips, and an outstanding shepherd's pie and Irish stew. Guinness is on tap, of course. The restaurant, across York Road from the Timonium fairgrounds, is open every day for lunch and dinner with live music almost every night.

Bel-Loc Diner $
1700 East Joppa Road, Towson
(410) 668-2525

No matter when you get hungry, the Bel-Loc Diner is there for you, serving breakfast, lunch, and dinner whenever you want it. The diner has been an institution for years, providing a place for travelers, businesspeople, nearby residents, and everyone else who stops by to visit, eat, and relax. The menu ranges from hot roast beef and fries with gravy to meat loaf, an omelet to pancakes, served at all hours, of course. Come as you are, because the coffee is always on, and there's always a slice of pie or maybe an awesome milk shake waiting for you.

Bill Bateman's Bistro $
7800 York Road
(410) 296-2737
www.billbateman.com

Located next to Towson University, this is a popular bar and restaurant for the college crowd as well as for families. The place has a sports bar feel, so it comes as no surprise that it is known for it chicken wings (so many flavors to choose from) and its wide selection of microbrews. The full menu is a broad offering of typical bar fare, with lots of burgers, sandwiches, and salads, as well as vegetarian options. A pool table and video games entertain restless kids. Open daily for lunch and dinner; a Sunday brunch is served. This popular restaurant has become a local chain with outlets from Severna Park to Hanover, Pennsylvania.

Selected Baltimore Firsts

In 1879 Constantine Fahlberg and Professor Ira Rensen of The Johns Hopkins University discovered saccharine, the first synthetic sweetening agent.

In 1848 William Young patented the first ice-cream freezer.

In 1891 Captain Isaac E. Emerson came up with the first formula for Bromo-Seltzer. The giant, stories-high blue replica of the Bromo bottle graced the Bromo tower building until the 1960s. The building now houses an art gallery.

In 1819 Thomas Kennett invented the first mode of preserving meats, fruits, and vegetables.

—Excerpted from Baltimore—America's City of Firsts, *a pamphlet published by Baltimore Bicentennial Celebration, Inc.*

Cafe Troia $$$
28 West Allegheny Avenue, Towson
(410) 337-0133
www.cafetroia.com

Here's a place for all those folks who miss their Italian mother. The food is good and the servings ample. One of the best things on the menu is the piatto misto, roasted red pepper, marinated eggplant, shaved prosciutto, arugula, goat cheese, and mozzarella. There's a full menu of Italian treats with fish, shrimp, chicken, veal, and steak bases. Osso buco served with a grilled polenta side order is a sure winner, recommended by the staff and by owner Gino Troia. Don't go in a rush. Plan to enjoy the semiformal setting in an apartment complex in the heart of Towson, about 8 miles north of the Inner Harbor.

Park at a municipal lot or on the street (bring change for the meter), and plan ahead with a reservation. The restaurant serves lunch Monday through Friday and dinner every day but Sunday.

Fractured Prune, the
Donut Shoppe $
8705 Harford Road, Parkville
(410) 661-9999

Donuts here are so fresh, they're made after you order them. You pick the glazes, the toppings, and the sugars, or choose one of their specialties, such as the black forest, a hot donut covered with raspberry glaze, coconut, and mini chocolate chips. The coffee's fine and there are a few breakfast sandwiches, too. The original shop in Ocean City frequently has customers waiting out the door and into the parking lot so the Baltimore outlets are a welcome arrival. Other local shops are in Arbutus (410-242-3515) and Columbia (410-531-6916), both southwest of the city in the suburbs. The shop is open daily from 6:00 a.m. on weekdays and 7:00 a.m. on weekends until mid-afternoon.

Jerry's Belvedere Tavern $
5928 York Road
(410) 435-8600

If you plan to take in a movie at the beautiful Senator theater (see The Arts chapter), which is about a block south of Jerry's on York Road, the food here offers the perfect match to the theater. It's your basic restaurant with a combination of Italian and American food; the favorites are a basic hamburger or cheeseburger. People come to Jerry's, about half a mile from the Baltimore City line, for everything from a big anniversary celebration to a family birthday celebration. You'll see sports fans as well as business executives dining here.

You'll hear Baltimoreans refer to it as Jerry's or Jerry's Belvedere often enough to make you realize what they know—there's something powerful that draws you back again and again. Jerry's serves breakfast, lunch, and dinner seven days a week. Parking is available behind the building. You don't need a reservation because everyone will make space for a few more to join in the fun.

The Milton Inn $$$$
14833 York Road, Sparks
(410) 771-4366
www.miltoninn.com

The Milton Inn is a bit of a drive out of the city, and technically is in Sparks, Maryland, but this staple of regional dining offers a wonderfully romantic getaway. You'll wind your way along York Road, past the developments and the minimalls to find a quaint home tucked in the pastoral landscape. Seasonal American fare (clams casino, porterhouse steaks, rockfish) is mingled with a touch of the European (seared foie gras), all served in an eighteenth-century farmhouse, replete with period decor and roaring fireplaces. The dress code is "business casual," which basically translates to no jeans and no shorts or collarless shirts. Open daily for dinner and weekdays for lunch.

Nichi Bei Kai $$$
1524 York Road, Lutherville
(410) 321-7090

Dine while seated around a Japanese hibachi, where the chef will be slinging your choice of shrimp, chicken, steak, or lobster into the air. Sushi is also prepared, but with not quite as much air in the cooking process. The restaurant serves lunch Tuesday through Friday only and dinner every day in a semiformal atmosphere, just outside of Towson off Interstate 83.

Pete's Grille $
3130 Greenmount Avenue
(410) 467-7698

A neighborhood diner is what you'll find at Pete's Grille. It serves breakfast and lunch; Pete's breakfast is hash browns, fluffy pancakes, and waffles made from scratch—tasty, down-home cooking, just like you'd expect from a good diner. Lunch offers more homemade family foods, such as sandwiches, a soup of the day, the usual meat loaf, and other American food. Parking is available on Greenmount Avenue, especially since lots of the people who visit live nearby and walk over.

The Prime Rib $$$$
1101 North Calvert Street
(410) 539-1804
www.theprimerib.com

You have to appreciate a restaurant that puts its best foot forward in its name. Guess what's the best thing on the menu? If you don't want to try your luck at its signature dish, you can try other steak and seafood offerings. But really, the prime rib's the thing, along with the buttery mashed potatoes.

If you're looking for a dark and classy atmosphere for your fine-dining experience, then this restaurant just north of Mount Vernon is for you. Black walls, carpets with leopard prints, and a baby grand piano lighted in neon are a feast for the eyes as much as the menu is a feast for the palate.

Parking is available on area streets at meters or for free. The restaurant only offers dinner. Be advised: Without a reservation, you will not get in. Jackets are required.

Tapas Teatro $–$$
1711 North Charles Street
(410) 332-0110
www.tapasteatro.net

Located next to the historic Charles Theater and just north of Penn Station, this restaurant is the perfect spot for a meal before or after a movie. The same owners also run The Helmand in Mount Vernon, and you'll find a few of their Afghan-inspired dishes on the menu, like the eggplant with yogurt. Overall, the food is a delicious mix of Spanish and international-inspired tapas cuisine. In the warm months outdoor seating lines the street. Reservations are not taken and the place is very popular, so if you're trying to eat before a movie, leave plenty of extra time. Open Tuesday through Sunday for dinner only; parking is available in a garage across the street or at meters. The garage offers discounted rates if you see a movie at the Charles (see The Arts chapter for more details).

Valentino's $$
6627 Harford Road
(410) 254-4700

Open 24 hours a day, this restaurant has a long list of regulars who make every visit a lesson in the history, economics, and sociology of the area—if you keep your ears open. The atmosphere at the cafeteria-style booths is informal and friendly for children. The menu offers Greek specials such as spinach pizza, Italian favorites such as lasagna (vegetable and meat varieties), and a full complement of foods that make this a good place for anyone at any hour. Breakfast, ranging from scrambled eggs to French toast, is offered at all hours. You can also get your hands and mouth on steaks, seafood, salads, and sandwiches as well as a few tasty cakes and pies for dessert. No reservations are necessary and parking is available on a parking lot behind the restaurant. No alcohol is served, nor are you allowed to bring any in.

NORTHWEST

The Ambassador Dining Room $$
3811 Canterbury Road
(410) 366-1484
www.ambassadordiningroom.com

This ranks as one of the best all-around dining experiences in the city. Located in the historic Homewood neighborhood in a 1930s-era apartment house, The Ambassador has a rich interior and a glass-enclosed terrace room that opens onto a gloriously landscaped city garden in the summer months. In the winter the terrace glows warm from the roaring fireplaces and the twinkling votive candles. Everything on the menu is superb, from the

samosas to the chana to the traditional unleavened naan bread. Don't know what to have? Come at lunchtime and try the famous buffet. White-glove service complements the delicious menu. Open daily for lunch and dinner, parking is on the street.

Cafe Hon $$
1002 West 36th Street
(410) 243-1230
www.cafehon.com

"Hon," rhyming with "gun" and short for "honey," is a term of endearment used by many Baltimoreans. This cafe, with its Hon's Much Better Than Mom's Meat Loaf and its assortment of homemade pies, is a tribute to the term and the people who use it. Located in Hampden in a more-than-100-year-old building that used to house a hardware store, the cafe is decorated in vintage and antique decor, with Formica tables and an antique chest for the liquor. The casual atmosphere is perfect for families and the neighborhood folks who make this a frequent gathering spot. The cafe, which opened in 1992, serves breakfast, lunch, and dinner every day.

Crepe du Jour $$
1609 Sulgrave Avenue, Mount Washington Village
(410)542-9000
www.crepedujour.com

The owner of the Crepe just knocked out a wall and expanded its dining room, but the crepe-making remains in full view of diners. Thank goodness. This bright yellow and blue creperie offers perfectly delicate crepes wrapping all sorts of treats from savory ratatouille to sweet ice cream or fruit. At dinner the menu includes steak, chicken, and seafood with a French accent. The restaurant is open Tuesday through Thursday for lunch and dinner; and for breakfast, lunch, and dinner on Friday through Sunday. On-street parking is fairly easy to find.

Ethel and Ramone's $$
1615 Sulgrave Avenue
Mount Washington Village
(410) 664-2971

Four restaurants are clustered here on this tiny side street of "the Village." Take your pick, they're all good, but if you like Cajun food, come here for a taste of New Orleans. A narrow dining room shares the first floor with the kitchen, but there's more seating upstairs too, and outside on the sidewalk and porch in warm weather. The spicy gumbo never fails to satisfy, and other Cajun concoctions are delightful, from jambalaya to blackened fish. Sandwiches are on the lunch menu. The restaurant is open for breakfast, lunch, and dinner Tuesday through Saturday. On-street parking is available.

Gertrude's at the BMA $$$
10 Art Museum Drive
(410) 889-3399
www.johnshields.com

Round out your cultural experience at the Baltimore Museum of Art with a culinary experience at the in-house restaurant, Gertrude's. John Shields, nationally acclaimed cookbook author, chef, and host of his own syndicated cooking program, brings his signature Chesapeake Bay cuisine to the restaurant. The menu evolves with the seasons to reflect the fresh produce and in-season seafood of the Chesapeake region. The Waterman's Oyster Stew is a hearty concoction and the grilled Maryland rockfish fillet with a roasted red bell pepper butter sauce on a bed of seafood hash is popular with diners. The wine list is extensive with an emphasis on Californian wines, although it also offers many local wines from Maryland and Virginia. Gertrude's is open for lunch and dinner Tuesday through Friday, with brunch also offered on Saturday and Sunday, but it is closed on Monday.

The Knish Shop $
508 Reisterstown Road, Pikesville
(410) 484-5850

A knish, an oven-browned and filled dough pocket, is the namesake and the attraction at this truly kosher deli in Pikesville. The spinach knish draws constant raves, and the potato knish is another winner. An assortment of kosher specialty sandwiches is also available. Don't miss the pickles—they have a personality all their own. The Knish Shop is open during the day, Monday though Friday and Sunday. Closed Saturday.

Mt. Washington Tavern $$
5700 Newbury Street
(410) 367-6903
www.mtwashingtontavern.com

The building goes back more than 150 years, with lots of dark wood-paneled rooms that give it a clubby feel. Indoor dining space upstairs includes the Chesapeake and Pimlico Rooms, decorated in hunting and lacrosse motifs. But if you yearn for the sun, ask for a table in the Atrium Room, a sun-drenched garden room with glass roof. Wherever you eat, there's a feast for the eyes as well as the stomach. The menu offers several seafood specialties, including crab soup with large, lump crabmeat, jumbo lump crab cakes, and a separate raw bar, featuring 2-inch-long shrimp. If you like steak, they have it here — huge and juicy or petite and topped with crab and béarnaise.

The restaurant offers lunch and dinner every day, with a Sunday brunch from 10:30 a.m. to 3:00 p.m. Parking is available for free at the Mount Washington Metro stop, just a few feet from the entrance to the restaurant, or at a private lot next door to the restaurant. Reservations are a good idea for weekends.

Oregon Grille $$$$
1201 Shawan Road, Hunt Valley
(410) 771-0505

A special-occasion restaurant situated in an old farmhouse in the horse country of Hunt Valley, the Oregon Grille offers well-prepared American food, mostly beef and seafood. There aren't many places to order caviar, but it's always on the menu here, along with a lobster martini, some traditional sandwiches, and a warm lobster salad that shouldn't be missed. The wine list has something for everyone. Service is attentive and the atmosphere is elegant and somewhat festive. Everybody here is celebrating something.

Papermoon Diner $
227 West 29th Street
(410) 889-4444
www.papermoondiner24.com

Imagine a restaurant filled with old toys—cars, trains, boats, and other items collected over the years. Though this casual and eclectic restaurant opened in 1993, the toys give the impression that it's much, much older. The Web site defines the Papermoon experience: "We think that everyday life is tough enough and you need to escape it sometimes." The food is distinctly American. Most people like the omelets and burgers. And leave room for one of their sinful cakes or pies. You can have beer and wine. Parking is easy to find on the street. Reservations aren't necessary for breakfast, lunch, or dinner, which are served every day. The restaurant is open 24 hours.

Petit Louis $$$
4800 Roland Avenue
(410) 366-9393
www.petitlouis.com

Chef Cindy Wolfe and her husband, wine expert Tony Foreman, were inspired by their extensive travels in France. The couple recreated the simple, robust cuisine of the French bistro in Roland Park. The seasonal menu boasts escargot in garlic and white wine and a rich foie gras terrine served with a crusty baguette. You can choose from small or large plates, so this is a good spot for a light meal or a five-course event. The bouillabaisse is popular with the regulars, as is the thoughtful wine list and the crème caramel dessert. Prix fixe lunches are offered as well as the a la carte menu.

Parking is available in a lot in front of the restaurant. Petit Louis serves dinner nightly and lunch Tuesday through Friday; brunch is served on Sunday. Reservations are highly recommended.

Stone Mill Bakery $$
10751 Falls Road, Greenspring Station
Lutherville
(410) 821-1358

A cup of strong coffee to jump-start your day, a hearty sandwich or homemade soup at lunch, and a loaf of focaccia for dinner—Stone Mill Bakery has it all. One refrigerated case features a few heat-and-eat dinner choices, too. Just a tiny space, though plans to expand were under way in 2007, the bakery offers lots of takeaway choices. There are also a dozen small tables for those who want to stick around. It's open every day but Sunday for breakfast and lunch. Once the second space is open, it will also open on Sunday and for dinner. There's plenty of parking in the adjacent lot; the shop is just inside this small shopping complex.

SOUTHEAST

The Acropolis $$
4718 Eastern Avenue
(410) 675-3384

You'll know you're in Greektown when you walk in the door: Murals and music of Greece and families dining make this a true ethnic find for casual dining in Baltimore. For a true taste of the culture, order the shrimp oregano, featuring jumbo shrimp sautéed in white wine and served over rice, or the Giouvetsi, a baby lamb braised in olive oil and baked with orzo, with a tomato, green pepper, and onion sauce. Rockfish and red snapper are also popular, and all portions are large.

Reservations are a good idea, especially on weekends. You can park on the streets near the restaurant. Lunch and dinner are served seven days a week.

Hull Street Blues Cafe $$$
1222 Hull Street
(410) 727-7476
www.hullstreetblues.com

If you were a fan of the gritty police drama *Hill Street Blues,* you probably think this restaurant's name is spelled incorrectly. Wrong, Bobby Hill. The name comes from the street on which it sits in Locust Point, the neighborhood near Fort McHenry that's becoming a trendy area. Inside this row house–style cafe with the bar in front is a relaxing environment for eating seafood and steaks with a true Maryland appeal. The restaurant serves lunch and dinner every day except Sunday, when lunch is replaced by brunch. Lite fare is also available in the bar.

Little Havana Restaurante y Cantina $$
1325 Key Highway
(410) 837-9903
www.littlehavanas.com

Little Havana is housed in a low, yellow, unpretentious building. But it boasts one of the few outside decks with a view of the Inner Harbor. On a nice day it's hard to find a seat and the service can be slow, but it's worth the wait to enjoy a mojito and a pulled pork sandwich with black beans and rice while watching the ships sail past. The interior decor includes Cuban-inspired murals and a large oval bar. The place has a starring role in the bar scenes of the Gene Hackman/Keanu Reeves film *The Replacements*. It's a convenient stop for visitors to Federal Hill and Fort McHenry. Little Havana is open every day for dinner and Friday through Saturday for brunch. A few parking spots are available out front, otherwise it's all metered on Key Highway. These meters run until 10:00 p.m., so bring quarters.

Matthew's Pizzeria $
3131 Eastern Avenue
(410) 276-8755
www.matthewspizza.com

Okay, recommending a pizza place is like picking someone's tailor, but this is one you have to try. Really. It seems everybody who goes to this Highlandtown spot comes out singing its praises. Established in 1943, the owners say this was the first pizzeria in Baltimore. The pizza is traditional (and called "pie" on their menu) with plenty of cheese and the usual toppings. The sauce and dough are made fresh here. There's other stuff on the menu, but it pales in comparison to the pizza, which is the appeal to many of the families and first dates that frequently make their way here.

Park on the street, and don't worry about your dress or the need for reservations. If you must rush, call your order in ahead of time. This is casual because everyone's committed to the goal of the mission—eating lots and lots of pizza. Lunch and dinner are served daily.

Nacho Mama's $
2907 O'Donnell Street
(410) 675-0898

With a giant statue of Elvis greeting you at the door and walls adorned with funky local art and oddities, this festive Tex-Mex restaurant in Canton is always hopping. The hot sauces are hidden in medicine cabinets mounted on the walls above the tables, and the tortilla chips are served in hubcaps. The inexpensive menu is chock-full of your basic Mexican eats, like enchiladas, quesadillas, and fajitas, while more traditional American dishes such as Mama's Meatloaf and baby back ribs offer dining options for those who don't feel like going south of the border. Be prepared to wait on a weekend night for a table. Nacho Mama's serves lunch and dinner daily.

Nick's Fish House $$
2600 Insulator Drive
(410) FISH123
www.nicksfishhouse.com

Where can you get a good crab cake in this town? Lots of places, of course, but this little South Baltimore waterfront restaurant in the shadow of the Hanover Street Bridge and I-95 never fails to satisfy the craving. All the usual crab dishes come unencumbered by fancy sauces to overwhelm the sweet crabmeat. There is, however, their burger with crab topping, an unusual combination for those of us who can't decide which to get. The dining room is traditional casual crab-house style, and the deck offers views of a local marina and the Patapsco River. And if all that good good food isn't enough, Nick's has karaoke Wednesdays and dance parties on Fridays, both on the deck. The parking lot here is big enough to accommodate just about everybody.

SOUTHWEST

Candle Light Inn   **$$$**
1835 Frederick Road, Catonsville
(410) 788-6076
www.thecandlelightinn.com
Situated in a largely residential area with lots of mature trees, the Candle Light Inn catches a visitor by surprise, its candlelit windows drawing the eye in the dark of the night. Once inside, the food draws the taste buds.

Chef Marc Lombardini, part of the International Culinary Olympics in 1992 and 1994, offers American food in a white-tablecloth environment. His favorites (as well as many of his visitors) are crab cakes and seafood bisque, although he won't discuss what makes them so special. Try to solve the mystery on your own. A sign that your experience will be memorable? Locals pack the numerous small dining rooms here on special occasions. So be sure to make a dinner reservation.

The restaurant serves lunch Monday through Saturday and dinner every evening, and reservations are mandatory on holidays and a good idea on weekends. The restaurant has a large bar serving light fare, and parking is available in a spacious lot next to the restaurant. In warmer months, the covered patio offers a more casual dining space.

NIGHTLIFE

Baltimore's nightlife has always thrived, but it seems the choice of things to do has exploded in the last few years. Ten years ago, you might have had difficulty finding late-night revelry on a Wednesday night, but all that has changed. Cruise Cross Street in Federal Hill or Broadway in Fells Point on any given evening, and you're bound to find the many bars, coffee shops, and music clubs filled with neighborhood friends. Flip through the latest edition of the *City Paper*, and you'll see pages and pages of concerts, theater performances, happy hours, and DJ sessions.

Nightlife is booming in part because of the influx of young business professionals working here and renting in our city's new loft and high-rise developments. Many 30-somethings are also taking advantage of low interest rates and are scooping up affordable property in up-and-coming neighborhoods, helping fuel a renaissance in club activity. Numerous artists and musicians choose to call Baltimore home because of the reasonable cost of living and the creative vibe that exists here. Nationally recognized recording artists such as Lake Trout and the Kelley Bell Band land here when they're not touring, and they frequently grace our music venues.

We are also a town of tourists, and the Inner Harbor is the mecca. Traversing Pratt and Lombard Streets on a Friday or Saturday night can be a traffic- and pedestrian-clogged hassle. But these crowds translate into packed clubs and restaurants, adding to the resurgence of Downtown nightlife. Power Plant Live!, a relatively new development within walking distance of the Inner Harbor, offers a number of nightclubs and restaurants in 1 square block. There are free outdoor concerts in the summer with popular national acts.

There is a wealth of jazz in the area, as one might expect of Billie Holiday's hometown. The city has also evolved a strong DJ culture, and the number of new clubs featuring turntables attests to the talent that exists in our quarters. These DJs have a strong pipeline to the clubs in D.C., and you'll frequently find talent from the famous 18th Street Lounge and the ESL recording label spinning here. Baltimore even merited its own sound designation; when flipping through the record stacks in places like New York City, you may run across a heading called "Baltimore breaks."

Beyond the clubs and the bars, we have a strong allegiance to literature, and you'll find national chains and local literary spots stay open late (flip through The Arts chapter for theater and fine-arts happenings). In this chapter you'll find a variety of offerings, ranging from the ideal dive bar to the high-end dance club. Most of these places exist in the city, although we have listed a few suburban hot spots. You can assume that all of the major hotels Downtown have some sort of adjacent bar for imbibing, so those have not been listed here. Neither have the chain clubs, like the Hard Rock Café, since those offer the same standard fare in every city.

Parking in Downtown basically comes in two varieties—on the street or in garages. Inner Harbor garages can run a couple of dollars an hour to $12 for the night. Outside of Downtown, most nightspots offer on-site parking, or spaces are available on nearby streets. In this chapter we've noted only when this is not the case.

The Inner Harbor at night. BALTIMORE AREA CONVENTION AND VISITORS ASSOCIATION

IMBIBING IN BALTIMORE

Maryland's alcohol laws are somewhat tricky. Municipalities, including Baltimore City and Baltimore County, have liquor boards that issue licenses for everything from full-service bars serving beer, wine, and alcohol to beer-and-wine-only establishments to places that allow people to bring their own but not purchase it at the facility. In this chapter we've tried to explain the rules where they apply, but if nothing is listed, assume that the facility offers beer, wine, and spirits.

To purchase or possess any form of alcohol in Maryland, you must be at least 21 years old—no exceptions. Increasingly, bar, club, and liquor store operators are checking ALL patrons to make sure they meet the legal-age requirements. Since they can face closures and fines if they violate the law, these operators figure an ounce of prevention is less of a pain than the cost of lost business time or fines. As a result, be prepared to be asked to show proof of age, even if you are a few years beyond your 21st birthday. Bartenders some-

times card up to age 40 just to be sure. Although it's always a pain to be carded, it ensures that the laws are followed. Therefore, you should carry a picture identification card with you. We recommend that you always have your driver's license with you if you plan to indulge, because it's rare that establishments don't ask for it.

The waiters and waitresses who work at bars and restaurants serving alcohol are required to be trained to identify people who have consumed too much alcohol. They are taught to handle these patrons before they become a menace to themselves and their surroundings. They're subtle but effective in these efforts, which are statewide.

Working hand-in-hand with the state's alcohol laws are increasing efforts to stop drunk driving. State, county, city, and marine police agencies have been making more drunk-driving arrests in recent years, fueled by the public's growing outrage over drunk-driving accidents and deaths. If you are planning to drink, do not plan to drive. It's not just a gamble that could lead to an expensive ticket and from two to four points on your driving record, but a gamble with your life and the lives of innocent people. Officers in marked and unmarked cars often patrol areas known for their entertainment and tourism. Be warned: During holiday weekends, the intensity of patrols increases, as do drunk-driving incidents.

If you plan to drink, bring along someone who will remain sober. A growing number of clubs offer designated-driver programs that enable people who pledge to remain alcohol-free to drink nonalcoholic beverages for free. Oriole Park at Camden Yards offers this program for all its home games. If you are a designated driver, ask when you enter the club if you're allowed to drink soft drinks or club soda for free.

If you've had too much to drink, hailing a taxicab or using public transportation are good options. If you need a taxicab, ask the bartender to get one for you. A number of clubs and bars have arrangements with taxicab companies that will get you where you need to be quickly and safely. Some tow truck companies also provide free towing, especially on holidays, of cars whose operators have consumed too much alcohol.

All of these programs have a simple goal: to protect people from the devastating effects of too much alcohol. Do your part by knowing when you've had enough or too much.

If you're staying in and plan on purchasing alcoholic beverages, remember that Baltimore City does not allow sales of beer, wine, or liquor in grocery or convenience stores. You will need to go to a liquor store, and most of these are closed on Sundays. Some bars offer carryout after hours and on Sundays, but be prepared to pay top dollar or plan to drive to an adjacent county, such as Howard or Anne Arundel, where liquor stores frequently stay open all weekend.

Downtown

Baja Beach Club
55 Market Place
(410) 752-7188
www.bajabeachbaltimore.com

A DJ plays Top 40 dance music every night as people fill the big dance floor and bikini-clad women in front of tubs of beer serve cold ones—beers, that is. There's just no denying the beach theme here. Want to leave your mark in Baltimore? Donate your bra to the collection hanging from the bar. It's a young crowd, and there's both a cover and a line on weekends. It's open Wednesday through Saturday.

Bay Cafe
2809 Boston Street
(410) 522-3377
www.baycafeusa.com

Located on the water in Canton, the Bay Cafe serves good food (like shrimp salad), but it is really known for its libations and great environment. The beach-themed space is the ideal location for cold cocktails and blended daiquiris on a hot, humid Baltimore day. Sit on the outdoor deck and watch the sailboats and tugs cruise by. Parking is available at a lot nearby.

Bedrock
401 West Baltimore Street
(410) 685-7665

Located next door to the Hippodrome Theatre, this old bank has been turned into a two-level bar with lots to do. The colored lights glowing from inside may attract your eye first. Once inside, order a drink or maybe a microbrew and look for the fun: board games, darts, billiards, pinball and video games, plus plenty of tunes from the jukeboxes. If you prefer cozy to the wide-open airy first floor, head downstairs to the more intimate lower level.

Some among us decide to go to church after a Saturday night out on the town. St. Vincent de Paul Church offers midnight Mass every Saturday night—although by then it's Sunday—in the historic church at the foot of the Jones Falls Expressway (just north of Little Italy) at 12:15 a.m. Everybody's welcome. Call (410) 962-5078 with questions.

Bertha's
Lancaster and Broadway, Fells Point
(410) 327-5795
www.berthas.com

The Fells Point restaurant known for its mussels is also known for its live music. You can count on jazz or blues most Wednesdays, Fridays, and Saturdays. Bands play from 9:30 p.m. to close. The bar has a good variety of beers, including their own Bertha's Best Bitter, an English-style ale.

Cat's Eye Pub
1730 Thames Street
(410) 276-9866
www.catseyepub.com

This Irish pub features a collection of flags from all over the world and live music every night, ranging from bluegrass to zydeco, jazz to Irish tunes. Two bars will keep your whistle whet, and a back room with games and chess tables—yes, chess tables—will keep your mind busy. Cover charges vary. They open their doors at noon every day.

Chesapeake Wine Company
2400 Boston Street, Canton
(410) 522-4556
www.chesapeakewine.com

Sometimes you just need a civilized place to have a glass of wine. This wine shop-cum-bar in the Can Company complex, a fun collection of restaurants and shops, offers a fine setting for a glass. Stop by for a Tuesday-evening wine tasting or even one Friday a month, when a house band plays rock and roll.

Club Charles
1724 North Charles Street
(410) 727-8815

You might bump into filmmaker John Waters at this Baltimore pillar of nightlife. Across from the Charles Theater and the Everyman Theatre (see The Arts chapter), the dark red, Art Deco–inspired bar was listed as one of the Top Dive Bars in *Details* magazine. This is an all-inclusive kind of club where you'll find a mix of funky artists, local musicians, and suburban Dockers wearers grabbing a cocktail before catching a movie across the street. A mural with a sandstone background and red brush strokes depicts Greek mythology scenes, and the bathrooms breathe fire and brimstone art. FYI: The clocks are all set a half hour ahead.

Club Orpheus
1003 East Pratt Street
(410) 276-5599

This two-level nightclub is known for industrial/Art Deco decor and techno,Gothic alternative, and progressive hits supplied by the DJ. A large screen on the first floor displays abstract images. Wednesday night is hip-hop night. Saturdays have a "fetish dance party." A cover of up to $5 is charged.

Comedy Factory
36 Light Street
(410) 547-7798
www.baltimorecomedy.com

About 2 blocks from the Inner Harbor and above Burke's Cafe (see the Restaurants chapter), the Comedy Factory brings in national and regional comedians Thursday through Sunday nights. Tickets are about $17. We suggest you plan ahead; tickets go fast. Don't be late. When the doors close, they stay closed.

The Crescendo
1225 Cathedral Street
(410) 528-5950
www.robertoliverseafood.com

Though it's only a bar attached to the Robert Oliver Seafood Restaurant, this has become the go-to place in Mount Vernon. Located across the street from the Meyerhoff Symphony Hall and the Lyric Opera House, you'd think it would be full of bluebloods and blue-hairs. Before and after the show, they certainly stop in for a drink and a bite to eat, but mostly the crowd here is young professional and the sound system plays more contemporary tunes. Lit by the colored bubble wall behind the bar, The Crescendo is a cozy place to meet with friends or a special friend for a couple of drinks and maybe one of Robert Oliver's very tasty appetizers or desserts. The restaurant has a jazz combo playing during dinner.

The 8X10
10 East Cross Street, Federal Hill
(410) 625-2000
www.the8x10.com
This Federal Hill establishment is known for its music, usually local and regional bands. The goal here is good music—an eclectic mix, but all good. There's something several nights a week, with Tuesdays often offering five bands for five bucks. Otherwise, tickets run up to about $10 and are available at www.ticket master.com. Be prepared to stand for the show, though there are bar stools around if you can snag one. Though this is a bar, the under-21 set is invited for $5 more.

Fletcher's
701 South Bond Street
(410) 558-1889
www.fletchersbar.com
Fletcher's, located in Fells Point, ranks as one of the city's best small clubs for live music. A cousin to the famed 9:30 Club in D.C. features national and local bands of note in its upstairs room. Local musicians often launch their new CDs here. Downstairs offers a comfortable bar with pool tables and couches and occasionally the AV Club with video and DJs. An updated list of concerts can be found on the home page of the Web site.

The best sources for up-to-the-minute nightlife activity are the "Live" section in the Thursday *Baltimore Sun*, a pullout section on what's going on for the weekend, or the *City Paper*, which offers an extensive collection of free events and outings in the area. The *Sun* is available everywhere for 50 cents. City *Paper*, which is published on Wednesday, is free and found in stores and on newsstands throughout the Baltimore area.

Full Moon Saloon
1710 Aliceanna Street
(410) 276-6388
www.fullmoon-saloon.com
There can't be a much better mix than historic Fells Point and live music every night. You can sit to watch the show or head out on the dance floor. A $5 cover is charged Friday and Saturday.

Grand Central
1001 North Charles Street
(410) 752-7133
www.centralstationpub.com
The Grand Central, which takes up the space of two bars in this Mount Vernon block, calls itself the "Distinguished Alternative." The pub offers pool and dance videos every evening of the week and there's karaoke on Monday and Tuesday. The dance floor, including high-tech lighting and sound, is open Wednesday through Sunday at 9:00 p.m. with regular special events, including a drag show, once a month. The lounge on the second floor is low-key compared to the rest of the place, with leather seating and tables outside in warm weather.

Havana Club
600 Water Street
(410) 468-0022
Located directly above Ruth's Chris Steak House, 2 blocks north of the Baltimore Inner Harbor, this is an upscale nightclub decorated with soft leather sofas, state-of-the-art sound,

and an extensive (and often expensive) wine and cigar list served from a 58-foot custom-designed bar. Dress is swanky at this Cuban-inspired place. The music Thursday through Saturday has a Latin beat. The owners also rent the space for private events, so keep this in mind if you're looking for a sophisticated setting for your next party. You can become a member of the Havana Club and get privileges like valet parking and VIP entrance when it's crowded.

The Hippo
1 West Eager Street
(410) 547-0069
www.clubhippo.com

This place is a three-for-one. The Eager Street Station bar, pinball, and pool tables are in the main room. A 14-foot video screen is the draw for the video dance bar, while the main dance floor has a sunken dance floor, elevated seating at tables, and top-notch sound and light systems to make the place rock and roll. The dance club and video bar are open Friday and Saturday nights, while each night brings something new in the main dance area, including dance party night on Saturdays, hip-hop on Thursdays, and the highly popular Bingo on Wednesdays. This is a gay-friendly club.

The Horse You Came In On
1626 Thames Street
(410) 327-8111
www.horsesaloon.com

This club in historic Fells Point is modeled after an English pub. Brick walls, wood floors, and a bar give way to a variety of live performances by local musicians on acoustic guitar and other instruments. There's no cover charge during the week and it's only $1 on Saturday nights.

Howl at the Moon
22 Market Place
Power Plant Live
(410) 783-5111
www.howlatthemoon.com/baltimore_tonight.html

Dueling rock 'n' roll pianists are the centerpiece of this Power Plant Live venue. The show starts at 7:45 p.m. on Wednesday and Thursday and at 5:45 p.m. on Friday and Saturday. It's a college party place on Thursdays, when students don't have to pay a cover if they show their student ID. The cover is usually $3 early in the evening and $5 or more after 9 p.m.

Ixia
518 North Charles Street
(410) 727-1800
www.ixia-online.com

Ixia Restaurant offers Jazz and Blues Night with musicians from the Baltimore–Washington scene on Friday nights. Though there is no cover charge, reservations for dinner are appreciated. The menu features modern fusion food with lots of small plates. Entree prices run from $20 to $30. The restaurant also features a sophisticated lounge that stays open long after the dinner hour for those who want a relaxed place to have a drink and share time with their friends.

Mick O'Shea's Irish Pub
328 North Charles Street
(410) 539-7504
www.mickosheas.com

Mick O'Shea's offers an authentic Irish pub experience with live entertainment Wednesday through Saturday nights. Conveniently located a few blocks from the Inner Harbor, here's a place to hoist a few with true green-blooded Irishmen.

ONE
300 East Saratoga Street
(410) 230-0049
www.onebaltimore.com

The chicest new club in Baltimore is in an unlikely location—tucked under Interstate 83. But this little corridor along Saratoga Street has become quite an enclave for clubs with Sonar a block away. ONE is inspired by the elements, and each floor in this transformed warehouse offers an interior-designed theme relating to earth, wind, air, and fire. Resident and guest DJs spin hip-hop, reggae, top 40, and classics. Salsa night is Wednesday, and Friday night's party is broadcast live on XM radio. ONE is open Wednesday through Sunday and the admission charge is usually $10 to $15. The dress code is called "club chic," described as fashionable and funky—no hats, shorts, or athletic wear. Reservations are accepted for the couches on the Water and Air levels.

The Ottobar
2549 North Howard Street
(410) 662-0069
www.theottobar.com

There's not much else in the way of bars around the Ottobar, but this is a destination spot for those looking for good live music. The two-story club has a bar and pool tables upstairs, and a stage for live music on the first floor. Since its inception in 1997, the Ottobar has consistently booked up to 100 local and national bands a month, primarily in the rock/punk/rap genres. The club is well-known around the country, and it's not unusual to see someone sporting Ottobar's signature T-shirt with the cat and martini logo as far away as Los Angeles. While touring bands appear from all over the world, Ottobar is a strong supporter of the local music scene. Their "Pretty in Pink" Prom has become an annual event. There is a paved lot with free parking behind the venue and usually plenty of street parking.

i If you want to find a lot of clubs in a small area, try Fells Point. Within a 4-block-square area are more than a dozen watering holes and clubs whose entertainment ranges from hard rock to jazz to acoustic hits and dance music. Most of the places charge a cover, but it's worth it if you stay for a drink or two.

The neighborhood has a questionable reputation, so remember not to leave anything in your car that might entice a break-in.

Paradox
1310 Russell Street
(410) 837-9110

Out of an industrial area warehouse near the Inner Harbor comes this tribute to a wild night. DJs spinning dance, hip-hop, rap, funk, and techno keep the dance floor in a constant state of excitement. Bleachers, a cafe, and even a basketball court are alternatives to the dance floor. There is also an outdoor area for enjoying a Baltimore summer night.

There's plenty of parking. A cover of up to $5 is charged some nights, but it's worth it just to take a look inside this converted warehouse.

Phillips Harborplace Restaurant
301 Light Street
(410) 685-6600

In addition to great seafood and a great location next to the Inner Harbor, Phillips offers some down-home, any-voice-will-do, sing-along action at its piano bar. Whether you want to belt out your favorite Sinatra, Dixieland, or jazz hit, Phillips is ready to encourage you seven days a week.

Park at one of the garages near the harbor, or if you're staying at one the hotels nearby, walk on over for a drink, a snack, and some good or bad music, depending on your ear. There's no cover.

Looking for a Baltimore happy hour experience? In the summer a narrow portion of Water Street evolves into a street party, where workers from nearby Legg Mason and Deutsche Bank crowd outdoor patios. Over in Federal Hill, the Cross Street Market offers a great happy hour in a unique setting throughout the year.

Power Plant Live!
Market Place and Water Street
(410) 727-LIVE
www.powerplantlive.com

Located at the intersection of Market Place and Water Street, just 2 blocks from the Inner Harbor, Power Plant Live! is the latest development in Downtown nightlife. To date, five bars and six restaurants circle a large, open plaza where bands play for free on warm summer evenings. This is a great place to come early with the kids for a bite to eat. After dinner hours it gets rowdy with revelers partying at places like Mosaic and The Lodge Bar. Valet parking is offered nightly from 5:00 p.m. to 2:00 a.m. There is the Harbor Park Garage off Lombard Street, or you can take your chances on the street.

Red Maple
930 North Charles Street
(410) 547-0149
www.930redmaple.com

A modishly sleek interior formed from teakwood, steel, and glass makes this one of the most architecturally stunning spots in the city. Opened in 2001, the modern lounge vibe fueled by the best resident and guest DJs earned the Red Maple a slot on *In Style* magazine's list of the top 60 nightspots in America. Linear benches offer seating for an Asian tapas menu or simply for people watching. Be aware that these seats are often reserved on weekends by diners, so check with the hostess before sitting during prime dinner hours. There is usually a cover at the door in support of the music. Once inside, there's no smoking at all, but an outdoor courtyard (home to the namesake red maple) allows smokers to light up. The attire is hip, not formal, but tennis shoes are not allowed. Open daily after 6:00 p.m. Reservations for dinner are recommended. Park on the street or pay to park on a surface lot for about $6.

Sidebar Tavern
218 East Lexington Street
(410) 659-4130
www.sidebartavern.com

A dive bar popular with the local punk scene, Sidebar features live hardcore and punk rock shows with the occasional rockabilly band most nights of the week. When the music isn't playing, the regulars head over to the pool table or pinball machines. Happy hour may be only for the 21 and older crowd, but shows are open to those 18 and older and sometimes all ages. Check the Web site. Sidebar also hosts a monthly Mod Party with music from the 1960s and 1960s-inspired music, and it features live music and DJs. Shows usually begin around 9:00 p.m.

Sonar
407 East Saratoga Street
(410) 327-8333
www.sonarlounge.com

Sonar, as the name suggests, is a place for new electronic music. The main stage, with room for 1,000 people, is the location for most of the club's live shows and special events. The lounge is mellower, with leather couches, a pool table, and a bar. The club holds 300 people. The cover runs from $5 to $20 for bigger acts. Check the Web site so you don't miss out on your favorite band. Shows do sell out. Indie-Electro dance parties are regular Friday-night events, and DJs are featured on Wednesdays.

The 13th Floor
The Belvedere, 1 East Chase Street
(410) 347-0881

On the 13th floor of The Belvedere condominiums complex, a posh accommodation near the center of the Downtown Baltimore area, is the Club 13, where the sounds of live music—oldies, jazz, blues, and dance—can be heard Thursday through Saturday. If you want to know what you'll see before you get there, call the hotline. The cover varies but is usually $5. Parking can cost you even more at the hotel. Street parking is sometimes available. Dress to impress if you want to fit in.

XS
1307 North Charles Street
(410) 468-0002
Deep house and Nu-Jazz DJs start playing music at 8:00 p.m. at this hip but relaxed downtown restaurant and bar. There's no cover, but come hungry and thirsty.

Northeast

The Barn
9527 Harford Road, Parkville
(410) 882-6182
Local rock groups perform on weekends at this bar with a dance floor that tends to draw a younger crowd. The bar has lots of baseball and football memorabilia. Park where you can in the area, but watch out for the NO PARKING signs. Police are on the lookout for violators. There's a minimal cover for live music.

Borders Books & Music
170 West Ridgely Road, Timonium
(410) 453-0727
www.bordersstores.com
In addition to the cavalcade of books, magazines, and CDs, Borders offers live entertainment on Friday nights at its Espresso Cafe. There's no cover charge, but it's hard to spend much time in this place without buying a book, CD, or homemade dessert. Parking is available on-site.

The Greene Turtle
408 York Road, Towson
(410) 825-3980
This neighborhood sports bar is usually the place to go for a hamburger and the Orioles game on one of their many TVs. But on Fridays after work, acoustic music gets the weekend started with a relaxing vibe. A DJ plays dance music later in the evening. DJs play music from the '70s, '80s and '90s on Tuesday.

New Haven Lounge
1552 Havenwood Road
(410) 366-7416
You've found a home for the classic style of jazz performed by Cab Calloway and Billie Holiday, whose images are preserved in murals along with other jazz greats. Bartenders don tuxedos to bring drinks to your table, while you listen to live jazz Tuesday, Wednesday, Friday, and Saturday or a DJ on Sunday. The cover is $5 most nights at this lounge near Morgan State University.

Parker's Tavern
1809 North Eastern Avenue
(410) 342-3468
Just about every type of popular and new music form is played live by local musicians at Parker's Tavern. Smooth blues, "unplugged" acoustical classic rock, trendy progressive, and alternative stuff get fair airings each week. There's no cover for this good look at Baltimore-area music talent.

Putty Hill Station
2531 Putty Hill Avenue, Parkville
(410) 882-0500
This is a typical neighborhood sports bar that also has a DJ Friday nights and live bands on Saturday. No cover is charged, and you can park in the shopping center lot outside.

i The first Thursday of the month is always a treat at the Walters Art Museum, 600 North Charles Street. In addition to free admission to the museum, you can hear live jazz in the arms and armory museum. It's the perfect way to get from an interminable Thursday to the weekend. (For more information, see The Arts chapter.)

Rascals
1630 East Joppa Road, Towson
(410) 825-1570
There's live rock and popular music for a 40-and-older crowd at this lounge with three bars. The small stage and a dance floor get quite a workout. A cover is charged to patrons, many of whom come in search of love.

The Recher Theatre
512 York Road, Towson
(410) 337-7178
www.rechertheatre.com
Housed in a former movie theater, this night-club offers about 10 pool tables, a full bar, and live music. It's an enchanting mix that draws many students from the nearby colleges. The cover charge varies with the entertainment, although pool playing in the afternoon and early evening requires no cover charge. Park in one of the municipal garages or parking lots in Towson or at Towson Town Center, a large mall just north of the site on York Road. Keep your eyes on the listings for this small club, as it sometimes attracts major touring acts.

Tracy's at the Bowman
9306 Harford Road, Parkville
(410) 665-8600
It's really an unlikely place for a comedy club, inside a formal restaurant, but Tracy's hosts quality local, regional, and national comedy acts at 9:15 p.m. Friday and 8:30 and 10:45 p.m. Saturday. Cover ranges from $9 to $15 with a two-drink minimum.

Tully's
7934 Belair Road, Overlea
(410) 665-9100
Just a few blocks outside the Baltimore Beltway's exit 32 (U.S. Highway 1) is a great bar for eats, chats, and dancing. The dance floor is small, but the atmosphere is perfect for a relaxed evening of food, drink, dancing, and fun. Most nights a DJ runs the show, while on Tuesdays karaoke is on tap. No cover is charged. Parking is available in the parking lot of Putty Hill Plaza.

Northwest

Baldwin's Station
7618 Main Street, Sykesville
(410) 795-1041
www.baldwinstation.com
The train doesn't stop by here anymore—though it sure makes a lot of noise when it speeds by—but music lovers make their way all the way out to Carroll County for the Baldwin's special events. Several times a month, usually on Wednesday, the restaurant features nationally known singers and songwriters who play folk and traditional music. Hard Travelers visit here, and recently one of the Monkees was here. (The booking agent is nonprofit.) Come early for dinner and stay for the show, but get your tickets in advance. They run about $15 to $20.

Gordon Center for Performing Arts
3506 Gwynnbrook Avenue, Owings Mills
(410) 356-SHOW
www.gordoncenter.com
One of the newer performing arts centers in the Baltimore area, the Gordon Center offers cultural programming ranging from theatrical productions to book readings, concert presentations to recitals. The clientele tends to dress up, wearing dresses or shirts and ties, to take in the action. Some events are free, but tickets can go as high as $30.

Southeast

Brewster's Saloon
303 East Furnace Branch Road
Glen Burnie
(410) 760-5239
Glen Burnie's House of Blues is Brewster's Saloon, where live blues music is performed Friday and Saturday. The cover charge is small but varies.

Southwest

Hull Street Blues Cafe
1222 Hull Street
(410) 727-7476
www.hullstreetblues.com
Hull Street has been a neighborhood saloon since 1889. The classic pub is sandwiched among blocks of row houses in South Baltimore's Locust Point, its crimson red front identifying it from the neighboring residences. A full menu of sandwiches, crab cakes, and bar snacks is served at the bar and at the few tables scattered in the back room. The famous Hull Street chili is the perfect antidote to a blustery winter day.

J. Patrick's Irish Pub
1371 Andre Street, Locust Point
(410) 244-8613
In the heart of Locust Point is a quaint little neighborhood bar where live Irish music is played Thursday through Sunday. No cover is charged, and parking is all over the roads along the bar.

SHOPPING

The Baltimore region offers die-hard shoppers an eclectic mix of shopping experiences. There are plenty of plain vanilla shopping malls that ring the city, usually just off the Beltway. You can count on these for chain shops and the department stores: Macy's, Sears, J.C. Penney, and the newest department store in Maryland, Boscov's, which took over three stores when Hecht's closed its doors in 2006.

A couple of regional malls offer bigger selections and a bit of variety in their assortment of shops. Arundel Mills, south of the city off Interstate 295 (Baltimore–Washington Parkway), is filled with factory outlets, a huge movie multiplex, and a Medieval Times dinner-entertainment venue. There's even space for bus parking and hotels—this place draws lots of out-of-towners.

Baltimore's neighborhoods offer an appealing variety of mom-and-pop shops and boutiques. Fells Point, Charles Street, Hampden, and Mt. Washington mix their shopping with charming streetscapes. Antique Row on Howard Street is equally intriguing, with a patina of age covering the inventory of Potthast furniture, Stieff silver, and assorted tchotchkes. Plus, at most shops, you have to ring the doorbell to gain access.

Then there are the newcomers. Harbor East's not only a brand-new neighborhood just east of the Inner Harbor, it's a new shopping destination with a Whole Foods Market and an ecofriendly home-decor store. And up Interstate 83 the Hunt Valley Towne Centre makes the old shopping center the new place to gather—and it's all outside.

Farmers' markets close down streets in Baltmore City and Towson. City markets keep Baltimoreans supplied with everything from crabmeat to Rheb's chocolates.

So where do you start?

Downtown offers visitors the Inner Harbor's Harborplace and the Gallery, as well as museum stores at the Science Center, National Aquarium, Reginald Lewis Museum, American Visionary Art Museum (maybe the most interesting of all the museum shops), and well, every tourist destination. It's an easy walk up Charles Street for a variety of small shops that offer prints and original art, fair-trade clothing, CDs, and jewelry, among other items. To the east, Harbor East, Fells Point, and Canton are a short drive (or water taxi ride) away for galleries and specialty shops that cater to the young and young at heart. South of the Inner Harbor, Federal Hill's shopping isn't as concentrated, but Light Street offers a few shops plus the wonderful Cross Street Market, great for fresh produce and flowers.

If you have to have a mall (besides Harborplace), there are plenty of options. Head north to Towson, where you'll find Towson Towne Center, the most elegant of the local malls with the added bonus of a Nordstrom's and a pretty good food court. Towson Circle next door offers a few extras, including Trader Joe's and Barnes & Noble. The mall is on the edge of the Towson shopping district on York Road, as well. The shops at Kenilworth are just down the street with another good mix of locally owned shops.

Or head northeast to White Marsh, with its own exit off Interstate 95. Here you'll come to the White Marsh Mall, the Avenue at White Marsh, an Ikea home furnishings store, and a big-box center with Best Buy and Target.

The northwest section of Baltimore County has Owings Mills Mall, a small mall with a big cineplex and chain restaurants. Reisterstown Road offers some of the best boutiques in the area. Also in the northwest in the city, just off Northern Parkway, is the Village of Cross Keys, a collection of upscale shops, many of them chains such as Williams Sonoma and Talbot's, and an Elizabeth Arden Red Door spa.

On the west side of town is Security Square Mall, most notable for its Korean market, Seoul Plaza. Out in Howard County is the Mall in Columbia, one of Columbia-founder James Rouse's first malls. Don't look for something decrepit from the 1960s, however. This is a mall that keeps reinventing itself to keep up with the city's needs.

Glen Burnie, to the south of Baltimore, is home to one strip center after another all the way to Annapolis, as well as the site of Marley Station Mall. Arundel Mills is nearby, too.

Arundel Mills is only the first of the outlet malls near Baltimore. If you're willing to cross the Bay Bridge, Prime Outlets in Queenstown is newly remodeled with some great outlets, including Oshkosh B-Gosh, St. John Company, and L.L. Bean. Other outlet centers are in Perryville on I-95, another Prime Outlets is in Hagerstown west on Interstate 70, and a nearly endless supply of outlets are in Rehoboth Beach, the nirvana of outlet shopping.

If that isn't enough, check out the next chapter, Antiques and Collectibles, for a variety of shops that sell all sorts of old stuff, junk, crafts, and other knickknacks. Some are also listed in the Day Trips chapter, designed to lure you to destinations a short drive from Baltimore. And if that isn't enough, check out the flea markets and yard sales listed in the local newspapers, the *Baltimore Sun* and the *City Paper*.

Somewhere you'll find the shopping of your dreams

All malls and shops are smoke-free in the state of Maryland. If you light up, you'll be thrown out. Parking is free at all the suburban malls, even in garaged space, but in most shopping districts, you'll find on-the-street, metered parking or, in the case of Downtown malls and districts, pay parking garages. Downtown garages usually charge a flat rate

for the first hour or two and then "x" amount for every hour thereafter. Sometimes, it will be $3.00 for the first hour and $1.50 for every following hour, or it might be $1.00 for the first hour and $2.50 for every hour thereafter. In any case if you stay all day, you're going to be paying between $10 and $15 for parking. There are some special day rates if you park before 9:00 a.m. or after 5:00 p.m., but they vary. On the other hand, all of Downtown can be accessed by public transit, whether by bus, Light Rail, or subway. (See the Getting Here, Getting Around chapter for details.)

We couldn't possibly list every space with a cash register and merchandise in and around the city. Instead, we've done our best to hit the high notes—the best buys, if you will. We've organized the malls, shopping districts, farmers' markets, under-roof markets, and music stores by our geographic divisions—Downtown, Northeast, Northwest, Southeast, and Southwest. Bookstores and thrift stores are not separated by geographic region since many of these stores have locations in different regions. You will, however, find the geographic region for each location in parentheses next to the street address.

MALLS

Downtown

Harborplace
Light and Pratt Streets
(410) 332-4191
www.harborplace.com
Sometimes it seems as if Harborplace is the most talked about shopping mall in the country. (It has even been mentioned in *National Geographic*!) Businesspeople come from far and wide to look at it and see if the concept could work in their hometown. Opened in 1980, Harborplace has become the focal point for Baltimore's "new downtown" at the head of the Inner Harbor and the main mover and shaker in Baltimore's harbor renaissance.

More than 10 million people a year come to peruse the 130 shops, restaurants, and eateries, many of which feature outside tables that face the Inner Harbor. Boaters can pull their vessels right up to the dock and eat lunch at their choice of waterside cafes. Or they can get carryout and sit on their boats to watch the street performers at the Harborplace Amphitheater between the two glass pavilions.

You'll find chain restaurants, like Cheesecake Factory or the California Pizza Kitchen. You'll also find Maryland traditions such as Phillips Harborplace Restaurant. The bottom line on food at Harborplace: If you want it, they've got it—Tex-Mex, Chinese, burgers, cheesecake, seafood, and pizza. It's all there.

The shops are as diverse as the eateries. Of course, there are a few standards. For women's clothes, you'll find Ann Taylor, The White House (the original store), and J. Crew. The Sports Shop has both men's and women's clothing with local team logos. A branch of The Body Shop is also there, as is Sunglass Hut International, but the bulk of the stores at Harborplace are more esoteric.

Hats in the Belfry, for instance, has Easter-type hats and everyday casual hats for both men and women. In the Light Street Pavilion, you'll find The Discovery Channel Store, with a wide selection of unique gifts for any member of the family.

Although there are lots of places to pick up souvenirs of your trip to Baltimore, Harborplace has a shop that deals strictly in that dimension. Destination Baltimore is a national chain of souvenir stores whose main focus is souvenir sportswear, such as T-shirts and hats.

There are also shops with a Baltimore flavor, such as Who You Calling a Crab?, which sells items that have a crustacean theme, and Larry Stevens World of Art, which displays works by local artist—you guessed it—Larry Stevens.

We could go on for pages about all the shopping opportunities here, but suffice it to say that Harborplace gives you a lot of choice without requiring you to walk for miles and miles to get it. The pavilions are large but compact.

There is no parking at Harborplace and no free parking Downtown, unless you are extremely lucky and find that odd place on the street. If you're driving, consider The Gallery's parking, which is above Pratt Street on Calvert Street, or at one of the many meters or lots nearby. An hour's parking will cost $1 in quarters. Harborplace and The Gallery shops, restaurants, and eateries offer a $2 validation stamp for valet parking with any purchase.

The Gallery
Pratt and Calvert Streets
(410) 332-4191
www.harborplace.com

Across the street from the Pratt Street Pavilion at Harborplace is The Gallery, four stories of glass that hold some of the more exclusive shopping opportunities in the area. The Gallery boasts more than 75 nationally known shops and eateries under a central skylight that makes you feel as if you're shopping in the National Arboretum.

The shops at The Gallery are not unique; you'll know almost every name—Coach, General Nutrition Center, and Godiva Chocolatier are just a few. There are several clothing stores to choose from. Brooks Brothers has a bi-level store here, and you'll find Banana Republic and J. Crew as well.

There are designer clothes at Ann Taylor and specialty shops for both men and women, including Johnson and Murphy and Downtown Locker Room for men and Bebe and Victoria's Secret for women. For the smallest among us, The Gallery's Gap store has Gap Kids.

There's also a fair number of shoe stores—9, to be exact—including such well-known names as Lady Foot Locker, Nine West, and Aerosoles. You'll also find some really interesting ancillary shops such as Bath and Body Works, which carries all those bath and body lotions and sweet-smelling stuff you'll want to put on under the new outfit you just bought.

The mall has its own underground parking, but there are also many lots nearby if that one should be full. Access to the parking lot is from Calvert Street, which is one-way north. Head east on Pratt Street and turn left. The parking lot entrance is on your right, as is The Gallery. The Gallery Garage offers both self-park (24 hours a day) and valet parking (5:00 p.m. to midnight Monday through Friday, 11:00 a.m. to midnight Saturday and Sunday).

Northeast

Hunt Valley Town Centre
118 Shawan Road, Hunt Valley
(410) 785-3770
www.shophuntvalley.com

Hunt Valley Mall just wasn't attracting shoppers, so what did its owners do? Tore it down and built Hunt Valley Towne Centre. A "main street" similar to the Avenue at White Marsh, this new concept has drawn plenty of teenagers, who come to shop at chic shops such as Box of Rain or discount stores like Wal-Mart, grab a snack at Panera Bread, and and then catch a movie.

Their parents are here, too, buying groceries at Wegman's Food Market (not your average grocery store), finding something stylish at Filene's Basement, and meeting friends at Greystone Grill. There's a funny combination of shops here, but everybody will find a place they love. Restaurants, women's apparel, a terrific gift and card shop, Greetings and Readings, and an equally fine wineshop, Calvert Wine and Spirits. Discount shoppers have their choice of Wal-Mart, Filene's Basement, Burlington Coat Factory, or Dick's Clothing and Sporting Goods. In all there are 54 shops and restaurants, including the 12-screen Regal movie theaters with stadium seating. Parking is plentiful, If you are early enough, you just might find a spot right in front of your favorite shop. If not, acres of parking surround the shopping center.

Towson Town Center
825 Dulaney Valley Road, Towson
(410) 494-8800
www.towsontowncenter.com

Towson Town Center started life in the 1950s as a simple neighborhood shopping center that had a shoe store or two, a ten-cent store, a drugstore, and a few other things. Its location, down the hill from the original suburban Hutzler's department store, at that time the biggest local department store around and currently being renovated as a new mall unto itself, made it a popular destination. Over the years, as Towson and the demand for services grew, the shopping center added levels, stores, and, eventually, a roof.

Hutzler's has long since closed, but Towson Town Center has been renovated and reorganized to become a major player in the mall arena. As it stands today, it boasts Macy's and Nordstrom's and more than 150 specialty stores. As with many of the malls, you'll find tons of clothing stores—about 40 of them. There are 20 or so stores that sell shoes, including Foot Locker, Nine West, and Aldo Shoes. The 18 kids specialty shops include Build-A-Bear Workshop and Gymboree.

If you're after books, Towson Town has a major bookstore, Waldenbooks. For music, Sam Goody should be able to accommodate anyone's groove.

If you need a briefcase or a wallet, Coach has a location in the mall.

For gifty things, try the soaps and scents of Crabtree & Evelyn or the tasty treats of Godiva Chocolatier. For everything else, you'll find things from the classic offerings of the The Bombay Company to the wonderfully classless offerings of Spencer Gifts.

You can have your hair cut at Bubbles Salon; purchase jewelry at 18 different stores, from the premium items of Radcliffe Jewelers to the fun stuff at Claire's Accessories. You can rent a tux, have your nails done, have your eyes examined, even send a letter (there's a post office on the first floor!). There is—literally—something for everyone here.

And when you're tired of all this variety, you can hunker down in the large food terrace that offers food choices from yogurt and salad to steaks and Boardwalk Fries.

Towson Town is easily accessible. It's right in Towson and just a long block off the Beltway. The mall has four levels, three major parking garages, and some open parking. All parking options are free.

White Marsh Mall and
The Avenue at White Marsh
8200 Perry Hall Boulevard, White Marsh
(410) 931-7100
www.whitemarshmall.com

White Marsh Town Center is the name given to an area of planned development, at the center of which is a megamall with five department stores (Macy's, Boscov's, JCPenney, Sears, and Lord & Taylor) and more than 170 specialty stores.

White Marsh is only two stories high, so it spreads out over a large area. It is easy to get around in, however, because there is only one main drag lined with shops. The only shops that shoot off this corridor line the entrances to the department stores and the one main entrance from the outside.

Like many megamalls, White Marsh's main focus is clothing, with 29 specific clothing stores in addition to the five department stores. Among those is a shop for larger women, Lane Bryant, one of five locations left in the Baltimore area.

White Marsh has more shoe stores than just about anywhere else—18 in all—including Bostonian, Rockport, Aldo, and Easy Spirit. The mall does have, however, its fair share of nonapparel stores.

You'll find a branch of Borders Express for books and Sun Coast Motion Picture Company for videos. White Marsh Mall has the traditional sporting goods offerings, such as Foot Locker and The Athlete's Foot. There is also Driving Impressions, which has neat stuff for your car as well as neat stuff about cars.

You might enjoy Things Remembered, where you can buy a simple silver cup or a gold pen—lots of gift ideas for weddings and have them engraved. White Marsh has one of the few Disney Stores in Baltimore.

White Marsh has more than its fair share of high-level jewelers, including Gordon Jewelers, Kay Jewelers, Littman Jewelers, etc., etc.,

but for inexpensive, fun jewelry we suggest Claire's Accessories.

The food court at White Marsh is a special treat for kids (and moms) because of the full-size carousel at its center. The food court itself is decidedly one of the largest in any of the malls around and always crowded. It offers 20 food booths. There are also a few sit-down restaurants within the mall.

The mall is centrally located between Baltimore to the west and the city of Bel Air to the north. It has easy access to I-95 and Interstate 695. Around the mall are strip shopping centers, industrial parks and business centers, a large hotel, eateries, a health club, and an adjunct facility called The Avenue at White Marsh (www.theavenueatwhitemarsh.com).

The Avenue is not a mall but neither is it a strip shopping center. It is, instead, a Main Street clone, complete with brick sidewalks, low-level streetlamps, and a giant marquee for its 16-screen movie house. Opened in 1997, The Avenue of White Marsh includes eight sit-down restaurants and cafes. Both White Marsh and The Avenue have free parking.

In addition to The Avenue, other stores and small strip shopping centers gather around White Marsh. Of special note is Ikea, the Scandinavian home-furnishing chain. This is its only location in the Baltimore area. Plants and planters, lamps and lamp shades, mugs, glassware, dishes—everything you could possibly want for floor, shelf, or porch and most of it made with natural fibers, clays, and wood—make up the stock here. There is a snack bar on the premises as well as a restaurant that serves terrific Swedish meatballs. If you have children under 2 feet tall, you'll love the giant-sized glassed-in play area that comes complete with babysitters.

Northwest

Mondawmin Mall
2401 Liberty Heights Avenue
(410) 523-1534
www.mondawmin.com

This mall was built 50 years ago on the site of Mondawmin, an estate owned by Alexander

Brown, founder of the first mortgage banking company in the United States. The mall currently has 110 retailers and a variety of fast-food eateries. It's about to get a face-lift in 2007. Existing space will get a makeover, and the mall will be enlarged to add new retail stores, a grocery store, and sit-down restaurants. Even parking and traffic patterns will be reworked.

You will, of course, find traditional stores such as Foot Locker and Payless for shoes. K-B toy stores has a location here, as does Lerner New York. Mondawmin is unusual among many of the malls around, however, because although it is a relatively large mall, it has no anchor department store. It is shops . . . lots and lots of shops.

Mondawmin is not lacking in clothing stores, with 24 to its credit, including Big & Tall Casual Male, Leather Man, Ashley Stewart, and Rainbow.

If it's music you're after, stop by FYE or Urban Knowledge. Hungry? There's Mondawmin Chicken and Seafood and Panda China and a variety of fast-food outlets.

Mondawmin also boasts many personal service–oriented stores. Most suburban malls will have one or two places to get your hair cut, and they might have one place that sells beauty supplies, but Mondawmin has three beauty salons, two barber shops, a wig store, two nail shops, and two beauty supply shops.

Outside the mall, you will also find the Motor Vehicle Administration office, an office of the Social Security Administration, and a well-used subway stop. Even with all the parking spaces that these organizations use, there's always plenty of free parking.

Owings Mills Town Center
10300 Mill Run Circle, Owings Mills
(410) 363-7000
www.owningsmillsmall.com
Owings Mills Town Center opened in 1987 to serve the affluent far west side of Baltimore and the county. With three major department stores (Boscov's, JCPenney, and Macy's) and almost 250 specialty shops, plus 20 eating places on the food court, Owings Mills is a mall of mammoth proportions. If that weren't enough, a 17-screen AMC theater boasts stadium-style seats and three premium screens.

Waldenbooks and Bath and Body Works are among the standard mall shops at Owings Mills. You'll also find some of the more high-end clothing shops, such as Cache, Express, and H&M. Gymboree, American Eagle Outfitters, and Victoria's Secret are also here. Owings Mills has one of the five Lane Bryant stores left in the area, and there are five electronics stores—Radio Shack and the Game Stop, plus other video game and phone stores. Owings Mills also sports 10 jewelry stores from the more exclusive shops that actually have "jeweler" in their name—Alta Jewelers, Littman Jewelers, Reeds Jewelers, and Zales Jewelers—to the inexpensive, fun costume jewelry shops, such as Claire's Accessories.

The food court has, among other establishments offering mainly snacks and drinks, Italian cuisine at Mamma Ilardo's Pizzeria and Asian fare at Dragon House Express and Sarku Japan. There is also traditional fast food available at McDonald's and Chick-fil-A. For those of us who are watching our weight, there's Everything Yogurt/Salad Cafe. You'll also find Bourbon Street Cafe and Ruby Tuesday's on the menu. Full-service restaurants from Don Pablo's Mexican Kitchen and Red Robin to Red Lobster and Tony Romas have sprung up in a new restaurant park near the entrance of the mall.

If you're driving, try to park near the JCPenney, which sits at the middle of the arc-shaped building. That way you won't have to walk so far to your car when you've finished shopping. Owings Mills is also served by mass transit. Light Rail does not have a stop at the mall, but there is a bus from the Owings Mills metro stop.

Reisterstown Road Plaza
6564 Reisterstown Road
(410) 358-2275
www.reistertownplaza.com
Opened in 1962, Reisterstown Road Plaza

started out as the then-biggest regional shopping center, and it has grown over the years. Its most recent overall renovation was completed in 2004, when a two-story office building was added to house the headquarters for the Maryland State Lottery and two new entrance wings were built.

Quantity of stores is not the benchmark of Reisterstown Road Plaza—variety is. In the words of a Plaza Insider, it's an "ethnic-oriented center that has everything from bras to post offices." It generally caters to four basic surrounding ethnic communities: African American, Russian, Jewish, and Latin American. For instance, its grocery store has a complete Russian aisle and a full kosher aisle, and, simply put, has everything from chitlins to borscht.

The two department stores at the mall are Burlington Coat Factory and National Wholesale Liquidators; both are medium-size stores with moderately priced goods. In fact most of the mall stores offer good bargains. For women's clothing you can find The Avenue, Shingar, Marshall's, and Gallo Clothing. Shoe-store bargains include Payless Shoes/Payless Kids, Economy Shoes, and Shoe City. There's a Giant Food and a liquor store, Mall Spirits. Several beauty supply houses are also here—Visions Beauty Outlet, Vogue Hair Supply, and Sally's Beauty Supply. There are also salons for your hair and nail needs, as well as five stores that sell jewelry and accessories. Two furniture stores, Furniture Palace and Rent-a-Center, offer items for the home. The one bookstore, Sepia, Sand & Sable Books, can order any title you want but specializes in African-American literature. Home Depot also has a store here.

There is plenty of free parking. If you'd rather not navigate Reisterstown Road, you can easily take the metro, which has a Plaza stop.

Southeast

Marley Station
7900 Ritchie Highway (Highway 2)
Glen Burnie
(410) 760-8900
www.shopmarleystation.com

With more than 130 specialty stores, nine restaurants, and four department stores (JCPenney, Macy's, Boscov's, and Sears) as well as an eight-screen Regal Cinema, Marley Station is easy to get to either by going straight down Ritchie Highway from Baltimore or heading down Highway 100 from I-695.

Under the auspices of the slogan "The Fun's Inside," Marley Station has turned itself into a family-oriented shopping center, with lots of amenities and activities for parents and kids. From programs that present country guitarists or African dancers to breakfast with Peter Rabbit, Marley Station goes out of its way to make itself a center for community as well as shopping.

The mall is laid out on two floors essentially in the shape of a printed M, with main entrances at the center of the "letter" and major department stores at each of its four "points."

Along this route, you'll find a bookstore, Waldenbooks; more than 16 women's clothing stores; and one of only two Frederick's of Hollywood stores in the area. There are almost as many specialty gift stores as there are women's clothiers, counting in at 19. Marley Station offers 10 jewelry stores, including Edward Arthur Jewelers, Kay Jewelers, and Zales. There are six shoe stores that carry children's shoes in addition to the department stores. You'll also find The Children's Place and the Limited Too for kids' clothes.

Marley Station has such food specialty places as Mrs. Field's Cookies, Pretzel Time, and Rita's Italian Ice. The mall is also rife with restaurants, both chain and fast food. Many are the popular mall fare, such as Sbarro's, with its thick-crust pizzas, and Boardwalk Fries, with some of the best fries in Baltimore, and a Taco Bell. This may not seem like a big deal to some, but to those of you who have vegetarian and meat-eating children in the same family, it can be very handy. Of course, if it's just Mom and Dad out shopping, they might want to try sitting down at Ruby Tuesday's or Rocky Run Tap and Grill.

Parking is free and plentiful, with more than 4,500 spots to choose from.

Southwest

Arundel Mills
7000 Arundel Mills Circle, Hanover
(410) 540-5100
www.arundelmills.com

Since Arundel Mills opened in November 2000, it has become a popular destination for shopping, dining, and entertainment. The center includes a mix of one-of-a-kind manufacturer and retail outlets, specialty retailers, and category-dominant stores. In fact, more than 200 specialty retailers share the space with entertainment venues and a variety of dining options.

Simply put, the mall is huge, at 1.3 million square feet of retail space. Anchors and major tenants include Bed, Bath & Beyond, Books-A-Million, Off Broadway Shoe Warehouse, Off 5th—Saks Fifth Avenue Outlet, Neiman Marcus Last Call, and Old Navy. A new addition is the popular H&M clothing chain.

It will be hard to not find what you're looking for at this megamall. For fashion there's a Banana Republic Factory Store, Eddie Bauer Outlet, Gap Outlet, United Colors of Benetton Outlet, and Ann Taylor Loft—just to name a few of the more than 40 apparel stores. Shoe stores are also easy to find and include Skechers USA, Cole Haan, Jarman, and a Nine West Outlet.

Handbags, leather, and luggage can be found at Leather Limited, Samsonite Company Store, and Wilson's Leather Outlet. Bath & Body Works, New York Perfumery Outlet, and Beauty Express offer the latest in health and beauty needs.

Jewelry and accessories can be found at 14 stores, including Reeds Jewelers Outlet, Claire's Accessories, Ultra Diamond and Gold Outlet, and Zales the Diamond Store Outlet.

Arundel Mills also offers some of the best shopping around when it comes to children's apparel, with Carters, Limited Too, Nautica Kids, and Osh Kosh B'Gosh all under one roof. Home furnishings can be found at Island Rattan, Kirkland's Outlet, World Accents, and Select Comfort.

Arundel Mills prides itself on its specialty shops. F.Y.E. For Your Entertainment, a huge music, video, and electronics store, has a large children's department. The Bass Pro Shops Outdoor World is an outdoor enthusiast's paradise, with fishing, hunting, and athletic apparel, gear, and other outdoor accessories.

Shoppers will never go hungry at Arundel Mills, with 27 places to grab a bite, including the classics like Burger King, Sbarro's, and Starbucks Coffee as well as the specialties like DuClaw Brewing Co., Café ReMomo, and Kelly's Cajun Grill.

Arundel Mills has three entertainment venues; movie theaters; Dave and Busters, a combination arcade and restaurant; and Medieval Times, which mixes knights, horses, and a Middle Ages–style dinner. Tickets are about $50 for adults. At the other end of the mall, Muvico Egyptian Theatres offers 24 stadium-seating theaters showing mostly Hollywood blockbusters, although occasionally there will be a foreign film, an independent art movie, or even a live broadcast from New York's Metropolitan Opera. (Plan well in advance for these tickets; they're hot.) Near the theaters, along restaurant row, you'll find Dave and Busters Grand Sports Cafe. Besides the usual bar food and cocktails, Dave and Busters has billiards and a "Midway" arcade, and it's open until midnight or 1:00 a.m.

Arundel Mills is located off I-95 and the Baltimore–Washington Parkway (Highway 295), heading south from Baltimore, via Highway 100 in Anne Arundel County. It is also just 2 miles west of the Baltimore–Washington International Thurgood Marshall Airport. There is plenty of parking available.

Security Square Mall
6901 Security Boulevard
(410) 265-6000
www.securitysquare.com

Security Square Mall has 120 stores and eateries inside, and two additional restaurants—International House of Pancakes and

Bennigan's—on its large parking lot. There are six main stores: Sears, Seoul Plaza, Model's Sporting Goods, Macy's, Old Navy, and Burlington Coat Factory. Sears has an auto service center. The mall has an AMC Cinema theater with eight screens that has access from outside the mall.

The mall is very community oriented, with ongoing special programs such as the Summer Theater for children, which presents a different children's production each month from June to August. But the most interesting thing about the mall is its signs.

You know how irritating it is to be heading for one store in the mall and inadvertently end up parking at the exact opposite end from where that store is located? Well, that can't happen at Security. From the moment you enter the parking lot, there are signs that tell you which way to go. Macy's this way; Sears Auto Center that way. Once you're in the mall, you don't have to search for a directory to figure out where you are and where you want to go. Signs point the way.

The only question you need answered, then, is which way do you want to go. The main entrance into the mall is by Macy's, but that will drop you into the food court and a long hall that has a lot of service spots on it, such as the U.S. Post Office, Shoe Repair, and Picture People.

The shortest way into the center of the mall is through Seoul Plaza. From there, you can determine which way you want to head.

You'll encounter two kid's shoe stores, a large Super Kids store, and a smaller Payless Kids. Men's and women's fashion boutiques cater to African American styles. Radio Shack, Karibu Books, K-B toys, and FYE are here as well.

Of course, Security Square has the usual mall shops and food court, but what makes it unique is Seoul Plaza, a sort of mall within a mall. Catering primarily to the large Korean community, which lives in the area, the plaza has two levels of shopping with a grocery store, eateries, clothing stores, and even a pool hall.

As with most suburban shopping centers, all parking is in open lots and free.

SHOPPING DISTRICTS

Because Baltimore is a city of neighborhoods, you'll find that every neighborhood has a shopping district. Each one will usually have some typical neighborhood stuff, such as a grocery store, at least one bank, a drugstore, sometimes a dollar store, a shoe store, and a haircutting place.

We can't possibly list every shopping area in Baltimore's more than 200 neighborhoods as well as all of the suburban shopping centers. What we have striven to do is note those that people visit from all over town.

Downtown

Charles Street Shopping District
Charles Street, from Pleasant Street to Mount Royal Avenue

Farther uptown, both north and south of Mount Vernon Square and the Washington Monument, you'll find the Charles Street Shopping District. This area was at one time where all the posh shops were—the furriers, the saddleries, the exclusive menswear shops. Over the years those stores left as the neighborhood became more peopled with students and young professionals. Now the Charles Street corridor contains the hippest of the hip. From the south at Brown's Market, which is arcade shopping tucked into one of Charles Street's magnificent buildings, to Mount Royal Avenue, you'll find some of the most interesting shops and restaurants in the city.

At the south end is **Woman's Industrial Exchange,** 333 North Charles Street, (410) 685-4388. Organized in 1882 to provide an opportunity for women to make a living through their crafts rather than have to face the low-paying sweatshops of the time, the Woman's Industrial Exchange opened its doors at this location in 1887 and ever since has been filled with goodies hand-crafted by Baltimore women. If you're in the market for quilted pillows, handmade dolls, and knitted booties, this place should be at the top or your list.

Down the street are a number of small art galleries and boutiques. **Beadazzled,** 501

North Charles Street, (410) 837-2323, is a jewelry-maker's paradise, with hundreds of colorful beads sold in bulk. On the same block you'll find **Foot Fetish**, 525 North Charles Street, (410) 962-8080, a shoe boutique specializing in high-end footwear. Across the street is **A People United**, 516 North Charles Street, (410) 727-4471, a collective that sells clothing, jewelry, and crafts from around the globe. Be sure to visit the furniture gallery in the basement. Around the corner on Centre Street is Ted's Music Shop (see Music later in this chapter).

On the other side of Mount Vernon Place, you'll run into **Donna's Coffee Bar**, 800 North Charles Street, (410) 385-0180. North of there is a block-long section that is sort of the neighborhood shopping spot, complete with drugstore and sub shop. Working your way north, you get to the University of Baltimore and the outskirts of the Maryland Institute College of Art, so the businesses and restaurants start to reflect the college environs. There are lots of vintage and secondhand stores with a rotating stock of yesterday's T-shirts and funky jewelry.

The Belvedere at 1 East Chase Street started life as a hotel but is now a condominium complex. It also has a couple of terrific restaurants, including the **Owl Bar**, (410) 347-0888, where H. L. Mencken used to hang out. In the other direction on Chase, you'll find **Architect's Bookstore**, 11½ West Chase Street, (410) 625-2585, a design and architecture–focused store run by the Baltimore Chapter of the American Institute of Architects.

The Charles Street Shopping District is 13 blocks of shopping, culture, and architectural wonders, and right in the middle of it at Mount Vernon Place is a cross-shaped park, whose centerpiece is the Washington Monument—the first monument built to honor ol' George. Mount Vernon Methodist Church, the Peabody Conservatory of Music, and The Gladding Mansion, which is now part of The Walters Art Gallery, are also nearby. There are also park benches, fountains, and marvelous shade trees to shelter the weary traveler.

All parking is on the street at meters or in lots on side streets. Our suggestion is to park at one of the side-street lots (there are two facing each other at Cathedral and Centre Streets, a block west of Charles Street), then walk Charles Street from south to north until you get tired, and take a cab or bus back to your parking lot. For more information about the cultural wonders of the area, see The Arts chapter.

Federal Hill Shopping District
Along and between Light and South Charles Streets, south of Key Highway

Federal Hill Shopping District has its center at Cross Street Market (see the listing later in this chapter), but it has been enhanced by the neighborhood's renaissance. Many of the corner stores that were once drugstores or grocery stores have been transformed into gift shops, clothing shops, and antiques and collectibles shops.

It's a great place to meander through, because it's within walking distance of Inner Harbor and attractions such as the American Visionary Art Museum (see The Arts chapter) and Federal Hill Park (see the Parks and Recreation chapter). The neighborhood also offers some of the best food around (see the Restaurants chapter).

The shops offer an interesting mix of neighborhood essentials such as dry cleaners, pharmacies, and shoe repair. There is **Smitty's Cut Rate Liquors**, 1044 South Charles Street, (410) 752-8288, and **Movie Time Video**, 1118 South Charles Street, (410) 528-8888. You can also find less traditional stores. **Zelda Zen**, 46 East Cross Street, (410) 625-2424, specializes in beautiful gifts and jewelry.

In Federal Hill specialty stores include **Patrick Sutton Home**, 1000 Light Street, (410) 783-1500, a storefront for one of Baltimore's top interior designers. You'll find exquisite touches for the sophisticated home. **Shofer's Furniture**, 930 South Charles Street, (410) 752-4212, has four levels of furniture and home accessory shopping.

Light Street Cycles, 1015 Light Street, (410) 685-2234, has everything for the cyclist—bikes, wheels, and helmets. **Charles Tiles,** 801 Light Street, (410) 332-1500, sells ceramic tile, handpainted and plain, for kitchens, baths, counters, tabletops, and floors. If you need a special piece of foam cut for a chair, a pillow, or a sofa, or if you'd like a dense foam mattress for your bed, **House of Foam,** 1108 Light Street, (410) 727-0982, has all that and more.

You're bound to get hungry and if you don't have time for a meal, don't miss Dangerously Delicious Pies at 1036 Light Street (410-522-PIES). The name may be offbeat but it's accurate. Fruit pies and specialty pies such as Chocolate Peanut Butter Chess or White Trash Crème Brûlée are the delicious creations of Rodney "The Pie Man" Henry. He loves rock 'n' roll but everybody loves his pies.

Federal Hill is one of the oldest neighborhoods in Baltimore, and many of the stores have been there just about as long. **Morstein's Jewelers,** 1114 Light Street, (410) 727-3232, celebrated its 100th anniversary in 1998. Grandfather William, a Russian immigrant, set up his first shop in East Baltimore in 1898. Sonny Morstein (pronounced More-steen), third generation of this still family-owned business, handles fine jewelry and does custom work, appraisals, and repairs.

Parking in Federal Hill is mostly on the street at meters. There is one parking ramp located just off of Cross Street between Charles Street and St. Paul Street.

Fells Point Shopping District
Broadway, from Eastern Avenue to Thames Street
Fells Point Shopping District grew up at the foot of Broadway around the Broadway Market

i Unless you park at a paid meter or have a residential parking sticker, most on-street parking in Federal Hill is restricted to two hours. During baseball and football games, however, parking is prohibited altogether on many streets, and you can get a steep ticket. Be sure to read parking signs carefully.

(see the listing later in this chapter). This is a must-see area of old buildings, cobblestone streets, the smell of salt water, and the cry of sea gulls. Yet, it is dichotomous. Working tugboats slosh at their moorings, while after-the-ater toffs in tails and gowns head for a drink at the Admiral Fell Inn. Johns Hopkins Hospital staff, just off a shift, as well as sailors just off the boat, are drawn into Jimmy's Restaurant for a true Maryland breakfast.

We talk extensively about Fells Point's antiques stores in our Antiques and Collectibles chapter and its fine restaurants and nightlife in those respective chapters, but you'll also find just some good old-fashioned shopping available here.

The area started out as a village for workers in the Fell shipyards, and it is still a place where you'll find craftspeople. **Brass Works Company,** for instance, at 1641 Thames Street, (410) 327-7280, sells brass items, but its stock in trade is brass restoration. From bed frames to candlesticks to bunged-up brass railings, Brass Works will bang it out, refit it, and make it shine like new.

Fells Point has a number of small, kitschy stores offering a variety of clothing, gifts, and home accessories. At **9th Life,** 620 South Broadway, (410) 534-9999, you'll find vintage T-shirts, funky jewelry, and retro lunchboxes. Fans of punk and hardcore music shouldn't miss **Reptilian Records,** 403 South Broadway, (410) 327-6853, while the **Sound Garden,** 1616 Thames Street, (410) 563-9011, ranks as the best local music store in the city, specializing in both new and used CDs. The staff of music aficionados can also give you the inside scoop on live rock shows. Across the street at **Su Casa,** 901 South Bond Street, (410) 522-7010, you'll find funky furniture and home accessories.

Down the street is **The Big Iguana,** 1633 Thames Street, (410) 675-3231, where you'll find imported clothing. **Ten Thousand Villages,** 1621 Thames Street, (410) 342-5568, is for anyone who likes handmade goods. Ten Thousand Villages is essentially a third-world outlet. It's a nonprofit organization opened by the North Baltimore Mennonite Church and the Society of Friends to provide an outlet for crafters in third-world countries. The shop carries jewelry from the four corners of the earth, toys, sarongs, woodcarvings from Kenya, and pottery from Vietnam and Bangladesh. There's also a year-round Christmas section.

Looking for a new tablecloth or some towels for the bride-to-be? **Super Linens**, 601 South Broadway, (410) 732-7900, has a large selection.

For some more exotic home decor, check out **Eclectic Elements**, whose two-level shop is located at 813 South Broadway, (410) 675-5105. Here you'll find rich leather sofas, finely textured throws and pillows, and a wide assortment of lamps, knickknacks, and whatnots. If your style is more, well, green, don't miss **blueHouse** at 1407 Fleet Street, (410) 276-1180. Bamboo floors, organic candles, lotions and aromatherapy products, trash recycled into decorative items, and a host of ecofriendly products pack this sleek and stylish space. There's a lunch counter, too.

Fells Point Shopping District is just like Fells Point, with top- and bottom-end shops throughout. You can pay a premium price or a low one. You can find the extremely esoteric or the more traditional—whatever fits your mood or your need at the moment.

Park and walk or simply take the Inner Harbor water taxi. It's a great way to spend an afternoon and still get all your shopping done.

Harbor East Shopping district
Aliceanna Street, from President Street to Caroline Street

A few years ago, this neighborhood didn't exist. It was a conglomeration of vacant lots, abandoned buildings, a virtual wasteland. Frankly, it was a dark and creepy place. Not anymore. Developers call it "the gold coast" now, and it boasts the new **Marriott** tower, the highly regarded **Charleston Restaurant**, office complexes, and brand spanking new condominiums. A **Four Seasons Hotel** is in the offing as well. With all that development comes, what else—shopping. A large por-

tion of the shops are on Exeter Street. **Benjamin Lovell Shoes**, 618 South Exeter Street, (410) 244-5359, offers a variety of comfortable and stylish shoes. **Handbags and the City**, at 612 South Exeter Street, (410) 528-1443, has upscale handbags from lots of well-known designers, including Cynthia Rowley, Lulu Guinness, and Juicy Couture. **Bin 604**, at 604 South Exeter Street, (410) 576-0444, is owned by the duo that runs some of Baltimore's best restaurants, including the nearby Charleston. Stop here for a bargain or a rare bottle.

Nearby is **City Sport**, 809 Aliceanna Street, (410) 837-4420, which offers a broad range of adult athletic gear. **Whole Foods Market**, 1001 Fleet Street, (410) 528-1640, offers organic and natural foods. **South Moon Under**, 815 Aliceanna Street (410) 685-7820, has clothing, swimwear, and jewelry for the young and the young at heart. **Gaines McHale Antiques and Home**, 700 South Caroline Street, (410) 625-1900, has moved their showroom to this new hot part of town. Details can be found in the Antiques and Collectibles chapter. **Urban Adventure Company**, 1500 Thames Street, (410) 534-4453, sits right on the edge of Harbor East and Fells Point and offers a range of outdoor gear, clothing, and shoes.

Northeast

Old Towson Shopping District
York Road, between Towsontown Boulevard and Joppa Road, Towson

As mentioned in the introduction to this chapter, Towson has one of the largest malls in the area, Towson Town Center (see Malls previously in this chapter), and is also the starting point of a shopping area that stretches east all the way to Perry Hall and north to Cockeysville. But Old Towson, the area north of Towsontown Boulevard to Joppa Road, is a little shopping district all to itself.

A block west of the district are the Towson Court House and business offices for financial and legal firms in Towson, which may account for the large number of eating places in this 2-

block-square shopping area. For instance, within just 2 blocks on York Road, you'll find **The Orient Restaurant,** 319 York Road, (410) 296- 9000; a **Ruby Tuesday's,** 401 York Road, (410) 825-1334; and **The Melting Pot Restaurant,** 418 York Road, (410) 821-6358.

All along this little corridor (and east and west of it) are interesting shops and sights to see. Your kids will enjoy **Ten Car Pile Up,** a secondhand clothing store for teens at 511 York Road, (410) 832-5246. If your family likes the outdoors, **Hudson Trail Outfitters,** 424 York Road, (410) 583-0494, has all the gear and apparel you'll need for a weekend in the woods.

Tucked in among other interesting shops is **Fader's Tobacconist,** 25 Allegheny Avenue, (410) 828-4555, one of the 10 oldest tobacconists in the country. In business since 1891 and in this Towson location for more than 35 years, Fader's carries more than 100 different types of tobacco, including Davidoff White Label Cigars, which are available in only 44 other retail locations across the United States.

The main branch of the **Baltimore County Library** is at the south end of the district.

In Towson Circle you'll find **Trader Joe's,** (410) 296-9851, a unique chain grocery store with great prices and more than 800 grocery items under their own label. **Pier 1 Imports,** (410) 296-4112, offers an interesting array of gift items, furniture, and art work. There is also a **Barnes & Noble** located here (see Book Stores later in this chapter).

Bahama Breeze Restaurant, at 100 East Joppa Road, (410) 821-7090, bridges the space between Towson Circle and the Towson Town Center mall. It features Caribbean-inspired lunch and dinner items and, of course, frozen drinks to wash down all that food. The nearby merchants get a tad testy about diners parking in the shops' spaces, so mind where you put your car. Free parking is available in the mall's parking lot, but not in the lower level of the Towson Circle's lot.

Area parking is on the street at meters, or you can park in two parking lots. The old Hutzler's parking lot is now part of the free parking system for Towson Town Mall. The Towson Commons parking garage costs about $5 for an average stay, but if you're going to the theater or to some of the shops around, that can be reduced if you get your ticket validated.

Northwest

Hampden Shopping District
36th Street, between Falls Road and Chestnut Avenue
www.hampdenmerchants.com
Twenty years ago hardly anybody in Baltimore knew about the little community of Hampden. But it has come of age since then, and the shopping district that runs for 4 blocks along 36th Street between Chestnut Avenue and Falls Road has become a very popular spot. This neighborhood was the backdrop to John Waters' film *Pecker* and its quirky mix of stores and street life has earned it ink in publications ranging from *Travel & Leisure* and the *New York Times* to *Lucky* and *Budget Living*.

Starting on the west end of "The Avenue," as it is known locally, you'll find **Atomic Books,** 1100 West 36th Street, (410) 662-4444, the best place for independent and underground literary finds. Across the street, **Antreasian Art Gallery,** 1111 West 36th Street, (410) 235-4420 is the state's largest privately owned venue for local and regional art.

For furniture, you'll find plenty of used and vintage stores, like **David's,** 914 West 36th Street, (410) 467-8159, or **Millbrook Antiques,** 859 West 36th Street, (410) 235-7655. Design-savvy hipsters will want to check out the latest clothing and accessories at **Shine Collective,** 3554 Roland Avenue, (410) 366-6100.

Cafe Hon, 1002 West 36th Street, (410) 243-1230, was probably the first place that appealed to a larger audience than just the neighborhood. It started out as hardly more than a counter and a coffeepot but has become one of the favored destinations for a taste of down-home cookin' and a good cup

You never know what you'll find for sale in Hampden's quirky little shops.
BALTIMORE AREA CONVENTION AND VISITORS ASSOCIATION

of brew (see the Restaurants chapter for more information). The souvenir shop across the street from the Hon is **Hometown Girl,** (410) 662-4438. It has cards and gifts of the Baltimore variety. You can buy Baltimore Oriole Checkers and Anne Tyler's latest bestseller, a Cafe Hon T-shirt, or the bottled version of Hon's Dill Vinaigrette.

Heading east you'll find **Ma Petite Shoe,** 832 West 36th Street, (410) 235-3442, where extraordinary shoes and indulgent chocolates come together under one roof. There's **Mud and Metal,** 813 West 36th Street, (410) 467-8698, which offers fine crafts from local artists and other "art to live with" items. **Holy Frijoles,** 908 West 36th Street, (410) 235-2326, offers a great Mexican menu. **Gotta Have Bags,** at 846 West 36th Street, (410) 243-5999, has all sorts of handbags, something for every taste and every pocketbook. Hampden has a number of shops that cater to the hungry among us. **New Systems Bakery,** 2400 Chestnut Avenue, (410) 235-8852, has traditional baked goods and an outstanding peach cake in summertime. Look for the **Wine Source** at 3601 Elm Avenue, (410) 467-7777; grab a grocery cart and load up on all kinds of liquid refreshment. Need advice? You've come to the right place. Plenty of knowledgeable people here can direct you to the right bottle of wine or spirits. **Mill Valley Garden Center,** 2800 Sisson Street, (410) 889-6842, offers produce and food products from local farmers, bakers, and producers. The shop is a bit south of the actual Hampden shopping district. Call if you need directions.

The **Golden West Café,** 1105 West 36th Street, (410) 889-8891, offers innovative breakfast, lunch, and dinner items.

Down near Chestnut Avenue you'll find three interesting shops clustered together. **Village Flower Mart,** 3601 Chestnut Avenue, (410) 235-0404; **In Watermelon Sugar,** 3555 Chestnut Avenue, (410) 662-9090; and the second location in Hampden for **The Turnover Shop,** at 3549 Chestnut Avenue, (410) 235-9585 (see the Antiques and Collectibles chapter for more information).

Mount Washington Shopping District
Kelly Avenue on the east to Smith Avenue on the west

Farther out Falls Road past Northern Parkway in the community of Mount Washington is a defined shopping district clustered before, after, over, and under the Kelly Avenue Bridge. When Falls Road narrows as you head north and you see the furniture refinishing shop on your left and the pizza place on your right, you're there. At the light, turn left over the bridge and make an immediate right onto Kelly Avenue once you're on the other side. You'll head right into a large metered parking lot. There are some nice restaurants, bakeries, clothing shops, and other interesting stores and restaurants tucked into four short streets.

Many of the shops have to do with keeping yourself looking good, from a simple haircut to an hour-long body massage such as **Studio 1612,** 1612 Kelly Avenue, (410) 664-3800. Around the corner is **Diana's European Skin Care,** 1501 Sulgrave Avenue, (410) 367-1866; **Europa International Salon,** 5701 Newbury Street, (410) 367-1111; and **Goldilocks Hair Studio,** 5600 Smith Avenue, (410) 664-4330.

Once you've gotten beautiful (or handsome, as the case may be), you can have a great lunch in the atrium room at the **Mount Washington Tavern,** 5700 Newbury Street, (410) 367-6903.

Along Sulgrave Avenue are little shops—one-room, stuffed-with-stuff places that are great to poke around in to find treasures, new and old. **Something Else,** 1611 Sulgrave Avenue, (410) 542-0444, is a mainstay in the community as it has been for almost 40 years, Something Else has imported clothing, jewelry, and bric-a-brac. All the clothing is made of natural fabrics, and the most popular currently is linen. The store boasts Naot Shoes, a line of comfort shoes from Israel; folk art from Mexico, including tin frames and clay sculptures; and other items from Indonesia and India. Also included in the village is **Baltimore Clayworks,** 5707 Smith Avenue,

(410) 578-1919, a nonprofit that promotes ceramics. Baltimore Clayworks is set in an old library building and offers classes as well as items for sale.

When you head out of this Mount Washington shopping district back over Kelly Avenue Bridge to Falls Road, a left turn onto Smith Avenue will take you to the Mt. Washington Grill that has been turned into shops and offices. Shops in the mill include a **Starbucks** coffee shop, **Framin' Place, Whole Foods** natural foods grocery store, and **Amazing Glaze** for you to practice your pottery skills. If all that shopping and pottery leaves your manicure in need of attention, visit **Giovanna Hair Skin Nail Salon**, 6071 Falls Road, (401) 367-3434. If you're not driving, however, and would like to meander through the Mount Washington shops, you can easily get there by Light Rail, which has a stop right on the edge of the shopping district.

The Village of Cross Keys
5100 Falls Road
(410) 323-1000

On the edge of Roland Park, so close to the Jones Falls Expressway you can hear it, is this upscale little mall with a good assortment of independent and chain shops. It's small with just 30 shops, but still worth a look. In addition to fine women's clothing chains, including **Ann Taylor, April Cornell, Chico's,** and **Talbot's,** there are some excellent independent clothing stores. **Ruth Shaw** is the local socialite's stop for designer clothing and Jimmy Choo shoes. **Chezelle** has upscale styles for upsize women. **Pied Piper** has that party dress you were trying to find for your daughter, and all the other adorable outfits she and your son need.

Need a gift? **The Store Ltd.** has Betty Cooke Jewelry, folk art, and plenty of interesting things for a kid or a business associate. **Barston's Childs Play** has toys; **Truffles and Tea** has tea and chocolate. **Williams-Sonoma** has everything for your kitchen. The second level of the center is mostly offices, but the **Elizabeth Red Door Salon** is a luxurious oasis

for relaxation and renewal. A second salon, **Carl Intercoiffure,** is also on the second floor, as is **Donna's Cafe,** a local chain.

Southeast

Canton Shopping District
Eastern Avenue to Conkling Street to the
Waterfront to Chester Street

Canton is the waterfront area south and west of Highlandtown and east of Fells Point. Turn-of-the-twentieth-century, two-and three-story row houses as well as new town houses and condominiums line the streets of Canton. This area is thriving amid the renovation fever that hit the city during the 1990s. Canton is filled with both innovative new housing and upper-income professionals as well as traditional row homes with blue-collar workers whose families have lived here for generations.

The shopping options in Canton seem to only get better with time. What started out as a renovation around O'Donnell Square has spread to redeveloped industrial buildings along the waterfront filled with specialty shops and restaurants.

Three hair salons with trendy and upscale service include **AKA Studios,** 2823 O'Donnell Street, (410) 276-6898, **Geometrics Hair Studio,** 2904 O'Donnell Street, (410) 563-3180, and **Sima's,** 2927 O'Donnell Street, (410) 276-7462. O'Donnell Square, the 2800 and 2900 blocks of O'Donnell Street, offer not only hair salons but also fun eats that should not be missed. Just to name a few, there's **Claddagh's Pub,** 2918 O'Donnell Street, (410) 522-4220, with a great mix of Irish food, Baltimore seafood, and steaks. **Helen's Garden Restaurant,** 2908 O'Donnell Street, (410) 276-2233; and **Nacho Mama's,** 2907 O'Donnell Street, (410) 675-0898, which is a local favorite for Mexican food and margaritas. Check out the Restaurant chapter for more information.

A popular spot to buy unique gift items is **2910 ON THE SQUARE,** 2910 O'Donnell Street, (410) 675-8505. It's worth a visit for American and international crafts, everything from wood to stained glass. It opens late (3:00 p.m.) so it can stay open until 10:00

> ℹ️ Chesapeake Wine Company in Canton's Can Company offers more than just carry-out wine, beer, and liquor; they also have a small tasting bar in the back with a selection of wines and cocktails. Try one of their signature margaritas.

p.m. Sunday hours are the usual 11:00 a.m. to 5:00 p.m.

The Can Company, (410) 558-CANC, a renovated industrial building at 2400 O'Donnell Street, offers the shopper an interesting mix of stores, studios, and restaurants. Inside Chesapeake Wine Company, (410) 522-4556, is the latest in wine and liquor, including one of the best selections of local wine, and at Cloud 9, (410) 534-4200, clothing for men and women is stylish and fun.

Highlandtown Shopping District
East Avenue on the west to Haven Street on the east, along Eastern Avenue and Conkling Street

Highlandtown's business district got a shot in the arm in the spring of 2007 when the city's first new library in 30 years opened here. State of the art, with wireless Internet connectivity, children's library, teens' study area, and even a Spanish-language section for the increasing number of Spanish speakers among us, the library is designed to bring people together here in the heart of Highlandtown at 3601 Eastern Avenue, (410) 396-1580. Around this strikingly modern glass and brick building is the traditional Highlandtown, a working-class neighborhood with all the shops and services the locals can count on and walk to.

What makes Highlandtown a well-used shopping area by the rest of the city is its penchant for formal-wear shops. In the 3000 block of Eastern Avenue, you'll find **Stella's Gifts & Bridals,** 3309 Eastern Avenue, (410) 522-7447, which takes up at least half the block and is jam-packed with dresses, veils, tuxedos, and books that will help you plan

your attire for formal occasions. This is the place you go when you want your shoes dyed to match your gown. At the corner of Highland and Eastern Avenues is **Tuxedo Zone,** (410) 534-1000, which rents and sells anything men would need for a formal event. The Highlandtown Shopping District also has traditional neighborhood stores like the **Walgreen Drug Store** (4000 Eastern Avenue, 410-534-8661). But Highlandtown also offers the unusual, like **D. J. Liquidation** (3825 Bank Street, 410-732-2245), which is a large discount variety store with weekly specials and a large selection of seasonal and holiday items. At 512 South Conklin Street, there's the **Restaurant Supply Store,** (410) 534-4500, with just about any item you can imagine for the restaurant or home kitchen.

Parking for the most part is on the street at meters, but since most of Highlandtown's patrons walk from home, it's usually pretty easy to find a spot. On the other hand, since Eastern Avenue is a main thoroughfare out of the city, it is often clogged with traffic.

UNDER-ROOF MARKETS

Baltimore's markets are our pride and joy. In continuous operation since the late 1700s, they provide a place to buy fresh foods, from garden lettuce to live crabs just off the boat, as well as serve as a central location for many neighborhood residents to meet and greet. The shopping is easy. The people are friendly. The prices are excellent. But what may be the most pleasant aspect of this kind of shopping is being able to control what you get and how much you take home with you.

It's a powerful feeling when the butcher asks you how you would like your fresh piece of meat cut, instead of just offering prepackaged, preweighed, dyed meats. It's wonderful to be able to have one and a half pounds of fresh cottage cheese scooped up for you, count out an odd number of chicken legs, or pick out a succulent rockfish and tell the fishmonger how you would like it filleted.

If you've never shopped in a market . . . if your life has been filled with Piggly Wiggly, Safeway, and Giant . . . indulge yourself by visiting one of the markets that follow.

A contact number has been provided for Lexington Market, but if you need more information about the other markets, call Baltimore Public Markets at (410) 276-9498. The markets listed here, unless otherwise noted, are open 7:00 a.m. to 6:00 p.m. Monday through Thursday and 6:00 a.m. to 6:00 p.m. Friday and Saturday. The Avenue Market opens at 7:00 a.m. Monday through Saturday.

Downtown

Broadway Market
1640-41 Aliceanna Street
Broadway Market is not the oldest market in Baltimore, but it is in the oldest market building, dating from 1785. In fact, there are two buildings to the market, both of which sit in the middle of Broadway in Fells Point, the northern building facing Fleet Street and the southern building facing Aliceanna Street.

The market, which hasn't been as successful as some of the other city markets in spite of its great location, is small and focuses on prepared foods with a few delis, but it also has produce and seafood vendors. Negotiations were going on at press time to sell or lease the north building to a developer who wanted to restore the building to its original two-story design for only one or two tenants. Current shopkeepers in that building would be given space in a newly expanded south building. If the plan proceeds, the new market will open by April 2009.

Cross Street Market
Cross Street between Light and Charles
www.southbaltimore.com/shop/cross.mkt.html
Cross Street Market is in the middle of the Federal Hill Shopping District, just south of the Inner Harbor. It's the neighborhood market for Federal Hill and surrounding South Baltimore as well as visitors to those areas. Cross Street

Market's 27 vendors sell everything from flowers to imported wines and cheeses. You'll also find a candy store, a sushi shop, three bakeries, and a tobacconist. Cross Street is a great place to go for fried chicken or to partake in the bounty of a raw oyster bar. Don't miss out on the fun at Nick's Inner Harbor Seafood. This local hot spot hosts a unique happy hour in Federal Hill. Nick's offers a large selection of seafood, including steamed and raw clams and oysters, steamed shrimp, and crab soup as well as a large selection of beer and wine. The market is open 7:00 a.m. to 7:00 p.m. Monday through Saturday.

Lexington Market
400 West Lexington Street
(410) 685-6169
www.lexingtonmarket.com
Lexington Market opened in 1782 at its present location. Then known as Howard's Hill, it was part of John Eager Howard's estate and donated by him for the purpose of creating a market. By the 1850s, when Baltimore was the second largest city in the United States, more than 50,000 people shopped here on market days.

Today, the market doesn't host quite so many shoppers day to day as it did in 1850, but for 225 years of its existence, it has served Baltimoreans as a central location to find just about anything. Lexington Market takes up 2 square blocks and has more than 120 dealers of both fresh produce and prepared foods. You can buy just-off-the-boat fish and crabs, farm vegetables such as tomatoes and corn, homemade bread, candy, or lunch. There are plenty of places to eat, but favorites include anywhere that offers the traditional Polish hot dog with sauerkraut and mustard.

The tale is told that in 1859, Oliver Wendell Holmes visited the market and afterward named Baltimore "The Gastronomic Capital of the Universe." Suffice it to say that if you know what you want to eat, you will find it at the market.

Lexington Market is open Monday through Saturday 8:30 a.m. to 6:00 p.m. Feel

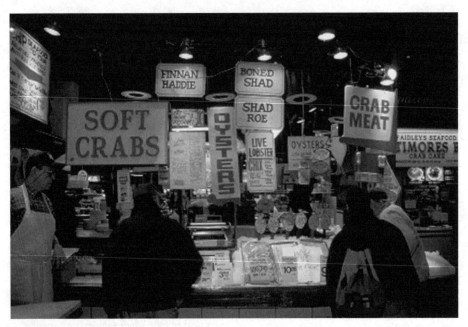

Lexington Market offers everything from crab cakes to fresh coconut to takeout. BALTIMORE AREA CONVENTION AND VISITORS ASSOCIATION

free to take public transportation—both Light Rail and buses have market stops—or drive. There are more than 4,000 parking spaces under roof. Parking is by the hour—$2 for the first hour and $1 for every additional hour.

Outside the market are licensed street vendors. They have clothing, jewelry, balloons, souvenirs, and other items of interest and are part of the old-world aura of shopping at Lexington Market.

Northeast Market
2101 East Monument Street
Northeast Market is near Johns Hopkins Hospital. It houses 40 vendors that offer fresh foods such as fresh chicken and meats, baked goods, and the like, as well as plenty of places to sit and eat. From the extensive salad bar at

i When shopping in one of Baltimore's indoor markets, remember to bring cash. Many of the produce and seafood stands do not accept credit cards.

Something Fresh to Japanese selections at Surf & Wok, you can find pretty much anything your tastes desire. It's open Monday through Saturday 7:00 a.m. to 6:00 p.m.

Northwest

Avenue Market
1701 Pennsylvania Avenue
The Avenue Market opened in 1996 (replacing the 100-year-old Lafayette Market) as a showcase market for the African-American community. Conveniently located next to the Upton subway station, the Avenue Market has 15 vendors offering meats, produce, seafood, and baked goods. The vendors range from Ma-Burt's Soul Kitchen to Community Produce, offering a large selection of delectable fruits and vegetables.

Southwest

Belvedere Square
540 East Belvedere Avenue
Just off the junction of Northern Parkway and

York Road, Belvedere Square has been attracting upscale foodies who come for Atwater's amazing organic soups and sandwiches, Moxley's locally made ice cream, and a variety of fresh produce, seafood, cheeses, and prepared items. The 100,000-square-foot complex, which revitalized a corner after the demise of a local department store, also has clothing and home furnishing shops, a Daedalus Books and Music outlet, as well as several small eateries—some casual, some serious. In summer, the market plays host to a Friday evening concert series. Plenty of neighbors bring a chair, grab something good from the market, and spend the evening listening to local music.

Hollins Market
26 South Arlington Avenue
Hollins Market is near Union Square, where H. L. Mencken lived. He was a regular at the market, as are Union Square neighbors today. Hollins offers 16 vendors of meats, produce, poultry, seafood, and baked goods. There are also three lunch counters and Custom Salads, which is pretty much self-explanatory. It is closed on Sunday and Monday.

FARMERS' MARKETS

In addition to our under-roof markets, the Baltimore area also has some farmers' markets that open at the same place and time every week.

Downtown

Downtown Farmers' Market
Jones Falls Expressway, at Holiday and Saratoga Streets
On Sunday mornings from June until mid-December, the Downtown Farmers' Market opens at 8:00 a.m. under the cover of the Jones Falls Expressway at Holiday and Saratoga Streets, just about at the expressway's end. It is a massive affair, attended by thousands every week. Vendors sell out around noon. Parking is easy, since there's metered parking under the expressway. You can also park on the street.

Northeast

Waverly Farmers' Market
32nd Street Market
32nd and Barclay Streets
www.32ndstreetmarket.org
Every Saturday morning, the metered parking lot at 32nd and Barclay Streets becomes the site of the 32nd Street Market. Hours are 7:00 a.m. to noon or until the goods are gone. About 30 vendors offer tailgate sales of fresh farm produce, homemade baked goods, and other goodies. The French bakery is a frequent stop—its chocolate croissants are the perfect treat to nibble on as you stroll among the booths. Or perhaps you'd prefer a grilled mushroom sandwich, made with fresh mushrooms of your choice. About $10 will buy you a shopping bag full of good food, but keep a few dollars for the street performers. You'll often hear blues riffs on a guitar or the haunting sound of Irish pipes.

Parking is on the street, but it's often crowded. Be prepared to go around the block a few times.

Towson Farmers' Market
Allegheny Avenue, between York Road and Washington Avenue, Towson
(410) 825-1144
Every Thursday from the last Thursday in June through the month of October, Towson blocks off Allegheny Avenue between York Road and Washington Avenue for a farmers' market. Between 11:00 a.m. and 3:00 p.m. you'll find vendors selling luncheon foods as well as more than 30 booths filled with fresh farm produce.

Park at Towson Commons and walk up a block to the market. (See the Old Towson Shopping District previously in this chapter.)

MUSIC

In almost every mall, you'll find places that sell new music. But there are stores around town that offer some special buying opportunities, such as old 45s for sale and places where you can trade as well as buy. Musicians will be interested in the shops we've listed below that offer instruments and sheet music as well as the knowledgeable advice that needs to accompany that kind of stock.

Downtown

An die Musik
409 North Charles Street
(410) 385-2638

Located in the Mount Vernon Shopping District, this store derived its name from a Franz Schubert composition from the early seventeenth century. It figures, then, that An die Musik specializes in classical, opera, jazz, and world music. Every member of the staff is an expert, and they welcome customer queries about obscure recordings.

Flashback
728 South Broadway
(410) 276-5086

Flashback buys, sells, and sometimes trades LPs. You will not find old 45s, and don't bother trucking in your ancient 78s. But if you've got long-playing vinyl—rock, blues, jazz, soul, or reggae—or if you're in the market for the same, then Flashback is your kind of place. Albums start at about $3, and the average price is between $3 and $10. The shop also sells some collectibles, videos, books, posters, and show souvenirs, such as programs. Parking is on the street.

Kentrikon Music Store
4704 Eastern Avenue
(410) 675-4100

Kentrikon means "center" in Greek, and Kentrikon Music Store has certainly been at the center of the Greek community since 1954, handling only Greek music, videos, books, and gifts. The music selections cover modern Greek selections and the pop music for the last 40 years, as well as folk. Parking is on the street.

Reptilian Records and Comics
403 South Broadway
(410) 327-6853
www.reptilianrecords.com

Reptilian was opened in 1989 to fill a void in the city's music offerings—there wasn't any one place to find a broad range of the thrashing sounds that hard rockers crave. Reptilian has since earned a reputation for its broad selection of punk, hardcore, noise, emo, grind, garage, and indie rock. You won't find mainstream label stuff here.

Sound Garden
1616 Thames Street
(410) 563-9011
www.cdjoint.com

Located in the heart of Fells Point, Sound Garden is the best independently owned record store in the city. Sound Garden carries an exhaustive selection of all styles of music, including new and used CDs, cassettes, vinyl, videos, imports, books, magazines, stickers, shirts, and more. There are more than 250,000 CDs, 10,000 imports, and 10 listening areas, where you can hear before your purchase.

Ted's Music Shop
11 East Centre Street
(410) 685-4198

Appropriately across the street from the Peabody Conservatory of Music, Ted's has been the place to go to either rent or buy (or rent-to-buy) new and used instruments for more than 35 years. Ted's has every kind of instrument under the sun, and most of them hang from the rafters. From ancient African drums to electronic keyboards, Ted's pretty much has it all. The shop is closed on Sunday.

Northeast

Music & Arts Center
1940 York Road, Timonium
(410) 453-0811
www.musicarts.com

Just south of Timonium Road is Music & Arts Center, which has or can order almost any piece of sheet music you want. The entire stock is on computer, so the salesperson can tell you whether what you want is on the shelf or not in a matter of moments. The fairly large collection includes classical, jazz, and rock. The store has a large selection of acoustic and electric guitars as well as horns. Instruction is also available.

Record & Tape Traders
736 Dulaney Valley Road, Towson
(410) 337-0002

7551 Ritchie Highway, Glen Burnie
(410) 760-4242

3003 North Charles Street (Midtown)
(410) 662-9610

10435 Reisterstown Road, Reisterstown
(Northwest), (410) 654-0711

1409 Merritt Boulevard, Dundalk
(Southeast), (410) 282-4362

806 Frederick Road, Catonsville
(Southwest), (410) 788-6767
Record & Tape Traders is a large, well-known shop with 10 locations around Baltimore. We've listed a few of the closer locations. The Towson shop is the biggest location with the largest selection, but no matter which Record & Tape Traders you're near, know that its mandate is to buy and sell CDs, tapes, DVDs, and LPs. CDs and tapes come in both new and used varieties. LPs are both new and used and offer selections from all genres. The store prides itself on having the hard-to-find items, including out-of-print CDs and a fair number of imports. Rock music is the biggest focus, but the store also carries jazz, country, Big Band, and music cut by local Baltimore artists, as well as ancillary rock items such as magazines, jewelry, posters, and T-shirts. Some records are priced as low as 50 cents; rarer albums can go as high as $30. New CDs are priced $10 and up, with used CDs priced $5.99 and up.

Northwest

Jazz House West
6037 Liberty Road, Randallstown
(410) 265-6060
Since 1976 Jazz House West has been finding those hard-to-find jazz albums that you're just dying to add to your collection. Names such as Billy Harper, Booker Ervin, and Doug Cam are available at Jazz House, which buys, sells, and trades CDs and vinyl. It has a huge selection of vinyl and one of the best special order sections in the area. Albums sell from 50 cents, with an average price being around $5; CDs range from $7 to $14. In addition to jazz, the shop also sells rhythm-and-blues selections and African-American collectibles. Jazz House is open Thursday and Friday 11:00 a.m. to 7:00 p.m. and Saturday 11:00 a.m. to 5:00 p.m.

Recordmasters
The Rotunda, 711 West 40th Street
(410) 366-1250
When this Baltimorean-owned company began in 1973, it was chock-full of records, both 45s and LPs. As it grew, it became known for having a truly eclectic selection. People came from all over to see if they could find this record or that record among the store's stock. If no one else in town had it, Recordmasters did. When videos became all the rage, it began renting videos, and its video section still carries some of the most esoteric, who-knew-that-was-on-tape kinds of movies as well as the latest hits. Recordmasters was also among the first stores in the area to carry CDs, then DVDs, and now those selections have completely elbowed out vinyl. Alas, Recordmasters has no records, but it is still the place to buy, sell, or trade musical selections of CDs and tapes. There is also a satellite store at the Shops at Kenilworth in Towson.

Shubert Music
518 Reisterstown Road, Pikesville
(410) 653-3196
In 1954 Herbert Froehlich started Shubert Music by offering piano tuning and repair. He still does that. His son, Myron, runs the shop, which carries all kinds of band instruments, guitars, and accessories that can be bought or rented. Shubert also offers lessons. The store's mainstay is sheet music—racks and racks of popular, classical, and jazz selections as well as instructional books. If you're looking

for it, Shubert Music probably has it; if not, Myron will be happy to special-order it and mail it out to you. The store is closed Saturday and Sunday. It is in a little strip shopping center that offers free lot parking, both in front of and behind the store.

Southeast

Alan's Roadhouse Oldies
5200 Ritchie Highway (Highway 2), Brooklyn
(410) 789-3142
www.roadhouseoldies.com
Baltimore loves rock 'n' roll. And Alan Lee, the radio personality who announces the longest-running oldies radio program in Baltimore on WQSR (105.7 FM), may be said to love it more than most. When he's not playing it, he's selling it here at Alan's Roadhouse Oldies. Alan carries music from the '50s, '60s, and '70s on 45s, LPs, cassettes, and CDs. Although he sells both new and used vinyl, a lot of old hits are available newly pressed, which means that Blue Suede Shoes is going to sound just as it did when Elvis cut it. The standard cost of a 45 is $2.98, but rare collector's items may run into the hundreds of dollars. The shop issues a catalog of all the best-selling 45s and CDs Alan handles. If you decide to stop by, call first, as days and hours open vary depending on Alan's schedule.

Southwest

Appalachian Bluegrass Shoppe
643 Frederick Road, Catonsville
(410) 744-1144
www.appalachianbluegrass.com
Appalachian Bluegrass specializes in acoustic instruments and is a great place to buy stringed instruments and have them repaired. The store also has sheet music and instructional tapes and booklets as well as Irish flutes and hand drums. It's closed Sunday.

Bill's Music House, Inc.
743 Frederick Road, Catonsville
(410) 788-8900
www.billsmusic.com
Bill's specializes in school band instruments

that you can rent, lease, or buy, but you can also find drums, guitars, and pianos. It's a large shop jammed with stuff that's new and used. You can also trade in used instruments or get them repaired. Lessons are also offered.

BOOKSTORES

All the bookstores mentioned here mostly sell new books. For antiquarian bookstores, see the Antiques and Collectibles chapter. And don't forget every mall has at least one bookstore to browse through.

Atomic Books
1100 West 36th Street (Northwest)
(410) 662-4444
www.atomicbooks.com
The tagline for this small, independently owned store is, "literary finds for mutated minds." Located on "The Avenue" in Hampden, Atomic has survived the influx of chain megabookstores by serving up a unique selection of literary works. Owners Benn and Rachel supply the city's literati with shelves of hard-to-find indie and micropress books and obscure magazines, as well as a solid selection from mainstream writers. Atomic also carries a small selection of CDs, many produced by local musicians who frequently pop by the store to visit.

Barnes & Noble Booksellers
4300 Montgomery Road,
Ellicott City (Southwest)
(410) 203-9001

8123 Honeygo Boulevard, White Marsh
(Northeast) (410) 933-9670

1 East Joppa Road, Towson (Northeast)
(410) 296-7021

601 East Pratt Street (Downtown)
(410) 385-1709
www.barnesandnoble.com
Barnes & Noble stores stock an impressive

The Book Thing

Perhaps you'll need a book for your return flight home? If you're visiting on a Saturday or Sunday, you might want to stop by The Book Thing, where you can get your books for free. Baltimoreans give their already-read books to The Book Thing and The Book Thing gives them away. You may not get the latest Tom Clancy thriller (or maybe you will), but you can take as many books as you want. The limit is 150,000 books per day per person. The doors are open 9:00 a.m. to 6:00 p.m. at their slightly worn "shop" at 3001 Vineyard Lane, just down the street from the corner of North Calvert Street and East 30th Street. Call (410) 662-5631 or check their Web site at www.bookthing.org for directions. Amazingly enough, there's parking on site.

selection of book titles and provide access to more than one million titles. If a book is not in stock at one of the local stores, the staff can usually get it in a matter of days. Barnes & Noble offers books from more than 50,000 publisher imprints with an emphasis on small, independent publishers and university presses. Barnes & Noble also offers a wonderful children's section with the latest puzzles, games, and educational resources, as well as the classic reading favorites. The newsstand includes more than 250 magazines and newspapers from around the world.

The Book Escape
805 Light Street, Federal Hill
(410) 576-8885
www.thebookescape.com
This tiny bookshop puts a premium on customer service while offering the latest best seller along with used and out-of-print books. They'll also order something if you can't find it on their shelves. There's even a couple of comfy chairs and a hidden courtyard for readers who just can't wait to get home to open their new books.

Borders Books & Music
170 West Ridgely Road, Timonium (Northeast)
(410) 453-0727

6151 Columbia Crossing Circle, Columbia (Southwest) (410) 290-0062
www.borderstores.com
Borders features a vast inventory of books, music, and videos. The selection is second to none, and the friendly atmosphere makes shopping for books even more enjoyable. The store regularly hosts in-store appearances by authors, musicians, and artists. Borders' knowledgeable staff can help you find whatever title you might be looking for. There is also a casual espresso cafe to make the shopping experience even more pleasurable.

The Children's Bookstore
737 Deepdene Road, Roland Park
(410) 532-2000
www.thecbstore.com
Since 1978 this bright and airy shop has been specializing in only the best in children's books. Whether it's a classic by Roald Dahl or the latest Harry Potter, this place has it, along with shelves full of beautifully illustrated storybooks and those related stuffed toys, books on tape and CD, and cards and posters that encourage reading. It's a good place to come if you need a child's gift but have no clue or want something special.

Daedalus Books and Music
5911 York Road, Belvedere Square
(410) 464-2701

9645 Gerwig Lane, Columbia (Southwest)
(410) 309-2730
In northern Baltimore, just off Northern Parkway, and also in Columbia, just off I-95, these warehouse stores hold 10,000 square feet of remaindered books and compact music. Books from Harper Collins, Random House, Simon and Schuster, and children's book publishers send their leftovers here. Readers have their pick of 20,000 fiction and nonfiction books as well as jazz, classical, and world music CDs, all at great discounts. The Baltimore store also has evening speaker and film series and a children's story time on Monday mornings.

Gordon's Booksellers
The Rotunda, 711 West 40th Street (Northwest) (410) 889-2113

The Shops at Kenilworth,
800 Kenilworth Drive,
Towson (Northeast) (410) 296-3500

2139 York Road, Timonium Shopping Center, (Northeast) (410) 308-1900
Gordon's is a locally owned bookstore that thrives on being able to provide the basics. This is no-frills shopping, but you'll always be able to pick up the newest best seller at the Rotunda location, which also has a good-size children's department, featuring everything from a simple counting book to the next in the series of Nancy Drew or Babysitters Club books your preteen is searching for. The other two locations are where Gordon's sells overstocked and out-of-print books at the discounted price of 70 percent off.

Greetings & Readings
118-AA Shawan Road
Hunt Valley Towne Center
Hunt Valley (Northeast)
(410) 771-3022

What was once a small bookstore and card shop over on Loch Raven Boulevard has become a two-level card/book/gift shop and cafe anchoring a corner of the shiny new Hunt Valley Towne Centre. G&R has every best seller in demand, the parlor games you can't get anywhere else, and a wide selection of cards and gifts, wrapping paper, and stationery. When all that shopping is done, celebrate with a cup of coffee at their cafe.

Ivy Bookshop
6060 Falls Road, Mount Washington
(410) 377-2966
The independently-owned and operated Ivy offers new fiction and nonfiction as well as art and cooking books, with a special emphasis on local authors. Customer service is key and the place is popular—it just doubled its floor space in 2007.

THRIFT STORES

One man's trash is another man's treasure it is said, and nowhere is this truth more evident than when you're scavenging for bargains at a thrift shop. Some people in Baltimore never shop anywhere but thrift stores. Their whole wardrobes are built from jackets they bought for $1.00 and jeans they bought for $2.50. Their homes are furnished with excellent finds that jumped out at them from piles of stuff in thrift stores.

Subsequently, we've listed the major thrift stores in the general area and noted their other locations around town. We have provided only a few specifics on each one because essentially a thrift store is a thrift store. At almost every one, you'll find clothing, furniture, bric-a-brac, and items such as cameras, stereos, tennis rackets, and bowling balls. What's in them depends on what treasures someone has donated that month. That is, of course, part of the fun. You can shop there today and go again tomorrow and find all kinds of new stuff.

Goodwill Industries
200 South Broadway (Downtown)
(410) 327-2211

3101 Greenmount Avenue (Northeast)
(410) 467-7505

5644 The Alameda (Northeast)
(410) 323-6638

5405 Loch Raven Boulevard (Northeast)
(410) 323-6634

1700 North Rolling Road, Wood Lawn
(Southwest) (410) 448-9368

11411 Reisterstown Road, Owings Mills
(Northwest) (410) 581-8960
Since 1919, Goodwill Industries has collected used goods and sold them to help put members of the community back to work. In addition to employing the poor and the disabled at its stores, Goodwill funds training programs as well. Items at the stores run the gamut from the totally practical to the gee-I-wish-I-had-this—anything from an English saddle to a humidifier, from skis, bikes, and in-line skates to infant car seats, crutches, and bed frames.

Salvation Army
905 West 36th Street
(410) 243-5916

West Patapsco and Gable Avenues
(Southwest) (410) 644-9750

1748 East Joppa Road (Northeast)
(410) 663-3915

8715 Liberty Road (Northwest)
(410) 655-9399

8001 Jumpers Hole Road (Southwest)
(410) 766-4841
The Salvation Army uses its income to help Baltimore's indigents. In addition to missions, for instance, the Salvation Army funds a drug rehabilitation center. Donations can be pretty much anything, including cars, trucks, boats, and trailers. But mostly what you'll find in SA's thrift stores are secondhand clothes, toys, furniture, and knickknacks.

St. Vincent de Paul
6 North Central Avenue (Downtown)
(410) 276-3277
St. Vincent de Paul Society has only this one location in Baltimore, but it's a busy place. Six days a week the store is open to not only help you find a great bargain to purchase but also to hand out free clothes, furniture, and housewares to people who have been victims of fire, eviction, or some other housing calamity. The Society also helps the poor with their gas and electric payments and uses the money you spend in its store to fund Camp St. Vincent during the summer months.

Value Village
3424 Eastern Avenue (Southeast)
(410) 327-5300

5013 York Road (Northeast)
(410) 433-9090
Value Village is a large thrift store chain that offers household items, toys, and such, but its main focus is clothing. Tons of it. Piles of it. Racks of it. The Eastern Avenue store, in fact, has three full floors of it! If you're looking for a new pair of jeans or a barely used pair of shoes for your two-year-old who's growing fast, this is the place to look.

The Wise Penny
5902 York Road (Northeast)
(410) 435-3244
Right next door to The Senator theater, you'll find The Wise Penny, a thrift shop owned and operated by the Junior League of Baltimore since 1970. All proceeds from the store go to support League projects in Baltimore, including such diverse projects as the Hampden Family Center and Done in a Day, which lends labor to other nonprofits when a project must be done and the organization doesn't have

enough personnel to handle it. Since the shop began, it has been responsible for raising more than $1 million for the Junior League's projects. The Wise Penny operates strictly on the charity of others, including the 250 members of the League who both pledge donations and their time as salespeople.

At The Wise Penny, you'll find clothing, housewares, jewelry, books, records, and small furniture items such as tables and chairs. The shop's best thing is its sales. There's one almost every month that features special items, such as the Treasure and Trinkets sale in February. There's a Baby Sale in September and a Toy Sale in December, but the most exciting events are the biannual clearance sales that begin the first week of February and June and last until the last week of those months, at which time you can fill a bag with anything in the shop for $5.

ANTIQUES AND COLLECTIBLES

There are more than 700 shops across the state of Maryland dedicated to antiques and collectibles, and many of them are in the Baltimore area. Fells Point alone has more than 40 shops. Main Street in Ellicott City, only 10 miles due west of Baltimore's center, is saturated with shops selling antiques, collectibles, and crafts. Cockeysville, north of Towson, is about 20 minutes away and has a considerable number of great finds along the York Road corridor. And Reisterstown, to the city's west, has been an antiques lover's paradise for more than 30 years.

In all these locations there are junk shops, secondhand shops, consignment shops, and furniture shops. Some specialize in vintage clothing; others, vintage jukeboxes. Some shops deal strictly in collectible items, such as Looney Tunes or Coca-Cola memorabilia; others handle primarily arts and crafts collectibles.

Some shops lay out their interiors as if they were a department store window; in others the inventory is stacked pretty high but is easy to maneuver and sift through. Still others require you to search out your treasure by climbing over or digging under piles of merchandise to find what you want. Shops where everything is very neat tend to be more expensive. The busy-but-findable way of setting things out usually offers some bargains without too much effort; and the everything-thrown-in-a-pile kinds of shops can offer great bargains if you can find something you want.

Most shops are wheelchair accessible on their first floors but have no ability to transport wheelchairs between floors, since almost all of the shops, except those in the malls, are in old houses. So if you are an antiquer on wheels, malls are your best bet. Malls also offer such amenities as public bathrooms and coffee bars or restaurants, perks the smaller shops do not. You'll most likely find them nearby but not within the shop itself.

What follows are some of the city and suburban hot spots and the major nearby malls, as well as some specialty shops that you might want to visit while you're in the neighborhood. They are listed first by area (Downtown, Northeast, Northwest, Southeast, Southwest) and then by the neighborhood or town. As with all other chapters in this book, unless designated otherwise assume these shops are in Baltimore. We do not list every shop in these areas but instead provide a kind of walking tour in which some of the shops are highlighted. Each tour begins at the suggested parking area and continues until you come back around to your car. The tour will give you a feel for the types of shops in the area and a general lay of the land.

In some cases you will find only one or two shops listed under an area title. These areas do not constitute meccas, but we didn't want you to miss these special shops. And see our Day Trips chapter for other antiquing destinations.

We've done our best to note when the shops are open. Unless we stipulate otherwise, assume a store is open seven days a week. If your heart is set on visiting a particular store, we suggest you call ahead to make sure it will be open.

If you're an antiquer, a junker, a collector, a lover of old classics or new masterpieces, then Baltimore is the place to be, and this chapter is the one you're looking for. Good hunting!

Baltimore Treasure

Baltimoreans consider Potthast Brothers furniture a local treasure and snap it up when they happen upon it in any of the local antiques stores. The four Potthast brothers founded their furniture shop in 1892 after coming from Germany, where a fifth brother remained and continued to make furniture. The brothers' store was located on North Charles Street until it closed in 1975. With a staff of highly skilled craftsmen, they specialized in reproducing eighteenth-century styles as well as original Potthast designs. They made everything from dressing-table mirrors to side chairs to dining tables. If you're looking for something special from Baltimore, this just might be it (if you can find it).

DOWNTOWN

Antique Row

Antique Row is in the 800 block of North Howard Street, south of Read Street and a few blocks west of the Maryland Historical Society. The Row—the oldest antiques district in the country—has been a factor in antiques collecting for more than 100 years and is still the place to find a wide range of specialty stores offering a variety of items like sterling silver and French furniture. Because these dealers are so well-known in the trade, many of them make their livings selling to other dealers and decorators, but shops are still open to the individual buyer. There are more than 20 dealers on The Row, as well as shops that specialize in ancillary services, such as restoration.

The easiest way to get to Antique Row is by Light Rail, which goes right down the middle of Howard Street. The Row is also just a short cab ride from Inner Harbor hotels. If you drive yourself, we suggest that you park on Park Avenue or Cathedral Street around Read Street or Monument Street and walk the few blocks west. There are plenty of off-Row shops on these streets that are also worth a look.

Beginning our tour at the corner of Read and Howard Streets, the first shop you'll come to is Regency Antiques.

L.A. Herstein and Company
877 North Howard Street
(410) 728-3856
Herstein's sells Tiffany lamps, has lamp parts, and does lamp repairs. It's one of those one-of-a-kind shops: The paint may be peeling on the sign, but it's the place to go if your Tiffany has begun to dim. The shop is open Monday, Friday, and Saturday from 11:00 a.m. to 4:00 p.m.

Connoisseur's Connection
869 North Howard Street,
(410) 383-2624
Connoisseur's considers its antiques specialty to be continental decorative arts of the Empire period. Connoisseur's has supplied period furniture and objets d'art as set pieces for movies made in Baltimore and elsewhere. One of its more down-to-earth attributes is the layaway plan. If you see something you like, just put a down payment on it, and your treasure will be sent to the layaway room to wait in peace and contentment until you can finish paying for it. Open 11:00 a.m. to 5:00 p.m. Monday through Saturday, 12:00 noon to 5:00 p.m. Sunday.

Imperial Half Bushel
831 North Howard Street
You can't miss the gleaming silver stashed inside the glass cases at this tiny shop. Silver's about all they sell. But what amazing

silver! The shop specializes in nineteenth- and twentieth-century European and American silver. You'll find Civil War–era coin silver, Baltimore's own Stieff Rose and Kirk Repousse flatware, tongs and cups, and desk sets all tucked on shelf after shelf. Open Monday through Saturday 10:30 a.m. to 5:00 p.m. August hours by appointment.

Antique Row Stalls
809 North Howard Street
There's 10,000 square feet of paintings, furniture, decorative thing-a-ma-bobs, and other treasures tucked into this converted bank. Multiple dealers display their wares here and there's quite a variety. You'll find Wedgwood, Chinese export porcelain, antique jewelry, and vintage toys and furniture from just about every period. The shop is open every day but Tuesday 11:00 a.m. to 5:00 p.m.

Drusilla's Books
817 North Howard Street
(410) 225-0277
Drusilla has been selling books on The Row since 1981. Her most recent incarnation is in a beautifully renovated, bright, and clean space where she sells a wide range of antique books. Her specialty is children's literature, but she does have a great spectrum of rare and unusual items such as pop-up and series books. If you cannot visit the store, Drusilla's sells online through an e-mail address: drusilla@mindspring.com. The store is open Tuesday through Saturday and by appointment.

Fells Point

Fells Point is a wonderful enclave of more than 40 antiques and specialty shops, five minutes from the Inner Harbor. There are also bookshops, junk shops, and clothing shops that offer everything from handmade and imported clothing to vintage items. The ambience can't be duplicated. Brick sidewalks, cobblestone streets, and railroad and trolley tracks that lead from nowhere to no place combine with breezes off the water and the sound of sea gulls, making for a pleasant journey.

i If you are planning an antiquing trip, remember that each fall the Maryland Antiques Show and the Hunt Valley Antiques Show bring national and international dealers to Baltimore (see Annual Events for more details).

To get to Fells Point from Downtown, take Pratt Street to President Street and turn right. Turn left onto Fleet or Aliceanna Street and head east until you get to Broadway, the heart of Fells Point. Park anywhere you can and walk.

Most of the shops are south of Eastern Avenue and within 3 blocks on either side of Broadway. Although they are scattered throughout the area, they seem to come in clumps—five here, eight there. (For more information about Fells Point, see the Relocation chapter.)

For our tour of Fells Point, park on the east side of Broadway on Fleet Street.

The Antique Man
1806 Fleet Street
(410) 732-0932
With 4,000 square feet jammed with a veritable treasure trove of rare items, this store is a combination antiques store and oddity museum. In one corner you may find good-quality antique furniture and Tiffany lamps, while across the room a two-headed giant mummy holds court with a full-size wooden horse. The Antique Man is open only on weekends and the hours vary, so we suggest you call ahead.

The Bowery of Antiques & Collectibles
1736 Fleet Street
(410) 732-2778
The Bowery is the place to go if you are looking for variety. Owner David Donovan says his store "runs the gamut" with everything from Arts and Crafts furniture to children's toys and trains to Victorian lamps. The Bowery is open seven days a week.

Mystery Loves Company
1730 Fleet Street
(410) 276-6708, (800) 538-0042

This bookstore carries only mysteries. For collectors the shop offers signed first editions of both new and older books as well as other out-of-print editions. It's a small shop with books lining the walls and piled on the floor. It's the kind of place where you will be welcomed with open arms, a friendly smile, and maybe even a cup of tea. It also has specialty gift items that relate to mysteries and will ship them anywhere. The shop is closed on Monday.

Another Period in Time
1708-1710 Fleet Street
(410) 675-4776
www.anotherperiod.com

Another Period in Time has 15 dealers and boasts, "We buy, sell, and ship." Tiffany lamps, silver chalices, a whole set of ruby dinnerware, and lots of unusual bottles met us as we wandered the shop. It also has furniture, old Victrolas, and advertising memorabilia. Another Period in Time is one of the largest shops of its type in Fells Point and the only one we've come across that has a discount area (on the second floor).

J&M Antiques
1706 Fleet Street
(410) 732-5339

J&M is a very small shop that specializes in jewelry—buying it, selling it, trading it, and repairing it. The store also offers rare pieces of Judaica. It is closed on Saturday.

Fells Point Antique Market
617 South Broadway
(410) 675-1726

Fells Point Antique Market is a medium-size co-op with only eight dealers but a lot of unusual and hard-to-find items. One dealer

i If you are planning an antiquing pilgrimage across the state, purchase a good state map and street maps as you go.

has a lot of ancient African items, such as hide drums and ceremonial masks; just down the aisle is a large section that contains mostly mannequins. The most overriding theme, however, was late 1950s/early 1960s furniture. Molded chairs as well as leatherette and wood armless waiting room furniture are in stock along with lamps and ashtrays—the kind that take up half the coffee table and come in the colors of the time, such as soft yellow and turquoise. You may also find stained glass, clothing, and jewelry. The market is closed on Wednesday.

Federal Hill

Federal Hill is a bustling city neighborhood just minutes from the Inner Harbor. On a warm day it is an easy walk from the shops and attractions of the waterfront to the cobblestone streets of Federal Hill. Walk south on Light Street, turn right onto Montgomery Street, and then right onto Charles Street, which serves as the hub of the area. Charles Street is filled with tiny shops, furniture stores, art galleries, and restaurants. Although Federal Hill does not have a concentration of antiques stores, there are several in the neighborhood worth mentioning.

Antique Warehouse at 1300
1300 Jackson Street at Key Highway
(410) 659-0663

A few years ago, 35 antiques dealers took over a 14,000-square-foot warehouse space on Key Highway, just east of the Inner Harbor. And are we glad they did—the dealers offer a one-stop shop, with a full spectrum of antiques, including furniture, glass, silver, and ceramics. There is no parking lot available, so find what you can on the street. The Warehouse is closed on Monday.

Gaines McHale
Harbor East
700 South Caroline Street
(410) 625-1900
www.gainesmchale.com

Baltimore has plenty of wonderful antiques

shops, but none as venerable as Gaines McHale. Always one to be where the action is, the shop moved from its Federal Hill digs to the newest block in town, Harbor East. Perhaps not a mecca for antiques, the neighborhood is nonetheless the up-and-coming place to be. In its huge new showroom, Gaines McHale offers antiques from throughout Europe and fine furniture and accessories, as well as reproduction pieces.

NORTHEAST

Cockeysville, Maryland

Cockeysville, named for the Cockey family, is the area north of Towson and Timonium but south of Hunt Valley. The easiest way to get to Cockeysville from Baltimore City is to take Interstate 83 north toward Timonium and York, Pennsylvania. Get off at Warren Road, then turn left at York Road. The main shopping area is on your left. Look for the small sign on the side of the building that says PARKING with an arrow pointing down.

Hunt Valley Antiques
10844 York Road
(410) 628-6869
This medium-size shop has two major specialties. The first is high-end fine china. There are stacks and stacks of it, both whole sets and odd pieces. If you're looking for a mate to a beautiful bone china cup and saucer your great-grandmother left you, this is where you should begin the search. The second specialty is Potthast furniture. Potthast is a Baltimore furniture maker who from 1892 to the 1950s created handmade reproductions of classic pieces. The owner, Lenis Barney, authenticates all pieces, so you know you're getting the real thing. The shop is closed on Monday.

The Pack Rat
10834 York Road
(410) 683-4812
The Pack Rat is not the junk shop its name implies; in fact, it's just the opposite. The Pack Rat's owners carry, almost exclusively, what

i Painted screens were popular in the 1950s and adorned many windows on Downtown row houses. Renovations displaced some of these screens, and now they are collectible finds at local antiques stores.

they call "traditional furniture," which is formal dining room and bedroom groups. You will find some Potthast pieces. When we were there they were showing a mint-condition formal dining table and chairs by Potthast, circa 1895. Co-owners Ric Davis and Posie Huppman do all of their own refinishing, so just about everything in the shop looks showroom new. The shop specialty is wall mirrors and fireplace equipment—screens, fenders, and tools. The Pack Rat is closed Monday and Tuesday.

Cuomo's Interiors and Antiques
10759 York Road
(410) 628-0422
Across the street from the other Cockeysville antiques dealers, you'll find this shop filled with European and American antique furniture and objets d'art. In business for nearly two decades, the shopkeepers will help customers put together an authentic period room.

Jumpin-Jim's Jukeboxes
10828 York Road
(410) 683-0500, (443) 463-2826
www.sycbp.com/jukebox
In the basement of Brindley and Company's Antiques, you'll find this jukebox outlet, where J. Colt Bloodgood sells new Wurlitzers with bubble lights or antique models that spin 45s. The shopkeeper sells and services Wurlitzers, Seeburgs, and Rock-olas. And if you want one for a party, he can set you up with that, too—including the music. See the man for slot machines and pinball games, too. Since the shop is open whenever Brindley's is open, you can always browse. But if you need to buy, call to be sure Joe will be there.

Brindley & Company Antiques
10828 York Road
(410) 666-7790

Ruth Ann Brindley owns this shop in Cock-eysville, which is an exceptional multidealer enclave. Brindley & Company specializes in more modern collectible pieces, such as 1920s wicker and 1930s bamboo, but also country and Victorian antiques. The shops are closed on Monday and Tuesday.

Tyrie Antique Village
11008-11010 York Road

Tyrie Antique Village is comprised of two shops (one with two buildings) north of the main antiques shopping area of Cockeysville. You'll need to get back in your car and head up York Road past the railroad tracks. The buildings are on your left.

European Delights, (410) 527-1422, needs two buildings to contain all its wares. Fans of the bright florals of Nicholas Mosse ironware from Ireland take note. You'll find it here, along with French antique pottery.

The Corner Cottage, (410) 527-9535, sells primarily early American, cottage and country antiques, and bric-a-brac in a low-ceiling, multiroom building with a history. Ask owner Nancy Moores to tell you about the building. Many of the items in the store, which is closed on Monday and Tuesday, are on consignment.

NEARBY . . .

Valley View Farms
11035 York Road
(410) 527-0700
www.valleyviewfarms.com

i Many smaller antiques stores are run by the owners. If an out-of-town show requires their attendance, or a great estate sale offers good buying opportunities, the owners may close shop for the afternoon or a few days. We highly recommend that you call ahead before visiting to check hours.

North of Tyrie on the right-hand side of York Road is Valley View Farms. A well-frequented roadside produce stand back in the 1950s, Valley View has grown to a giant-size place with tons and tons of flowers and plants, everything you could possibly need for gardening. A major claim to fame, however, is its Christmas Shop. Starting in late September, Valley View's main display room lights up with more than 125 decorated trees. In the International Room, a smaller display area that opens on Labor Day and stays open until January, you can find handblown glass ornaments, nutcrackers, and outstanding manger scenes from Germany, Israel, and other European and Middle Eastern countries.

Timonium, Maryland

If you decide to trek out to Cockeysville, you might want to make a quick stop in Timonium, to visit Clearing House Ltd.

Clearing House Ltd.
200 West Padonia Road
(410) 561-4546

Clearing House Ltd. is a consignment shop, pure and simple, but it has some of the best stuff around. Be warned: It is the devil to find. Take the Padonia Road exit off I-83 North. You'll see the sign on Padonia Road, about 1 block west of York Road. But once you've turned in to where it says it is, there are two things you need to know: It is in the shopping center, but its entrance is at the back of one of the buildings. Clearing House Ltd. is open Tuesday through Sunday and by appointment.

Parkville, Maryland

Parkville, east of Towson, doesn't have the numerous shops of Antique Row or Fells Point, but it does have The Dusty Attic, a must-see for any Coca-Cola enthusiast.

The Dusty Attic
9411 Harford Road
(410) 668-2343

The Dusty Attic handles only Coca-Cola memorabilia. There are Coke trays, Coke ads, Coke bottles, Coke machines, Coke anything you can possibly think of. The Attic is closed on Monday and Tuesday. To get to The Dusty Attic, take Interstate 695 to Harford Road toward Carney. The shop is on your right within a block of the exit, before you get to Joppa Road.

NORTHWEST

Hampden

If you've already read the Shopping chapter, you're familiar with the 36th Street shopping district in Hampden. The shops that follow are north of 36th Street by just a few blocks, almost to 41st Street. If you're on an antiques-and-crafts hunt, you won't want to miss them.

Tomlinson Craft Collection
711 West 40th Street, The Rotunda
(410) 338-1572

118 Shawan Road, Hunt Valley Towne Centre
(443) 578-4130
Once a small framing shop, Tomlinson now features the handiwork of some 140 artisans of glass, sculpture, tinwork, and clothing in two shops. The original shop is housed in The Rotunda, a small mall inside a restored turn-of-the-twentieth-century insurance office building. The second shop is in the new Hunt Valley Towne Centre. Both shops have unique pieces created by talented people from all over the country. Need something unusual? You'll probably find it here.

The Turnover Shop
3855 Roland Avenue
(410) 235-9585
The Turnover Shop has been at this location since 1943. The oldest consignment shop in Maryland, its treasures come mainly from nearby neighborhoods—not only Hampden and Roland Park, but also Homeland, Guilford, Charles Village, Remington, Woodbury, and

Waverly. You'll find exceptional furniture, glassware, sterling silver, jewelry, and china. A second shop is located at 3549 Chestnut Avenue, (410) 366-2988. Both locations have two floors of goodies. The shops are closed on Sunday and Monday.

Reisterstown, Maryland

Settled by German immigrants before the American Revolution, Reisterstown escaped the suburbanization of the 1950s and '60s, perhaps in part because it had already become a haven for antiques shops, and Baltimoreans enjoyed the drive out into the country.

The road to Reisterstown has since become the typical suburban sprawl all the way along. Shopping centers, housing developments, and industrial parks have replaced farms, rolling fields, and cottages by the side of the road. But the original Reisterstown is still an excellent destination for antiquers and seekers of the unique.

Only 35 minutes from Baltimore, it's easy to find by simply heading west from I-695 on Reisterstown Road. If you'd like at least a partially scenic drive, however, you can exit I-695 (or I-83) at Falls Road and turn onto Greenspring Valley Road. Follow it through all its twists and turns through the valley; you'll end up at Reisterstown Road. You'll know you're in Reisterstown proper when modern road signs give way to old-fashioned streetlamps and brick sidewalks. Along this strip are 22 shops. Your best parking strategy is to pick a shop, park in its parking lot, and then walk.

Tina's Antiques
237 Main Street
(410) 833-9337
Tina's main focus is jewelry, including antique, modern, and vintage look. There isn't any nickel-free jewelry, but the choice of earrings is truly staggering. You may also find other small gift items. Tina's is closed Monday.

The Scratching Post
237 Main Street
(410) 833-6369
The Scratching Post, which shares space with Tina's Antiques, handles collectibles that have to do, primarily, with cats, although there are some elephants, giraffes, and bears. The shop also carries dolls and marionettes, some of which are 3 feet tall. The Scratching Post is closed on Monday.

Relics of Olde
237½ Main Street
(410) 833-3667
Relics of Olde is a small furniture shop that doesn't have a large selection but is obviously doing something right since it's been open since 1979. Chests, wicker, and a fair amount of painted country furniture are on display Wednesday through Friday afternoons and Saturday and Sunday, 10:00 a.m. to 5:00 p.m. It's best to call ahead.

The New England Carriage House
218 Main Street
(410) 833-4019
This small shop is filled with unlikely treasures, both antique and reproduction. One of its specialties is country crafts. There are all sorts of gift items here. It's closed on Monday and Tuesday.

Derby Antiques
239 Main Street
(410) 526-6678, (410) 848-4863
Derby has some antique furniture but what it specializes in is pottery. You'll find all kinds of china and stoneware, Flow Blue, Weller, Roseville, and Nippon pieces. Furniture and jewelry round out the inventory. The shop is closed Monday and Tuesday.

Things You Love . . .
234 Main Street
(410) 833-5019
When you first walk in, you'll be sure you're in a medium-sized shop. But after you've looked at the jewelry and gifts in the front rooms, walk through the hallway. In the back and upstairs is a gigantic room filled with furniture and glass—everything from movie posters to sleds. It's open Friday, Saturday, and Sunday only.

SOUTHEAST
Hanover, Maryland
Hanover is mostly known as the location of Fort Meade. Otherwise, it is a rather sleepy place about 25 minutes south of Baltimore. Access is easy from either the Baltimore–Washington Parkway (Highway 295) or Interstate 95.

AAA Antiques Mall
2659 Annapolis Road
(410) 551-4101
www.kaleden.com
AAA Antiques Mall is the largest mall of its type in Maryland, with more than 400 dealers. It is actually housed in an old grocery store building at the end of a strip shopping center. If you're looking for antiques, this is a don't-miss-it destination. Each dealer booth is about 12 by 12 feet, but some of them have taken over three or four areas for their shops. We saw everything from modern McDonald's collectibles to Victorian furniture. There were trains and toys, clothing, glassware, silver flatware, and just too much other stuff to note. It took us two hours just to walk around the whole mall once.

To reach AAA, just take Highway 175 east to Odenton off Highway 295. After about a mile, you're in Hanover and on your right in the shopping center is AAA. It's open every day except Christmas and Easter.

SOUTHWEST
Ellicott City, Maryland
Ellicott City's original town is a showplace. Even if it didn't have one shop, it would be worth seeing. Its old stone and brick buildings are a step back in time, untouched in many ways. However, Ellicott City does have tons of

shops, including three large antiques malls. We've picked out the places that we like best, but there are also plenty of others that are worth your time. Celebrate Maryland, for instance, is all Maryland souvenirs and features crab cakes "packed for traveling." Maryland Wine Cellars stocks bottles of Maryland's finest, and all the things to go with them, such as buckets, corkscrews, and recipe books. There's an oriental rug shop on Main Street, and right down the street from it is The In Store, which has more modern rugs as well as lots of bric-a-brac.

The easiest way is to get to Ellicott City proper is to take the Beltway (I-695) to the Frederick Road exit heading toward Catonsville. Within about 10 minutes, you'll be right in the heart of Ellicott City. Once you go under the railroad bridge, turn left on Maryland Avenue. There are only a few metered parking spaces there, but you can usually find a vacant space. There are also seven other parking lots at various spots around the city. The Maryland Avenue lot is nice, though, because it is so convenient to one of the largest antiques malls in town, Antique Depot.

Antique Depot
3720 Maryland Avenue
(410) 750-2674
Antique Depot lays claim to more than 100 dealers of antiques and collectibles under one roof, and the whole place is cluttered with tons of good stuff. The first floor is wheelchair accessible and has enough room between stalls to get around. You could meander here for hours; every stall has something of value to consider. Stalls with records and comic books round out the offerings.

Discoveries
8055 Main Street
(410) 461-9600
Discoveries is a craft store. There are no antiques here, but there are one-of-a-kind artists dolls, hand-rubbed wooden bowls, handblown glass, and even some wearable

art. There are new artists being showcased all the time, and a Discoveries Insider said that some real bargains can be found here on newly discovered crafts artists. Teenagers love their racks of party dresses in the back.

Caplan's of Ellicott City
8125 Main Street
(410) 750-7678
www.caplans.com
Caplan's is one of the most interesting places you'll ever visit, starting with the antique sign hanging out front that says CAPLAN'S DEPARTMENT STORE. Caplan's has furniture and books and a large corner space filled with nothing but stained-glass windows and doors that have been salvaged from old houses. It specializes in mahogany furniture and estate liquidations. Caplan's also has an auction gallery at 8307 Main Street, just a little ways away in Oella, (410) 750-7676.

Taylor's Antique Mall
8197 Main Street
(410) 465-4444
Taylor's is a very large antiques mall that meanders over the whole corner at the top of the hill where Main Street meets Old Columbia Pike. Taylor's has Fiesta dinnerware reproductions, Autumn Leaf china, mahogany sideboards, and composition dolls among its stock and even more unusual items. (On the first floor, in the right-hand back corner, there are some macabre oddities—a full human skeleton and two shrunken human heads. Steer clear if you or your small children are prone to nightmares.) Taylor's is one of the few shops that asks you to check your bags when you enter the store. So, if you can't bear to part, even for a moment, with the $200 vase you just bought at another shop, consider hitting Taylor's first.

Maxine's Antiques
8116 Main Street
(410) 461-5910
Maxine's is a tiny shop, but if you're looking for jewelry or glassware, it's definitely a place

Unique in antiquing is the town of New Market, just about one and a half hours west of Baltimore and completely given over to antiques shops and shopping. (See the Day Trips chapter for details.)

you should poke into. We particularly liked a pair of pink, milk-glass candlesticks that were shaped like fish and appeared to be 1920s vintage. Maxine's is closed on Monday.

Ellicott's Country Store
8180 Main Street
(410) 465-4482
The building is the real antique here, a four-story duplex, the oldest duplex in the country. Inside you'll find furnishings for your country estate: antiques, art glass, Early American primitives, country furniture built in Ellicott City, and everything a country kitchen needs. The store also offers interior design service.

Country Crafters
8080 Main Street
(410) 203-2618
This country store offers a variety of quaint furniture, floral arrangements, and crafts, but its specialty is American Girl accoutrements. If you are a collector or have a child who loves American Girl, this is the place to find the dolls and the accessories.

The Forget-Me-Not Factory
8044 Main Street
(410) 465-7355
The Forget-Me-Not Factory nourishes the inner child in all of us. It is three floors of fantasy. Fairies, mermaids, unicorns, and all manner of undersea and oversea creatures can be found here. The whole place glitters—literally—but what's best about it is that the shop is filled with practical gifts and collectibles. Items such as wrapping paper and cards, tree decorations, and wall hangings are prevalent. Toys, games, and ethereal clothing are also in evidence. It's crowded with stuff, so little ones

who tend to touch everything could make shopping here a bit precarious. For kids whose fingers are not as prone to do the walking, however, it's a dream come true.

Gramp's Attic Books
8304 Main Street
(410) 750-9235
Need a book? Whether it's a local history, a children's tale, or an old best seller that's been collecting dust, this is the place to look for it. They also specialize in maritime, architecture, and medical books.

Savage, Maryland

Antique Center at Historic Savage Mill
8600 Foundry Street
(410) 880-0918
Savage Mill was built in 1822 as a textile mill. Its beautiful old buildings, which once supported a 30-foot water wheel that powered the mill, have been restored to house a giant mall with more than 225 select dealers.

Savage Mill has all the amenities, such as a cafe and meeting rooms, and excellent wheelchair access. It also has a lot of charm, with exposed brick walls, hand-rubbed wood, and high ceilings. Oddly enough, what it does not have are really exorbitant prices.

The Mill's buildings are named by their original purpose: New Weave, Old Weave, Cotton Shed, Spinning, and Carding. The New Weave building, for example houses **Artcraft,** a shop filled with crafts and furniture and **Hands of Time Clocks and Collectibles.** Antiquers will head to the Old Weave building for the **Antique Center,** where more than 100 dealers offer furniture, jewelry, and accessories. If you want international antiques don't miss the Cotton Shed Building's **International Antique Design Center.**

Other shops sell Finnish gifts, games, and quilting materials. Throughout the complex, you'll find shops filled with unique items, as well as salons and saloons. A French bakery offers a civilized way to take a break from all that shopping. And you may well need the break. Seeing everything here can easily take a whole day (but it sure is fun).

Don't be blinded by the dealers. Take some time to admire the mill itself and the 17 acres that surround it. For instance, the last Bollman Truss semi-suspension bridge in the world still stands at Savage Mill. It was erected across the Little Patuxent River in 1860 by the B&O Railroad.

The best and easiest way to get to Savage Mill from Baltimore is to simply go south on U.S. Highway 1—best because there are small antiques enclaves on your way, such as Historic Elkridge, and easiest because it is a straight shot out of town. No turns, no confusion. You'll see the signs on your right in about 30 minutes, right after you pass under Highway 32. Once you turn, you'll enter the town of Savage. Almost totally restored, it boasts turn-of-the-twentieth-century country homes, some traditional brick duplex mill houses (similar to those you'll find in the mill valleys in Baltimore City), and at the end of Baltimore Street where you turn to go toward the mill, one of the most glorious mansard-roofed Victorian homes you'll ever see.

ATTRACTIONS

As one of the nation's oldest cities, Baltimore has an edge when people are looking for museums, historical sites, and attractions to visit. Many buildings from the area's early roots—churches that played a major role in developing the nation's religious tolerance and houses where famous local and national leaders lived—still exist and are open for tours. Close enough to the Inner Harbor for a quick stop for even the busiest person is the home of Mary Pickersgill, who sewed the famous U.S. flag that Francis Scott Key saw, to his relief, from the harbor after a long night of war in 1814, and the house where writer Edgar Allan Poe lived.

While historical sites abound, newer tourist attractions and cultural offerings in Charm City continue to grow. In 1998 Port Discovery, a museum for children, opened near the Inner Harbor, offering yet another way for children and adults to experience science. Several new museums tell the story of local heroes: The Reginald F. Lewis Museum of Maryland African American History and Culture opened just north of Little Italy, bringing to the public stories of local African Americans from Supreme Court justice Thurgood Marshall to Olympic gymnast Dominique Dawes. Sports Legends Museum opened near Oriole Park at Camden Yards with tales of athletes in every sport from baseball to duckpin bowling. In Fells Point, the Maritime Museum recalls the heroics of sailors and shipbuilders of the city's early days.

Some older museums are new again, too. The Baltimore and Ohio Railroad Museum, seriously damaged during a snowstorm in 2003, has been repaired, though many of the valuable trains still on display also need to be restored. The Catholic Basilica of the Assumption of the Blessed Virgin Mary celebrated its bicentennial with a total restoration that returned the nation's oldest cathedral to the design Benjamin Latrobe original planned.

More than two decades after the Inner Harbor was transformed from an old and tired industrial stretch on the waterfront into a tourist tour de force, the city continues to work hard to meet the interests and needs of an increasingly sophisticated tourist market. This trend is most evident in the Power Plant. Long dark and empty, the old power plant is now a hub of entertainment. It is the home of the Hard Rock Cafe— you can't miss the giant guitar gracing the triple smokestack—as well as the hugely-popular ESPNZone, a Barnes & Noble bookstore, other shops, and offices. Now the Power Plant is a thriving spot for tourists and locals alike. The Power Plant idea went a step further with the nearby development of Power Plant Live!, which houses galleries and restaurants for daytime excursions and bars and clubs that rock late into the evening (see the Nightlife chapter).

Despite these modern developments, the area still boasts some exciting landmarks and attractions from centuries past. Lots of cities have something for everyone; Baltimore has lots of things for everyone. Interests as diverse as visiting the graves of the famous dead or viewing a submarine or diesel engine will be satisfied by the Baltimore area. As we've done in most of the other chapters in this book, we've organized the attractions by geographic location—Downtown, Northeast, Northwest, Southeast, and Southwest. (For insight into the boundaries and general areas that these regions cover, see the How to Use This Book chapter.) In this chapter we've included homes of famous Baltimoreans, spectacular examples of architecture in the area, maritime exhibits, museums, monuments, and memorials.

You'll find green spaces profiled in the Parks and Recreation chapter and art museums and galleries in The Arts chapter. Be sure to glance through the Kidstuff chapter if you have little ones in tow.

Finally, keep in mind that attractions have been known to close down, and exhibits and admission prices can change. If you're planning to visit an attraction that isn't as entrenched along the beaten path as Fort McHenry or the National Aquarium, it's worth a phone call to verify it's still open and how much it costs to visit. Note also that if no city is listed for a site, you can assume it's inside Baltimore's city limits. Sites outside the city have the town name included with the street address.

DOWNTOWN

Babe Ruth Birthplace and Museum
216 Emory Street
(410) 727-1539
www.baberuthmuseum.com
Although the Sultan of Swat made his name as a New York Yankee (hiss!), Babe Ruth was born in Baltimore on February 6, 1895. A museum now resides in the house where Ruth was born at 216 Emory Street. The house almost came under the wrecking ball in 1968 until the mayor and the Greater Baltimore Council rallied to save the historic site. Now Ruth's home is a shrine to baseball's greatest legend.

Artifacts and photographs tell the story of a phenomenal life. There are also exhibits pertaining to both the Baltimore Colts and the Baltimore Orioles. The museum celebrates Ruth's birthday each year on February 6 with free admission from 11:00 a.m. to 1:00 p.m. and a champagne toast and cake. It's open Tuesday through Sunday 10:00 a.m. to 5:00 p.m., November through March and daily 10:00 a.m. to 6:00 p.m. April through October, with hours extended to 7:30 p.m. when the Orioles have a home game. Admission is $6 for adults, $4 for seniors, $3 for children age 5 through 16, and free for those younger than age 5.

Baltimore City Fire Museum
414 North Gay Street
(410) 727-2414
This 117-foot tower was built in 1853 by the Independent Fire Company so volunteers could keep watch over the city. The building, inspired by Giotto's Campanile (Bell Tower) in Florence, Italy, was an operating firehouse for Engine Company No. 6 for more than a century. Today the museum offers a look back at early firefighting in cities as well as the Great Fire of 1904, which claimed no lives but destroyed about 70 blocks of Baltimore's central business district. The museum exhibits five pieces used to fight the 1904 fire, as well as film shot by Thomas Edison during the blaze. A new Acoustiguide tour of the museum is available. Free tours are offered on Sunday from 1:00 to 4:00 p.m., Thursday from 9:00 a.m. to 1:00 p.m., and Friday from 7:00 to 9:00 p.m. or by appointment.

Baltimore Maritime Museum
Piers 3 and 5 in the Inner Harbor
(410) 396-3453
www.baltomaritimemuseum.org
Experience history on the water on three historical ships that depict the story of American naval power from 1930 to 1986. Tour the bridge of a 337-foot-long U.S. Coast Guard cutter *Roger B. Taney* (WHEC-37), named after the Marylander who was the chief justice of the United States. It's the last warship still afloat that survived the attack on Pearl Harbor in 1941. It continued its work in the Korean and Vietnam Wars. In the drug war it seized a record 180 tons of marijuana. Pass through the narrow and submergible corridors of the U.S.S. *Torsk*, a Tench Class submarine that sank the last Japanese combatant ships of World War II, and see what it's like to work on the lightship *Chesapeake*, a 1930s floating lighthouse. Hands-on exhibits and tours offer a firsthand look at these historic seafaring vessels. The museum is open from 10:00 a.m. to 5:00 p.m. (6:30 p.m. on Friday and Saturday); winter hours are Friday to Sunday from 10:30 a.m. to 5:00 p.m. The ticket booth closes a half

Harbor Pass

One way to see the Inner Harbor's highlights is to get a Harbor Pass. For one price, you can visit the National Aquarium in Baltimore, the Maryland Science Center, Port Discovery Children's Museum, and the Top of the World observation deck plus get a day of travel on Ed Kane's Water Taxi. Now this pass doesn't include the dolphin show at the aquarium or the Imax theatre at the Science Center, but it does include everything else, as well as discounts for Orioles' tickets, other museums, and harbor cruises.

Tickets are $49 for adults and $35 for children age 3 through 12. Buy them at the visitor center at the Inner Harbor or online at www.baltimore.org. Call (877) BALTIMORE for information.

hour earlier than the ships. Admission is $8 for adults, $6 for seniors, $4 for children, and free to children younger than age 6.

Baltimore Museum of Industry
1415 Key Highway
(410) 727-4808
www.thebmi.org

Located in an 1865 oyster cannery on the west side of Baltimore's Inner Harbor, this museum allows visitors to experience the industries that made the city one of the busiest ports in the nation. Learn about the long workdays at a belt-driven machine shop, a garment loft, a print shop, and aboard the historic 1906 steam tugboat the *S.T. Baltimore*. The museum is open Monday through Saturday 10:00 a.m. to 4:00 p.m. Admission is $10 for adults and $6 for those age 5 through 18 and senior citizens.

Baltimore Public Works Museum
751 Eastern Avenue
(410) 396-5565
www.baltimorepublicworksmuseum.org

Below the city streets lies a maze of pipes and drains moving our water and waste. Opened in 1982 in the historic Eastern Avenue Pumping Station at the east end of the Inner Harbor, this one-of-a-kind museum features the history of public works and the development of urban infrastructure. While it is a museum,

it remains a working pumping station, with 30 million gallons of wastewater passing through here every day. The highlight of the museum is the outdoor Streetscape, a model where guests can walk through the maze of pipes and drains that exist belowground. Kids love the changing exhibits, with names like "What's Beneath the Streets?" and "The Rotten Truth About Garbage." There is also a computer room where games bring city works to life. The gift shop, though tiny, has some interesting items, all recycled. The museum is open Tuesday through Sunday 10:00 a.m. to 4:00 p.m. Admission is $3 for adults and $2.50 for seniors and children age 6 through 17.

Baltimore Streetcar Museum
1901 Falls Road
(410) 547-0264
www.baltimorestreetcar.org

Although there are few traces of them left, streetcars played a major role in the city's transportation history. This museum, founded in 1966, traces the 104-year history, starting with the first horsecars in East Baltimore in 1859 through to the end of the streetcar era in 1963. Feel what it was like to ride a streetcar during a 1.5-mile round-trip ride aboard one of the restored streetcars. The museum offers operating layouts, displays, and a video on local streetcar history. It's open from noon to 5:00 p.m. Sunday year-round and Saturday and Sunday from June to October. Admission is $6 for adults and $3 for children age 4 through 11 and senior citizens, with a family maximum of $24.

Baltimore Tattoo Museum
1534 Eastern Avenue
(410) 522-5800
www.baltotat.com

Tattoos may be back in favor with the fashionistas, but the art of body ink never went out of style in Baltimore. Both a full-service tattoo and piercing shop and a museum of classic tattoo art, this is the place to go for a lasting souvenir of your trip to Baltimore. Open noon to 8:00 p.m. Sunday through Thursday and noon to 9:00 p.m. Friday and Saturday.

The Basilica of the Assumption
Cathedral and Mulberry Streets
(410) 727-3565
www.baltimorebasilica.org

The first metropolitan cathedral in the United States has been the mother church for Baltimore's Roman Catholic population since 1806. Designed by Benjamin Henry Latrobe, designer of the Capitol in Washington, the cathedral features a grand organ dating from 1821 and a high altar from 1822. The entire cathedral underwent a complete restoration that was completed in late 2006. The stained-glass windows were removed; the dark colors were replaced with cream, yellow, and rose. Galleries that were reserved for cloistered nuns and slaves were uncovered. Memorials to two of the cathedral's most beloved and famous visitors—Pope John Paul II and Mother Teresa of Calcutta—were added, as was a small museum, gift shop, and new access to the undercroft. Across the street from the Enoch Pratt Free Library main branch, this example of neoclassical architecture also holds the remains of Bishop John Carroll, America's first Catholic bishop, who placed the cornerstone. Guided tours are given on Sundays at noon and by appointment. The basilica is open daily 8:30 a.m. to

4:30 p.m. Tours are offered at 9:00 and 11:00 a.m. and 1:00 p.m. Monday through Saturday and on Sunday around noon, after the 10:45 a.m. Mass. The gift shop is open Monday through Saturday 9:00 a.m. to 4:00 p.m. and Sunday 11:00 a.m. to 4:00 p.m.

Brown Memorial Park Avenue Presbyterian Church
1316 Park Avenue
(410) 523-1542
www.brownmemorialparkavenue.org

Baltimore has many fine churches with stunning architecture and distinctive Louis Tiffany and John LaFarge stained-glass windows, but Brown Memorial may very well house one of the largest collections of Tiffany windows in their original setting anywhere. The 11 Tiffany windows circle a Gothic Revival interior with a magnificent vaulted dome that was recently painted a rich blue during a major restoration of the church. The two Tiffany windows in the transept are among the largest and finest stained-glass windows to ever come out of the master's studio in New York. Call for hours.

Carroll Museums
800 East Lombard Street
(410) 605-2964
www.carrollmuseums.org

Two historic properties only a block apart make up this attraction. The Carroll Mansion was the home of Charles Carroll, the last surviving signer of the Declaration of Independence. (He's the man inaccurately portrayed as having passed on a secret to Nicolas Cage's family in *National Treasure*.) The mansion was closed for several years while undergoing restoration, but several rooms are now open. A first-floor gallery space has changing exhibits of local artists' work. Gallery openings are announced on the Web site. Admission to these exhibits is free. Also free is the Jonestown Welcome Center for visitors on the Heritage Walk through Jonestown, the surrounding neighborhood. Historic exhibits are on display here, and the space also offers visi-

When The Basilica of the Assumption renovated its back section in the mid-20th century, architects could not find the same Italian stone used in the original 1806 structure. If you look closely, you will see that this section of the church is actually composed of formstone, a concrete mixture designed to mimic the look of the original stone.

tors a place to rest and buy a bottle of water. Upstairs the tour of the mansion begins, telling the story of the home's first owner as well as the history of the house when it was the German Working Men's Club, a tenement for Russian tailors, and a recreation center for Little Italy—complete with a basketball court inside the mansion. Visitors can see four rooms on the second floor and the bedroom where Charles Carroll died at age 95 in 1832 on the third floor.

A short walk down Front Street takes you to the Phoenix Shot Tower, an 1828 tower built to produce "drop" shot; molten lead was poured through colanders at the top of the shaft, which then fell down the column and became perfectly round before it fell into vats of water to cool. This 215-foot structure was the tallest building in the United States until 1846. Visitors learn the story of the tower through a simple but interesting light and sound show. It's worth a look whether you've lived in Baltimore all your life or are visiting for the first time. Be warned: It's not air-conditioned so it can get quite warm in summer.

The Carroll Mansion is open year-round but the shot tower is open only April through October. Opening hours are Wednesday through Sunday, noon to 4:00 p.m. or by appointment. All tours begin at the mansion. Admission to the mansion is $5 for adults and $4 for students and seniors. A visit to the shot tower costs $1. A limited number of parking permits are available at the museum for free parking on the street beside the mansion. Additional metered parking is also available.

The Dr. Samuel D. Harris National Museum of Dentistry
31 South Greene Street
(410) 706-0600
www.dentalmuseum.umaryland.edu

Get ready for a brush with the world's first dental school, which opened on the campus of the University of Maryland at Baltimore in 1839. The museum building, which opened in 1904, houses collections of artifacts and educational exhibits dealing with the history and lore of teeth and dentistry.

The museum offers a look at the evolution of the toothbrush, temporary offices for a traveling dentist, and an interactive exhibition, "32 Terrific Teeth," featuring George Washington's dentures and a tooth jukebox. The museum is open Wednesday through Saturday 10:00 a.m. to 4:00 p.m. and Sunday 1:00 to 4:00 p.m. Admission is $4.50 for adults, $2.50 for children age 7 through 18, and free for children age 6 and younger.

Enoch Pratt Free Library
400 Cathedral Street
(410) 396-5430
www.prattlibrary.org

Since 1886 this branch has served as the central library for "The City That Reads," as former Mayor Kurt Schmoke once dubbed Baltimore. Among its more than two million volumes are extensive collections of writers Edgar Allan Poe and H. L. Mencken and a library of lyrics and music sheets for more than 100,000 songs. The library's benefactor, Enoch Pratt, set out to educate the common man by establishing this neighborhood library system, which has served Baltimoreans for more than 100 years. All the libraries in Maryland benefit from Pratt's gift, as it lends out its extensive collection to county library systems when requested. The library is open Monday through Wednesday 10:00 a.m. to 8:00 p.m., Thursday 10:00 a.m. to 5:30 p.m., Saturday 10:00 a.m. to 5:00 p.m., and Sunday 1:00 to 5:00 p.m. Admission is free.

Eubie Blake National Jazz Institute and Cultural Center
847 North Howard Street
(410) 225-3130
www.eubieblake.org

Honoring Eubie Blake (1883–1983), the famous ragtime piano player and musical theater composer of Shuffle Along and songs "I'm Just Wild About Harry" and "Memories of You," the center's museum educates and explains the legacy of jazz greats from Baltimore, including Cab Calloway, Billie Holiday, Chick Webb, and Avon Long. Monthly exhibits in the gallery highlight renowned and aspiring artists. The museum is open Tuesday, Thursday and Friday 10:30 a.m. to 5:30 p.m. and Saturday 10:00 a.m. to 2:30 p.m. Admission is $2 for adults and $1 for age 6 through 18.

The Flag House and Star-Spangled Banner Museum
844 East Pratt Street
(410) 837-1793
www.flaghouse.org

Mary Pickersgill sewed by hand the 30-foot-by-42-foot flag that flew over Fort McHenry during the British bombardment in 1814. Built in 1793, this house was her home during her adult years. The adjacent museum commemorates the War of 1812 and features an audio-visual program about Pickersgill's life and her role in the war. Living-history programs are offered here on Saturdays. The house is open Tuesday through Saturday 10:00 a.m. to 4:00 p.m. Admission is $7 for adults, $6 for seniors, and $5 for students.

George Peabody Library
17 East Mount Vernon Place
(410) 659-8179
www.library.jhu.edu/collections

George Peabody was a benefactor to Johns Hopkins University and is the namesake of Baltimore's Peabody Conservatory of Music. In this building owned by Johns Hopkins University are about 300,000 volumes, mostly covering the period from the sixteenth century to the early twentieth century. You'll find no books on music here; subjects include archaeology, British art and architecture, British and American history, science, and geography. The library is open to the public for reference only—none of the books may be checked out.

The building is famous for its interior architecture, including five stories of ornamental cast-iron balconies. Baltimore is the backdrop for many Hollywood films, and this library is a popular setting in several major films. Its gracious interior and exterior recently underwent a major renovation. The library is open to researchers and readers Tuesday through Friday 9:00 a.m. to 5:00 pm. and Saturday 9:00 a.m. to 1:00 p.m. Visitors who just want to take a peek at this magnificent room may stop by Tuesday through Saturday 10:00 to 10:15 a.m. or Tuesday through Friday 3:00 to 3:15 p.m. No admission is charged.

Geppi's Entertainment Museum
Camden Station
301 West Camden Street
(410) 625-7060
www.geppismuseum.com

On the second floor of the old Camden train station, local entrepreneur Steve Geppi has installed a portion of his amazing collection of comic books, animation cels, movie posters, and antique toys, arranging them by era. Audio commentary introduces visitors to each room. Interactive screens let comic book fans leaf through some of the classics or listen to music and radio programming from the World War II era. Perhaps what makes this a must-see is the presentation of items we remember from our own childhoods. The museum made an effort to include all kinds of items—cereal boxes, decoder rings, cowboy hats, Star Trek board games—that will trigger a memory from the past. Of course, many of these items are older than most of us: a 1568 broadsheet from Germany, comics of the 1930s, newspaper comic strips of "Yellow Kid" and "Buster Brown." Tickets are $10 for adults, $9 for seniors, and $7 for children age

5 through 18. Combination tickets with Sports Legends are available for $18 for adults, $15 for seniors and $11.50 for students. The museum is open daily 10:00 a.m. to 6:00 p.m. April through October and Tuesday through Sunday 10:00 a.m. to 5:00 p.m. the rest of the year. It's wheelchair accessible and parking is available on-site.

The Great Blacks in Wax Museum
1601-3 East North Avenue
(410) 563-3404
www.greatblacksinwax.org
The first and only museum of its kind, The Great Blacks in Wax Museum opened in 1983 to pay tribute to African Americans by exhibiting more than 100 lifelike statues in one place. You'll be standing next to Dr. Martin Luther King Jr., Supreme Court Justice Thurgood Marshall, Baltimore neurosurgeon Dr. Ben Carson, known for his lifesaving surgeries on infants at Johns Hopkins Hospital, and Kweisi Mfume, a former Baltimore congressman who took over the helm of the National Association for the Advancement of Colored People (NAACP). A model slave ship offers an in-depth look at the 400-year history of the slave trade, while another gives a picture of black youths' contributions to the civil rights movement. Don't miss the gift shop, where you can pick up everything from postcards to posters and tote bags.

Hours from January 15 through October 14 are 9:00 a.m. to 6:00 p.m. Tuesday through Saturday and noon to 6:00 p.m. Sunday. Hours from October 15 through January 14 are Tuesday through Saturday 9:00 a.m. to 5:00 p.m. and Sunday noon to 5:00 p.m. Admission is $9 for adults, $8 for college students and senior citizens, $8 for kids age 12 through 17, and $6 for children age 2 through 11.

Greenmount Cemetery
1501 Greenmount Avenue
(410) 539-0641
Here lie many of Baltimore's greats, including Civil War generals, poet Sidney Lanier, and philanthropists Johns Hopkins, Enoch Pratt, Moses Sheppard, and William and Henry Walters. Napoleon's sister-in-law, Betsy Patterson Bonaparte, and the spymaster of the CIA, Allen W. Dulles, also share the cemetery with the infamous John Wilkes Booth. The cemetery is free to visitors and open Monday through Saturday from 9:00 a.m. to 3:45 p.m. for the grounds. Visitors can get a list and map of the seventy-three most visited graves from the gate office, which has the same hours as the cemetery, except Saturdays, when it closes at 11:45 a.m.

Holocaust Memorial
Corner of Water, Gay, and Lombard Streets
(410) 752-2630
Near the Inner Harbor, this outdoor memorial and sculpture center is designed to remind visitors of the six million Jews murdered by the Nazis in Europe from 1933 to 1945. The memorial is open 24 hours a day.

Jewish Museum of Maryland
15 Lloyd Street
(410) 732-6400
www.jhsm.org
The largest Jewish history museum in the United States was formed in 1960 to preserve the Lloyd Street Synagogue, built in 1845, making it the third oldest in the country. The B'nai Israel Synagogue, built in 1876, has also been restored by the museum and now houses exhibitions, a library, archives, and collections about regional Jewish history as well as adult and children's educational programs and events. The museum is open Tuesday through Thursday and Sunday from noon to 4:00 p.m. Tours run at 1:00 and 2:30 p.m. Admission is $8 for adults, $4 for students, and $3 for children younger than age 12.

National and local figures from sports, politics, and medicine are featured in the Great Blacks in Wax Museum. BALTIMORE AREA CONVENTION AND VISITORS ASSOCIATION

Lacrosse Museum and National Hall of Fame
113 West University Parkway
(410) 235-6882
www.uslacrosse.org

If you love lacrosse, or if you know someone who loves lacrosse, stop here for a bit of history and a celebration of those who have made it the exciting sport it is. Sitting on the edge of the Johns Hopkins University campus, the museum has artifacts from the game as it is played now by both men and women and from the way it was played in the past. (Equipment sure has changed over the years.) The museum is open June through January Monday through Friday 10:00 a.m. to 3:00 p.m. From February through May, it is open Tuesday through Saturday 10:00 a.m. to 3 p.m. Admission is $3 for age 16 and older and $2 for age 5 through 15.

Lovely Lane United Methodist Church
2200 St. Paul Street
(410) 889-1512
www.lovelylane.net

This lovely old church, newly restored in recent years, was designed by Stanford White in 1884 as a centennial monument to the founding of the Methodist Episcopal Church. The original Lovely Lane church on Redwood Street was the site where the denomination was established in 1784. "The Mother Church of American Methodism" is open to visitors Monday through Friday 9:00 a.m. to 3:00 p.m. Tours are offered after Sunday worship services. From Labor Day through July, tours begin around noon after the 11:00 a.m. service. In August, since the church service begins at 10:00 a.m., the tour begins at 11:00 a.m. Call the church at (410) 889-1512 to confirm times. On the ground floor of the church is the American Methodist Historical Society Museum and museum shop. Call the museum for information at (410) 889-4458.

Maryland Historical Society Museum
201 West Monument Street
(410) 685-3750
www.mdhs.org

The original draft of "The Star-Spangled Banner," the world's largest collection of paintings by Charles Wilson Peale and his family, and the nation's largest collection of nineteenth-century American silver are among the attractions in this independent museum and library of Maryland history. There's also a great collection of decorative arts and galleries with image depicting the Civil War and War of 1812. Museum hours are Wednesday through Sunday from 10:00 a.m. to 5:00 p.m. The H. Furlong Baldwin Library hours are Wednesday through Saturday from 10:00 a.m. to 4:30 p.m. Admission is free to members, $8 for adults, $6 for seniors, students with valid ID, and children age 13 through 17, and $4 for children age 3 through 12. Admission to the library is $6 for adults and $4 for students with ID. Parking is available in the Monument Street lot.

Maryland Science Center and IMAX Theater
601 Light Street
(410) 685-5225
www.mdsci.org

The world of science comes alive with interactive exhibits and live demonstrations explaining light, mechanics, and sound. In addition to the hundreds of hands-on exhibits about science, the center houses DinoQuest, a room filled with life-size recreations of the giant lizards that once roamed the earth; the Davis Planetarium, which mixes stargazing with history and story-telling; and an IMAX movie theater that features a five-story-high screen that shows films ranging from the just-plain-fun *Happy Feet* to the awe-inspiring *Space Station 3D*.

For kids, this is a must. Everything is interactive, meaning they can be touching things that other museums and science centers put behind glass. The result is happier, better educated kids (and adults who want to be kids again). It's not uncommon for people to leave saying, "I wish they had this when I was a kid!" Exhibits on the Human Body have been designed with kids in mind: gross is cool here as well as educational. Dig for bones after staring up at the Giganotosaurus. Check out all the interactive displays that help us understand our place in the world and in space with image from the Hubble Space Telescope and the National Oceanic and Atmospheric Administration. Little ones who might grow bored with exhibits designed for older children have their own Kid's Room where they can play with blocks, crawl around the Room to Grow area, or explore a Baltimore streetscape.

The Maryland Science Center is open fall through spring Tuesday through Thursday 10:00 a.m. to 5:00 p.m., Friday 10:00 a.m. to 8:00 p.m., Saturday 10:00 a.m. to 6:00 p.m., and Sunday 10:00 a.m. to 5:00 p.m. From Memorial Day weekend through Labor Day, hours are Sunday through Thursday 10:00 a.m. to 6:00 p.m. and Friday and Saturday 10:00 a.m. to 8:00 p.m. The IMAX Theater also has evening shows, and the observatory opens afterhours on Friday nights for stargazing. Admission prices vary, depending on what you want to see. For the museum only admission is $14.50 for adults, $13.50 for seniors, and $10 for children 3 through 12. Adding an IMAX film costs an extra $4 for all ages. Special exhibits, such as recent shows on the Titanic and "Grossology," have an additional charge. Evening IMAX presentations are $8.

The Mother Seton House
600 North Paca Street
(410) 523-3443
www.mothersetonhouse.org

Home of America's first native saint, the house is adjacent to the Old St. Mary's Seminary Chapel, where Elizabeth Ann Seton took her first religious vows in March 1809. Born in New York City in 1774, Mother Seton came to Baltimore in 1808. She had been a devout

Episcopalian with five children when she was widowed at the age of 28. She turned to Catholicism and later opened an elementary school at the house—the first boarding school for Catholic girls—that is regarded as the basis for the nation's parochial school system. In 1809 she founded the Sisters of Charity, the first U.S. religious society. She died in 1821 and was canonized a saint in 1975.

The house and chapel are open on Saturday and Sunday from 1:00 to 3:00 p.m. and by appointment. The house is closed on Easter, Christmas, and New Year's Days. No admission is charged.

National Aquarium in Baltimore
Pier 3/501 East Pratt Street
(410) 576-3800
www.aqua.org

Sharks, dolphins, puffins, stingrays, poisonous dart frogs, piranhas, electric eels, and reef fish are just some of the thousands of marine creatures awaiting you here. The four corners of the globe are represented in Baltimore's Inner Harbor attraction—the frosty Icelandic coast, a misty rain forest, a coral reef, and an ocean. The aquarium has more than 14,000 animals and a dolphin presentation. There's lots to see and do as you wander through the many exhibits. Visitors can't miss the two most prominent architectural features: the glass pyramid atop the aquarium and the giant glass cube at the front. Though the fish tanks that fill the building are fascinating, these two sections house the aquarium's best exhibits, the Rain Forest and Animal Planet Australia: Wild Extremes. The Amazon Rain Forest exhibit is home to a flock of colorful birds, iguanas, and sloths. The view of the Inner Harbor is well worth seeing, too. The Australia exhibit has a short path, so take your time to be sure to see all the inhabitants here. A lot is packed into this glass cube. Of course, dolphin fans make a beeline for the Marine Mammal Pavilion behind the aquarium's main building. Elsewhere in the aquarium are the lovable puffins, the fierce-looking sharks, and a ring tank filled with jewel-tone tropical fish. Perhaps you'll be visiting when the scuba divers feed the fish; that's always fun to see. Tickets are $21.95 for adults, $12.95 for children age 3 through 11 and $20.95 for seniors. The dolphin show and new 4-D Immersion Theatre cost an extra couple of bucks. Tickets are available online at www.aqua.org and at www.ticketmaster.com, but be aware there are "convenience" fees. Go to the aquarium early and buy your tickets. You'll be given an entry time and can visit another attraction until your time comes to visit the aquarium. Early in the day and later in the afternoon, crowds are smaller. Friday evenings, when the aquarium is open later, is a good time to avoid crowds, too. If you are bringing children, remember that you will have to check your stroller. The aquarium provides child carriers, which give the children a better view. Several eateries and gift shops are available in the aquarium. The food's fine but you might prefer the wide range of foods available at the Inner Harbor or in the Power Plant complex. The gift shops, however, have some terrific souvenirs. Hours are generally 9:00 a.m. to 5:00 p.m. daily with extended hours on Friday and weekends. Extended hours vary by season, so it would be best to call or check the Web site for details. The staff recommends you beat the crowds by visiting on weekdays after 3:00 p.m. On weekends, arrive between 10:00 and 11:00 a.m. to stay ahead of the crowds. Be prepared for the new security measures in place; all bags are subject to search upon entry. The building closes one-and-a-half hours after the last entry time so latecomers still have time to enjoy the sights.

Nine North Front Street
9 North Front Street
(410) 837-5424

In Baltimore's Shot Tower Park, this three-story brick house is the only surviving member of a group of homes built for merchants, artisans, and gentlemen in the 1790s. Thorowgood Smith lived in the house when

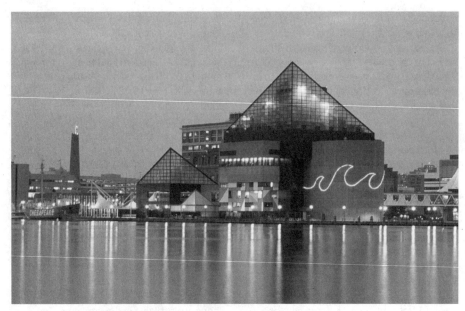

The National Aquarium at dusk. GEORGE GRALL, NATIONAL AQUARIUM IN BALTIMORE

he became the second mayor of Baltimore. The Women's Civic League, which rescued the home from demolition and restored it, now keeps its headquarters in the house, which features a colonial kitchen and an art gallery. The house is open Tuesday through Friday from 9:30 a.m. to 2:00 p.m. and by appointment Saturday and Sunday. Admission is free. Parking is available on site.

Old Otterbein United Methodist Church
112 West Conway Street
(410) 685-4703
In a city with lots of century-old churches, Baltimore's oldest surviving church is the home to exhibits showing the role in founding

United Brethren in Christ, the first all-new American religious denomination. It is also the last standing church in the city where Bishop Francis Asbury preached. The church is open Saturdays April through October from 10:00 a.m. to 4:00 p.m. Admission is free.

Old St. Paul's Church
Charles and Saratoga Streets
(410) 685-3404
www.osp1692.org
The mother church of the Episcopal church in Baltimore since 1856, Old St. Paul's was designed in the basilica style by Richard Upjohn. Tiffany windows and inlaid mosaic work capture the eyes, while ringing church bells capture the ears. The bells were part of a carillon given to the church by residents of Baltimore. The church is open on weekdays from noon to 1:00 p.m. Admission is free, but donations are welcome.

> **i** The Inner Harbor's indoor attractions, the Maryland Science Center, Harborplace, and the National Aquarium in Baltimore, fill quickly when the weather is poor. The Maryland Zoo and Fort McHenry are good places to go if a few raindrops won't bother you.

Pride of Baltimore II
Inner Harbor
(410) 539-1151
www.pride2.org

When it's in port, this replica of an 1812 clipper ship offers great insight into the nineteenth-century-style Baltimore clipper ships that plied the waters of the Chesapeake throughout the century. The *Pride II* has sailed all over the world, extending a dose of Baltimore charm and history wherever it docks. It's usually at sea more than half of the year. Hours vary for tours, which are conducted by the paid and volunteer staff that man it during journeys. No admission is charged. Call in advance to see when the boat is in dock. The *Pride* offers sailing trips around the Baltimore harbor and between Baltimore and Annapolis (one-way only). They cost $45 to $65.

Reginald F. Lewis Museum of Maryland African American History and Culture
830 East Pratt Street
(443) 263-1800
www.africanamericanculture.org

The Lewis Museum makes an impression right from the street. A strikingly modern building with a bright red accent wall, it is far different from the low, traditional buildings nearby. Inside the exhibits detail the personal stories of African Americans throughout Maryland history. All sorts of Marylanders are represented here: politicians and artists, religious leaders and physicians, working people and celebrities. The goal here is to tell stories of African Americans who have made a difference in spite of poverty and racism that will inspire children to greatness of their own. Admission is $8 for adults and $6 for children

The Pride of Baltimore II. PRIDE OF BALTIMORE, INC.

older than age 7, students, and seniors. The museum is open Tuesday through Saturday 10:00 a.m. to 5:00 p.m. and Sunday noon to 5:00 p.m. A parking garage is available across the street from the museum.

Robert Long House and Gardens
812 South Ann Street
(410) 675-6750
www.preservationsociety.com

Robert Long was an early eighteenth-century merchant who built what is now the city's oldest urban residence, in 1765. Long's house in Fells Point has been restored to its original appearance so that visitors can learn about the life of a city merchant. Among the highlights are its proximity to the docks, the simple furnishings, and the intriguing design of its gardens. Tours of the house are available daily at 1:00 and 2:30 p.m. Admission is $3, children younger than age seven are admitted free.

St. Jude Shrine
512 West Saratoga Street
(410) 685-6026
www.stjudeshrine.org

Shortly after World War II began, the shrine became the center of St. Jude devotions. People from all over the United States keep in touch with the center through the mail, while people from Baltimore and beyond require there to be four novena services each Wednesday. Every year, thousands of people enroll themselves and their living and dead loved ones in the League of St. Jude, the patron saint of impossible causes. Perpetual novena services are held Wednesdays at 7:45 a.m., noon, and 5:45 and 7:45 p.m., while Sunday Masses are celebrated at 8:00, 9:00, and 11:30 a.m., with Sunday novena after the latter two Masses. The church is open daily for visitations. No admission is charged.

Sports Legends Museum at Camden Yards
Camden Station
301 West Camden Street
www.baberuthmuseum.com

If you love sports—any sport, baseball, lacrosse, horseracing—this is your place. Home of the Maryland Athletic Hall of Fame and the Orioles Museum, there are shrines to the Baltimore Colts and Johnny Unitas; tributes to baseball greats such as Cal Ripken Jr., Babe Ruth, and Jimmy Foxx; and memorabilia from girls soccer teams, college sports programs, the Preakness, and baseball's Negro Leagues. Try on a uniform in the Locker Room, too. Since this museum occupies two stories of the historic Camden Station, the Gentlemen's Waiting Room is set aside to recall the building's railroad history. The museum is open Tuesday through Sunday 10:00 a.m. to 5:00 p.m. November through March and during baseball season daily 10:00 a.m. to 6:00 p.m. (until 7:30 p.m. on home game days). Tickets are $10.00 for adults, $8.00 for seniors, and $6.50 for those age 3 through 12. Combination tickets with the Babe Ruth Birthplace and Museum are available and discounts are given to visitors with tickets for the Oriole Park stadium tour. A discount coupon is available on the Web site, too.

Top of the World Observation Level
World Trade Center
401 East Pratt Street
(410) 837-8439
www.bop.org/topoftheworld/topofthe
world.aspx

The 27th floor of the World Trade Center in Baltimore offers a stunning 360-degree view of Baltimore's skyline. Stationed binoculars and photo maps enhance the experience, offering a detailed look at the Inner Harbor, the surrounding city, and the lapping waters of the Chesapeake Bay. Guides offer anecdotes about Baltimore's history and happenings. The Top of the World Observation Level

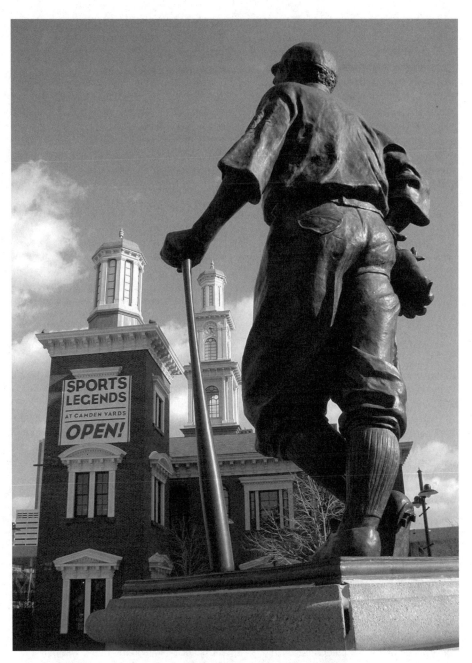

A statue of Babe Ruth faces the Sports Legends Museum at Camden Yards from its place of honor. PHOTO PRO-
VIDED COURTESY OF THE BABE RUTH MUSEUM

is open September through May from 10:00 a.m. to 6:00 p.m. Wednesday through Sunday. From Memorial Day to Labor Day, the observation level is open seven days a week from 10:00 a.m. to 9:00 p.m. Admission is $5 for adults, $4 for seniors, and $3 for children age 3 through16. Special rates apply during events. Security measures require searches of purses, briefcases, package, and backpacks. For your convenience, the Trade Center staff suggests that you leave nonessential items at home or in your hotel.

USS *Constellation*
Pier 1
301 East Pratt Street
(410) 539-1797
www.constellation.org
Docked at the Inner Harbor, this majestic 1,400-ton, 179-foot sailing sloop is the only surviving Civil War–era naval vessel and all-sail warship. Built in 1854 by the navy, the *Constellation* has a colorful history of active duty. The ship was dry-docked in 1999 and given a complete historic restoration. It's now open every day except Thanksgiving, Christmas, and New Year's Day. A ship's store sells memorabilia. Open daily April through October 10:00 a.m. to 5:30 p.m. and November through March 10:00 a.m. to 4:00 p.m. Admission is $8.75 for adults, $7.50 for seniors, and $4.75 for children age 6 through 14.

Washington Monument
Mount Vernon Place
(410) 396-1049
The view from the top of the first architectural monument to honor George Washington is worth the climb—228 steps (but who's counting?). Beyond being able to say you did it, the sights from atop the monument are breathtaking. The climb costs $1, but the ground-floor museum, explaining the history and construction of the monument, begun in 1815, is free. The monument is open Wednesday through Sunday from 10:00 a.m. to 4:00 p.m.

Westminster Hall and Burying Grounds
519 West Fayette Street
(410) 706-2072
www.westminsterhall.org
Established in 1786, this cemetery is the final resting place of writer Edgar Allan Poe, among others. The cemetery, open Monday through Friday from 8:00 a.m. to dusk, is free, while the catacombs, open only by reservation, cost $4 for adults and $2 for children age 12 and younger and seniors.

NORTHEAST

Baltimore County Historical Society
9811 Van Buren Lane, Cockeysville
(410) 666-1878
www.hsobc.org
In an old almshouse, where the poor and destitute were housed before public welfare programs, is the county's Historical Society headquarters, including a library that provides information about county residents and history. The library is open to the public. Six of the original rooms of the 1872 house have been furnished to reflect life in Baltimore County during the nineteenth century, including the Parkton General Store and Post Office, a Victorian grandmother's house, and a farmhouse. The museum is open by appointment only; admission is $3. The library is open Tuesday through Saturday from 10:00 a.m. to 4:00 p.m.

Evergreen House
4545 North Charles Street
(410) 516-0341
www.museums.jhu.edu/evergreen
Listed on the National Register of Historic Places, this Italianate home on 26 wooded and landscaped acres was owned by Baltimore's Garrett family from 1878 to 1942. John W. Garrett was the president of the Baltimore & Ohio Railroad, and this house was purchased for his son, T. Harrison Garrett. The mansion, the carriage house, and the gardens have been returned to their original settings. The Garretts' collections of more than 5,000

pieces, including post-Impressionist paintings, rare books, Japanese netsuke and inro, Tiffany glass, and Baltimore's only private room featuring colorful Russian designs, offer a wide array of art and history in one place. The house, which is closed on major holidays, is open 11:00 a.m. to 4:00 p.m. Tuesday through Friday and noon to 4:00 p.m. Saturday and Sunday. The last hourly tour begins at 3:00 p.m. Admission is $6 for adults, $5 for senior citizens, and $3 for children age 13 through 17.

Fire Museum of Maryland
1301 York Road, Lutherville
(410) 321-7500
www.firemuseummd.org

Learn how fires are fought, including the Great Fire of 1904 in Baltimore, while viewing this extensive collection of fire equipment and vehicles spanning the years of pumpers to hook-and-ladder trucks to today's sophisticated and advanced technology. Open on Saturday March through December and Tuesday through Saturday June through August from 10:00 a.m. to 4:00 p.m. Admission is $8 for adults, $4 for children age 2 through 12, and $7 for seniors and firefighters.

Hampton National Historic Site
535 Hampton Lane, Towson
(410) 823-1309
www.nps.gov/hamp

This 40-room Georgian mansion, built by Capt. Charles Ridgely just after the Revolutionary War, has original furnishings and is surrounded by gardens and 26 outbuildings, including original slave quarters. Owned by the same family for 160 years, the house is a great stop for people who love old houses, antiques, and early American history. A major renovation project was completed in November 2007. Operated by the National Park Service, this 63-acre site is open from 9:00 a.m. to 5:00 p.m. daily, except Thanksgiving, Christmas, and New Year's Day. Entry to the grounds is free, but tours are $5 for adults, $2 for seniors, and free for children younger than age 12.

i Many attractions and museums offer discounts on regular admission. AAA members, for example, get a break on entrance fees at the Mount Clare Museum House, while the National Park Service at Fort McHenry accepts passes such as the National Park Pass and the Golden Age Pass. Remember to ask about special discounts—it may save you a few bucks!

Jerusalem Mill/Jericho Covered Bridge
2813 Jerusalem Road, off U.S. Highway 1, Kingsville
(410) 877-3560

Part of Gunpowder Falls State Park, a 16,000-acre park in northern Baltimore County, the mill was built on the Gunpowder River in 1772. The renovated second floor serves as headquarters for the park, while the first floor features historical artifacts, paintings, photographs, old stone, and the old mill. The museum is open Saturday and Sunday from 1:00 to 4:00 p.m. for free. Don't miss the Jericho Covered Bridge, a long single-span bridge over the Gunpowder River that is open to traffic.

Sherwood Gardens
Between Stratford, Highfield, Underwood, and Greenway Streets

About 80,000 tulip bulbs are planted each year, along with a variety of other spring-flowering bulbs that illuminate this park with color and beauty. The display is most spectacular in late April and early May. A small park in the neighborhood of Guilford, Sherwood Gardens has on-street parking nearby, and the site is perfect for quiet meditation, a picnic, or reading a book. Bring a blanket to sit on. The gardens are open dawn to dusk, with no admission charge.

NORTHWEST

Cylburn Arboretum
4915 Greenspring Avenue
(410) 367-2217
www.cylburnassociation.org

It's hard to believe that these 207 acres of beautiful formal and woodland gardens and trails outside the historic Cylburn mansion house are in Baltimore City. Operated by the city Department of Recreation and Parks after being started by Baltimore businessman Jesse Tyson, the Victorian mansion offers a horticultural reference library and a bird and nature museum. The grounds are open daily dawn to dusk, while the mansion is open weekdays 7:30 a.m. to 3:30 p.m. The museum, library, and gift shop, operated by the Cylburn Arboretum Association, are open Tuesday and Thursday from 1:00 to 3:00 p.m. Call ahead or visit the Web site to arrange for a guided tour.

Homewood House Museum
3400 North Charles Street
(410) 516-5589
www.museums.jhu.edu/homewood

One of Baltimore's oldest buildings, Homewood House and its 122-acre farm was the residence of Charles Carroll Jr., a member of the important Carroll family (see our History chapter for information about the Carrolls). The house, built in 1801 for $40,000 with the finest materials and workers, is one of the best examples of Federal architecture of the early nineteenth century. Carroll received the money to build the five-part house as a wedding gift from his father, Charles Carroll, a signer of the Declaration of Independence. In 1987, after 12 years of research, archaeological excavation, and restoration, the museum opened as part of Johns Hopkins University. The house, which is closed on major holidays, and the beautiful gardens are open Tuesday through Friday 11:00 a.m. to 4:00 p.m., Saturday and Sunday noon to 4:00 p.m. The last tour begins at 3:00 p.m. Admission is $6 for adults, $5 for senior citizens, and $3 for children age five and older. AAA members get $1 off.

Howard Peters Rawlings Conservatory and Botanic Gardens
Druid Hill Park, 12 Druid Park Drive
(410) 396-0180

The Baltimore Conservatory and Botanic Gardens is located in the historic Druid Hill Park, where 1.5 acres erupt in colorful flower gardens. A Victorian Palm House (circa 1888) and three display greenhouses are open Tuesday through Sunday 10:00 a.m. to 4:00 p.m. The outdoor gardens are open to the public from dawn to dusk.

The Maryland Zoo in Baltimore
Druid Hill Park, 1 Druid Park Lake Drive
(410) 366-5466
www.marylandzoo.org

For more than 130 years, Baltimoreans have been coming to this little green patch to see the animals. They came to see four swans back in the first days. Now they come to see more than 1,500 animals on the 160-acre site. The zoo is divided into several sections, including Africa Journey (where you'll find the baby chimpanzees, lions, and giraffes), the Children's Zoo and Polar Bear Watch, home to Alaska and Magnet. The Children's Zoo has won accolades from professional organizations and the thousands of kids who roam through the farmyard, visit the animals, or jump like a frog over the lily pads. The polar bears are probably the most popular animals, though the penguins, giraffes, and elephants have their own following.

The zoo has been undergoing construction the past few years, one reason the oldest part of the zoo is currently closed to the public. A welcome change to the zoo is the new tram to take tired visitors around the zoo; it's free. The zoo is open daily 10:00 a.m. to 4:00 p.m., but closed on Thanksgiving, Christmas, and the second Friday in June, as well as the entire months of January and February. Tickets are $15 for adults, $12 for seniors, and $10 for children age 2 through 11. Parking onsite is free. (See the Kidstuff chapter.)

Soldiers Delight Natural Environmental Area
5100 Deer Park Road
(410) 922-3044
www.dnr.state.md.us/publiclands/central/
soldiers.htm
About 25 miles northwest of Baltimore's Inner Harbor, this 1,900-acre park contains 39 rare, threatened, or endangered plant species as well as rare insects, rocks, and minerals. The only source for the fringed gentian, a fall-blooming wildflower, the natural park features the largest area of serpentine barrens, green mineral or rock composed of hydrous magnesium silicate, on the East Coast. A nature center provides information about serpentine barrens and how the property was used in the past. The park also has 7 miles of marked hiking trails and is open during daylight hours. The visitor center is open Wednesday through Friday from 9:00 a.m. to 4:00 p.m. and from 10:00 a.m. to 4:00 p.m. on weekends. There's no admission fee.

SOUTHEAST

Ballestone Manor
1935 Back River Neck Road, Essex
(410) 887-0218
Guides dressed in period clothing lead visitors through this manor house built in 1780 overlooking Back River. Furnishings reflect the Federal and Victorian styles. In June to August only, tours are available from 2:00 to 5:00 p.m. by appointment. A donation of $3 for adults and 50 cents for children younger than age 12 is requested.

Battle Acre Monument
3219 Old North Point Road, Dundalk
(410) 583-7313
This monument commemorates the Fifth Regiment's defensive position against an attack by the British in 1814. It was here that a ragtag group of soldiers fought a better prepared and larger British military force. The monument is open 24 hours daily.

Fort McHenry National Monument and Historic Shrine
End of East Fort Avenue
(410) 962-4290
www.nps.gov/fomc/
This place gives "The Star-Spangled Banner" its meaning. A 15-minute slide presentation recalling Francis Scott Key's penning of the song during the War of 1812 while he watched from the water as the city was bombarded is a stirring reminder of our past. The presentation closes with the playing of the anthem and the unveiling of the "flag [that] was still there." Its position at the point of the harbor leading into Baltimore's port made Fort McHenry a strategic military site. The fort looks as it did that night in 1814 though displays recall its history through the Civil War and the two World Wars. Good times to visit are near sunset when visitors are asked to help lower the 30-foot by 42-foot flag or for one of the twilight "tattoos" held in the summer. These combine music and historic military pageantry. In addition, the grounds offer a beautiful place to walk and see ships heading in from or out to the Chesapeake Bay. Don't forget a jacket because the wind can be strong. The park is open every day except Christmas and New Year's from 8:00 a.m. to 5:00 p.m., with extended summer hours. Admission to the historic fort is $7 for adults and free for children younger than age 16. The park also accepts various national park passes.

SOUTHWEST

The B&O Railroad Museum
901 West Pratt Street
(410) 752-2490
www.borail.org
The B&O Railroad Museum, which houses the largest railroad collection in the Western Hemisphere, reopened in 2006 following repairs needed after a 2003 snowstorm caused the roof to collapse onto the museum's historic train collection. Though the trains are still on display many of them still need extensive repairs. The museum, an affili-

ate of the Smithsonian Institution, looks better than ever. Train buffs will thrill to see some of the best historic trains in the world, and to ride the rails laid for the very first trains. Children will love climbing aboard the trains and seeing the model trains. Between Thanksgiving and New Year's Eve, model railroad hobbyists bring some pretty extensive layouts to the museum—well worth a visit. The museum is open Monday through Friday 10:00 a.m. to 4:00 p.m., Saturday 10:00 a.m. to 5:00 p.m., and Sunday 11:00 a.m. to 4:00 p.m. It is closed for most major holidays. Admission is $14 for adults, $12 for seniors, and $8 for children age 2 through 12. Admission includes a short train ride. The train runs about twice a day in good weather and not at all in January, February, and March. Combination tickets are available for the B&O Railroad Museum and the Ellicott City station about a half hour away by car.

Benjamin Banneker Historical Park and Museum
300 Oella Avenue, Catonsville
(410) 887-1081

The 142-acre park recalls the legacy of this African-American man of science. A self-taught mathematician and astronomer, he corresponded with Thomas Jefferson, wrote almanacs, and surveyed the land that would become Washington, D.C. The museum pays tribute to his history; the park—part of Banneker's own property—preserves the culture and natural history of the colonial period with a series of walking trails. The museum is open Tuesday through Saturday from 10:00 a.m. to 4:00 p.m. Admission is free but a $3 donation is suggested.

Catonsville Historical Society
1824 Frederick Road, Catonsville
(410) 744-3034
www.catonsvillehistory.org

The Townsend House has eighteenth- and nineteenth-century antiques as well as local historical exhibits and genealogical resources. Open by appointment. Admission is free.

Historical Electronics Museum
1745 West Nursery Road, Linthicum
(410) 765-0230
www.hem-usa.org

This is a specialized museum with seven small galleries exhibiting the history of electronic technology. The vast displays of equipment put a particular emphasis on radar, countermeasures, and communications. Visitors can see the lunar TV camera that transmitted Neil Armstrong's first steps on the moon, and the German Enigma, which encoded messages in World War II. Open Monday through Friday 9:00 a.m. to 3:00 p.m. and Saturday 10:00 a.m. to 2:00 p.m. Admission is free.

Mount Clare Museum House
1500 Washington Boulevard
(410) 837-3262
www.mountclare.org

Furnishings of the eighteenth and nineteenth centuries belonging to Charles Carroll, a colonial barrister and one of Maryland's leaders in the cause for independence, and his wife, Margaret Tilghman, fill Baltimore's only pre–Revolutionary War mansion. Located in beautiful Carroll Park, the house offers a great example of Georgian architecture in Maryland. Open Tuesday through Saturday from 10:00 a.m. to 4:00 p.m. The house is closed on major holidays. Admission is $6 for adults, $5 for senior citizens, and $4 for students age 18 and younger. A discount coupon is available on the Web site. Parking is available at the house.

Poe House and Museum
203 North Amity Street
(410) 396-7932
www.eapoe.org/balt/poehse.htm

This is Baltimore's smallest museum, but it offers a big punch. One of America's most famous poets, Edgar Allan Poe, who also wrote short stories and criticism, lived in the house from 1832 to 1835. The museum features Poe memorabilia, exhibits, and a video presentation highlighting Poe's life and career. Period furniture gives visitors a sense of the time in which the poet wrote such great works as "The Raven" and "The Fall of the House of Usher." Don't miss the nearby Westminster Hall, where he was buried after his death at age 40 in 1849 (see the listing previously in this chapter). The museum also hosts the annual World's Biggest Poe's Birthday Celebration in January (see the Annual Events chapter). The museum is open April through July and October through December Wednesday through Saturday from noon to 3:45 p.m. and August through September Saturday noon to 3:45 p.m. The house is closed January through March. Admission for adults is $3, and for children younger than 12, it's free. The museum is located on a very narrow, one-way street that can become very slick (or freeze) after a snowfall. Use caution when visiting here. Visit when you can park close to the house and call ahead to verify the house will be open.

KIDSTUFF

Whether your kids go crazy over planes, trains, or ponies, or get revved up over go-karts, science experiments, or baseball, you'll find someplace for them to expend their energies in Charm City. A multitude of exhibits, activities, programs, and historical sites offer the younger set a mindful of things to consider and be fascinated by. And though the focus of this chapter is stuff for kids, we're sure that kids at heart will be equally entertained at these attractions.

To make sure your excursions are more fun than fretful, remind your children to stay close. Some exhibits and activities can get really crowded, and a short distance between Mom and Dad can seem like miles in a sea of unfamiliar faces. Show your kids the entrance or information center when entering an attraction and remind them to go there if they lose track of you. (You know how parents tend to wander off.)

We've divided the following activities by geographic location. These attractions are traditional favorites with kids, but be sure to look to other chapters, such as Attractions and Parks and Recreation, for more outings to share with the little and not-so-little ones. You may also want to pick up a free copy of *Baltimore's Child,* a monthly publication with information about services, resources, and events for parents and children in the Baltimore metropolitan area. Copies are distributed free throughout the city, and most libraries carry them.

DOWNTOWN

Baltimore Museum of Industry
1415 Key Highway
(410) 727-4808
www.thebmi.org
Docents here do an excellent job of gearing their presentations to children. And what school-age child doesn't like to see machinery at work or step into an old-fashioned grocery store or drugstore and imagine working there? Life-size photos of children working in industries around Baltimore add to the experience. For more on this museum dedicated to the industries that kept Baltimore so busy a century ago, see the listing in the Attractions chapter. The museum is open Monday through Saturday 10:00 a.m. to 4:00 p.m. Admission is $10 for adults and $6 for children age 5 through 18 and senior citizens.

The Ducks sightseeing tours
Light Street Pavilion waterfront, Harborplace
(877) 887-8225
www.baltimoreducks.com
Is it a boat or a bus? The odd-looking "ducks" touring Baltimore's attractions go from land to water to land to give visitors a unique tour of Charm City. What other way can a visitor see the Washington Monument by land and Fort McHenry by sea? The tours are fun. Since everyone gets a "quacker" they can also be loud. Tours run daily mid-March through December. Tickets are available on-line and at the kiosk near Harborplace. Tickets are $24 for age 13 through 52, $23 for seniors, and $14 for age 3 through 12.

Enoch Pratt Free Library
400 Cathedral Street
(410) 396-5430
www.prattlibrary.org
The Pratt programs for children feature movies, crafts, and read-aloud sessions conducted by librarians at the main branch and at smaller branches throughout the city. The programs offer kids a welcome intellectual respite, especially if the day turns inclement.

It's best to call ahead if you're looking for a kids' program, but if you're really desperate, the kids will find plenty of books with which to wile away the hours in the library's children's section. Programs are free and open to all.

The library's hours are 10:00 a.m. to 8:00 p.m. Monday through Wednesday, 10:00 a.m. to 5:00 p.m. Thursday through Saturday, and 1:00 to 5:00 p.m. Sunday. During the summer hours often change. The central branch can offer information about other branches' hours and programs for children. On-street metered parking is usually available within a few blocks of the main branch on Cathedral Street. (See the Attractions chapter for more information about the library.)

Geppi's Entertainment Museum
Camden Station
301 West Camden Street
(410) 625-7060
www.geppismuseum.com
Geppi's museum is set up for adults, primarily, but its toys and comics from the last 100 years or so appeal to children, too. Interactive videos give kids the chance to play a game, listen to old-time radio broadcasts, or flip through a comic book. Otherwise, everything is behind glass, but the artifacts range from century-old mechanical banks to decoder rings from the 1950s to lunch boxes from 1970s television shows. Get in there with your kids and show them some of your childhood. More on the exhibits can be found in the Attractions chapter.

Tickets are $10 for adults, $9 for seniors, and $7 for children age 5 through 18. Combination tickets with Sports Legends are available for $18.00 for adults, $15.00 for seniors, and $11.50 for students. The museum is open daily 10:00 a.m. to 6:00 p.m. from April to October and Tuesday through Sunday 10:00 a.m. to 5:00 p.m. the rest of the year. It's wheelchair accessible and parking is available on-site.

M&T Bank Stadium
1101 Russell Street
(410) 230-8000
www.baltimoreravens.com
A Ravens football game is not the only attraction at M&T Bank Stadium. For children and the young at heart, a tour through this amazing stadium is entertainment enough. The almost 69,000-seat stadium has more than one million hand-laid bricks throughout its innovative design. The only catch is you need a group of 20, say your scout troop or your swim team. Admission is $5 per person for the tour, which lasts up to 90 minutes. Visitors see the field up close, as well as the locker rooms and suite. Make a reservation at least two weeks in advance. Tours are offered Monday through Friday 9:00 a.m. to 5:00 p.m. and Saturday before noon. Fewer tours are available during the Ravens season. For information or reservations, call (410) 261-7283.

Maryland Science Center and IMAX Theater
601 Light Street
(410) 685-5225
www.mdsci.org
Additions to the Maryland Science Center in 2004 made this even more fun for kids than it was before—and this is really a museum aimed at children. The new dinosaur exhibit has children looking up at their favorite Tyrannosaurus Rex; the human body exhibit takes a close look at all the things that will make a kid scream with delight, "Eww, gross." The IMAX theater now has 3-D capability and offers movies in both three- and two-dimensions that appeal to younger attention spans from the just plain fun *Happy Feet* to the awe-inspiring *Space Station 3D*. The Davis Planetarium's shows add stories to the nighttime sky displays to capture children's imaginations. The world of science comes alive with interactive exhibits and live demonstrations explaining light, mechanics, and sound. For kids, this is a must. Everything is interactive, meaning they can be touching things that other museums and science centers put behind glass. The result is happier, more edu-

cated kids (and adults who want to be kids again). Check out all the interactive displays that help us understand our place in the world and in space with images from the Hubble Space Telescope and the National Oceanic and Atmospheric Administration. Little ones who might grow bored with exhibits designed for older children have their own Kid's Room, where they can play with blocks, crawl around the Room to Grow area, or explore a Baltimore streetscape.

The Maryland Science Center is open fall through spring Tuesday through Thursday 10:00 a.m. to 5:00 p.m., Friday 10:00 a.m. to 8:00 p.m., Saturday, 10:00 a.m. to 6:00 p.m., and Sunday 10:00 a.m. to 5:00 p.m. From Memorial Day weekend through Labor Day hours are Sunday through Thursday 10:00 a.m. to 6:00 p.m. and Friday and Saturday 10:00 a.m. to 8:00 p.m. The IMAX Theater also has evening shows, and the observatory opens after hours on Friday nights for stargazing. Admission prices vary, depending on what you want to see. For the museum only, admission is $14.50 for adults, $13.50 for seniors, and $10.00 for children age 3 through 12. Adding an IMAX film costs an extra $4 for everyone. Special exhibits, such as recent shows on the *Titanic* and "Grossology" have an additional charge. Evening IMAX presentations are $8.

National Aquarium in Baltimore
Pier 3/501 East Pratt Street
(410) 576-3800
www.aqua.org
Walk into the world of the briny deep at Baltimore's National Aquarium. Five levels exhibit several habitats, ranging from tidal marshes along the coast of Maryland to the dense tropical foliage of a South American rain forest.

i Place a slip of paper or a business card in the pockets of each of your children's clothes so that if they get lost the authorities can contact you or will at least know whom to look for.

Level 1 features stingrays and small sharks in a 265,000-gallon pool as well as Animal Planet Australia: Wild Extremes. Kids will love the new "4–D" movie theater that opened on Level 1 at the end of 2007. On Level 2, Mountains to the Sea, you can trace the water cycle from a freshwater pond in the mountains of western Maryland through the Tidal Marsh, into the Coastal Beach, and out into the waters of the Atlantic shelf. Visitors to Level 3 are shocked by the voltage created by an electric eel and entangled by the magnificence of a giant Pacific octopus. Patient people in this gallery are rewarded by the sight of tiny jawfish that live in small burrows that they dig.

On Level 4 visitors can see one of the aquarium's exhibits that recreates a section of the blackwater Amazon River tributary and the forest that it seasonally floods. Along a 57-foot-long acrylic wall, visitors can see schools of tropical fish, giant river turtles, dwarf caimans, caiman lizards, and a giant anaconda. Level 4 also offers the Atlantic Coral Reef, where visitors are surrounded by a rainbow—hundreds of vividly colored tropical fish.

Level 5 offers the Tropical Rain Forest, where careful observers can view colorful birds, golden lion tamarins (monkeys), red-bellied piranhas, and lizards. Other treats at the aquarium include a 1,300-seat aquarium that hosts daily dolphin shows.

A food court and The Aqua Shop, the aquarium's gift shop, round out the offerings here. Tickets are $21.95 for adults, $12.95 for children age 3 through 11, and $20.95 for seniors. Hours are generally 9:00 a.m. to 5:00 p.m. daily with extended hours on Fridays and weekends. Extended hours vary by season, so it would be best to call or check the Web site for details. Also see the Attractions chapter for more information.

Oriole Park at Camden Yards
333 West Camden Street
(410) 547-6234
www.theorioles.com
A baseball game is only part of the attrac-

Divers hand feed the skates and rays at the National Aquarium. GEORGE GRALL, NATIONAL AQUARIUM IN BALTIMORE

tion of Oriole Park at Camden Yards, but unfortunately the beloved O's only play 81 home games from April to October each year. For most kids a 90-minute guided tour of the stadium is equally exciting. This railroad warehouse-ballpark is a mere 12 minutes west by foot from the Inner Harbor and only 2 blocks from the birthplace of baseball's most legendary hero, George Herman "Babe" Ruth (see the Attractions chapter for more on the Babe Ruth Museum). During the tour kids get to sit behind the dugout and at the helm of the control room while getting the behind-the-scenes scoop on the facility, the team, and the history of this classic stadium. Tour schedules vary, but public tours usually are conducted daily from February 15 to December 23, except on days of afternoon home games. Private tours can be arranged. You can purchase tickets in advance or on the day of a tour from the ticket office in the ballpark warehouse adjacent to gate H. Tickets are $7 for adults and $5 for children younger than age 12 and seniors. Parking is free during the weekends when the team is away. There is lot parking available during the week for $5. It's best to call ahead for details.

Port Discovery
35 Market Place
(410) 727-8120
www.portdiscovery.org

Since opening its doors on December 29, 1998, Port Discovery, the kid-powered museum, is one of the ultimate experiences in fun and learning for children and their families in the Baltimore area. Designed in collaboration with Walt Disney Imagineering and a team of educators, Port Discovery takes education and entertainment to a new level and brings a new vision to the idea of a children's museum. Located in the historic Fishmarket Building, Port Discovery is one of the largest children's museums in the country. On Meet and Greet Street free fun and entertainment, including live performances and special exhibits, is offered. In Kidsworks, children can crawl, jump, slide, swing, and swoosh through a three-story urban tree house. MPT Studioworks allows kids to watch TV and find out how it works. There is also a learning library designed to enhance the museum experience. Port Discovery is open Monday through Saturday 10:00 a.m. to 5:00 p.m. and Sunday noon to 5:00 p.m. Admission is $10.75 for age 2 and older. Parking in the adjacent Harbor Park Garage is $7 on weekends.

Reginald F. Lewis Museum of Maryland African American History and Culture
830 East Pratt Street
(443) 263-1800
www.africanamericanculture.org

Through its exhibits of African-American history and accomplishments, the Lewis Museum is designed to inspire children. The exhibitions about politicians and artists, religious leaders, and athletes are people oriented, with memorabilia and stories of individual Marylanders. The three major galleries focus on family and community; labor (including slavery), and art and intellect. Some exhibits are harrowing, just as some portions of African-American history are harrowing, but most exhibits relate stories of great achievement. The exhibits appeal mostly to older children and adults. The museum's goal is to reach out to children and inspire them to achieve their own dreams. Admission is $8 for adults, and $6 for children age 8 and older, students, and seniors. The museum is open Tuesday through Saturday 10:00 a.m. to 5:00 p.m. and Sunday noon to 5:00 p.m. A parking garage is available across the street from the museum.

Sports Legends Museum at Camden Yards
Camden Station
301 West Camden Street
www.baberuthmuseum.com

This is no dry hall filled with glass between you and the artifacts. Go ahead and pick up the phone and hear Johnny Unitas get a call to become a pro football player. Put your hand in the enormous catcher's mitt. Stand next to Cal Ripken Jr. and see how you measure up. Best of all, go into the locker room and try on that Raven's jersey. (Bring your camera.) There's an exhibit for every sport here; some exhibits—the Orioles Hall of Fame and the Gentlemen's Waiting Room, for instance—are more formal. But the emphasis here is on fun, the way we like our sports. More on the exhibits is in the Attractions section. The museum is open Tuesday through Sunday 10:00 a.m. to 5:00 p.m. November through March and during baseball season daily 10:00 a.m. to 6:00 p.m. (until 7:30 p.m. on home game days). Tickets are $10.00 for adults, $8.00 for seniors, and $6.50 for children age 3 through 12. Combination tickets with the Babe Ruth Birthplace and Museum are available and discounts are given to visitors with tickets for the Oriole Park stadium tour. A discount coupon is available on the Web site.

USS Constellation
Pier 1
301 East Pratt Street
(410) 539-1797
www.constellation.org

The Constellation has a special program for children, the Powder Monkey tour. Youngsters age six and older can come aboard to learn about the lives of youngsters who served as powder monkeys during the Civil Wars. They're going to "work" on this tour, handling lines and such. Tours are scheduled every Saturday and Sunday at 1:00 and 3:00 p.m. and included in the price of admission. For more on the ship, see the Attractions chapter. The ship is open every day except Thanksgiving, Christmas, and New Year's Day. A ship's store sells memorabilia. Open daily April through October from 10:00 a.m. to 5:30 p.m. and November through March from 10:00 a.m. to 4:00 p.m. Admission is $8.75 for adults, $7.50 for seniors, and $4.75 for children age 6 through 14.

Washington Monument
Mount Vernon Place
(410) 396-0929

Here's a guaranteed way to wear down those overactive kids. The first monument built to honor the nation's first president is 178 feet tall. The monument has 228 steps to climb, and your kids will love the challenge and the payoff—a view of the city from atop the structure, completed in 1829 after 14 years of work. Tour the base of the monument and see "The Making of the Monument," an exhibit chronicling the history of the monument and Mount Vernon Place. Don't even think about taking kids who won't make it all the way up because it's a long climb for adults, especially with a kid in your arms or on your back; strollers are an absolute no-no. Hardy climbers can give it a try for a $1 donation (a small price to pay to use up some of your children's energies) from Wednesday to Sunday from 10:00 a.m. to 4:00 p.m. and on the first Thursday of the month from 10:00 a.m. to 8:00 p.m.

NORTHEAST

Anita C. Leight Estuary Center
700 Otter Point Road, Edgewood
(410) 612-1688
www.otterpointcreek.org

Indoor exhibits designed to teach children about the Chesapeake Bay, the world's largest estuary, include an indoor turtle pond and habitats for reptiles, amphibians, and fish. The Anita C. Leight Estuary Center is the research and education facility of the Chesapeake Bay National Estuarine Research Reserve. It is part of a national reserve system established by Congress in 1972 to protect estuarine areas as natural field laboratories for long-term research and monitoring. Programs include Critter Dinners, where children can learn about turtles, snakes, and fish that live at Otter Point Creek. It also offers a chance to see the captive critters eat.

The reserve also has a pontoon boat that offers an exciting way to explore the waters of Otter Point Creek. Anyone with a minimum weight of 30 pounds is invited on Spring boat rides for a small fee. There are also canoe trips available to explore the marsh. Check out the Web site or call ahead to find out program times and availability.

The facility is about 30 miles north of Baltimore City, off U.S. Highway 40 in Edgewood (exit 77). It's a 40-minute drive but worth the travel time for kids and adults. The center is open Saturday from 10:00 a.m. to 5:00 p.m. and Sunday from noon to 5:00 p.m. No admission is charged.

Baltimore County Public Library
320 York Road, Towson
(410) 887-6100
www.bcplonline.org

The main branch in Towson and the other 14 branches throughout the county provide programs several times a week that target children's interests and books. It's best to contact the main branch to get information about events at the branch closest to you. There is usually no charge, although increasingly libraries have been asking for reservations to control the number of kids participating. Programs include read-alouds, sing-alongs, and activities tied to holiday events. Hours vary from branch to branch, but most children's programs are in the morning or early afternoon.

Go-Kart Track, Inc
10907 Pulaski Highway, White Marsh
(410) 335-6393
www.baltimoregokarts.com

Two go-kart courses (one fast and one slow) keep the kids behind the wheel and on the track. Five cars make their way around each track in a four-minute ride that costs $5. Bumping or crashing are not allowed. Minigolf is also available. The best time to go is early in the day. The tracks are open from 10:00 a.m. to 11:00 p.m. on weekdays from May to September and until midnight on weekends during those months. From October to January and in March and April, the hours are noon to 8:00 p.m. daily.

Reading with Sneaks

The Baltimore County Public Library's summer reading program offers kids plenty of rewards (besides the sheer joy of reading) for reading when they don't have to. The summer reading club, open to any child at any county library, is free, except for the t-shirt. And buying that is optional. As they read and record their books on a special activity sheet, they collect points that they can turn in for trinkets and gift certificates throughout the summer. There are usually drawings for special prizes. Toss in the special events starring authors, storytellers, and even magicians for extra fun. Separate programs are geared to preschoolers and middle schoolers.

Irvine Nature Center
8400 Greenspring Avenue, Stevenson
(410) 484-2413
www.explorenature.org

The Irvine Nature Center, located just north of the city, is the place to take children for a real exploration of the outdoors. Children, families, and adults are invited to explore Maryland Piedmont habitat at the nature center. Irvine features a self-guided nature trail, demonstration gardens to attract wildlife, a natural history museum, live animal exhibits, hands-on exhibits, and a special children's corner. There are also programs, lectures, special events, and other activities. A nature store offers specialty books on gardening, birds, and ecology for all ages, birdfeeders, science kits, binoculars, and selected children's toys. Hours at Irvine are 9:00 a.m. to 4:00 p.m. Tuesday through Saturday and noon to 4:00 p.m. on Sunday. The trails, museum, and gift shop are free to the public, but guests are encouraged to consider a donation to the center. Programs and special events may have a fee. Call ahead of time for information on the various programs. The program is scheduled to move to a new 1,200-acre site in 2008. Check the Web site for details.

NORTHWEST

The Maryland Zoo in Baltimore
Druid Hill Park, 1 Druid Park Lake Drive
(410) 366-LION
www.marylandzoo.org

The third-oldest zoo in the nation has more than 2,250 birds, reptiles, and mammals. Programs such as Keeper Encounters, EdZOOcation classes, behind-the-scenes tours, and zoo camps teach children about endangered wildlife, their habitats, and life cycles. The programs change from day to day, so it's best to call for specific details. The exhibits and cages housing the animals have low sight lines designed to allow kids of all ages to check out the action. The reptile house is a favorite, while the African Safari section offers an insight into life on another continent and is inhabited by elephants, chimpanzees, giraffes, and lions. The Children's Zoo focuses on animals that call Maryland home—from the hills and caves of the western part of the state to the waters and marshes of the Chesapeake Bay. The Children's Zoo, rated number one in the country, also includes hands-on KidZone, where children can hop across lily pads, perch in an oriole's nest, and jump over a frog.

On hot summer days, shaded areas can be at a premium. Benches are available throughout the zoo, and almost every stretch is designed for stroller-pushing families. Refreshments, including beverages, pizza, hot dogs, and snacks, are available at several locations. There's also a carousel in the Village Green section. But don't spend too much time with the fiberglass menagerie. The real McCoys are much more entertaining.

The zoo is open daily, except on Thanksgiving, Christmas Day, and one Friday in June for an annual fund-raising event, from 10:00 a.m. to 4:00 p.m. It's completely closed in January and February. Adults pay $15, while children age 2 through 11 pay $10, and seniors 62 and older pay $12. Children younger than age 2 are admitted free.

Had enough of the rumbles and roars? Druid Hill Park, a marvelous spot for letting the kids run free, surrounds the zoo. Open areas around a large, fenced-in lake are perfect for everything from a quick game of ball to flying a kite or flying a radio-controlled airplane. The park is free and open daily. (See the Parks and Recreation chapter for more about Druid Hill Park.)

Northwest Family Sports Center Ice Rink
5731 Cottonworth Avenue
(410) 433-2307

This year-round ice-skating rink provides everything from private, group, and family lessons to pickup hockey games to figure skating and speed skating instruction. For those who just want to try an all-skate, there is plenty of time, mostly on weekends and holidays, for that. Refreshments are available, and parking is on-site. Admission is $6 per person, with an additional $2 charged for skate rental. Hours vary, with two-hour blocks open for free skating several times a day. Generally the rink is open daily 10:00 a.m. to 10:00 p.m.

Pumpkin Theatre
Ruxton Towers
8415 Bellona Lane, Suite 115
www.pumpkintheatre.com

Baltimore children have had their own theater (although the actual location has changed a number of times) since 1967. Begun as part of the College of Notre Dame's theater depart-

i The free monthly magazine for families, Baltimore's Child, offers tips and suggestions on how to fill hours with entertaining and educational activities. It's available at bookstores, convenience stores, and other locations in the Baltimore area.

ment, Pumpkin Theatre struck out on its own and continues to dazzle young audiences with all kinds of family entertainment. The shows, which regularly sell out, are produced with attention to detail for the most demanding audiences. A cool feature for kids are the "talk-back performances" held during a matinee when the audience can ask questions of the actors and staff after the show. Plays hit the boards at St. Timothy's School for Girls, 8400 Greenspring Avenue in Stevenson. It's just outside the Beltway off exit 22. Tickets at the door are $12, $11 in advance. If your child is stagestruck, Pumpkin offers a variety of theater classes and summer camps, too.

SOUTHEAST

Fort McHenry National Monument and Historic Shrine
End of East Fort Avenue
(410) 962-4290
www.nps.gov/fomc

Forget all the history and exhibits inside detailing the writing of "The Star-Spangled Banner" by Francis Scott Key. Holding cells for prisoners, living quarters within the fort, and cannons lining the perimeter of the facility hold the most interest for young visitors here. Weapons and munitions sit ready for review, while a walkway outside the perimeter of the fort serves as a great vantage point for spotting ships coming into the Inner Harbor. Bring along your binoculars.

There is a free, 15-minute informational film shown every 20 minutes from 9:00 a.m. to 4:00 p.m. The entrance fee to the park is $7 for adults and free for children younger than age 16. Bring a jacket—the winds coming up the Patapsco River make it about 15 degrees colder than expected. Also, keep an eye on your brood. Though kids often think the munitions resemble playground equipment, climbing on them is not allowed. Fort McHenry is open from 8:00 a.m. to 5:00 p.m. daily, except Christmas and New Year's Days. On-site parking is free and within close walking distance of the fort and indoor exhibits. (See the Attractions chapter for the historical presentations at Fort McHenry.)

SOUTHWEST

The B&O Railroad Museum
901 West Pratt Street
(410) 752-2490
www.borail.org

The history of trains, beginning with the first use in Baltimore more than a century ago, could seem bland on the surface. But at the B&O Railroad Museum, where visitors can walk among and board these big, beautiful machines, history comes alive and mesmerizes all those within earshot of a train whistle. A devastating winter storm in 2003 caused the roundhouse roof to cave in; repairs have made the building better than ever but some of the historic trains haven't yet been restored. They remain on display. The kids probably won't care, but they will like the short train ride that goes over the country's first railroad tracks. And they'll probably like the model trains and the play area built to look like a train. The wide-open space of the roundhouse makes for a fun place to explore and get lost, while keeping Mom and Dad within their line of vision the whole time. The museum is open Monday through Friday 10:00 a.m. to 4:00 p.m., Saturday 10:00 a.m. to 5:00 p.m., and Sunday 11:00 a.m. to 4:00 p.m. It is closed for most major holidays. Admission is $14 for adults, $12 for seniors, and $8 for children age 2 through 12, and it includes the train ride. Be sure to call ahead for the train schedule if this is an important part of your visit; sometimes the trains don't run.

BWI Airport Observation Gallery
Interstate 195, Linthicum
(410) 859-7111
www.bwiairport.com

Everyone knows how intoxicating an airport can be—the sights, the sounds, the power, the takeoffs, the landings. The Baltimore-Washington International Thurgood Marshall Airport has an observation lounge between Wings B and C for kids of all ages to enjoy the scenes of a busy airport. In addition to large windows for viewing the action outside, there's a mockup of an airplane, a baggage train, and a gas truck for kids to climb through and practice their flying and driving skills. On the second floor is an aviation exhibit that includes sections of a real airplane. You can't crawl into the cockpit, but you can look through the glass and push buttons to light up specific cockpit lights. It's the closest kids can get to an airplane without shelling out big bucks for a seat on the next flight out. A play area is adjacent to all this fun. Parking is the only cost, with the airport garage charging no fee for the first half hour and $2 per half hour afterward. Just remember to keep the kids close by because airport activity is fast and furious, and the opportunity for kids to veer away from parents is often great.

The airport is at the end of I-195. (See the Getting Here, Getting Around chapter for information about adult pursuits at BWI.)

Clark's Elioak Farm
10500 Clarksville Pike, Ellicott City
(410) 730-4049
www.clarklandfarm.com

This is no ordinary petting zoo. This 540-acre farm tended by the Clark family for generations opened its doors to families several years ago with pigs and goats and calves willing to be petted and hayrides and pony rides available. The extra attraction here, however, are the fairy-tale structures that were once part of Enchanted Forest, a theme park built in Ellicott City in 1955. The old theme park did indeed enchant. Until it closed in the late 1980s, generations of families went there to climb in Mother Hubbard's shoe and explore Cinderella's pumpkin coach. The park has given way to a shopping center, but these beloved attractions were preserved and moved to the farm. Storybook Time is on Tuesday and Thursday in June and July, held four times during each day. Admission is $4.50 per person. Hayrides and pony rides are an additional $2. The farm is open April through October 10:00 a.m. to 4:00 p.m. and is located by traveling Highway 29 to Highway 108 west; it's about 45 minutes from Baltimore.

Playwise Kids
6570 Dobbin Road, Columbia
(410) 772-1540
www.playwisekids.com

Here's the giant dream playroom every kids wishes for. The fire truck they can play on is real and so are the firefighter uniforms. The grocery store has shopping carts. Or try the game room, arts and crafts area, or dress up area. Tap on the dance floor. Special areas are set aside for toddlers, including slides and tunnels, soft blocks, and a medieval castle with ball pit. Drop in for playtime Monday through Friday 9:30 a.m. to 5:00 p.m., Saturday 9:30 a.m. to 7:00 p.m., and Sunday 11:30 a.m. to 6:00 p.m. No reservations are required, but adults must stay with the children. Admission is $8.95 for children age 2 through 10, $5.95 for children age 12 to 23 months, and $3.00 for those age 11 and older. There's a cafe open on weekends, school holidays, and summer days. When it's not open, feel free to bring your own lunch. Vending machines carry drinks and snacks, too. Call ahead to be sure. Playwise Kids used to be known as ExploraWorld; the same owners have continued on but changed the name to better reflect the mission.

Thomas A. Dixon Jr. Airport Observation Area
Dorsey Road, Linthicum
(410) 859-7111
www.bwiairport.com

Near Baltimore-Washington International Thurgood Marshall Airport, off Interstate 97 at exit 15, is an outdoor parking area for observing airplane takeoffs and landings. Located to the south of one of the airport's busiest runways, the parking area provides kids of all ages with an up-close view of planes in motion. The planes fly about 200 feet over the site. You'll also find a playground area. During the summer months, stop there to enjoy hot dogs, snowballs—a shaved ice and flavor mixture that truly quenches anyone's thirst on a hot, humid day—and other refreshments. The area is part of a 12½-mile scenic trail that encircles the airport property. Watch all you want—there's no admission fee.

ANNUAL EVENTS

Baltimore is a happening place. From family backyard crab feasts to Artscape, our yearly arts and crafts fair that draws crowds of more than one million, we have fun wherever and whenever we can.

These events and festivals are just some of those that occur every year in the Baltimore community. We cannot list them all. In any given week, there are thousands of things to do in the Baltimore area. Our most widely distributed free paper, *City Paper*, devotes about one-quarter of its pages every week to what to do in Baltimore. *Baltimore* magazine does likewise on a monthly basis.

In addition to print publications, three Web sites offer up-to-the-minute information about area events and attractions; the Baltimore Office of Promotion serves as our city's party planners, and it maintains a comprehensive calendar of Baltimore events at www.promotionandarts.org. The Maryland Office of Tourism has a statewide calendar that highlights activities throughout Maryland at www.mdisfun.org. Finally, the Baltimore Area Convention and Visitors Association keeps a list of happenings at www.baltimore.org.

Each listing that follows tries to answer the questions what, where, when, why, and how, but in an attempt to cut out the extraneous or repetitive information, there are a few things you'll want to know up front. Most festival and event locations are user friendly; therefore, they are wheelchair accessible and bathrooms of some sort are on-site. If an event does not have a bathroom, we'll tell you. Otherwise, assume it does. We'll tell you if an event is free or list the admission fees. Prices often go up from year to year, so if price is a determining factor as to whether or not you'll attend an event, call the contact number provided to get the most recent fees.

Parking Downtown can cost as little as $1.50 an hour to about $30.00 a day. The closer you get to the Inner Harbor, the more expensive the parking. So, if you have no aversion to walking a few blocks, parking a few blocks north will save you some bucks. Coming early will also save you money. In most harbor lots, checking in before 9:00 a.m. will net you almost 50 percent in savings; if you're parking all day, that's $11 versus $30.

For specific dates of annual festivals and information on other events, concerts, and celebrations in Baltimore, consult the Media chapter for where to find publications that carry these up-to-the-minute details. Or contact the following organizations: the Baltimore Area Convention and Visitors Association, 100 Light Street, 12th Floor, (877) BALTIMORE or (800) 282-6632; Baltimore Office of Promotion, 200 West Lombard Street, (410) 752-8632; and Maryland Office of Tourism, 217 East Redwood Street, (866) MDWELCOME.

JANUARY

Edgar Allan Poe Birthday Celebration
Westminster Hall and Burial Grounds
Fayette and Green Streets
(410) 396-7932
www.poecelebration.tripod.com
Throughout the entire weekend closest to Poe's January 19th birthday, Poe House sponsors a celebration in honor of the life and works of Edgar Allan Poe. Events vary from year to year but include such goodies as theatrical presentations of Poe's stories, musical renditions of his poems, a bagpipe tribute and a graveside toast—after dark, of course. More than 1,000 people attend the celebration, which begins Friday evening with repeat performances Saturday evening and Sunday

afternoon. Prices vary, but tend to run in the $18 to $25 range, and they are usually available at the door. Parking is on the street or in a nearby garage.

Reverend Dr. Martin Luther King Jr. Birthday Celebration Parade
Parade route follows Martin Luther King Jr. Boulevard, between Eutaw and Russell Streets
(877) BALTIMORE
www.promotionandarts.com

Baltimoreans love a good parade, and this is no exception. The city takes to the streets of Downtown to celebrate the birth of civil rights leader Reverend Martin Luther King Jr. Many of Baltimore's own living legends participate in the parade, including past civil rights activists and prominent community and political figures. Floats, marching bands, choirs, and dancers add to the festive commemoration. This is a free event.

Fishing Expo and Boat Show
Maryland State Fairgrounds
2200 York Road, Timonium
(410) 838-8687
www.fishingexpo.com

Maryland is a state crisscrossed with lakes, rivers, and streams, and our proximity to the bay and the ocean make angling and water sports a major pastime. It makes sense, then, that the East Coast's largest fishing expo is held here each year in mid-January. Bass, saltwater, and fly-fishing retailers sell their goods while boat companies and fishing supply manufacturers display their latest toys. Seminars and demonstrations help reel in the crowds, and patrons can try their hand at pulling in a live trout. Discount coupons for admission are frequently offered on the Web site. Prices are $10 for adults and $5 for children age 10 through 14; children younger than age 10 admitted free. Parking is free.

Horse World Expo
Maryland State Fairgrounds
2200 York Road, Timonium
(301) 916-0852
www.horseworldexpo.com

Marylanders love the field as much as the stream, and our state boasts an impressive history of steeplechase and horse races. This event, usually held mid-January, is a must for horse lovers. Hundreds of vendors boast a plethora of horse products and services for every breed of horse and every discipline of riding. A parade of breeds, educational seminars, and demonstrations are scheduled throughout the three-day event. Admission is $8 for adults and $4 for children age 10 through 14; children younger than age ten are admitted free. Admission prices may go up, so it's worth calling in advance to confirm. All activities are indoors and heated. Parking is free.

Fridays After Five National Aquarium
Pier 3/501 East Pratt Street
(410) 576-3800
www.aqua.com

The National Aquarium is one of the many treasures not to be missed at Baltimore's Inner Harbor, and now you can visit the denizens of the deep for a discounted price. For several years, on Fridays after 5:00 p.m. from mid-September to early March, the aquarium opens its doors to patrons for more than half off the regular admission price. Because of the event's popularity, tickets are sold in timed blocks. This means you can enjoy the miracles of the sea without getting crushed by overwhelming crowds, but it may also mean you'll have some time to kill before your ticket is valid. Not to worry—the aquarium is a stone's throw from the Harbor's restaurants and shops. On Friday evenings tickets can be purchased until 8:00 p.m., and the aquarium stays open until 9:30 p.m. to accommodate visitors (see the Attractions chapter for admission). The aquarium is on a pier at the harbor so there is no adjacent parking. Parking is available at Inner Harbor i Baltimore is divided into north and south by Baltimore Street and east and west by Charles Street. The first block in any direction from those streets is what's known as the unit block. The 100 block is actually the second block away from those streets, so 10 East Baltimore Street is in the unit block east of Charles Street—the first block—and 101 East Baltimore Street is in the second block.

parking garages, nearby metered lots, or on the street. A semicircle drive off of Pratt Street allows you to drop off individuals who prefer not to walk from the parking lots.

FEBRUARY

Black Heritage Art Show
Baltimore Convention Center
1 West Pratt Street, Baltimore
(410) 521-0660
www.aavaa.org
February is Black History Month, and there is no better way to celebrate than with a weekend of cultural activities and the nation's best African-American visual artists. The second weekend of the month, the African American Visual Arts Association brings together visual and performing artists, lecturers, jazz and gospel singers, and poets for a showcase of contemporary arts and crafts. This is a rare opportunity to meet internationally and nationally acclaimed African-American artists and to purchase their work. Admission is free. There are no food vendors at this event, so do not come on an empty stomach! The Baltimore Convention Center does not have parking on-site, but several garages are nearby. Tickets are $5.

Hunt Valley Antiques Show
Holiday Inn Select
(410) 366-1980, ext. 253
www.armacostantiqueshows.com
Looking for that special something to make your house a home? For more than 30 years,

the Hunt Valley Antiques Show has offered an exquisite lineup of the country's most reputable antiques dealers. Fifty-plus merchants sell a mix of items such as furniture, Oriental rugs, jewelry, and ceramics. These antiques are rare, and the prices reflect the quality of the goods. Those interested in learning more about the fine art of collecting may wish to participate in one of the many lectures or guided show tours. Tours are free with general admission, while lectures are $50. A $15 general admission fee includes a show catalogue with dealer biographies and informative articles. Parking is free and there are several restaurants on-site for a sit-down meal or a quick snack. The show benefits a local child welfare agency.

The ACC Craft Fair of Baltimore
Baltimore Convention Center
1 West Pratt Street
(410) 583-5401, (800) 836-3470
www.craftcouncil.org/baltimore
For more than 20 years, The American Craft Council fair has provided crafters space to exhibit their work. The more than 700 crafters you'll see have to go through an arduous judging process to be allowed to exhibit. Artists come from all over the country—Baltimore included. Unlike some judged shows, where the artist can send a representative to man his booth, at the ACC Fair, the artist/crafter must attend the event; and all of the items must be handmade in the United States. Crafts include ceramics, glass, wood, metal, jewelry, fiber, and leather. Although the American Craft Council hosts these fairs in six other cities across the country, each one invites different artisans. So, if you've attended one in Atlanta, you haven't necessarily seen it all. The ACC Craft Fair is usually held over a weekend in late February but sometimes meanders into early March, so call for exact dates. Admission is $12 for adults, and there is a two-day pass that can be purchased for $18. Kids younger than age 12 get in free. The Convention Center has no parking on-site, but parking is available in nearby garages or at Camden Yards.

Travel and Golf Expo
Baltimore Convention Center
1 West Pratt Street
(410) 332-6470
www.sunspot.net/travelexpo
This mammoth consumer travel show takes place the last weekend in February or the first weekend in March and attracts an average of 12,000 people over two days. More than 70 exhibitors representing the U.S. and most international countries stand ready to help you realize your ultimate holiday getaway. Savvy travelers should be able to strike exceptional deals. Local entertainment—like a popular steel drum band—adds to the flavor of the show. The Convention Center's in-house caterer provides basic concession food for an additional cost. Admission is $5 for individuals and $10 for a family of four; children younger than age 12 are admitted free.

Fridays After Five National Aquarium
Pier 3/501 East Pratt Street
(410) 576-3800
www.aqua.org
Come and party with the fishes every Friday night from mid-September through early March. Special guest appearances each week in honor of Black History Month. See the January "Fridays after Five" entry for more information.

MARCH

Maryland Spring Craft Show and
Maryland Home and Garden Show
Maryland State Fairgrounds, 2200 York Road, Timonium
(410) 863-1180
www.mdhomeandgarden.com
Held over two weekends toward the middle of March, the Home and Garden Show is a gigantic show, with more than 500 exhibits of professionally landscaped gardens and home products. There are two sides to the fairgrounds—one is completely outdoor landscaping, for which prizes are given, the other is crafts and home improvement items. Free

seminars on gardening and home crafts are offered, and there's a huge plant sale. There's also lots of good food and garden benches to rest on. The entrance fee for adults is $9 (seniors are $8), and for kids age 6 through 12, it's $3. Children younger than age 6 are admitted free. There's no charge to park at the fairgrounds. Pick up coupons on the Web site.

St. Patrick's Day Parade and 5-K Run
Downtown city streets
www.irishparade.net
The Sunday closest to the annual Irish holiday includes a parade and a 5-K Shamrock Run through Downtown. The parade forms in Mount Vernon at the Washington Monument and steps off around 2:00 p.m., heading south on Charles Street. Thirty Irish organizations, 20 marching bands, pipe and drum corps, and politicians wind their way through the city heading east on Pratt Street and disbanding at Market Place. The 5-K race follows the parade route and starts at 1:35 p.m. Preregistration is required for the race and costs $22 before March 1, $25 after March 1, or $35 the day of the race. Watching the parade and the race is free. Some years a brunch is held before the parade; iin recent years it has been held at the Camden Club in Camden Yards. Tickets are very limited. Rain or shine.

Contemporary Print Fair
Baltimore Museum of Art (BMA)
10 Art Museum Drive
(410) 396-6345
www.artbma.org
For over a decade the Print & Drawing Society of the Baltimore Museum of Art (BMA) has coordinated one of the only fairs dedicated to the sale of contemporary prints, drawings, photographs, and other works on paper. Twenty distinguished national art dealers offer a wide range of museum-quality images at this biennial one-day event, which takes place on a Sunday in mid-March in even-numbered years. Admission to the fair also affords you access to the BMA's extraordinary

i Spring is horse season in Maryland, with a race just about every weekend. The tailgate drink of choice at the Hunt Cup is the South Side (equal part South Side mix, dark rum, and club soda) while at the Preakness the favorite is the Black-Eyed Susan (bourbon and lemonade). But if you want to look like a true native, imbibe a "Natty Boh, hon" (National Bohemian beer).

collection, so plan on spending the day at the museum (see the BMA listing in The Arts chapter). And since it takes place on Sunday, you should plan to partake in the spectacular brunch menu at the museum's in-house restaurant, Gertrude's, featuring the best in Chesapeake Bay and Southern cuisine (reservations are recommended). Admission to the show is $5 for BMA members, $8 for students and seniors, and $10 for nonmembers. The museum has two free parking lots and the adjacent Johns Hopkins University frequently opens its lots to museum guests on Sundays.

The Great Train Expo
Maryland State Fairgrounds
2200 York Road, Timonium
(630) 279-4048
www.greattrainexpo.com

Three times a year Baltimore is treated to intricate displays of model trains. This hobby-specific show is ideal for families looking for a fun outing as well as the expert model train fanatic looking for the latest addition for a serious collection. At least 100 exhibitors offer a one-stop shop for trains, parts and accessories, and decals. "Meet the Masters" clinics provide practical advice from experts about starting, maintaining, and developing your very own train collection and building your own model railroad. Complex model railroad displays are one of the event's more popular attractions, and a few hands-on layouts even let the kids run the action. On-site food vendors offer snacks and beverages. This is a traveling show that goes up and down the East Coast, but it does hold three

shows locally. This first one is in mid-March, the second show happens during the summer months, and the third usually takes place in early December. Parking is free. Admission is $7 for anyone older than age 12. Admission usually goes up each year, so call or visit the Web site for the most recent information.

Smith College Book Sale
Maryland State Fairgrounds
2200 York Road, Timonium
(410) 821-6241

The Smith College Club of Baltimore, founded in 1917, has been holding its Smith College Book Sale in late March or early April for more than 40 years to raise money for scholarships to help local girls attend Smith. All yearlong, when sorting and cleaning, we pile up any books and records we can no longer use and trot them over to the Smith College Club. The sale is a great motivator to clean off shelves. Items are reasonably priced all weekend, but be advised that on Sunday all books and records are half-price noon to 5:00 p.m., after which the sale closes for an hour. It re-opens at 6:00 p.m., and from then until closing, it's all you can carry in your arms for $2! There is no food served, but drink vending machines are available.

On Friday the sale opens at 10:00 a.m., but to get in the door that first hour (when your pickings are greatest), the price is $5. At 11:00 a.m., the doors open for free, and the sale has no entrance fee from that point on. Saturday hours are 10:00 a.m. to 6:00 p.m., and Sunday the sale opens at noon. Parking is available on the street or at public parking garages nearby. No credit cards or checks are accepted.

Maryland Day
Maryland Historical Society
201 West Monument Street
(410) 889-4488

March 25 doesn't just mean nine more shopping months until Christmas. It's the anniversary of the 1634 founding of Maryland down in St. Mary's City near the southernmost tip of the state. State and city officials gather at the historical society near the actual anniversary for addresses and a wreath laying at the monument to Cecilius Calvert, one of the state's founders. On the actual anniversary, other celebrations are held in Annapolis, the state capital, (www.annapolis.org) and in St. Mary's City (www.stmaryscity.org.)

Lunch with the Elephants
Lexington Market
400 West Lexington Street
(410) 685-6169

When the circus comes to town, Lexington Market invites the elephants to lunch.

The Ringling Brothers and Barnum & Bailey's Circus usually arrives at the Baltimore Arena sometime in March. Lunch with the Elephants is a tradition. Look for an announcement in the local newspapers. The elephants march from the Baltimore Arena up Eutaw Street to the market's south parking lot around noontime. Live music and the circus clowns add a festive air to an already dazzling event. And then these pachyderms chow down on 1,100 oranges, 1,000 apples, 500 heads of lettuce, 700 bananas, 400 pears, and 500 carrots. (Nobody has to coax them to eat their veggies!) Other cities may invite the elephants to lunch, but only in Baltimore is it an annual affair—and children and their parents are always invited. It's free, and parking is usually available in a nearby garage.

Fridays After Five National Aquarium
Pier 3/501 East Pratt Street
(410) 576-3800
www.aqua.org

Joy to the fishes in the deep blue sea . . . and everyone else who comes to enjoy this after-work party at the Aquarium. Discounted tickets on Friday evenings from mid-September through early March. See the January entry for admission prices.

APRIL

The Baltimore Symphony
Decorators' Show House
Location varies annually
(410) 783-8023
www.baltimoresymphony.org

Each year for more than a quarter of a century the Baltimore Symphony Associates have taken one of Baltimore's architecturally renowned homes and updated its interior with the help of the area's finest designers. In addition to a tour of the exquisitely redecorated manor, visitors may shop at an on-premises boutique and dine at a small tearoom. There are some restrictions to the show: Because this is a private residence, it is not wheelchair accessible. Also, no cameras are allowed and no high heels. No children younger than 10 are allowed, including infants.

The Show House runs from mid-April to mid-May. Admission is $20. Advance tickets can be purchased from area stores for $15. Specific information on where to purchase discounted advance tickets is made available on the symphony's Web site by February or by calling the contact number.

Johns Hopkins University Spring Fair
Homewood Campus,
Johns Hopkins University
(410) 516-7692
www.jhuspringfair.com

The Spring Fair is a three-day event planned, organized, and run exclusively by John Hopkins students, and it attracts members of the student body and the community at large. Food, music, and art vendors round out carnival rides, children's shows, and activities.

There are usually two or three musical stages featuring daytime concerts and entertainment and larger evening concerts. Admission is free, and the fair runs from noon on Friday through Sunday evening in early April. Parking lots are available on campus, but be sure to read the signs carefully—some spots are reserved for faculty and staff, even on the weekends and in the evenings. Additional

The Second Sundays Antique Markets

The Second Sundays Antique Markets bring out dealers and antiquers to the Broadway Market Square in Fells Point from 8:00 a.m. to 5:00 p.m. every second Sunday April through October. About 50 dealers bring their wares, with buyers coming from all over the city and beyond. The Preservation Society, a nonprofit organization formed to maintain the character of Federal Hill and Fells Point, sponsors the antiques markets.

parking can be found at the meters along University Parkway or on the streets in the adjacent Charles Village neighborhood.

The Maryland Hunt Cup
Glyndon, Maryland
(410) 527-9299
www.marylandhuntcup.com
The last weekend in April for more than 100 years has seen the running of the Maryland Hunt Cup. This cross-country steeplechase, which is thought by many racing Insiders to be the most difficult race of its kind in the world, is held on private land. Amateur competitors come from all over the Mid-Atlantic region as well as from places as far away as England. Tickets to the race, which are $35 to $75 per car, must be purchased in advance. Bring a picnic lunch and plan to tailgate with pitchers of South Sides (if you don't know about this Southern tradition, see our Insiders' Tip in this chapter). Call the Maryland Historical Society, (410) 685-3750, for information about its luncheon held under tent for an additional fee.

The Mayor's Billie Holiday
Vocal Competition
Meyerhoff Symphony Hall
(410) 752-8632
www.promotionandarts.com
In celebration of Baltimore's own jazz legend Billie Holiday, this is the city's search for the state's perfect set of pipes. Each singer gets to perform a rendition of a Lady Day signature song, as well as a melody of her own choosing. Admission to the show is free and open to the public, but tickets are required and available in advance and on the day of the competition (see The Arts chapter for more information on Center Stage). Only two tickets are allowed per person.

MAY

Flower Mart
Mount Vernon Square
Under the Washington Monument
(410) 323-0022
www.flowermart.org
Put on your nicest hat (you know, the one with all the flowers) and head down to the Washington Monument for a day of flowers, lemon sticks, crab cakes, and the sounds of children singing. The Flower Mart closes a section of Charles Street the first weekend in May and fills the area around the monument and throughout the parks with some 200 tables laden with crafters' wares, bedding plants sold by local charities, and lots of other garden goodies. Concerts by local schoolchildren are held throughout the celebration. This annual event (held for more than 90 years) was once a garden club ladies' event, but now that it's spread over a weekend everybody comes out to buy some flowers, look at the crafts, and enjoy the spring day. Parking is a nightmare, but a few lots and garages usually have space a couple of blocks away. Don't plan to drive on this section of Charles Street any time that weekend, and usually the Friday before and the Monday after, either.

Baltimore Waterfront Festival
Inner Harbor and Rash Field
Key Highway
(877) BALTIMORE
www.baltimoreevents.org
Baltimore's waterfront comes alive in early
May for a celebration of the sea. Live music
and entertainment are backgrounds to an outdoor adventure area that boasts a simulated
rock wall. Visitors can learn how to hoist a sail
or visit an environmental village that highlights life on the Chesapeake Bay. A Chesapeake Kitchen features popular chefs
whipping up delicious seafood dishes. You
can also taste the nation at the international
ports of call—booths that allow visitors to
explore food and traditions from nations far
and wide. The event runs for one weekend,
Friday through Sunday, and is free. Hours are
usually Friday and Saturday 7:00 to 10:00
p.m., and Sunday 4:00 to 8:00 p.m.

Maryland Film Festival
Locations vary
(410) 752-8083
www.mdfilmfest.com
This four-day festival is Maryland's own Sun-
dance, bringing world-renowned filmmakers
and movies to Baltimore, usually the first
weekend in May. Not that we have to look far
outside our own city limits for great motion
picture art; Baltimore has a ripe filmmaking
scene, with talented natives like John Waters
and Barry Levinson using the city as inspira-
tion. But the Maryland Film Festival extends
its reach globally and presents more than 120
foreign and domestic feature films and shorts.
Films are primarily screened at the Charles
Theater and the Senator theater as well as the
University of Baltimore and Maryland Institute
College of Art (see The Arts chapter for more
information.) Screenings include an introduction by the director or the producer with a Q
& A session after. Special lectures and presentations take place throughout the weekend.
Waters and Levinson have been guest speakers in the past. Admission to one film is $10, a
three-show pass is $20, and an all-access pass

for the entire event is $250. Student and sen-
ior discounts may be applicable.

Towsontown Spring Festival
In and around the Old Courthouse Plaza
1 block west of York Road and
Pennsylvania Avenue
(410) 825-1144
www.towsontownspringfestival.com
This spring fair has been entertaining visitors
and residents for more than 30 years. It's a
large event (attracting 200,000 people) that
always has local as well as national bands as
live entertainment on various stages throughout the fairgrounds. (The "fairgrounds" are a
4-block area between Allegheny Avenue on
the north to Susquehanna Avenue on the
south.) Every year features local microbrew-
eries, more than 40 food vendors, and many
arts and crafts booths. There are plenty of
children's activities, including a children's
stage and the Annual Towsontown Spring Festival Youth Art Show, in which young artists
get to show off their best work. This free
event is held the first full weekend in May. All-
day parking is available for around $8.

The Preakness Parade and
Preakness Week
East on Pratt Street to Market Place
(877) BALTIMORE
www.preaknesscelebration.org
The Preakness Parade (held the Saturday
before the Preakness) begins Preakness
Week, a celebration in early to mid-May that
often includes a hot-air balloon ascension,
outdoor concerts, schooner races, benefit

i Many local antiques shows are benefits for area not-for-profits. To raise
additional funds for their cause, event
planners frequently offer a preview party
the day before the show officially begins.
Admission to these parties can be steep,
but the trade-off is the chance to buy the
objects for sale before the onslaught of
the public, a real boon if you are a serious collector.

galas, fireworks, and more, and culminates in the running of the Preakness Stakes, "the second jewel in horse racing's triple crown." (See the Spectator Sports chapter for more about the Preakness.) As always, we hope for a fast, dry track and a warm sunny day for the race. If we're lucky, we get the same for the parade. The weather mat be iffy. So, put on a jacket, buy some cotton candy, and watch the equestrian units, the marching bands, the clowns, and the floats. Admission is free. (See the *Baltimore Sun* and other local publications the week before the parade for lists of activities during Preakness Week or call the Preakness Celebration number, (410) 837-3030, to receive a booklet that has it all.)

The Preakness Stakes
Pimlico Race Course
5201 Park Heights Avenue
(410) 542-9400
www.preakness.com
The third Saturday in May marks the annual running of the Preakness Stakes and has for more than 125 years. Gates usually open at 8:30 a.m. for the infield, which is the area inside the track. Infield seats are popular, first because you are right at eye level with the horses; second, because seats are less expensive; and third, because it's a great all-day picnic. When you look at the infield on television, it looks as if infielders are trapped, since the races run around them; but, in fact, there is a tunnel under the track that allows you to come and go as you please, but why would you want to go? Concession stands, betting windows, and the all-important portable toilets are available for infielders. Clubhouse and grandstands seats are more expensive (from $75 to $275), but you don't have to fight the crowd to see the racing, since all seats are reserved. The clubhouse, which is under roof, is the most posh seating, and guests dress for the occasion. (If you purchase a clubhouse seat, don't go in jeans.) Racing begins at 10:30 a.m., but the Preakness goes off at around 6:05 p.m. and is the next to last race of the day. For standing-room-only, clubhouse

admission is $25. Infield admission is $45 in advance or $60 on Preakness Day. Call for reserved seating prices. Parking can be difficult. Traffic backs up for miles, so give yourself plenty of time to get there if you're driving and wear your walking shoes. Sometimes you can find inexpensive parking on someone's front lawn, but you might have to walk more than a mile. Parking at the track costs $60 to $115. (More for your limo.) However, public transportation is available, including Light Rail and MTA Preakness buses.

Market Day
Cylburn Arboretum
4915 Greenspring Avenue
(410) 367-2217
www.cylburnassociation.org
For more than 20 years, the Cylburn Arboretum Association, the volunteer group that keeps the 207-acre nature reserve running smoothly, has held Market Day on the day before Mother's Day. The group's main fundraiser, Market Day is an opportunity for us to get out in the fresh spring air and look over a selection of plants for this summer's backyard or window box. Baltimore's horticulturists are out in full force with their best offerings of flowers, vegetables, and, as one Insider put it, "just about any plant you can imagine." Crafters are also in evidence with crafts constructed on a gardening theme. While you wander through the booths or down one of Cylburn's many nature trails, you will not go hungry. Common Market Day fare includes crab cakes, fried chicken, hamburgers, and hot dogs. But don't stay out among the trees too long or you'll miss the annual maypole dance. Gates open at 8:00 a.m. and the formal closing is 4:00 p.m. Parking is $4; admission is $2.

The Baltimore Symphony
Decorators' Show House
Location varies annually
(410) 783-8023
www.baltimoresymphony.org
Come see how the other half lives at this

event sponsored by the Baltimore Symphony Associates. For more than two decades, the group has given one of Baltimore's homes to designers to decorate. See the April entry for more information.

BALTICON: Maryland Regional Science Fiction Convention
Marriot Hunt Valley Inn
(410) 563-2737
www.balticon.org
More than 300 science fiction authors, artists, musicians, aficionados, and actual scientists—of which we have plenty in Baltimore—meet to talk about what they're doing, reading, and thinking at this convention held over a weekend in late May. Tickets prices are based on how far in advance they are purchased, ranging from $37 several months from the event, to $52 just a few weeks before the event. For more information, call the Baltimore Science Fiction Society at the listed number or write to P.O. Box 686, Baltimore, MD 21203. Beam on in if you can, and may the force be with you in your quest.

JUNE

Maryland Rose Society, Inc.
Annual Rose Show
Cylburn Arboretum
4915 Greenspring Avenue
(410) 367-2217
www.cylburnassociation.org
In early June Maryland's roses are in full bloom at the Annual Rose Show. Growers, both members of the Rose Society and others, come to the mansion at Cylburn to display their beauties. All registered categories of roses may be entered, and the roses are judged by a panel of experts for their perfection. Members of the Rose Society staff a booth to answer questions about growing roses, and information is available that you can take home. If nothing else, the Rose Show gives anyone who visits a gift of the scent of summer—without the bees. Parking and admission are free.

Greek Festival
St. Nicholas Church
520 South Ponca Street
(410) 633-5020
www.greek-fest.com
One of Baltimore's most popular festivals, the Greek Festival is an immersion into all things Greek. Food is always a major draw at the ethnic festivals. At the Greek Festival, it's the stuffed grape leaves and the baklava you'll find us hunting down first. If you'd like to learn how to make such treats the Greek way, the festival offers cooking lessons and cooking demonstrations. To work off what you eat, there's Greek dancing. The festival is held the second weekend of the month. Admission is free.

Between 20,000 and 30,000 people descend on this small community, and parking is difficult, because it is all on-street parking. In recent years, organizers have utilized the Downtown trolley system. Festivalgoers can park Downtown and hop on the trolley on Pratt Street to bring them over to the festival grounds. Call to confirm before relying on the trolley—some years it does not run.

Gay Pride Festival
Various locations
(410) 837-5445
www.baltimorepride.org
Toward the middle of June, the Gay, Lesbian, Bisexual, and Transgender Association of Baltimore sponsors a weekend celebration to which all are invited. On Saturday a Gay Pride Parade heads north on Charles Street, through the Mount Vernon neighborhood, and disbands at Eager Street for a rowdy block party. The festivities continue on Sunday when the gay community hosts a festival at Druid Hill Park beginning at 11:00 a.m. Under the trees on the grassy lawn of the park you can listen to live music, taste ethnic food, and visit more than 100 booths full of information, arts, and crafts. More than 20,000 people attend this function, making it one of the largest gay pride events on the East Coast. The festival is free.

Latino Fest
Patterson Park
(410) 783-5404
www.eblo.org

The Latino Fest is a celebration of folk music, dance, arts, and crafts from all of Central and South America. Groups perform folk music of the Andes, Latin jazz, and salsa. Arts and crafts displays and demonstrations include handcrafted pottery, silver from Peru, and woolens from Ecuador and Bolivia. Sponsored by the education-based Latino Outreach, all funds raised support children's educational and cultural programs for the Latino community. There is always plenty of dancing, as well as a dance contest. So, if you consider yourself a mambo expert, put on your dancin' shoes and come on down.

The Latino Fest, which usually takes place over a weekend in late June, also has a Baltimore County venue. It is held at the Courthouse Square in Towson in August.

JULY

Baltimore's Fourth of July Celebration
Inner Harbor
(877) BALTIMORE
www.promotionandarts.com

The rockets' red glare—and blue and white—casts its sparkles on the water within sight of where "The Star-Spangled Banner" was penned. If you've never seen fireworks over water, push your way into the crowd for this. It's beautiful. It's as if the sea opens up and shows another world below, exploding into magical lights. Here's a hint, however, if you decide to go. Any spot along the Inner Harbor is a good one. Plan to stand. Almost everyone does. The free show begins at 9:30 p.m. Parking can be a nightmare, so arrive early and be patient.

Baltimore Playwrights Festival
Various locations
(410) 276-2153
www.baltplayfest.org

Every summer for more than 20 years Balti-more's Downtown community theaters have hosted the Baltimore Playwrights Festival, a celebration of the best Maryland playwrights. The festival has premiered more than 160 plays since its inception, and usually highlights 10 to 12 productions a year in seven theaters around town. Plays are selected by the end of March through a rigorous judging process, and open auditions for actors are held in April. Individual ticket prices vary from theater to theater, but an advanced subscription package (six tickets for $45) can be purchased.

Artscape
West Mount Royal Avenue,
beginning south of North Avenue
(877) BALTIMORE
www.artscape.org

Artscape is a city-sponsored free event that was started in the mid-1980s and is now the country's largest public arts celebrations. Strung out along Mount Royal Avenue from The Maryland Institute College of Art, bending around in front of the Lyric Theatre and around the Meyerhoff Symphony Hall are hundreds of arts and crafts vendors and 30 food vendors. There are potters and woodworkers, glassworkers and ironworkers—just about every kind of worker you can imagine. You can buy tiny origami earrings or a 6-foot carved statue. There are paintings, drawings, and etchings. Galleries abound, as do live theater productions and poetry readings. There's great kidstuff at the Maryland Institute, and it's different every year. Through it all, local and national talent provide continuous music. Everywhere you turn, you find food from traditional pit beef to delicately flavored crepes. Since more than a million fairgoers come over these three days during the third or fourth weekend of July, parking is difficult as people jockey for spots on the street or in lots. One of the most sensible ways to get there is by Light Rail, as there is a Light Rail stop right in the middle of the "fairgrounds." It can get hot on the city streets in July, so dress appropriately.

Baltimore celebrates the arts at Artscape with three days of performances, exhibits, and the always popular artist market. BALTIMORE OFFICE OF PROMOTION AND THE ARTS

The Inner Harbor is the name given both to the actual harbor in the center of Baltimore and the area that surrounds it. The main activity center is at the head of the Inner Harbor, in and around the Harborplace shopping area at the corner of Pratt and Light Streets.

AUGUST

Gospel Music Crab Feast
Oregon Ridge Park, Beaver Dam Road, 1 mile south of Shawan Road, Hunt Valley
(888) 375-0080
www.crabfeast.com

The Dixie Hummingbirds once performed at this all-day, outdoor gospel event usually held in early August. Essentially a picnic with music, the fare includes hamburgers, hot dogs, pit beef, as well as crabs. Admission, which costs about $60, includes the music as well as the fabulous fare. People come from all over to attend this event, so reservations are required at least 48 hours in advance, but group discounts are available, if you want to reserve space for two busloads of folks from your church. Note: If you're not into gospel music, this same group hosts a number of different themed crab feasts throughout the city.

India Day
Center Plaza, Charles Street
(888) 225-8466

Toward the middle of August the India Forum, in conjunction with the Baltimore Office of Promotions, puts on a free festival that not only celebrates Indian heritage but also provides information about Baltimore to the community at large. Information booths concern local schools and businesses, but the main focus is the Indian culture. The smell of curry, the whirling dancers, and the sound of ankle bells fill the square. Vendors offer Indian jewelry and decorated silks. Kids will enjoy the face painting, but decorative handpainting is also available for the older "kids," as is palmistry. The best fun is the closing ceremonies,

in which all present are invited to learn and dance the Dandia Dance in celebration.

The Maryland Renaissance Festival
Crownsville, 20 minutes south of the city off Highway 97
(800) 296-7304
www.rennfest.com

The Maryland Renaissance Festival is habit-forming. Fondly called "The Renny" by some of those addicted, its permanent Renaissance village is truly a step back in time. Many of the crafters who attend actually reside in the village for the festival's duration. Attendees often dress up in medieval costume, but if you don't have one and want one, there are booths where costumes can be rented or bought. You can see glass blown and etched, metal work, clay work, leather craftsmen, and much more. The food is very Henry VIII—whole turkey legs, french-fried sweet potatoes, soup in bread bowls. But not everything is dinner. You can also buy a fresh glass of ice-cold milk and a pile of homemade chocolate chip cookies for about a buck. Or how about a homemade apple dumpling smothered in vanilla ice cream? There's jousting, Shakespeare, magic, madrigals, and more. One of the most interesting things about the Renny is the history lessons. For every year that passes, the festival moves forward one year in history. Recently, Henry VIII took the throne.

The Renaissance Festival is held on weekends from late August to late October. Admission fees are $8 to $18. No weapons (costume or real).

Baltimore Playwrights Festival
Various locations
(410) 276-2153

The Baltimore Playwrights Festival has been a city tradition for more than 20 years. The performances are hosted by Downtown community theaters. See the July entry for more information.

Maryland State Fair
Maryland State Fairgrounds
York and Timonium Roads, Timonium
(410) 252-0200
www.marylandstatefair.com

For 11 days in late August and early September, the state of Maryland puts its best foot forward at the Maryland State Fair, and the Maryland State Fairgrounds are allowed to fulfill the purpose for which this permanent site was created. Every exhibition hall is filled with displays and shows. Maryland's citizens from the western counties to the Eastern Shore bring their best pigs, cows, chickens, quilts, jams, pies, wine, honey—you name it—to try to win a blue ribbon. The open area is jammed with traditional three-balls-for-a-dollar kind of games where you can win a stuffed toy, a live goldfish, or a myriad of other goodies. There's even horse racing for 10 days at Timonium Racetrack.

Rides dominate the fairway and cost from 75 cents for the smaller kiddie rides to $3.25 for the more grandiose. On some special days there are bulk ride offers, where you only pay one flat fee and can ride all the rides. Parking, which is usually free at Timonium during other events, costs $2 during the fair. Free parking is available at a Park and Ride off Deereco Road, west of the fairgrounds. Parking is a real zoo: York Road is always jammed with cars. More and more people are opting to take the Light Rail. In fact, Insiders at the fair note that it's becoming the biggest entrance gate.

The entrance fee is $6 per person, with children younger than age 12 entering for free. Gates essentially open at 10:00 a.m., but some special livestock shows begin as early as 8:00 a.m. The fair closes at 10:00 p.m. every evening.

American Indian PowWow
Patterson Park
400 South Linwood Avenue
(410) 675-3535
www.baic.org

Baltimore has a large American Indian population. This PowWow, sponsored by the Baltimore American Indian Center (113 South Broadway in Fells Point), is the last of the year and by far the biggest. There's plenty of good food and vendor booths with leather goods, silver jewelry, and other crafts, but, by far, the most exciting sight is American Indians in full costume competing in the dance competitions that are held throughout the weekend, usually the last one in August. Traditional dances tell stories or are more ceremonial in nature, and the regalia worn has meaning to the dancer about the aspects of his or her tribe, family, and beliefs. There is also competition in "fancy dancing," which is a more contemporary style of dance, originated by the Ponca people. Admission is generally $5, and a three-day pass is $10.

International Festival
Poly/Western High School parking lot
Falls Road and West Cold Spring Lane
(410) 396-3141

Baltimore's summer of ethnic festivals winds up with the International Festival, kind of a melting pot of cultural diversity with plenty of music, dancing, and ethnic foods and a two-day international soccer competition. The event is held the first weekend in August at the high schools right off Interstate 83 at the Cold Spring Lane exit. Admission is free.

> **i** A lemon stick is half of a fresh lemon that has been cored and into which a peppermint stick has been inserted as a straw. When you're eating one, keep squeezing the lemon. It helps secure the peppermint stick and ensures you're sucking juice, not pulp. When the end of the stick in the lemon starts to melt, take it out, turn it over and start again.

SEPTEMBER

Maryland State Fair
Maryland State Fairgrounds
York and Timonium Roads, Timonium
(410) 252-0200, ext. 226
www.marylandstatefair.com
The Maryland State Fair is a feast for the senses. Popcorn, cotton candy, and hot dogs are a delight for both the nose and taste buds. Games of skill test the eyes and hands for coordination. And the ears revel in pipe-organ music and the laughter of hundreds of people coming together. It's 11 days of pure fun for everyone. See the August entry for more information.

Defenders' Day
Fort McHenry and the Flag House
and Star Spangled Flag Museum
(410) 962-4290
www.nps.gov/fomc
Baltimoreans commemorate the night our citizens saved the city from the British and Francis Scott Key wrote the "Star Spangled Banner" with a weekend of festivities held at the fort and the house where Mary Pickersgill sewed the flag Key saw flying over the fort during the War of 1812. There are re-enactments at the fort, along with artillery firings, evening fireworks, concerts, and children's programs at the fort as well as special events at the Flag House. These events are held the first weekend after Labor Day. Parking at the fort is free; the parking garages near the Flag House and in Little Italy usually have space available.

Annual Plant Sale Day
Cylburn Arboretum
4915 Greenspring Avenue
(410) 367-2217
www.cylburnassociation.org
If you've wondered where to go to buy a palm tree to put in your living room or a beautiful fern for your window box, Cylburn Arboretum Associations Plant Sale Day is the place. All manner of exotic and native plants are for sale from local nurseries on the grounds of the arboretum. The sale is either the weekend before or the weekend after Labor Day. Both parking and admission are free.

Constellation Turn Around
Pier 1
Inner Harbor
(410) 539-1797
www.constellation.org
The USS *Constellation* is generally too delicate to sail anymore. So for 364 days of the year, she floats regally beside Pier 1. But once a year, she takes a ride out to Fort McHenry just to turn around. The thinking is that this way, she wears evenly on both sides. The *Constellation*'s caretakers schedule the annual cruise on a Friday in early September, about 3:00 p.m. Most people never see this event, but it's worthwhile heading to the Inner Harbor to see this huge and ancient vessel leave her pier (under power, not sail, alas) and take the short trip down to the fort, turn around, and come back. Throw in an ice cream or dinner at the Inner Harbor and perhaps a visit to the Aquarium or Maryland Science Center and it could be a very nice afternoon. After all, if you've paid for parking, you might as well get your money's worth. Don't be late, of course; the trip isn't very long.

The Irish Festival
Maryland State Fairgrounds
York and Timonium Roads, Timonium
(410) 747-6868
www.irishfestival.com
Fill up on Irish champ (potatoes and onions) and Guinness while tapping your foot to the lively music of the Irish folk groups that perform continuously on stage. And, although you'll find the usual kinds of souvenir-type items to buy, there are also some educational opportunities, such as a lecture on twentieth-century Irish literature. The festival, held in mid-September, is sponsored by Irish Charities of Maryland, Inc. The entrance fee is $10 for adults, $7 for seniors, $5 for kids age 12 through 17, and free for kids younger than 12.

Baltimore Book Festival
Mount Vernon Place
Charles and Monument Streets
(877) BALTIMORE
www.baltimorebookfestival.com
The mid-Atlantic's premier celebration of the literary arts offers well-known authors, local bookstores, publishers, children's writers, storytellers, author signings, crafts, refreshments, and entertainment. The cobblestone streets around the Washington Monument in Mount Vernon are cordoned off and filled with vendors, food, books, and crowds of people milling about. In the past Elmo (Kevin Clash), Ruby Dee, and John Sheilds have read from their books. Live music and a beer garden take over one quadrant of the festival, while a Kid's Corner fills the Mount Vernon square park with plenty of activities to keep the young ones busy. The food is always good—definitely try the souvlaki from the Greek stand! The Book Festival runs in mid-September Friday 5:00 to 9:00 p.m. and Saturday and Sunday 11:00 a.m. to 7:00 p.m. Admission is free.

Fridays After Five National Aquarium
Pier 3/501 East Pratt Street
(410) 576-3800
www.aqua.org
Fridays. Five. Fish. Fun. What do these things have in common? YOU!—if you're smart and looking for a good, though maybe a little wet, time on a Friday evening. See the January entry for details.

The Maryland Renaissance Festival
Crownsville, 20 minutes south of the city off Highway 97
(800) 296-7304
www.rennfest.com
Join peasants and princes at this event held from late summer through midfall. Food, costumes, crafts, and performances are all a step back in time to a period of mighty kings, fair ladies, and noble knights. See the August entry for more information.

OCTOBER

Maryland Oktoberfest
5th Regiment Armory
Howard and Division Streets
(410) 522-4144
www.md-germans.org
The doors open at noon, and the oompahs start at 1:00 p.m. Polka until you drop or just sit at the communal tables and drink, eat, and sing. German imports as well as sauerbraten, sauerkraut, schnitzel, and all the respective wursts are there for the gobbling. There's also a wine garden for those with more refined tastes and crafts and souvenirs for those who want to bring a little taste of Germany home with them. Oktoberfest is usually held the second weekend of the month. Admission is $5. Free parking in state of Maryland lots.

Baltimore Marathon
M&T Bank Stadium
And various locations around town
(410) 605-9381
www.thebaltimoremarathon.com
The marathon, known officially as the "Baltimore Running Festival-Under Armour Marathon," brings out hundreds and serious runners—and plenty of not-so-serious runners willing to give it a go for this 25K held on a Saturday in mid-October. Streets are closed throughout town and lined with well-wishers and fans waiting to see the runners zip by—or stumble by depending on the spot on the route. If you are early, you'll see world-class runners. If you're late, you might see the woman who jogs through your neighborhood toughing it out to the end no matter what. Runners take part in the full marathon, a half marathon, a team relay, and, for the weekend jogger, a 5K and kids' fun run. It lasts from about 8:00 a.m. to 4:00 p.m. If you aren't interested in the race, pay attention to the route anyway; you may not be able to use some of the streets you usually take.

Chocolate Festival
Lexington Market
400 West Lexington Street
(410) 685-6169
www.lexingtonmarket.com

For three days toward the middle of October, Baltimoreans get the opportunity to experience chocolate. We may be able to pick up a candy bar any day of the week during the year, but at the Chocolate Festival, statues are carved from it. You can watch it being melted and molded and dipped or linger at the fudge-making demonstration. If you are a chocoholic, there is no better place to go to feed your addiction. It's free, unless you buy a three-pound box of something, and parking is available in the Lexington Market parking garage ($4 all day).

ZooBoo
The Maryland Zoo
1 Druid Park Lake Drive
(410) 366-LION
www.marylandzoo.org

At Halloween, Charm City turns into Boo City. Houses are rimmed in orange lights. Ghosts made from sheets and white plastic bags float from trees. Haunted houses abound. And the zoo has ZooBoo. Be sure to have your little one dress up, as there is a costume contest. Other things of interest include 25 different booths with various attractions, trick-or-treating, a Creepy Class where they can make spooky things, and the Haunted Barn for the older and braver. All kids get an activity coloring book and a Halloween bag. Entrance to ZooBoo is the regular zoo entrance fee of $15 for adults and $10 for kids age 2 through 11 and $12 for seniors. The entrance fee includes the Children's Zoo. The event is usually held the two weekends before Halloween, rain or shine.

The Maryland Renaissance Festival
Crownsville, 20 minutes south of the city off Highway 97
(800) 296-7304
www.rennfest.com

Oyez! Oyez! Come one, come all to this festival of food, theater, and crafts. Enjoy archery and jousting, magic and music here weekends from late August through late October. See the August entry for details.

Fridays After Five National Aquarium
Pier 3/501 East Pratt Street
(410) 576-3800
www.aqua.org

Come party with puffins and piranhas, do the electric slide with an electric eel, or mambo with other marine creatures at this get-together that celebrates the end of the workweek. See the January entry for more information.

NOVEMBER

Thanksgiving Parade
From Camden Yards to Market Place, along Pratt Street
(877) BALTIMORE
www.artsandpromotion.com

Santa Claus and his reindeer make their first seasonal appearance, surrounded by marching bands, equestrian units, and hosts of clowns. Bundle up and bring a folding chair. It's a short route, but usually a fairly long parade. Admission is free. Held on the Saturday before Thanksgiving, the first bands usually step off at 11:00 a.m.

Fridays After Five National Aquarium
Pier 3/501 East Pratt Street
(410) 576-3800
www.aqua.org

Friday evenings from mid-September to early March the Aquarium brings Baltimoreans and marine life together during this celebration of the end of the workweek. Discounted admission prices make this a real bargain as well as a real good time. See the January entry for more details.

Christmas in Hampden
700 block of West 34th Street
www.Christmasstreet.com

Here's a miracle on 34th Street that shouldn't be missed. The residents on this one little block of row houses string up thousands of Christmas lights, stretching them across the street, lining their roofs, and covering every square inch with color. Then they fill their yards with every kind of Christmas decoration they can think of: snow globes, nativity scenes and, a popular favorite, the hubcap tree. It's all kitschy. And it's definitely fun. Residents spend their evenings on the porch, talking to the passersby. Some displays extend into the house and you may be invited in to see these. The display goes up Thanksgiving weekend and lasts until New Year's Day. Cars drive through the display or when the weather's nice, Baltimoreans park nearby and walk to see the decorations. Come New Year's Eve to count down the seconds to the new year. The display has gotten national attention; once you see it, you'll understand.

Festival of Trees
Maryland State Fairgrounds
200 York Road Timonium
(800) 830-3976
www.festivaloftrees.kennedykrieger.org

Organizers of this fund-raiser for the Kennedy Krieger Institute turn the fairgrounds' Cow Palace into a winter wonderland. Some 300 decorated trees are on display (and for sale), along with holiday crafts and dozens of beautifully trimmed wreaths, and there are dozens of choirs singing throughout the weekend. The festival takes place the weekend after Thanksgiving. Friday and Saturday hours are 10:00 a.m. to 9:00 p.m., and Sunday hours are 10:00 a.m. to 6:00 p.m. Tickets are $10 for adults and $5 for children age 5 through 12 and senior citizens. Tickets are available at the door. Parking on the fairgrounds lots is free. Proceeds benefit the institute's young patients who are undergoing treatment for neurological disorders.

Holiday Festival of Trains at the B&O
B & O Railroad Museum
901 West Pratt Street
(410) 752-2490
www.borail.org

Who knows why trains have become a Christmas tradition, but once you see the displays in the B&O roundhouse, you'll be glad to be part of the festivities. The turntable in the center of the roundhouse is filled with an enormous train garden. It takes a dozen train enthusiasts to keep all the trains running, but they'll be happy to tell you their stories about the trains and the different parts of the garden. Other train gardens are on display in the O #725 passenger car and in an outside layout that features the large "G" scale trains. Once the kids get tired of teeny trains, climb aboard an operating train for a short round-trip on some of the oldest track in the country. Santa arrives on Friday in a locomotive and is happy to visit with children on Saturdays and Sundays until Christmas. The exhibit is open Monday through Friday 10:00 a.m. to 4:00 p.m., Saturday 10:00 a.m. to 5:00 p.m., and Sunday 11:00 a.m. to 4:00 p.m. It is closed on Christmas Day, New Year's Eve, and New Year's Day. Admission is the same as any other day at the B&O Museum: $14 for adults, $12 for seniors, and $8 for children age 2 through 12.

DECEMBER

A Monumental Occasion
Washington Monument
Mount Vernon Place
(877) BALTIMORE
www.promotionandarts.com

Baltimore, once dubbed Monument City for its number of, well, monuments, sets its most prominent monument aglow for the holiday season. The first Thursday in December the city hosts the official lighting of the Washington Monument—which features entertainment, fireworks, and refreshments. The event is always festive and gets the city in the mood for the holiday season. The program begins right after work on a Thursday, around 5:30

p.m. The event is held in conjunction with First Thursday, the Baltimore event where neighborhood museums and galleries open their doors to the public for an evening of free art and entertainment. So plan to make an evening of it.

Baltimore's New Year's Eve Spectacular
Various locations downtown
(877) BALTIMORE
www.promotionandarts.com
Baltimore rings in the New Year in a big way—and all without alcohol. This nonalcoholic celebration started a few years ago and caught fire. There are live music and countdowns around the Inner Harbor and Fells Point. The party begins at 9:00 p.m. and culminates with fireworks at midnight, as we enter the new year. All outdoor events are free. It's a grand time, particularly if it's a balmy night. But be prepared. You could need your winter woollies.

Fridays After Five National Aquarium
Pier 3/501 East Pratt Street
(410) 752-8632
www.aqua.org
Dolphins, and stingrays, and dart frogs, oh my! You're sure not in Kansas anymore. Enjoy one of Baltimore's most popular attractions at discounted prices during Fridays After Five. See the January entry for more information.

Hampden Holidays

Nobody does Christmas decorations like Hampden, hon! Every house on the 700 block of 34th Street is decorated from Thanksgiving to New Years. And when we say decorated, we mean decorated. Hubcap Christmas trees, Yule flamingos, train sets galore. Even strings of lights stretch from row house roofs on one side of the street to the other. Everybody gets in the holiday spirit one way or the other. Homeowners even sit on their front porches and welcome guests in to see the decorations on the porch, the train tracks that run through the living room, or the animated scenes lining their front walk. People drive down the street or in nice weather track down a parking space and walk so they can savor all this holiday fun. Lights are on every night until 11:00 p.m. through New Year's Day. Visit on New Year's Eve and you can watch the ball drop. It's just like Times Square, only different.

THE ARTS

Baltimoreans are known as a discerning audience. There was a time when no Broadway show would open in New York until its company had played in Baltimore. If Baltimore's audiences didn't like the show, then producers could be sure New York audiences wouldn't either.

Theater is still very big in Baltimore and includes some pre-Broadway entries as well as Broadway touring company offerings. Community theater offerings are diverse, and prices are low. You can often see experimental efforts or the works of new authors that you would not be privy to in a larger, more professional venue. In fact, during July and August of every year, many of the community theaters focus entirely on new scripts as they present the works of entrants in the Baltimore Playwrights Festival (see the Close-up in this chapter). We've listed the major professional theaters and a few of the older or unique community theaters and groups later in this chapter.

If you're looking for a music recital or a concert, Baltimore has many groups, some professional and some amateur, that perform on a continuing basis. Many of these do not have permanent performance venues, but if you call the contact numbers we've provided, the individual organizations will give you current performance information, including what, when, where, and how much.

Of course, there are some performance groups that do have permanent venues, such as the Peabody Institute. Students of the Peabody mount more than 60 concerts per year, most of which are recitals and public performances. (For concert information, call the Concert Office at (410) 659-8100. For more information about the school, see the Education chapter.)

Next to theater and music, Baltimore's biggest love is probably movies. Until the early 1960s Baltimore claimed a fair-size theater in every neighborhood as well as magnificent downtown movie houses. The Stanley, The Mayfair, The Hippodrome, and The Century-Valencia were the most splendid. Baltimore was a stop on the promotional tours of all the big production houses, and local theaters played host to big movie names like Errol Flynn and the Marx Brothers. The accoutrements they boasted for such entertainers send today's lavish lifestyles into the pale. Consider, for instance, an Olympic-size swimming pool beneath the Hippodrome Theatre that rumor has it was completely made of marble and designed in the style of a Greek temple. Many of the neighborhood houses and major downtown theaters are gone now, victims of urban renewal or simply ground down by urban decay. We've listed some of the unique ones as well as a more complete listing of family theaters later in this chapter.

The good news is the Hippodrome has been reborn as a venue for Broadway Across America. Restored to its former glory, with a backstage big enough to back in a 16-wheeler, the theater has become Baltimore's premier location for Broadway's traveling shows. We no longer have to head to New York or D.C. to catch "Wicked" or "Spamalot." All the national shows have been stopping in Baltimore since the Hippodrome reopened in February 2004. (See the entire write-up later in this chapter.)

With all of these museums, galleries, and performances going on, how can you possibly choose between them? Well, what are you doing Thursday? The first Thursday of the month in summer features a continuing Downtown art celebration known simply as

First Thursdays. First Thursdays takes place along the Charles Street corridor, both above and below Mount Vernon Place, the acknowledged center of Baltimore art and culture. All the galleries, museums, shops, and restaurants are open late, with some providing special entertainment, either inside or out on the sidewalk. Live music is a mainstay, whether classical, jazz, or Dixieland. It's a great way to sample a lot of the city's arts offerings. For more information about First Thursdays, call the Downtown Partnership of Baltimore at (410) 244-1030.

VISUAL ARTS
Museums and Centers
American Visionary Art Museum
800 Key Highway
(410) 244-1900
www.avam.org
CNN called the AVAM "one of the most fantastic museums anywhere in America." The museum features artwork produced by self-taught individuals, usually with no formal training. "Visionary" art, according to the museum, "arises from an innate personal vision that revels foremost in the creative act itself. Visionary art begins by listening to the inner voices of the soul, and often may not even be thought of as 'art' by its creator." In this spiraling, four-story gallery space you will discover inspirational creations made by extraordinary people. The museum is open Tuesday through Sunday 10:00 a.m. to 6:00 p.m. Admission is $12 for adults and $8 for seniors and students.

Baltimore Museum of Art
10 Art Museum Drive
(443) 573-1700
www.artbma.org
Maryland's celebrated art museum houses a permanent collection of more than 100,000 objects, ranging from ancient mosaics to contemporary art pieces. The Cone Collection features the works of Matisse, Picasso, Cezanne, van Gogh, Gauguin, Renoir, and others from the Modernist era, while the New Wing boasts post-1945 artwork, including a gallery of major works by Andy Warhol. The John Russell Pope Building houses furniture, decorative arts, paintings, and miniature rooms, while the sculpture gardens boast works by artists such as Rodin and Calder. Hours are Wednesday through Friday from 11:00 a.m. to 5:00 p.m. and Saturday and Sunday from 11:00 a.m. to 6:00 p.m. The museum is closed Monday, Tuesday, New Year's Day, July 4, Thanksgiving, and Christmas. Admission is free.

Contemporary Museum
100 West Centre Street
(410) 783-5720
www.contemporary.org
The Contemporary Museum is "dedicated to creating education programs and cultural experiences that reach an exceptionally wide range of constituents." Contemporary exhibitions and educational programs are on show at the gallery space on Center Street, just 1 block from the Maryland Historical Society and the Walters Art Museum. Hours are Wednesday through Saturday noon to 5:00 p.m., Call before visiting as it closes between exhibitions.

Creative Alliance at the Patterson
3134 Eastern Avenue
(410) 276-1651
www.creativealliance.org
The Creative Alliance is a member-based non-profit group that presents and promotes the arts throughout the city. Founded in 1995 as the Fells Point Creative Alliance, the original goal of this group was simply to be a guild for the active community of local artists. The organization soon broadened its mission by developing performance, video, film, and music series. The Creative Alliance organizes at least six exhibitions a year as well as the popular Big Show, an open members' exhibition. The alliance is an integral part of our community; each summer it holds Open

Movies under the Stars

What could be better on a warm summer night than a movie under the stars? Both the community of Little Italy and the American Visionary Art Museum schedule them.

In Little Italy the movies usually have an Italian theme—*Moonstruck* is a regular—and they are shown on the side of a building over a parking lot on summer Fridays when it is finally dark enough. The neighbors bring their kids and their chairs (and their bug spray) for a night out.

In Federal Hill, the museum shows movies on the side of its building and Baltimoreans spread their blankets on the hill. The museum also stays open until 9:00 p.m.—with free admission after 5:00 p.m.—and also schedules an activity for families to go along with the movie's theme. Everybody is invited to both.

Minds, a free art education program for children at the Enoch Pratt Free Library. Exhibitions, performances, classes, and other programs take place in the restored Patterson Park Arts Center, a theater, gallery, artist studio residencies, media lab, and cafe in the former Patterson movie theater. Situated on Eastern Avenue 1 block east of Patterson Park, the Creative Alliance at the Patterson serves as an anchor for the revitalization of this historic neighborhood.

Maryland Art Place (MAP)
38 Market Place
(410) 962-8565
www.mdartplace.org

Maryland Art Place is the place to see contemporary art in Baltimore. The nonprofit arts center has garnered support for local artists and has facilitated exchange between the community and the art world through thought-provoking exhibits and educational outreach programs. Located right in Power Plant Live, this is the best place to go to see the rising stars of the art world. MAP also sponsors the 14 Karat Cabaret, a place for scintillating performance art. Hours for MAP are Tuesday through Saturday from 11:00 a.m. to 5:00 p.m.

The Maryland Institute, College of Art
1300 West Mount Royal Avenue
(410) 669-9200
www.mica.edu

All around The Maryland Institute, art abounds. On the lawns, in the median strip down Mount Royal Avenue, and just about anywhere there is space to put sculpture. But, if you're after a more formal structure for viewing, the institute has four galleries that mount between 60 and 90 exhibitions a year. Three major galleries— the Decker Gallery in Mount Royal Station, the Meyerhoff Gallery in the Fox Building, and the Pinkard Gallery in the Bunting Center— are supplemented by student galleries.

The Pinkard Gallery is at the Bunting Center at 1401 West Mount Royal Avenue, and the Decker Gallery is in Mount Royal Station at the corner of Cathedral and Dolphin Streets, right across the street from the Lyric Theater. The Mount Royal Station is a magnificent space that was once a train station for the main line of the B&O Railroad, which still runs through tunnels under the street there. The station, hence the gallery, is tucked down into a gully that in the summer serves as a natural amphitheater for live musical entertainment during Artscape (see the Annual Events chapter).

The Cone Sisters

Etta and Claribel Cone, Baltimore sisters blessed with education, wealth, and extremely good taste, are largely responsible for the fabulous collection of Matisse paintings now owned by the Baltimore Museum of Art (BMA). Etta bought her first work by Henri Matisse during a visit to the Salon d'automne in 1905.

The sisters became one of Matisse's first patrons, collecting some 500 works of the French painter—the largest and most comprehensive collection in the world—during their lives. Their 40-year acquaintance blossomed into friendship with the artist. When Claribel died in 1929, Matisse came to Etta's apartments to extend his condolences.

The sisters were avid collectors. Their collection included paintings by American impressionist Theodore Robinson, 144 works by Pablo Picasso, as well as other paintings by Paul Cezanne, Paul Gauguin, Vincent van Gogh, and Pierre-Auguste Renoir.

In all, the Cone Collection at the BMA numbers some 3,000 items. Most of it is artwork, but the museum also has the sisters' personal library and archive, furniture, travel souvenirs, and jewelry.

The Cone Wing, most recently redesigned in 2001, includes a virtual tour of their home with an exhibition of some of their things. It's a fascinating glimpse into the lives of these most fascinating women.

The sisters were 2 of 13 children born to German emigres. Claribel was born in 1864; Etta in 1870. The family, who had lived in Tennessee, moved to Baltimore in 1871 to open a wholesale grocery. About 10 years later, they moved to an elegant apartment on Eutaw Place, located in what was a fashionable residential district and the center of a vibrant German-Jewish community. Etta and Claribel took an active part in the social scene of the day. Claribel studied medicine after high school, eventually doing advanced reserarch at Johns Hopkins Medical School and becoming president of her alma mater, the Women's Medical College of Baltimore. Etta took on the responsibilities of running the family household.

Along with their friends Leo Stein and his sister, writer Gertrude Stein, both Baltimoreans, the sisters became passionate about travel and art. With the Steins, they traveled frequently to Europe and the Far East. In fact, Claribel remained in Munich for the duration of World War I. During that period she was deeply involved in her research and did not buy a single painting. Neither did Etta.

Claribel Cone (left) and her sister Etta Cone (right) enjoy a summer afternoon in Italy in 1930 with their friend Baltimorean Gertrude Stein. THE BALTIMORE MUSEUM OF ART: BMA CONE ARCHIVES

But beginning in 1922, the sisters' collecting began again in earnest. Though Claribel's collection emphasized the Matisse work, Etta focused more on works that explored the creative process. Their luxurious apartments in Baltimore were soon filled with memorabilia and great works of art. Etta promised the Baltimore Museum of Art her collection in 1940, with the stipulation that the museum promote a better appreciation of modern art in the city. The BMA got to work on that request right away. When Etta died in 1949, the art collections of both sisters were bequeathed to the museum.

All the galleries display student and faculty art as well as other exhibits. The Thesis Gallery is especially busy during the spring semester of each year, when the exhibitions of graduate work change every week. The Pinkard Gallery is primarily dedicated to faculty works. All galleries are free and open to the public. Hours are Monday through Wednesday and Saturday 10:00 a.m. to 5:00 p.m., Thursday and Friday, 10:00 a.m. to 9:00 p.m., and Sunday noon to 5:00 p.m. (See the Education chapter for more information about The Maryland Institute.)

The Walters Art Museum
600 North Charles Street
(410) 547-9000
www.thewalters.org

The Walters collection is one of only a few worldwide to present a comprehensive history of art from the third millennium B.C. to the early twentieth century. This collection is renowned in the cultural community for its breadth of pieces, including a rare sarcophagus from second-century Rome, Fabergé eggs, rare Ming vases, and a large collection of ivories. The museum also plays host to major traveling exhibitions, such as a recent show featuring works by Edouard Manet.

The museum has undergone a major facelift in the recent years and has transformed its space in the heart of Mount Vernon into a well-planned, aesthetically thoughtful place to see its extraordinary collection. Free docent-led tours are offered Saturday at 11:30 p.m. and Sunday at 2:00 p.m. Hours are Wednesday through Sunday 10:00 a.m. to 5:00 p.m.; on Friday it is open until 8:00 p.m. Extended hours may apply for special exhibitions. Admission is free except for occasional special exhibits.

Commercial Galleries

Downtown

Angeline's Art Gallery
1631 Thames Street
(410) 522-7909

Angeline Culfogienis paints Baltimore scenes and pieces that concern female themes. She offers signed and numbered Baltimore prints, many scenes from around the area. Her gallery also shows and sells ceramics, sculpture, crafts, and exotic jewelry from around the world.

Art Gallery of Fells Point
1716 Thames Street
(410) 327-1272
www.fellspointgallery.org

This is a cooperative gallery of local artists. You'll find watercolors, oils, pastels, landscapes, portraits, and still-life offerings. The artists are also available for private commissions. Ann Rupert, a local sculptor, has some pieces available through the gallery, as do some local jewelry artists and potters. Several large shows each year include national and Mid-Atlantic artists as well. The gallery is generally open Tuesday through Friday from noon. to 6:00 p.m., and Saturday and Sunday from 10:00 a.m. to 6:00 p.m., but because the gallery is a co-op and, hence, staffed by volunteers, hours sometimes vary. Be sure to call ahead if this is your primary destination.

C. Grimaldis Gallery
523 North Charles Street
(410) 539-1080
www.cgrimaldisgallery.com

If you're interested in abstract art, you'll want to head to Grimaldis, which handles primarily post-World War II contemporary painting and sculpture from American artists. The gallery deals with local and national artists and sculptors, including Anthony Caro, Grace Hartigan, and Elaine De Kooning. You'll find lithographs and etchings alongside oil paintings. Individual artists are shown separately, and the featured artist changes every month. The gallery is closed on Sunday and Monday.

Craig Flinner Gallery
505 North Charles Street
(410) 727-1863
www.flinnergallery.com

Located in the Mount Vernon Cultural District, this expansive gallery specializes in original vintage posters and maps. Everything is original—you'll find posters dating from the 1890s Belle Epoque to the designs of the 1960s. Prints, lithographs, and engravings line the wall as do a number of original and intricate maps. The Flinner gallery also carries some contemporary work and a great collection of vintage food labels. Custom framing is done on the premises.

Ludwig Katzenstein
729 East Pratt Street
(410) 727-0748
Since 1941 Katzenstein has been providing a venue to view and purchase paintings, prints, and watercolors by local artists. Framing is also a big part of the business here. The gallery is closed on weekends.

School 33 Art Center
1427 Light Street
(410) 396-4641
www.school33.org
Housed in an old schoolhouse newly renovated in 2007, School 33 Art Center has fostered contemporary art in this city for more than 20 years. Administered by the Baltimore Office of Promotion and the Arts, its gallery space mounts 18 shows per year, featuring the work of local artists in its three galleries. The center's Studio Artist Program provides inexpensive studio space for working artists, while affordable, year-round classes and special weekend workshops taught by professional artists bring art to the masses. Each fall the center sponsors the Open Studio Tour, which takes us around the city and allows us to peek into the magical spaces where the artists create their work. The gallery is open Tuesday to Saturday from 11:00 a.m. to 4:00 p.m.

Northeast

Bendann Art Galleries
The Shops at Kenilworth,
834 Kenilworth Drive, Towson
(410) 825-0585
www.bendannartgalleries.com
In 1859 Bendann opened as a simple portrait photography studio on West Baltimore Street. The gallery today, still owned and operated by the Bendann family, shows and sells fine art, including oil paintings and watercolors. The 45 regional artists represented offer items in styles from classical realism to contemporary impressionism. In addition, the gallery has historic Maryland and Baltimore prints, restores paintings, and offers framing. Bendann is closed on Sunday.

Northwest

Antreasian Gallery
1111 West 36th Street
(410) 235-4420
www.antreasiangallery.com
Established in June 1998, this funky gallery on "The Avenue" in Hampden represents more than 60 artists and features affordable art in a comfortable atmosphere. The artwork for sale runs the gamut from painting, mixed media, collage, sculpture, and ceramics to jewelry, pastel, watercolor, handmade paper, stained glass, textiles, and decorative furniture. There is a separate exhibition space in the back with a rotating cast of featured artists. These exhibits occur approximately every six weeks and highlight a particular theme, medium, or individual. Opening receptions for these shows happen on the first Thursday of the exhibit from 6:00 to 9:00 p.m. The gallery is open Wednesday through Sunday.

Goya Contemporary
Mill Center, Studio 214
3000 Chestnut Avenue
(410) 366-2001
www.goyacontemporary.com
Goya Contemporary features the works of many contemporary artists, including Baltimore's own Joyce J. Scott, a multimedia artist known for her bold colors and fantastical sculptures. The gallery is open Tuesday through Friday 10:00 a.m. to 5:00 p.m. and Saturday noon to 5:00 p.m.

Wild Yam Pottery
863 West 36th Street, Hampden
(410) 662-1123
www.wildyampottery.com
Before Hampden was cool, the potters of Wild Yam set up shop here to work and display their stoneware and porcelain art. The pots, plates, teapots, and other clay works are functional pieces, with styles as varied as their creators' personalities. The potter's wheel is visible behind the counter, and you'll often see an artist up to her elbows in clay. The potters are happy to talk as they work. And they'll take custom orders, too.

PERFORMING ARTS

Music

Baltimore Opera Company
110 West Mount Royal Avenue
(410) 727-6000
www.baltimoreopera.com
"Opera: it's better than you think. It has to be," goes the wry slogan for the Baltimore Opera. And it is. Four times a year, the classic operas of Puccini, Verdi, Wagner, and Gounod fill the beautiful old Lyric Opera House with magic. Supertitles above the stage keep operagoers in the loop through all that adultery, love affairs gone wrong, murders, and executions. The romantic music and creative sets keep the audience entranced. And if you love an aria, it's okay to jump up, clap wildly, and scream "Bravo," ("Brava" to the soprano, of course). The Baltimore Opera attracts musicians and singers from all over the world, especially the Metropolitan Opera in New York. Dress up in your fanciest clothes, or wear a clean pair of slacks. Come an hour early for a short lecture to clue you in on the music and the story (too many people don't know about these and they're pretty good). Opera, unfortunately, is expensive. Orchestra seats run about $100 each. But even if you sit in the last row of the balcony (about $45), you'll hear every heartbreaking note. Acoustics here are terrific. Each of the four

productions gets five presentations spread throughout two weeks.

Baltimore Symphony Orchestra (BSO)
Joseph Meyerhoff Symphony Hall
1212 Cathedral Street
(410) 783-8000
www.baltimoresymphony.org
In the 2007–2008 season, the BSO became the first major American orchestra to appoint a female music director. During her year as a music director designate, Baltimoreans fell in love with their new Maestra, Marin Alsop, who has been interviewed in the local media many times and whose concerts are a delight. The BSO does all it can to attract an audience to its concerts: a series of all of Beethoven's symphonies, Soulful Symphony with an emphasis on African-American musicians, Symphony with a Twist for young adults, as well as a summer series in Oregon Ridge Park and several series for children. Check out the Web site and you're bound to find something you like. Concerts are held in the Meyerhoff, which has great sight lines and good acoustics. Get a seat in the orchestra or any of the side boxes for the best experience.

Concert Artists of Baltimore
1114 St. Paul Street
(410) 625-3525
www.cabalto.org
Since 1987, founder and artistic director Ed Polochick has organized a group of professional chamber orchestra musicians and vocal ensembles to present engaging, accessible classical music programs throughout the state. The group, which ranges from duos to a full cast of 65 musicians, performs operettas, pops concerts, and classical favorites in a number of venues around town. Performances are frequently followed by informal question-and-answer sessions with the audience. Tickets for seniors and students are $5; adult admission is $8. Call for concert schedules and locations.

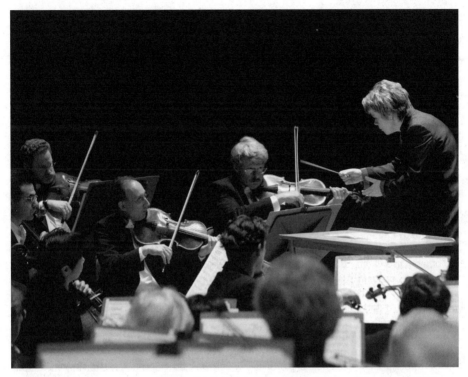

The Baltimore Symphony Orchestra's music director, Marin Alsop, wields the baton during her inaugural season. TRACEY BROWN

Handel Choir of Baltimore
3600 Clipper Mill Road
(410) 366-6544
www.handelchoir.org
The Handel Choir, directed by Melinda O'Neal, is probably best known for its rendition of Handel's masterpiece, *The Messiah*. In fact, the Handel Choir has performed this work every year since 1934. In addition, the 46-voice community oratorio ensemble performs approximately 15 other concerts during the year that include not only Handel's choral works but also those of other classical composers, such as Gabrieli and Bach. Public performances are held at local concert halls and houses of worship, with at least one concert every year at the Basilica of the Assumption. Children's and family concerts are a regular part of the schedule. Anyone, including children, may audition to become part of this nonprofit choir. Auditions are held in late summer.

Hopkins Symphony Orchestra
Shriver Hall, Johns Hopkins University
3400 North Charles Street
(410) 516-6542
www.jhu.edu/~jhso/
The Hopkins Symphony began as a creative outlet for Johns Hopkins students in the 1980s. It has grown over the years into a true community orchestra. Only about one-third of its 90-plus performers are students at the university. The orchestra performs two subscription series at Johns Hopkins' Shriver Hall during the year. One features four major concerts with a full orchestra, and the other entitles you to attend two chamber music concerts throughout the year.

The chamber group is not the typical five or six people, but rather a large chamber orchestra of 13. The group's size allows the musicians to play such pieces as *Appalachian Spring* by Aaron Copland. The group also provides educational concerts for Baltimore's youth and donates tickets to senior centers and schools in the Baltimore area. The orchestra holds auditions annually in the fall. General admission is $10.

Peabody Ragtime Ensemble
3226 Midfield Road
(410) 484-5200
www.peabodyonline.com

The Peabody Ragtime Ensemble began in 1974 when its members were students at the Peabody Conservatory of Music. It has continued not just because its members put on a great show but also because they are dedicated to their stated mandate: "to preserve the roots of American jazz through research, arrangement, and performance of the vintage repertoire." The group's history includes such honors as performing with Eubie Blake, Baltimore's own ragtime legend, as well as appearing with the Baltimore Symphony Orchestra and such notables as Aaron Copland and Hal Linden. Under the direction of Ed Goldstein, the ensemble has toured other countries and won numerous competitions and awards. Put all that aside, however, and you'd still have one great band that plays authentic ragtime, Dixieland, jazz, and 1940s swing year-round. Just give them a call to find out where, when, and how much.

Pier Six Concert Pavilion
731 Eastern Avenue
(410) 244-1131
www.piersixpavilion.com

The tent on the Inner Harbor just beyond the National Aquarium is the site for many pop, blues, and rock concerts during warm weather. Many national and international acts have played here, including the B-52s, the Goo Goo Dolls, Linda Ronstadt, and B.B. King. Summer concerts can be steamy, so dress appropriately. Tickets are available at the Pier Six box office, though it's open only on show days, as well as at Rams Head at either location in Baltimore 410-244-1131 or Annapolis 410-268-4545 or at Ticketmaster outlets. Or go online to the Web site piersixpavilion.ramsheadlive.com or www.ticketmaster.com.

Rams Head Live
20 Market Place, Power Plant Live!
Restaurant: (410) 244-8856
Box Office: (410) 244-1131
www.ramsheadlive.com

You never know who'll play next at Rams Head Live. It could be Ice-T or Pat Benatar, India.Arie or Weird Al Yankovic, or maybe an up-and-coming band. All kinds of acts come to play in this 26,000-square-foot concert hall/tavern/restaurant. Although Rams Head's Annapolis and Rehoboth Beach locations are all about both music and food, music has been number one here since its opening in December 2004. Food is served here, of course, but people are coming for the music. The schedule is posted on the Web site, and tickets run anywhere from $15 to $60, depending on the act. It's big, it's loud, and it draws a crowd.

Professional Theater

Arena Players
801 McCulloh Street
(410) 728-6500
www.arenaplayersinc.org

Arena Players is one of the nation's oldest continuous African-American theater companies. Begun in 1953, its first production was William Soroyan's one-act drama *Hello Out There*. By 1961 the company had found its permanent home and has since continually reshaped the space to create a modern theater. Five plays are presented every season, with productions by playwrights such as William Inge, August Wilson, and Lorraine Hansberry. In addition to this mix of comedy and drama, the young actors of Youtheatre perform four times a year, usually a lavish musical such as *The Lion King,* or *Once on This Island*. Tickets are about $15.

Baltimore Shakespeare Festival
Roland Avenue, Hampden
(410) 366-8596
www.baltimoreshakespeare.org
This professional troupe has turned a little Tudor-style church into a living shrine to the Bard. Summer productions are staged on the grounds of Evergreen House at 4545 North Charles Street. The nonprofit theater survives on a shoestring but manages to produce several Shakespeare plays a year, as well as plays inspired by Shakespeare, such as *The Complete Works of William Shakespeare (abridged)* and *Rosencrantz and Guildenstern are Dead*. Tickets are about $25, with discounts for seniors, students, and artists (with proof of artistry.)

Center Stage
700 North Calvert Street
(410) 332-0033
www.centerstage.org
Center Stage is the State Theater of Maryland and has been in business for some 45 years. The theater is in the Mount Vernon neighborhood, just 2 blocks east of the Washington Monument, in what was once the building for Loyola College and Preparatory School. The building was donated by the Jesuits in 1974. There are actually two theaters in the building, the Pearlstone Theater and the more intimate Head Theater. The larger Pearlstone has only 541 seats. Sight lines are excellent, and no seat in the house is a bad one. Center Stage mounts six shows every year—some Broadway, some classic, some more avant-garde. A recent season featured Sondheim's "A Little Night Music" and August Wilson's "Joe Turner's Come and Gone." There are also always offerings by new writers as well. Irene Lewis is the company's resident director. The season runs from October to June, but the theater is never really dark.

Children's Theater Association (CTA)
1055 Taylor Avenue, Suite 200
(443) 901-0835
Children's Theater Association has been a Baltimore fixture for more than 40 years. CTA offers three public performances every year for general audiences at the Baltimore Museum of Art theater, as well as performances in schools and community settings. The season runs from September through May. Recent performances include such educational pieces as *Stay Tobacco Free* and *Teddy Roosevelt*. CTA also offers acting classes to students throughout the year at the Loch Raven Library, 1046 Taylor Avenue.

The Hippodrome Theatre at the France Merrick Performing Arts Center
12 North Eutaw Street
(410) 837-7400
www.france-merrickpac.com
We just call it the Hippodrome, Baltimore's newest venues for Broadway-style musical theater. Occasionally, there's a straight drama—Richard Thomas and George Wendt performed here in *Twelve Angry Men* in 2006—but this is the place for lavish musicals. About a dozen are scheduled here each year. We've seen *Wicked, Spamalot,* and *Lion King* in the last few seasons. The theater was once one of Baltimore's most popular vaudeville houses, so it's a happy event to have the old place packing them in again. The season runs from September through June, but special events keep the Hippodrome hopping most of the year. There's a tiny cafe, the Hipp, on-site. Parking is available in several nearby garages. Park in the garage at 5 North Paca Street; it connects directly into the theater lobby.

Lyric Opera House
140 West Mount Royal Avenue
(410) 685-5086
www.lyricoperahouse.com
The Lyric presents all manner of theatrical and musical entertainment. One can see a Broadway road company production, national comedy acts, and performances by the Baltimore Opera Company. *The Nutcracker* is a Christmas tradition; but *Stomp* has also been on stage here. All told, the Lyric hosts 25 to 30

productions a year. The Lyric was built in 1894 and today seats 2,564 (1,000 orchestra, 206 boxes, and 1,358 balcony). Although its antique facade has been replaced by a more modern front and a gallery-type outer lobby, the theater remains as it was built, including perfect acoustics and excellent sight lines, even for those in the last row. The old lobby, which is now the inner lobby, has been renovated to look as it did when the theater first opened—which is to say, spectacular. The theater and its continuing history are part of Baltimore's pride.

Theatre Project
45 West Preston Street
(410) 752-8558

The Theatre Project brings to Baltimore some of the best, cutting-edge theater in the country, maybe the world. Its founder started the theatre in a run-down building with makeshift seating and passed a hat at the end of the performances. It's come a long way since then. The space is much more professional; the seats are comfortable and you can buy a real ticket or even a whole subscription. The theater is still pretty amazing, and still right on that very sharp edge. In a recent season, theologian Dietrich Bonhoeffer and Albert Einstein's dreams were the subjects of two plays. Circus, women's empowerment, and dark comedy were among the choices, too. You may have to look to find the theater. It's just down the street from the Joseph Meyerhoff Symphony Hall. The season runs September through June, with an occasional special event during the summer.

Dinner Theater

Lorenzo's Timonium Dinner Theatre
9603 Deereco Road, Timonium
(410) 560-1113, (877) 560-1113
www.timoniumdinnertheatre.com

Timonium mounts musicals and comedies for adult audiences five days a week and children's productions every Saturday. Tickets to the show and buffet dinner range from $20 to $45. Parking is free. To get to the theater, take Interstate 83 north to Timonium Road, then go east toward York Road. The first light is Deereco Road.

Toby's Dinner Theatre
Best Western Hotel
5625 O'Donnell Street
(410)649-1660, (866) 99TOBYS
www.tobysdinnertheatre.com

Toby's Dinner Theatre has been a fixture in nearby Columbia for nearly 30 years and now founder Toby Orenstein brings her mix of musical theater and a hearty buffet to this unlikely spot, a hotel off Interstate 95 beside a bus station. The season is ambitious, with plays year-round. In its opening season in 2006–2007, Toby's produced *Fiddler on the Roof*, *Grease* and *Dreamgirls*. Productions change every two to three months. Everybody will find something they like on the buffet, including the sundae bar. Sunday plays begin with brunch. Tickets run about $45.

Community Theater

The Baltimore Theatre Alliance
100 East 23rd Street
(410) 662-9945
www.baltimoreperforms.org

The Baltimore Theatre Alliance (BTA) is an invaluable resource to the 43 community theaters in Baltimore that are its members. BTA gives member theaters a central clearinghouse for theater information, actors, and technicians. For instance, once a year, BTA holds major auditions to which all member theaters send representatives. If you were interested in acting at the community-theater level in Baltimore, instead of auditioning for every single play at every single theater in the city, you could become one of the 250 people who audition at BTA for all the theaters. If a theater needs a lighting tech for a particular play, it calls BTA. If you are a lighting tech who wants work at the community-theater level, you can get on the list by sending your resume to BTA.

A Summer for Playwrights

When theaters would typically be going dark, Baltimore's non-professional theaters are gearing up for a summer of original plays. The Baltimore Playwrights Festival takes over theaters from all corners of the city—and neighboring suburbs.

Around 10 plays are produced, all written by local writers. Dramas, comedies, and musicals, one-act plays, and full-scale productions are submitted for judging by members of local theater companies. Some get a reading, and ultimately the final plays are chosen for production. Theater staff members also attend the public readings so they can decide which play they want to produce.

A play usually runs two to three weeks, with runs scattered throughout the season so theater lovers have a chance to see as many as they want. All this drama ends with an awards ceremony in September. But the best part has to be the chance to see so many new plays in just a few weeks.

The schedule is posted at www.baltimoreplaywrightsfestival.org in April or early May, just in time to order a subscription—or just see what's going to be playing this summer. Baltimore Playwrights Festival is headquartered at Fells Point Corner Theatre, 251 South Ann Street in Fells Point.

Everyman Theatre
1727 North Charles Street
(410) 752-2208
www.everymantheatre.org

Everyman has made quite a name for itself, producing high-quality professional theater since 1990. The resident repertory company of Equity actors and guest artists perform in five plays a year as well as an Explore Everyman series. Education programs bring children into the theater throughout the school year. Beginning with the 2009–2010 season, all that will move to a renovated space across the street from the Hippodrome Theatre. The Town Theatre, located at 315 West Fayette Street, will give Everyman a 250- to 300-seat auditorium with plenty of rehearsal rooms, artisan shops, and classroom space. Everyman's season offers a variety of shows, such as Sheridan's *The School for Scandal,* Shakespeare's *Much Ado About Nothing,* and David Auburn's *Proof.* Explore Everyman serves as a laboratory for new plays, and even a cabaret series.

Fells Point Corner Theatre
251 South Ann Street
(410) 276-7837
www.fpct.org

Fells Point Corner offers two theaters, one up, one down. Both are small: 65 seats up, 85 seats down. The upstairs theater has stadium seating and even in the top row at the back, you can easily see the expressions on the actors' faces. Of course, sometimes this kind of intimacy makes it difficult for audience members not to feel that they're part of the action. (A former actor at the theater tells a great story about how he was in a bar scene on stage, his table downstage near the first row. His character had just lit a cigarette when an elderly lady in the first row leaned over and asked him to please put it out.)

The season runs from September to the middle of June, after which the actors go into rehearsal for two shows for the Baltimore Playwrights Festival, which is in residence at the theater. Fells Point Corner also offers acting and directing classes for adults and children. The first-floor theater is wheelchair accessible.

Mobtown Players
3600 Clipper Mill Road, Suite 114
(410) 467-3057
www.mobtownplayers.com
The Mobtown Theater is a 68-seat auditorium, and the players put on a variety of shows, some classical, including Shakespeare, and some modern, including Edwin Albee's *The Goat*. The season usually features four productions. Tickets are $12 general admission, $10 for students and seniors. No credit card purchases are yet available, although online purchases are. Tickets may be available at the door, but remember this is a tiny theater, so the best thing to do is get them in advance. Likewise, if you have a ticket and can't attend, call so they can use your seat for one of the poor souls waiting in the lobby to see if there's a space for them.

Pumpkin Theatre
Ruxton Towers
8415 Bellona Lane, Suite 115
www.pumpkintheatre.com
Baltimore children have had their own theater (although the actual location has changed a number of times) since 1967. Begun as part of the College of Notre Dame's theater department, Pumpkin Theatre struck out on its own in the mid-1980s and continues to dazzle young audiences with all kinds of family entertainment. The shows, which regularly sell out, are produced with attention to detail for the most demanding audiences. A cool feature for kids are the "talk-back performances" held during a matinee when the audience can ask questions of the actors and staff after the show. Plays hit the boards at St. Timothy's School for Girls in Stevenson. Tickets at the door are $12, $11 in advance. If your child is stagestruck, Pumpkin offers a variety of theater classes, too.

Spotlighters Audrey Herman Theatre
817 St. Paul Street
(410) 752-1225
www.spotlighters.org
Spotlighters is a true community theater. There are open auditions for every play, and actors' and stagehands' backgrounds span the gamut from acting student to doctor or lawyer. Some of the actors who began here have gone on to become professional actors. A few names you may recognize include Howard Rollins, who was nominated for an Oscar for *Ragtime,* and Edwin McDonogh, who made it to Broadway in *Moon for the Misbegotten.* The theater itself has been in the basement of the Madison Apartments since October 1962, when the group severed its ties with Baltimore City's Department of Recreation and opened as an independent theater company capitalized with a whopping $600. Since then, the theater never goes dark, except for the week between Christmas and New Year's. The company mounts 12 plays a year, including two plays in July and August from the Baltimore Playwrights Festival, and, in the winter, *Scrooge, the Musical*, which it has produced every year since the early 1980s.

Vagabond Players
806 South Broadway
(410) 563-9135
www.vagabondplayers.com
The Vagabond Players are so-called because for most of its 90-plus years the group had no permanent home. In 1974, however, as Baltimore's housing renaissance was just beginning, the group took over a seedy bar/hotel near the foot of Broadway in Fells Point and turned it into a theater. For 20 years, the members made do, happy just to have a place to call home in an area that has grown into one of the most popular and artistically inclined neighborhoods in the city. In 1995 the space was completely renovated. Now the Vagabond Players perform in a modern theater with 106 seats and such unheard of community-theater amenities as wheelchair

accessibility and a sprinkler system. Vags, as the theater is known around town, does seven shows a year during the regular season (September through July) and then joins in the Baltimore Playwrights Festival, performing one or two plays in August. If you're interested in seeing true classic theater, Vags is the place. A recent season included, among others, *Enchanted April* by Mathew Barber and Moliere's *Tartuffe*. All actors and stage crews are community volunteers. Vags is only open weekends—Friday and Saturday for an 8:00 p.m. curtain and Sunday with a performance at 2:00 p.m.

AT THE MOVIES

Bengies Drive-in Theatre
3417 Eastern Boulevard, Bowleys Quarters
(410) 687-5627
www.bengies.com

In the 1950s drive-in theaters were all the rage across the country. If you've never experienced a drive-in movie, do it while you're here. It gives a whole new meaning to the term "big-screen" (it's the largest on the East Coast, measuring 52 by 120 feet) and offers you such amenities as playgrounds for the little ones who get antsy from sitting too long. And, of course, since seating is in your own car, you can smoke, eat, drink, nurse babies, do just about anything you darn well please, and no one can say nay.

Don't think, however, that you can bring a barbecue or let your kids run wild. Bengies has some strict rules about behavior and about what food may be brought in. A food and beverage permit costs $7.

Bengies is open Friday through Sunday. The box office opens at 7:15 p.m. Prices are $5 to $8 for those age 12 and older, depending on whether it's a single, double, or triple feature. Children in your car who are age 11 and younger are admitted free. The theater opens in the spring for shows. Call in advance to confirm showings.

The Charles Theater
1711 North Charles Street
(410) 727-3456
www.thecharles.com

This is our city's premier cinema for international and rare films. Housed in a renovated 108-year-old Beaux-Arts building, The Charles has five screens, most with stadium seating. The lobby is spacious and comfortable and it attaches to the adjacent Tapas Teatro cafe (see the Restaurants chapter), which is the perfect spot for a premovie meal. Every year The Charles helps host the Maryland Film Festival and on Sundays it offers a film series called Cinema Sunday, which begins with a simple brunch of bagels, coffee, tea, and includes a speaker after the film. Doors open at 9:45 a.m. for brunch and conversation. The film begins at 10:35 a.m.

IMAX Theater
601 Light Street
(410) 685-5225

Part of the Maryland Science Center in the Inner Harbor, the IMAX Theater shows short films about nature, culture, and science on a five-story, 70-foot-wide screen that makes you feel as though you're right there in the middle of the action. Admission is $8 for the evening films. Admission to the Science Center is separate. (See the Attractions chapter for more details on the Maryland Science Center).

The Rotunda Cinemateque
711 West 40th Street, Hampden
(410) 235-4800
www.senator.com

This independent theater, a sister to the hallowed Senator, shows a mix of classic and newly released movies on two screens at this refurbished old movie house. Tickets are $6 Monday through Thursday and $8 on weekends for everyone. Children younger than age five are not admitted except for the occasional children's flick. Plenty of free parking is available behind the Rotunda.

The Senator
5904 York Road
(410) 435-8338
www.senator.com

For mainstream movies with ambience, you'll want to go to The Senator, which is just south of Northern Parkway on York Road. Though average size for a neighborhood theater when it was built, it now is counted among the largest in greater Baltimore, with seating for 900 and a screen about 40 feet tall. Its 1939 Art Deco ambience is intact and preserved for posterity, right down to the etched, oval, blue-glass mirror over the water fountain and marble stalls in the ladies' room. Listed on the National Register of Historic Places and named one of the best movie theaters in the country by *USA Today*, The Senator is still a first-run house. It has had the distinction of hosting the world premieres of many of the movies that have been made here in Baltimore. Outside the theater is a Baltimore-style walk of fame, where stars and producers have their names in the cement.

Admission is $8 for everyone. Children younger than age five are not admitted unless the film showing is a children's movie. However, babes in arms are never admitted.

Private skyboxes, which include an Art Deco lounge and two private viewing rooms, are available for parties of 15 to 40 people for a separate fee. Call (410) 323-1989 to reserve the space.

A Theater Near You

The following list provides the location and contact numbers for major movie houses in Baltimore, which, with the exception of the Downtown houses, are located at or near suburban malls. Most of these theaters have at least two screens, and often several more.

Ticket prices usually run $8.00 to $9.50 for adults, with matinee prices and ticket prices for children and seniors hovering around $5.00 to $6.00.

Downtown

The Charles Theater
1711 North Charles Street
(410) 727-3456

Landmark Theatres' Harbor East Cinema 7
645 President Street
www.landmarktheatres.com

Northeast

AMC White Marsh Theatre
The Avenue at White Marsh
8141 Honeygo Boulevard
(410) 933-9034

Regal Hunt Valley 12
11511 McCormick Road, Hunt Valley
(410) 329-9800

The Rotunda Cinemateque
711 West 40th Street, Hampden
(410) 235-4800

The Senator
5904 York Road
(410) 435-8338

Northwest

Loews Valley Centre 9
9616 Reisterstown Road
(410) 363-4194

AMC Owings Mills
10100 Mill Run Circle, Owings Mills
(443) 394-0060

Southeast

Bengies Drive-In Theatre
3417 Eastern Boulevard, Bowleys Quarters
(410) 687-5627

Eastpoint 10
7938 Eastern Boulevard
(410) 284-3100

Southwest

Hollywood Theatre
5509 Oregon Avenue, Arbutus
(410) 242-1188

Hoyts Cinema 14
1591 West Nursery Road, Linthicum
(410) 850-4097

Muvico Egyptian 24
Arundel Mills Mall
(443) 755-8992

Security Square 8
1717 Rolling Road
(410) 265-6911

PARKS AND RECREATION

A great deal of attention is paid to Baltimore's developed areas, often without fair consideration of all its open space. Greater Baltimore is dotted with areas where development has intentionally been forbidden so that people can picnic, play sports, or party with nature. Virtually every community has a park, a playground, school fields, or some kind of green space that allows for getting out among trees and grass.

Maryland has been a leader in efforts to ensure that property remains available for recreation through its Program Open Space, which for more than three decades has been targeting one half of 1 percent of the sale price of all real estate to protecting and enhancing the green areas within the state. These funds have gone to establish an ambitious network of greenways—natural corridors of open space that meander along streams and rivers—so that people can peacefully coexist and commune with all things flora and fauna.

These greenways offer areas for people to hike, bike, ride horses, fish, canoe, and kayak and act as buffers between development and nature. These buffers also protect wildlife, fish, and plants from stormwater runoff and other potentially harmful effects of development. As of 2007, Maryland has more than 1,500 miles of protected greenway corridors, including more than 600 miles of land trails and 350 miles of water trails. A greenway stretch is within a half hour of where anyone lives in the area, according to the state Department of Natural Resources, which regulates the national model program. In addition to greenways, Program Open Space funds have been used to create more than 3,000 county and municipal parks and conservation areas.

The funds are also used to buy land for state parks and state forests. Maryland boasts 47 state parks and forests, areas where people can take part in activities ranging from hiking and biking to hunting and camping, swimming and boating to birding and fishing. About a third of these areas are within the Baltimore area, while other parks, operated by the city and counties and acquired using the same funds, fill the area.

Plan an extended stay with more than 2,000 campsites and 120 full-service and camper cabins to choose from. Campsites, cabins, and shelters can be reserved from May 1 through September 30 by calling (888) 432-2267 or online at www.dnr.state.md.us/. From October 1 to April 30, call the specific park for information.

In this chapter parks are categorized by region within the Baltimore area—Downtown, Northeast, Northwest, Southeast, and Southwest. Descriptions of the parks include information on playing fields, trails for hiking, biking, and skating, and playgrounds. Recreational opportunities are listed in this chapter by jurisdiction. Groups and organizations providing organized recreational opportunities, which are too, too numerous to list individually, are grouped by organizations, which usually serve as clearinghouses for information, registrations, and referrals. Your best bet is to contact the appropriate group or agency and ask that a schedule of upcoming activities be sent to you by mail. These schedules explain the breadth of activities available in your area as well as some of the offerings that might be worth a drive.

Most recreational programs have a fee, which can range up to $5 a session, depending on what it is and how involved it is. Because these fees change frequently from

season to season and community to community, we cannot accurately include them here,
except to let you know when a fee applies.
Call the department or center for specific fees
involved.

Waterfront activities, such as fishing and
boating, are contained in the On the Water
chapter. Activities and locations geared
especially toward children are in the Kidstuff
chapter. And for all you duffers out there
looking to hit the links, we've given golf its
own chapter.

Most of the parks in this chapter do not
charge an admission fee and are open year-
round, usually from dawn to dusk. You can
assume these parameters to be true unless
we note otherwise.

PARKS

Downtown

Federal Hill Park
Key Highway at Battery Avenue
Overlooking the Inner Harbor, Federal Hill isn't
the area's largest park, but it certainly offers
one of the best views. There's a playground, a
small basketball court, and an open section
for throwing a ball or a Frisbee. For a real
walking workout, try climbing the 100 steps
from Key Highway to the hilltop a few times.
You'll definitely feel the burn. Benches are
available for a post-workout rest. Park on the
street or at the harbor and walk over.

Patterson Park
Eastern and Patterson Park Avenues
Patterson Park provides a welcome respite
from the demands of city life. Sports fields, an
ice-skating rink, and open areas where the
bothers of urban living seem to take a back-
seat await you when you head toward East
Baltimore's crown jewel of parks whose centerpiece is the 1890 Pagoda. There's even a
small stadium, named Utz Towardowicz after
the person who gave the funds for it, that
hosts big-time baseball and softball competitions. Parking is available on the streets surrounding the park.

Northeast

Cromwell Valley Park
2002 Cromwell Bridge Road, Towson
(410) 887-2503
www.co.ba.md.us
Just minutes from Interstate 695's exit 29, this
park consists of a farming area along Minefield
Run that dates from the 1700s and a small
stream feeding into the Gunpowder River; it
encompasses 367 acres of pasture, open
fields, woods, cultivated fields, and floodplain.
It was purchased in 1993 by Baltimore County.

The park plays host to concerts and other
functions, but it's Mother Nature who usually
takes center stage here. Among the natural
actors are raptors such as the redtailed hawk,
kestrel, and great horned owl, which prey on
small mammals such as rabbits and deer
mice. Other actors are deer, foxes, and song-
birds, including Baltimore orioles (a local
favorite, obviously), bobolinks, meadowlarks,
indigo bunting, and great blue herons.

Parking is available on-site and best
accessed from I-695 at Loch Raven Boulevard
(exit 29).

Double Rock Park
8211 Texas Avenue, Parkville
(410) 887-5300
About 3 miles inside I-695's exit 32, two small
baseball fields that double as fields for football and lacrosse, some trails along a stream,
and a playground and picnic area are parts of
this park within a quiet and serene Parkville
neighborhood. The playground is small, but
the seesaw, swing, and a slide with a collection of holes where children can drop sand
(simple, but quite the pastime for kids) are big
hits. Picnic tables and restrooms are also
available. Parking is free on-site. The picnic
tables are often reserved for groups on weekends and summer days, but there's plenty of
grass for spreading a blanket.

Gunpowder Falls State Park
2813 Jerusalem Road, Kingsville
(410) 592-2897
www.dnr.state.md.us

One of Maryland's largest state parks takes up about 18,000 acres of Baltimore and Harford Counties, heading west to east along the Big Gunpowder and Little Gunpowder Rivers. Horseback riding, mountain biking, hiking, bird-watching, canoeing, tubing, and fishing (especially fly fishing) are among the favorite activities of the thousands of visitors to the park. Maps of specific park areas are available at park headquarters and provide a lot of helpful information.

The best places for entry are along U.S. Highway 1 about 8 miles north of Baltimore City, where there's a parking area right on the river, and in the Cockeysville area, off Interstate 83, along York Road, about 12 miles north of the city near Hunt Valley. The Hammerman area in Chase, off U.S. Highway 40 north of Baltimore City, requires admission of $3 a person, but in return for the fee, you get access to a beach (one of only two public beaches in the area) for swimming (Memorial Day through Labor Day) and sunning, an open picnic area, and numerous stretches of hiking trails. The Northern Central Rail Trail, also near Hunt Valley and off York Road near I-83, offers a 19-mile flat hiking and biking route, safe and serene, like no other in the area.

Herring Run Park
Belair Road at Parkside Drive
www.belair-edison.org/parks.html
Like so many other parks in Baltimore, Herring Run was established along a waterway. Herring once ran through the waters here, hence the park's name. Trash and other obstacles would have impeded their passage over the past few years, but recent efforts are pushing forward to improve the water quality and restore the herring. The park is accessible from Harford Road, Sinclair Lane, and Belair

Road in Northeast Baltimore. Park benches, picnic tables, open areas for playing ball or walking dogs, and trails along the run are within a few blocks of those main road intersections with the run. Parking is available on streets within the communities nearby. Beneath the Harford Road bridge near Argonne Drive is an area with lots of picnic tables and trails, a perfect getaway for a few hours. No admission is charged.

Lake Montebello
Hillen Road and Argonne Drive
A paved walking, running, and in-line skating trail goes around Lake Montebello, one of the drinking water collection lakes for the city. From dawn to dusk, people of all ages take to the street, which also has traffic running alongside it. The circular path is a great place to meet people of all sorts and sports. Parking is available on side streets.

Loch Raven Reservoir
12101 Dulaney Valley Road
(410) 887-7692
www.co.ba.md.us
The Loch Raven Reservoir is a 2,400-acre watershed that provides drinking water to a large portion of Baltimore City, even though it is located in Baltimore County. No matter. Because the water must be as clean as possible, the surrounding acres are open for recreation, not development, giving people who visit the area the chance to participate in everything from hiking to biking to fishing to equestrian activities. A portion of Loch Raven Drive, from Providence Road to a parking lot about a mile to its north, is closed from 10:00 a.m. to 5:00 p.m. on Saturday and Sunday so that bikers, hikers, in-line skaters, skateboarders, and others can enjoy the park without worrying about traffic. The Loch Raven Fishing Center rents boats and offers docking on the reservoir from April through October (see the On the Water chapter for more information). Picnic tables are near the Providence Road entrance, while open stretches for flying a kite, reading a book, or communing with nature are

i Insta-parks at colleges and other school facilities are often overlooked for what they offer—great open spaces for running, walking, or taking in a free and enjoyable environment, especially in the evening and on weekends.

all over the park. No refreshments are available, so bring your own. Park only in designated areas; police issue lots of tickets to folks who fail to obey the parking regulations.

Putty Hill Park
8600 Hoerner Road, Parkville
(410) 887-5300
www.baltimorecountyonline.com
One large baseball field and a spread-out playground provide a welcome respite to residents of Parkville. Just minutes from I-695's exit 31, the park is convenient to Towson, White Marsh, and other areas just north of Baltimore City. Parking is available on the street, and restrooms are on-site.

Northwest

Druid Hill Park
Druid Lake Drive near I-83
(410) 396-6106
The park, one of the largest inner-city parks in the country, surrounds the Maryland Zoo in Baltimore.

In one of the greater ironies of Baltimore, the animals remain confined inside the zoo, while people are welcome to roam freely about the outer area surrounding Druid Lake. (See the Kidstuff chapter for more information about the zoo.)

Tennis courts and a public swimming pool are also part of the park. Although access to the lake is prohibited, the fields, trails, and hardwoods are ideal for picnicking, hiking, and bird-watching. Tables and cabanas that date from the last century have been restored and are strategically located around the park for picnickers and weary revelers. Druid Hill Park also offers a fantastic view of the city as it is on one of the highest promontories in the area.

Oregon Ridge Park and Nature Center
13555 Beaver Dam Road, 1 mile south of Shawan Road, Hunt Valley
(410) 887-1815
www.oregonridge.org
Just west of I-83, Oregon Ridge Park used to have a short ski lift, long before some of the more popular skiing locales opened in Pennsylvania. Now the 1,036-acre park offers a hill for running, hiking, climbing, and hang gliding, mostly afternoons and weekends. A large playground, an amphitheater where the Baltimore Symphony Orchestra performs about a dozen shows each summer, and an indoor banquet facility round out the offerings at the main park. Hiking trails are also on-site. The park is open seven days a week from dawn to dusk. Admission is free, and parking is available outside the banquet center.

There is also a swimming beach available 10:00 a.m. to 8:00 p.m. Memorial Day through Labor Day. The park charges $6 for adults and $2 for children younger than age 12 for the swimming area.

Visitors also enjoy the Oregon Ridge Nature Center, where recreational and educational programs are offered to the public and school groups. Full-time naturalists and volunteers offer a wide range of activities for children and adults, including moonlit hikes, bird-watching trips, bee-keeping demonstrations, and maple syrup making, mostly on weekends. The center is open from 9:00 a.m. to 5:00 p.m. Tuesday through Sunday.

Seminary Park
1414 Burton Avenue, Lutherville
(410) 887-7684
www.co.ba.md.us
Just east of I-83 north of Towson, this facility has several lighted baseball fields that also offer space for adult softball, youth football, soccer, and lacrosse. A playground with slides, suspension bridges, swings for children and infants, a tunnel, and a sandbox is at the back of the park, far from the on-site parking lot. Restroom facilities and picnic tables are also available.

Southeast

North Point State Park
2813 Jerusalem Road, Kingsville
(410) 592-2897
www.dnr.state.md.us
This Chesapeake Bay waterfront park could

be the best-kept secret in Baltimore as far as parks go. It is more than 1,300 acres located in southeastern Baltimore County and is rich in history and natural resources. The Defenders' Trail, used during the War of 1812, goes through the park. This is also the site of the former Bay Shore Amusement Park.

With more than 6 miles of shoreline, visitors to this park can find rarely used areas for biking, cross-country skiing, fishing, flatwater canoeing, and hiking. A portion of North Point State Park has been designated as a Wildlands Area. There is also one of the finest examples of tidal marsh on the Upper Chesapeake found here.

Rocky Point Beach and Park
801 Back River Neck Road, Essex
(410) 887-3873
www.co.ba.md.us

Pick your poison—a beach, five picnic areas, a historic waterfront house, a fishing and boating pier, or two boat ramps for watching the serene waters off Rocky Point, located at the confluence of the Back and Middle Rivers. A somewhat secret place with 375 acres for getting away from the heat and humidity in the summer, Rocky Point offers great views of eagles, osprey, and great blue herons. Fishing, boating, and swimming have been part of the menu at Rocky Point since 1969.

Swimming is an option at the beach from 10:00 a.m. to 6:00 p.m. every day from Memorial Day through Labor Day. Parking can get somewhat tight on hot summer weekends, but a short delay is worth what awaits you, especially when it's really hot and humid—like throughout July and August.

Southwest

Catonsville Community Park
501 North Rolling Road
Catonsville
(410) 887-0959

Catonsville Community Park boasts a sand-lined volleyball court, fields for outdoor sports, and a playground featuring a tire swing and a high, high swing. Picnic tables

are also available, and parking is on-site. Bathroom facilities are available.

Gwynns Falls Park/Leakin Park
Edmondson Avenue at Hilton Parkway
Franklintown
(410) 396-7931
www.gwynnsfallstrail.org

Spread out among several miles of eastwest land along the Gwynns Falls, this park offers hiking, biking, bird-watching, sightseeing, and relaxing spaces. It serves as a stop on the Gwynns Falls Trail. Formed to protect the Gwynns Falls from development all around it, the park at one point housed an amusement park, but those days are long gone. In its place are grass, trees, and other natural amenities that provide a strong contrast to the housing close by. You can access the park from a variety of sites along Edmondson Avenue. Leakin Park, a portion of the facility, offers tennis courts, a track, abundant parking, and a ropes course, which tests even the best athletes with climbing, balance, and endurance testing. The ropes course is operated by the city and several other agencies, primarily for children in summer camps and school day trips.

Patapsco Valley State Park
8020 Baltimore National Pike, Ellicott City
(410) 461-5005
www.dnr.state.md.us

Patapsco Valley State Park is one of Maryland's largest parks and its oldest—dating from 1907—offering more than 14,000 acres of open space along the Patapsco River. The park has five separate recreation areas, including the Hilton Area, off Hilton Avenue, south of Rolling Road in Ellicott City; the Hollofield Area, off US 40 just east of Ellicott City; and three other areas in Baltimore, Howard, and Anne Arundel Counties.

One of the best features of Patapsco Valley is the Thomas Viaduct, the world's longest multiple-arched stone railroad bridge. Also, a visit to Bloede Dam is always a fun hike for kids and kids at heart. Or hike the McKeldin Area Trail system for an unparalleled look at the natural valley and river rapids. The Hilton Area tire park is always a kid pleaser. Admission is $2 per person, $3 for out-of-state visitors.

Western Hills Park
1437 Rolling Road and Crosby Road
Woodlawn
(410) 887-0962
An open area in which to run around accompanies picnic tables and playground equipment, such as slides, tunnels, ramps, and bridges at Western Hills. Parking is on-site.

RECREATION
Departments and Centers

Baltimore City

Baltimore City Recreation Centers
3001 East Drive
(410) 396-7900
www.ci.baltimore.md.us
Baltimore City operates 45 recreation centers in virtually every neighborhood within the city limits. The programs range from after-school activities, including study groups and tutorial sessions, to more recreational offerings and summer camp programs.

The recreation centers also operate programs for toddlers, children, adults, and senior citizens in recreation and therapeutic care. These programs include sports such as baseball, softball, lacrosse, tennis, table tennis, pool, swimming, football, and track and field. Indoor sports are played within the centers, either in gyms or activities rooms, in schools and on fields at schools and parks. More sedate programs, including crafts, art, painting, and dance, are also offered.

The fees for these programs vary, with most costing less than $20 for a full season in a sport. Call to receive a schedule of the activities available.

<table>
<tr><td>i</td><td>Most of the larger hotels in the area have relationships with fitness centers or have their own facilities so you can easily find a way to exercise, even in the worst weather.</td></tr>
</table>

Baltimore County

Baltimore County Department of Recreation and Parks
44 locations
(410) 887-3871
www.co.ba.md.us
Baltimore County's Department of Recreation and Parks operates 44 separate facilities throughout the county broken into six areas. Programs are available for all ages, with a heavy emphasis on programming for children ranging from gymnastics and arts and crafts to music and sports. Some of the more popular sports are baseball, softball, floor hockey, volleyball, football, soccer, tennis, basketball, and tumbling. Fees to participate usually cost less than $20 for lessons or a season of play. Registrations are typically held at the schools, where activities are held within the gymnasiums, classrooms, and outdoor fields. Call the department for a booklet that lists what programs are offered when.

Baltimore County Police Athletic League Recreation Centers
700 East Joppa Road, Towson
(410) 887-5864
www.co.ba.md.us
The Baltimore County Police Department operates nine recreation centers, offering video games, karate, weight lifting, table tennis, tutoring, and field trips for children age 7 through 17. Check the Web site for the listing of centers. Most programs are free of charge.

Baltimore County Y.M.C.A.
600 West Chesapeake Avenue, Towson
(410) 823-8870
www.ymcamd.org
Seven Y.M.C.A.s offer programs for all ages, including swimming, aerobics, tennis, weight

Where to Take Pets

Baltimore's Charm City moniker extends from the way it treats people to its ability to accommodate pets, especially dogs. The area offers a variety of locations for taking Fido for a run, walk, or sense of the outdoors, and all of the places are just as rewarding for the person on the other end of the leash.

Whether you treat Rex like the king, Tiffany like the queen, or Butch like the annoying house pet he really is, there's a place around town for getting out and treating your pet to a whiff of the outdoors. Here are a few things to keep in mind when you take your pet out on the town.

• All jurisdictions require that pets be leashed.

• All jurisdictions require that pets be cleaned up after, and these requirements are maintained with fines ranging from $5 to $15 for violators. More important than a possible fine is the fact that some of the places where pets are allowed to visit are relatively pristine parks and open spaces that will continue to remain so only if people protect them from litter and animal wastes. Do your part to keep the area looking pretty.

• Watch out for ticks. Small deer ticks can lie in the woods around Baltimore, so it's a good practice to check your pet after each visit— even if they've never had one before or are wearing the latest and greatest tick collar. Favorite sites for ticks on pets are the collar area (even under the collar), ears, where the legs and torso meet, and on the tail. For people—yes, ticks are attracted to people, too—the best places to

look are the hair, neck, legs, ankles, and other areas that tend to be warm. Light-colored clothing can make them easier to spot, and wearing a hat, long sleeves, long pants, socks, and shoes can help prevent them from finding a piece of skin to burrow into. If you see one, remove it completely with a pair of tweezers. If it's on your pet, you might also want to keep it in a sealed envelope or plastic bag just in case something happens and doctors need to check on its size at the time it was removed to determine how long it lived on your pet.

• Not everybody's dog is as friendly as yours, and not everyone is as willing to experience the ritualistic love/hate relationship between pets on first encounter. Make sure the person with a pet ahead or behind wants your dog rubbing elbows or whatever else before you allow it. It's best to keep your dog on its leash when around other people or near the water.

Unless otherwise noted, the following sites are within Baltimore City limits. No admission fee is charged at any of these locations.

In the northeast **Herring Run Park** at the intersection of Harford Road and Argonne Drive is a 4 mile-long area along the watershed for Lake Montebello. It has easy-to-follow trails and provides dogs and owners with lots of cool sights, smells, and sounds. A playground, restrooms, and parking are all on-site.

Robert E. Lee Park at Lakeside Drive and Hollins Avenue offers a place for single dogs and cats to go in search of a mate or someone to hang with for a few hours. Owners of pets also have been known to find a mate with similar interests—namely, pets—at this park along Lake Roland. Dozens and dozens of dogs roam this park or take a plunge. On a warm afternoon or on weekends, it's the place to be. Parking is available on the street.

Northeast of the city on Ebenezer Road about a mile east of US 40 in the White Marsh area is the Dundee Fishing Area of **Gunpowder Falls State Park**. What could be better than calm surf, white sands, and marsh grasses? You'll find all that and convenient on-site parking at this underused section of the state park. Although originally intended for anglers and boaters, it's a perfect place to take pets. Bring a towel—few canines can resist a romp in the waves.

Another section of Gunpowder Falls State Park is north of the city and on US 1 near Kingsville at Belair Road. About 20 minutes outside of Baltimore City, this section of the park offers pet owners a place for hiking and swimming. Along both shores of the river are narrow trails with pull-offs leading into the water. Most pet owners favor the south side, heading east, where they don't have to compete with mountain bikers, fly fishers, and others using the area. Occasionally, a dog even pulls out a fishy treat from the trout-filled waters. Take a towel and a change of fur because it's hard to keep them out of the water. Parking is available on-site, although it can fill quickly. Hint: Don't park on the highway, because you'll get a quick and expensive ticket. Be patient and wait a few minutes—a spot will open up.

In the Northwest area **Druid Hill Park,** at the intersection of McCulloh Street and Druid Hill Avenue, sports open fields for people and pets. This area outside The Maryland Zoo in Baltimore is perfect for a quiet picnic with a loved one and pet. In the back area of the park, away from the on-street parking, are trails lined with trees, but the open areas are more than large enough to accommodate even the largest and most rambunctious dogs.

Soldiers Delight Natural Environment Area is on Wards Chapel Road about 8 miles west of Interstate 795 in Owings Mills about 8 miles outside the Baltimore city limits. Several small streams compete with pines and other trees at this largely unnoticed, open, and protected stretch of land. The trails are not well marked, adding more mystique to this area that is used by snowmobilers and equestrians. Don't forget the bag and scoop. Because it remains natural, the need to clean up after pets is even more necessary. Make sure you check your pets for needles and briars after the trip. Parking is available on Wards Chapel Road.

Oregon Ridge Park, off Beaver Dam Read in the Hunt Valley area about 12 miles north of Baltimore City, is a former short-hill skiing area that has given way to a county park, with tulip poplars stretching up high and a tall hill for walking. Below, dogs can venture across open fields while hang gliders, kite fliers, ballplayers, and picnickers enjoy the day. Bathroom facilities and vending machines are available on-site. You'll find ample parking throughout the area.

CONTINUED

If Your Bow-Wow Gets a Boo-Boo
In case Fido gets to feeling a little under the weather, we've included some basic information about the local emergency veterinary clinics. Here's hoping you don't need one, since there's nothing worse than a sick pet—except maybe the smell of a wet pet.

In the **Northeast the Animal Emergency Center,** (410) 252-8387, at 1711 York Road in Timonium, a community just north of Towson, has a veterinarian on-site 24 hours a day, seven days a week.

The **Harford Emergency Veterinary Service,** (410) 836-5173, is at 2105 Laurel Bush Road in Bel Air, a community about 20 miles north of Baltimore City off Interstate 95 in Harford County. A vet is available from 5:00 p.m. to 8:00 a.m. Monday through Thursday and from 8:00 p.m. Friday to 8:00 a.m. Monday.

About 10 miles northwest of Baltimore is the **Reisterstown 24-Hour Veterinary Complex,** (410) 833-0500, at 501 East Main Street. This clinic offers a vet on-site 24 hours a day, seven days a week for emergencies.

In the Southwest corner of the area is **Emergency Veterinary Clinic,** (410) 788-7040, at 32 Mellor Avenue in Catonsville. Just outside the Baltimore Beltway (I-695), this office has a veterinarian on-site from 6:00 p.m. to 8:00 a.m. Monday through Friday and 24 hours on Saturday and Sunday.

lifting, racquetball, driver's education, dance instruction, softball, basketball, and karate. The newest Y is located on the site of the now-gone Memorial Stadium: Harry & Jeanette Weinberg YMCA at Stadium Place, 900 East 33rd Street, (410) 889-YMCA, with other locations at 101 Walter Ward Boulevard in Abingdon, (410) 679-YMCA, 1719 Sykesville Road in Westminster, (410) 848-3660; 1609 Druid Hill Avenue in Baltimore, (410) 728-1600; 4331 Montgomery Road in Ellicott City, (410) 465-4334; and 850 South Rolling Road in Catonsville, (410) 747-9622. A fee is required for some programs. Call for a schedule of activities.

Anne Arundel County

Recreation and Parks
44 Calvert Street, Annapolis
(414) 222-7000, (410) 222-7300
ww.aacounty.org
A wide range of programs is administered by the county's recreation and parks department in every neighborhood. Swimming, baseball, basketball, football, lacrosse, softball, and other activities are offered for children; many of the same activities and others, including more sedentary pursuits, are offered to adults and senior citizens. Fees ranging from $2 to $50 are charged for most programs, and advanced registration is suggested. The county publishes a booklet of activities; call to get a copy.

Howard County

Recreation and Parks
7120 Oakland Mills Road, Columbia
(410) 313-7275
Various recreational programs are offered by the county through neighborhood recreation councils. Sports include baseball, basketball, swimming, gymnastics, and lacrosse. There are a number of indoor programs as well. Fees, topping out at $40, are charged for most programs. Call for a schedule.

ACTIVITIES

Archery/Bowhunting

Baltimore Bowmen
Harford Road, north of Cub Hill Road
Parkville
www.baltimorebowmen.com
Based on a large property north of Baltimore, this group holds archery competitions, shoots, and educational programs throughout the year.

Maryland Bowhunters Society
(800) 434-0811
www.bowsite.com/mbs
The Maryland Bowhunters Society was organized to promote safe and successful bowhunting in the area. It offers information on where to hunt, when hunting is allowed, safe procedures, and other information about bowhunting in the state.

Billiards

Baltimore remains faithful to billiards, or pool as we usually call it. Area players compete as often as they can for such prizes as pride, beer money, or cash.

Not a rowdy crowd by any stretch, most of these players, whether experts or beginners, savor the challenge that comes from trying to sink balls into the pockets in the midst of friends and like-minded spectators.

Unless otherwise noted, expect to find smoking and alcohol available as well as plentiful parking outside. Billiards tables are available in a number of Baltimore nightclubs. See the Nightclubs chapter earlier in this book. See also the Shopping chapter for information about Dave and Busters, a club at Arundel Mills.

Downtown

Baltimore Billiards
7701 Eastern Avenue
(410) 282-7968
Fifteen tables await players here—four of them 9-footers, the rest 8-footers. Most of the players are beginners, although its location

i A quick, cheap, and fun way to exercise and see the sights up-close is to take a brisk walk or run through the area where you are staying. Besides getting a good cardiovascular workout, you get a real sense of the community.

makes it attractive to out-of-towners who are in the area. More experienced players often help newcomers to improve their skills, making this a good place to meet people and play better.

In addition to pool, Baltimore Billiards provides a full bar as well as burgers, chicken sandwiches, and other food for less than $5. Friday and Saturday nights are busiest.

Parking is available on the street outside the club, which is open from 4:00 p.m. to 2:00 a.m. daily.

Edgar's Billiards Club
1 East Pratt Street
(410) 752-8080
www.edgarsclub.com
Less than a block from the Inner Harbor, between the Hyatt Hotel and the Baltimore Convention Center, this club is perfect for the dressed-up businessperson who needs to cut loose for a few hours. Edgar's provides patrons 16 9-foot Olhausen pool tables for play as well as a full restaurant and bar. Smoking and nonsmoking sections are available for pool players.

Edgar's is busiest after work on Thursdays and Fridays. Saturday afternoon and evenings are also busy, especially when the Orioles or Ravens are in town. Over the past few years of its operation, Edgar's has developed a strong reputation as providing all the joys of billiards in a family-friendly environment. Dress ranges from casual to just-getting-off-of-work, depending on the day and hour.

Tables can be rented for $8.00 an hour before 6:00 p.m. and $12.50 an hour afterward. The club is open from 11:00 a.m. to 2:00 a.m. daily. Parking is available, but you will have to pay an hourly rate at several of the Inner Harbor's parking garages.

Northeast

Champion Billiards
Perring Plaza Shopping Center
1969 East Joppa Road at Perring Plaza
Parkville
(410) 665-7500

In what more than a decade ago was a popular Parkville nightclub, Champion today offers nine 9-foot tables in its downstairs area as well as 12 6-foot bar-size tables and three 9-foot tables in its upstairs area. Champion, part of a four location chain in Maryland and Washington, D.C., offers a pleasant, upscale environment for its patrons, who often find themselves dining or imbibing at the 10 booths or 8 tables in the dining area. Smoking and nonsmoking areas are available.

Champion is open every day from 11:00 a.m. to 2:00 a.m. The cost is $4.95 per person per hour, but call to get a listing of daily specials. Champion offers a lot of specials on drinks, on specific game types, such as eight-ball or nine-ball, and on food, so make sure you check them out before you hit the table.

Should you find yourself with a group where some members would prefer to shop, a strip center and a small mall are within convenient walking distance of Champion.

Kelly's Cue Club
Parkville Shopping Center
7713 Harford Road, Parkville
(410) 661-4308

In Parkville Shopping Center, less than a mile from Champion Billiards, is Kelly's Cue Club, a smaller facility allowing players to use its six 9-foot Brunswick tables for $2 per person per hour before 6:00 p.m. and $3 after 6:00 p.m. Open from 10:00 a.m. to midnight Sunday through Thursday, and 10:00 a.m. to 1:00 a.m. on Friday and Saturday, the club is busiest on weekend nights. Most of its customers are folks who gather each week or every few days to play a little pool and get away from life for a while. Smoking is allowed, and no food or drinks are available for sale. Patrons can bring in food and nonalcoholic beverages. When Champion's is busy, Kelly's offers a good, nearby alternative.

Rec Room Billiards
512 York Road, Towson
(410) 337-7178

Located next to the Recher Theatre and the Rec Room Restaurant, Rec Room Billiards plays host to all levels of billiard players, including men and women, adults and children, and lots of college folks from Towson University and Goucher College, both less than a mile from this Towson hot spot.

The Rec Room, as most people call it, provides players with eight 9-foot tables and video games. Busy times tend to correspond to the nightclub acts the place brings in most nights.

Visitors can dine on everything from steaks and crab cakes to submarine sandwiches and pizza. Most main courses cost between $7 and $15. There's also bar food and a full-service bar. Smoking is allowed throughout the facility. Parking is available at metered spots (25 cents an hour, with no fee charged after 8:00 p.m.).

Rec Room Billiards is open from 10:00 a.m. to 2:00 a.m. every day.

Top Hat Cue Club
8809 Satyr Hill Road, Parkville
(410) 665-1906

Yet a third pool-playing option in Parkville is at Top Hat, where billiard aficionados will find 31 pool tables, including four bar-size 7-footers, two 8-footers, and one billiard table featuring no pockets. If you have to ask about the last one, you probably shouldn't even visit this home for local pool players. Everyone pays the same—$2.75 an hour to play on any table, including its 24 9-foot regulation-size tables.

Management provides free coffee to players along with a selection of sandwiches, meatballs, hot dogs, and Italian sausages. A vending machine and soda machine are also on-site. No beverages, including alcohol, can be brought into the club. Weekend nights are busiest, but a short wait (or a stroll to use the three $2.50 an hour Ping-Pong tables) will usually be all that is required to get a pool table.

The place is open from 10:00 a.m. to 2:00 a.m. Sunday through Thursday and from 10:00 a.m. to 4:00 a.m. Friday and Saturday.

Southwest

Jack and Jills
Building 11, Crain Industrial Park
512 North Crain Avenue
Glen Burnie
(410) 766-4444
The play is serious here in Glen Burnie at the 18 9-foot regulation tables and the snooker table. Featured in *Playing Off the Rail,* Jack and Jills never closes, even on Christmas. The "money boys" usually arrive between 5:00 and 10:00 p.m. Friday and hang around until dawn or Sunday, depending on how the games are going. Management has an open approach to its customers. Order and peace are always present inside the building, which offers sandwiches, snacks, and soft drinks. No alcohol is served or permitted inside.

Play costs $4 an hour.

Boardsailing

Baltimore Area Boardsailing Association
(410) 315-8481
www.windsurfbaba.org
The membership association organizes regular competitive boardsailing events with prizes at Gunpowder Falls State Park's Dundee Creek area. Membership for a year is $20.

Camping

Maryland has 47 state parks, 11 of which offer facilities for camping in cabins, on gravel or grass, or in primitive areas far from bathrooms and other conveniences. The state park system accepts campers on a first-come, first-served basis, although some exceptions apply. Contact the Maryland Association of Campgrounds, which can offer referrals and other information about facilities, at (301) 271-7012.

Patapsco Valley State Park
8020 Baltimore National Pike
Ellicott City
(410) 461-5005
www.dnr.state.md.us.com
The closest park to Baltimore City offering camping is Patapsco Valley State Park in Ellicott City. The Hollofield Area of Patapsco Valley State Park, off US 40 just east of Ellicott City, has more than 100 campsites, some with electricity, on several wooded loops. There's a pump-out station, a shower house, and a pet loop for campers. Rates range from $10 to $50, depending on your needs and the season. Spots can be reserved, and weekends become quite busy with tourists and folks wanting an affordable way to visit the Baltimore area.

Dancing

Charm City Swing
charmcityswing.com
Charm City Swing is operated by a U.S. Naval Academy math professor and a doctor who met while swing dancing in 1999. Learn swing dancing at the Austin Grill, 2400 Boston Street in Canton, on Monday night from 8:00 to 9:00 p.m. and then get dancing. Or come on Wednesdays to learn and dance at Red Square in the Belvedere, 1023 North Charles Street. Classes are $10. When you get hooked, there are intermediate and advanced classes.

Greater Baltimore Swing Dance Committee
www.baltimoreswing.org
This nonprofit group hosts dances on second Saturdays around town. Lessons precede the dances. Tickets are $12. Check the Web site for details.

The Friday Night Swing Dance Club
8520 Drumwood Road
(410) 583-7337
www.fridaynightswing.com
The Friday Night Swing Dance Club promotes Swing, Latin, and social dancing in the greater

ℹ️ Youth recreational programs can fill quickly—especially soccer, basketball, baseball, softball, and lacrosse. So if you want the kids to play, don't delay when it's time to register.

Baltimore area. It encourages dancers of all levels to participate and has weekend dances that are regularly attended by 300 to 400 people. With more than 6,800 people on the mailing list and more than 3,500 on the e-mail list, this is one of the largest dance groups on the East Coast.

Fencing

The Chesapeake Fencing Club
201 Homeland Avenue
(410) 532-7445
Just north of the College of Notre Dame in North Baltimore, this club offers open practice Monday nights, with supervised junior practice Monday, Thursday, and Saturday evenings for kids age 6 through 12 years. Foil, saber, and epee lessons are conducted by Moniteur Ray Gordon by appointment and for a varying fee.

Baltimore County Fencing
(410) 532-7445
Baltimore County Parks and Recreation Councils offer fencing lessons for children age 8 through 13 in Parkville and Lutherville. Call for the schedule of classes.

Gymnastics

Baltimore County Gymnastics
5811 Allender Road, White Marsh
(410) 335-4646
www.baltocogym.com
Instructional gymnastic classes and tumbling programs are offered to children age 3 through 12, and cheerleading instruction is offered to high school-age girls. Rates vary, and sessions start several times a year.

Gerstung
1400 Coppermine Terrace
Mount Washington
(410) 337-7781
www.gerstung.com
In northern Baltimore City, Gerstung offers gymnastics programs and movement education to children from 1 through 13 years of age in a large building off Falls Road near I-83. Skills classes are also presented to children age 5 through 13. Dance classes and rock climbing are also available. Call for rates and information on special summer programs.

Gymnastics Elite
899 Airport Park Road, Glen Burnie
(410) 590-3547
Tumbling and gymnastics for children age 18 months through 18 years are offered at this site south of Baltimore City, off I-695. There is also a 40-foot spring floor and 30-foot tumble mount as well as the standard vault, beam, and bars. Dance classes and toddler programs are also available.

Horseback Riding

Maryland is horse country, so horsebackriding opportunities abound. Among the starting points are the Equiery at www.equiery.com or (410) 489-7826 and the Maryland Horse Show Association at (410) 552-1701, www.mdhsa.org.

Running

Baltimore Area Triathlon Club
www.tribmore.org
This local organization offers support to athletes who like to run, swim, and bike fast. Track workouts are held weekly and their Web site includes area races.

Baltimore Road Runners Club
P.O. Box 9825
Baltimore, MD 21284
(410) 377-7327
www.brrc.com
For more than 30 years, this club has pro-
moted running for both recreational and
competitive runners. Some members run
occasionally, others are marathoners. There
are plenty of runs, some 100 meters and others 10 or 20 miles. Relays are on the schedule, too.

Howard County Striders
(410) 964-1998
www.striders.net
More than 1,000 runners in the Baltimore-
Washington area are part of this group that
holds weekly "bagel runs" at the Swim Center
at Wilde Lake in Columbia, about 10 miles
south of Baltimore in Howard County. The
runs start at 7:00 a.m. on Saturday, and
bagels are frequently part of the post-run
meal. The group also organizes races
throughout the region and has many other
weekly runs.

GOLF

Golf in the Baltimore area is undergoing a renaissance.

Young players and older couples are hitting the links, extending the reach of a sport that has traditionally catered to middle-aged men. More people find the challenge of chasing a small, white ball around on sun-drenched fields of green a relaxing way to unwind. Other duffers are using the links for business, making deals on the greens or in their carts, and still others are seeking to follow in the footsteps of Tiger Woods.

In the quest for the green, Baltimore has for decades offered a variety of courses, including several municipal tracks that for more than 40 years have provided hackers with big challenges in urban settings. During the 1950s and early '60s, several of Baltimore's municipal courses played host to the Eastern Open, one of the Professional Golfer's Association's premier events.

Those dependable courses remain a bargain for beginners and intermediate players, while some of the publicly owned courses and a newer municipal course in Baltimore County, Greystone Golf Course, provide challenges for even the best golfers.

Don't get us wrong. Baltimore isn't Myrtle Beach, South Carolina, yet. But you can find good courses and some real bargain plays in the city and the surrounding parts of Maryland. In fact, there are good courses in practically every section of the state, especially near major roadways such as Interstate 70 and Interstate 68 to the west, Interstate 95 to the north and south, and U.S. Highway 50 to the east.

The area's weather is good for golf, though the hearty golfers play in any weather, including snow. The best seasons for teeing off are spring and fall, but winter play is not that uncommon or uncomfortable. With the average winter temperature in the 40s, and occasional days in the 50s and even the 60s, Insiders keep a close eye on the weather forecast, hoping for a warm front that will allow more comfortable play.

At the other extreme is summer, when the three Hs—hazy, hot, and humid—can make for a long day on the links, even if you're shooting par. The best way to avoid as much of the three-H treatment as possible is to tee off before 10:00 a.m. or after 4:00 p.m., but be forewarned: During the hottest part of summer (mid-July through August), these are typically the most coveted tee times. Hot days can also scorch the grass on even the most immaculate fairways and greens; that might make the course especially good for low liners, but the humidity can actually lessen the length of a good tee shot.

Like most areas, foursomes are mandated at most courses, meaning you're probably going to be paired up with others if you don't have enough friends to fill two carts. Most courses are too crowded to allow for walking, though exceptions are noted in this chapter.

There are a few semiprivate courses available in the immediate Baltimore area. Almost every private course requires that you play with a member; there's practically no chance to buy your way onto the private course of your choice.

The listings for each course include the cost of greens fees for one player; these prices are subject to change. Prices include the cart fee except where otherwise noted; again, carts are almost always mandated. In cases where a higher fee is charged on weekends than on weekdays, an average has been given. Yardages are from the white tees (middle markers).

All courses listed have pro shops with clubs, tees, and other essential and nonessential golf equipment.

No guide can tell you as much as you will learn by playing a course, but our goal is to help you choose the right place for you to tee it up. A great Web site for information on all Maryland courses is www.marylandgolf.com. Fore!

NORTHEAST

Bulle Rock
320 Blenheim Lane
Havre de Grace
(410) 939-8887

This Pete Dye-designed course has been host to the McDonald's LPGA Championship in 2005, 2006, and 2007. It's considered one of the state's best—if not the best—public courses. What makes it challenging are plenty of par 5 holes and a killer 18th hole with water all the way down the left side. It's a hike from Baltimore to this Havre de Grace course, about an hour's drive up I-95. But the challenging play and the beautiful vistas make it worth the trip. Regular rates, including greens fee, cart, and use of driving range and putting green, are $145.

Clifton Park Golf Course
2701 St. Lo Drive
(410) 243-3500

A good course for beginning and intermediate players, this Baltimore City-owned, 5,714-yard course has no water and just a few trees. At a price of $26 to $29, it's a good bargain for people in the city, especially golfers who like to walk. The cost is the same whether you ride or walk. Giving this par 70 course an urban flavor are the several roads that run nearby (all of which are out of bounds). Golf pro Mark Paolini offers lessons, while the course provides practice greens, a restaurant, and a snack bar.

Forest Park Golf Course
2900 Hillsdale Road
(410) 448-0734

i Advance notice needed to reserve tee times varies from two to seven days. Make sure you do it as soon as possible, especially for Friday and weekends.

Watch out for what is the largest sand trap on the East Coast, according to the operators here. The mega-bunker on this 5815-yard course used to be a water hazard but was covered with cement and sand some years ago. The 18th hole features a par 5 double-dogleg, forcing you to avoid the slice for two successive shots; if you can't, you're in big trouble trying to make par at 71. A round costs $23 to $26. Tim Sanders offers golf lessons at the course, which features a snack bar and shower facilities.

Greystone Golf Course
2115 White Hall Road, White Hall
(410) 887-1945
www.baltimoregolfing.com

A little farther away than most other courses listed, this 6,925-yard course is worth the drive if you are looking for a challenge. *Golf Week* named it one of America's best municipal courses. To make par (72), you're going to have to successfully negotiate your ball through a 140-foot elevation change and 85 bunkers lining the fairways and surrounding the greens—average-size at about 5,000 to 6,000 square feet. It's one of the only bent grass courses in the area.

Designed by Joe Lee, who designed the Doral's Blue Monster and Disney courses, the toughest hole is the 150-yard No. 4. Water lines the shot, with a bulkhead to the right for this distinct downhill shot. Miss it and you'll lose your ball to the water, which comes into play on about five holes on the back nine. An average round costs $54 to $74, a real bargain for a tough-playing course. After you finish your round, you can enjoy lunch or dinner in Greystone's dining room or a cold drink on the patio deck overlooking the course.

Greystone is an easy 30-minute trek from Baltimore City. To get there, head north on ℹ️ If paired with people you don't know, any of the following topics are good Baltimore conversation starters: the weather, the Orioles, the Ravens, rush-hour traffic, and did we mention the weather?

Interstate 83 north past Towson to the White Hall exit, where signs point the rest of the way.

Gunpowder Falls Golf Course
11101 Raphel Road, Kingsville
(410) 592-9165
www.baltimoregolfing.com

Head north on I-95 to this small suburb north of White Marsh for a mid-length course with par set at 60. The course, formerly called Mt. Vista, is a perfect spot for new golfers or those who want to squeeze a game into their busy schedule. There are novice tees for the newbies and several par 4s for those who want a few challenges. And all of this is set on 65 lush acres by the park. Lessons are also available. The place is a bargain, too, with greens fees running about $20, $22 on weekends.

Longview Golf Course
1 Cardigan Road, Timonium
(410) 887-7735
www.baltimoregolfing.com

An ideal, short course for beginners, this 5,880-yard masterpiece opened in 1971 on top of a landfill. No signs of the previous life lurking under the surface are present—not even to the deer and foxes that are common sights for golfers on the back nine. There's practically no water and very few trees, so errant shots don't necessarily prevent a golfer from finding the green quickly on this par 70 course. A round costs $23 to $30. Pro John Lazzell offers lessons. A snack bar is on-site.

Mount Pleasant Golf Course
6001 Hillen Road
(410) 254-5100

Here's your chance to play on the course where the great Arnold Palmer won his first PGA tournament, the old Eastern Open. Sam Snead also won on this 6,003-yard course, which played host to the Eastern until 1962. Designed by maintenance employees for the City of Baltimore, this par 71 municipal course pits golfers against mature trees and lots of hills, meaning few flat lies. On a breezy day, the back nine can be a duffer's nightmare. It's one of the busiest courses in the area; 85,000 rounds of golf are played each year, so reservations are necessary. A round of golf will cost you $32 if walking and $38 with a cart on weekends. Golf pro Jim Deck provides lessons. A snack bar is on-site.

Pine Ridge Golf Course
2101 Dulaney Valley Road, Lutherville
(410) 252-1408

Built in 1958, this mature, 5,954-yard course hasn't lost its luster. Located next to the Loch Raven Reservoir, the par 72 course features lots of fully grown trees, moderate hills, and more than 100 bunkers. It played host to the Eastern Open on occasion during the 1950s and '60s and offers golfers of all skill levels a moderate challenge on a course where every hole has a dogleg. At $36 to $49 a round, it's still a definite bargain. Pro Kim Hand offers lessons at the course created by Alex "Nipper" Campbell and Gus Hook. A locker room, showers, and a snack bar are available.

NORTHWEST

Francis Scott Key Golf Club
1900 River Downs Drive, Finksburg
(410) 526-2000, (800) 518-7337
www.fskgolfclub.com

Francis Scott Key Golf is one of the most scenic and at the same time challenging courses in the Baltimore area. Designed by renowned architect Arthur Hills, the par 72 golf course offers four par 3 and four par 5. Located about 25 miles outside Baltimore, this semi-private course welcomes public customers. This course, just less than 6,500 yards, was selected the 1995–1996 Best Course (Honorable Mention) in the Baltimore-Washington,

D.C. area by *Washington Golf Monthly Magazine*. Daily fee rates can vary greatly. Based on the day of week, season, and time of day, rates can range from $27 up to $55. The director of golf on this course is Bill Labrozzi.

Mitchell's Golf Center
301 Mitchell Drive, Reisterstown
(410) 833-7721

A nine-hole executive course, the Golf Center draws beginners and good golfers alike, most of whom want a quick golf fix. Playing it through twice, it's almost impossible to make par, which is set at 61 for the total 3,772 yards. The toughest holes are No. 5, which is a 150-yard water shot that looks much easier than it is, and No. 14, a 205-yard par 3 shot over a pond. The facility also features batting cages, three miniature golf courses, and a driving range to keep the kids or others busy while you hit the links. A round costs $18 to $20 with a cart. There is also a snack bar.

Waverly Woods Golf Course
2100 Warwick Way, Ellicott City
(410) 313-9182
www.waverlywoods.com

Located just 9 miles west of the Baltimore Beltway, Waverly Woods offers a 7,000-yard championship design through farmland and beautiful wooded areas. Opened in 1998, this par 72 course was designed by world-renowned golf course architect Arthur Hills. There is a 9,000-square-foot putting green, a separate short game practice area with practice bunkers, and an eight-acre practice range complete with a grass teeing area of over 60,000 square feet. When the golfing is done, the course offers an outdoor patio on the clubhouse with views of the 1st, 10th, and 18th holes. The Kirsch Mathews Golf Academy offers lessons and clinics. A round of golf in the summer, including cart, costs $64 Monday through Thursday and $84 Friday through Sunday.

ℹ Dress in layers. Baltimore's weather is notoriously fickle. In summer, an umbrella isn't a bad idea. Sudden, sometimes severe, late afternoon showers and thunderstorms can hit when cold fronts meet a prevailing warm front. They usually go as quickly as they come.

Willow Springs Golf Course
12960 Livestock Road, West Friendship
(410) 489-7700
www.willowspringsgolfcourse.com

Willow Springs is an 18-hole, par 62 links-style golf course that is both playable for the occasional golfer and satisfying for the serious golfer. The course offers a quick play if you're on a tight schedule. Willow Springs boasts undulating greens, grass mounds, sand bunkers, and water hazards. Tee time reservations may be made up to seven days in advance. And while Willow Springs does not require reservations, it does recommend them. The facility also offers a 32 station, full-length lighted driving range, a practice sand bunker, and putting green. It will cost you $40 to play all 18 holes at Willow Springs, but call ahead for specials.

Worthington Valley Country Club
2425 Greenspring Avenue, Owings Mills
(410) 356-9890

Worthington Valley seems wide open, but this course is narrow (20 to 30 yards wide) and tree-lined. It remains one of the area's best-kept secrets, often because people assume wrongly that its name means it's a private course. This par 70, 6,145-yard course is a real challenge, designed in 1952 by its late owner James Dukes, a local professional golfer. Set on 110 acres, this course is an easy walk, as tees and greens are set close together. Many golfers find they're in good shape until they get to the 14th hole. It's a 600-yard par 5 followed by No. 15, a 240-yard par 3, No. 16, a 440-yard par 4; and No. 17, a 450-yard par 4. A round costs $30.

SOUTHEAST

Rocky Point Golf Course
1935 Back River Neck Road, Essex
(410) 887-0215
www.baltimoregolfing.com

This 6,750-yard, par 72 course reminds some players of a British Open site. Golfers here enjoy breathtaking views of the Chesapeake Bay from several of the holes that border this body of water. When it's windy out, particularly in the fall, the course becomes really tough, especially on No. 10 and No. 11, which are right along the shoreline. Owned and operated by the Baltimore County Revenue Authority, this is a great walking course that rewards players who keep the ball in the wide fairways. Rocky Point has a front nine that is fairly open, while the back nine is fairly tight. Beginners will find the four doglegs a big challenge. A round costs $25 to $30.

SOUTHWEST

Carroll Park Golf Course
2100 Washington Boulevard
(410) 685-8344
www.bmgcgolf.com

The only 10-hole course in the area, Carroll Park's 3,214-yard course is good for beginners and intermediate players and is a growing favorite among women. It's a good course to walk, featuring eight par 4 holes and four par 3s. The course's newest hole, the 232-yard No. 4, requires a low, down-the-middle approach to set you up for a slight right dogleg. For an afternoon golfer looking for a quick game, this course can be completed in about two hours, even when it's busy. A round costs $10 to $16. Cart rental is $6.

Diamond Ridge Golf Course and The Woodlands
2309 Ridge Road, Woodlawn
(410) 887-1349
www.baltimoregolfing.com

Diamond Ridge features two fine tracks for enthusiasts. Try the new Woodlands, so named because of the 3,000—yes, 3,000—white dogwoods lining the fairways. As one pro put it, "It's like Christmas lights all around you when those dogwoods are in bloom." Lindsay Ervin designed this 6,500-yard, par 72 course that opened in 1998. Dramatic elevation changes offer a unique hole-by-hole mix. Check out the No. 17 par 5 hole that drops into a valley for a tough second shot. The No. 1 is a 470-yard par 4 that promises to get a fair number of golfers off to a subpar start heading to the second tee. The pro on this course is Chris Hanson.

The older, 6,300-yard, par 72 Diamond Ridge course features rolling hills and open stretches. The lush fairways and rolling terrain has made Diamond Ridge a favorite of local golfers for more than 30 years. The 10th hole takes you over the water, while other holes have you battling the trees. Frank Blind, Joe Rahnis, and Tim Butlerand are the pros at Diamond Ridge. The courses share a clubhouse and state-of-the-art practice facility. A round costs $26 to $31 at Diamond Ridge and $50 to $70 at the Woodlands.

ON THE WATER

Since settlers first encountered what is now Baltimore, a main attraction has been its waters, hundreds of big and small tributaries to the Chesapeake Bay. Beautiful rivers, gentle and serene coves, an open harbor, and streams perfect for spending time with a fishing pole or a rudder in hand—these are some of the area's most respected and protected resources for anglers, boaters, windsurfers, and personal watercraft operators.

If you're looking for a place to fly fish, the Gunpowder River offers one of the best trout streams on the East Coast. If you're eager to practice steering a catamaran, there are few better spots than the rivers lining eastern Baltimore County. Their many coves and inlets offer calm and shallow waters that enable the novice or the most experienced skipper to practice his or her skills.

If you want tidal waters, the Chesapeake Bay and some of its larger tributaries provide what you're looking for. If you seek nontidal waters, some of the rivers flowing in eastern Baltimore County are your best bet.

In this chapter we introduce you to Baltimore's waters and their attributes, including marinas, services, charters, and rentals. You'll also find information on boating, fishing, crabbing, and other watersports in the area.

SAFETY ON THE HIGH SEAS

With water comes responsibility, and Maryland's Natural Resources Police (a division of its Department of Natural Resources) keeps a close watch over the surrounding waters to make sure activities follow these rules and regulations. They are joined by marine police teams from Baltimore City, Baltimore County, Howard County, and Anne Arundel County as well as U.S. Coast Guard units from Curtis Bay,

an area near the Inner Harbor on the Patapsco River.

The number of people boating in Maryland has been on the rise in recent years, with explosive growth in the personal watercraft category. In the wrong hands, these sleek and slick boats can mar any boating adventure. Whether using a Jet Ski or Sea-Doo or passing by one on the water, remember to keep your guard up.

And remember that people are not the only living things out there. The bay and the rivers and creeks leading into it are full of marine life that would prefer—if they had the choice—not to share the waters with plastic bags, empty beer cans, and paper cups. So, in an effort to grant the wishes of the fishes, so to speak, we Marylanders are trying to "Save the Bay." The outgrowth of this program has been to expand the protection and restoration in the last few years into the hundreds of tributaries that feed into it. As a result, we look unkindly on those who pollute its waters, whether they drop a piece of trash into Minebank Run, a small feeder stream into the larger Gunpowder River, or pump out their on-board sewage system into the bay itself. Help us to keep the bay clean, safe, and fun, because it's our only one. And the area wouldn't be nearly as nice without it.

WATERWAYS

Consider this your formal introduction to the bodies of water that surround Baltimore. Here we've outlined the activities they welcome, the sights that dot their shorelines, and the hazards you should be aware of. For more information about boating, fishing, and water sports, see those sections later in the chapter.

Numbers to Know

If you experience marine problems, contact the Maryland Natural Resources Police, (800) 419-0743, or use Channel 16 VHF on your on-board radio.

For general information from the Department of Natural Resources, call (877) 620-8DNR

Boating emergencies, channel 16 VHF (monitored by Coast Guard, city, state, and county police)
Coast Guard Search and Rescue, (410) 576-2525
Baltimore County Fire Department, 911 or (410) 887-5974
Baltimore County Police Department, 911
Maryland Natural Resources Police, (410) 260-8881 or (800) 628-9944
Local Weather, (410) 936-1212
Coast Guard Station Curtis Bay, (410) 576-2625
Coast Guard Station Stillpond, (410) 778-2201
Coast Guard Boating Safety Hotline, (800) 368-5647
Coast Guard Auxiliary Flotilla boating class, (800) 336-BOAT

The Chesapeake Bay

The origins of the world's largest estuary, the Chesapeake Bay, date from the last Ice Age, more than 20,000 years ago, when a colder climate prevailed on earth. Back then, sea level was more than 300 feet lower than it is today.

Now, the bay has an average depth of 21 feet, with its deepest point in the middle bay, near Bloody Point, where it drops to 174 feet. The bay's length is 195 miles, and it draws water from a 64,000-square-mile area, extending to the headwaters of the Susquehanna River, 441 miles away from its mouth in the northern bay in Otsego, New York. Water flowing from New York to Pennsylvania to Maryland makes its way to the bay. As hard as it is to believe, the bay's shoreline at 4,000 miles is longer than the shoreline of the Pacific Ocean on the West Coast. Really.

The bay's 55-foot channel makes it a favorite for shipping companies sending ore, vehicles, coal, and other materials from all over the world to the port of Baltimore as well as Hampton Roads, Virginia, which is closer to the Atlantic Ocean and Baltimore's competitor to the south.

Because of the intense amount of commercial traffic, operating recreational vessels on the bay can be more challenging than on some of the rivers. Keep in mind that the larger commercial vessels should always have the right of way because of their size, which prohibits them from being able to maneuver easily in the channel. In foul weather, give them a wider berth and heed their horn blows.

In addition to larger vessels, the bay's depth can be a hazard. Shallow waters with unpredictable shifts, especially in side creeks, can run you aground. Furthermore, dredging of channels isn't always done as often as necessary, and sometimes the depths reflected in maps can be fluid, to say the least.

Weather conditions can also challenge boaters. Sudden changes in weather are frequent in summer, although variances occur in spring and fall, too. Although the bay tends to offer good boating weather most of the time, sudden storms can bring high winds, thunderstorms, and heavy downpours in areas where the sun was shining brightly just a few minutes prior. Keep an ear to the radio to monitor situations as they develop, and when signs of possible trouble appear, heed them quickly. Don't wait for the storm to hit—act beforehand.

If you're planning to fish for striped bass (rockfish), you'll want to be in the deeper waters of the lower bay rather than northern sections. The fish seem to favor the deeper areas, with Bloody Point being among the best sites for them. You also might want to talk to other mariners to see where they're hitting. Just watch out for the occasional lie, designed to keep you out of their special spot.

Susquehanna River and Flats

From the city of Havre de Grace, where the Concord Point Lighthouse still stands below the Conowingo Hydroelectric Plant's dam, to the head of the Chesapeake Bay are the Susquehanna Flats, an open and expansive area known for its calm waters and marvelous natural sights. American bald eagles nest on the small islands and can often be seen in the early morning hours among the power lines and trees near the flats. A keen eye is the key to seeing these symbols of America.

In the summer fish lifts carry American and hickory shad, two protected species, over the dam on their spawning tour to the Harrisburg area of Pennsylvania. Largemouth bass, feeding on the shad and other brackish water species, are prevalent in the waters of the Susquehanna throughout the year. Crabs, however, are not too prevalent in this river.

Aberdeen Proving Ground Restricted Waters

The lower Susquehanna, Gunpowder, and Bush River, from Spesutie Island to the mouth of the Gunpowder River is closed off to boaters from 7:00 a.m. to 5:00 p.m. Monday through Friday, except on national holidays. As part of Aberdeen Proving Ground, established in 1917 after the Sandy Hook, New Jersey, proving ground became inadequate, anchoring, swimming, and going on shore are prohibited. Military patrols aboard white boats with orange stripes keep stray boats from restricted spaces, where tank and munitions testing occurs on weekdays and weekends. The sound of the blasts can carry for miles over the water, often scaring those who hear it for the first time. The busiest testing days are Tuesday and Thursday. When the cloud cover is good, testing is more intense.

Sections of Aberdeen house military functions and are therefore restricted to visitors. Guests are invited to tour the United States Army Ordnance Museum, which has one of the world's leading collections of military ordnance, ranging from small arms to 240 large armored vehicles, tanks, and artillery pieces, some of the last survivors of their type. The outside includes a 25-acre tank park.

Gunpowder River and Bush River

In Harford County, the Bush River is among the more quiet, supporting a variety of local boaters and many visitors from Pennsylvania, Delaware, and other areas to the north. The Bush River feeds into the Gunpowder River, and because of a low Amtrak railroad bridge, the river has a 12-foot vertical clearance, prohibiting large sailboats from entering. The Gunpowder, farther north and west, offers excellent fishing and recreation and is protected as part of the 16,000-acre Gunpowder Falls State Park. Farther east, where the water is deeper, the Gunpowder plays host to a variety of boating and aquatic recreational activities, including swimming, waterskiing, and scuba diving. The Gunpowder River channel runs at 11 feet for 2 miles, from 6 to 8 feet for 3.5 miles, and about 5 feet in a dredged section below Joppatowne. Throughout the river, fishing is excellent, with stocking of brown trout in the spring and fall bringing the species total to an astounding 150 to 200 fish per acre. With those numbers, it's hard to miss, assuming you can find a place to cast. Word of stockings brings out the masses, so head out early or during the off season, such as winter and hot summer days, for the best results. You can also find some carp and catfish among the trout.

Middle River

An active boating area near Baltimore, Middle River is home to a number of marinas, waterfront restaurants, and boatyards. The river has several creeks, including Galloway Creek, Frog Mortar Creek, Stansbury Creek, Dark Head Creek, Hopkins Creek, Sue Creek, Hog Pen Creek, Norman's Creek, and Seneca Creek. These creeks provide quiet, calm, and protected waters where waterskiing, swimming, and personal watercraft are allowed. Crabbing and fishing are frequent activities of residents and visitors to the area. Bass, carp, and catfish are frequent visitors to these waters. On weekends and holidays, a 6-knot speed limit is enforced upstream of Galloway Point.

Back River

Back River is between Middle River and the Patapsco River, an area that used to be home to a great deal of industry and still shows signs of the industrial age. The river is home to a number of recreational anglers and boaters who moor their boats along the shorelines. Back River has a poor reputation in the area because of the Back Water Treatment Facility, which can offer a pungent aroma.

Despite this problem—far larger in reputation than in reality—the river is a peaceful getaway from the more widely used Gunpowder, Middle, and Patapsco Rivers.

A favorite place for crabbers, moving among the crab lines or the people checking them can sometimes require effort. The area supports the same bass, carp, and catfish populations as its fellow rivers to its north.

Patapsco River

The Inner Harbor overshadows the Patapsco River by name and opportunity, but in spite of this, the river claims its own recognition. Many of the area's finer marinas are in the Inner Harbor, Fells Point, and Canton areas, where big-ticket boats dock during weekends and summer nights. Closer to the Inner Harbor are paddleboat rentals for $8 to $11 a half hour and sightseeing tours. (For more information about sightseeing tours, see the Charter Boat and Sailing sections later in this chapter as well as the By Water section of the Getting Here, Getting Around chapter.) These vessels, including pontoon boats, water taxis, and larger boats that head to Annapolis, can make for challenging traveling, although passing by the ports and industrial complex built up along both shores is fascinating. The Francis Scott Key Bridge is another site to behold heading up the river, as is the Domino Sugar sign. Stony Creek, Bodkin Creek, home of the Curtis Bay Coast Guard yard, and Rock Creek are peaceful inlets along the river.

Don't expect to find easy docking and mooring along the Patapsco. Most people plan well in advance for the right to dock

Selected Baltimore Firsts

In 1788 the *Chesapeake* was the first American vessel to raise the colors of the United States above its billowing sails.

Our *Constellation* was the first ship to capture an enemy ship after the Revolution in 1797.

Isaac McKim of Fells Point built the first clipper ship, the *Ann McKim*, in 1833. The first steamship made wholly of American steel, the *DeRosset*, was registered here in 1839.

—*Excerpted from Baltimore—America's City of Firsts, a pamphlet published by Baltimore Bicentennial Celebration, Inc.*

along the Inner Harbor piers or the commercial piers nearby. To expect last-minute accommodations is to underestimate the popularity of the area and the need for those with great boats to cruise the Inner Harbor on a hot summer's night. To reserve a space, contact the Baltimore Harbormaster's office at (410) 396-3174. Larger boats should make a reservation all the time, while smaller boats should reserve spaces at either the Harbor or Canton sites a few days in advance for weekends or summer weekdays.

Farther up, the Patapsco River provides fishing opportunities in Patapsco Valley State Park, a 14,000-acre recreational area in western Baltimore County. The park offers fishing, tubing, canoeing, and other waterside activities throughout the summer months, while anglers find their way to the river throughout the year. (See our Parks and Recreation chapter for more information about Patapsco Valley State Park.) Crabbing in the Inner Harbor is relatively poor and not recommended, as the crabs have been exposed to the pollution from trash and commercial vessel activity.

Loch Raven Reservoir

This sprawling water-collection area for much of Baltimore County is on Loch Raven Drive in Towson, (410) 887-7692. It's a great spot for fishing for largemouth bass in the spring, especially in the thick bed grasses of the smaller coves, and smallmouth bass and crappie in the summer, especially toward the end of the summer when waters warm up significantly. Fishing from the shore or by boat can be rewarding and relaxing, especially to those who covet quiet and peaceful spots removed from the more urbanized area nearby.

Rowboat rentals at $14 for a day, are available. (See the Parks and Recreation chapter for more information about the reservoir.)

Loch Raven Fishing Center, near Dulaney Valley Road, www.co.ba.md.us, is operated by the Baltimore County Department of Recreation and Parks. Fishing, boating, and docking are offered on a daily or seasonal basis. Rentals include rowboats, canoes, jon-

i Tide Point, a former Proctor and Gamble Plant built in the 1920s, recently benefited from a $67 million redevelopment. Located on the harbor in South Baltimore, the office park has a lovely waterfront promenade replete with Adirondack chairs for lounging. Grab a cup of coffee from the nearby cafe and enjoy Baltimore's working waterfront.

boats, and electric-powered boats; rates start at $14 a day. You can not have more than three people in one boat at a time. A valid driver's license is required. Anglers make up the bulk of the rental business, but sightseers can also rent boats. Keep in mind that it can be difficult to get a boat in the afternoon when the weather is good. Call (410) 887-7692 for more information or to check on the availability of boats during the day.

The facility is open April through Labor Day from 6:00 a.m. to dusk. After Labor Day and through October, the center is closed on Tuesday and Thursday. It opens at 7:00 a.m. all other days. Gasoline-powered boats are prohibited. No boats are rented after 4:00 p.m.

Boating

Give Baltimoreans a body of water larger than a puddle, and they'll try to sail or motor a boat over it. Especially popular are the Chesapeake Bay, the Susquehanna, Gunpowder, and Bush Rivers, and the Middle and Patapsco Rivers (see the Waterways section for more information).

What follows is a roundup of some of the marinas, ramps, and boat rental providers in the area.

Marinas

Gunpowder River

Gunpowder Cove Marina
510 Riviera Drive, Joppatowne
(410) 679-5454
www.gunpowdercove.com
Since 1969 this marina has been providing service to the Joppatowne area, where at

least half of the mariners come in for week-ends. The marina on the Gunpowder River at Taylor's Creek has 294 protected slips and a mean depth of 5 feet. Electricity and showers are provided, along with marine supplies and engine and hull repairs. Gas, but no diesel, is available on-site. A convenience store and other amenities are within walking distance in Joppatowne. Transient slip rates vary.

Back River

Weaver's Marine Service
730 Riverside Drive, Essex
(410) 686-4944
www.weaversmarine.net

A full-service marina since 1945, Weaver's offers 96 slips and a variety of services to boaters. Among its amenities are gas, show-ers, and pump-out facilities as well as a marine supply service and marine repair and mechanic services. The marina, which is 5 miles from the Chesapeake Bay on the Back River, has a depth of up to 6 feet. Weavers offers all kinds of sales and services, including a marine store, pump-outs, washing and wax-ing, gas dock, haul-outs, parts department, and insurance repairs. Wi-fi is available here.

Middle River

Anchor Bay Marina
202 Nanticoke Road, Essex
(410) 574-0777
www.bayboatsupplies.com

On Hopkins Creek, about 2.5 miles from the mouth of Middle River, this 6-foot-to-8-foot-deep facility provides uncovered slips for up to 42-foot vessels and covered slips for yachts measuring up to 50 feet. Among the ameni-ties are showers, restrooms, restaurants next door, and grocery stores within a few blocks of the marina. Boating services include gas and diesel fuel pumps, generators, AC and electrical service, which can be done at the slip, and parts and accessories available at the Ships Store.

Chesapeake Yachting Center
114 Carroll Island Road, Essex
(410) 335-4900
www.chesapeakeyachting.com

Designed for yacht owners, this marina fea-tures a calm, sheltered harbor on Frog Mortar Creek on Middle River. With more than 200 slips, ranging from 24 feet to 70 feet long, the center caters to yacht owners and motorboat operators. It features a complete marine maintenance and repair facility as well as 24-hour, on-site staff, pump-out facilities, travel lifts, sail lofts, mast and rigging service, engine shop, and a fuel dock for gas and diesel fill-ups. The site also offers lots of park-ing, with convenient access to Interstate 695 (the Baltimore Beltway) just a few miles away.

Maryland Marina
3501 Red Rose Farm, Middle River
(410) 335-8722
www.marylandmarina.com

This 360-slip marina along Frog Mortar Creek lives up to its slogan "Unique Among Mari-nas." The facility offers all the usual amenities, including electricity and water at all slips, a store, bathhouses, shower and laundry facili-ties, yacht care, sailboat hardware and rig-ging, pump-out facilities, and spaces for up to 200 boat trailers. Maryland Marina also offers a restaurant, the Wild Duck Cafe. The nightly rate for transients is $1 a foot, with a $22 min-imum, at the 4-foot-to-6-foot draft facility.

Porter's Seneca Marina
918 Seneca Park Road, Middle River
(410) 335-6563
www.porterssenecamarina.com

At the mouth of Seneca Creek, giving boaters direct access to the Chesapeake Bay, this 125-slip marina offers a quiet resting place, espe-cially for families. Proclaiming itself a "family marina," Porter's offers picnicking facilities, including tables, grills, a play area, and a swimming pool. Conveniently located near Hart-Miller Island, the marina has a variety of amenities, including haul-out and winter storage, a ship's store with ice, a gas dock, mechanics, supplies, a 30-ton open-end travel lift, and a cement launching ramp. Its showers and restroom facilities are available 24 hours a day.

Patapsco River

Anchorage Marina
2501 Boston Street, Canton
(410) 522-7200
www.anchoragemarina.com
This Canton marina offers slips for a night or a year. It's located near the Promenade. It's a long walk to the Inner Harbor, but you can catch a water taxi to either the Inner Harbor or Fells Point. Or just stay in the area; it's an easy stroll to the restaurants of Canton. The daily docking rate is $2.25 per foot.

The Baltimore Inner Harbor Marine Center
400 Key Highway
(410) 837-5339
www.baltimoreinnerharbormarinecenter .com
The Baltimore Inner Harbor Marine Center has been serving Baltimore boaters and visitors for more than 20 years. Its convenient location in the heart of Downtown makes it a great place to dock and enjoy the sites. Both overnight and day docking are available. Amenities include 24-hour security and customer service, 24-hour dock and pump-out facility, and a 24-hour convenience and marine store. There is also a laundry facility, Wi-fi, pool and health club access, concierge service, and business center.

Baltimore Marine Center
2738 Lighthouse Point East, Inner Harbor
(410) 675-8888
www.baltimoremarinecenter.com
Baltimore Marine Center at Lighthouse Point has 500 slips on the south side of the Inner Harbor, as well as indoor boat storage, a health club, and a pool. Wi-fi and fuel dock are available.

Baltimore Public Docking
Patapsco River at Baltimore Harbor and Canton
(410) 396-3174
The city's docks are always crowded, but the locations at the Inner Harbor and Canton can be among the best for sightseers or for those seeking to be seen. High visibility comes at a high price at this 16-foot-deep marina. Electricity and showers are available, along with ice. Other services, including grocery stores, pharmacies, shopping, and restaurants, are near each dock.

Inner Harbor East Marina
801 Lancaster Street
(410) 625-1700
www.innerharboreastmarina.com
This marina offers just about everything a boater could ask for, including 200 state-of-the-art floating boat slips. Located in the heart of the Inner Harbor, this marina has a 24-hour staff, ship store, on-site parking, fuel pier, water, and electricity hook-up. There is also an on-site restaurant with observation deck. Transients are welcome. This is also home of the Canton Kayak Club (www.canton kayakclub.com).

Middle Branch Marina
3101 Waterview Avenue
(410) 539-2628
www.middlebranchmarina.com
Under the Hanover Street Bridge, about 1 mile directly across the Patapsco River from the Inner Harbor, this 365-slip marina is one of the most affordable for all the amenities it provides. With a transient rate of $1 per foot and facilities for everything from a dinghy to a 60-footer, it's hard to go wrong. The 6-foot-deep, protected cove provides safety, security, and access. A security fence surrounds the place, free parking is available to all users, and it's convenient to the Light Rail system, which allows access to the airport and Baltimore's Inner Harbor area. Among the amenities are water and electricity connections to

each slip, shower rooms, a full-service repair yard, and a ships store as well as a do-it-your-self service area, where tools are provided at an hourly rate. Gas and diesel service and pump-out facilities are also available.

Boat Ramps

Baltimore County operates five public boat ramps, where fees are $5 a day or $15 for the year. The sites include:

Cox's Point, (410) 887-0255, leading into the Back River from Essex

Inverness Park, (410) 887-7536, which leads into Bear Creek and Middle River in Dundalk

Merritt Point Park, (410) 887-7155, off Bullneck Creek and leading into the Patapsco River

Rocky Point, (410) 887-3873, off Back River Neck Road and leading into the bay in Essex

Southwest Area Park, (410) 887-1439, off Hollins Ferry Road in Baltimore Highlands, leading into the Patapsco River

Turner Station, (410) 887-7536, off Broening Highway in Dundalk, leading into the Patapsco River.

Marine Services

Deckelman's Boat Yard
201 Oak Avenue, Middle River
(410) 391-6482, (410) 850-2993 (beeper)
If your boat's in need of a tow, Deckelman's is the place to go. They're quick, efficient, and reasonably priced. They're also available 24 hours a day. They'll tow your boat where you want it to go, or they'll do the work them-selves.

Tidewater Yacht Service Center
321 East Cromwell Street
(410) 625-4992
www.tysc.com
If you can float it, Tidewater Yacht Service Center can fix it—at a guaranteed rate established before the work begins. Located now at the Port Covington Maritime Center, Tidewater specializes in cleaning and detailing, bottom

painting, engine and generator repairs and sales, fiberglass and blister repair, woodwork-ing, awlgrip refinishing, varnishing, air condi-tioning and refrigeration, electrical service, sail repair, and canvas installation and repair. Since 1965 the facility has provided service to boats weighing as much as 60 tons or with beams as long as 20 feet. Towing services are also avail-able. The fuel dock is still located near the DOMINO SUGAR sign at Key Highway.

Sailing

Getaway Sailing
2700 Lighthouse Point (Suite 905)
(410) 342-3110, (888) 342-3709
www.getawaysailing.com
Getaway Sailing offers a fleet of sailboats from 9 feet to 34 feet at the Lighthouse Point Marina, on the Patapsco River in Canton. Rentals vary depending on the size and type of boat and on how long you decide to spend sailing it—so call ahead for details. Both bare-deck and skippered charters and cruises are available. Owner Dick Mead also offers after-noon and overnight cruises to the Eastern Shore. In addition to rentals, the company provides lessons, beginning at about $200 to $500 for an eight-hour day of instruction. If you think you might be visiting often, a mem-bership for between $300 and $5,000 a year might be more economical.

Sail Baltimore
1809 Thames Street
(410) 522-7300
www.sailbaltimore.org
Sail Baltimore is a nonprofit, community serv-ice organization located in Baltimore City and works as a great resource for boating and sail-ing activities in the area. It was founded as the Mayor's Official Committee on Visiting Ships to host Baltimore's first tall ship gather-ing in the summer of 1976 and is responsible for coordinating Baltimore's waterfront activi-ties. Sail Baltimore also supports other mar-itime events, such as the Great Chesapeake Bay Schooner Race, the Fells Point Yacht Club Lighted Boat Parade, the Blessing of Balti-more's Work Boats, and OpSail Baltimore.

FISHING

Largemouth bass, smallmouth bass, and brown trout, oh my! Baltimoreans are fascinated by marine life, and we enjoy hauling it over the side of a boat just as much as visiting it at the National Aquarium. The Chesapeake Bay as well as the Susquehanna, Middle, and Patapsco Rivers are great places to drop your line. Gunpowder River is stocked with brown trout every spring and fall offering you, the cunning angler, 150 to 200 fish per acre, and Loch Raven Reservoir has its own fishing center. (See the Waterways section for more information about fishing these areas.)

Here we've provided information for obtaining a license in Maryland and highlighted some of the charter boats in the area.

Licenses

Maryland's fishing license fees depend on whether you're from the state or from outside the state. Licenses, necessary for anyone age 16 or older, can be obtained from a number of sports and tackle shops around the state as well as at several regional service centers operated by the Maryland Department of Natural Resources. For more information, call (410) 260-3220 or visit www.dnr.state.md.us.

Maryland residents pay $20.50 for a nontidal license or $15.00 for a tidal license, which is applicable to fishing in the Chesapeake Bay and its tidal tributaries. Those hailing from outside Maryland pay their state's fee for a nontidal license or $15 for a tidal license.

All other licenses, stamps, and permits are the same regardless of residency. A short-term nontidal license, which is valid for five days from the date of issuance, is $7. A trout stamp is $5. A pleasure boat decal to fish, which allows fishing from a boat by all the people on board, is $40. No license is require to fish from a charter boat.

Charter Boats

Associated Bay Captains
5980 Rockhold Creek Road, Deale
(410) 269-1115
Since 1973 the Associated Bay Captains have been providing anglers with access to the Chesapeake Bay's best fishing areas. All of its captains know the places to find trout, drum, flounder, bluefish, Spanish mackerel, spot, and croakers through chumming, trolling, bottom fishing, and jigging. Boats with six or fewer passengers cost $380 for a six-hour day and $480 for an eight-hour day. For boats with 6 to 10 passengers, the cost is $650 for an eight-hour day.

Blue Goose Yacht Charter Service
2501 Boston Street
(410) 647-2583
www.bluegoosecharters.com
This charter service, based out of the Baltimore Harbor in historic Canton, specializes in diesel trawler yachts, not sailboats. The yachts come fully equipped—complete with linens, towels, and utensils. Early boarding is allowed the night before, at no additional charge, if the schedule permits. Discounts for charters lasting longer than one week and for repeat customers are offered. Blue Goose operates from late April through the end of October.

Baltimore Rowing Club
3301 Waterview Avenue
(410) 355-5659
www.baltimorerowing.org
Get up and go near the Hanover Street Bridge south of the Inner Harbor and you might see the slim rowing boats of the Baltimore Rowing Club—or the sculls of local high school and college teams—breaking the still waters of the Patapsco River. If you've ever seen these graceful vessels and wanted to take your turn at an oar, the Baltimore Rowing Club offers lessons and regattas. You've got to get up early; classes begin at 5:00 a.m.

Chesapeake Charters, Inc.
Taylor's Island
(410) 320-4550
www.bayfishing.net
From April to November, Captains Chad and Kerry Muse steers his 48-foot fiberglass *Darlene II* through the Chesapeake Bay so that anglers can catch striped bass, sea trout, flounder, perch, or other fish of the bay. The charge for up to eight people is $550 and $50 for each additional person, including weekends, which, however, are difficult to book on short notice. Half-day and evening trips are also available. The boat can carry up to 34 passengers, but Muse suggests no more than 20 for a fishing trip. The boat leaves at 6:00 a.m. for its eight-hour trip, which begins from Taylor's Island on the Eastern Shore.

OTHER WATER SPORTS

Captain Don's Fishing Charter
Henderson's Wharf Marina
1001 Fell Street, Fells Point
(410) 342-2004
www.captdonscharters.com
The 46-foot *Lady Luck* has room for six passengers and leaves for the Chesapeake Bay from Fells Point. Fishing tackle and licenses are provided, but bring your own food and beverages. The boat goes on a variety of trips, from eight-hour rockfishing expeditions for $450 to two-hour Inner Harbor cruises for $220. Less-serious fishermen might like the three-hour fishing trip for $250. In the fall the boat goes out on hunting expeditions for sea ducks or Canada geese.

Chesapeake Paddlers Association
P.O. Box 341, Greenbelt, MD 20768
www.cpakayaker.com
With more than 300 members from the Maryland, Delaware, and District of Columbia areas, the Chesapeake Paddlers Association offers a forum for sea kayakers who'd like to discuss techniques and common interests, improve paddling skills, and experience the beauty of the Chesapeake Bay region's waters. Membership costs $10, and while the organization has no telephone number, you can learn more about it by sending a letter to the previously listed address or by checking the Web site.

Ultimate Water Sports
Hammerman Area of Gunpowder Falls State Park
7340 Greenbank Road
(410) 335-5352
www.ultimatewatersports.com
From May to September, Owner Hal Ashman operates a wonderland for newcomers and experienced water enthusiasts in a calm and protected 2-foot- to 3-foot-deep stretch of Dundee Creek off Maxwell Point. This location boasts some of the most spectacular natural scenery and pristine beauty the bay has to offer. Ultimate Water Sports offers kayak lessons, rentals, and tours, as well as sailing lessons, sailing rentals, windsurfing lessons, and windsurfing rentals. There is also a kids' water sport camp and other group programs available.

To reach the sports center, you must pay a $2 state park entrance fee; frequent visitors might want to purchase a $75 annual pass allowing unlimited visits to the park throughout the year.

DAY TRIPS

Maryland is called America in Miniature because every type of land configuration that exists in the United States exists to some degree in Maryland. To the west are the Allegheny Mountains; to the east, flat plains, sandy beaches, and marshlands. In central Maryland, you'll find green valleys, grasslands, and gently rolling foothills.

At the approximate center of all this lies Baltimore. Three hours from Ocean City to the east, three hours from the Cumberland Gap to the west, a little more than an hour's distance from the Mason-Dixon Line to the north and the Virginia border to the south, Baltimore makes an excellent jumping-off point for day trips and weekend getaways in the mid-Atlantic.

We've organized this chapter as usual in this book, leaving out Downtown but including Northeast, Northwest, Southeast, and Southwest. We've also added three more directions—North, South, and West. This creates a wheel-like configuration that has Baltimore as its hub and state and interstate highway routes as its spokes. Using these main spokes as the basis for your driving directions out from the city makes the directions simple.

If you'd rather not hit the highways, a typical Maryland map will show you that most of these routes coexist beside older roads that will take you to the same place and more often than not offer a more scenic drive. Interstate 83, for instance, runs almost parallel to York Road—actually in sight of it for most of the ride. So, if you'd rather go through small towns, drive more slowly, and stop when you feel like it, these roads are a viable alternative.

Almost all of the trips noted in this chapter can be taken in a day. Maryland is, after all, a relatively small state. It doesn't take too many hours of driving before you are out of this state and halfway through another. (It is, for instance, only a three-and-a-half-hour drive to New York City from Baltimore.) However, since a trip to the beach or the mountains takes three hours, you may want to plan a weekend getaway. So, if you decide at 4:00 p.m. that you don't want to drive back to Baltimore, you'll know the lay of the land. If you're thinking national parks, Maryland has plenty of them, but you'll find them listed in the Parks and Recreation and On the Water chapters. The day trips that follow take you across Maryland's roads and tracks rather than its trails and rivers.

So, buckle the kids in the back seat, pack up the cooler, and dog-ear this page. You're on your way!

NORTH

To reach points north, use I-83, the interstate highway that begins (or ends, depending on how you look at it) at Fayette and President Streets in Baltimore City. It is I-83 that takes you quickly out of the city (except at evening rush hour) to local destinations such as Towson, Lutherville, Timonium, Cockeysville, and Hunt Valley. North of Hunt Valley, Baltimore County becomes country. There are plenty of little towns along the way that offer their own kinds of charm. White Hall, with its country shops and roadside stands, is a simple destination if all you're after is an afternoon's drive through the countryside. Get off I-83 at Hunt Valley, head east about a mile to York Road, and turn left. It will take you through or near many little towns and lots of scenic farmland and horse country.

If you want a true northern destination, however, the first ones are not in Maryland at all but just over the Mason-Dixon Line in Pennsylvania or in northern Delaware.

York, Pennsylvania
Exit 9 off I-83
50 miles from Baltimore

York was the nation's capital when the British troops occupied Philadelphia during the American Revolution. The Historical Society of York County, 250 East Market Street, has a museum with exhibits that depict York County from those times as well as a reproduction of the original York village square. The museum is open 10:00 a.m. to 4:00 p.m. Tuesday through Saturday. Cost is $6 for adults and $5 for seniors and children older than age 12. This allows entrance into four other sites of historic interest in the area: Bonham House, the Golden Plough Tavern, General Gates House, and Bobb Log House.

You may also find the York County Colonial Court House of interest. This reproduction of the original courthouse has a presentation that recounts the signing of the Articles of Confederation, adopted by the Continental Congress in the original building. Call (717) 848-1587 for more information or visit www.yorkheritage.org.

Hershey, Pennsylvania
I-83 north to U.S. Highway 322
90 miles from Baltimore

"The sweetest place on earth" combines 60 rides, shows, a special exhibit on how chocolate is produced, and chocolate for sale in every conceivable manner. Hersheypark, which celebrated its centennial in 2007, isn't on a par with Walt Disney World, but if you love chocolate, spending a day here is a must. If you even want to bathe in chocolate, then make an appointment at the Chocolate Spa at the Hershey for a whipped cocoa bath and maybe a chocolate bean polish.

Admission to Hersheypark is $45.95 for people age 9 to 54 and $26.95 for seniors and children age 3 through 8. Seniors older than age 70 pay $18.95. Come two hours before closing and you can visit the park on your admission ticket the next day also.

That means you're going to spend the night. Plenty of chains have hotels here. Hershey has its own lodging, the Hershey Lodge and the posh Hershey Hotel. Information about all of this is available at www.hersheypa.com. The operators at (800) HERSHEY can help with reservations and information

NORTHEAST

Our northeast route is Interstate 95 North, which is easily accessed by taking I-83 to Interstate 695 East, which at that point parallels U.S. Highway 40 East. Don't let this confuse you. The upper end of the Chesapeake Bay gets in the way of US 40's progress east, so it heads more northerly for a time. Both I-95 and US 40, if you keep going, can take you straight toward Newark, New Jersey, and points north; or you can head south on the other side of the bay down U.S. Highway 301 to Eastern Shore points in both Delaware and Maryland. (See the East section later in this chapter for Eastern Shore destinations.)

Whether you drive up I-95 or US 40, you'll find yourself fairly quickly near Havre de Grace.

Havre de Grace
I-95 North to Highway 155
28 miles from Baltimore

Just before the Susquehanna River, you'll find Havre de Grace, the town that came in second on the list of choices for the nation's capital in 1791. Sitting on the point of land where the Susquehanna meets the Chesapeake Bay, close to its northernmost tip, one would think that it would have given the capital a well-protected harbor. However, the founders chose well, for during the War of 1812, Havre de Grace was essentially burned to the ground by British invaders.

The town continued due in large part to the location that put it in peril. Being at the mouth of the Susquehanna made it a trading location for points north from its earliest days. From 1839 to the turn of the next century, barges drawn by mule made their way up the Tidewater Canal 45 miles to Wrightsville, Pennsylvania. The lock house at the canal's head is still extant and can be visited from 1:00 to 5:00 p.m. on weekends May through October. Call (410) 939-5780. Admission is $2 for adults.

At one end of the town's waterfront Promenade you'll find the Concord Point Light House, which is one of the oldest East Coast lighthouses in continuous operation. The lighthouse is open on weekends April through October from 1:00 to 5:00 p.m. Admission is free. Call (410) 939-9040. The Promenade, a half-mile wood boardwalk at the water's edge, provides a picturesque route to two of the town's museums. The Havre de Grace Decoy Museum is at 215 Giles Street, open daily 11:00 a.m. to 4:00 p.m. Stop in for a glimpse at genuine American folk art. Admission is $6 for adults. Also on the Promenade is the Havre de Grace Maritime Museum, at 100 Lafayette Street, (410) 939-4800. It's a tiny place, filled with artifacts from local residents, telling the story of Havre de Grace's maritime history. It's also home to the Chesapeake Wooden Boat Builders School. Admission is $2 for adults and $1 for seniors and students. If you decide to stay for the night, Havre de Grace has some lovely bed-and-breakfasts, including the Currier House near the Promenade (410-939-7886), and the charming Spencer Silver Mansion (410-939-5200). A number of chains have hotels on US 40.

If you'd like more information about Havre de Grace, call the Havre de Grace Tourism Commission at (800) 851-7756, or visit the Web site at www.hdgtourism.com.

Perryville Outlet Center
I-95 North to exit 93
32 miles from Baltimore
The outlet center in Perryville isn't the biggest, but if you're already on I-95, it's convenient. It is located north of Havre de Grace, past the Susquehanna River. Prime Outlets has some 20 stores, including Liz Claiborne, Jones New York, Bass, Osh-Kosh B'Gosh, Claire's Acces-

sories, Mikasa, Book Cellar, and Nike. Prime Outlets is open Monday through Saturday 10:00 a.m. to 9:00 p.m. and Sunday 11:00 a.m. to 6:00 p.m. To find out more, call (410) 378-9399 or visit www.perryvilleoutlet center.com. (If you're looking for really great outlet shopping, plan a visit to Rehoboth Beach, Delaware, to visit the 130 stores of Tanger Outlets, where shopping is tax free, or go to Prime Outlets in Queenstown, about a half hour east of the Chesapeake Bay Bridge. Newly expanded, this is the best and closest outlet shopping for Baltimoreans. More information on these may be found later in the chapter.)

Brandywine Valley
I-95 North to Highway 52
72 miles from Baltimore
The hills and valleys between Philadelphia and Wilmington, Delaware, welcome visitors with beauty both natural and man-made. The Brandywine River gives the area its natural beauty; the castles built by the duPont family rightly give the area the nickname Chateau Valley. If you have only a day, you've got a tough choice ahead of you.

Longwood Gardens on U.S. Highway 1 in Kennett Square, Pennsylvania, offers 1,050 acres of gardens designed by Pierre S. duPont. The Conservatory makes this a place worth seeing in any season; the Christmas lights are worth bundling up against the cold. Tickets are $14 during the growing season, $15 between Thanksgiving and New Year's Day, and $12 during off-season. Tickets are discounted on Tuesdays except during the Christmas season. The gardens are open the usual business hours except during the Christmas light displays when the gardens are open until 9:00 p.m. Call (610) 388-1000 or visit www.longwoodgardens.org.

Winterthur Museum and Country Estate, on Highway 52 north of Wilmington, offers both an enormous mansion which can be seen on several tours as well as a 60-acre garden with the fairy-tale garden for children known as Enchanted Woods. Tours of the house require reservations and cost about $20 each. The Yuletide Tours are immensely popular for their fanciful recreations of Christmas past. Call (800) 448-3883 or visit www.winterthur.org. The Hagley Museum, Delaware Highway 141, Wilmington, at first glance is a gracious place on a verdant riverbank. But they made gunpowder here (with plenty of explosions) and that was the beginning of the duPont fortune. The scenery is enough reason to visit, but the house and what's left of the gunpowder mills are fascinating. Even children like to visit here. Tickets are $11 for adults, $9 for students and seniors, and $4 for children. The house and grounds are open 9:30 a.m. to 4:30 p.m.

These are only the highlights of the Brandywine Valley's treasures. If you want to make a weekend of it, there are plenty of great bed-and-breakfasts, inns, and restaurants. The nearby Inn at Montchanin Village, (800) COWBIRD, was once home to the workers at Hagley. Now it is a luxurious inn with a first-rate restaurant, Krazy Kats. For other choices visit www.wilmcvb.net or call (800) 489-6664.

Lancaster, Pennsylvania
I-95 North to exit 93, U.S. Highway 222 North
70 miles from Baltimore

Lancaster County is Amish country, the land of the Pennsylvania Dutch. To reach Lancaster hang a left off I-95 onto US 222 toward Lancaster, the city.

Keep your eyes peeled—road signs in the Amish country are not the large, green markers we are used to. They are much smaller, usually requiring drivers to slow down to read them. As much of the "traffic" along these roads is horse-drawn buggies, traveling about 2 miles an hour, you'll have plenty of time to read the signs and enjoy the sights of this beautiful, green countryside.

There are plenty of places to shop in Lancaster, including a large number of factory outlets stores. The Rockvale Square Factory Outlet Village has about 119 stores, making it

one of the largest outlet malls in the mid-Atlantic. You can find everything from Jones New York to Black & Decker, from Waterford Wedgwood to L'eggs. To reach it, you'll actually want to turn off US 222 before you get to the city of Lancaster. A right on Pennsylvania Highway 372 and a left on Pennsylvania Highway 896 should get you there with no difficulty. The mall is open Monday through Saturday 9:30 a.m. to 9:00 p.m. and Sunday 11:00 a.m. to 5:00 p.m. Call (717) 293-9595 for more information, or visit www.rockvale outletslancaster.com.

On U.S. Highway 30 east of Lancaster is the Tanger Outlet Center, with more than 60 stores. These include Izod, Banana Republic, J. Crew, Skechers, Liz Claiborne, Polo Ralph Lauren, Noritake, and Movado. The outlet is open 9:00 a.m. to 9:00 p.m. Monday through Saturday and 10:00 a.m. to 6:00 p.m. Sunday. Call (717) 392-7260 for more information, or visit www.tangeroutlet.com.

To immerse yourself in the Amish way of life, visit the Amish Farm and House on US 30. This is a working farm, so all tours are guided, but you will get an opportunity to see the inside of an 1805 Amish farmhouse, barns, and grounds. Food is also available on-site from April through October. The tour costs $7.50 for adults, $6.75 for seniors, and $5 for children age 5 through 11. Call (717) 394-6185 for more information, or visit www.amishfarm andhouse.com. The Amish Village, also on US 30, has not only a house and barn but also a schoolhouse, blacksmith shop, store, and picnicking area. Admission to the village is $6.75 for adults or $2.75 for children age 6 through 12. Call (717) 687-8511 or visit www.800padutch.com for more information.

If all this doesn't satisfy your interest in the Amish culture, consider taking a tour of Amish farmlands and the countryside through Amish Country Tours. Tours leave daily from 3121 Old Philadelphia Pike. Call (717) 768-3600 for information.

About 10 minutes north of the Rockvale outlet mall is the little town of Strasburg. Hardly more than a post office and a general

Welcome Centers

If you get lost while taking in Maryland's sights or find that you need more information on where you're heading, you can call or visit a Maryland Welcome Center.
In addition to the centers listed here, Maryland also has approximately 65 picnic
areas, scenic overlooks, and minor rest areas available to motorists. A complete list
of these facilities is located on the Maryland Official Highway Map, which is available at any welcome center or by visiting the State Department of Transportation
online at www.marylandroads.com.

Youghiougheny Overlook Welcome Center, (301) 746-5979. Located on Interstate
68 East 1.5 miles east of Friendsville in Garrett County, Maryland.

Sideling Hill Interpretive Center, (301) 678-5442. Located on I-68 West, approximately 10 miles west of Hancock in Washington County, Maryland.

I-70 East and I-70 West Welcome Centers, Located at mile marker #39, Myersville,
Maryland. Interstate 70 West: (301) 293-4161. Interstate 70 East: (301) 293-2526.

U.S. 15 South Welcome Center, (301) 447-2553. Located just south of the Pennsylvania state line in Frederick County, Maryland.

I-95 South and I-95 North Welcome Centers. Both centers are located in Howard
County south of Baltimore and north of Washington, D.C. The Southbound site
serves traffic heading toward Washington, D.C.: (301) 490-2444. The Northbound
site serves traffic heading toward the Baltimore/Annapolis area: (301) 490-1333.

Crain Memorial Welcome Center, (301) 259-2500. Located approximately 2 miles
north of the Potomac River on northbound US 301 in Charles County, Maryland.

Bay Country Welcome Center, (410) 758-6803. Located on US 301 in Queen Anne's
County, Maryland, approximately 15 miles north of its junction with U.S. Highway 50.

U.S. Highway 13 North Welcome Center, (410) 957-2484. Located on US 13 northbound, just north of the Virginia state line in Worcester County, Maryland.

In addition to the above facilities, the Maryland Transportation Authority operates two full-service facilities on the toll portion of I-95 (JFK Memorial Highway):
The Maryland House. Located on the median of I-95 and accessible to both northbound and southbound traffic, approximately 24 miles north of Baltimore City in
Harford County, Maryland. Food and fuel are available.

Chesapeake House Welcome Center, (410) 287-2313. Located 14 miles north of the
Maryland House and 12 miles south of the Delaware state line.

store, the town is notable for its Strasburg
Railroad, with a train ride across beautiful
Pennsylvania countryside and a pleasant picnicking stop in the middle. Chartered in 1832,
the Strasburg line is now just a few cars pulled
by an ancient steam locomotive, but it is
great fun. The entire trip takes 45 minutes, if
you don't get off midway at the picnic
grounds. Round-trip fare on the coach is $11
for adults and $6 for children. Open-air cars,
deluxe lounge cars, first-class cars, and a dining car are also available for slightly higher
fares. Call (717) 687-7522 or visit www
.strasburgrailroad.com for details.

The best way to tour Dutch country, however, is to get in your car and go. For information about other destinations, call the Pennsylvania Dutch Convention and Visitors Bureau at (800) 723-8824 or (800) PA-DUTCH or visit www.padutchcountry.com.

Ladew Topiary Gardens
I-95 North to exit 74, Highway 152 North

Ladew Topiary Gardens and Manor House is located on Highway 152, about 20 miles off US 1. The 15 seasonal gardens spread across 22 acres are ranked among the finest topiary gardens in America. The restored manor house is a telescoping house, built in sections, with the oldest section dating from almost 300 years ago. The house contains Harvey S. Ladew's collection of English antiques and paintings. Much of his collection concerns fox hunting and riding. The house and gardens are open mid-April through October 31 from 10:00 a.m. to 4:00 p.m. Monday through Friday and from 10:30 a.m. to 5:00 p.m. Saturday and Sunday. The last house tour leaves at 3:00 p.m. on weekdays and 4:00 p.m. on weekends. Admission to both is $13 for adults, $11 for seniors and students, and $5 for children younger than age 12. To tour only the gardens, the cost is $10, $8, and $2, respectively. Call (410) 557-9466 or visit www.ladewgardens.com for more information.

SOUTHEAST

Our southeast route takes Interstate 97 south off I-695 to US 50. (The parallel road to I-97 is Highway 2, Ritchie Highway, but it is not a scenic route, clogged as it is with shopping centers all the way to the Severn River.

Annapolis
I-97 South to US 50
49 miles from Baltimore

Maryland's capital city is situated at the mouth of the Severn River, which makes it not only our political and historical capital, but also our sailing capital. Some say it is the sailing capital of the world. Die-hard sailors can argue that one, but for day-trippers, this is one trip worth making.

Annapolis is one of the oldest cities in both the state of Maryland and the United States. Originally called Anne Arundel Town, 100 acres was laid out for its creation in 1684, and it was chartered in 1708. In addition to being made the capital city of Maryland in 1694, it was the first peacetime capital of the United States, when in 1783 and 1784 the United States Congress met there. When George Washington resigned his commission as commander in chief, he came to the Maryland State House where Congress was meeting. In fact, the State House has been in continuous legislative use since those times. You can visit the State House free of charge on weekdays from 9:00 a.m. to 5:00 p.m. or from 10:00 a.m. to 4:00 p.m. Saturday and Sunday, or call (410) 974-3400 for information. Guided tours are offered at 11:00 a.m. and 3:00 p.m. Adults need to bring ID to gain entry.

The city of Annapolis holds dear the flavor of those earlier days. The area that surrounds the waterfront is known as the City Dock, and the buildings that line its cobblestone streets date from earlier times. Along Main Street, Maryland Avenue, and West Street, as well as the two circles, State and Church, almost every building houses a shop or eatery. Actually you could just eat your way around Annapolis; there are more than 30 restaurants in the historic district alone. Strolling through Annapolis is a lovely way to spend an afternoon because Annapolis offers living history as well as an old-fashioned ambience.

Another option on a pretty day is to stop in the Annapolis Market right at the City Dock for its many carryout options. Then find a spot along the City Dock for lunch alfresco. It's a favorite lunchtime activity for both visitors and locals.

Annapolis is the home of the United States Naval Academy, in session for the full brigade from August to June. Plebes (freshmen) arrive for their orientation summer in early July. Don't even think about trying to tour Annapolis during Commissioning Week—the Naval Academy's yearly pregraduation celebration. The city is always full to bursting.

Guided tours of the Naval Academy leave the Armel-Leftwich Visitors Center every half hour from 10:00 a.m. to 3:00 p.m. Monday through Saturday and from 12:30 to 3:00 p.m. on Sunday. Additional tours are offered in summer; fewer in January and February, depending on the demand. Tours take you through the grounds, with a stop at the crypt of John Paul Jones, and another at a model midshipman's dorm room. No advance reservation is required; simply show up at the visitor center inside the main gate of the Naval Academy and wait for the next tour to begin. The cost is $8.50 for adults, $7.50 for seniors, and $6.50 for students. Children age three and younger are admitted free. For more information, call (410) 263-6933 or visit www.navyonline.com. Parking is not available except for handicapped and those with military ID. Visitors age 16 and older need ID to enter the Academy grounds, known as the Yard.

St. John's College, which was founded in 1696 as King William's School and whose campus boasts what is noted as the third-oldest academic building in the United States—McDowell Hall, is also in Annapolis. St. John's also has the Carroll-Barrister House. Built in 1722, it is the birthplace of Charles Carroll, who was on the committee that drafted the Maryland Declaration of Rights in 1776. An appointment to take a campus tour may be made by calling (410) 263-2371.

Various guided walking tours of the city are available from Watermark Tours, which conducts them from and in conjunction with the Annapolis Visitor Center. There are two points of departure, one at the visitor center at 44 Calvert Street and one at History Quest, 99 Main Street. Tours focus on such attractions as colonial homes and the Naval Academy; some are thematic, such as the African American Tour, which highlights important African-American sites, including the Banneker-Douglass Museum, which is named for Benjamin Banneker and Frederick Douglass and which mounts exhibits on prominent black Marylanders. Tours, which are presented by guides in period costume, are $12 to $14 for adults and $4 for children age 3 through 11. For more information call (410) 263-5401 or visit www.annapolis-tours.com.

For a different view, consider taking a water tour of Annapolis. A 40-minute cruise around the Annapolis harbor on various boats costs between $8 and $15 for adults and $4 to $8 for children younger than age 12, depending on the boat. Longer cruises are also available. Visit www.watermarkcruises.com or call (410) 268-7601 for information. Watermark also offers several boat tours of Annapolis's harbor, nearby lighthouses, and even a pirate tour. An all-day (close to eight hours) water tour on the *Annapolitan II* not only views Annapolis sites, such as the Naval Academy, from the water but also takes you across the bay to the Chesapeake Bay Maritime Museum at St. Michaels. (More on St. Michaels appears later in the chapter.) Although St. Michaels can also be reached by land, the water access is eminently more fun, especially on a warm, sunny day.

Annapolis has plenty of accommodations, from hotels to inns and bed-and-breakfasts, for those who think they need more that a single day to visit. In fact, in the historic district alone, there are more than 25 licensed bed-and-breakfasts. Visit www.visitannapolis.org or call (410) 216-9382 for information.

SOUTH
Southern Maryland

If you head towards Washington on US 50 to US 301 and then turn south on Highway 4, you come to the oldest part of Maryland. Tobacco used to be king here but farmers have turned to other crops—or they've sold their land to developers building new Washington, D.C., suburbs. Two areas are worth a visit: Solomons and St. Mary's City.

Wine Centerpiece

No matter what direction you head when taking off on your day trip, most likely you will not be far from one of 12 Maryland vineyards spread out across the state. Coaxing visitors with tempting outdoor celebrations, the wineries are consistently releasing new wines, offering special activities and festivals, and, of course, tours and tastings. The award-winning wineries help to showcase Maryland's prolific and growing winemaking industry.

"Spring is one of the most exciting times to visit a winery," said Bert Basignani of the Maryland Wineries Association. "Visitors can see the budding vines—the start of the winemaking process. Maryland winemakers are thrilled to share vineyards and wineries with our guests."

The Maryland Wineries Association includes 20 wineries that produce more than 200 varieties of wines. And the list is growing with another eight wineries to open by 2008. Maryland wines consistently win prestigious national wine competitions, are served at the region's finest restaurants, and are available at several retailers throughout the United States.

Maryland wine has a rich history dating from the mid-1600s, when then-governor Charles Calvert, at the prompting of Lord Baltimore, planted 200 acres on the east bank of the St. Mary's River, using vines he had received from several countries in Europe. These were later supplemented by another 100 acres. In 1768 Charles Carroll established a vineyard in Howard County that included some natural hybrids and some European varieties, but by 1800 all but the indigenous vines died. In the early 1940s, Philip Wagner, then an editorial columnist with the *Baltimore Sun* and later editor of the *Evening Sun,* acquired as many different hybrids as he could lay hands on and planted them at his home in Riderwood. The success of his efforts signaled a turning point in the Eastern wine industry. In addition to making his own wine, he propagated the vines and sold them throughout the East Coast.

Then in 1945 Wagner opened Boordy Vineyards, Maryland's first bonded winery, producing wines made from the hybrid grapes. Most were simple, easy-to-drink wines, and it was his philosophy that the winemaker's goal should be to make inexpensive everyday wines for consumption with meals. Wagner also produced the first up-to-date winemaking text, *American Wines and How to Make Them,* which was later revised as *Grapes Into Wine* and has become a classic in the field. He also wrote *A Wine-Growers Guide,* which has remained a staple in the vineyard establishment repertoire. During the 1940s and '50s, 15 additional wineries opened, 8 of which are still in business today.

In 1981 the Maryland Grape Growers Association was formed. The primary purpose of the organization was to support the Maryland wine industry by encouraging commercial growers. Since then, its perspective has broadened to include many small-scale, "backyard" vineyardists, many of whom sell their produce to amateur winemakers. MGGA produces a quarterly newsletter and a vineyard establishment manual and sponsors several on-site activities during the year.

In 1984 the Maryland Wineries Association was founded, the purpose of which is to coordinate winery activities and deal with legal and commercial issues involving the production and distribution of Maryland wines. Currently the association focuses on ways to promote the broader use of Maryland wines by Marylanders.

Maryland wines are celebrated at the annual Maryland Wine Festival held every September at the Carroll County Farm Museum. The local chapter of the American Wine Society sponsors amateur wine judgings, wine education seminars, and winemaking demonstrations, and the Maryland Grape Growers Association dispenses grape juice and provides grape-growing information.

Maryland Wineries Association
P.O. Box 173, Timonium
(800) 237-WINE
www.marylandwine.com

Basignani Winery
15722 Falls Road, Sparks
(410) 472-0703
www.basignani.com

Berrywine Plantations/
Linganore Winecellars
13601 Glissans Mill Road, Mount Airy
(410) 795-6432, (301) 831-5889
www.linganorewines.com

Black Ankle Vineyards
14463 Black Ankle Road, Mount Airy
(301) 829-0579
www.blackankle.com
Opening in mid 2008

Boordy Vineyards
12820 Long Green Pike, Hydes
(410) 592-5015
www.boordy.com

Cove Point Winery
755 Cove Point Road, Lusby
(410) 326-0949
www.covepointwinery.com

Cygnus Winecellars
3130 Long Lane, Manchester
(410) 374-6395
www.cygnuswinecellars.com

Deep Creek Cellars
177 Frazee Ridge Road, Friendsville
(301) 746-4349
www.deepcreekcellars.com

Elk Run Vineyards
15113 Liberty Road, Mount Airy
(410) 775-2513
www.elkrun.com

Fiore Winery
3026 Whiteford Road, Pylesville
(410) 879-4007
www.fiorewinery.com

Frederick Cellars
Everedy Square/Shab Row
221 North East Street, Frederick
(301) 668-0311
www.frederickcellars.com

Fridays Creek Winery
3485 Chaneyville Road, Owings
(410) 286-WINE
www.fridayscreek.com

Little Ashby Vineyards
27549 Ashby Drive, Easton
(410) 819-8850, (410) 822-6027
www.littleashbyvineyards.com

CONTINUED

Loew Vineyards
14001 Liberty Road (Highway 26)
Mount Airy
(301) 831-5464
www.loewvineyards.net

Penn Oaks Winery
11 Midhurst Road, Silver Spring
(301) 562-8592
PennOaksWinery@aol.com

Solomons Island Winery
515 Garner Lane, Lusby
(410) 394-1933
www.solomonsislandwinery.com

St. Michaels Winery
605 South Talbot Street #6
St. Michaels
(410) 745-0808
www.st-michaels-winery.com

Sugarloaf Mountain Vineyard
18125 Comus Road, Dickerson
(301) 605-0130
www.smvwinery.com

Tilmon's Island Winery
755 Millington Road, Sudlersville
(443) 480-5021
www.tilmonswine.com

Woodhall Wine Cellars
17912 York Road, Parkton
(410) 357-8644
www.woodhallwinecellars.com

We are grateful to the Maryland Wineries Association for supplying the contact information above and the history of winemaking in Maryland.

Solomons
US 50 to US 301 to Highway 4 South
85 miles from Baltimore

Everywhere you look on Solomons you'll see water. Part of this water-oriented town is Solomons Island, but it has since spread out with additional hotels, marinas, shops, and restaurants. Visitors come for the water views, the seafood, and the Calvert Marine Museum (800-735-2042). Exhibits feature local animal life including seahorses, a lighthouse, fossils from Calvert Cliffs nearby, and local maritime history. The museum is open daily 10:00 a.m. to 5:00 p.m. Admission is $7 for adults, $6 for seniors, and $2 for children age 5 through 12. In addition, a promenade along the Patuxent River has boat rentals, an ice-cream stand, and access to several restaurants.

Cross the soaring Gov. Thomas Johnson Bridge to St. Mary's County for a visit to St. Mary's City.

St. Mary's City
Route 4 to Route 5 South

This site along the St. Mary's River was the state's first capital, founded in 1634. The city is long gone—it slowly disappeared after politicians moved the capital to Annapolis in 1694. But through the efforts of archaeologists, historians, and craftsmen, a recreated city is emerging along this picturesque riverbank. The result is a historical attraction where visitors can easily spend a day touring the recreated State House, tobacco plantation, Print Shop, and Brick Chapel. The waterfront is a lovely place for a picnic and a visit to the Dove, a reproduction of the square-rigged merchant ship that brought Maryland's first settlers to this site. Interpreters, especially at the Godiah Spray tobacco plantation, help bring the history here to life. Walking trails through the area's woodlands and near the water give visitors a place to stretch their legs and let the children run.

Admission is $10.00 for adults, $8.00 for seniors, $6.00 for children age 13 through 18, and $3.50 for children age 6 through 12. In spring and fall, the exhibits are open 10:00 a.m. to 5:00 p.m. Tuesday through Saturday with limited hours on Sunday. In summer the exhibits are open Wednesday through Sunday 10:00 a.m. to 5:00 p.m. In January through mid-March, most of the exhibits are closed but the visitor center exhibits and the grounds are open. There's no admission charge then. For information call Historic St. Mary's City at (800) 762-1634 or visit www.stmaryscity.org.

Facilities here are better than they were in the 17th century, but it is best to remember to bring water, insect repellant, and sunscreen, and perhaps your own snacks and picnic lunch. While driving through Solomons, a good place to stop for picnic items is the Woodburns market (410-326-3284), right on Highway 4. It has a salad bar and deli counter with lots of lunch choices.

In St. Mary's City, Farthings Ordinary has a limited menu, and there are a few other options for dining around here. Of course, when college is in session, you could stop by St. Mary's College of Maryland's dining hall right across Highway 5 from St. Mary's City parking lot. For cafeteria food, the food here is pretty good. The menu and price are scaled back in the summer when the dining hall is open for lunch on weekdays.Lodging choices in southern Maryland include all the chain hotels on Highway 4 near the Patuxent River Naval Air Station, the Brome-Howard Inn near St. Mary's College, and a variety of accommodations in Solomons.

The Brome-Howard Inn (pronounced broom-Howard), a restored 1840 farmhouse nestled in the center of 30 acres of farmland, offers five to six unique sleeping rooms, as well as dinner Thursday through Sunday and Sunday brunch to the general public (reservations recommended). Room and breakfast runs $125 for weekdays and up to $185 per night on weekends.

For reservations, at the Brome-Howard,

call (301) 866-0656 or visit www.brome howardinn.com. For accommodations in Solomons call (410) 257-5381 or visit www.ecalvert.com. Information about lodging closer to St. Mary's City is available by calling (800) 327-9023, or visit www.co.saint-marys .md.us/tourism.

EAST
Eastern Shore

The land east of the Chesapeake Bay is known as the Eastern Shore. Although parts are too quickly becoming suburbia, it is still home to many of the Chesapeake's watermen and farmers and the locale of some of the state's prettiest small towns. There are plenty of places to drop a fishing line, swing a golf club, or paddle a kayak. To get there you have to cross the Chesapeake via the Bay Bridge. The bridge has a per-car toll of $2.50 eastbound. No toll is collected westbound.

A warning about traffic: Lines can stretch out for several miles from the bridge —eastbound on Friday and Saturday and westbound on Saturday and Sunday from May through Labor Day. Your best bet is to get an EZ Pass (visit www.ezpassmd.com for information) so you can bypass as much of the toll traffic as possible and plan to cross the bridge at an off-peak time. That would mean crossing early on Friday or late on Saturday. Call the bay bridge hotline (877-229-7726) for traffic updates, too.

Prime Outlets at Queenstown
Junction of US 50 and US 301
43 miles from Baltimore

Once you've crossed the bay, you have to decide whether to head north or south. Continue on US 50 east to the split with US 301. Prime Outlets at Queenstown is located at the junction.

After getting a complete makeover in 2007, this popular outlet center now added 20 stores, good ones like BCBG Max Azria, Eddie Bauer, and Coach. There's also a St. John Company Store, L.L. Bean, and plenty of other apparel and home furnishings stores. The Book Cellar, full of discount-priced books, is a good place to stop for a beach book. Parking is plentiful. Strollers and wheelchairs are available at the visitor services office. (410-827-8699). The center is accessible from both US 301 and US 50, but the safest way is to continue on US 301 and turn right into the parking lot.

Chestertown
US 301 north to Highway 213
65 miles from Baltimore

Drive north through Queen Anne's County, cross the Chester River, and you'll find yourself in a colonial college town. Chestertown dates from 1706, when it was a major port for its surrounding counties. A great Web site to find out more about the town is www.chestertown.com, or call the town office at (410) 778-0500. One of Chestertown's claims to fame from those early years was its own "tea party," when the townspeople dumped the cargo of tea from the brigantine *Geddes* into the Chester River to protest the tax on tea in 1774. Every Memorial Day weekend, the town holds the Chestertown Tea Party Festival at which, among other things, reenactors ceremoniously dump tea into the harbor to commemorate that day.

Chestertown is also the home of Washington College, founded in 1782. The college conferred an honorary doctorate degree on George Washington in 1784. It is the only college using Washington's name with his express permission.

Chestertown's biggest attraction, however, is its eighteenth-century architecture. The Kent County tourism office has brochures for self-guided tours at their visitor center at 122 North Cross Street, (410) 778-9737. It's open year-round 9:00 a.m. to 4:00 p.m. on weekdays and 10:00 a.m. to 4:00 p.m. on weekends. You can also get a brochure online at www.kentcounty.com/tourism/. Or just park and meander through the historic district stopping in the more than 35 little shops and restaurants along the way.

Easton
US 50 east to Easton
59 miles from Baltimore

US 50 stretches all the way to Ocean City. Plenty of sunseekers skip all the charming towns along the way to get to Ocean City or Rehoboth Beach. But you don't have to. Here are three towns worth visiting for their charming streets, shops, and restaurants. Easton is landlocked, but both St. Michaels and Cambridge have lovely riverfront vistas. All three towns inspired James Michener as he penned his historical novel *Chesapeake*, which he actually wrote while living in St. Michaels.

Easton is considered the colonial capital of Maryland. Its historic downtown district boasts 200-year-old architecture as well as several small-town museums. The Historical Society of Talbot County, 25 South Washington Street, (410) 822-0773, features local industry such as boat building and duck decoy carving and has a Federal-style garden in back. Admission is free and the museum is open Monday through Saturday 10:00 a.m. to 4:00 p.m. The society offers tours, too.

The Academy Art Museum, 106 South Street, (410) 822-2787, www.art-academy.org, offers special exhibitions, sometimes from the National Gallery of Art, as well as a treasure trove of local art. Admission is $3 for adults and children younger than age 12 are admitted free. Shopping is fun here, too, with crafts, antiques, and home furnishings stores along Harrison and Washington Streets. Foodies take note: Restaurants here keep getting better. You can get a good crab cake, of course, as well as French fare, Australian specialties, and a wood-fired pizza.

If you fall in love with the town, go ahead and spend the night at one of the chain hotels along US 50 or the newly restored Tidewater Inn (800-237-8775), the swank Inn at Easton (888-800-8091), or the Inn at 202 Dover (866-450-7600). Rooms run from $100 to $400 a night.

St. Michaels
US 50 east to US 322 to Highway 33
80 miles from Baltimore

St. Michaels is located on a peninsula jutting out into the Chesapeake Bay, but its waterfront is on the Miles River. This is serious sailing territory, home to a fleet of racing log canoes and stopping place for many a weekend sailor. In fact, the harbor can be quite clogged with boats on a sunny summer weekend. No matter, if you've come by car. Hunt down a parking place, which is usually easier to find than a spot to moor your boat.

St. Michaels offers visitors fine dining, lots of gift shops, and the Chesapeake Bay Maritime Museum, home to the picturesque Hooper Strait Lighthouse. This is a good place to see some of the historic boats that once worked on the bay. The grounds are open as a waterfront park after the museum closes for the day. Admission is $13 for adults, $10 for seniors, and $5 for children age 6 through 17.

If you visit on a summer weekend, you might get to see the log canoe races. These are sailboats with what looks like way too much sail. The boats have been racing here for more than 100 years. For the schedule of races, visit www.logcanoes.com.

If you prefer shopping, Talbot Street is your goal. If you're hungry, there are a number of restaurants in town, mostly specializing in seafood. For waterfront dining, you'll have to go to the Crab Claw (410-745-2900), St. Michael's Crab and Steak House (410-745-3737), or the Town Dock Restaurant (410-745-5577).

If you want to spend the night, St. Michaels has many lodging choices, including the highly regarded Inn at Perry Cabin (800-722-2949), the modern St. Michaels Harbour Inn (800-955-9001), and the old-fashioned Wades Point Inn on the Bay (888-923-3466). Contact the Talbot County Office of Tourism for details on both Easton and St. Michaels at (410) 770-8000 or visit www.tourtalbot.org. All three are waterfront.

Cambridge
US 50 East to Cambridge
74 miles from Baltimore

Sharpshooter Annie Oakley once lived here in a house facing the Choptank River. Now lots of people want to live here as the town experiences a renaissance. Besides the waterfront views and easy access to the Chesapeake Bay, visitors come for the historic downtown district, the Hyatt resort, and the Blackwater National Wildlife Refuge south of town.

If you stop here, don't miss the beautiful homes of High Street, Water Street, Mill Street, and Hambrooks Boulevard. Or stop by one of the local museums. The Dorchester Arts Center at 120 High Street, (410) 228-7782, exhibits the works of local artists. The center will move to 321 High Street in mid-2008. Local history is on display at La Grange Plantation, at 902 LaGrange Avenue, (410) 228-7953. It is open Monday 10:00 a.m. to 1:00 p.m., Tuesday through Friday 10:00 a.m. to 4:00 p.m., and Saturday 11:00 a.m. to 4:00 p.m. Watermen are honored at the Richardson Maritime Museum at 401 High Street, (410) 221-1871. It is open March through October on Wednesdays and weekends 1:00 p.m. to 4:00 p.m. and weekends only November through February. Harriet Tubman Museum pays homage to the celebrated Underground Railroad conductor at 424 Race Street, (410) 228-0401, and is open Wednesday through Saturday 10:00 a.m. to 3:00 p.m.

Nature lovers must visit the Blackwater National Wildlife Refuge, (410) 228-2677. It's open year-round and quite popular with the waterfowl. Osprey and eagles make their summer homes here. Ducks and geese fly here by the thousands in spring and fall. Humans can drive through or stop on the hiking path to see them. Biking, boating, and fishing are popular activities here, as well as limited hunting. Check the refuge's Web site (www.fws.gov/blackwater) for the details.

If one day isn't enough for your visit, chain hotels line US 50, which is also where to find the Hyatt Regency Chesapeake Bay, (800) 233-1234, a 342-acre resort with 400 hotel rooms, a golf course, marina, pools, spa, and restaurants. In town are a handful of bed-and-breakfasts, including the Cambridge House, (410) 221-7700, and the Mill Street Inn (410-901-9144). Contact the Dorchester Tourism office at www.tourdorchester.com or call (410) 228-1000.

Atlantic Beaches

US 50 East ends at Ocean City, Maryland's ocean resort. Ocean fans have several other options in Delaware, the most popular of which is Rehoboth Beach. Both resorts boast wide, white sandy beaches, a boardwalk lined with shops, restaurants, and hotels, water sports from surfing to sailing, and lots of entertainment for all ages. Beyond these similarities, each city has its own style. They are laid out differently and each has unique attractions.

Rehoboth Beach, Delaware
Off US 1
120 miles from Baltimore
To get to Rehoboth (pronounced Reh-HO-beth), stay on US 50 until you see the sign for Highway 404. (There's a left-turn lane. You can't miss it.) Then turn left at Highway 16 and right onto Delaware Highway 1. This is the quickest way to Rehoboth and will take you through miles of flat, open country. It's a beautiful drive through farmlands and small towns.

Rehoboth Beach's central city near the water stretches about 10 blocks along the water's edge. The rest of the city wraps around it. There are two large lakes (one north, one south) and a great many shade trees. Most homes, particularly near the lakes, are substantial, year-round homes.

Most summer tourists stay in the central or western areas of the city. On season or off, however, Rehoboth is primarily a family place where most people rent an entire house or an apartment for long-term stays. The Boardwalk by the beach offers visitors amusement rides, games, miniature golf courses, restaurants, and small shops. Out on US 1, you'll find the bulk of the restaurants, hotels, and shopping

centers, including movie theaters and the outlet malls for plenty of tax-free shopping.

Rehoboth is a great place to relax. It's relatively quiet and a safe place for children to feel free to go places and do things without always needing a parent along as protector. While Rehoboth is a place to spend relaxing, its neighbor, Dewey Beach, is a place to let loose at its many happening restaurants and bars.

If you decide to stay over, there are usually vacancy signs even in season, and housing can be found on the spur of the moment. On a weekend, hotel rooms are harder to come by. If you plan to stay a couple of days, check out www.visitsoutherndelaware.com for a wide variety of beach accommodations. The Web site will give you information about all of Delaware's beaches from Lewes to Fenwick. For information specific to Rehoboth and Dewey, contact the Rehoboth Beach Dewey Beach Chamber of Commerce at (302) 227-2233 or (800) 441-1329 or visit www.beach-fun.com.

Your overnight options include everything from a room in a rooming house to a two-bedroom suite at a modern hotel, from a bed-and-breakfast to a house or apartment. Costs vary depending on what accommodations you choose, how close those accommodations are to the beach, whether it is the weekend, and whether it is peak season (July and August). Obviously, peak season, weekend, beachfront accommodations would be the most expensive.

Nonweekend in-season hotel prices in Rehoboth begin at about $85 a night; weekend prices at about $120 a night; and houses at about $600 a week.

Ocean City, Maryland
eastern end of US 50
135 miles from Baltimore
For Marylanders a trip to Ocean City conjures up images of wide sandy beaches; fierce rolling waves; deep-sea fishing for white marlin; pizza and seafood dinners; sunsets over Sinepuxent Bay; and evenings spent on the Boardwalk or playing miniature golf or meet-

Junebugs at the Beach

Ocean City attracts thousands of newly minted high school graduates in early June. The town calls them "Junebugs." They fill up the beach and the hotels that are willing to take them (plenty turn them down, as do almost all condo rental offices). But they don't fill up the restaurants and they can't go to the bars since they're still underage. So the rest of us don't have to wait an hour for a table at dinner time or need to squeeze ourselves into a corner at our favorite nightspots.

If you don't use the buses and can tolerate a bit of speeding on Coastal Highway, this is a surprisingly good time to visit the beach. The Boardwalk is crowded—and loud until late at night. But the rest of town is relatively quiet.

For high school graduates visiting Ocean City, the town has a variety of activities from free windsurfing lessons to a beach volleyball tournament. The goal is to keep them safe while ensuring a good time for every visitor.

ing friends at one of the dozens of nightspots. It's a family resort, a party town for single visitors, a retirement town for seniors. Though it's just a narrow barrier island less than 10 miles long, hundreds of thousands of people spend time here in the summer. This is one of Maryland's most popular destinations. A sleepy town of 10,000 in mid-winter, by mid-summer, it's the second largest city in the state with 300,000 temporary residents. They rent condos or reserve hotel rooms—and more and more are buying second homes here.

Ocean City stretches from Fenwick Island, Delaware, to the north, down to the inlet that divides Ocean City from Assateague Island with Coastal Highway bisecting the island. On the east is the beach and Boardwalk (up to 27th Street) and on the west is a mix of hotels and condos, restaurants taking advantage of sunset views over Sinepuxent and Assawoman Bays, and plenty of shop for bikinis, surfboards, and groceries.

Deep-sea fishing is a big draw here in the White Marlin Capital. In fact, the White Marlin Open in August draws 400 boats for its million-dollar-plus purse. You can charter a boat just for you and your family or you can grab a place on one of the head boats that troll the seas.

If you don't like fishing, there are also pleasure cruises available. Landlubbers can check out the many miniature golf courses or the championship golf courses west of Ocean City, as well as the amusement rides on the Boardwalk, on the fishing pier, and at Jolly Roger or Frontier Town (one of the country's oldest theme parks).

Day-trippers who want to be in the middle of the action should plan on parking in the paid Inlet lot at the south end of the city. The beach here is the widest, and the pier rides, the Boardwalk, and plenty of fishing and cruise boats are within walking distance. If you want to go to a restaurant farther north than you are willing to walk, you can catch a ride on the Boardwalk tram for $2.75 per trip or ride the bus on Coastal Highway all day for $2.

Visitors who want to stay overnight should stop at one of the two visitor centers. They know where the empty rooms are in a town where NO VACANCY signs are common. They can also work out a one-night stay when hotel owners say they require a two-night minimum.

In Ocean City, stop by Ocean City Convention and Visitors Bureau at the convention center on 40th Street. Or call (800) OC-OCEAN or visit www.ococean.com. West of Ocean City on US 50 at the junction of Highway 707, the Ocean City Chamber of Commerce's visitor center provides the same service. Contact

them at (888) OCMD-FUN or visit www.ocean
city.org. Both visitor centers have piles of
brochures about area attractions, hotels, and
restaurants—even menus.

A night in Ocean City will set you back
about $70 or $100 off-season. In season,
expect to pay $200 to $350 for a room with
an ocean view.

Assateague and Chincoteague

Just before you reach Ocean City on US 50,
you'll see signs for Assateague Island National
Seashore, which includes 19,000 acres on
Assateague Island, and the Chincoteague
National Wildlife Refuge. Chincoteague's wild
ponies are descendants of sixteenth-century
horses who swam to safety from a sinking
Spanish galleon off the coast.

One of the best-known events at Chincoteague is the annual pony roundup, which
takes place the last Wednesday and Thursday
in July. The horses are herded across the
quarter-mile channel from Chincoteague
Island to Chincoteague, Virginia, where foals
are auctioned off. The story of one foal who
makes the journey is the classic Misty of Chincoteague, by Marguerite Henry.

The National Park Service has a visitor
center at the north end of Assateague Island
that is accessible from US 50, with exhibits
about the history of the islands and the
wildlife refuge. A lot of people who would
rather not pay hotel prices at Ocean City
camp at the park. The park itself offers opportunities to boat, crab, clam, fish, swim, take
guided walking tours, and sing around the
campfire. Admission to the park via car is by a
seven-day private-vehicle permit that costs
$10 or, if you're going to be around awhile or
return, you can purchase a $20 annual per-

i At the beach, don't get overconfi-
dent about water safety. The riptide,
also called the undertow, can be treacher-
ous, grabbing hold of those who have
strayed too far and placing them in life-
threatening situations.

mit. For more information, call (410) 641-
1441. For specific camping information, call
(410) 641-3030 or visit www.nps.gov/asis/.
Assateague also has a state park with 2 miles
of beach, bathhouse, and snack bar. Admission is $3 for Maryland residents and $4 for
out-of-state visitors. Seniors and children in
car seats are free. Visit www.dnr.state.md.us/
publiclands/eastern/assateague.html. If you
decide you want to see the ponies on the
Chincoteague side, visit the U.S. Fish and
Wildlife Service's Web site www.fws.gov/
northeast/chinco/. Chincoteague is 52 miles
from Ocean City.

SOUTHWEST

Our southwest road of choice is U.S. Highway
29, which can be accessed from US 40 or I-70.
The drive south on US 29 is slower than I-95,
and it has more trucks than the
Baltimore–Washington Parkway, on which
trucks are not allowed. But US 29 has one
thing those routes don't—a straight shot from
Baltimore to Silver Spring, Maryland, just outside of Washington, D.C. Once in Silver
Spring, you can follow the signs to the Metro
station, then park and ride the subway into
our nation's capital.

If you doubt the wisdom of this idea,
remember that Washington, D.C., was
designed to confuse strangers to the city—
originally British troops—and it serves the
same function today. Unlike Baltimore, which
is laid out in a simple north-south, east-west
grid, D.C. has circles, squares, tunnels, and
diagonal roads that will send your head spinning if you're not accustomed to them.

If you're planning a trip to the nation's
capital, you might want to consult The Insiders' Guide to Washington, D.C., which
includes information on northern Virginia and
suburban Maryland, for an overall picture of
what awaits you. What follows are just a few
highlights.

Our Nation's Capital
38 miles from Baltimore

If you followed our suggestion and took the Metro's Red Line in from Silver Spring, there are two ways to get to the National Mall. The one that doesn't require you to transfer trains is to simply get off at Union Station and walk out the main station doors. You'll see Capitol Hill essentially straight ahead of you, beyond the circle. Walk around the circle and head for Capitol Hill. When you get there, you'll see the Mall stretching ahead of you, and you'll be within walking distance of most of the things that you'll want to see. The Washington Monument and the United States Capitol face each other; between them are the Smithsonian Institutions' museums, including the National Museum of Natural History, the National Gallery of Art, the National Air and Space Museum, the Freer Gallery, and the National Museum of African Art.

Your other Metro option is to take the Red Line to Metro Center, where you'll go downstairs to get on either the Blue Line or the Orange Line. Both lines will take you to the Smithsonian–National Mall stop. Just make sure you're taking the train heading toward the Mall, not away from it.

Within walking distance of the Mall on the north is the White House, the Tidal Basin, where the cherry blossoms bloom in spring, and the large reflecting pool that is opposite the Lincoln Memorial. South, at the Capitol end, you're within an easy walk of the U.S. Botanical Garden and the Library of Congress.

If you'd like to shop while you sightsee, Georgetown beckons. From the Smithsonian–National Mall Metro stop, take either the Blue Line or the Orange Line to Foggy Bottom–GWU; you'll be about a half mile from Georgetown. Home to Georgetown University, the neighborhood, off its main drag of Wisconsin Avenue NW, is still the picture-perfect vision of the eighteenth century. You can almost see the ladies in their mob caps preparing to hail down a hansom cab.

The history doesn't stop with the elegant homes, however. Georgetown also has the C&O Canal National Historic Park, Dumbarton

i Maryland boasted a large free black population long before the Civil War, and much of Maryland's heritage is vested in our African-American ancestors who lived, fought, and died in Maryland. Baltimore Black Heritage Tours, Inc., offers tours of historic sites across the state. Tours must be set up in advance by calling (410) 783-5469.

Oaks, and Hillwood Museum. On Wisconsin Avenue, you'll find some great shopping at both elegant and esoteric boutiques. There are also restaurants, coffee shops, and nightclubs.

Across the Potomac: Arlington and Mount Vernon
50 miles from Baltimore

Arlington National Cemetery can be reached by Metro from Georgetown by taking the Blue Line from Foggy Bottom directly to the cemetery. Arlington's 612 acres serve as the resting place for more than 175,000 American military as well as John F. Kennedy, Robert Kennedy, the Tomb of the Unknowns, and Pierre Charles L'Enfant, who designed Washington, D.C. The grounds were once part of Arlington House, the home of Robert E. Lee, which still stands here.

The Blue Line of the Metro can also take you to King Street, right in the heart of Alexandria, which is also across the Potomac River in Virginia. The center city, known as Old Town, has been restored throughout the past 30 years. It offers lots of unique shopping, with more than 200 stores clustered along Washington Street and the waterfront. At Union and King Streets, you'll find a popular Old Town destination, the Torpedo Factory Art Center (www.torpedofactory.org, 703-838-4565), which, though originally built to manufacture torpedo casings during the World Wars, now has 84 studios and six main galleries with the works of more than 160 artists. The Alexandria Archaeology Museum is also under the Torpedo Factory's roof. The Archaeology Museum displays items from the Alexandria area that date from 3000 B.C. The museum is open Tuesday through Sunday year-round. Call (703) 838-4399 for hours and information, or visit www.alexandria archaeology.org.

Down the road, you may want to take in a tour of Mount Vernon, George and Martha Washington's home. Acquired in 1754 by the Washingtons, they enlarged and improved the estate that had been in George's family for years. The main house has been restored to its former glory, as have more than 12 of the outbuildings and the formal gardens. Some of the original furniture is on display, including the bed in which Washington died, his sword, and a present from Lafayette—the key to the Bastille. Washington is buried on the grounds. Mount Vernon is open year round. Admission is $13 for adults and $6 for children age 6 through 11. Call (703) 780-2000 or visit www.mountvernon.org for more information, but be prepared to drive. The Metro doesn't go all the way to Mount Vernon. From Baltimore, it's about a two-hour trip by car. Travel south on I-95 (which becomes the Beltway). As you cross the Potomac River on the Woodrow Wilson Bridge, move to the far right lane. Take the first exit after the bridge, marked Mount Vernon. At the light, turn right onto the George Washington Parkway. Mount Vernon is 8 miles south, at the large traffic circle at the end of Parkway.

NORTHWEST

Our northwest route is Highway 140, otherwise known as Reisterstown Road, which is accessible from the Baltimore Beltway, I-695. At Reisterstown (see the Antiques and Collectibles chapter for more about Reisterstown), there is a fork in the road. Stay on Highway 140.

On Pilgrimage
Emmitsburg
57 miles from Baltimore
To visit the National Shrine of St. Elizabeth Ann Seton, travel up Highway 140 past Westminster about an hour to the town of Emmits-

burg, which lies just south of the Mason-Dixon Line and is home to Mount St. Mary's College. The shrine of our first native-born American saint is at 333 South Seton Avenue. A museum at the shrine holds some of Mother Seton's personal items, and the chapel houses her tomb. Other restored buildings are part of the tour that lasts approximately two hours. There is no entrance fee, and, except for major holidays, the shrine is open year-round from 10:00 a.m. to 4:30 p.m. (daily from April through October and Tuesday through Sunday November through March; the shrine closes most of January and for major holidays). Call (301) 447-6606 for more information.

The National Shrine Grotto of Lourdes, also in Emmitsburg, is a replica of the Grotto of Lourdes, France, created in 1805 by Father John Debois. The grotto is open dawn to dusk, daily, throughout the year. There is no entrance fee. If you would like more information, call (301) 447-5318.

If you have time for a picnic, Cunningham Falls State Park offers a lake big enough to swim in and canoe on, a 78-foot-high waterfall and plenty of hiking trails. The park is located between Emmitsburg and Frederick on US 15. Day-use fees are $3 per person in the Houck area where the falls and lake are located. Fees in the Manor area, which has a number of hiking trails, is $3 per carload. Visit www.dnr.state.md.us/publiclands for details or call (301) 271-7574.

WEST

Our western route out of Baltimore is I-70, which is easily accessed from I-695, the Beltway. I-70 heads initially into Howard County, where the scenery is plentiful after you pass all the nearby developments between Baltimore and Columbia.

Antiques, Antiques, Antiques
New Market
I-70 West to Highway 75 North
40 miles from Baltimore

After about an hour you will see signs for the town of New Market. New Market itself is an antique, dating from 1793. It was a trading town originally because it sat right on the Baltimore National Pike, which was a main road even back then and is now US 40.

Today's New Market is still a trading place. Only today New Market trades in antiques and collectibles and, in fact, is billed as the Antiques Capital of Maryland. There are more than 50 shops on Main Street and down the side streets. Park in the large parking lots down the hill and walk.

All shops are open on weekends, with fewer than half open Wednesday through Friday. Learn more at www.townofnew market.org.

North Meets South
Frederick
I-70 West to US 15
47 miles from Baltimore

About 20 minutes farther on from New Market is Frederick, which was occupied by both Union and Confederate forces during the Civil War. Today's Frederick is a thriving city and Washington, D.C., suburb, but it is steeped in history. It was here that Barbara Fritchie approached Confederate forces waving the Stars and Stripes and said, according to the poet John Greenleaf Whittier, "Shoot if you must this old gray head, but spare my country's flag!"

Barbara Fritchie's house, barely bigger than a dollhouse, was reconstructed early in the twentieth century, and it contains many original furnishings and artifacts from the Civil War. The cost is $2.00 for adults and $1.50 for children younger than age 12, but call in advance, (301) 698-0630, as hours vary depending on the day of the week and time of year. The Barbara Fritchie house is open Friday and Saturday 10:00 a.m. to 4:00 p.m. and Sunday 1:00 to 4:00 p.m.

It's set along the 1.3-mile Carroll Creek Park, which combines green space with shops and restaurants along the narrow creek. Frederick also has other museums and some very good restaurants and bed-and-breakfasts.

If you're a cemetery buff, you might want to visit the graves of Mr. and Mrs. Francis Scott Key, Barbara Fritchie, and others at Mount Olivet Cemetery at the end of Market Street. It's open daily from 8:00 a.m. to dusk. Call (301) 662-1164 for more information. Or take a walking tour through Frederick's historic district. From May through October tours depart from the Frederick Visitor Center at 19 East Church Street on Saturday and Sunday at 1:30 p.m. Tickets are $7 for adults, $6 for seniors. and $5 for children age 2 through 12. If you can't make the tour, be sure to get a self-guided tour brochure at the center. Call (800) 999-3613 or visit www.fredericktourism .org for details and brochures. History buffs will enjoy the Historical Society of Frederick County, Inc., at 24 East Church Street, call (301) 663-1188 or visit www.hsfcinfo.org. The building, constructed early in the nineteenth century, housed an orphan asylum from the 1880s until the 1950s. Docents offer tours from 10:00 a.m. to 4:00 p.m. Monday through Saturday and 1:00 to 4:00 p.m. Sunday. Admission is $3.

Many of the western cities in Maryland emphasize their antiques stores and malls in an effort to draw tourists, and Frederick is no different. Frederick has more than 40 antiques shops across town, and much like Baltimore's Antique Row, Frederick has Antique Walk at South Carroll and East Patrick Streets, where a fair number of shops can be found.

If you'd like to stay over in Frederick so that you can seek out points farther west on subsequent days, there are a number of hotels and bed-and-breakfasts in the area. Fairfield Inn (301-631-2000, www.fairfieldinn .com), Hampton Inn (301-698-2500, www.hamptoninn.com), and Holiday Inn (301-694-7500, www.ichotelsgroup..com) are all available. Prices range from $79 at the Holiday Inn to a top price of $104 at the Hampton Inn for a room with two double beds.

Frederick is a good stopping point for Civil War buffs. It housed plenty of soldiers during the War as they headed to nearby Monocacy, Harpers Ferry, Antietam, and Gettysburg. Monocacy National Battlefield (pronounced Mah-NAH-kah-see) marks the last attempt by Southern troops to march on Washington, D.C. The visitor center at 4801 Urbana Pike is the best place to begin the self-tour. Call (301) 662-3515 or visit www.nps.gov/mono.

Harpers Ferry
70 miles from Baltimore

About 20 minutes southwest of Frederick, down U.S. Highway 340 across the Potomac River into West Virginia, you'll find Harpers Ferry. This historic town is part of Harpers Ferry National Historical Park. Look for signs to the park's visitor center just after you cross into West Virginia.

Much of the town of Harpers Ferry has been restored, with exhibits, museums, and shops throughout. Among the specific attractions you might be interested in are John Brown's Fort at Old Arsenal Square, which was the old brick armory firehouse where John Brown was captured. There is also a monument to John Brown near the main line of the B&O Railroad.

Wear your walking shoes and take your walking stick because Harpers Ferry rises up from the confluence of the Potomac and Shenandoah Rivers at a steep angle. Everything, save for the main corner of the town, is either up or down. You do not have to worry about parking, however, for even though there is no parking in town, there is a shuttle bus that will take you from the parking lot at the visitor center to the town.

Admission to Harpers Ferry National Historical Park, which includes the town, John Brown's Farm and Fort, other museums and exhibits, and the shuttle bus from the parking lot is $6 a car and is good for three days.

The park is open from 8:00 a.m. to 5:00 p.m. daily except on Thanksgiving, Christmas, and New Year's Days. Shuttle buses to the visitor center run for a half hour to 45 minutes after closing times. For information, call (304) 535-6223 or visit www.nps.gov/hafe/.

Antietam
I-70 West to Exit 29, Route 65 South
84 miles from Baltimore

West of Frederick and south of Hagerstown, equidistant from both on Highways 34/65, is Antietam National Battlefield, 960 acres of rolling Maryland countryside that witnessed the bloodiest day of the Civil War. On September 17, 1862, battle began between Confederate and Union troops who, at the end of the day, saw more than 23,000 men killed or wounded. Not only did this place see the bloodiest day of the Civil War, but the bloodiest day in any other single day of combat, including D-Day.

Antietam is of particular interest to Marylanders not just because the battle was fought on Maryland soil but also because Maryland had sons on both sides of the battle. The Maryland Monument is the only monument in the world to pay homage to fallen dead on both sides of a battle—eight Union regiments from Maryland and two Maryland Confederate regiments. All together, more than 54,000 Marylanders fought in the Civil War.

Open dawn to dusk, Antietam Battlefield is dotted with monuments to those who fell there, which you can stop and read on your drive along the 8.5-mile trail. On weekends June through October, guides in period costume are present to show how soldiers lived at camp and to demonstrate military drills. Throughout the summer months, there are also special presentations and events.

For information, call (301) 432-5124 or visit www.nps.gov/anti. A charge of $4 for individuals or $6 for a family admits you to the battlefield as well as Antietam National Cemetery and the visitor center, where you start the tour. The visitor center is open 8:00 a.m. to 7:00 p.m. Memorial Day to Labor Day and 8:30 a.m. to 5:00 p.m. the rest of the year.

Gettysburg, Pennsylvania
I-70 west to US 15 North
60 miles from Baltimore

From Emmitsburg, take Highway 140 to Pennsylvania Highway 116 in Pennsylvania, to get to Gettysburg, best known as the site of one of the major, bloody battles of the Civil War. More than 50,000 men were killed or wounded at Gettysburg over the battle fought July 1 to July 3, 1863. About 5,700 acres of open fields where 160,000 Americans met to do battle are now consecrated as Gettysburg National Military Park.

The park, which virtually surrounds the town of Gettysburg, is dotted with more than 1,300 state memorials to the fallen. Markers allow you to follow the battle from the first volley to Pickett's Charge. Gettysburg National Cemetery, on the battlefield, was dedicated by President Lincoln in 1863. The speech he gave at the dedication, the Gettysburg Address, is one of the most famous speeches of American history. The National Park Visitor Center, which is open daily from 8:00 a.m. to 5:00 p.m. except for major holidays, is a good starting point for self-guided tours. Entrance to the park is free. A new museum and visitor center is set to open in 2008, located between Highway 134 and Baltimore Pike (Route 97). For park information, visit www.nps.gov/gett or call (717) 334-1124, ext. 431.

In addition to the battlefield, there are other museums and historic sites concerning the battle in the area. For a complete list, call Gettysburg Convention and Visitors Bureau at (717) 334-2106 or visit the Web site www .gettysburg.com.

THE MOUNTAINS

Nestled in the heart of the Appalachian Mountains, called the Alleghenies hereabouts, is the city of Cumberland. To get there from Frederick, take I-70 until it turns into U.S. Highway 68/40/144. It's a straight shot from Frederick; just follow the signs. The name and the town are descended from Fort Cumberland, which was headquarters to General Edward Braddock and then-Lieutenant George Washington during the French and Indian War. Because of its location on the other side of Cumberland Narrows, also known as Cumberland Gap, Cumberland became the natural

jumping-off place before heading farther west. It was the western terminus of the Chesapeake and Ohio Canal, the eastern terminus of the National Road (Baltimore National Pike, now US 40), and during the nineteenth century, its economy was fueled by the railroad. Coal was brought down from the mountains and "gold" was returned.

The city is essentially cut in half by the railroad, which runs over the mountain and down through the center of the valley in which Cumberland sits. Homes and streets are carved up and into the surrounding mountains on either side of the tracks. The most impressive side of the city and the historic district is along and around Washington Street, which is often called Washington Hill. The City Hall, library, and the stately homes of the railroad's original rich line Washington Street. Everything from sprawling Victorian mansions to conservative Federal and Georgian Revival may be seen there.

Riding up Washington Street from the center of town, you'll pass the Western Maryland Railway Station which now serves as a railroad museum and place of departure for trips on the Western Maryland Scenic Railroad to the countryside, around Piney Mountain, through Brush Tunnel, and into Frostburg. Scenic rides with either diesel or steam engines pulling the train depart from the depot. Fares range from $25 to $75, depending on whether there's a meal, a murder mystery, or just a pleasant 32-mile excursion. For information about when and where, call (800) 872-4650 or visit www.wmsr.com.

Downtown Cumberland is only about 3 blocks long, but offers a few must-see attractions, as well as shopping at Canal Place and along the pedestrian mall on Baltimore Street. The tiny log cabin that was used by George Washington during the French and Indian War has been preserved and is located in Riverside Park. Stop by even if you can only peek in the windows and listen to an audio description.

Because Cumberland sits at one of the narrowest areas of Maryland's western counties, West Virginia is just across a short bridge from Washington Street, literally a five-minute trip. Within minutes you'll be in the country. Pennsylvania is only about 20 minutes north on U.S. Highway 220.

If you've gotten to Cumberland, you've been on the road a minimum of three hours. After a full day of antiquing or enjoying all things Cumberland, you might decide to stay over. There are some bed-and-breakfasts around the area, but the main hotel in town is the Holiday Inn, which sits by the railroad tracks in the center of town at 100 South George Street. Rates run between $80 and $109 a night. A high-rise hotel built in the 1960s, it offers 130 rooms in six stories. There is a restaurant in the hotel, but there are also some nice eateries within walking distance. For reservation information at the Holiday Inn, call (301) 724-8800, or visit www.holidayinn .com.

Another option is located just east of Cumberland at Rocky Gap Lodge and Golf Resort. Set on Lake Habeeb, the 218-room hotel also has a restaurant, pool, lakeside water activities, health club, and 18-hole Jack Nicklaus golf course. Rooms run from $79 to $650, depending on the size of the room or suite. For information, call (800) 724-0828 or visit www.rockygapresort.com

For more information about Cumberland, call the Allegany County Visitor's Bureau at (800) 508-4748 or visit www.mdmountain side.com.

Deep Creek Lake
I-70 West to I-68 West to
U.S. Highway 219 South
181 miles from Baltimore

Unlike any other destination in Maryland, Deep Creek Lake is the state's four-season outdoor resort. It's home to a ski resort, white-water rapids, a 12-mile-long lake, and 100,000 acres of protected wilderness spread over the Appalachian Mountains. What do you like to do outdoors? Fishing? Kayaking? White-water rafting? Skiing? Dogsledding? Horsebackriding? You'll find it here. Garrett County, with Deep Creek Lake as its center-piece, offers the outdoors-lover just about every possible activity. About 100 inches of snow falls here every year, drawing thousands to Wisp Ski Resort for a day or weekend of ski-ing. The parks attract hikers, fly fishermen, and mountain bikers In spring, the white waters of the Youghiogheny River bring out the adventure seekers. A new white-water rafting course at the top of the 3100-foot Marsh Hill Mountain that opened in mid-2007 gives thrill seekers a taste of the Yough in a controlled environment. And the lake offers swimming, boating, fishing, and waterskiing. There's even a polar-bear plunge in the dead of winter here. One could conceivably visit Deep Creek from Baltimore in one day—but it would be a long day. Weekend getaways are the way to go here. Wisp Ski Resort, (301) 387-4911 or www.skiwisp.com, has its own hotel. Railey Mountain Lake Vacations, (800) 544-2425 or www.deepcreek.com, has all kinds of town houses and mountainside and lakeview homes available to rent for a week-end or a week. For information about the area's other hotels and bed-and-breakfasts, see www.visitdeepcreek.com.

SPECTATOR SPORTS

Sports in Baltimore is a weird mix, to say the least.

Long before it became commonplace, Baltimore lost its football team, the Colts. On a snowy night in March 1984, owner Robert Irsay packed up the team's belongings in moving vans to head for a better deal and a bigger stadium in Indianapolis. Thirteen years later, certain Baltimore higher-ups wooed Cleveland's Browns to town and renamed them the Ravens (referring to the main character of a poem by Edgar Allan Poe), doing essentially the same thing to Cleveland that was done to Baltimore in the 1980s. But of course, Cleveland was able to keep its team name and colors—something that Baltimore Colts fans could only dream about. Then there's the Baltimore Arena, which was called the Baltimore Civic Center when the NBA's Bullets ruled there. The Bullets moved to Washington, D.C., and are now called the Washington Wizards. The civic center is now called an arena. It plays host to indoor soccer but not basketball or hockey because professional teams in these sports have failed here.

Yet we consider ourselves a big-league town, where home football or baseball games can significantly affect sales at the movies, restaurants, and other venues. We drop everything for a Saturday in May when the Preakness, the second jewel in horse racing's Triple Crown, comes to town.

Our sports stars are still our heroes, and our teams—pro, college, and high school— are part of our families.

For many of us, Cal Ripken Jr., the Orioles infielder who played in 2,632 consecutive baseball games before ending the streak on September 20, 1998—a major league record—is a symbol of what we demand of ourselves. Through Cal we see ourselves—working hard, playing hard, having fun, getting better and better, facing adversity. It's hard to forget Cal catching the final out as shortstop in the 5-0 victory over the Phillies in Philadelphia on October 16, 1983. The catch, the raised arms, the jumping up and down, the thrill of the moment. Then there's the night time stood still in baseball—September 6, 1995. All the world's sports fans watched as the banner proclaiming 2,131—the record number game—was unfurled on the warehouse past right field. In a scene seemingly out of *The Natural*, Cal took an impromptu victory lap at Camden Yards, slapping and shaking hands of the fans in the front row, as though each was a close friend.

It's hard to forget the arm of Johnny Unitas launching touchdown passes to Raymond Berry heading down the sidelines toward the closed end of the field at Memorial Stadium more than three decades ago, or when a game between the Pittsburgh Steelers and the Colts or the New York Jets and the Colts practically paralyzed the town all day Sunday.

Then there's more heartbreak. More than 50,000 fans filled Memorial Stadium in 1988 to celebrate the end of a 21-game losing streak for the Baltimore Orioles, a record that brought the city ridicule and attention from local, national, and international sports fans. When the streak ended, the fans were there, another sellout, as if they had been a part of the streak, even though it was something they would have rather forgotten.

We live and breathe with the players— they aren't just the team. They're family, people who would be welcomed with open arms at a family picnic or birthday dinner. To love an athlete is a concept that is all too often thrown around without meaning, but in Baltimore there is truth to the statement that we love our teams. They form a big part of who and what we are—to ourselves, to our friends, and to the world. When ESPN shows the score of the Ravens' game, we take heart in the team's success or failure. They are our teams, and we love them as if they were our brothers or children. So feel free to share them with us, but don't ask us to part with them. We've learned our lesson.

BASEBALL

Baltimore Orioles
Oriole Park at Camden Yards
333 West Camden Street
(410) 685-9800
www.orioles.mlb.com

When it comes to baseball, the black and orange of the Baltimore Orioles are all that matters in this city. Since 1954 the team has been giving fans something to cheer about from April through September . . . and some years even into October, when the playoffs and World Series take place.

You've probably heard about one of the team's standouts. Name's Cal Ripkin Jr. He grew up about 30 miles north of Baltimore in Aberdeen, and he played in more consecutive games than any other player in professional baseball history. On September 20, 1998, he ended his streak that lasted 2,632 consecutive games. Ten years later, Cal remains a hero to us Baltimoreans. When he was inducted into the Baseball Hall of Fame in July 2007, diehard fans rearranged their entire lives to be in

i The Baltimore Orioles, routinely referred to as the Os or the Birds, roost in the dugout on the first-base side of the field, even though it gets the afternoon sun. So if you're looking for shots of someone on the team, it's best to get seats in the outfield or on the third-base side. If you're on the first-base side for an afternoon game or before the sun sets for a night game, take a hat, sunglasses, and suntan lotion—the sun is going to be hitting you hard.

Cooperstown, New York. When he makes a public appearance, he still draws a crowd. Hey, we cheer for the minor league Ironbirds up in Aberdeen, partly because it's Cal's team.

In the meantime, we keep hoping one day Cal will be the Orioles' owner and make them a winning team again. That doesn't mean we give up on the Orioles, of course. What kind of Os fans would we be if we did that? Sam Perlozzo has been the latest in a string of managers to try to take this young team to the top of the American League East standings. We cheer for some pretty talented young men, too: pitchers Erik Bedard and Daniel Cabrera and infielders Melvin Mora, Brian Roberts, and Miguel Tejada. We keep cheering them on—with every win we think this could be the season. When we lose, we wait for the next game, the next weekend series, the next season.

After all, it could happen again. The team that once boasted Hall of Famer Brooks Robinson at third, Frank Robinson in the outfield, and pitchers Jim Palmer, Dave McNally, and Mike Cuellar won the World Series in 1966, 1970, and 1983. Since then they've only made it as far as the divisional championships (in 1996 and 1997) before losing the American League Championship Series.

Maybe next year . . .

Oriole Park at Camden Yards

Since its opening in 1992, Oriole Park at Camden Yards' reputation has grown to the point that it is considered one of the best venues in the country (if not the absolute best) for watching baseball. Each season, fans from all over the world come to Camden Yards (locals tend to drop the Oriole Park), a 48,876-seat (including standing room) stadium that successfully mixes the old and new. Practically every seat has a great view of the whole field.

The old B&O Railroad warehouse runs along Eutaw Street behind the right-field seats. The seven-story brick building, built around the turn of the century, is the longest warehouse building on the East Coast; it extends an amazing 1,016 feet, although it is only 51 feet wide.

At 439 feet from home plate, the warehouse is a long shot away for a batter. No player has hit the warehouse during a game, although Ken Griffey Jr., then the Seattle Mariners' star outfielder, nailed it during a home-run hitting contest the day before the 1993 All-Star Game, which was hosted by the Orioles in their year-old stadium. As you walk among the shops and offices along Eutaw Street beside the warehouse, look down and you'll see round, bronze markers where home runs have landed as players continue to tee up for the warehouse.

Inside the ballpark, the field is set 16 feet below ground level, giving the park a more intimate feel than its predecessors. Conveniently located about 6 blocks west of the Inner Harbor, on land a block from where Babe Ruth, the Bronx Bomber himself, was born and raised, the stadium integrates the skyline and feel of today's Baltimore with some of the classic features of old ballparks. Steel, rather than concrete, trusses and an arched brick facade call to mind bygone playing grounds like Ebbetts Field in Brooklyn and Shibe Park in Philadelphia. Other distinctive features, some copied at Jacobs Field in Cleveland, Turner Field in Atlanta, and the Ballpark at Arlington in Texas, include an asymmetrical playing field and low outfield walls. On every aisle is a reproduction of the logo used by the Baltimore Orioles of the 1890s, a National League team that won consecutive pennants from 1894 to 1896.

Camden Yards even welcomes rain. The field features Professional Athletic Turf, an irrigation and drainage system below the natural grass that ends rain delays about 30 minutes after the rains stop. The field can remove as much as 75,000 gallons of rainwater from the field each hour.

Recent renovations included replacing the entire playing surface and changing the field dimensions of the ballpark. Home plate was moved about 7 feet closer to the backstop, bringing fans closer to the action, providing better sight lines from hundreds of seats, reducing obstructions near the foul poles, and increasing

safety for spectators behind home plate.

The foul line measurement increased from 318 feet to 320 feet in right field and from 333 feet to 337 feet in left. The center field distance increased from 400 feet to 406 feet and the deepest part of the ballpark, left center field, increased from 410 feet to 417 feet.

In addition to repositioning the foul poles, the Orioles replaced the left-field foul pole with the original left-field foul pole used by the Orioles at Memorial Stadium from 1954 through 1991. The Memorial Stadium foul pole is shorter (70 feet) and requires a smaller support structure that will allow more fans in the lower club and upper decks to have an unobstructed view of the field. The Orioles have used the original right-field foul pole from Memorial Stadium since Camden Yards opened in 1992.

The bleacher seats in right field and center field are really good seats, although you're looking over the shoulders of the outfielders. Standing-room-only tickets, which enable spectators to watch from an outfield porch in right field or to fill seats left unoccupied, are another bargain (see the following section on Tickets). You'll also notice the 72 luxury boxes, where movers and shakers can watch the game, sip champagne, and eat from expensive platters. They're great seats and great eats when you can get them, but don't hold your breath.

The club level is the place for those who want to be treated like royalty but can't afford to own a luxury box. In these seats, just a few feet higher than the Press Box, waiters and waitresses will get your hot dogs, turkey sandwiches, or crab cakes. Another advantage of club seats: There is access to indoor facilities with air conditioning, a bar, and TV lounges.

Tickets

Tickets for Orioles games are available at the Camden Station ticket office, at the intersection of Howard and Camden Streets.

Getting tickets on game day is possible but can be difficult on weekends. But planning in advance is best as the stadium is often filled to capacity from June through September, even if the Os aren't fighting for a playoff spot.

Close-up

Baseball

If you love baseball, you've gotta love Baltimore. The birthplace of Babe Ruth has (we think) the greatest baseball stadium in the world, two museums dedicated to the sport, and a ring of minor league stadiums surrounding it out in the suburbs.

Oriole Park at Camden Yards is, of course, the shrine to the majors. So what if the Orioles can't seem to pull out a winning season? As the team of Ironman Cal Ripken and Hall-of-Famers Brooks Robinson, Luis Aparicio, and Eddie Murray, we know they'll win one of these days. Meanwhile, we're proud of our downtown stadium, an homage to old-fashioned stadiums, with plenty of good seats, a beautiful brick facade, and lots of stands selling crab cakes, hot dogs, and CrackerJacks. Regulars know the beer man by name, and everyone is happy to stand and sing "Thank God I'm a Country Boy" during the seventh-inning stretch. John Denver even came and led the crowd the year just before he died.

Tours of Oriole Park are available for groups and individuals. It's a great way to take a seat in the Orioles dugout, see the press box, and see the controls for the scoreboard. Ninety-minute tours run at 11:00 a.m., noon, and 1:00 and 2:00 p.m. Monday through Saturday and Sunday at 12:20 p.m. and 1:00, 2:00, and 3:00 p.m. Tickets are $7 for adult and $5 for children and can be purchased online at baltimore.orioles.mlb.com or at the stadium box office. Call (410) 547-6234.

The Babe Ruth Birthplace and Museum, 216 Emory Street, (410) 727-1539, has preserved the tiny row house where this baseball giant was born. It recalls his discovery of the game when he was a student at St. Mary's Industrial School in southwest Baltimore and celebrates his tremendous talent as a ballplayer—even if he was a Yankee. (We forgive you, Babe).

In Camden Station, next door to the stadium, Sports Legends Museum, 301 West Camden Street, (410) 727-1739, houses the Orioles and Colts (the Baltimore team) Halls of Fame, as well as displays for other local sports teams, from soccer's Baltimore Blast to the Johns Hopkins University lacrosse team. Cal Ripken Jr., Brooks Robinson, Frank Robinson, and Jim Palmer are among the greats remembered here.

Tickets can be obtained by mail by writing to Oriole Mail Order Form, 333 West Camden Street, Baltimore, MD 21201, or by calling the Orioles at (888) 848BIRD. You can also order online through ticketmaster.com. Tickets can be charged using MasterCard or Visa and can be picked up at the "will call" window on game day (note that there might be a line and a wait). It's better to arrive early, get your tickets, then either visit the Inner Harbor or head in to watch batting practice, which is open to the public usually 90 minutes to two hours before game time. Tickets can also be printed from the ticketing Web site.

Ticket prices range from $55 for box seats right behind the Oriole dugout to $15

Historic Camden Station (foreground) welcomes visitors to Oriole Park at Camden Yards.
PHOTO PROVIDED COURTESY OF THE BABE RUTH MUSEUM

As for the minor leagues, a number of stadiums are close enough to get to a game. Cal Ripken's Ironbirds, an Oriole farm team, play at the stadium in Aberdeen, about 30 minutes north on I-95. The Frederick Keys, another O's affiliate, play at Harry Grove stadium, about an hour from the city. And down in Bowie, south on US 50, The Bowie Baysox, a Class AA affiliate, play in their ballpark. Two other teams are about two to three hours away. Orioles farm team, the Shorebirds, play in Salisbury, just outside of Ocean City, and the Hagerstown Suns, newly selected as a Washington Nationals farm team, play farther out Highway 70 in Municipal Stadium, one of the oldest Minor League stadiums in the country.

For details of the museums, see the Attractions chapter. The minor league teams have their own Web sites, as well.

for an upper reserve seat behind home plate. Cheap seats out in left field are $9. Standing room is $8. Prime games, i.e, the Yankees and the Red Sox, have a surcharge of $5 to $10 a ticket. Bostonians and New Yorkers come down and fill the stadium since they can't get tickets at home.

Getting There and Parking

About 5,000 parking spaces were lost in 1997 when construction of the football stadium for the Baltimore Ravens began. The loss made an already bad parking situation that much worse. Don't expect to park at the stadium's lots unless you have a license plate denoting a handicap or you managed to obtain a parking ℹ️ Good places to meet up with people at Oriole Park at Camden Yards include the front of Camden Station or in front of the statues outside the Eutaw Street entrance. Both are easy to find and even easier to get directions to.

pass from a season-ticket holder. Area parking garages, including the ones at Sheraton Inner Harbor and the Gallery shopping center, offer parking that ranges in price from $5 for a walk of up to 15 blocks to $15 for parking near the stadium.

Getting to the game is made easiest by using one of the variety of mass transit options. Not only do you avoid the bumper-to-bumper drive through the city, but you also get to meet and greet like-minded fans. The stadium is only 6 blocks from the Inner Harbor.

The state's MARC commuter rail runs a bus from the Greenbelt Station to the ballpark on game days and nights. Tickets are $10 or a regular MARC train ticket. Light Rail lines also carry passengers from Hunt Valley Mall, about 15 miles north of Baltimore City, to Camden Yards. From the south, rail lines transport fans from the Baltimore-Washington International Thurgood Marshall Airport and Cromwell Station in Anne Arundel County, about 20 miles away. The Light Rail, which stops at several locations between Hunt Valley Mall and the ballpark, costs $3.20 for a round-trip pass for games or $1.60 for the regular one-way fare. The entry points north and south get crowded about 90 minutes before game time, but it's still a quick and easy way to get to and from the park. Trains usually run every 17 minutes, but more trains are put in service for games.

Park 'N' Ride lots around Interstate 695 (the Baltimore Beltway) also offer parking and bus transport to the games. This can often be an affordable and enjoyable option, usually costing $10 for adults and $5 for children age 6 through 16. To find more commuter information, check the MTA Web site at www.mta.maryland.com.

Ballpark Rules

The following rules apply at all Orioles home games.

- No alcoholic beverages, cans, or glass can be brought into the park. Containers, including coolers and bags, are checked as spectators enter.
- Food can be brought into the stadium, meaning those peanut and pretzel vendors outside the ballpark make good money. Their prices are lower than what you'll find inside.
- All entrants must pay, except infants sitting on the same seat as parents.
- Smoking is prohibited in all areas, except the concourses outside the playing field and seating area.
- Selling tickets for more than face value is illegal, and undercover police stings targeting offenders are not unusual.

The Os on the Air

If you can't get to the park, Orioles games are carried on television through a unique arrangement. All games are broadcast by the mid-Atlantic Sports Network, either on WJZ-TV Channel 13 or a cable channel.

Radio broadcasts are carried on WHFS (105.7 FM) and in Washington on WETM (980 AM), as well as on smaller stations throughout Maryland, Pennsylvania, Virginia, and West Virginia.

FOOTBALL

Baltimore Ravens
M&T Bank Stadium
1101 Russell Street
(410) 230-8000
www.ravenszone.net
Over the past few years Baltimore area residents have steadily developed a love for purple. The cause—the Super Bowl XXXV Champion Ravens. Since the team came from the city of Cleveland, where they had been the Browns until 1995, Baltimore embraced them and the chance to have the NFL back in Baltimore. The Ravens, a name honoring the title of

the classic Edgar Allan Poe poem, wear purple, black, and gold, and area residents are sporting those colors with pride. Although the reflexive urge to call our football team anything but the Colts is hard to break, the Ravens have made it easy to fall in love with them.

After decades during which the exploits of the greats—"Golden Arm" Johnny Unitas, Raymond Berry, Lenny Moore, and Bert Jones—cemented fans' love of the team, people are starting to find new heroes to focus their football fandom on.

After several years of rebuilding, team owner Art Modell's hard work to put together a first-rate team paid off. On January 28, 2001, under supervision of Head Coach Brian Billick, the Ravens defeated the New York Giants by a score of 34-7 at Super Bowl XXXV.

During the glory years of the 1960s and '70s, Baltimore football fans were known to skip church or go to early services to allow proper time for, er, game preparation. Now, many fans are again carrying out the tradition and of course starting their own.

In 1998 a new era began for the team, as it opened a football-only stadium, built across from Oriole Park at Camden Yards in downtown Baltimore, about 6 blocks from the Inner Harbor. After closing the book on Memorial Stadium—a 60,000-seat grande dame among outdoor stadiums, used by the Colts, Ravens, and the Canadian Football League's now-defunct Baltimore Stallions (not to mention the Baltimore Orioles until 1992)—the team's move to what is now called M&T Bank Stadium has brought more of the historic charm that came with Camden Yards. The new digs provide the team, its owner, and fans with the state-of-the-art facilities considered so essential to a winning football organization these days.

M&T Bank Stadium

The 69,084-seat stadium brought new life to the team and the city's Downtown. It follows by several years the incredible success of neighboring Oriole Park at Camden Yards, and football fans will find similarities to the base-ball stadium. But there are new features, including a "split" upper-seating bowl designed to serve as an architectural signature while offering football fans a great view of the city's skyline.

The stadium has several unique characteristics, including a distinct upper-seating level with notched corner. There are 62 over size restrooms located throughout the stadium. The stadium also features close to 250 permanent points of sale for food and beverages that are complemented with several specialty food and beverage carts throughout the stadium. Extra-wide concourses and unobstructed views place this stadium in a class of its own. But perhaps the most spectacular feature are the two Smartvision boards, each measuring 25 by 100 feet and utilizing the most advanced technology, that give every visitor the feeling of being right on the field in the middle of the action. The spectacular visual effect is enhanced with a state-of-the-art sound system.

There are seven levels, including five with seating. The facade has brick arches at its base, aluminum trim at the grid lines, and a frame of concrete supported by pewter structural steel rakers. Throughout the project, dark, rich brick and mortar, manufactured in Maryland and similar in appearance to other buildings in the area, were used.

Stadium Rules

The following rules apply at all Ravens home games.

- No alcoholic beverages, cans, or glass can be brought into the stadium. Fans must be age 21 or older to purchase or consume alcoholic beverages at the stadium. This includes any parking lots designated as tailgating zones.
- Smoking is not permitted in the seating areas or restrooms. Smoking is allowed on open concourses and ramps.
- Umbrellas are not allowed in the stadium so as not to interfere with the sightlines of other guests.
- Cameras and video equipment are permitted

Selected Baltimore Firsts

The first baseball player to be named Most Valuable Player in both the American and National Leagues was Frank Robinson of the Baltimore Orioles (1966).

Baltimore is the first city to win championships in the National Football League, the United States Football League, and the Canadian Football League. This distinction became ours when we locked up the Canadian trophy, The Grey Cup.

—Excerpted from *Baltimore—America's City of Firsts*, a pamphlet published by Baltimore Bicentennial Celebration, Inc.

in the stadium during Ravens' games but cannot be used to reproduce the game.

• Selling tickets for more than face value is illegal.

Tickets

Although season-ticket holders control most of the seats to a Ravens game, the team does reserve about 6,000 tickets for each game to sell to the general public. These tickets generally go on sale in mid-July and can be purchased at the Ravens box office at the stadium, through TicketMaster Phone Charge, or online at www.tickemaster.com. Ticket prices for a single seat start at $50 and go up from there. Selected group sales package plans (for 25 or more people) are sometimes available by contacting the Ravens ticket office at (410) 261RAVE (7283).

To purchase a season ticket in M&T Stadium, the purchase of a Permanent Seat License is required. This is a one-time purchase that transfers the rights of the seat from the team to the individual licensee. The one-time permanent seat fee is either $750 to $8,000. Season tickets start at $450 and can go up to $3,400 for the top club level seat.

Raven games are broadcast on the mid-Atlantic Sports Network, a local cable/broadcast television network. Fans can see games on an MASN cable station or on WBFF (Channel 45) or WNUV (Channel 54). Radio broadcasts of all Raven games are on WBAL (1090 AM) and 98ROCK (97.9 FM).

Getting There and Parking

Ravens fans will experience similar parking woes as the folks heading to one of the 81 home games played by the Orioles. Look for the Ravens bird at Downtown parking locations. There are more than 30,000 spaces in garages within walking distance of the stadium. Some to look for include the Market Center Garage at Paca and Lexington Streets, Fayette West Garage at Howard and Fayette Streets, and the Redwood Street garage at Eutaw and Baltimore Streets. These lots can charge from $5 to $30 for parking.

But mass transit is the name of the game. About 6 blocks from the Inner Harbor, the stadium offers easy access to most mass transit options. The state's MARC commuter rail runs between Union Station in Washington and the ballpark on game days and nights. Light Rail lines carry passengers from Hunt Valley Mall, about 15 miles north of Baltimore City, to Camden Yards, and from the Baltimore–Washington International Thurgood Marshall Airport and Cromwell Station in Anne Arundel County, about 20 miles south of Baltimore City. The Light Rail costs $3.20 for a round-trip pass or $1.60 regularly one way. The entry points north and south get crowded about 90 minutes before game time but are a quick and easy way to get to and from the stadium.

HORSE RACING

Maryland's roots in horse racing go back a long, long way. In fact, the Maryland Jockey Club, which owned Pimlico Race Course for most of its history, was established in 1743—more than 30 years before the Revolutionary War! The Annapolis Subscription Plate is the second-oldest racing trophy in America.

If you head out into horse country—the open and largely undeveloped land north and northwest of Baltimore—you'll see sprawling horse farms, their long, beautifully painted white fences leading the way to tomorrow's race champions.

Baltimore is also home of the Preakness Stakes, the middle jewel of horse racing's Triple Crown. Each May, the eyes of all horseracing fans as well as all those people who get caught up in the annual quest to win the three big races turn to Pimlico, where horses and jockeys race for the crown.

Pimlico Race Course
5201 Park Heights Avenue
(410) 542-9400
www.pimlico.com

On 140 acres in northwest Baltimore City sits a mile-long, 70-foot-wide track with a stretch distance (from the last turn to the finish line) of 1,152 feet. That means lots of excitement as the horses head for the wire.

Bettors are serviced by 750 betting windows and automated betting machines. The new grandstand holds up to 5,692 people, while the old grandstand accommodates 5,926. The clubhouse has space for 1,269 people. The stables offer accommodations for up to 500 horses, plus tack, feed, and sleeping rooms. Quarters for the male jockeys are behind the paddock, and female jockeys' quarters are located near the paddock.

Pimlico's race days are mid-April to early June. The track's live days are Wednesday and Thursday. Admission is $3 for the grandstand, the clubhouse, and the sports palace, an enclosed lounge where simulcasts of other races are shown, except on weekends and holidays when it's $7. Inside box seats (two

i Seabiscuit became a legend when he defeated the Triple Crown winner War Admiral in the 1938 Pimlico Special. Pictures from that race—voted the Race of the Century by Sports Illustrated—can be seen at the Maryland Jockey Club at Pimlico

seats in each box) in the grandstand are $2.50 a seat. Likewise, outside box seats (four seats in each box) in the grandstand are $2.50 a seat. Sports palace seats (weekends and holidays only) are $2.50 a seat. Tickets are available at the entrance on Preakness Way; MasterCard and Visa are accepted.

Getting to Pimlico is relatively easy. Take Interstate 83 to Northern Parkway, head west about 2 miles, and the race track is on the left. Parking is all on-site, with 7,522 spaces available; except on Preakness Day, there are a total of 2,100 general parking spots available for free on Preakness Way and Rogers Avenue, 1,500 clubhouse parking spaces cost $2 each, and valet parking, in 620 spots, is offered at $3.

The Preakness

The Preakness Stakes is a big, big event. People come from around the country to watch the run for the second jewel of the thoroughbred racing industry's Triple Crown. For the Preakness, Pimlico's capacity grows to 109,398, including 22,000 standing-room-only patrons and 60,000 people filling the infield, where visitors tend to see little of the race but usually leave feeling no pain. That comes the next day, if you know what we mean. Demand for tickets gets pretty fierce as Preakness Day approaches. Tickets go on sale the October before the May race day. Clubhouse seating ranges from $25 for general admission to $95 for the best grandstand boxes. Of course, if you want to head to the infield for the giant party (and it is possible to see the horses, too, if you want) tickets are $50 in advance or $60 if you buy them at one of the BP gas stations. They are usually available until race day at the gas stations.

Close-up

Maryland's State Sport—Jousting?!?

Ask most Baltimoreans, and they'll tell you the state sport is lacrosse, a high-speed, bone-crunching sport played by young men and women with webbed sticks. Lacrosse is huge in the northeastern United States, and Johns Hopkins University and the University of Maryland are two local powerhouses.

But the state sport (and Maryland is the only state with a designated state sport) is actually jousting, a medieval test of bravery and skill that pitted knight against knight in battle, often for the hand of a fair maiden.

In Europe between the tenth and twelfth centuries, jousting required that an armor-clad rider on horseback knock another knight from his mount using a long pole. Jousting was an occupation and the widely accepted method throughout Europe for competing knights to prove their mettle to the fair maiden of the day, while making some money for beating an able competitor.

Thankfully, riders don't square off against each other anymore. Instead, they compete in the "running at the rings," the name given to the new approach to the sport created about the time of James I of England. It was this form that Cecil Calvert, the first Lord Baltimore, brought to the colonies in the early 1700s.

Today, as in colonial times, jousting riders take three runs at the rings, which in the first round are an inch in diameter, roughly the size of a quarter. The rider steers toward three small rings with a 5- to 7-foot-long wooden pole, designed specifically for the rider. The pole must be crafted to provide perfect balance when on the rider's arm. Inserted into the end of the pole is a 2-foot lance, handmade of aluminum, stainless steel, or steel. Riders who

Parking is a lot more difficult to find on Preakness weekend, and it's best to get to the track early. It's also a lot more expensive, with general parking going for $45, VIP parking for $150, and valet parking for $85. Limos cost more. (See the Annual Events chapter for more information about the Preakness.)

Laurel Race Course
Race Track Road and Route 198, Laurel
(410) 792-7775
www.laurelpark.com
Located on 360 acres midway between Baltimore and Washington, D.C., Laurel Race Course offers live racing on Wednesday through Sunday with post time at 12:40 p.m. Live race days are held most of August and September through December. Some racing is held in spring, as well. The dirt track is a 1⅛-mile oval with a 7-furlong chute. The length of the stretch from the last turn to the finish line is an exciting 1,344 feet.

Bettors at Laurel are serviced by 350 betting windows and automated betting machines.

In 1988 Laurel Park was the site of a complete rebuilding of the racing strip at a cost of almost $2 million. The park also received a face-lift in 1985 when the Sports Palace was built with the ambience of a plush casino succeed in collecting nine rings (three in each of three rounds) compete at the next level, where the rings are about the size of a nickel. A subsequent round has rings a quarter-inch in diameter, about the size of a dime.

The rings are suspended from arches 30 yards apart, with a 40-yard starting area for the horse and rider to get their timing and approach perfect. Competitors are given nine seconds to complete a regular round, eight seconds for a championship round. They are timed from when they cross a starting line 20 yards from the first ring until they gather the third ring. Taking more time than allotted eliminates the competitor, regardless of whether the rider succeeds in gathering the rings on his pole.

The winner is crowned at an elaborate closing ceremony, where the winning knight chooses the lady to be crowned "Queen of Love and Beauty." When women win, and they increasingly compete in this skill event, they choose the "King of Love and Beauty."

In keeping with the medieval tradition, riders male and female take names like Knight of One-Thousand Days or Maiden of Misery, often using humor or their real family names as sources for their monikers. These modern-day knights have chosen brightly colored costumes of the period over the medieval armor of centuries past.

Because the rider must focus all attention on the rings, the movements of the horse must be exact. For this reason, horses typically go through at least two years of formal training with riders before entering competitions.

Few formal jousting tournaments are held, though exhibitions are often performed at county fairs and the Maryland Renaissance Festival (see the Annual Events chapter). A careful eye to the open stretches of farmland in northern Baltimore County can often reveal the telltale arches where would-be lords practice for the opportunity to be Lord of the Rings.

complemented with state-of-the-art technology featuring computerized handicapping and a video library.

The clubhouse has space for 1,216 people and the grandstand has space for 2,964 people. The stables offer accommodations for 880 horses. Jockeys' quarters are located next to the racing secretary's office across from the paddock.

Admission to the grandstand and clubhouse is $3 and night and simulcasting seating is free. Seats on weekdays are also free with a few exceptions. Box seats on weekends and holidays are $2.50 per seat for grandstand and clubhouse (four seats to a box).

Getting to Laurel Park is easy; it is located just 22 miles from Baltimore on Route 198. Just take Interstate 95 south toward Washington, D.C., and get off at exit 33, Route 198, heading east and follow the signs. General parking for live racing is free, preferred is $2, valet is $5, and park and lock is $5 during the day and free at night. Parking for simulcasting is free, except park and lock is $2 and valet parking is not offered.

Steeplechase Season

For most people April means showers and the start of warmer weather. But for many of us in Baltimore it really only means one thing—the i The crown adorning the winning horse in May's Preakness Stakes isn't really made of black-eyed Susans. They're daisies with centers that have been handpainted black to resemble black-eyed Susans, which don't bloom until late summer. Shhhh, it's a secret!

start of steeplechase season. During the first four Saturdays in April a different steeplechase is held on four farms in northern Baltimore and Harford Counties. If you've never experienced a steeplechase, it's an exciting opportunity to view—usually up-close—a traditional point-to-point race. But remember these events are held outside, rain or shine, so be sure to wear proper attire. A few stores in close proximity to the races usually sell steeplechase tickets; a good bet is the Butler Store and Liquors (410-771-4383) at 14921 Falls Road.

One of the first races of the season, held the first Saturday of April, is the **Elkridge Harford,** run over Atlanta Hall Farm in Monkton. This race has served over the past 50-plus years as the testing ground for riders and horse. Its placement on the calendar and its inviting course have attracted such worldrenowned horses as Jay Trump and Ben Nevis II, both of whom went on to capture the English Grand National in Liverpool. This is the smallest of the races, so observers can really get in close to the action. There are six races, both timber and flat races. General admission tickets are $25 per carload. To get there, take I-695 to exit 27/Dulaney Valley Road. Cross Loch Raven Reservoir and bear left onto Jarrettsville Pike. Continue through the light at Jacksonville and go 4 miles to Pocock Road. Left on Pocock Road and follow parking signs.

On the second Saturday of April the **My Lady's Manor Steeplechase Races** are held to benefit Ladew Topiary Gardens. Gates open at noon and post time is 2:30 p.m. This is Harford County's largest annual sporting event, with an estimated crowd of anywhere between 2,000 and 6,000 people attending.

The day includes three races, 3 miles over timber. People may bring coolers, picnics, or charcoal stoves. Because of danger to the horses, all glass containers should be deposited only in receptacles provided. General admission tickets are $30 and family parking is $35. These are both available on race day at the gate or ahead of time at local stores. You can call Ladew Topiary Gardens for more information at (410) 557-9570. To get there take I-695 to Dulaney Valley Road, north. Keep left to Jarrettsville Pike. Go to Pocock Road and follow signs.

On the third Saturday in April, the **Grand National Steeplechase** is held starting at 3:15 p.m., with gates opening at noon. This race, second in age only to the Hunt Cup, began as an outgrowth of a boys' race that was instituted in 1898. In 1900 the race, which is restricted to amateur riders, became an annual event. The Grand National has moved four times before finding its present home in Butler. The day includes three races. General admission tickets are $20 per car. Tickets can be optained by writing to: Grand National Steeplechase, P.O. Box 1, Butler, MD 21023. To get to the race, take I-83 north to Belfast Road west. Follow to Falls Road and make a right. Go less than a mile, making a left onto Butler Road. Go out Butler Road a little over a mile, until you see signs for parking.

On the fourth Saturday in April is the most popular and largest of the races, the **Maryland Hunt Cup.** This race ranks with the English Grand National as one of the two greatest steeplechase races in the world. It was originally run as a rivalry race between the Green Spring and Elkridge hunt clubs but in 1903 opened to any recognized hunt club in the United States and Canada. The race is run over Worthington Farms, a distance of 4 miles, and gates open at 11:00 p.m. Parking passes must be obtained prior to the day of the race by sending $35 and a self-addressed, stamped envelope to: The Maryland Hunt Cup Association, P.O. Box 3606, Glyndon, MD 21071. No sales are made on race day. The schedule, as well as ticket and parking information, for the steeplechase season, can be found at www.marylandsteeplechasing.com. Tickets can also be picked up at many local stores. To get there take I-83 north to Shawan Road. Follow Shawan Road west until you see signs for parking.

Shawan Downs, a new equestrian center in Cockeysville, was established to save 300 acres of farmland and preserve the horsey traditions in an area quickly being swallowed up by suburbia. From March through September the center holds a series of equestrian events that benefit local charities. These include the Green Spring Valley Point to Point and the Maryland Junior Hunt Cup for young riders, as well as horse shows. The course's premiere event is its final event of the season, the Legacy Chase, held in late September. The event combines the steeplechase with country fair and events for children—even a stick horse race. Tickets go on sale in the summer. Check www.shawandowns.org for the schedule and ticket prices. Or call (410) 666-3676 to order. Ticket prices range from $10 to $30 per carload.

INDOOR SOCCER

Baltimore Blast
Baltimore Arena
201 West Baltimore Street
(410) 732-5278
www.baltimoreblast.com
The Baltimore Blast may be a top-scoring soccer team but Baltimoreans often don't seem to notice. Usually disappointed by the Baltimore Orioles or engrossed by the Baltimore Ravens, city residents don't seem to notice that right there in the Baltimore Arena, the local franchise of the National Professional Soccer League is winning games—and they're making it look like a lot of fun. Though the 2006–2007 season ended in disappointment, this is a championship franchise that topped the rest in 1984, 2003, 2004, and 2006. Baltimore has had a professional indoor soccer team since 1980. Indoor soccer is played November through March on a modi-

fied hockey rink covered with artificial turf.

The team features mostly American players, often drafting players from college. While the team is international, a couple of local boys are on the roster. One of the top scorers on the team, Giuliano Celenza (#4), holds the University of Maryland Baltimore County's record as the number two scorer in school history. A graduate of both UMBC and Archbishop Curley High School, he lives with his family in Perry Hall. Billy Nelson (#2) hails from Bel Air, a northern suburb, and played for UMBC before joining the Blast in 2003. He even coaches for Boys Latin, taking the team there to the local championship in 2006. And Mike Lookingland (#24) is from Fallston, Maryland, and played for Loyola High School, winning the team's MVP award both his junior and senior years.

The Baltimore Blast fans can rock the Baltimore Arena, which has room for 11,400 fans. Unfortunately, average game attendance fills about half the seats. So there's usually space available for those who want to join in the fun at the last minute.

Home games start at 7:35 p.m. Tickets are available at the arena box office, (410) 732-5278, or through Ticketmaster at (410) 547SEAT. They are available online at www.ticketmaster.com. Tickets are $20 for prime seats, $17 for upper levels, and $14 behind the goal line. Games are broadcast on WCBM (680AM) radio.

ROLLER DERBY

Charm City Roller Girls
722 Dulaney Valley Road, Towson
www.charmcityrollergirls.com
Founded in 2006, the Charm City Rollers Girls league fields four flat-track roller derby teams (the Night Terrors, Mobtown Mods, Junkyard Dolls, and Speed Regime), as well as a travel team, the Mobtown Maulers. The teams' members have names as, well, dainty, as their teams' names, with such monikers as Amazon Disaster, Pistol Whip, Large Marge, and the Mexican Fury. In only its second year, the

Close-up

Lacrosse

Marylanders love lacrosse, and Baltimore, with its concentration of colleges and universities, is the lacrosse center for the state. Drive by any prep school at 3:30 p.m., and you'll see loads of boys and girls carting their lacrosse sticks and helmets to the fields. Many graduate to play at the collegiate level, and Maryland boasts some of the top schools for NCAA lacrosse. The game is primarily a collegiate sport with nearly 25,000 men playing lacrosse at more than 400 colleges and universities.

The earliest accounts of lacrosse date from the first French missionaries and English explorers who came to the New World around 1630. The Native American tribes playing the stick and ball game intrigued explorers in the Great Lakes area, along the northeastern seaboard, and in Canada. Lacrosse was given its name by early French settlers, using the generic term for any game played with a curved stick (crosse) and a ball. There is no evidence of non–Native Americans taking up the game until the mid-nineteenth century, when English-speakers in Montreal adopted the sport from the Mohawks. For some classic history lessons about lacrosse, you may want to pick up George Beers' book about the Mohawk playing techniques entitled *Lacrosse* (1869) or James Mooney's *American Anthropologist* (1890), which describes in detail the Eastern Cherokee game and its elaborate rituals. *American Indian Lacrosse: Little Brother of War* (1994) by Thomas Vennum Jr. offers a good contemporary look at the history of the game.

The sport of lacrosse is a combination of basketball, soccer, and hockey. Like hockey, a small semicircle called the crease protects the goalie, and offensive players cannot step inside this area (there is a sports bar and grill on York Road in Towson that honors the game with its name, "The Crease"). The cardinal rule of lacrosse is that your hands can never touch the ball. Players handle the ball with a long stick that has a net on the end. Quickness and agility are essential skills for this fast-moving sport. Players frequently sprint down the field making fast precision passes. Men's and

Division III roller girls were ranked eighteenth nationally. The Women's Flat Track Derby Association has 37 leagues from Stamford, Connecticut, to Seattle. Teams play 60-minute games, or bouts, on a flat track at the Putty Hill Skateland on Dulaney Valley Road, (410) 661-7778. The league is owned and operated by the women athletes themselves, who hold day jobs, such as mothers, teachers, artists, and other ordinary occupations. The season runs from April through October, with special events throughout the year. Tickets are available through Brown Paper Tickets (www.brown papertickets.com) and at Dangerously Delicious Pies in Federal Hill and Atomic Books in Hampden (more on those two shops in the Shopping chapter). Tickets are usually available on the day of a bout, but they sell out quickly. These girls have quite a following.

women's lacrosse were played under virtually the same rules, with no protective equipment, until the mid-1930s. At that time, men's lacrosse began evolving to the game that exists today, one of more physical contact. Men wear helmets and padding to protect from the occasional stick jab or elbow that comes from an opposing team member.

If you've never watched live lacrosse you are missing an exciting game. The adept skill with which the men and women play the sport coupled with the advances in sports equipment makes for a fast, graceful game that is a thrill to watch. Spring weekends at Homewood Field at the Johns Hopkins University are packed with lacrosse fans cheering the men's lacrosse team. With Loyola, Towson University, and the University of Maryland competing in the same division, hometown rivalries can get fierce. Friendly jabs at opposing team's fans are common, but it's all in good fun. The lacrosse season begins in the spring, and everyone looks forward to enjoying the breezy Baltimore weather, the blue skies, and the sunshine at an afternoon lacrosse game and the inevitable tailgates that go with it. But even the most inclement weather won't keep the diehard fans from braving the elements to watch the game.

If you don't know the rules of the game, don't worry. The uninitiated are sure to find a friendly lacrosse fan willing to share the details of the game. If you really want to do your homework and know what you're watching before you get to the game, visit the U.S. Lacrosse National Hall of Fame and Museum located on the Johns Hopkins University campus. There you can get a crash course in the history and glories of lacrosse. You'll learn that lacrosse is considered one of the quickest growing team sports in the United States today.

Collegiate lacrosse is attracting major league–sized crowds. M&T Bank Stadium in Baltimore hosted the 2003 and 2004 NCAA Lacrosse Finals and Championship over Memorial Day Weekend, attracting a record breaking 108,000 people from around the country. The Finals were also played at M&T Bank Stadium in 2007, and the games attracted even larger numbers of attendees.

COLLEGE SPORTS

Baltimore is a hotbed of college sports action, where you can often find good competition at family rates. Several area teams garner national attention for their exploits. Call the numbers listed to learn more about each school's sports teams and see our Education chapter for information about these institutions.

Towson University (410-704-2759, www.towsontigers.com), plays its indoor sports in the Towson Center, a 5,000-seat arena, and outdoor sports at Johnny Unitas Stadium. Although it competes in more than 15 collegiate sports, its best include lacrosse, men's basketball, baseball, and women's gymnastics, where its teams frequently are among the top in the nation.

Johns Hopkins University (410-516-7490, www.hopkinssports.cstv.com) plays a variety of sports but is best known for men's lacrosse, in which it frequently competes with other powerhouses such as Syracuse, Rutgers, Towson, and the universities of Maryland, Virginia, and North Carolina. The school's outdoor field features artificial turf with concrete grandstands on both sides of the playing surface. The Bluejays rarely miss the NCAA lacross tournament, and they won the 2007 title right here in Baltimore.

Morgan State University (443-885-1522, www.morganstatebears.com) fields teams in most college athletics. Morgan's best sports include football, track and field, and basketball.

Coppin State University (410-951-3000, www.coppinstatesports.com) fields men's and women's teams in a number of sports but is known for its top-notch men's basketball program. Under head coach Fang Mitchell, Coppin plays against some of the best teams in the nation (usually on the road, unfortunately) and every now and again scores a big upset win and a trip to the NCAA tournament.

University of Maryland, Baltimore County (UMBC, 410-455-1000, www.umbc.com), is part of the University of Maryland system. The ACC-affiliated Terrapins in College Park, outside Washington, gain national attention for basketball and lacrosse play. UMBC competes in Division I, fielding good teams in basketball, including a top-notch women's basketball team, baseball, soccer, and lacrosse. The men's lacrosse team reached the NCAA finals held in Baltimore in 2007.

CHILD CARE

Baltimoreans needing child care are a lucky lot. We have the support and services of the Maryland Committee for Children. This is the place to call for referrals for in-home child care as well as advice about finding child care. In the greater Baltimore area, child-care facilities run the gamut from Grandmother to family day-care homes to child care centers. Several services will even put families in touch with au pairs and nannies.

Named one of the top ten states for child care for six consecutive years by *Working Mother* magazine, Maryland keeps winning excellent marks for the quality and safety of its child care.

At present about 36 percent of Maryland's 911,000 children younger than age 12 are in some kind of day care. And it is estimated that by 2011, the number who could need child care could skyrocket to 75 percent.

Child care isn't cheap. Families spend about 20 percent of their income on child care, anywhere from $13,000 in Baltimore City and $15,000 in Baltimore County to $19,000 in Montgomery County.

The state of Maryland subsidizes child care for families in need, with about 22,000 families receiving aid in 2007. More than 4,000 children are cared for by relatives. It is estimated that 11.9 percent of families with children have incomes below the poverty level, according to demographics data collected by the Maryland Committee for Children.

How many children overall who are cared for by non-regulated care providers isn't really known, though the estimate could be as high as half a million. Of course, care in a child's own home doesn't need to be regulated; nor does care by a relative, noted a state Department of Education official.

In addition, summer vacation means even more children needing child care. To meet the demand, many schools have after-school programs and summer camps provide working parents with plenty of options to keep their children safe and busy. There are city- and county-sponsored programs as well as many camps offered by local high schools, colleges, and many private schools. A wintertime Summer Camp Fair, sponsored by *Baltimore's Child* magazine, is usually held in early March. The actual date and time are publicized in the magazine from December until the month of the fair. A summer camp directory is available online at www.baltimoreschild.com.

The popularity of au pair programs nationwide speaks to the cost issue of child care. With working parents looking at sacrificing about a fifth of their pay every week to the cost of child care, the live-in au pair looks like a good alternative. Minimal salary plus room and board gives a foreign student the opportunity to live abroad in a family environment while providing the host family virtually one-on-one child care for the children.

Nannies are another well-used alternative in the Baltimore area. Live-ins and day nannies are the norm, but there are also some circumstances in which trained, licensed nannies are available on a per-diem basis for travelers in town just for a few days. On a per-diem basis, nannies seem relatively inexpensive, charging as little as $88 for an eight-hour day. On the other hand, when parents progress from using a nanny as an occasional answer to a necessary part of life at 10 to 12 hours per day, five days a week, the cost can increase significantly ($660 to $960).

Licensed programs in Baltimore take children as young as six weeks to as old as 12 years. Though many parents believe that their 12-year-old does not need child care, in the city of Baltimore, it is illegal for any child age 12 or younger to be left home alone for any amount of time, for any reason.

It would be terrific if we could simply list all the child-care facilities in the Baltimore area in this chapter, but in this case we're going to defer to child-care Insiders who can tell you a great deal more than we could, given our limitations of space. These are the organizations listed under Child-Care Location Services. They include information services as well as regulators and placement agencies.

We've also provided some information on licensing in the state and the groups that regulate those licenses because all of the agencies noted here deal only with licensed providers and certified personnel.

Licensed child-care providers have fulfilled the state's parameters for acceptable care and are ongoing, dependable sources for child care. Those parameters include regulation space allotted, access to outdoors, numbers of safety exits, child-teacher ratios, type of care, activities and equipment provided, how snack foods are kept, and myriad other things. Admittedly, licensing doesn't guarantee that the child-care provider is without flaw, but it does go a long way toward that goal.

For instance, all personnel who work at licensed child-care centers must be certified. These requirements are often minimal, but they can save lives. At the very least, workers receive training in CPR, how to handle choking emergencies, and general first aid.

If you decide to hire independent, unlicensed child-care help, be prepared to ask applicants about their training and abilities. Get names and phone numbers of former

---

i Don't be fooled by perfect surroundings. It's how your child is treated that counts. Ask permission for you and your child to spend a sample day at the center; if after that you like what you see and enroll your child, make surprise visits from time to time just to check that all is going well.

---

employers, and call those people to chat about how their kids felt about that worker. If the child-care worker is being recommended through a friend, see if he or she will let you talk with the child and see how the child feels because it is, ultimately, the kids whose feelings are important in this matter.

When hiring a child-care worker or deciding on a child-care facility, one overall item to watch out for, however, is "fit." What kind of child is your child? Is he quiet, enjoying board games, card games, and blocks? Or is she boisterous and physical, needing lots of space for climbing, dancing, and roughhousing? Does she need continual reassurance? Does he require a bit of independence? These questions and more like them will help you define what kind of child-care situation you're looking for and help the location and placement services help you find just the right opportunity for your child.

Child-care advocates recommend that parents begin the search for child care as soon as they discover they'll need it. Care for infants can be difficult to find because regulations allow only two infants in a home at one time. Care for school-age children can also be difficult for parents who need to find care close to school. The other factor, of course, is having enough time to check references, conduct interviews, and be sure your child will be happy with the day-care provider.

LICENSING

One of the reasons why, in the main, child care in the Baltimore area may be considered above average is the state licensing requirements. Unlike most states that only regulate multichild situations, Maryland's Child Care Administration laws cover any situation in which even one child is being cared for by someone other than a parent. Maryland's Child Care Administration's Office of Licensing inspects, reviews, and documents the activities of existing child-care facilities and personnel through 13 regional and two field offices while actively seeking to develop new child-care options for Maryland's parents. The Office of Licensing also investigates complaints.

It is extremely important when seeking child care, whether a one-day drop-in or a permanent situation, to make sure that the person or center that you are leaving your child with is licensed. Don't assume that just because there's a sign on the front door that says DAY CARE CENTER that the center is, in fact, licensed. Ask to see the license if it is not posted in plain view. Family day cares, in which a person cares for a few children in his/her own home, must possess a child-care home license.

For child-care personnel, the Office of Licensing of the Child Care Administration approves trainers, both individuals and organizations, in the child-care arena. Specialized training in core subjects such as infant care and caring for children with special health needs is available as are some curricular subjects such as art for preschoolers.

Recent information shows that a child's environment, both physical and social, has a major influence on the child's ability to learn and think. Actual brain development is hindered if the early environment is poor, and the effects of such poor environments are both long-lasting and cumulative.

If you would like to know all the licensing regulations in Maryland, you may request more information from the Child Care Administration. In greater Baltimore there are two offices of the Child Care Administration, (800) 322-6347, www.dhr.state.md.us: Baltimore City Regional Office, 2700 North Charles Street, Suite 203, (410) 554-8300; and Baltimore County Regional Office, 409 Washington Avenue, Suite LL8, Towson, (410) 583-6200. The administration also produces a pamphlet to help parents find regulated child care, *A Parent's Guide to Regulated Child Care.*

CHILD-CARE LOCATION SERVICES

The Maryland Committee For Children
608 Water Street
(410) 752-7588
www.mdchildcare.org

The Maryland Committee For Children (MCC) was created in 1946 when, at the end of World War II, the federal government rescinded funds for day-care centers and preschools for working mothers. Rosie the Riveter may have no longer been needed by the government, but in many cases Rosie's husband didn't come home from the war, and it was up to her to put a roof over her children's heads and food on the table. The MCC was founded to help her do just that. Currently, the MCC, a private nonprofit organization, serves as a clearinghouse for information about child care—where, how, and from whom to get it—as well as a training and research organization. The committee's informational arm is the Maryland Child Care Resource Network, noted below, but you can also call the MCC for information about such things as conferences, lectures, and training, as well as to request more information.

The Maryland Child Care Resource Network
(410) 625-1111
www.mdchildcare.org/mdcfc/

The Network, which is managed by the Maryland Committee For Children, includes a statewide center that is based at MCC headquarters (noted previously) and at 13 regional centers in surrounding counties. The statewide center also has two local affiliates, one in the city and one in Baltimore County, both of which offer resources and referral services at no charge. The Network also provides technical training to child-care providers. The Network helped 307,860 callers find child care for 419,539 children between September 1990 and June 2003. It has also trained more than 130,285 individuals interested in providing care or improving their programs.

Network's most dynamic service, however, is LOCATE. LOCATE is a computer database, created by MCC and available through the Maryland Child Care Resource Network and its resource centers. The database can address specific needs for the care of a specific child. For instance, if you have a child who has a learning disability and you live in Baltimore City and know that you can pay only $80 a week for child care, LOCATE can find appropriate care for your child within those parameters. Parents are given the name, address, and telephone numbers of up to 10 child-care providers or programs when they call for a referral. Other topics available through LOCATE include employers that have child care on-site, child care available through schools, and child care for children with special needs.

To reach a LOCATE counselor, call (410) 625-1111 for a 24-hour recorded message for the closest resource center or contact the Resource Center numbers that follow.

Baltimore City Child Care Resource Center
1645 Ridgely Street, Suite 200
(410) 685-5150
(410) 539-2209 (LOCATE)
www.mdchildcare.org/bx/
The Baltimore City Child Care Resource Center, one of the offices of MCC's Maryland Child Care Resource Network, can help you find child care through the LOCATE database. In addition, the center offers courses for parents in child growth and development, how to deal with childcare service providers, and other topics. This is also the place to call if you are interested in becoming a child-care provider or in starting your own child-care center. Office hours are 9:00 a.m. to 5:00 p.m. Monday through Friday. LOCATE hours are 9:30 a.m. to 3:30 p.m.

Baltimore County Child Care Links
1101 North Point Boulevard, Suite 112
(410) 288-5600 (LOCATE)
www.childcarelinks.net
Affiliated with the MCC through its LOCATE

database, Children's Services can provide a listing of all licensed child-care programs in Baltimore County, which include 1,400 family providers and 400 independent and school-based centers. A LOCATE counselor is available from 9:30 a.m. to 3:30 p.m. Monday through Friday. Because of the vast area that the office serves, however, it is sometimes difficult to get through the line. If you can't get through, call the statewide number, (410) 625-1111, and ask about listings in Baltimore County.

Because Baltimore County is so large, there are two additional offices. In the Woodlawn area in the southwest county, the office is at Campfield Early Learning Center/School at 6834 Alter Street. In Pikesville, in the northwest county, the office is at 915 Milford Mill Road.

NANNIES AND AU PAIRS

Nannies and au pairs are not licensed in Maryland, but if you choose your nanny through a referral service, he or she will receive an extensive background check.

A Choice Nanny
201 West Padonia Road, Suite 304
(410) 823-8687
This nanny referral service that has been in the area since 1983 first interviews nanny candidates for their suitability, at which time their three most prominent child-care references are checked. If the nanny is hired by one of the member parents, the company performs an extensive background check. Nanny training is also provided to both hired nannies and those interested in receiving such training. Parents interested in hiring a nanny are first interviewed for a needs assessment. Once that is complete, the parent pays a membership fee, after which the company will refer nannies for interview that it believes can fulfill the parents' needs. When a nanny is hired, parents pay an additional referral fee, usually between $900 and $1,300, depending on the parameters and salary of the job. Of course this fee is subject to change. Hourly rates are around $11 to $16 per hour.

The Nanny Network Inc.
521 East Joppa Road, Towson
(410) 321-1566
www.nanny-network.com
The Nanny Network is an independent nanny referral service serving Baltimore and surrounding counties. A member of the International Nanny Association, the Nanny Network refers nannies to families for in-home care on a permanent or temporary basis for one day, one month, or even overnight. It conducts a thorough background check of all nannies that includes credit and criminal conviction records in counties the nanny has resided in for the past five years. The Nanny Network even offers a three-month guarantee. There is no finder's fee unless you hire a nanny from the network. There is a one-time, nonrefundable application fee of $225 and a finder's fee based on the hours a nanny is hired to work. Nannies are paid $11 to $15 per hour.

Au Pair in America
(800) 928-7247
www.aupairinamerica.com
Au Pair in America is an au pair placement service under the auspices of the American Institute of Foreign Studies in Greenwich, Connecticut. It sponsors student study-abroad programs, hiring programs both here and abroad as well as other cultural and student exchange opportunities. According to Insiders at Au Pair in America, au pairs are "international visitors" who come to America for no more than 12 months to help gain a "better understanding and appreciation of American life while living with an American family and caring for their young children." The family provides room and board and a $282 weekly stipend to the au pair in return for no more than 45 hours of work per week. There is also a fee of $6,955 paid to Au Pair in America. This fee includes the au pair's travel expenses, medical, and liability insurance, and a four-day orientation. The au pair's work does not include housekeeping or other chores unless they are directly related to taking care of children. The standard au pair is not professionally trained or licensed but has child-care experience and is a young person (aged 18 to 26) who has accepted the duties associated with the care of children while he or she visits America. There is another program at AIFS called Au Pair Extraordinaire that places au pairs who have a minimum of two years of professional child-care training or two years of work experience as nannies. Call for details.

EDUCATION

Baltimore is chock-full of schools. In fact, institutions of higher learning are one of Baltimore's main draws. Such names as the Johns Hopkins University, Goucher College, Loyola College, and the University of Maryland are known worldwide for the quality of the education provided. Our private and parochial school systems are widespread as well, and our public schools offer some surprises in vocational training and the arts.

Outside of these traditional educational institutions, the Baltimore area lays claim to specialty schools that run the gamut from institutions for physically challenged children to courses that specialize in haute cuisine.

All elementary and secondary systems across the state, both public and private, have advanced courses for academics, usually known as gifted and talented or honors programs. Most systems also offer some kind of technical course or a school-to-work program. The Maryland State Department of Education requires that all students take high school assessments. They must take these tests in order to receive a Maryland diploma, and students must be in attendance for the entire duration of the test in order to receive credit for the course.

Most schools sponsor opportunities in the arts, but there are some in which the arts are the main focus, such as the Baltimore City School for the Arts, a public high school. The Polytechnic Institute specializes in engineering, offering courses for either future engineers whose grades reflect the fact that they actually enjoy doing integral calculus or for kids who just want a college-prep environment with an emphasis in math and science. Kenwood High School Sports Science Academy is for those who want to coach as well as those who are considering a career in sports medicine.

Newcomers to the area are struck by the way Baltimore's middle-aged adults identify with their high schools more than their colleges. We remain Poly boys and Western girls essentially forever. High school affiliations create instant bonding or distrust. We carry on our historic high school rivalries long after most communities would think reasonable. Gilman vs. McDonogh, Calvert Hall vs. Loyola, Poly (Polytechnic Institute) vs. City (Baltimore City College), Dunbar vs. Lake Clifton, IND (the Institute of Notre Dame) vs. Mercy—all are historic rivalries known citywide. Such rivalries heat up the competitions and make them as exciting as watching the Orioles trounce the Yankees or the Ravens beat the Redskins! Schools in Baltimore and surrounding counties have extensive intermural competition in such areas as soccer, basketball, football, and lacrosse.

Though we love a good game, Baltimore has always placed more emphasis on academics than sports. Many of our Baltimore Firsts have been in education. The first parochial school to educate African-American children was opened here, as were the first parochial schools for girls. (See Selected Baltimore Firsts in this chapter.)

In this chapter we provide an overall picture of the public school system in Baltimore City and the counties of greater Baltimore, as well as a more intimate look at some of the popular private and specialty schools, community colleges, and four-year institutions.

Among the information presented, you will occasionally find student-teacher ratios. It is important to note that these are average figures that do not necessarily reflect exact class size. For instance, in a school with an average ratio of 22 to 1, you may find some seminar classes for seniors that have only 10 students and a science class with 35. However, the ratios provide a general idea of class size, which is why we've included them.

Tuition for private schools varies considerably, depending on the school and courses selected, financial aid eligibility, etc. Therefore, we haven't included tuition rates in our listings. Most schools (not all) list tuition on their Web sites. Generally, expect to pay between $2,000 and $6,000 for Catholic elementary school and up to $20,000 for other private elementary schools. The rates go up to about $10,000 for Catholic high school and hover near $20,000 for other private high schools.

All private and parochial schools have either a strict dress code or a required uniform. Many public schools, particularly elementary schools, have uniform options, and most public high schools have some rules about acceptable attire. Call the individual school to resolve questions about uniforms and costs.

When you visit a prospective school, either private or public, elementary or university, don't just go to admissions and administration. Hang around if you can and talk to faculty and students about curricula, after-school programs and activities, and the school's approach to academic and social discipline. Their enthusiasm or lack thereof gives the best insight into what the school is really like.

PUBLIC SCHOOLS

Public education in the greater Baltimore area, as in Maryland generally, is supported by our property taxes. In past years this meant that if you were in a poorer area, such as Baltimore City or a rural county, your schools did not get as many dollars for education as those in a more affluent area. In recent years, however, the state of Maryland has tried to help the counties and the city achieve economic equality to provide needed services. Recently, the per child expenditures for a school year in greater Baltimore were $9,600 in Baltimore City; about $9,500 in Baltimore

County; $11,496 in Howard County (the third richest county in the country); and $10,721 in Anne Arundel County.

What is really helping public education reach toward excellence, however, is its growing focus on what's going on in the classroom. Maryland's systems are in the process of making area schools more accountable for the education received.

Maryland recently adopted a new set of standards for marking a school's performance, and it also issues an annual School Performance Report, which takes a comprehensive look at individual schools' success in meeting basic educational requirements. These reports are in downloadable form on the Web site, www. marylandpublicschools.org.

Baltimore Public Schools
Baltimore City Department of Education
200 East North Avenue
(410) 396-8700
www.baltimorecityschools.org
Baltimore City's schools are in the process of a rebirth. Test scores and measured skill levels are rising among the city's children, and it is expected that this trend will continue.

Baltimore City has about 86,000 students enrolled. Among the schools these are 15 extended elementary schools, which are essentially elementary/middle schools with grades K through 8, and 20 citywide schools. Among the citywide schools are some specialty schools: the Baltimore City School for the Arts, the Polytechnic Institute, the Merganthaler Vocational Technical Center, and the Carver Vocational Technical Center, just to name a few.

Whereas the School for the Arts prepares students to play for the Baltimore Symphony or head for Broadway and Polytechnic grounds college-bound engineering students in the basics of their field, the vo-tech schools offer a focus in commercial trades as diverse as carpentry and commercial art as well as an Occupation Prep program that deals with skills such as cosmetology and drafting.

Other classes allow students to pursue a

more specialized path at nonspecialty schools. The Tech Prep program permits high school students to take courses in biotechnology, business technology, electronics/computer repair technology, child care, travel and tourism, and machine tool technology in addition to their regular coursework. Tech Prep was created in conjunction with Baltimore City Community College and is meant to help a student take courses relating to a chosen career as early as the ninth grade.

ROTC and CollegeBound are also offered at the high school level. The individual school listings book, *Planning Your High School Program*, is available free from Baltimore City Schools; it can tell you which schools offer what. Contact the Department of Education at the previously listed number for a copy to be sent to you.

Staffing Baltimore's schools are more than 6,600 teachers and nearly 1,000 school-based support staff and schoolbased administrators, who account for more than 60 percent of the employees of the Baltimore school system. Overall, student-teacher ratios are 25 to 1. The late 1990s saw significant betterment in the Baltimore City school system. Several national foundations, including the Bill and Melinda Gates Foundation, contributed some $20.75 million, fueling the transformation of nine large Baltimore City neighborhood high schools into smaller learning communities. The city's Master Plan II has goals, through the 2008 school year, for improving student achievment with clean, safe schools, more parent involvement, and better instruction.

Communities have the go-ahead to institute programs that they feel are needed for their children, and they're acting quickly to put new elements into play for their kids. Elementary schools, for instance, have already created after-school enrichment and/or tutoring programs that extend the school day, thereby helping out with child care and also

Selected Baltimore Firsts

John Archer was the first medical student ever to be granted a degree from an American medical school. The year was 1768.

The Baltimore College of Dental Surgery, the first dental college in the world, opened in February 1840.

The first Catholic school for African-American girls in the United States, St. Frances Academy, opened in 1828. Today a coeducational institution, the school is still in operation at 501 East Chase Street.

Eastern High School and Western High School opened in 1844. They were the first publicly supported high schools for girls in the United States.

The Baltimore Female College, the first women's teaching college in the United States, opened its doors in 1849. It is now known as Goucher College, a premier coed liberal arts college.

Thanks to the prodding of Hugh Bond, the owner and resident of Mount Royal Mansion in the mid-1800s, Baltimore was the first city to create publicly supported schools for African-American children. This was particularly important to Baltimore because by 1865 its citizenry included the largest population of black freemen in the country.

In 1895 the first Catholic college for women in the United States, The College of Notre Dame of Maryland, opened its doors in Baltimore.

—*Excerpted from* Baltimore—America's City of Firsts, *a pamphlet published by Baltimore Bicentennial Celebration, Inc.*

creating another avenue to improve student performance. Nearly all of Baltimore City's elementary schools have such programs, and their success is helping test results move upward—sometimes in double digits.

Baltimore County Public Schools
6901 North Charles Street, Towson
(410) 887-5555
www.bcps.org

The Baltimore County Public School System is the 25th-largest in the United States. It serves 107,000 school-aged children. Choices of study include many options outside traditional academic areas, from carpentry to quilting and everything in between.

The county uses in all its schools a program called Values Education and Ethical Behavior that seeks to address values and ethics issues in the curricula, to speak to their practical application. The program is not a laundry list of values and ethics, but, as the county schools' yearly report noted, a "process of inquiry to help students pose and understand . . . ethical questions and dilemmas." A relatively unusual program, it covers everything from encouraging students to be honest and compassionate to asking larger ethical questions about scientific discovery and what constitutes responsible citizenship.

Of the county's 163 schools, 25 are magnet schools. Magnet schools offer special programs that draw students from all over a particular geographic area. At the elementary levels, it is area alone that determines if your child may enter a particular magnet school. At the middle school level, entrance is determined by prior academic achievement, student interest, and geographic location. At the high school level, geographic area still plays a part in most cases, but that area is either county-wide or a large general area, such as northern Baltimore County. And if for some reason the student is not in the chosen area but has the qualifications and desire for the education offered at the site, then he or she may be admitted by special permission. Magnet programs of study at the high school level include

such offerings as the Lansdowne Academy of Finance, the Kenwood High School Sports Science Academy, and the Towson High School Law and Public Policy Program.

The county also has four alternative schools for students with emotional and behavioral difficulties.

Academically, Baltimore County offers a relatively competitive environment, which includes advanced placement courses and testing. Using the state standards for performance, Baltimore County matched or exceeded state standards in 97 percent of the areas measured.

Baltimore County spends $9,500 on each pupil annually, and the student-teacher ratio is 22 to 1. The average dropout rate is 4.1 percent.

Anne Arundel County Public Schools
2644 Riva Road, Annapolis
(410) 222-5000
www.aacps.org

The Anne Arundel County school system is the fifth-largest school system in Maryland and among the 50 largest systems in the United States. Anne Arundel has more than 5,300 teachers teaching 75,000 students in 118 educational sites. Because of the county's size and primarily rural/suburban configuration, more than two-thirds of those students are bused to school. The county spends about $10,721 per student.

The system offers a pre-K program in selected schools as well as traditional kindergarten through twelfth grade education across the board. In addition to the basics, Anne Arundel schools offer instruction in art, music, physical education, health, library media, family and consumer sciences, computers, and technology.

The county also has two centers of applied technology at which secondary students may specialize in career and technology education. The International Baccalaureate Program is offered at three high schools: Annapolis, Old Mill, and Meade.

Howard County Public Schools
10910 Maryland Highway 108,
Ellicott City
(410) 313-6600
www.hcpss.org
Howard County Schools continually rank as one of the top public school systems in the state. In 2006 more than 90 percent of its high school graduates went on to higher education. In 2006 the average score for a Howard County high school junior on the SAT was 1,096, which is higher than the overall Maryland average and higher than the national average.

The system serves 48,221 students, but projections foresee a 20 percent increase in student population, at about 1,000 students per year. Student-teacher ratios, however, average 23 to 1. Already the largest employer in the county, Howard County Public Schools employs more than 4,000 teachers, 50 percent of whom hold master's or doctorate degrees.

PRIVATE SCHOOLS

Baltimore has an extensive system of private and parochial institutions. Subsequently we've listed the high schools and K through 12 institutions. We have not listed private or parochial elementary and middle schools, but you can usually expect to find at least one of each serving your neighborhood. And these are not just Catholic schools, but Christian schools of many denominations as well as other religion-based schools and those classed as alternative. If you need information on a parochial elementary school in your area, it is best to contact your house of worship or simply look under Schools in the Yellow Pages.

Downtown

Institute of Notre Dame (IND)
901 North Aisquith Street
(410) 522-7800
www.indofmd.org
IND is a college preparatory high school for girls run by the School Sisters of Notre Dame. The school offers three degree programs:

general academic, college preparatory, and Theresian Honors. Advanced placement courses are also available. Basketball, crew, soccer, baseball, theater, chorus, and many, many more extracurricular activities and service clubs tend to keep the girls way past their normal school hours, but there are few complaints. The school boasts a 20-to-1 student-teacher ratio for its 423 students and a competitive academic environment. The school consistently achieves the statistic of 100 percent of IND graduates moving on to additional education. IND is the only all-girls school in the country that can count two members of United States Congress among its alumnae: Senator Barbara Mikulski (class of 1954) and Speaker of the House Nancy D'Alesandro Pelosi (class of 1958). (For more information on IND, see the Close-up in this chapter.) IND has recently increased its scholarship program.

St. Frances Academy
501 East Chase Street
(410) 539-5794
www.sfacademy.org
St. Frances Academy was founded in 1828 by Mother Mary Lange, foundress of the Oblate Sisters of Providence, who is currently being considered for sainthood by the Roman Catholic Church. The building in which St. Frances is housed once served as the mother house for the Oblate Sisters as well as an orphanage and a boarding school for young women. St. Frances was the first parochial school to be created to educate African-American children and currently serves a coeducational student body of about 280 in a college preparatory curriculum in grades 9 through 12. St. Frances serves what's deemed the "disenfranchised" student, i.e., that student who has not been performing up to his or her intellectual or social potential. The school's instructional success can be measured by the fact that more than 90 percent of its graduates go on to post-secondary education. Though a historically African-American school, the school is open to students of all

Close-up

How to Apply to Private Schools

Private and Catholic schools schedule school fairs to give prospective students an informal look at a variety of schools at one time. The Association of Independent Maryland Schools, a group of more than 100 private college preparatory schools, holds their school fair in late September. A wide variety of schools, including religious schools, are represented here. For the actual date and listing of schools, visit www.aimsmd.org.

The Archdiocese of Baltimore's Division of Catholic Schools holds two high school fairs in September. The first is held the Sunday after Labor Day at the University of Maryland Baltimore County west of Baltimore City from 3:00 to 5:00 p.m. The second is usually held the next Sunday at another location, frequently at College of Notre Dame, on the northern edges of the city. It is also held from 3:00 to 5:00 p.m.

During the summer, schools with openings in any grade take part in a school fair held at Archbishop Curley High School in east Baltimore. It is usually held on a weekday in mid-July from 6:00 to 8:00 p.m. These schools are still accepting students for the upcoming school year.

All of the Catholic high schools coordinate their placement test date so prospective students may take the test at any school the second Saturday in December at 8:30 a.m. The test comes just before applications are due to the schools. For details, visit www.archbalt.org/schools or call (800) 5CATHOLIC.

races and economic backgrounds. Class size averages about 25 or less.

Northeast

Archbishop Curley High School
3701 Sinclair Lane
(410) 485-5000
www.curley.loyola.edu
www.archbishopcurley.org

"Curley" is an all-male college preparatory high school with a well-developed arts program. The school opened on its 33-acre site in 1961 to serve its surrounding, then densely Catholic, neighborhoods, but it now accepts students from all over the state, some coming from as far away as northern Baltimore County, Carroll County, Harford County, and Cecil County. For a boy who is interested in math but would also like to play trumpet, Curley is made to order. The school has professional-quality orchestra, dance, and jazz bands. They rock the house! There are also newer visual arts programs for budding painters, photographers, and other artists. The school encourages parent involvement and is proud of the fact that many of its parents continue to work with and for the school long after their own boys have graduated. Current enrollment is 621. The student-teacher ratio is 13 to 1.

Calvert Hall College
8102 Lasalle Road, Towson
(410) 825-4266
www.calverthall.com

Calvert Hall College was the first Christian Brothers school in the country, established in

Close-up

Learning in the Midst of Ghosts and History

The Institute of Notre Dame (IND) has ghosts. A Union soldier is seen walking post in an upstairs hall. In the old dormitories, a 40-year-old candle left on a side table by its last occupant spontaneously erupts into flame. A mother trying to find the school offices gets lost and is shown the way by a soft voice that comes from the direction of a large statue of the Virgin Mary. No one else is there.

Stories like these abound at IND, and it's no wonder. The school and its building share a palpable connection with the spirits of the young women who have trod its halls. A short walk up the central staircase, its slate stairs deeply indented by more than 100 years of footsteps, will transport you to another time. Like the city of Baltimore itself, IND is infused with history.

IND's history began when Mother Theresa of Jesus Gerhardinger, who helped found the School Sisters of Notre Dame (SSND) in her native Germany, crossed the Atlantic with four others intent on educating immigrant girls. The school's original mission included only German immigrants, but it very quickly reached out to serve all Catholic girls and has, for many years now, focused simply on girls without regard to race or faith. A typical class at IND is an eclectic mix: 4 percent from the city and the remainder from surrounding areas as far as an hour's drive.

When the site for the school was chosen in 1847, it was outside the city's limits, with rolling hills and ancient trees. The Baltimore & Ohio Railroad was still laying new track when the modern marvel of the telegraph had just been discovered, and the United States of America was only 60 years old.

The initial buildings for the school were little more than large cabins, which between 1852 and 1925 were changed and added on as growth demanded, to become the blocklong complex of buildings that is still used

1845 by the first American Christian Brother who was himself barely out of seminary at 17 years old. The first year it was in operation, the school had 100 students. In operation for more than 150 years and at its 33-acre campus in Towson for about 40 years, this all-boys college preparatory school serves approximately 1,200 students today. Academically competitive, Calvert Hall also has a full complement of arts and athletics. The Activities Center, for instance, houses Calvert Hall's art studios and learning resource center as well as its swimming pool and weight training room, and Calvert Hall's marching band is as well known as its football team. The student-teacher ratio is 12 to 1, with an average class size of 21.

The Catholic High School of Baltimore
2800 Edison Highway
(410) 732-6200
www.thecatholichighschool.org
Catholic High, begun in 1939 and currently

today. Although a new gymnasium was added in 1902, the buildings look much as they did at the turn of the last century. SSND sisters still reside in the original brick convent, with its stunning stained-glass windows and tongue-in-groove wainscot. And the school building is as it was, complete with underground catacombs and stables, although students are no longer allowed access to these last two.

The student dormitories, which had not been used for more than 30 years, were rehabilitated in 1996 and 1997 to become the Caroline Center, a job training center for neighborhood women in East Baltimore. But this was just IND's most recent community outreach program.

IND was one of Baltimore's many stops on the Underground Railroad, in which former slaves on their way to freedom were housed, fed, and clothed, then passed on to those who could see them to safety.

When Civil War battle raged, the catacombs beneath the school served as an infirmary, where nuns nursed both Union and Confederate soldiers back to health or, if that was not possible, buried them.

As the city grew up around it, IND surmounted city problems. The school suffered through the Great Baltimore Fire of 1904, which decimated the area all around it but left the school unscathed. It has also survived two World Wars and the Depression and was left untouched by the riots of 1968.

Through it all, safe within, have been the girls. The study is intensive; the homework, extensive. Students spend their days learning through aggressive instruction and thoughtful debate, and their evenings pouring through Faulkner. As in any school, there is time to relax, places to make friends. There are games to cheer, places to serve.

IND is not so different from many schools in Baltimore that have a long history and an ongoing mission, but the fact that it remains constant, viewing all from its unique vantage point, provides a subtle thread that ties together generations of women under one spirited umbrella of tradition and history.

serving 277 students, is an areawide college preparatory school for girls. The school offers two primary focuses: technology and the arts. Fine-arts offerings include advanced-placement opportunities in art and chorus, but the technology side boasts not only state-of-the-art equipment but also state-of-the-art teachers. Every week teachers are trained in the latest technological offerings, so that students in their turn receive, literally, up-to-the-minute knowledge. This unique competitive curriculum offers a general academic degree, a college preparatory degree, and the McAfferty Honors program, but what is most interesting about the school is its individualized approach. Courses are mixed and matched depending on the ability of the student, so that a freshman with talent in math could be placed in pre-calculus, rather than having to wade through the typical freshman math. Catholic High's student-teacher ratio is 17 to 1.

Loyola Blakefield
500 Chestnut Avenue, Towson
(410) 823-0601
www.loyolablakefield.org

Loyola was founded in tandem with Loyola College in 1852 by the Jesuit order of the Catholic Church. The college broke off from the school in 1921 and by 1934 the high school had moved to its present site at Blakefield. Today's Loyola is a competitive college preparatory middle and high school (grades 9 through 12) serving 1,005 boys. The school's stated mission is to "teach boys to be men for others." In that regard, the school fosters mentor/adviser relationships between the boys and their teachers and coaches and offers opportunities for retreats, service projects, and athletics in addition to a regular academic curriculum. The student-teacher ratio is 15 to 1, and about 7 percent of the teachers are Jesuit priests or scholars.

Mercy High School
1300 East Northern Parkway
(410) 433-8880
www.mercyhighschool.com

Mercy High School, run by the Sisters of Mercy, was built in 1960 to serve a burgeoning Northeast city population. On a campus that takes up most of the large block between Loch Raven Boulevard and The Alameda, Mercy serves 553 female students with a college preparatory curriculum. One of Mercy's offerings is the Advisor Program, in which the school has created a new relationship between adviser and student. Typically, advisers are apart from students, sitting in their offices, waiting for the students to come to them with questions. Also, typically, advisers are attached to a particular graduating class, so that one adviser serves 100 or more students. In Mercy's Advisor Program, an adviser is attached to only 15 or so students whom she follows through their four years at the school. She acts as homeroom contact, mentor, and sometimes mediator, but over the students' high school careers, she becomes a vested part of each girl's success. In the past Mercy's graduating seniors received close to $4.2 million in scholarships and grants, and 95 percent entered college. The student-teacher ratio is 19 to 1.

Notre Dame Preparatory School (NDP)
815 Hampton Lane, Towson
(410) 825-6202
www.notredameprep.org

Founded in 1873 by the School Sisters of Notre Dame to complement the Institute of Notre Dame, NDP opened in 1874 as the Notre Dame Collegiate Institute for Young Ladies on what was then wilderness acreage where the College of Notre Dame now stands. At its current campus on Hampton Lane, NDP offers a competitive, college preparatory curriculum to more than 740 girls in grades 6 through 12. NDP boasts an active social service program, which includes the students' working with abused children at Villa Maria, spending time with patients at AIDS hospices, and working with Habitat for Humanity, among other projects. Its student-teacher ratio is 16 to 1.

Towson Catholic High School
114 Ware Avenue, Towson
(410) 427-4900
www.towsoncatholic.org

Founded in 1922, Towson Catholic is the oldest coeducational Catholic high school in greater Baltimore. Once staffed entirely by nuns, Towson Catholic is now taught entirely by lay faculty with a student-teacher ratio of 11 to 1. A small private school with only 275 students, Towson Catholic considers its size an advantage in creating a healthy environment in which young men and women can get to know one another and feel comfortable enough to actively compete with one another. Close to 98 percent of Towson Catholic's graduates go on to higher education.

Northwest

Bais Yaakov School for Girls
11111 Park Heights Avenue, Owings Mills
(410) 363-3300
www.baisyaakov.net

Bais Yaakov School opened in 1942 to provide a comprehensive education to Jewish girls of all backgrounds. Bais Yaakov has a lower school (grades pre-K through 6) as well as an upper school (7 through 12) that teaches a competitive college preparatory curriculum. In addition, Bais Yaakov's Hebrew Department provides extensive study in Jewish history, customs, the Hebrew language, problems, ethics, and philosophy as well as study of the Torah. The school is open to all without regard to race, color, or national or ethnic origin, but it does require that the girl seeking admission be of the Jewish faith. More than 1,300 students attend Bais Yaakov. The overall student-teacher ratio is 8 to 1.

Beth Tfiloh Dahan Community School
3300 Old Court Road
(410) 486-1900
www.btfiloh.org

Beth Tfiloh Community School opened on its 20-acre campus in west Baltimore County in 1942 with only five students in kindergarten. Currently, the school provides the only coeducational college preparatory curriculum in greater Baltimore for Jewish study in grades pre-K through 12. Because of its comprehensive course of Jewish study, the school has never had a student of another faith attend, but it does not prohibit such attendance, and it openly encourages participation of all Jewish denominations. Beth Tfiloh offers advanced-placement classes and an honors track for its high school students as well as some interesting internships and study opportunities, including Senior Seminars in Israel. Enrollment is about 1,037. The student-teacher ratio is 7 to 1 with a staff of 150 teachers.

Boys Latin School of Maryland
822 West Lake Avenue
(410) 377-5192
www.boyslatinmd.com

Boys Latin School, a college preparatory day school, began in the mind of Evert Marsh Topping, a professor of long-standing at Princeton University, who over time had come to believe that standard teaching methods of the time did not teach students to think and understand, and that only through understanding did children truly learn. This revolutionary idea prompted him to come to Baltimore and open his own private school in 1846. The current Boys Latin School, which straddles the city-county line just west of our east/west dividing line of Charles Street, has more than 600 boys in grades K through 12. The school's educational focus is to build on each boy's strengths and not harp on his weaknesses. The median SAT score is 1120. The student-teacher ratio is 15 to 1.

Bryn Mawr School
109 West Melrose Avenue
(410) 323-8800
www.brynmawr.pvt.k12.md.us

Bryn Mawr was founded in 1885 on the belief that women were entitled to the same classical education that boys were receiving at the time. Bryn Mawr today has a competitive college preparatory curriculum, while still providing its girls with extensive opportunities in art, music, and athletics. Bryn Mawr has a comprehensive language department and is one of the few schools that teaches more than just Spanish and French in its middle and upper schools. Greek, German, Russian, and Chinese are also available. Enrollment is about 796 in grades K through 12 and in a coed preschool group and day care. An eclectic group of students just around the corner from Roland Park Country and Gilman schools, Bryn Mawr coordinates some classes with both of those schools in grades 9 through 12. The student-teacher ratio averages 15 to 1.

Friends School
5114 North Charles Street
(410) 649-3200
www.friendsbalt.org

Friends School is the oldest school in Baltimore. Founded in 1784 by the Quakers, it originally stood on Aisquith Street but had many incarnations until it found its present location in 1925. Halfway between Towson and the Inner Harbor on a well-traveled stretch of road, and now nonsectarian, the school has a large campus that includes woods and stream and the use of the Roland Park swimming pool for its summer camp. The school and the camp make good use of the dance studio, fitness room, two gymnasiums, outdoor tennis courts, five playing fields, and two practice fields. Students attend Meeting on a regular basis and are encouraged in critical thinking and problem solving as well as academics. Nearly 1,000 students attend the school, pre-K through 12. The student-faculty ratio is 17 to 1, with 113 teachers.

Garrison Forest School
300 Garrison Forest Road, Owings Mills
(410) 363-1500
www.gfs.org

Garrison Forest was founded in 1910 as a day school for the girls of families living in Greenspring Valley, which at that time was very far away from city schools. By 1912 the school had established a boarding program, and it still offers boarding for girls in grades 8 through 12 as well as day school for girls K through 12 and a coeducational pre-K for students from age two. Approximately 660 students from all over the world, including the Pacific Rim, Latin and Central America, the Caribbean, and parts of Europe, are enrolled. The school has a new performing arts center, new lower school, and new riding and athletic facilities. Garrison Forest underwent a campus-wide rewiring that allows students to access the school's computers from anywhere, dorm to classroom. The student-teacher ratio is 10 to 1.

Gilman School
5407 Roland Avenue
(410) 323-3800
www.gilman.edu

Gilman School, the first country day school in the United States, turned 100 years old in 1997. The school was conceived by Anne Galbraith Carey, who also founded the Women's Civic League in Baltimore and worked to help found the Girl Scouts in Maryland. At the time Carey was simply looking for a healthy educational environment in which to place her eight-year-old son that was not attached to a military or religious discipline. Approximately 970 boys attend Gilman on its 64-acre campus in Roland Park. Because of the country school concept, which seeks to educate the body as well as the mind, athletics at Gilman are almost as important as the academics. Gilman is competitive academically, as evidenced by the number of seniors moving on to top colleges and universities.

Maryvale Preparatory School for Girls
11300 Falls Road, Brooklandville
(410) 252-3366
www.maryvale.com

Begun in 1945 by the Sisters of Notre Dame De Namur as a boarding school, Maryvale had only 12 students when it opened. That was OK by the sisters, however, whose mission was to set up a school that was small by design so each girl would receive a lot of individual attention. Staying true to the sisters' mission, only 370 day students are enrolled in grades 6 through 12, and the student-teacher ratio is only 9 to 1. Citing a very competitive college preparatory curriculum, Maryvale's academic focus encourages girls in mathematics and the sciences. A Science and Student Center was completed in 1997 and houses computer and science labs. Maryvale boasts a championship-winning athletic department, strong in field hockey, basketball, volleyball, lacrosse, and softball. Its choruses produce two musicals each year. Community service is an important part of every Maryvale girl's life, with ample opportu-

EDUCATION
nities to take part in fund-raising for breast
cancer research, foreign missions, and other
charities. Girls also serve meals at a Fells Point
soup kitchen at least once a month.

McDonogh School
8600 McDonogh Road, McDonogh
(410) 363-0600
www.mcdonogh.org
The American Civil War orphaned thousands
of children and destroyed much of the South,
including its schools. Philanthropist John
McDonogh must have had this on his mind, for
when he died, he willed money to fund a public school system in Louisiana and the
McDonogh Farm School for orphaned boys in
Maryland. McDonogh opened in 1873 on its
800-acre campus with a multiracial student
body that worked the farm, growing vegetables, raising pigs, and milking cows. The original headmaster, Col. William Allen, who had
fought with the Confederacy under Stonewall
Jackson, imposed a military discipline and the
military uniforms the boys wore were Confederate gray. Today, the school's original mandate to serve students in need is still very
much in evidence, but the school has changed
a lot in the last 35 years. Now coed, with day
students as well as five-day boarders, the
semimilitary atmosphere was dropped in
1971, and the farm no longer exists, save for
the horse barn and riding facilities. Every
McDonogh student learns to ride, and horsey
amenities include riding rings and yearly horse
shows. Other athletic pursuits include the
more conventional football, lacrosse, tennis,
golf, and swimming. Teachers, as well as students, live on campus, eat in the dining hall,
and take part in campus life. The college
preparatory curriculum is competitive, and virtually 100 percent of McDonogh's graduates
now go on to further education. The student-
teacher ratio is 15 to 1.

The Park School
2425 Old Court Road, Brooklandville
(410) 339-7070
www.parkschool.net

The Park School was founded in 1912 as a
progressive school. A progressive school is
one in which children are guided toward
moral behavior, self-discipline, and intellectual
achievement. Park is a nonsectarian, independent, coeducational day school. A 27,000-
square-foot science, math, and technology
center opened in 1997, and both the middle
and upper schools have been renovated to
better support Park's seminar style of teaching. Approximately 875 students are enrolled
in grades pre-K through 12. The student-
teacher ratio is 15 to 1.

Roland Park Country School
5204 Roland Avenue
(410) 323-5500
www.rpcs.org
Roland Park Country School (RPCS) began in
1894 as a neighborhood school housed in a
private home. By 1901 it had won sponsor-
ship from the Roland Park Company and eventually became the first fully accredited
independent school for girls in Baltimore City.
RPCS places emphasis on both academic
achievement and athletic accomplishment. It
fields teams in traditional sports such as field
hockey and lacrosse as well as more unusual
ones for girls, such as crew. There are 710
girls in grades K through 12, who are, according to *U.S. News & World Report*, consistently
admitted into the nation's 25 most selective
liberal arts colleges and universities. One of
its 1996 graduates made headlines when she
achieved a perfect score on her SAT. The
student-faculty ratio is 14 to 1 in the upper
school and 18–20 to 1 in the lower school.

St. Paul's School, 11152 Falls Road,
Brooklandville
(410) 825-4400
www.stpaulschool.org

St. Paul's School for Girls, 11232 Falls Road,
Brooklandville
(410) 823-6323
www.spsfg.org
St. Paul's School, an all-boys school, and St.

319

Libraries

Downtown

The Enoch Pratt Free Library is one of the oldest free public library systems in the United States. Over a span of 120 years, the Enoch Pratt has established 24 branches throughout the city and the county and has evolved a reputation as one of the finest resources in Baltimore. Book loans are just part of the services. The library offers technology centers, kids' events, and career assistance. Research rooms carry reference books with up-to-date census information and crime stats, which can be very helpful when deciding where to buy a home.

Enoch Pratt Free Library Main Branch
400 Cathedral Street
(410) 396-5430

Surrounding Counties

The Baltimore County Public Library system has 18 branches peppering the five counties surrounding the city. A full list of all branches is available on the Web site www.bcplonline.org or by calling the administrative offices at (410) 887-6100. Here are a few of the larger branches:

Towson Branch
320 York Road
(410) 887-6166

Catonsville Branch
1100 Frederick Road
(410) 887-0951

Pikesville Branch
1301 Reisterstown Road
(410) 887-1234

White Marsh
8133 Sandpiper Circle
(410) 887-5097

Paul's School for Girls are separate schools, with separate campuses, budgets, and boards of directors. They are, however, closely associated, not only because their campuses adjoin but also because both schools share day-care, kindergarten, and lower school facilities. The coeducational day care and kindergarten, called St. Paul's Plus, is administered by the girls' school. The lower school, administered by and located at the boys' school, provides primary education for boys and girls planning to attend middle and high school (grades 5 through 12) at both St. Paul's schools.

St. Paul's School
www.stpaulsschool.org
Founded in 1849 by Old St. Paul's Church as a school for poor boys in Baltimore's down-

town, the school moved to its 68-acre campus in Brooklandville in 1952. A private school that still enjoys association with Old St. Paul's, St. Paul's School offers a single-sex Episcopal education with the added benefit of coeducational classes and activities with St. Paul's for Girls at the high school level. St. Paul's welcomes students of all races, cultures, and religions, noting that its focus is to help students realize their spiritual selves and to enable them to participate in all parts of their lives. St. Paul's student body numbers 867 students in the lower, middle, and upper schools. The student-teacher ratio is 9 to 1. The campus includes the Ward Center for the Arts, a 28,000-square-foot facility for the dramatic, vocal, and fine arts, jointly operated with St. Paul's School for Girls.

St. Paul's School for Girls
www.spsfg.org

The history of St. Paul's School for Girls goes all the way back to 1799, when the Benevolent Society of the City and County of Baltimore founded a school for poor and orphan girls under the auspices of Old St. Paul's Church. After many incarnations, the current school was founded in 1959. More than 480 girls participate in a college preparatory curriculum and a strong athletic program at the 38-acre campus. One of St. Paul's most interesting instructional features is its morning gathering called prayers, in which all students and teachers share concerns and school news. The student-teacher ratio is 9 to 1.

St. Timothy's School
8400 Greenspring Avenue, Stevenson
(410) 486-7400
www.sttims-school.org

St. Timothy's was founded in 1882. In 1974, Hannah More Academy, the oldest Episcopal girls' boarding school in the country, merged with St. Timothy's. Today, the expanded St. Timothy's offers boarding and day school from grade 9 through postgraduate studies for 136 girls on a stunning 234-acre campus in Greenspring Valley. With 70 percent of its students living on campus and a student-to-faculty ratio of 4 to 1, St. Timothy's girls receive close attention in a community atmosphere that seeks to "develop each person's ability to live thoughtfully in a community of diverse and unique individuals."

Academically, St. Tim's is competitive, with virtually 100 percent of its graduates heading for higher education. Average SAT scores hover around 1120. Not all learning is in the classroom, however. Throughout the students' tenure, the school offers off-campus experiences through a program called Connections, in which students study the political, social, economic, and cultural aspects of Baltimore, Annapolis, and Washington, D.C. And in the senior year, students perform three weeks of independent study in which they become corporate interns.

> **i** The Enoch Pratt Library loans more than just books. The downtown branch on Cathedral also offers an extensive video and music collection, and the rental fees are about half that of major video rental stores

Students interested in athletics have the opportunity to compete in eight interscholastic sports, including tennis and riding. And students who tend toward the artistic have at their disposal a theater complete with costume shop, dance studio, and music practice rooms as well as the Art Barn, which boasts darkrooms and kilns.

Talmudical Academy of Baltimore
4445 Old Court Road, Pikesville
(410) 484-6600
www.talmudicalacademy.org

Talmudical Academy is the oldest Jewish day school in the United States outside of New York. Founded in 1917, its intent was to provide young Jewish boys with an Orthodox environment in which they could receive a secular education as well as a religious one. It still serves this need. Boys in pre-K through grade 12 spend mornings in study of the Hebrew alphabet, the Torah, and other sacred Hebrew texts. In the afternoon, they pursue the reading, writing, and arithmetic part of their education.

Talmudical serves 625 students in classes of 16 to 20 students. The student-teacher ratio is 10 to 1.

Southwest

The Cardinal Gibbons School
3225 Wilkens Avenue
(410) 644-1770
www.cardinalgibbons.com

The Cardinal Gibbons School was established in 1959 on the site of Babe Ruth's alma mater, St. Mary's Industrial School. Originally chosen because it provided space for athletic fields and a convent, the large campus and school serves more than 200 boys in a college preparatory program for grades 6 through 12. Gibbons students average 16 points higher than the national average on SAT scores. The student-teacher ratio is 10 to 1.

Mount Saint Joseph High School
4403 Frederick Avenue
(410) 644-3300
www.msjnet.edu

St. Joe's, as it is lovingly called, began in 1876 on the prayer of one Brother Bernardine, who asked for the intervention of Saint Joseph to help him and his Xaverian Brothers find the money to start the school. Although St. Joe's has a balanced college preparatory curriculum, the focus in its advanced-placement courses is on science. The school recently added a 30,000-square-foot, state-of-the-art media and technology building to its pastoral 31-acre campus and is set to upgrade its athletic facilities. The school serves approximately 1,100 boys and has a student-teacher ratio of 12 to 1.

Seton Keough High School
1201 South Caton Avenue
(410) 646-4444
www.setonkeough.com

Seton Keough is a hybrid that was created in 1988 when Seton High School, a midtown city high school for girls founded by the Daughters of Charity in 1865, merged with Archbishop Keough High School and moved out to its 30-acre campus where Keough had been since its founding by the School Sisters of Notre Dame in 1965. Seton Keough offers a comprehensive college preparatory program for all its girls that includes advanced-placement classes as well as the Marillac Program, for students with special needs, and the Focus program, for students who enter the school achieving below their grade level in major subject areas. More than 550 students are enrolled at Seton Keough. The student-to-faculty ratio is approximately 12 to 1.

COLLEGES AND UNIVERSITIES

College of Notre Dame of Maryland
4701 North Charles Street
(410) 435-0100
www.ndm.edu

The College of Notre Dame (CND) handed out its first baccalaureate degrees in 1896. An all-woman's college, CND began when graduates of Notre Dame Preparatory School cried out for post-secondary education. A two-year then a four-year college grew from this need, and CND still stands on the land that was originally set aside for Notre Dame Prep. CND focuses on liberal arts in its full-time, weekday program and offers 22 majors. CND also offers a Weekend College and a flexible master's degree program for men and women with full-time jobs. The college also offers a continuing education program for older women who are seeking their bachelor of arts degrees. Full-time day students on the Charles Street campus number 825, but overall enrollment is more than 3,000 in 27 major fields of study. Dormitory facilities house 440 students. The school also offers educational opportunities through community colleges in surrounding counties, including an "RN to BSN" program in Frederick County.

Goucher College
1021 Dulaney Valley Road, Towson
(410) 337-6000
www.goucher.edu

Goucher was founded in 1885 as a liberal arts college for women in midtown Baltimore. It moved to its 287-acre Towson campus in 1953 and began accepting male students in 1986. Goucher counts among its student body about 1,200 undergraduates and 700 graduate students from all over the United States and 20 foreign countries. It offers undergraduate majors in 18 departments and five interdisciplinary areas; students can also design their own majors. Study abroad is now a Goucher requirement. Internships and independent study and research are encouraged and in some cases required for graduation.

Approximately 75 percent of Goucher's graduates pursue advanced degrees. Master's degrees in education, teaching, historic preservation, and creative nonfiction as well as a postbaccalaureate premedical program are available through Goucher. The college recently broke ground for its Athenaeum, a 24-hour library and community building. It opens in 2009.

The Johns Hopkins University
Charles and 34th Streets
(410) 516-8000
www.jhu.edu

The Johns Hopkins University (JHU) was founded in 1876 when, upon his death, Johns Hopkins willed $7 million to create it and The Johns Hopkins Hospital. Then, as now, the hospital and the university work hand in hand, so that research, instruction, and practical application are all put together in one neat package. JHU was the first university in the United States to employ this all-encompassing method of teaching that was modeled after the European research teaching methods of the time.

Originally an all-white male facility, JHU admitted its first African-American student in 1887, but admitted women only sparingly over the years until 1970, when it officially became a coeducational facility. More than 16,000 full- and part-time students of both sexes and all colors are enrolled at its three major mid-Atlantic campuses and campuses in China and Italy. The Homewood campus in Baltimore serves almost 5,000 of those students in its two major schools: the Krieger School of Arts and Sciences and the Whiting School of Engineering, which offer master's and doctorate degree programs as well as bachelor's degrees of both arts and science. The East Baltimore campus where the hospital is located also houses the schools of Medicine, Nursing, and Hygiene and Public Health.

Some of Hopkins' special divisions include the Paul H. Nitze School of Advanced International Studies and the Applied Physics Laboratory, and Hopkins also now runs the Peabody Institute (see the Peabody's entry under Specialty Schools later in this chapter).

A highly competitive private university, JHU has extensive community outreach. Intercollegiate sports are well attended, particularly lacrosse and football, and the annual Hopkins Fair (see the Annual Events chapter) is always crowded. JHU, which is the largest private employer in Baltimore, has its fingers in many pies, including building and renovating city buildings in cooperation with Habitat for Humanity on the volunteer level and through Dome Corporation, a Hopkins subsidiary, on the corporate level.

Loyola College in Maryland
4501 North Charles Street
(800) 221-9107
www.loyola.edu

Loyola College in Maryland was founded in 1852 by the Jesuit order as an all-male postsecondary institution. In 1971 it merged with Mount St. Agnes College (an all-women's college) and became a coeducational facility. Loyola includes the College of Arts and Sciences and the Sellinger School of Business and Management, which offer undergraduate, graduate, and professional development programs. Loyola has more than 3,400 undergraduates in on-campus and study-abroad programs and 2,600 graduate students. Its eclectic student body includes students from 41 states and 48 foreign countries, 77 percent of whom live on the main campus. However, Loyola also offers classes at campuses in Columbia and Hunt Valley, Maryland, as well as Belgium, Thailand, and England. Classes are also offered through community colleges in Anne Arundel, Harford, and Cecil Counties, and graduate classes are accessible through a site in Timonium. A competitive school, more than 58 percent of Loyola's students graduated from high school in the top fifth of their classes.

Morgan State University
1700 East Cold Spring Lane
(410) 885-3333
www.morgan.edu

Morgan State University was founded in 1867 by members of the Baltimore Methodist Episcopal Church to educate African Americans and prepare them for the Methodist clergy. Its mission quickly expanded to include educating teachers. For almost a century, Morgan functioned as a private college, but in 1968 it was accepted under the umbrella of the University System of Maryland, and with its resources became a university in 1975. Oddly, however, enrollment dwindled down to 2,000 students, until 1984 when in an effort to save itself, the school once again became independent. With current enrollments at 6,000 and a full-time faculty of 300, it has become one of the fastest growing campuses in the state. An independent state university, Morgan offers master's and doctorate programs as well as baccalaureate degrees in the arts and sciences but notes particular strengths in science and engineering, where it has seen it greatest growth. Although a historically African-American college, Morgan welcomes students of all colors, cultures, and backgrounds. It is home to the well-regarded new Carl Murphy Fine Arts Center.

St. Mary's Seminary and University
5400 Roland Avenue
(410) 864-4000
www.stmarys.edu

This private university began in 1791 by the Society of St. Sulpice to educate students for the priesthood and was the first Catholic seminary in the United States. The equivalent of a high school and community college by today's standards, it grew in importance when the Sulpicians were granted recognition as a Pontifical Theological Faculty in 1822 by Pope Pius VII and gained the ability to grant pontifical degrees. St. Mary's Seminary is one of only six seminaries in the United States that are allowed to grant such degrees. St. Mary's also offers graduate education for those not interested in ministry. The Ecumenical Institute of Theology, which opened in 1968 to persons of all faiths, continues to provide a platform for investigation and argument of religious and philosophical topics as well as award master's degrees in theology and religious education. Within its School of Theology, St. Mary's opened the Center for Continuing Formation in 1995, which hosts priests on sabbatical as well as provides learning opportunities in religion and philosophy for the general public.

The University System of Maryland

The University System of Maryland (USM) is comprised of both previously independent schools that have come under its umbrella and schools that have historically been branches or campuses of the University of Maryland. There are 13 degree-granting institutions in all enrolling some 130,000 students worldwide in 600 degree programs.

The value of the University System of Maryland for residents of Maryland falls into two categories: convenience and cost. It is convenient not only because of the many campuses and educational centers that are easily accessible within the area but also because of the worldwide academic flexibility it offers. A student in the University System, for instance, may earn credits at various campuses and have all of them count toward a degree. You could do your freshman and sophomore years at University of Maryland, Baltimore County and then transfer to Towson or UB, and your credits would go with you. You may have to take additional courses to make up requirements for a particular school or program, but you will not lose the credits already earned.

Or perhaps you'd like to move to Europe or Asia for your junior and senior years. The University of Maryland University College has campuses in Heidelberg, Germany, and on several American military bases in Japan, including Okinawa and Yokota. Perhaps you've decided on military service and would like to take advantage of one of the University College's offerings at more than 160 U.S. military bases in Europe, East Asia, and the Pacific.

Whatever your needs, academic transfer within the University System is relatively easy, and assimilation into graduate school, though not guaranteed, is often uncomplicated as a baccalaureate program in a specific discipline is direct preparation for the graduate or professional schools. For instance, a student might major in pre-med at College Park and that would prepare him or her directly for the medical professional school at the Baltimore campus.

Costwise, the University System is much, much cheaper than the private colleges in Maryland. Tuition with student fees at Johns Hopkins is currently about $35,900; at Loyola, $31,270; and at Goucher, $29,000. In-state residents at the University of Maryland, Baltimore County pay $6,500 for the same number of credit hours. This means, of course, that you could pay for four years at the University of Maryland and a few postgraduate courses besides for what it will cost to go to most private universities for a year. You can make that money go even further if you take your first two years of education at one of the local community colleges, which have transfer and scholarship programs that work with the University System and at which a full-time local student pays about $2,000. So, if you were to receive an associate's degree from Catonsville Community College of Baltimore County and then go on to finish your bachelor's degree at UMBC, your total cost for the four years would be less than $15,000.

But students are not the only beneficiaries of the USM umbrella. For participant schools, USM offers access to the financial support of the state of Maryland, the prestige of being part of this well-respected international institution, and access to a steady stream of students seeking a good education for the least amount of money.

Listed below are those colleges and campuses that are in the greater Baltimore area. If you would like more information about the main campus in College Park, Maryland, call (301) 445-2756. For the University College at College Park or other campuses worldwide, call (800) 888UMUC, or for the Baltimore City Community College call (410) 462-8000. For an overview of USM, visit the Web site at www.usmd.edu.

Coppin State University
2500 West North Avenue
(410) 951-3000
www.coppin.edu

Coppin State University is a historically African-American college that was established in 1900 as a private normal school to train elementary school teachers. Coppin, which became a part of the University System in 1988, currently offers degrees and certification programs in dentistry, engineering, pharmacy, criminal justice, and social work as well as teaching. It also offers graduate degrees in the arts and sciences, including nursing and teacher education. Originally a day school, most of Coppin's 3,700 students are still day-trippers, but a new 300-bed residence hall attracts students from out of state to the 50-acre campus.

Towson University
8000 York Road, Towson
(410) 704-2000
www.towson.edu

Towson University began as the State Normal School, a state-sponsored teaching school in Baltimore City. It moved to its Towson campus in 1915, and the majestic building in which it was housed is still used by the university. Since then, the school has gone through many incarnations, ending up as the present Towson University. The university grants baccalaureate degrees in 100 majors and master's degrees in 25 programs through its eight colleges: the College of Business and Economics; the College of Education; the College of Fine Arts and Communication; the College of Graduate and Extended Education; the College of Health Professions; the College of Liberal Arts; the College of Natural and Mathematical Sciences; and the Honors College. Enrollment numbers around 19,000 full- and part-time students. There's residential space for 3,300. The school boasts state-of-the-art facilities in radio and TV and a growing reputation in the mass-media industry. It is the second-largest university in Maryland.

University of Baltimore
1420 North Charles Street
(410) 837-4200
www.ubalt.edu

The University of Baltimore (UB) began in 1925 as a private, coeducational, two-year school of business. In 1975 it went public and became part of the Maryland system. UB offers baccalaureate study for all four years beginning in 2007 granting bachelor's degrees in the arts and sciences as well as postgraduate degrees through the Neil Kleinman Institute for Language, Technology and Publications Design; the Robert G. Merrick School of Business; and the Yale Gordon College of Liberal Arts. It is also well-known for its School of Law. UB has also been reaching out to more distant sites to centers in Harford and Howard Counties, and it also offers a virtual degree. You can get your bachelor's degree by studying with UB online from anywhere in the world. More than half of UB's 4,600 students attend evening classes. There is no campus housing for UB, whose campus is across city blocks instead of rolling hills. But sitting as it does on the edge of the Mount Vernon/ Belvedere neighborhood and near Bolton Hill, there is plenty of apartment space for out-of-towners. The new 38,000-square-foot Student Center houses a theater, meeting space, study space, offices, and cafe.

University of Maryland, Baltimore
737 West Lombard Street
(410) 706-3100
www.umaryland.edu

Although the University of Maryland's main campus is in College Park, Maryland, the university actually began here in Baltimore in 1807 with the founding of the School of Medicine. Davidge Hall, a lecture hall and operating theater built in 1812 and now a National Historic Landmark, is the oldest building in the United States in continuous use for medical teaching. In 1816 a School of Law was added. In 1840 the Baltimore College of Dental Surgery, Dental School opened as the first dental college in the world. In 1841, the Maryland College of Pharmacy was begun; and in 1889, the School of Nursing opened. The most recent addition was the School of Social Work, in 1961. This Baltimore campus of the University of Maryland focuses on professional graduate school programs. It has close to 5,400 students served by more than 1,600 faculty members. There are 42 graduate programs offered.

University of Maryland, Baltimore County
1000 Hillltop Circle
(410) 455-1000
www.umbc.edu

The University of Maryland, Baltimore County (UMBC) was founded in 1966. A separate school, not just a satellite campus of the University of Maryland, College Park, UMBC has more than 10,000 undergraduate and graduate students studying in the liberal arts and sciences at its 500-acre campus. The focus is on cutting-edge science and technology as well as the visual and performing arts, but it bills itself as a "public research university." In this regard, UMBC has nine separate research institutes located on campus that include everything from the Joint Center for Earth Systems Technology, a NASA/UMBC partnership that studies the global environment, to the Center for Education Research and Development, where model science programs for Maryland schools are created. There are 11,700 undergraduates.

Community Colleges

Baltimore City Community College
600 East Lombard Street
(410) 986-5599

2901 Liberty Heights Avenue
(410) 462-8000
www.bccc.edu

Baltimore City Community College (BCCC) has two main campuses in the city. Its Downtown campus, whose center is only a few blocks from the Inner Harbor, is convenient and well used by Downtown residents and workers. Its Liberty Road campus was the original site of the school when it was known as Baltimore Junior College, and its popular radio station, WBJC, still bears the original acronym. The school, however, has come a long way since the BJC days. More than 15,000 students pursue both credit and noncredit courses in 35 associate degree career programs and eight associate degree transfer programs.

The only state-sponsored, two-year college in Maryland, BCCC enrolls more city residents than any other college in Baltimore. Such popularity may be due to the emphasis the school places on preparing people for work. BCCC has 25 certificate programs, with special emphasis on health, human services, and business, though not all of its offerings are so mundane. BCCC offers an Apparel Technology Program, which was cited by the American Textile Manufacturers Institute for its innovative curriculum design and teaching excellence.

One of BCCC's most interesting features is that its education comes with a guarantee. "If a graduate of a career program . . . does not have a full-time job within 90 days after graduation, BCCC will provide 12 additional credits of course work and other support services at no cost to the student." To the graduates' future employers, the guarantee provides that BCCC students will be "competent in their work."

To help prepare the community at large for work and the world, BCCC offers the Business and Continuing Education Center. Located at 710 East Lombard Street, the center is the largest provider of literacy education in Baltimore. The center offers three main programs: Adult Basic Education, which provides opportunities for adults to hone literacy skills; General Education Development, which prepares students of all ages for the GED high school equivalency exam; and English as a Second Language, which helps prepare new immigrants to further their education and become productive citizens.

The Community Colleges of Baltimore County

There are three community colleges in Baltimore County, each of which grew up separately, responding to the needs of their respective communities. Within the last few years, however, they have been bundled under the umbrella name and administration of a new entity, The Community Colleges of Baltimore County (CCBC). Through this act of centralization, Baltimore County hopes to be able to enhance offerings while reducing overall costs through reorganization. The three original schools that now serve as CCBC's main campuses are at 800 South Rolling Road, Catonsville, (410) 455-6050; 7200 Sollers Point Road, Dundalk, (410) 282-6700; and 7201 Rossville Boulevard, Essex, (410) 682-6000. The CCBC also offers classes through neighborhood centers in Owings Mills and Hunt Valley.

Through all its campuses and centers, CCBC serves more than 70,000 students and offers 6,600 credit courses and 7,000 continuing education courses, including employee training courses that the county offers to employers in the area at more than 90 locations. Various certificates of completion are available for specific course offerings, but, overwhelmingly, students seek associate of arts degrees and transfer to a four-year institution.

Associate degrees are offered in more than 75 programs in the arts and sciences, business administration, computer sciences, engineering, general studies, and teacher education. Certificate programs include such ℹ️ Schools such as Baltimore City College and Calvert Hall College are not, in fact, colleges but high schools. Established in the middle of the nineteenth century, both schools were denoted as colleges because they were degree-granting institutions.

options as computer graphics and visual communications, printing management technology, environmental technology, chemical dependency counseling, retail floristry, and varied allied health programs. Visit the Web site at www.ccbc.md.edu.

SPECIALTY SCHOOLS

Baltimore Actors' Theatre and Conservatory
300 Dumbarton Road
(410) 337-8519
www.baltimoreactorstheatre.org
If you have a five-year-old who can really belt out a song or a 15-year-old who can make you believe he's Hamlet, then you might want to consider approaching Baltimore Actors' Theatre and Conservatory to see if your child can become one of the select few who get admitted every year. The K-12 student body at the conservatory numbers only 30, with an equal number of students pursuing a three-year baccalaureate degree and postgraduate studies. These 60 students work hand-in-hand with the resident professional performance company of 100 to produce a minimum of 12 plays per year, while pursuing a rigorous academic curriculum. High school degrees are accredited by the state of Maryland, but the baccalaureate and master's degrees offered are through Trinity College in London, although students do not study abroad.

The Baltimore Actors' Theatre and Conservatory is less expensive than many traditional private K-12 institutions and many area colleges because much of the school's expenses are paid for through performance receipts.

Baltimore International College (BIC)
17 Commerce Street
(410) 752-4710
www.bic.edu
BIC was founded in 1972 to offer certificates in culinary arts. It has grown to include bachelors and associates degrees in culinary arts as well as hospitality business and management. Graduate degrees in hospitality are also available. Classes are hands-on for all students, who can be seen heading to class in their chef's jackets and carrying their knife cases. They get to test their skills every weekday at lunchtime during the semester—and we get to see how good they are. The Bay Atlantic Club is staffed by students and open Monday through Friday 11:30 a.m. to 2:00 p.m. at 206 East Redwood Street. Call ahead if you want to go, both for a reservation and to be sure the restaurant is open. They close for school holidays.

The Maryland Institute, College of Art (MICA)
1300 West Mount Royal Avenue
(410) 669-9200
www.mica.edu
The Maryland Institute, selected by *U.S. News & World Report* as one of the top four visual arts colleges in the nation, was established in 1826 and has the distinction of being the oldest independent, degree-granting, fully accredited art college in the United States. The campus is made up of 16 buildings, most of which line Mount Royal Avenue from North Avenue to Park Avenue, adjacent to Mount Royal Terrace. Two of the buildings—the main building at 1300 and Mount Royal Station, a historic train station that the institute renovated for gallery and workspace—are on the National Register of Historic Places. In the winter of 2004–2005, MICA opened its new Brown Center, filled with classrooms, labs, and an auditorium. In 2008, the Gateway Building, housing dorms, and a performing arts center, will open.

But what is really most important about the institute is the education it offers its students. Undergraduate degrees are available in all major areas of artistic endeavor. All programs incorporate the use of the computer, offering state-of-the-art opportunities in design. A digital embroidery machine is available to material artists, and sculptors may now use computers to play with ideas and actually create their pieces digitally before they ever take chisel in hand.

The master's programs include six main areas of study, but the school offers two unique programs. One is the five-year, BSA/MAT program through which a student may study for five years and graduate with not only a bachelor of science degree in art, but also a master's degree in teaching. The second program is called Fine Arts in Studio for Art Educators. This program is designed for the practicing art teacher. Study is arranged so that the master's candidate may work during the teaching year, then go to class during the summers. Study is intensive, but a master's degree can be achieved in four summer sessions.

The institute also offers a plethora of options for continuing studies in everything from interior design to computer art, both for those seeking degrees and those simply wanting to learn.

Maryland School for the Blind
3501 Taylor Avenue
(410) 444-5000
www.mdschblind.org

The Maryland School for the Blind was founded in 1853. It moved from the city to its present location in 1906, because the children needed a place to run that had no obstacles. From its inception until the 1970s, the school served primarily blind and visually impaired students with a basic academic curriculum and specialized courses in Braille and orientation mobility. Daily living skills, such as personal hygiene, food preparation, and table etiquette, were also taught.

Since the 1970s when the federal government handed down a national mandate that required all states to provide education for handicapped children, the Maryland School has adapted its curriculum and services to include children that have not only visual disparities but also physical and emotional ones.

More than 300 professionals and 140 volunteers help the Maryland School's 185 students learn how to lead normal lives. Some 140 students live on campus five days a week and are supported by house parents, who live with them, and a 24-hour nursing staff on campus.

Students who are residents of Maryland pay nothing for their room, board, and tuition. Students from outside the state pay tuition and fees, but these are often picked up by their respective states that may have no facilities that fulfill the federal mandate. The Maryland School also helps public school systems develop programs within their schools for children with visual and/or physical handicaps and boasts an outreach program to an additional 800 students across Maryland. The school has also begun working with babies and toddlers in basic skills to give them a head start.

The Peabody Institute
1 East Mount Vernon Place
(410) 659-8100
www.peabody.jhu.edu

The Peabody Conservatory of Music, now the Peabody Institute of the Johns Hopkins University, was founded in 1857 with a bequest from George Peabody. It has become over the intervening years one of the premier music schools in the country. The Peabody has a preparatory division in music and dance that is open to people of all ages. The Conservatory offers high school, college, and advanced degrees in music. Close to 600 full-time and 40 part-time students are accepted into the Conservatory versus the almost 6,400 students in the preparatory school. The Peabody is performance oriented, and its students stage almost 60 public concerts every year.

St. Elizabeth's School and
Rehabilitation Center
801 Argonne Drive
(410) 889-5054
www.stelizabeth-school.org
St. Elizabeth's was started in 1961 as an out-growth of St. Francis for Special Education, which opened in 1953. St. Elizabeth's is what is known as an Intensity 5 school, meaning that 100 percent of the student's day is spent in specialized education. Children from age 11 through 21 receive education that focuses on academics, social/emotional growth and development, and vocational skills. There is athletic competition for those who are able to participate. A high school diploma is available through the school, as is a certificate of completion for specialized vocational curricula, which include such diverse areas as cosmetology, carpentry, and commercial cooking. Because apprenticeship and volunteer experience are a large part of the vocational focus, students often graduate with a job already in hand. This nonresident day school for the physically and emotionally handicapped has around 125 students. The student-teacher ratio is 2 to 1.

STUDENT SERVICES

Sylvan Learning Center
1001 Fleet Street
(888) EDUCATE
www.educate.com
Sylvan Learning Systems was founded in 1979 in Portland, Oregon, but has recently located its worldwide corporate headquarters in the Inner Harbor East. Sylvan has three divisions: Sylvan Learning Centers, Hooked on Phonics, and Catapult Learning.

Sylvan Learning Centers consists of approximately 1,000 franchised centers in the United States, 38 of which are in Baltimore. Each center provides tutoring and supplemental study in reading, writing, and mathematics for children in grades K through 12. The tutoring is focused and child specific. Although Sylvan's teaching methods are standard across the board, what they teach each child is not. If you are interested in getting in contact with a Sylvan Learning Center near your home or school, the previously listed toll-free number will connect you with Sylvan's location center. When you call, you may find that there is a Sylvan Learning Center in your school, as Sylvan provides in-school services to some of Maryland's districts through its Contract Services Division.

In addition to its numerous tutoring programs, Sylvan's parent company, Educate Inc., also produces Hooked on Phonics, a system of CD-ROMs, flash cards, and books designed to help young readers, and Catapult Learning, a service for schools and school districts to reach the goals of the No Child Left Behind Act. They also operate the Progressus Therapy subsidiary, which provides language, occupational, and physical therapists at schools.

HEALTH CARE

Baltimore is dotted with great hospitals, ranging from the world-renowned Johns Hopkins Hospital in East Baltimore and University of Maryland Medical System near the Inner Harbor to hospitals with increasingly impressive records and accomplishments, including Greater Baltimore Medical Center, St. Joseph Medical Center, and Mercy Medical Center.

More importantly, Maryland has been a leader in caring for critically injured people since the 1970s. The Maryland Shock Trauma Center at the University of Maryland Medical Center, which involves paid and volunteer firefighters and ambulance crews, state police, and their helicopters and every hospital in the state, ensures that people who need the most serious forms of care as a result of car accidents, shootings, falls, or other injurious acts get that care quickly. The success of the system is in the number of critically injured people who live to tell the tale of their serious accident. (See the Close-up in this chapter.)

And hardly a week goes by that a doctor associated with some hospital in the Baltimore area doesn't make national or international headlines for his or her lifesaving discoveries or successes in the operating room. Dr. Ben Carson, a neurosurgeon at Johns Hopkins Hospital, has saved hundreds of children through his surgical skills and is particularly well-known for separations of united twins.

Dr. Robert Gallo, a scientist and leader in the research of AIDS, opened a facility at the Institute of Human Virology at the University of Maryland School of Medicine in 1996, bringing to Baltimore a first-rate warrior against one of the era's most fatal and devastating diseases.

While advertisements and promotional materials make it seem as if there's great competition among the hospitals, a good deal of their success is in working together to help patients. Patients are routinely sent from one hospital to another for consultations, second opinions, and surgeries. The hospitals in the area play host to thousands of patients from all over the world, who come to the area seeking the best care possible.

One thing unique to Maryland's hospital system is capitation, a system of state regulation designed to ensure that all hospitals have enough patients to be effective. Capitation also ensures proper pricing, although critics will argue that regulated pricing prevents individual hospitals from setting a rate that would encourage competition among peers. The system also forces hospitals making a profit in one year to put those revenues into capital improvements. The result is better hospitals with state-of-the-art facilities and equipment, even at smaller hospitals and those removed from the more urban areas. For a hospital to expand or contract its existing services, capitation requires the hospital to obtain permission from state regulators, meaning the area's hospitals at times can lag behind newer needs of patients. However, most of these issues are resolved in board rooms and regulators' offices, not in hospitals or at the bedside.

Beyond the traditional forms of medicine practiced in hospitals, the area has seen growth in the holistic approaches to medicine, including alternative healing methods such as acupuncture, aromatherapy, and other forms of care practiced for centuries elsewhere but only now gaining wider acceptance in this country.

What follows is a listing of the area's hospitals and specialty services, including psychiatric hospitals. Hospice services are also listed. Like most sections of the book, these are categorized by regions. If no city is listed, then the hospital is within the confines of Baltimore City. Hospitals outside the city limits are noted with the town, after the street address.

HOSPITALS

Downtown

Baltimore VA Medical Center
10 North Greene Street
(410) 605-7000
www.maryland.va.gov

Part of the VA Maryland Health Care System, the Baltimore VA Medical Center offers veterans some of the most state-of-the-art facilities available through the military. The 221-bed medical center is home to the world's first filmless radiology department, which allows doctors nearly instant access to patient imaging from throughout the facility.

Conveniently located near the Inner Harbor and next door to the University of Maryland Medical System, the center offers a full range of inpatient, outpatient, and research programs for veterans. The Geriatric Research, Education and Clinical Center, offering research on strokes and cardiovascular disease prevention through exercise, smoking cessation, and nutrition therapy for older veterans, is one of only 21 VA system providers of these services in the country.

The hospital has opened a new center for the growing population of multiple sclerosis patients and one of the VA's 10 Mental Illness Research Education and Clinical Centers.

The center in Baltimore offers a wide range of specialties, including a state-of-the-art endoscopic suite; inpatient and outpatient mental health services; MRI, mammography, and CAT scan facilities; a home-based primary-care program; a refractory congestive heart failure program; an outpatient spinal cord injury support clinic; and a senior exercise rehabilitation facility.

The medical center offers free parking for outpatients only in its parking lot below the facility on Greene Street. A shuttle service taking patients to and from Perry Point and Fort Howard medical centers, separate facilities that are part of the same network of veterans services, is provided on weekdays.

Bon Secours Hospital
2000 West Baltimore Street
(410) 362-3000
www.bonsecours.org/baltimore

Cardinal James Gibbons, the ninth archbishop of Baltimore, asked the Sisters of Bon Secours to come from Paris in 1881 to provide health care to the sick in their homes. Through the financial support of philanthropist George Jenkins, they opened the first Bon Secours Hospital in Baltimore in 1919. Now, with 208 beds and 973 employees, that mission has spread to include an intense community commitment, involving 10 primary-care centers around West Baltimore; the largest outpatient renal dialysis program in the city; the New Hope Treatment Center, offering drug treatment and counseling; and Operation Reach-Out, a community development program. The hospital merged in 1996 with Liberty Health System to form Bon Secours Medical System. Among Bon Secours Hospital's specialties are cardiology, podiatry, surgery, substance abuse services, and home health.

The Johns Hopkins Hospital
600 North Wolfe Street
(410) 955-5000
www.hopkinsmedicine.org

The hospital opened in 1889, and since that time its recognition and groundbreaking work have grown with the years. Established as part of philanthropist Johns Hopkins' gift to form Johns Hopkins University, the school of medicine and hospital revolutionized American higher education, medical education, and health care by establishing an intense teaching and learning environment where doctors, teachers, and students work hand in hand. Hopkins was the first medical school to require an undergraduate degree for admission and the first to combine science learning

Important Numbers and Web Sites to Know

Police, fire, ambulance, or other emergencies, 911
(in Baltimore City, call 311 for nonemergency matters)
Maryland Natural Resources Police (maritime emergencies), (410) 260-8888,
(800) 628-9944, www.dnr.state.md.us
Poison Control, (410) 528-7701, (800) 222-1222

Departments of Mental Health and Hygiene

These numbers will lead you to people who can make referrals to specialists ranging from community health centers to centers dealing with specific types of care.

State of Maryland, (410) 767-5300, www.mdpublichealth.org
Anne Arundel County, (410) 222-7095, www.aahealth.org
Baltimore City, (410) 396-4398, www.baltimorehealth.org
Baltimore County, (410) 887-3740, www.co.ba.md.us
Howard County, (410) 313-6300, www.co.ho.md.us

Other Aid Agencies

Associated Black Charities, (888) 450-5836, www.abc-md.org
Associated Catholic Charities, (410) 547-5490, www.catholiccharities-md.org
Episcopal Community Services, (410) 467-1264, www.escm.org
Jewish Family Services, (410) 466-9200, www.jfs.org
Lutheran Social Services in Maryland, (410) 558-3168, www.lssnca.org

Crisis Intervention

Family Crisis Center, (410) 828-6390, www.familycrisiscenter.net
First Step (suicide intervention), (410) 521-3800 or (800) SUICIDE,
www.suicidehotlines.com/maryland
House of Ruth (domestic violence), (410) 889-0840; 24-hour hotline:
(410) 889-7884, www.hruth.org
Maryland Network Against Domestic Violence, (800) MDHELPS, www.mnadv.org
Maryland Youth Crisis Hotline, (800) 422-0009
Family Stress Line, 24-hour hotline, (800) 243-7337; www.familytreemd.org

Referral Sources

Maryland Psychiatric Society, (410) 625-0232, www.mdpsych.org
Maryland Psychological Association, (410) 992-4258, www.marylandpsychology.org

Substance Abuse

Al-Anon and Alateen, (410) 766-1984, www.md-al-anon.org
Alcoholics Anonymous, (410) 663-1922, www.baltimoreaa.org
Narcotics Anonymous, (410) 566-4022; hotline, (800) 317-3222, www.freestatena.org

and intensive clinical mentoring, thus creating a model for medical education that remains in use throughout the world today. Among the firsts the hospital can claim is the first major medical school in the country to admit women, the first to use rubber gloves during surgery, and the first to develop renal dialysis and CPR.

The hospital has 1,017 beds and draws seriously ill patients from all over the world who seek the cures for which Hopkins is renowned. Employing 25,000 people, the hospital features marvelous accommodations for those having to spend time in the hospital. Travel agents, concierges, several types of dining, and other amenities ease the tough times, and the hospital is located on the city's subway system, meaning transportation from the train station or airport doesn't require a taxicab ride. Its children's ward features games, movies, and a giant stuffed animal zoo that makes kids feel like they're not so far away from home. Among its specialties are AIDS care, anesthesiology, critical care, asthma and allergies, cancer, cardiology and cardiac surgery, dermatology, digestive disorders, emergency medicine, endocrinology, immunology and infectious diseases, kidney disorders, neurology and neurosurgery, pediatrics, pulmonary medicine, reconstructive and plastic surgery, transplant surgery, and urology.

Maryland General Hospital
827 Linden Avenue
(410) 225-8000
www.marylandgeneral.org

Founded in 1881 by a group of Baltimore doctors as a university-affiliated teaching hospital, the Baltimore Medical College, as it was called back then, became Maryland General after becoming affiliated with the University of Maryland School of Medicine. In 1965 it again merged, this time with the Baltimore Eye and Ear Hospital to become the premier teaching hospital for eye, ear, nose, and throat problems. Now, the 243-bed hospital provides those same services, as well as rehabilitation, transitional care, mental health, and obstet-

rics and gynecological services. In 1997 the hospital opened its Obstetrical Center, which allows each mother to remain in her one, well-furnished, home-like room throughout the entire childbirthing process. The hospital's rehabilitation facility provides typical subacute services, as well as a unique brain injury program.

Mercy Medical Center
301 St. Paul Place
(410) 332-9000
www.mdmercy.com

The 285-bed hospital started as a 20-bed clinic for the poor and indigent of Baltimore. It was run by one doctor and a couple of medical students in an abandoned schoolhouse in 1867. At that time, the hospital was part of Washington University School of Medicine. In 1874 City Hospital, named for the nearby City Springs, a public fountain and park, was taken over by six Sisters of Mercy, who continued to care for the city's poor, while opening the Mercy Hospital School of Nursing in 1899. Since that time, the hospital has continued to grow into one of the area's larger hospitals, employing 2,033 people and having an operating budget of about $147 million.

The Weinberg Center for Women's Health and Medicine is headed by world-class gynecologic oncologist Dr. Neil Rosenshein and breast cancer surgeon Dr. Neil B. Freidman heads the Hoffberger Breast Center. The newest additions are institutes for surgical oncology and foot and ankle reconstruction. In recent years the hospital has been making arrangements with a number of area businesses and government agencies to provide first-line health care to injured workers, giving it a new niche to fill in the Downtown area. The hospital provides care in internal medicine, surgery, obstetrics, pediatrics, urology, cardiology, oncology, cosmetic surgery, hospice, transitional care, and emergency medicine. The Cardinal Shehan Center/Stella Maris geriatric care facility and Mercy Ridge retirement community, both in Timonium, are Mercy affiliates.

University of Maryland Medical System
22 South Green Street
(410) 328-8667
www.umm.edu

Calling itself "Maryland's other great hospital" in deference to the more widely recognized Johns Hopkins Hospital, Maryland's largest hospital serves more than 250,000 patients a year. Established in 1807, the affiliated University of Maryland School of Medicine is the nation's fifth-oldest medical school. In 1823 the medical school built the Baltimore Infirmary, which later became University Hospital. Just blocks from Camden Yards and the Inner Harbor, the hospital has 747 beds, served by 5,500 employees.

A private, nonprofit teaching hospital, the first teaching hospital in the state, the University of Maryland Medical Center often assists with referrals and the handling of difficult cases from the region's doctors and smaller hospitals. The Maryland Shock Trauma Center was the first of its kind for providing critical care to those in immediate need of medical attention, using state police helicopters and the region's ambulance systems. The Greenebaum Cancer Center opened in 1996 and serves thousands of people in the region suffering from all types of cancer. The Gudelsky Building, featuring a unique 12-story atrium to provide comfort and solace to patients and their loved ones, transcends the typical hospital environment, while rooms in the building are mostly private. Specialties include neurosurgical care, cardiac care, and transplant surgery, as well as cutting-edge research and surgical advancements, including pioneering work in transplants, video-assisted surgery, and the Gamma Knife, a radiological procedure that requires no surgery to destroy brain tumors and repair vascular malformations.

Northeast

Good Samaritan Hospital of Maryland
5601 Loch Raven Boulevard
(410) 532-8000
www.goodsam-md.org

Good Samaritan was founded in 1968 through a gift from Thomas O'Neill, a local merchant and philanthropist. O'Neill set the condition that all activities at the hospital conform to the Catholic Principles, as set by the U.S. National Conference of Catholic Bishops. This means that abortions and in vitro fertilizations are not performed here. Through an arrangement with Johns Hopkins School of Medicine, the hospital provides orthopedics, rehabilitation medicine, and rheumatology. A Med-Star hospital, it is located on a 43-acre site in northeastern Baltimore City, where its 346 beds and 2,300 employees provide care to northern Baltimore City and the greater Towson area. The Emergency Department sees more than 23,000 patients a year, and the hospital's Good Health Center offers free and low-cost preventative medical services. The hospital also offers 69 rehabilitation beds and a 24-station renal dialysis unit. Specialties include medical/surgical care, obstetrics and gynecology, pediatric care, and emergency care. Good Samaritan is one of the top 10 hospitals for complex knee surgery.

Greater Baltimore Medical Center
6701 North Charles Street, Towson
(443) 849-2000
www.gbmc.org

Formed from the Presbyterian Eye, Ear and Throat Hospital and the Women's Hospital of Maryland, both of which opened in the 1880s, GBMC opened on its 106-acre wooded campus in 1965. The 292-bed, nonprofit community hospital performs more surgeries—44,000—than any other hospital in the state. Its emergency room sees more than 60,000 patients a year, while its obstetrics wing delivers the most babies in the region. The hospital, which has been recognized nationally for its gynecological surgeries, was the first to bring laser surgery to Maryland in the mid-1970s and has continued to revolutionize the use of lasers in laparoscopic surgical techniques. The hospital has also been active in breast cancer awareness and care, providing all services—from consultation to X-rays to

Selected Baltimore Firsts

The first Department of Public Health was established here in 1793.

Granville Stanley Hall established the first psychology laboratory at Johns Hopkins University in 1881.

In 1894 Dr. Williams Halsted, chief surgeon at Johns Hopkins Hospital, was the first to use rubber gloves for surgery.

In 1942 Johns Hopkins Hospital was the first to identify the polio virus.

The first intensive care unit was established at Johns Hopkins in 1955; the first shock-trauma unit, at the University of Maryland Hospital in 1961.

—Excerpted from Baltimore—America's City of Firsts, *a pamphlet published by Baltimore Bicentennial Celebration, Inc.*

treatment—through its Comprehensive Breast Care Center. It's a one-stop approach to breast health. The F. Barton Harvey Institute of Human Genetics, endowed with a $1 million gift and directed by nationally known geneticist Maimon Cohen, is working to bring practical applications of genetic research, especially on the adult onset of Alzheimer's and Parkinson's diseases, to patients. Through its GBMC HealthCare program, it offers all levels of medical care, including hospice through its Hospice of Baltimore center and the Gilchrest Center.

Specialties include emergency care, obstetrics and gynecological services, cancer care, ophthalmology, otolaryngology, and laparoscopic surgery.

St. Joseph Medical Center
7601 Osler Drive, Towson
(410) 337-1000
www.sjmcmd.org
Operated by the Sisters of St. Francis of Philadelphia, this Catholic hospital in Towson has 374 beds and employs 2,385 people. Its primary service area is Baltimore County, from Towson north to the Pennsylvania line. Specialties include cardiovascular services, open-heart surgery, obstetrics, women's services, minimally invasive surgery, and orthopedics.

Union Memorial Hospital
201 East University Parkway
(410) 554-2000
www.unionmemorial.org
The Union Protestant Infirmary was founded in 1854 to provide shelter and medical care to the sick, poor, and disabled. In 1923 its name was changed to honor the people who contributed to its founding and development. One of the first community hospitals in the nation to support graduate medical education, the hospital supports about 85 residents and fellows in areas ranging from sports medicine and orthopedics to foot surgery and obstetrics and gynecology. The hospital is nationally known for its orthopedic program, including the Curtis National Hand Center and the Sports Medicine Program. It's also the Baltimore Raven's official medical team. Union Memorial's more than 2,000 employees serve the people of northern Baltimore and greater Towson. The hospital is close to Johns Hopkins University and the other colleges in the area. Specialties include mental health services, oncology, cardiac and surgery services, and women's services at the Calvert Women's Group Center.

Northwest

Kernan Hospital
2200 Kernan Drive
(888) 4KERNAN, (800) 492-5538
www.umm.edu/kernan
Part of the University of Maryland Medical System, the 152-bed hospital began more than a century ago as a home for children with orthopedic deficits. The hospital has evolved into a site for innovative orthopedic and rehabilitation services for children and adults. Located on the border of Baltimore City and Baltimore County on a 90-acre wooded site, where founder James Kernan's original Victorian mansion still stands, the hospital, employing about 500 people, treats patients suffering from a variety of orthopedic and neurological conditions, including spinal cord and brain injury rehabilitation as well as sports medicine. The pediatric orthopaedics department focuses on the wide variety of growing children's problems, such as scoliosis and club feet.

Levindale Hebrew Geriatric Center and Hospital
2434 West Belvedere Avenue
(410) 601-2400
www.lifebridgehealth.org/Levindale
Started as the Hebrew Friendly Inn for the Old in the 1890s, the 172-bed facility is now a specialty hospital. Named after Louis H. Levin, executive director of the Associated Jewish Charities from 1921 until his death in 1923, the hospital observes all Jewish laws and rituals and is strictly kosher. Now part of the Lifebridge Health System, of which Sinai Hospital is also a part, Levindale has 202 nursing home beds, 50 specialty long-term-stay beds, 20 psychiatric-rehab beds, and 16 comprehensive rehabilitation beds. Employing about 600 people, the hospital also provides subacute care.

Liberty Village Urban Medical Institute
2600 Liberty Heights Avenue
(410) 362-3000
www.bonsecours.org/baltimore

The Liberty Heights campus of Bon Secours is unusual in that it emphasizes wellness and rehabilitation as well as treatment. Patients come here on an outpatient basis for rehabilitation, including physical therapy, occupational and speech therapy, cardiac rehabilitation, and social work services. The fitness center has cardiovascular equipment and exercise classes; the Tele-Heart Program helps patients with congestive heart failure recover.

Mount Washington Pediatric Hospital
1708 West Rogers Avenue
(410) 578-8600
www.mwph.org
Founded in 1922, the 102-bed facility provides pediatric care as well as helps the children's families learn and cope. Employing about 500 people, the hospital is part of the University of Maryland Medical System. The hospital's specialties include inpatient and outpatient care for infants and children with rehabilitation and special medical needs.

Northwest Hospital Center
5401 Old Court Road, Randallstown
(410) 521-2200
www.lifebridgehealth.org/northwesthospital
This 254-bed hospital employs about 600 doctors and serves Northwest Baltimore and the Randallstown and Pikesville areas. Specialties are minimally invasive surgery, general medical/surgical, cardiology, gynecology, and internal medicine. It is part of the Lifebridge Health System.

Sinai Hospital
2401 West Belvedere Avenue
(410) 601-9000
www.lifebridgehealth.org/sinaihospital
Founded in 1866 as the Hebrew Hospital and Asylum, the hospital is now part of the Sinai Health System. It is Maryland's largest community hospital and the third-largest teaching hospital in the state. With 467 beds and 2,543 employees, the hospital's residency program includes doctors from Johns Hopkins University

School of Medicine and other schools in Baltimore and elsewhere. Among its accomplishments are the introduction of a procedure to heal corneal epithelial glaucoma, showing the benefits of administering magnesium to speed recovery times after open-heart surgery, development of a Minimally Invasive Direct Cardiac Artery Bypass, and the invention of Automatic Implantable Cardioverter Defibrillator, both of which improve patient's success after heart problems. The hospital has opened a state-of-the-art Emergency Center, called ER7, which offers seven separate patient-care centers under one roof. The goal of the center is to reduce the anxiety of patients and their families while delivering the necessary and best care possible, including concierge service, 24-hour valet parking, and 22 private waiting rooms. An agency of the Jewish Community Federation of Baltimore, the hospital's specialties include heart services, cancer care, neurosciences, rehabilitation services, and women's and children's health care.

Southeast

Franklin Square Hospital Center
9000 Franklin Square Drive, Essex
(410) 777-7000
www.franklinsquare.org
The founding hospital in the growing MedStar Health System, this 357-bed facility is the third largest in Baltimore, offering subacute and acute care to eastern Baltimore County. It features one of the busiest emergency departments in central Maryland, treating more than 98,000 patients in 2006. A teaching hospital, Franklin Square has more than 750 physicians and 2,800 employees. Students at Essex Community College, located next door, receive clinical training in radiography and respiratory therapy. Its heart center is the third-largest, in terms of cases handled, in the area, while its OBTLC (Obstetrics Tender Loving Care) program, featuring home-like accommodations for birthing, makes it one of the busiest obstetrics programs in the area. Its Psychology and Behavioral Medicine section handles inpatient adult, adolescent, and child psychiatric care services. Specialties include cardiology, oncology, emergency medicine, labor and delivery, and general medicine.

Johns Hopkins Bayview Medical Center
4940 Eastern Avenue
(410) 550-0100
www.hopkinsbayview.org
Formerly known as Francis Scott Key Medical Center, this 700-bed community teaching hospital has evolved, since 1773, from an alms house to an asylum to a municipal hospital before having its ownership transferred from the city to Johns Hopkins Hospital and University in 1984. Staffed by physicians who are primarily full-time faculty at Johns Hopkins University School of Medicine, the hospital serves as a satellite to the bigger Hopkins hospital campus, although it has its own areas of specialty, too. Bayview's 2,880 employees work on a beautiful and growing 130-acre campus, featuring jogging trails and a community park-like environment. The hospital's Francis Scott Key Burn Center does amazing work for people suffering from serious burns. The hospital is home to one of Maryland's most comprehensive neonatal intensive care units, a sleep disorder center, an areawide trauma center, and a geriatrics center.

Southwest

Baltimore Washington Medical Center
301 Hospital Drive, Glen Burnie
(410) 787-4000
www.bwmc.org
Part of the University of Maryland Medical System, this 286-bed facility in northern Anne Arundel County employs about 2,400 people. Specialties include orthopedics, psychiatry, cardiology, and emergency medicine. The Tate Cancer Center, an outpatient facility, opened in 2003. The emergency room sees about 85,000 patients a year.

Harbor Hospital
3001 South Hanover Street
(410) 350-3200
www.harborhospital.org
Another member of the MedStar System, Harbor Hospital Center started when Dr. Harry Peterman founded the South Baltimore Eye, Ear, Nose and Throat Clinic in the industrial area of South Baltimore in 1901. Two years later, a growing population serving the industrial area, especially Bethlehem Steel shipyard, turned his clinic into a hospital that by 1918 had "an accident room" for sudden injuries, many resulting from workplace dangers. Fifty years later, in 1968, South Baltimore General Hospital moved from its home on Light Street to South Hanover Street, looking over the Patapsco River, where it continues today. Now called Harbor Hospital, the 182-bed teaching hospital offers about 30 specialties, which are provided by more than 1,500 employees, many of whom are affiliated with the University of Maryland School of Medicine. Focusing on primary and secondary care, the specialties include neonatology, a chest diagnosis center, obstetrics and gynecology, pediatrics, medical/surgical, oncology, and diabetes.

St. Agnes Hospital
900 Caton Avenue
(410) 368-6000
ww.stagnes.org
The first Catholic hospital in Baltimore, St. Agnes was founded by the Daughters of Charity in 1823 so they could provide nursing care to the poor. The 323-bed hospital moved to its present location, Caton Avenue at Wilkens Avenue, in 1876 and reorganized into a full-service hospital in 1906. Part of St. Agnes HealthCare, an integrated delivery system for all levels of medical care with numerous off-site centers, the hospital's 3,086 employees are part of the Maryland Health Network, which provides health services to about three million residents of Maryland and the Washington suburbs. Specialties include obstetrics, cardiology, orthopedics, and cancer services and pediatrics.

i If you're heading to a hospital for the first time, call for directions to the nearest parking lot rather than driving around. People with mobility impairments can often find up-close parking by planning ahead.

SPECIALTY FACILITIES
Downtown
Kennedy Krieger Institute
707 North Broadway
(443) 923-9200
www.kennedykrieger.org
Next door to Johns Hopkins Hospital, this facility serves more than 12,000 children annually. It specializes in the needs of children, while performing educational and research services designed to improve the lives of children. Besides providing multiple-day, home-based, and outpatient services to children suffering from disorders of the brain, either of congenital onset or acquired through injury or illness, the hospital has an internationally renowned neurogenics program that draws children from all over the world. With specialists in more than 14 disciplines, the center's scientists have identified the genes responsible for disorders including Tay-Sachs disease and adrenoleuikodystrophy (ALD). In recent years the center has been a leader in lead-paint poisoning prevention and treatment as well as infant eating disorders. Valet parking is available.

Planned Parenthood of Maryland
330 North Howard Street
(410) 576-1400
www.plannedparenthoodmd.org
Planned Parenthood organizations offer affordable access to a wide range of high-quality reproductive health-care services. Medical clinics in Annapolis, Baltimore, Frederick, Owings Mills, Salisbury, and Waldor offer health care, testing, education, and counseling.

Close-up

Shock Trauma—"The Golden Hour"

Dr. R. Adams Cowley theorized in the 1970s that if a person suffering a serious trauma could reach specially trained doctors within an hour of suffering a life-threatening injury, the chances of survival would increase greatly.

Once he got the support of Maryland officials, Cowley set out to create the first of its kind, critical-care system. The result of his groundbreaking work is a trauma center in Baltimore that now bears his name. Baltimoreans may grow uneasy when they hear the whirring of the helicopters rushing someone to "shock trauma." But almost everyone knows of a patient treated there—and so they speak of the center with awe and gratitude.

The R. Adams Cowley Shock Trauma Center, which is part of the University of Maryland System, has been responsible for saving the lives of thousands of people who probably would otherwise have died from injuries received in car crashes, violence, or other traumas to the brain and body.

More than 6,000 patients are treated at the center every year, about a third of them arriving by helicopter. Fire and rescue personnel evaluate whether a helicopter ride to Shock Trauma would mean the difference between life and death. Since speed is key, rescuers often request a helicopter from the central dispatching system moments after arriving on the scene of an incident if the person appears to have experienced any form of trauma, such as injuries to the head, upper torso, or spinal cord. A small percentage of the "flyouts" turn out to be unnecessary but rescuers choose to be safe rather than sorry. In fact, about half of the patients are treated and released.

University Specialty Hospital
601 South Charles Street
(410) 547-8500
www.specialtyhospital.org
Part of the University of Maryland Medical System, this 380-bed facility provides specialty care for the chronically ill, with programs in wound management, traumatic brain injury, respiratory care, terminal care, clinical diatetics, and IV therapy. It was formerly Deaton Specialty Hospital and Home.

Northeast

Sheppard Pratt Health System
6501 North Charles Street, Towson
(410) 938-3000
www.sheppardpratt.org
Moses Sheppard bequeathed his entire estate to start the Sheppard Asylum in 1862. Several years later, Enoch Pratt, who gave more than $1 million to create the free library in Baltimore bearing his name, asked that the 322-bed facility be changed to the Sheppard and Enoch Pratt Hospital after giving $1.6 million to complete the building. Today, the facility provides inpatient and outpatient behavior

While rescuers go about the business of freeing injured persons from a car or machine or beginning first aid and stabilizing the patients before they can fly, a separate fire truck is sent to a clearing where the helicopter can land safely. Shopping center parking lots, ball fields, and other open areas near the accident site are usually chosen.

Medevac pilots, many of whom have served in the armed forces, often land in places where it seems impossible for them to reach. High-speed helicopters are kept in seven strategic locations around the state to minimize the time it takes the teams of two medically trained state troopers to reach the scene. The multimillion-dollar helicopters have specially-equipped compartments with room for stretchers, emergency medicine personnel, and thousands of dollars of medical equipment.

Once the helicopter lands on the roof of the University of Maryland Hospital, a shock trauma team arrives to begin the specialized care that will, everyone hopes, lead to the patient's recovery. Patients may spend only a few days in Shock Trauma before their release or transfer to another hospital or rehabilitation center. Or they could spend long weeks under the care of these dedicated doctors, therapists, and nurses.

About 40 percent of Shock Trauma's patients were injured in vehicle crashes. Twenty-one percent were hurt in falls and 24 percent were injured by violence. The vast majority of patients are ages 20 to 40 and nearly three-quarters are male. Amazingly enough, in spite of their terrible injuries, some 97 percent of patients who arrive at Shock Trauma survive.

Because of this success rate, Baltimoreans are justly proud of—and thankful for—the work of so many dedicated men and women at the R. Adams Cowley Shock Trauma Center.

health, addiction services, crisis intervention, special education schools, and employee assistance programs. Through a partnership with the University of Maryland Medical Center, the facility operates a fellowship program in child and adolescent psychiatry. Its alcohol and drug addiction services have drawn notables from all over the world who seek help at the sprawling campus in Towson in anonymity. Sheppard Pratt employs 2,100 people and has programs in 11 counties of Maryland.

HOSPICE CARE

Hospice care in Baltimore is a growing industry, fueled in large part by the area's religious and familial histories. Hospice care enables people with terminal illnesses to remain in their natural settings during the final days of their lives. Instead of measures to prolong their lives with machines and technology, hospice care focuses on providing people with the medicines and services to make them as comfortable as possible. The benefits, according to proponents, are more peaceful experiences for the ill person as well as for family members and friends, who can share the final, important days of someone's life in the safety, protection, and security of a familiar surrounding.

Nurses, aides, and others who can ease the experience for these patients and for their families are available through the following agencies, all of which have been certified by the state and the Hospice Network of Maryland. To find out more information on hospice care in Maryland, contact the network at (410) 729-4571 or visit the Web site at www.hnmd.org.

Downtown

Joseph Richey Hospice Inc.
838 North Eutaw Street, (410) 523-2150
www.josephricheyhospice.org

Northeast

Hospice of Baltimore
6601 North Charles Street, Towson
(443) 849-8200
www.hospiceofbaltimore.org

Johns Hopkins Home Care Group
2400 Broening Highway
(410) 288-8080

Stella Maris Hospice Care Program
2300 Dulaney Valley Road, Timonium
(410) 252-4500
www.stellamarisinc.com

Northwest

Levindale Hebrew Geriatric
Center and Hospital
2434 West Belvedere Avenue
(410) 601-2400
www.lifebridgehealth.org/levindale

VNA Hospice of Maryland
7008 Security Boulevard, Woodlawn
(410) 594-2600

Southwest

Heartland Hospice Services, Inc.
4805 Benson Avenue
(410) 247-2900

St. Agnes Home Care and Hospice
3421 Benson Avenue
(410) 368-2825
www.stagnes.org

ALTERNATIVE HEALTH CARE

With a long and storied history in traditional medicine, the Baltimore area has been somewhat slow to accept alternative forms of health care. However, that is changing. New offices for holistic health providers, acupuncturists, and aromatherapists are opening all the time.

Check out the Web site www.maryland info.com/Medical_and_Health/Alternative _Healthcare.

RETIREMENT

Lots of people land in Baltimore, live here for a while, and before they know it, they find it hard to imagine leaving. What grows on them is Baltimore's collection of neighborhoods. There's a feeling of home among the brick row houses, the marble steps, and roads like Hillen that begin, end, begin, end. There's a sense of familiarity that develops that is not easily purged. It's unfathomable to think of leaving an area where everyone from friends to the waitress serving them dinner at the local watering hole is familiar.

Many of Baltimore's retirees, if they aren't longtime residents of the area, once visited the city for a day, a weekend, or a week in the past, liked what they saw, and decided to retire here. Maybe they were run through the Bainbridge Naval Training Center in Cecil County while serving in the military. Maybe they were employed by a government agency such as the Social Security Administration, headquartered in Baltimore, or myriad other government agencies less than an hour south in Washington, D.C. Still other retirees are drawn to the area because of their children or grandchildren who have come to Baltimore for its colleges, its medical facilities, or its job opportunities.

Baltimore's population of people age 65 and older is expanding rapidly. An estimated 12 percent of the city's 608,000 residents—73,000 people—have celebrated at least 65 birthdays. By 2020 the number of people blowing out at least 60 candles will make up just less than a quarter of the city's residents, following the national trend of baby boomers reaching retirement age. Even more amazing is that the fastest growing segment of this senior population is people older than 85.

This influx of older people has not been lost on developers of retirement communities and providers of services for the elderly. Retirement communities for independent seniors are huge. Enormous complexes complete with cafes, walking trails, swimming pools, and more activities than one person could possibly handle have cropped up all over town—mostly in the suburbs just outside the Beltway. Adults-only villa-style housing is the newest thing—for those "55 or better." Grandma doesn't have to give up her garden and move into a tiny apartment when she sells her house anymore. She has plenty of options.

Coinciding with this increase in facilities is an ever-expanding list of activities, programs, and support services catering to older people. Everything from vouchers for transportation to a Maryland Gold Card that allows the user to obtain valuable discounts at numerous merchants in the state is available, while each jurisdiction in the state provides a "one-stop service number" for people looking for information on services and programs geared toward keeping them happy and healthy. Maryland state parks offer reduced rates to seniors, enabling them to take in the beautiful sights and sounds of nature all over the state.

Area merchants are also joining in by offering senior discounts, special senior sales, and special senior merchandise.

But don't fool yourself. This isn't Florida or Arizona—nor is it Kansas, for that matter. The area's constantly changing weather, our hazy, hot, and humid summers, and those nasty, cold, and wet winters can exacerbate everything from arthritis to asthma. But for many, good growing seasons for tomatoes and the abundance of crab cakes are reason enough to endure Mother Nature's occasional tantrums.

Even when the weather is bad, it's hard not to want to go out to take in the varied offerings of Baltimore's culture. There are matinees at the Baltimore Symphony Orchestra, at the Hippodrome Theatre and at Center Stage, and the dizzying number of church, senior-center, and community group day trips to New York, Philadelphia, Atlantic City, the mountains of western Maryland, and dozens of other travel spots within the region keep older people busier than when they were working full-time.

In this chapter you'll find information on various resources, services, and senior centers in the area.

RESOURCES

Eldercare
(800) 677-1116
Calls to this toll-free number put seniors in touch with services and facilities in their area, including health care and housing options.

Home Team Program
(410) 887-4141
For seniors who want to remain in their homes but cannot be completely independent, this program offers help with friendly visits and telephone conversations, escorts to conduct personal affairs, help with shopping, chores, and maintenance, light housekeeping, and help with keeping up correspondence.

Senior Expo
(410) 887-3094
www.seniorexpoonline.com
This annual two-day information and resource expo held in mid-October and sponsored by

i Little orange and white buses zip all over Baltimore County, taking county residents age 60 or older as well as disabled adults to medical appointments, shopping, and other stops in both the county and the city. The buses are designed so those using a wheelchair can ride. A ride costs $2.50 to $5.00 one way, depending on where the rider wants to go. For information, call (410) 887-8281.

the Baltimore County Department of Aging features a wide variety of products and community services geared to make life easier for seniors and their families. More than 200 exhibitors attend this event, along with some 10,000 seniors, at the Timonium Fairgrounds.

Senior Information and Assistance Program
34 Market Piace
(410) 396-1341
CARE, which stands for Baltimore City's Commission on Aging and Retirement Education, staffs this hotline that offers referrals, assistance, and special programming information to seniors in the city. It's a good stop for people who can't find the answers to tricky questions about senior care or for those who don't know where to start their search.

Senior Information & Assistance
(410) 887-3094
www.baltimorecountymd.gov
This should be the first place you look for answers to questions about seniors in Baltimore County. Billed as a gateway to information for seniors, their families, and caregivers, the trained staff members of the Baltimore County Department of Aging help county residents age 60 and older with answers to questions, referrals and screenings. The agency operates 18 senior centers in the county. The service can also help with applications for energy assistance, homeowners/renters tax credits, and food stamps. Senior I&A also keeps a computerized directory of local senior services that can be used to access the best sources for help in your area.

Senior Digest is a large-print newspaper filled with information for seniors about local, state, and national issues of interest in Baltimore County. Issues come out eight times a year and cost $5 a year for a mail subscription. To subscribe, call (410) 887-3050 or go to the Web site at www.baltimorecountymd.gov.

Senior Citizen's Guide to Baltimore
www.seniorcitizensguide.com/baltimore

Log on to this Web site for a variety of resources. Need information on Alzheimer's disease? Want to find an eye doctor? Looking for a place to volunteer a few hours a week? This Web site—which has similar sites for a number of cities around the country—has plenty of info.

SENIOR CENTERS

In all parts of the Baltimore area, senior centers offer activities, classes, special events, trips, guest speakers, and other programs geared toward people age 60 and older. Fees range from free to a few dollars to cover the cost of supplies or a meal during a trip. A listing of senior centers is available on the Maryland Department of Aging's Web site, www.mdoo.state.md.us/srcenterlist.html.

Baltimore City

The city's 16 senior centers offer courses on computers, the Internet, financial planning, retirement savings, foreign languages, and lots of other areas of interest. The centers also sponsor trips to local and regional historical and cultural events and locations as well as visits by guest speakers and opportunities to volunteer in the community. Most centers require annual registration, costing just a few dollars, although exact amounts are set by each center.

The Baltimore City Commission on Aging (10 North Calvert Street, 410-396-4932, www.baltimorecity.gov) provides general information as well as locations of senior centers. The office can match your interest in a particular program with the senior center closest to you. Call for housing information.

If you are looking for health-screening services, contact the Waxter Senior Center, 1000 Cathedral Street, (410) 396-1295. University of Maryland Medical System staff provide primary care health services for free or reduced rates. Seniors needing help with their Medicare, especially the prescription drug plans, may call (410) 396-2273.

i Baltimore City sponsors several programs for seniors. The main number for the City Hall operator is (410) 396-3100. They can direct you to the right office.

Baltimore County

Baltimore County operates 19 senior centers throughout the area. They provide training and educational programs, including courses in foreign languages, crafts, the Internet, computers, and financial planning. Senior centers also provide leads on volunteer opportunities, community events and activities, reduced-rate trips and travel, and other programs and activities of interest to people age 60 and older. Several senior centers also provide fully equipped workshops with tools for use by registered members. Five centers have fitness centers. There are no dues, though some classes have fees. Offerings vary from center to center, so it's best to call to learn what's being offered where. Call the Baltimore County Aging Department, 611 Central Avenue, Towson, (410) 887-2594, for locations of senior centers in the county.

ADULT DAY CARE

Active Day Inc.
(443) 548-2200, (800) 805-7430
www.activeservices.com
Active Day centers are sprinkled around Baltimore County, with centers in the city and Carroll and Anne Arundel Counties as well. These adult day health-services centers are designed to help the frail elderly and disabled with their personal needs while injecting fun activities into their day.

Downtown

The Hooper Center
2601 East Baltimore Street
(410) 396-8067
The Hooper Center is a city-run facility that offers adult day care to those suffering from Alzheimer's disease.

i Many of the fine- and performing-arts organizations in the area value seniors as docents and volunteer leaders. These duties are frequently rewarded with free passes to shows and exhibits.

Southeast

Harbor Church Adult Day Care
3001 South Hanover Street
(410) 350-8260
www.harborhospital.org

The center located at Harbor Hospital provides up to 65 participants with a wide range of programs, from meals and nursing care to activities designed to promote an active mental and physical life. Nursing care services provided include appointment scheduling, medication administration and education, exercise classes, crafts, trips, therapy, escort services, and transportation. The staff is friendly and efficient and works to provide you with the services you need.

EDUCATIONAL PROGRAMS

Baltimore County Public Library
(410) 887-6100
www.bcplonline.org

The branches of the county library system offer programs during the day and evenings on a host of topics that may be of interest to seniors, including starting new hobbies, financial planning, and traveling on a budget. These free programs usually require advanced reservations but are free to all visitors. Programs vary from library to library.

i Community colleges in the area offer numerous noncredit courses for between $10 and $150, depending on the number of class meetings and the topic. The daytime courses attract lots of seniors who try their fancy at writing, art, photography, music, economics, foreign languages, bonsai, and dozens of other activities.

HEALTH SERVICES

Baltimore City Health Department
(410) 396-4494
www.baltimorehealth.org

Geriatric evaluation services, senior planning, and other programs are available to seniors through the city's health department. The department also offers fairs and local screenings and prevention programs, including influenza vaccines each year at senior centers, schools, libraries, and shopping centers.

HealthScope
(410) 887-2594

Seniors can obtain health education, screenings, and help in managing their medicines through a variety of free seminars and programs offered all over the region by Baltimore County Department of Aging.

LEGAL AID

Legal Services for Senior Citizens Program
(410) 951-7777
www.mdlab.org

If you need free legal assistance, consultations, or representation for health care issues, income maintenance, housing and utilities, protective services, unemployment benefits, or other matters, contact this service. Area lawyers provide free services to seniors in need or in risk of losing property, assets, or civil rights.

Sixty-Plus Program
(410) 539-3112, (410)337-9100
www.peoples-law.org/senior-citizens/sixty_plus.htm

The Sixty-Plus program is designed to provide assistance to the elderly who have moderate income with simple cases including wills, living wills, powers of attorney, small estates, and deed changes. Lawyers in private practice volunteer for the service, which includes one free meeting and reduced fees for those who decide to have a lawyer represent them.The program is part of the Maryland

State Bar Association's Elder Law Section, the Legal Aid Bureau, and local bar associations.

NUTRITION SERVICES

Eating Together in Baltimore City
(410) 664-0700
At senior centers throughout the city, this free service to those older than age 60 brings seniors together for nutritious meals and socializing. Call to register.

Meals on Wheels
(410) 558-0827
www.mealsonwheelsmd.org
If you're looking for a meal to be delivered to your door, Meals on Wheels is the ticket. Meals are provided to people in their homes five days a week through this free service.

TRANSPORTATION

CountyRide
(410) 887-2080
Low-cost transportation to doctors' appointments and to conduct other business is available to seniors regardless of what part of the county they live in. CountyRide provides door-to-door service and help to those with mobility impairments.

Elderly and Handicapped Taxi Program
(410) 664-1123
Free taxi vouchers are offered to low-income senior citizens through this program.

VOLUNTEER OPPORTUNITIES

Ages on Stages
(410) 396-4932
Seniors have an opportunity to work with the talented teens from the Baltimore School for the Arts to produce a variety of plays and skits to perform at schools, senior centers, and community organizations. Not only do participants have a chance to act in up to 80 productions a year, they also join in activities designed to teach a lesson while increasing tolerance, erasing stereotypes, and throwing fun into the mix.

Baltimore City Commission on Aging
10 North Calvert Street, Suite 300
(410) 396-4932
www.baltimorecity.gov
In addition to health services, senior-center locations, and a plethora of planned events, this one-stop shop for seniors in the city can help direct you to volunteer opportunities.

Retired and Senior Volunteer Program
(410) 396-8146
(410) 396-5253 (Baltimore City)
(410) 887-2059 (Baltimore County)
Seniors who want to offer something to their communities are matched with volunteer positions that enable them to use their previously obtained skills and experience to help others. Volunteers are also sought to help other seniors. Some seniors assist with tax preparations while others serve in schools as librarians, teachers' aides, and career counselors.

i Throughout Maryland, dialing 911 gets emergency help from police, fire departments, and ambulance crews. In Baltimore City, however, an "emergency with no urgency" phone number of 311 has been put into place for people who have been victims of crime but are not in immediate danger. The remainder of the state has not adopted the controversial 311 system.

MEDIA

Baltimore's media, like the city itself, has both an international and a neighborhood focus. On the same local TV news broadcast, you're likely to hear how neighbors are taking up a collection to help a family whose home was destroyed by fire as well as coverage of the latest developments in China and the bills that were passed in Washington that day. Newspapers will run 2-inch headlines about a local high school's football victory right next to a story about the recent congressional corruption scandal.

Our port status and our location right in the center of the Eastern seaboard, spitting distance from the nation's capital, tend to make AM talk radio big in Baltimore. Music is FM radio's main focus. You can find any kind of music you like on Baltimore radio, including classical, Big Band, blues, jazz, Dixieland, country, gospel, and, of course, rock.

Baltimore has always been very big on rock 'n' roll. Back in the 1950s and '60s, we had local dance-party shows on both radio and TV. Buddy Dean and his teenage committee were the ones to watch when you got home from school every day. We watched and learned all the new dances so that at the weekend's record hop we would be in the know. (John Waters spoofed this semi-religious dedication to *The Buddy Dean Show* in his movie and Broadway musical *Hairspray*.) Baltimore stations carried *Dance Party* and other national dance shows on radio, but the local show on Friday nights was *Lee Case and the HiFi Club*, on WCBM and sponsored by Coca-Cola. Kids could go down to the studio and be part of the show; they'd talk about local high school functions and dances and then win prizes. On Saturday nights there was always a HiFi Club record hop somewhere in town.

Print media is one of Baltimore's true passions. We have some large publishing houses, many of which are strictly book publishers and oriented toward educational or medical publishing, such as Lippincott, Williams & Wilkins, and the Johns Hopkins University Press. Agora Publishing is appreciated locally not only for the quality of its many publishing franchises but also because it embraced Baltimore's love of the past by restoring four stunning mansions in the Mount Vernon neighborhood for its headquarters. The company further ingratiated itself in the community by opening the lobbies of these buildings during neighborhood festivities such as the Flower Mart and the Baltimore Book Festival. (See the Annual Events chapter.)

Baltimore has only two daily newspapers, the *Baltimore Sun,* and the tabloid-sized the *Examiner,* which started in 2006. There is also one main business daily, the *Daily Record,* the many free citywide weeklies and monthlies tend to make up for the loss a few years ago of the *Baltimore News American* and, more recently, the *Baltimore Evening Sun.* Baltimore also boasts newspapers that focus on specific neighborhoods, such as the *Dundalk Eagle* and the *Charles Villager,* or even a specific religion, such as the *Catholic Review* and *Jewish Times.*

We also have two monthly four-color magazines that are Baltimore-centric, *Baltimore* and *Style,* as well as some area-specific ones, such as *The Urbanite,* which chats about urban living. Baltimore's active arts and culture scene is covered in two publications, *Link* and *radar.*

Subsequently we've listed some of the major players in the Baltimore media market.

NEWSPAPERS

Dailies

The *Baltimore Examiner*
400 East Pratt Street
www.examiner.com

Since April 2006, Baltimore is now a two-daily town again. The *Examiner*, which also has newspapers in San Francisco, Washington, D.C., and Denver, was started by Qwest founder Philip Anschutz to tap into the huge population which doesn't read the *Sun*. The *Examiner* is distributed in affluent neighborhoods in parts of Baltimore City, and Baltimore, Anne Arundel, and Howard Counties for free. Some 250,000 newspapers are delivered Monday through Saturday. Local news and sports coverage, with a number of Baltimore-based columnists, are emphasized, though there are plenty of pages devoted to national and international news. Scoops are a big thing with the tabloid-size *Examiner*, which tries to find stories the *Sun* isn't covering.

The *Baltimore Sun*
501 North Calvert Street
(410) 332-6000
www.baltimoresun.com

A. S. Abell originally created the *Sun* in 1837 as a penny paper to appeal to and serve Baltimore's middle class. The *Sun*'s first foreign correspondent left the harbor in 1887, and its in-depth coverage of the international scene continues today with firsthand accounts from its five foreign bureaus and through the Associated Press, of which it was a founding member. The *Sun* is well-known nationally for its investigative reports, and in 1997 it won particular attention for its three-part series on the continuing slave trade in Africa. Over the years the *Sun*'s journalism has won more than 15 Pulitzer Prizes, and the company has grown into Maryland's largest news-gathering operation.

From 1920 to 1995 A. S. Abell Company also published the *Evening Sun*, which many Baltimoreans still mourn. Its focus was more community-oriented and its tone slightly more irreverent—a legacy of H. L. Mencken, Baltimore's most famous curmudgeon and founder of the *Evening Sun*'s editorial page.

The *Sun*, bought by a private investor in 2007, enjoys a circulation of nearly a half million for its Sunday editions. The *Sun* has a daily press run of 430,000 copies. It offers county-specific editions for Anne Arundel, Howard, Carroll, and Baltimore Counties and also owns Patuxent Publishing (see the listing under Weeklies in this chapter). Weekly tabs include Thursday's "Live," a pullout that lists Baltimore happenings, while Sunday's edition has large real estate and employment sections.

The daily paper is 50 cents a copy; 25 cents if you buy it late in the day from a street vendor and $1.66 on Sundays. One-year subscription is $176.80.

The *Daily Record*
11 East Saratoga Street
(410) 752-3849
www.mddailyrecord.com

In business since 1888, the *Daily Record* delivers business and legal news to 30,000 professionals and the general public Monday through Friday. Founded by Edwin Warfield, who was the governor of Maryland in the early 1900s, the *Daily Record* continued as a family-run printing and publishing company until 1994, when Edwin Warfield IV sold the company. Not much has changed, although a Saturday publication, the *New Daily Record*, which hits the high spots of the week's events, has been added. The *Daily Record* has been in the same building for 70 years. The paper can be received through the mail by subscription ($199 per year), received online ($79 a year), or bought at a newsstand for 75 cents.

Weeklies

The *Afro-American*
2519 North Charles Street
(410) 554-8200
www.afro.com

The *Afro-American* has been a family-run publication for more than 100 years. The *Afro's*

Selected Baltimore Firsts

The American Turf Register & Sporting Magazine, the first magazine dedicated to the subject of sports, was published here in 1829.

Ms. Dorothy Brunson became owner of WEBB–AM in Baltimore in 1979 and with that purchase became the first black woman in the United States to own a radio station.

The first telegraph line in America was completed in 1844.

—*Excerpted from Baltimore—America's City of Firsts, a pamphlet published by Baltimore Bicentennial Celebration, Inc.*

first owner, John Henry Murphy Sr., was a former slave who gained his freedom with the Emancipation Proclamation of 1863. The original *Afro* was a church paper produced by the Rev. William Alexander for members of Sharon Baptist Church. John Murphy bought the name and equipment in 1882 so that he could publish church information for the Hagerstown District of the AME Church, of which he was Sunday School Superintendent. In 1900 he joined with St. James Episcopal Church to begin publishing the *Afro-American Ledger.* By 1907 the paper was incorporated into the *Afro-American* Company of Baltimore City. The paper has a distinguished history of challenging racial and political issues in its editorial pages. Today the *Afro* enjoys a weekly circulation of 100,000 and is the best source for what's happening in the black community, both locally and nationally. Look for it every Wednesday. Newsstand price is 50 cents.

The *Baltimore Business Journal*
111 Market Place, Suite 720
(410) 576-1161
www.bizjournals.com/baltimore
The *Baltimore Business Journal (BBJ)* has been in business since the mid-1980s. It publishes a weekly newspaper-print magazine about business happenings in Baltimore as well as business guides that may be purchased separately, such as its *Book of Lists,* an indispensable guide to the top companies and their decision makers. *BBJ* is owned by American City Business Journals, which publishes similar journals for 41 other cities, including Washington, D.C.

Individual copies of the *BBJ* can be purchased for $1.25, or subscriptions are available for $93 per year.

The *Baltimore Jewish Times*
1040 Park Avenue, Suite 200
(410) 752-3504
www.jewishtimes.com
The *Baltimore Jewish Times* has been published every Friday since 1919. The paper covers general national news as well as local news and issues in Baltimore's Jewish community, including social, political, educational, and sports topics. The paper circulates to 20,000 subscribers. It takes pride in being able to touch all members of the Jewish population from reformed to conservative. The *Jewish Times* is sold mostly by subscription ($46.15 per year). Newsboxes can be found around Pikesville and Mount Washington. The *Jewish Times* also publishes the full-color magazines *Style* and *Chesapeake Life* and frequently offers free copies with a subscription to the newspaper.

The *Catholic Review*
880 Park Avenue
(443) 524-3150
www.catholicreview.org
The *Catholic Review* provides the Catholic perspective on local and national news. The

most popular section is "Spotlight," which features a different regional archdiocesan parish or school each week. The *Catholic Review* has been published by the Cathedral Foundation Press since 1913; its precursor, the *Catholic Mirror,* began in 1833. It is the largest-selling weekly newspaper in Maryland, with a circulation of more than 72,000. Individual copies are available at many 7-11 stores for 75 cents a copy. Subscriptions are available for $40 a year, or you can request that a single copy be mailed to you for $1.75. The paper comes out every Thursday.

City Paper
812 Park Avenue
(410) 523-2300
www.citypaper.com

City Paper was started in 1977 by two students at Johns Hopkins University. Their goal was to create a liberal alternative to the mainstream papers in Baltimore, and they were very successful. Successful enough that the paper was bought by Times-Shamrock Communications in 1987. The paper is currently owned by the *Scranton Times. City Paper* still keeps a young voice, but it speaks honestly to the whole city and is the place Baltimoreans go to find out what's happening this week. Its calendar of events is pages and pages in length and covers everything from arts galas to movie times to yard sales. The paper prides itself on its in-depth investigative reporting and its arts coverage. The personals listings are also extensive. The paper has a circulation of 91,000 and a total readership of 300,000 and is distributed free at more than 1,800 locations in the metropolitan area. New editions come out Wednesdays; look for copies in the bright yellow boxes, at some corner stores, and at magazine stands. Subscriptions for home delivery are $75 per year. Individual copies are free.

Patuxent Publishing Company
10750 Little Patuxent Parkway
(410) 730-3990
www.patuxent.com

Patuxent Publishing creates area-specific newspapers in the greater Baltimore area that are delivered free right to your door once a week. The *Messenger* is for residents who live in the northern neighborhoods of Baltimore City, such as Roland Park, Homeland, and Guilford. Towsonians receive the *Towson Times;* in Owings Mills residents receive the *Owings Mills Times.* In all, Patuxent Publishing creates more than a dozen weeklies and in 2001, started publishing *Maryland Family Magazine.* These are excellent sources of information, especially if you're planning to move to a particular area. They provide in-depth cover stories, letters to the editor, crime logs, commentaries, and bulletin boards. The Enoch Pratt Library keeps back issues of these publications. Some of the papers will deliver outside their coverage areas for free or for a minimal yearly rate.

Monthlies

Baltimore's Child
11 Dutton Court
(410) 367-5884
www.baltimoreschild.com

Baltimore's Child is a free monthly newspaper that's been in business since the early 1980s. The paper covers topics on the diaper set as well as teens and focuses on the dissemination of practical, usable information through 52,000 monthly copies. A recent issue, for instance, had a round up of birthday party resources and several stories on Moms who work from home or own their businesses. *Baltimore's Child* publishes annual schools, summer camp, and parents' guides. You can find *Baltimore's Child* at newsstands, in grocery stores, street boxes, all area libraries, and other places where free papers are available.

Gay Life
241 West Chase Street
(410) 837-7748
www.baltimoregaylife.com

Gay Life, part of the *Mid-Atlantic Gay Life Newspaper,* is the oldest gay paper in the region, serving the needs of this community for more than two decades. It is published by the Gay and Lesbian Community Center of Baltimore and includes breaking news, in-depth cover stories, entertainment and music information, classifieds, and regular columns written by local activists. It is published on alternate Fridays.

MAGAZINES

Baltimore
Inner Harbor East
1000 Lancaster Street, Suite 400
(410) 752-4200
www.baltimoremagazine.com
Started in 1907, *Baltimore* magazine is the oldest continuing city magazine in the country. It comes out monthly, and in it you'll find information that runs the gamut from who wore what at the latest charity gala to feature information about Baltimore personalities and places. A yearly subscription is $15.00, or you can purchase individual copies for $3.95.

Chesapeake Life Magazine
1040 Park Avenue, Suite 200
(443) 451-6023
www.chesapeakelifemag.com
This magazine was purchased by the *Jewish Times* and *Style* magazine in 2001, and the editorial content and graphic layout are much improved. A lifestyles magazine that focuses on food, travel, home and garden, architecture, waterfront recreation, and the arts, this is the dominant upscale magazine for the Chesapeake Bay region. It costs $4.95 an issue; a yearly subscription (seven issues) is $15.00.

Maryland Family
10750 Little Patuxent Parkway, Columbia
(410) 730-3620
www.marylandfamilymagazine.com
Maryland Family, published monthly by Patuxent Publishing Company, covers topics of interest to the average young family. For instance, a recent issue had articles on Lyme disease and picnics, among other things.

They also produce *Maryland Family's Baby Steps,* which focuses on prenatal to pre-school. Pick up a free copy at area grocery stores or your local doctor's office. Subscriptions are $19.95.

Mason Dixon Arrive
1242 Paper Mill Road, Cockeysville
(410) 584-9960
www.mdarrive.com
This bright little tourism magazine covers all kinds of things to do around the state, as well as nearby states. Special events, such as art shows, concerts, historical commemorations, and festivals, are listed in the calendar. Features focus on antiques, food and wine, tourist destinations, and shopping. The magazine is free and available at lots of antiques shops, coffee shops and restaurants, libraries, and tourism offices in Baltimore and the northeast part of the state. If you don't want to look for it, get a year's subscription for $28.

RADAR
209 B Oak Avenue, Pikesville
www.radarreview.org
Produced through the support of local arts organizations, *RADAR* is a free, pocket-sized print publication reviewing the arts and culture in Baltimore. *RADAR* comes out six times a year, and local artists and journalists write the content. The publication is available at area arts venues, coffee shops, restaurants, bookstores, and the Baltimore Area Convention and Visitors' Association.

Style
1040 Park Avenue, Suite 200
(410) 332-1951
www.baltimorestyle.com
Style magazine is well named. The monthly itself has glitz. It is published monthly by the *Baltimore Jewish Times* and features comprehensive articles about living in Baltimore. In fact its subtitle is "Smart Living in Baltimore." Issues are $3.95 apiece. Yearly subscription is $15 for seven issues.

The *Urbanite*
2002 Clipper Park Road, 4th Floor
(410) 243-2050
www.urbanitebaltimore.com

The *Urbanite* isn't like other magazines. The editors pick a theme and look for talented wordsmiths to address the theme in their own way. Readers have their own spot in the magazine for essays, too. The ideas are fresh—so you won't find yet another photo spread of pretty clothes on tired, thin women. Local arts, environmentalism, the city's future, and the effects of Baltimore's latest wave of immigration were the themes of recent issues. The magazine is free, and it's available at coffee shops, restaurants, and lots of local businesses. Subscriptions are $18 a year.

The *Valley Times*
P.O. Box 614, Timonium, 21094
(410) 828-9070

The *Valley Times* is small enough to fit in your Kate Spade or the back pocket of your jodhpurs. And it's chock-full of valley sensibilities: articles on the coming steeplechase season, news about antiques, the local party scene, gardening, and food. Printed in black and white since its founding in 1986, the *Valley Times* is a must for getting to know the northern Baltimore way of life. Some 9,000 copies are produced every month and are available in shops and restaurants around the Towson/Mount Washington/Roland Park area. It's free.

TELEVISION

Baltimore is considered a medium-size market with a city population of 625,000. We get all the main network channels, including Fox and Warner Brothers. Baltimore has been the launchpad for many nationally recognized talents, such as Gary Moore, Jim McKay, and Oprah Winfrey. Just as writer Anne Tyler, producer/director Barry Levinson, and writer/producer John Waters are still just neighbors to us, many remember Oprah reading the news on Channel 13.

If that sounds like downhome sentimentality, it is. Baltimore's full of sentimental schtick—just watch the morning news on WJZ Channel 13, where you will see faces that have been in this town for the better part of their careers, if not their lives. And while local flavor still exists in many newsrooms, Baltimore is keeping pace with the national trend of upgraded, sophisticated broadcasting. Cable news and media mergers threaten smaller stations, and many newscasts have revamped both their staff and their sets in a constant battle for viewer ratings. So far the reviews are mixed. Some welcome the fresh-faced anchors and reporters, others mourn the loss of the local veterans they replaced. The upside to this increased competition is more news to choose from.

Local Stations

WJZ Channel 13 (CBS)
WBAL Channel 11 (NBC)
WMAR Channel 2 (ABC)
WBFF Channel 45 (FOX)
WNUV Channel 54 (CW)
WMPT Channel 22
(Maryland Public Television)
WMPB Channel 67
(Maryland Public Television)

Cable Services

Baltimore City and Baltimore County are served by Comcast Cable. Cable services have been getting a run for their money from the burgeoning satellite TV trend. Call Comcast Communications at (410) 649-9000. DirectTV's phone number for satelite dish service is (410) 727-9580.

i All Orioles' games, as well as Washington Nationals' games, are broadcast on local TV; Comcast channel 62 in Baltimore City and channel 64 in Baltimore County. On the rare occasion when the two teams play simultaneously, the second game is shown on channel 17 for both city and county fans.

RADIO

Baltimoreans still listen heavily to radio in our cars, while we work, while we hold on the telephone, while we eat. For talk, the public radio programs are available on WYPR all day, or you can do as many Baltimoreans do and tune into the personality radio on WBAL and WCBM. You'll find everything from former Governor Bob Ehrlich and his wife, Kendel, Saturday 9:00 to 11:00 a.m. on WBAL to a national feed of Rush Limbaugh's daily talk fest (noon to 3:00 p.m. on WCBM). The Mark Steiner Show on WYPR, our NPR affiliate, offers substantive conversations on local politics, culture, and lifestyle and is heard daily on 88.1 FM from noon to 2:00 p.m.

Every music station in Baltimore has a specialty. In the old days of radio, all stations did what they called "block" programming, in which each block of time was programmed separately with music, talk, game shows, or dramatic programs. Now, it's as if each station is a block of its own. We've noted the local stations under a particular category of music, and if the station's music preferences are even more specific, we've noted that in parentheses.

Big Band/MOR
WLG 1370 AM

Christian
WAVA 105.1 FM
WAVA 780 AM
WBGR 860 AM (gospel)
WCAO 600 AM
WRBS 95.1 FM

Classical
WBJC 91.5 FM

Jazz
WEAA 88.9 FM
WSMJ 104.3 FM
WYPR 88.1 FM

Country
WPOC 93.1 FM

Rock
WERQ 92.3 FM (hip-hop)
WIYY 97.9 FM
WQSR 102.7 FM (oldies)
WRNR 103.1 FM (alternative)
WTMD 89.7 FM (alternative)
WWMX 106.5 FM (pop)
WXYV 102.7 FM (hip-hop/pop)

Easy Listening
WLIF 101.9 FM

All Talk
WBAL 1090 AM
WCBM 680 AM
WOLB 1010 AM

Talk and Music
WYPR 88.1 FM (National Public Radio affiliate)

For bad-weather closings, listen to WBAL 1090 AM or WWMX 106.5 FM.

WORSHIP

When we think of the American colonies, we think of them as a religious haven. We often forget that, although many people emigrated to the colonies as a way to escape religious persecution in their homelands, some faced similar problems once they landed. Maryland was the first state to decree the tolerance of religion.

The decree was welcomed with a sigh of relief, and thousands of people seeking the free practice of their religions swept into the state, both from within the colonies and from other lands.

Immigrants who landed at the port of Baltimore embraced the opportunity, language, and prevailing culture of both city and country but were loath to release the religion and traditions of their ancestors. Holding on gave them security in uncertain circumstances. In many cases, building a church was one of the first things immigrants worked for as a community. Hence, historic churches color the Downtown landscape—the Lloyd Street Synagogue, the Basilica of the Assumption (see Attractions chapter), Mount Vernon Methodist Church, Old Otterbein Church, and Old St. Paul's Episcopal as well as scores of other massive or intimate, stunning or simple, places of worship.

Away from Downtown, in areas that were still considered country in the 1800s, there are some fascinating "country" churches, like St. John's Church of Huntingdon in Waverly, originally built in 1846, or the chapel at the Church of the Redeemer in Charles Street, which is a Victorian masterpiece. (See the Attractions chapter for more information about visiting historic churches.)

Of course, not all of our houses of worship are old. A great many were built in the 1950s and '60s, when postwar building was at its height. We may boast the first Catholic Cathedral in the United States (the Basilica of the Assumption, see the Attractions chapter), but we also have the Cathedral of Mary Our Queen, dedicated in 1959. We may be the cradle of Methodism in the United States, but our 290 Methodist locations show that the baby has grown up.

The fact is that, historic or modern, Gothic cathedral or one-room country chapel, Baltimore boasts more than 2,100 churches and 55 synagogues.

The Society of Friends has two large meeting houses in North Baltimore. The Church of Jesus Christ of Latter-day Saints has six churches scattered across town. Historic Baptist and African Methodist Episcopal congregations abound, and the Catholic Church is pretty much everywhere. (Don't forget we began as a Catholic state.) If you are Jehovah's Witness, Pentecostal, Mennonite, or Eastern Orthodox, you'll find places to worship here. Muslims, Buddhists, and Hindus are also among our numbers. And in almost every inner-city neighborhood, there are soldiers of the Salvation Army.

If the city were cut up into square-mile portions, it would be doubtful that there would be an area that did not include at least one house of worship. Sometimes, as you ride through the city, it seems as if there is a church on every block!

Baltimore's houses of worship are very neighborhood-oriented, very community-oriented. Particularly in the ethnic neighborhoods, the life of the neighborhood revolves around the church. For instance, although there are Greek Orthodox churches in other locations, in Greektown, everyone knows St. Nicholas, whose full name is St. Nicholas Church-Greek Orthodox Community. It's

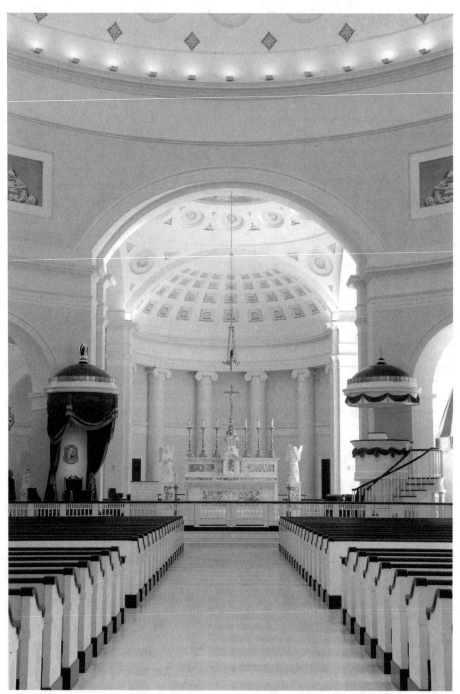

The Basilica of the Assumption is the oldest Catholic cathedral in the United States (see Attractions chapter).

where the Greek Festival is held every year, and where neighbors celebrate their culture, as well as their faith (see the Annual Events chapter).

Northwest Baltimore has a large Jewish population. Within that area there are neighborhoods that are Hasidic, neighborhoods that are Reformed, neighborhoods that are Conservative. They wrap around, for the most part, those synagogues that cater to their needs.

In tandem, there are large areas in West Baltimore that are almost exclusively African American. In these neighborhoods, you will find some of the largest and most socially and politically active African Methodist Episcopal churches in Baltimore.

On the other hand, there are a great many neighborhoods that are totally eclectic in race, culture, ethnicity, and religion. These neighborhoods use their churches, synagogues, and meeting houses as centers for community functions, such as covered-dish suppers, flea markets, and community meetings. Churches in the inner-city and midtown areas have big halls, big parking lots, and big sanctuaries where many people can gather. Worship centers also tend to be right in the middle of the community and easy to get to, as well as nonthreatening to people who might otherwise be shy of attending a large group function.

Community doesn't always mean the physical community that surrounds a church, however. It can also mean a spiritual community that is bound by some other common element besides where one lives. The Rock Church, an Evangelical church near Towson, is said to boast parishioners from as far away as northern Virginia. Korean Methodist, Catholic, and Presbyterian churches serve far-flung communities. Other churches serve special groups, such as the gay community.

And we do mean serve. All religious communities contribute to life in the city. There are houses of worship that have after-school care for children, those that have reading programs, health programs, and just provide a social center, particularly for the community's

youth, that is safe and supervised. Even small churches like St. Vincent de Paul Church in Jonestown reach out into the community weekly. St. Vincent distributes more than 300 bags of food every week. It also sponsors a day-care center and provides cosponsorship to two East Baltimore, primarily African-American, parochial schools.

Another church-created service organization is Tri-Churches Housing, Inc. It's a 20-year-old housing development corporation that was formed in the interests of the Washington Village and Pigtown neighborhoods by three neighborhood churches, St. Jerome Roman Catholic, Dorguth Memorial United Methodist, and St. Paul the Apostle Episcopal. (Scott Street Baptist has since joined the group.) Its ecumenical mandate is to create housing that is affordable for low and moderate income levels. In other words, members renovate. The service turns vacant housing into resident-owned housing, which makes the neighborhood safer. It also benefits the city since resident-owned housing means another taxpayer on the rolls.

One of the largest charity enterprises in the city, and the largest soup kitchen in the state, began with the simple charitable act of handing a homeless man a bologna sandwich. The pastor at the Basilica of the Assumption made it a practice to hand out sandwiches to the hungry, but by the mid-1970s, he was handing out more than 200 a day. By 1979 Catholic Charities was discussing the need for a soup kitchen nearby, and, in 1981, Our Daily Bread opened its doors. Although run by Catholic Charities, more than 6,000 volunteers from 80 churches, synagogues, groups, and businesses staff the facility, everyday rain, shine, snow, or cold. Our Daily Bread, which serves some 650 free hot lunches every day, moved to new quarters just outside of the Downtown area in May 2007. Business and church leaders, bowing to criticism about the soup kitchen in its Downtown location, built a new center to house Our Daily Bread as well as an employment center and referral and aid services for those who are poor.

Close-up

Tiffany Windows in Baltimore

Baltimore boasts two fine collections of Tiffany stained glass.

Brown Memorial Church in Bolton Hill commissioned stained-glass windows at the apex of Tiffany's career. The 11 windows are among the finest collection of Tiffany windows "in the country, and quite possibly the world," according to James E. Hauser, whose Minnesota firm restored the windows several years ago. The Smith and Babcock Memorial windows, both in the transepts, measure 16 feet wide and 32 feet tall. Brown Memorial Presbyterian Church, located at 1316 Park Avenue, is open for tours. For information or directions, visit or call (410) 523-1542.

Downtown, Old St. Paul's Episcopal also has several Tiffany stained glass and mosaics. Though not as large as the Brown windows (this is a small church) they should not be missed. St. Paul's is located at the corner of Charles and Saratoga Streets. The rose window above the entrance is a jewel, and the "Three Marys at the Tomb" window is breathtaking. The church is open to visitors during normal business hours. For information, visit www.osp1692.org or call (410) 685-3404.

Such interfaith action in behalf of the community is common in Baltimore and in Maryland. We take pride not just in our tolerance, as our forefathers decreed, but also in our acceptance of one another.

RESOURCES

The following resources can provide you with specific information about houses of worship in greater Baltimore. Specific times of services are listed in the Saturday edition of the *Baltimore Sun*.

Baha'i Faith
(410) 521-0841
www.greaterbaltimorebahais.org
The Baha'i Faith does not have a center in the Baltimore area, but there are prayer meetings and study groups that meet at homes in Baltimore City and nearby communities almost every night of the week. If you call the contact number and leave a message, a member of the Baltimore Community will call you back and provide you with information about upcoming meetings.

Baltimore Baptist Association
8203 Harford Road
(410) 882-0000
www.bbasbc.org
The Baltimore Baptist Association (BBA) serves as a resource for 74 Southern Baptist churches in the greater Baltimore area. When you call, you can request the name of a Baptist church in or near your neighborhood. BBA also offers outreach ministries to different parts of the city, including a port ministry that serves sailors. It also has a counseling service for those in need, (410) 426-2359 or (410) 882-1988.

Baltimore Eckankar Center
2318 North Charles Street
(410) 235-0073
The Baltimore Eckankar Center offers worship

services Sundays at 11:00 a.m. and book discussions Mondays at 7:00 p.m. The center also serves as an informational resource for anyone who is interested in finding out more about Eckankar and its religion of light and sound. Call (410) 666-2065 for information.

Baltimore-Washington Conference United Methodist Church
7178 Columbia Gateway Drive
Columbia
(410) 309-3400, (800) 492-2525
www.bwcume.org

The Baltimore-Washington Conference represents 700 United Methodist congregations in Baltimore, Washington, D.C., and West Virginia. It acts as a clearinghouse for information about what those churches are doing. It provides the location of churches in the area through its District Office (ext. 440), and it reports church happenings through its newspaper, *United Methodist Connection*. The conference also offers a prayer line at (800) 936-6893, which during off-hours has a tape recording but Monday through Friday from 9:00 a.m. to 5:00 p.m. has a live person at the end of the line who will be happy to chat with you and/or pray with you. The Web site offers a church location, complete with service times and mission statements.

Catholic Center, Baltimore Archdiocese
320 Cathedral Street
(410) 547-5555
www.archbalt.org

The Catholic Center houses the administrative and service units of the Archdiocese in Baltimore. Through the previously listed number you can reach the Office of the Archbishop, the offices of Catholic Charities, the Department of Catholic Education Ministries, the Department of Management Services, and the Department of Human Resources Development. The operator will direct you to the correct department or give you another number to call. A parish directory is available on the Archdiocese's Web site.

A directory of Catholic churches in Baltimore is available from the *Catholic Review*. Call (888) 768-9555 for information. The price of the directory is $15.00 if you pick it up and $22.50 if you have it sent to you.

Central Maryland Ecumenical Council
4 East University Parkway
(410) 467-6194

The Central Maryland Ecumenical Council is in the business of promoting Christian union. To this end, the council organizes ecumenical worship services, puts on ecumenical concerts, and helps day camps organize ecumenical services for children. In addition, the council keeps a database of more than 1,900 churches in the Central Maryland area (Baltimore City and its five surrounding counties). Churches are listed by both location and denomination, and anyone is welcome to request information.

The Ecumenical Institute of Theology
5400 Roland Avenue
(410) 864-4200
www.stmarys.edu

Part of St. Mary's Seminary and University (the training center for Baltimore's Catholic priests), the institute offers graduate programs and events for the community designed to promote dialogue between persons of different faiths. These have included a Holocaust remembrance service and lectures by historians and theologians.

Islamic Society of Baltimore (ISB)
6631 Johnnycake Road
(410) 747-4869
www.isb.org

The society has been around since 1969, but its growth has been tremendous in the last decade. Established as a way for a handful of Muslim immigrants to gather for Friday prayer, the ISB now boasts a mosque in southwest Baltimore county, a school, a community hall, and a variety of services for both Muslims and non-Muslims.

Jewish Community Federation of Baltimore
101 West Mount Royal Avenue
(410) 727-4828
www.associated.org
The Baltimore Jewish Council is what you might call a resource for resources. It has information about congregations as well as local and national agencies. It also serves as the community relations and political arm of the Jewish community.

Jewish Information Service
5750 Park Heights Avenue
(410) 466-4636
www.jirs.info
The local Jewish Iinformation Service offers all kinds of information for the Jewish community, including Shalom Baltimore, designed to welcome newcomers with information about local synagogues, Jewish schools, and other pertinent information. The Web site Baltimore .planitJewish.com provides a listing of activities for the Jewish communities, including lectures, fund-raisers, and festivals.

Selected Baltimore Firsts

Baltimore claims the first Methodist church in American and the first American Methodist Bishop. The Lovely Lane Meeting House, now at the corner of St. Paul and 22nd Streets, is the oldest continuously active Methodist congregation in the United States. The Reverend Francis Asbury became bishop in the same year the original Lovely Lane Meeting House was built, 1774.

The first Catholic Diocese in the United States was established here in 1789. This being the case, it seems appropriate that Baltimore also boasts the first Catholic Cathdral in the United States. The Basilica of the Assumption of the Blessed Virgin Mary—simply known around town as The Basilica—was completed in 1821. It was designed by B.H. Latrobe.

Elizabeth Ann Seton is the first native-born American citizen to be canonized a saint. Born in 1809, she achieved sainthood in 1975.

The Oblate sisters of Providence, the first black Catholic religious order of nuns, was founded by Mary Elizabeth Lange in 1829. She is currently being considered for sainthood.

America's first independent Unitarian Church was founded here in 1817.

The first Annual Conference of the African Methodist Episcopal (AME) Church met here in 1817.

In 1834 Baltimorean William Douglas became the first black man to be ordained to the Episcopal Ministry.

The first Young Men's Christian Association building was erected in Baltimore in 1859.

The Young Men's Hebrew Association, founded in 1854, erected the first Jewish Community Center. This may have been the work of the first ordained rabbi to come to the United States, Rabbi Abraham Rice, who served the Baltimore Hebrew Congregation beginning in 1840.

Henrietta Szold was the first woman to study at the Jewish Theological Seminary in America. She graduated in 1902 and went on to establish a few Baltimore firsts of her own, such as the first chapter of Hadassah.

—Excerpted from Baltimore—America's City of Firsts,
a pamphlet published by Baltimore Bicentennial Celebration, Inc.

Theosophical Society in Maryland, Inc.
523 North Charles Street
(410) 727-3471
The Theosophical Society is a world organization that encourages the comparative study of religion and philosophy. A taped message notes the week's offerings as well as provides you with contact numbers for more information.

INDEX

ABOUT THE AUTHOR

Mary K. Tilghman, a Baltimore native, has lived in Maryland her entire life. A journalist for more than 25 years, she has worked for a wide variety of newspapers and magazines and written on everything from local schools to agriculture to travel. In addition, as a graphic designer she has worked for local education organizations, designing brochures, annual reports, and other publications. She earned her degrees from the University of Maryland Baltimore County and the University of Baltimore. She and her husband have three almost-grown children.

Help Us Keep This Guide Up to Date

Every effort has been made by the author and editors to make this guide as accurate and useful as possible. However, many things can change after a guide is published—phone numbers change, facilities come under new management, etc.

We would love to hear from you concerning your experiences with this guide and how you feel it could be improved and be kept up to date. While we may not be able to respond to all comments and suggestions, we'll take them to heart and we'll also make certain to share them with the author. Please send your comments and suggestions to the following address:

The Globe Pequot Press
Reader Response/Editorial Department
P. O. Box 480
Guilford, CT 06437

Or you may e-mail us at:
editorial@GlobePequot.com

Thanks for your input, and happy travels!